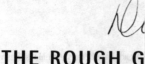

THE ROUGH G

Venice & the Veneto

jewellry shop Gloria Astolfo
www.gloriastolfo.com
near St. Mark's Square S. Marco 1581

There are more than two hundred Rough Guide titles
covering destinations from Alaska to Zimbabwe
and subjects from Acoustic Guitar to Travel Health

Forthcoming travel guides include

Chicago • Corfu • First-Time Round the World
Grand Canyon • Philippines • Skiing & Snowboarding in North America
South America • The Gambia • Walks Around London

Forthcoming reference guides include

Chronicles series: China, England,
France, India • Night Sky

Rough Guides Online

www.roughguides.com

Rough Guide Credits

Text Editor:	Jonathan Buckley
Series Editor:	Mark Ellingham
Editorial:	Martin Dunford, Jo Mead, Kate Berens, Ann-Marie Shaw, Paul Gray, Helena Smith, Judith Bamber, Orla Duane, Olivia Eccleshall, Ruth Blackmore, Geoff Howard, Claire Saunders, Gavin Thomas, Alexander Mark Rogers, Polly Thomas, Joe Staines, Richard Lim, Duncan Clark, Peter Buckley, Sam Thorne, Lucy Ratcliffe, Clifton Wilkinson, David Glen, Alison Murchie, Matthew Teller (UK), Andrew Rosenberg, Stephen Timblin, Yuki Takagaki, Richard Koss (US)
Online:	Kelly Cross, Anja Mutić-Blessing, Jennifer Gold, Audra Epstein, Suzanne Welles (US)
Production:	Susanne Hillen, Andy Hilliard, Link Hall, Helen Prior, Julia Bovis, Michelle Draycott, Katie Pringle, Mike Hancock, Zoë Nobes, Rachel Holmes, Andy Turner
Cartography:	Melissa Baker, Maxine Repath, Ed Wright, Katie Lloyd-Jones
Picture Research:	Louise Boulton, Sharon Martins
Finance:	John Fisher, Gary Singh, Edward Downey, Mark Hall, Tim Bill
Marketing & Publicity:	Richard Trillo, Niki Smith, David Wearn, Chloë Roberts, Birgit Hartmann, Claire Southern (UK), Simon Carloss, David Wechsler, Kathleen Rushforth (US)
Administration:	Tania Hummel, Demelza Dallow, Julie Sanderson

Acknowledgements

Jonathan would like to thank Susanne and Bruno for assistance in Venice, Elaine Pollard for proofreading, and all those readers who sent their comments on the previous edition of this guide, particularly: Pat Bartrup-Jones; Donna G. Bauer; Chad and Tracy Briggs; Tim Burford; Michael Burton; Tom Crow; Kenneth Haltman; Pat Hattersley-Smith; Ann Hecht; Tony Kay; Andrew and Sarah Knightly-Brown; Tom Lewis; Silvester Mazzarella; Dr Richard G. McWilliams; John Morgan; Dr Francis O'Gorman; Neil Penny; David Pitman; George E. Scott; The Right Reverend Lord Sheppard of Liverpool; Lord Markus Spann; Audrey Winter. James would like to thank Cristina Marinetti, Kate Davis, Carla de Nicola, Mauro Sambo, Vanessa Palomba, Elaine Mullings, Federico and Caterina for all their help and advice in Venice; thanks also to Daniella and Monica in Verona.

This fifth edition published June 2001 by Rough Guides Ltd, 62–70 Shorts Gardens, London WC2H 9AH. Reprinted June 2002

Distributed by the Penguin Group:
Penguin Books Ltd, 80 Strand, London, WC2R ORL.
Penguin Putnam, Inc. 375 Hudson Street, New York, NY 10014, USA.
Penguin Books Australia Ltd, 487 Maroondah Highway, PO Box 257, Ringwood, Victoria 3134, Australia.
Penguin Books Canada Ltd, 10 Alcorn Avenue, Toronto, Ontario M4V 1E4, Canada.
Penguin Books (NZ) Ltd, 182–190 Wairau Road, Auckland 10, New Zealand.
Printed in England by Clays Ltd, St Ives PLC.
Typography and original design by Jonathan Dear and The Crowd Roars.
Illustrations throughout by Edward Briant.

ISBN 1-85828-720-0

THE ROUGH GUIDE TO

Venice
& the Veneto

Written and researched by

Jonathan Buckley

With additional contributions by
James McConnachie and Hilary Robinson

ROUGH GUIDES

Help us update

We've gone to a lot of trouble to ensure that this fifth edition of *The Rough Guide to Venice & the Veneto* is accurate and up-to-date. However, things inevitably change, and if you feel we've got it wrong or left something out, we'd like to know: any suggestions, comments or corrections would be much appreciated. We'll credit all contributions and send a copy of the next edition – or any other Rough Guide if you prefer – for the best correspondence.

Please mark letters "Rough Guide to Venice & the Veneto" and send to:

Rough Guides, 62–70 Shorts Gardens, London WC2H 9AH or
Rough Guides, 4th Floor, 345 Hudson St, New York, NY 10014.

Email should be sent to:
mail@roughguides.co.uk

Online updates about Rough Guide titles can be found on our Web site at www.roughguides.com

The author

Jonathan Buckley is the co-author of the Rough Guides to Tuscany & Umbria and Florence, and has published three novels: *The Biography of Thomas Lang*, *Xerxes* and *Ghost MacIndoe*.

Rough Guides

Travel Guides • Phrasebooks • Music and Reference Guides

We set out to do something different when the first Rough Guide was published in 1982. Mark Ellingham, just out of University, was travelling in Greece. He brought along the popular guides of the day, but found they were all lacking in some way. They were either strong on ruins and museums but went on for pages without mentioning a beach or taverna. Or they were so conscious of the need to save money that they lost sight of Greece's cultural and historical significance. Also, none of the books told him anything about Greece's contemporary life – its politics, its culture, its people, and how they lived.

So with no job in prospect, Mark decided to write his own guidebook, one which aimed to provide practical information that was second to none, detailing the best beaches and the hottest clubs and restaurants, while also giving hard-hitting accounts of every sight, both famous and obscure, and providing up-to-the-minute information on contemporary culture. It was a guide that encouraged independent travellers to find the best of Greece, and was a great success, getting shortlisted for the Thomas Cook travel guide award, and encouraging Mark, along with three friends, to expand the series.

The Rough Guide list grew rapidly and the letters flooded in, indicating a much broader readership than had been anticipated, but one which uniformly appreciated the Rough Guides' mix of practical detail and humour, irreverence and enthusiasm. Things haven't changed. The same four friends who began the series are still the caretakers of the Rough Guide mission today: to provide the most reliable, up-to-date and entertaining information to independent-minded travellers of all ages, on all budgets.

We now publish 200 titles and have offices in London and New York. The travel guides are written and researched by a dedicated team of more than 100 authors, based in Britain, Europe, the USA and Australia. We have also created a unique series of phrasebooks to accompany the travel series, along with the acclaimed series of music guides, and a best-selling pocket guide to the Internet and World Wide Web. We also publish comprehensive travel information on our Web site: *www.roughguides.com*

Contents

List of maps

MAP SYMBOLS

═══	Road	ⓘ	Tourist office
━·━	Railway	✉	Post office
- - -	Chapter division boundary	■	Building
··········	River	⊞	Church
— —	Ferry route	₊⁺₊	Cemetery
———	Wall	▨	Park
▲	Mountain peak	▨	Beach
✕	Airport		

Introduction

Nobody arrives in Venice and sees the city for the first time. Depicted and described so often that its image has become part of the European collective consciousness, **Venice** can initially create the slightly anticlimactic feeling that everything looks exactly as it should. The water-lapped palaces along the Canal Grande are just as the brochure photographs made them out to be, Piazza San Marco does indeed look as perfect as a film set, and the panorama across the water from the Palazzo Ducale is precisely as Canaletto painted it. The sense of familiarity soon fades, however, as details of the scene begin to catch the attention – an ancient carving high on a wall, a boat being manoeuvred round an impossible corner, a tiny shop in a dilapidated building, a waterlogged basement. And the longer one looks, the stranger and more intriguing Venice becomes.

Founded fifteen hundred years ago on a cluster of mudflats in the centre of the lagoon, Venice rose to become Europe's main trading post between the West and the East, and at its height controlled an empire that spread north to the Dolomites and over the sea as far as Cyprus. As its wealth increased and its population grew, the fabric of the city grew ever more dense. Very few parts of the hundred or so islets that compose the historic centre are not built up, and very few of its closely knit streets bear no sign of the city's long lineage. Even in the most insignificant alleyway you might find fragments of a medieval building embedded in the wall of a house like fossil remains lodged in a cliff face.

The melancholic air of the place is in part a product of the discrepancy between the grandeur of its history and what the city has become. In the heyday of the Venetian Republic, some 200,000 people lived in Venice, not far short of three times its present population. Merchants from Germany, Greece, Turkey and a host of other countries maintained warehouses here; transactions in the banks and bazaars of the **Rialto** dictated the value of commodities all over the continent; in the dockyards of the **Arsenale** the workforce was so

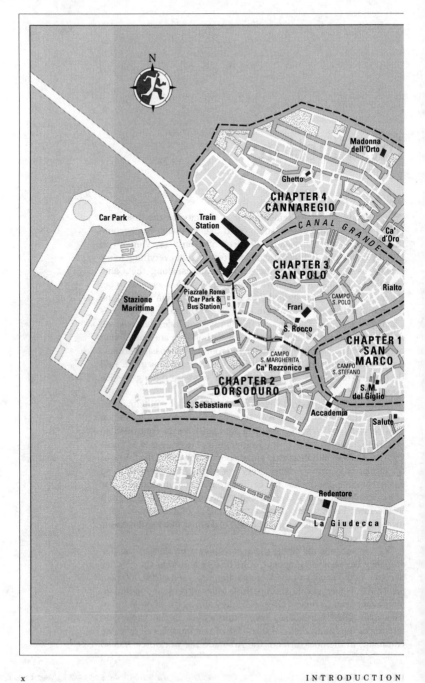

N

Madonna
dell'Orto

Ghetto

CHAPTER 4
CANNAREGIO

Car Park

Train
Station

CANAL GRANDE

Ca'
d'Oro

CHAPTER 3
SAN POLO

Rialto

Stazione
Marittima

Piazzale Roma
(Car Park &
Bus Station)

Frari

CAMPO
S. POLO

S. Rocco

CHAPTER 1
SAN
MARCO

CAMPO
S. MARGHERITA

Ca' Rezzonico

CAMPO
S. STEFANO

CHAPTER 2
DORSODURO

S. M.
del Giglio

S. Sebastiano

Accademia

Salute

Redentore

La Giudecca

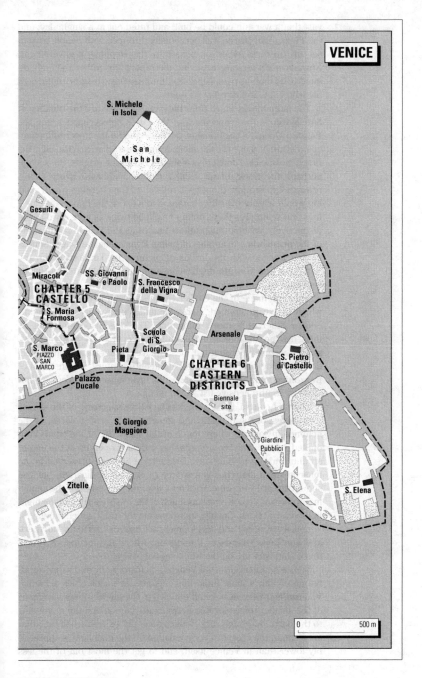

VENICE

S. Michele
in Isola

San
Michele

Gesuiti

Miracoli
SS. Giovanni
e Paolo
S. Francesco
della Vigna
CHAPTER 5
CASTELLO
S. Maria
Formosa
Scuola
di S.
Giorgio
Arsenale
S. Marco
PIAZZO
SAN
MARCO
Pieta
CHAPTER 6
EASTERN
DISTRICTS
S. Pietro
di Castello
Palazzo
Ducale
Biennale
site
S. Giorgio
Maggiore
Giardini
Pubblici
Zitelle
S. Elena

0   500 m

vast that a warship could be built and fitted out in a single day; and the **Piazza San Marco** was perpetually thronged with people here to set up business deals or report to the Republic's government. Nowadays it's no longer a living metropolis but rather the embodiment of a fabulous past, dependent for its survival largely on the people who come to marvel at its relics.

The monuments which draw the largest crowds are the **Basilica di San Marco** – the mausoleum of the city's patron saint – and the **Palazzo Ducale** – the home of the doge and all the governing councils. Certainly these are the most dramatic structures in the city: the first a mosaic-clad emblem of Venice's Byzantine origins, the second perhaps the finest of all secular Gothic buildings. Every parish rewards exploration, though – a roll-call of the churches worth visiting would feature over fifty names, and a list of the important paintings and sculptures they contain would be twice as long. Two of the distinctively Venetian institutions known as the Scuole retain some of the outstanding examples of Italian Renaissance art – the **Scuola di San Rocco**, with its dozens of pictures by Tintoretto, and the **Scuola di San Giorgio degli Schiavoni**, decorated with a gorgeous sequence by Carpaccio.

Although many of the city's treasures remain in the buildings for which they were created, a sizeable number have been removed to one or other of Venice's **museums**. The one that should not be missed is the **Accademia**, an assembly of Venetian painting that consists of virtually nothing but masterpieces; other prominent collections include the museum of eighteenth-century art in the **Ca' Rezzonico** and the **Museo Correr**, the civic museum of Venice – but again, a comprehensive list would fill a page.

Then, of course, there's the inexhaustible spectacle of the streets themselves, of the majestic and sometimes decrepit palaces, of the hemmed-in squares where much of the social life of the city is conducted, of the sunlit courtyards that suddenly open up at the end of an unpromising passageway. The cultural heritage preserved in the museums and churches is a source of endless fascination, but you should discard your itineraries for a day and just wander – the anonymous parts of Venice reveal as much of the city's essence as the highlighted attractions. Equally indispensible for a full understanding of Venice's way of life and development are expeditions to the **northern and southern islands** of the lagoon, where the incursions of the tourist industry are on the whole less obtrusive.

Venice's hinterland – the **Veneto** – is historically and economically one of Italy's most important regions. Its major cities – **Padua**, **Vicenza** and **Verona** – are all covered in the guide, along with many of the smaller towns located between the lagoon and the mountains to the north. Although rock-bottom hotel prices are rare in the affluent Veneto, the cost of accommodation on the mainland is appreciably lower than in Venice itself, and to get the most out of the less

accessible sights of the Veneto it's definitely necessary to base yourself for a day or two somewhere other than Venice – perhaps in the
northern town of Belluno or in the more central Castelfranco.

When to go

Venice's tourist season is very nearly an all-year affair. **Peak season**
is from **April to October**, when hotel rooms are virtually impossible
to come by at short notice; if possible give the central part of this
period a miss, and at all costs don't try to stay in July and August,
when the crowds are at their fullest, the climate becomes oppres-
sively hot and clammy, and many of the restaurants close down anyway. The other two popular spells are the **Carnevale** (leading up to
Lent) and the weeks on each side of **Christmas**; again, hotels tend to
be heavily booked, but at least the authentic life of the city isn't submerged during these festive periods, as it is by the summer inundation.

For the ideal combination of comparative peace and pleasant climate, the two or three weeks **immediately preceding Easter** is perhaps the best time of year. The days should be mostly mild – though
the weather can be capricious – and finding accommodation won't
present insuperable problems. Climatically the months at the end of
the high season are somewhat less reliable: some **November** days
are so clear that the Dolomites seem to start on the edge of the mainland, while others bring fogs that make it difficult to see from one
bank of the Canal Grande to the other. However, the desertion of the
streets in winter is magical, and the sight of the Piazza under flood-
water is unforgettable. This **acqua alta**, as Venice's seasonal flooding is called, is an increasingly common occurrence between
October and March, and you should anticipate a few inconvenient
days in the course of a two-week visit in winter. Duck-boards enable
people to move dry-footed around the busiest parts of the city, but
some low-lying areas – such as around Campo San Polo – become
impassable to anyone without gumboots, and on certain freakish
days the water rises so high that boats can be rowed onto the Piazza.

If you want to see the city at its quietest, **January** is the month to
go – take plenty of warm clothes, though, as the winds of the Adriatic
can be savage, and you should be prepared for some rain.

Average temperature and rainfall				
	Temp		Rainfall	
	°C	°F	mm	in
January	3.8	38	58	2
April	12.6	54	77	3
July	23.6	74	37	1
October	15.1	59	66	3

Part 1

The Basics

Getting to Venice from the UK

Flights

Direct flights take a few minutes over two hours from London. Nearly all scheduled services go to Marco Polo airport, 13km from the centre of the city, on the edge of the lagoon, while most charters and Ryanair's scheduled flights arrive at Treviso, 30km to the north of Venice (see p.32 for details of arrival at both airports).

Scheduled flights are operated three times daily from Gatwick to Marco Polo by Alitalia and British Airways. Prices vary enormously according to availablility, flexibility and so on, but both airlines run occasional offers from as little as £100 in low season. In high season, prices usually hover around £200 and can climb higher still if you book late in the day. The "low-cost" airlines nearly always beat the prices of the mainstream carriers. Go operates a daily flight (2 daily in summer) from London Stansted to Marco Polo, which usually costs around £100, with special reductions as low as £60 at slack periods, but the most spectacular deals, from as little as £19, have been advertised on Ryanair, which flies daily from London Stansted to Treviso. Unfortunately, prices as low as this are often unavailable unless you book a long time in advance.

Inexpensive charter flights to Treviso are sold through numerous **agencies** (see box on p.4) which undercut the major carriers by selling off the seats unsold by package holiday firms. If you scout around, a pre-Easter flight to Venice can be found for around £120, going up to £160 in summer. Sources are numerous: look in the classified sections of the Sunday newspapers (*The Sunday Times* especially) and, if you live in London, *Time Out* magazine or the *Evening Standard*. If you're online, check out the Cheap Flights website (*www.cheapflights.co.uk*), a very good source of low-cost flights from the UK.

Packages

Venice's high accommodation costs can make a flight-plus-hotel **package** a very attractive proposition, as the preferential hotel rates given to the holiday firms usually offset the slightly higher price of the flight. The brochures are dominated by three- and four-star hotels, sometimes offering rooms at discounts as high as 30 percent, and there's often a limited choice of one- and two-star rooms as well. Discounts at the lower end of the market are rarely dramatic, however, and the package firms tend not to deal with the older and more characterful budget hotels. You can expect to pay from around £400 per person per week for a three-star double room in low season; the same deal in peak season (from Easter right through to October) will cost anywhere between £100 and £250 more. At the upper end of the market, packages offering four nights at a top-notch establishment such as the *Gabrieli* will cost you between £800 and £1000 per person, depending on the season.

If you can find a particularly conscientious travel agent, they might contact the package company for you to find out if any of the hotels have rooms cheaper than advertised – something they're more likely to do in the winter months. Special offers do crop up from time to time, but very rarely between April and October. You might, though, come across early-summer reduced packages to Padua, Vicenza or Verona, the first two of which are near enough to Venice for you to commute.

Trains

Travelling **by train** to Venice will usually end up costing more than the plane, but it can be a

AIRLINES

Alitalia ☎ 0870/544 8259, *www.alitalia.co.uk*

British Airways ☎ 0345/222 111, *www.britishairways.com*

Go ☎ 0845/6054321, *www.go-fly.com*

Ryanair ☎ 0541/569569, *www.ryanair.com*

CHARTER COMPANIES AND AGENCIES

Alpha Flights 37 King's Exchange, Tileyard Rd, London N7 9AH ☎ 020/ 7609 8188.

APA Travel 138 Eversholt St, London NW1 ☎ 020/7388 1732.

CTS Travel 44 Goodge St, London W1P 2AD ☎ 020/7290 0620.

Flight File 46 Victoria Rd, Surbiton, Surrey KT6 4JL ☎ 020/8296 0309.

Italflights 125 High Holborn, London WC1V 6QA ☎ 020/7405 6771.

Itavia Travel 152 Bury Old Rd, Manchester M7 4QY ☎ 0161/740 5095, *www.itavia.co.uk*

LAI Travel 185 King's Cross Rd, London WC1 ☎ 020/7837 1477.

North South Travel Moulsham Mill Centre, Parkway, Chelmsford, Essex CM2 7PX ☎ 01245/608291.

STA Travel Telesales Europe ☎ 020/7361 6161, *www.statravel.co.uk* Branches in London, Aberdeen, Brighton, Bristol, Cambridge, Cardiff, Edinburgh, Glasgow, Leeds, Liverpool, Manchester, Newcastle, Oxford, Southampton and Exeter, as well as on university campuses throughout Britain.

Trailfinders European Flights ☎ 020/7937 5400, *www.trailfinders.co.uk* Branches in Birmingham, Bristol, Cambridge, Glasgow, London, Manchester and Newcastle.

Travel Bug 597 Cheetham Hill Rd, Manchester M8 5EJ ☎ 0161/721 4000.

Usit CAMPUS Call Centre ☎ 0870/2401010, *www.usitcampus.co.uk* Branches in London, Aberdeen, Birmingham, Brighton, Bristol, Cambridge, Coventry, Edinburgh, Glasgow, Manchester, Oxford, Sheffield and in YHA shops and on university campuses all over Britain.

---

leisurely way of getting to the country and you can stop off in other parts of Europe on the way. As you'd expect, the choice of routes and fares is hugely complex, but the most direct route is to take the Eurostar from London under the Channel, then pick up the overnight service from Paris to Venice, which runs via Milan; the whole journey will take at least fifteen hours and cost upwards of £200. A boat train from London to Paris will of course save money, but adds many hours to what is already a lengthy trip.

Prices on Eurostar vary significantly according to how far in advance you book, but the fare is usually between £90 and £160 for a return from

---

SPECIALIST OPERATORS

Abercrombie and Kent Sloane Square House, Holbein Place, London SW1 ☎ 020/7730 9600, *www.abercrombiekent.co.uk*

Citalia 3–5 Lansdowne Rd, Croydon CR9 1LL ☎ 020/8686 5533, *www.citalia.co.uk*

Crystal ☎ 020/8939 5405, *www.crystalholidays.co.uk*

Italian Connection 77 Oxford St, London W1 ☎ 020/7486 6890, *www.italian-connection.co.uk*

Italian Escapades 227 Shepherds Bush Rd, London W6 ☎ 020/8748 2661.

Italiatour 9 Whiteleaf Business Village, Whiteleaf, Surrey, CR3 0AT ☎ 01883/623363, *www.alitalia.it/italiatour*

Magic of Italy 227 Shepherds Bush Rd, London W6 ☎ 020/8939 5453, *www.magictravelgroup.co.uk*

Sunvil Sunvil House, Upper Square, Old Misleworth Middlesex TW7 7BJ ☎ 020/8568 4499, *www.sunvil.co.uk*

Thomas Cook 45 Berkeley St, London W1X 5AE ☎ 0990/666222, *www..thomascook.com*

Time Off 1 Elmfield Park, Bromley, Kent BR1 1LU ☎ 020/7235 8070.

TRAIN INFORMATION AND TICKET OFFICES

Eurostar EPS House, Waterloo Station, London SE1 8SE ☎ 0870/5186186, *www.eurostar.com*

Italian State Railways ☎ 020/7724 0011, *www.fs-on-line.com*

Rail Choice Delta House, 175 Borough High St, London SE1 1XP ☎ 020/7939 9915, *www .railchoice.com* Internet and telephone rail ticket agency.

Rail Europe 179 Piccadilly, London W1V 0BA ☎ 0870/584 8848, *www.raileurope.co.uk* Rail ticket agency.

International Rail Centre Victoria Station, London SW1V 1JY Rail tickets and passes for Italy; tickets can only be bought over the counter.

Ultima Travel 424 Chester Rd, Little Sutton, South Wirral L66 3RB ☎ 0151/339 6171.

London to Paris. From Paris to Venice a return ticket in a couchette (shared with five others), costs around £120; sleeper cars (single or double) are nearly twice as expensive. Be aware that advance-booked fares, discounts (including for under-26s) and special offers are legion. Travelling in the daytime is more expensive – than the overnight couchette, at least – as you are almost obliged to take the super-fast TGV south through France. Bear in mind also that if you travel via Paris you'll have to change both trains and stations which means lugging your bags on the metro from the Gare du Nord to the Gare de Lyon.

If a trip to Venice and the Veneto is only part of a longer exploration of the continent, you might consider investing in an **InterRail** pass. You'll need the two-zone version (£235, £169 for under-26s) to get from Britain to Italy; if you want to explore further afield than this, get the all-zone version (£309/£209). The pass gives one month's unlimited rail travel throughout Europe, plus discounts of up to 50 percent on cross-Channel services and trains in the UK. InterRail passes are

available from all main British Rail stations and youth/student travel agencies, and you need to have been resident in Europe for at least six months to qualify. Senior citizens holding a Senior Citizen Railcard can purchase a **Rail Europe Senior Card** for £5, which allows thirty-percent discounts on rail fares throughout Europe, including Italy.

Details on all international rail tickets and passes are best obtained by calling personally at major train stations or contacting the agencies listed in the box above.

Coaches

Travelling to Venice and back by **coach** will appeal only to those with phobias about planes and trains. National Express Eurolines (☎ 08705/808080, *www.eurolines.co.uk*) run a thrice-weekly all-year service from their Victoria terminal; the journey takes around 30 hours (changing at Milan) and the ticket costs around £140, with a small reduction for under-25s and students.

Getting to Venice from Ireland

Aer Lingus and Alitalia are the only airlines to fly non-stop from Ireland to Italy, the former flying daily from **Dublin to Milan**, and four times weekly to **Rome**; from November to March, there are just four flights per week to Milan, and two week-ly to Rome. Flights on **to Venice** from both airports are frequent and won't add much to the cost, which is generally around IR£300, though special deals are frequently on offer, bringing the price down by as much as IR£50.

Alternatively any good agent will be able to arrange a flight from Ireland to Venice **via London**, from where there are many different services (see p.3), though bear in mind that changing airports in London, added to Britain's high airport taxes, will increase the cost significantly. There are daily flights from Dublin to London, operated by Ryanair, Aer Lingus and British Midland. The cheapest is Ryanair (which also flies from Kerry, Cork and Knock), usually starting from around IR£60 for a return to Stansted, though special offers can be as low as £IR30.

From **Belfast**, British Airways and British Midland fly to Heathrow, but the cheapest options are the British European flights to Gatwick and Stansted, starting at around £60 return, though prices depend very much on availability.

AIRLINES AND TRAVEL AGENCIES IN IRELAND

AIRLINES

Aer Lingus Belfast ☎ 0845/9737747 Dublin
☎ 01/886 8888 Cork ☎ 021/4327155 Limerick
☎ 061/474 239, *www.aerlingus.com*

Alitalia Dublin ☎ 01/677 5171,
www.alitalia.co.uk

British Airways Belfast ☎ 08457/222111
Dublin ☎ 1800/626747,
www.britishairways.com

British Midland Belfast ☎ 0870/6070555
Dublin ☎ 01/283 8833,
www.britishmidland.co.uk

British European Belfast ☎ 0870/567 6676

Ryanair Belfast ☎ 0870/1569 569 Dublin
☎ 01/609 7881, *www.ryanair.com*

Virgin Express Limerick ☎ 061/704470,
www.virgin-express.com

TRAVEL AGENCIES

Budget Travel 134 Lower Baggot St, Dublin 2
☎ 01/661 1866

Italiatour! 4–5 Dawson St, Dublin 2 ☎ 01/671 7821.

Thomas Cook 11 Donegall Place, Belfast BT1
5AJ ☎ 028/9088 3900 118 Grafton St, Dublin 2
☎ 01/677 1721, *www.thomascook.co.uk*

United Travel Stillorgan Bowl, Stillorgan,
County Dublin ☎ 01/283 2555.

Usit 19 Aston Quay, O'Connell Bridge, Dublin
☎ 01602/1600 Fountain Centre, College St,
Belfast BT1 6ET ☎ 028/9032 7111, *www.usit.ie*

Getting to Venice from the US and Canada

There's a wide choice of flights from North America to Venice, but currently only Delta fly direct, with one daily flight from New York to Venice. Regular services operated by Alitalia, British Airways, Lufthansa, KLM, Delta, Trans World and United Airlines involve an interconnection either at Rome or Milan, or at one of the European hub cities – usually Frankfurt or Amsterdam.

Shopping for tickets

Barring special offers, the cheapest of the airlines' published fares is usually an **Apex** ticket, although this will carry certain restrictions: you will, most likely, have to book – and pay – up to 21 days before departure, spend at least seven days abroad (and be limited to a maximum stay of three months), and you tend to get penalized if you change your schedule. On transatlantic routes, there are also winter **Super Apex** tickets, sometimes known as "Eurosavers" – slightly cheaper than an ordinary Apex, but with, perhaps, further limits to your stay. Some airlines also issue **Special Apex** tickets to people younger than 24, often extending the maximum stay to a year. Many airlines offer youth or student fares to under 26s; a passport or driving licence are sufficient proof of age, though these

tickets are subject to availability and can have eccentric booking conditions. It's worth remembering that most cheap return fares involve spending at least one Saturday night away and that many will only give a percentage refund if you need to cancel or alter your journey, so make sure you check the restrictions carefully before buying a ticket. From time to time, the major carriers also have special limited offers. These fares may be substantially cheaper than the cheapest Apex fares, have fewer restrictions on travel and often require no advance purchase.

You may be able to cut costs further by going through a **specialist flight agent** – either a **consolidator**, who buys up blocks of tickets from the airlines and sells them at a discount, or a **discount agent**, who in addition to dealing with discounted flights may also offer special student and youth fares and a range of other travel-related services such as travel insurance, rail passes, car rentals, tours and the like. Bear in mind, though, that penalties for changing your plans can be stiff. Remember too that these companies make their money by dealing in bulk – don't expect them to answer lots of questions. Some agents specialize in **charter flights**, which may be cheaper than anything available on a scheduled flight, but again departure dates are fixed and withdrawal penalties are high (check the refund policy). If you travel a lot, discount travel clubs are another option – the annual membership fee may be worth it for benefits such as cut-price air tickets and car rental.

Don't automatically assume that tickets purchased through a travel specialist will be cheapest – once you get a quote, check with the airlines and you may turn up an even better deal. Be advised also that the pool of travel companies is swimming with sharks – exercise caution and *never* deal with a company that demands cash up front or refuses to accept payment by credit card.

Regardless of where you buy your ticket, fares will depend on the time of year, which is

AIRLINES IN NORTH AMERICA

Alitalia US ☎1-800/223-5730 Canada ☎1-800/361-8336, *www.alitaliausa.com* Daily flights via Rome or Milan from New York, Boston, Miami, Chicago, LA, Toronto and Montreal.

British Airways US ☎1-800/247-9297 Canada ☎1-800/668-1059, *www.britishairways.com* Daily flights via London from most major North American cities.

Lufthansa US ☎1-800/645-3880 Canada ☎1-800/563-5954, *www.lufthansa.com* Daily fights via Frankfurt from a large number of North American cities.

Delta Airlines ☎1-800/241-4141, *www.delta.com* Daily flights from New York (some of which are direct to Venice), Chicago and Los Angeles, mostly via Paris.

Northwest/KLM US ☎1-800/374-7747 Canada ☎1-800/361-5073, *www.klm.com* Daily flights via Amsterdam from over twenty North American cities.

United Airlines ☎1-800/538-2929, *www.ual.com* Daily flights via Frankfurt from several US cities.

DISCOUNT AGENTS, CONSOLIDATORS AND TRAVEL CLUBS

Air Brokers International 150 Post St, Suite 620, San Francisco, CA 94108 ☎1-800/883-3273, *www.airbrokers.com* Consolidator.

Air Courier Association 15000 W 6th Ave, Suite 203, Golden, CO 80401 ☎1-800/282-1202 or 303/278-8810, *www.aircourier.org* Courier flight broker, often with flights from New York to Milan or Rome.

Airhitch 2641 Broadway, 3rd Floor, Suite 100, New York, NY 10025 ☎212/326-2009, *www.airhitch.org* Standby-seat broker: For a set price, they guarantee to get you on a flight as close to your preferred destination as possible, within a week.

Cheap Tickets 115 E 57th St, Suite 1510, New York, NY 10022 ☎1-800/377-1000, *www.cheaptickets.com* Discounted tickets for international destinations.

Council Travel Head Office: 205 E 42nd St, New York, NY 10017 ☎1-800/2COUNCIL or ☎212/822-2700 in New York, *www.counciltravel.com* Student and youth travel organization offering discounted air fares, rail passes and travel gear. For those over 26, it acts like a regular travel agency.

Educational Travel Center 438 N Frances St, Madison, WI 53703 ☎1-800/747-5551, *www.edtrav.com* Student/youth

---

typically divided into "low", "shoulder" and "high" seasons. Naturally, the seasonal boundaries differ from airline to airline and are regularly subject to change. Moreover, carriers like Alitalia have a different set of published fares for just about every other week of the year (distinguishing between low shoulder, high shoulder, etc etc). However, you can expect fares to be highest over the summer months (June through mid-September) and lowest during the winter (November through March excluding the two weeks before Christmas). The rest of the year (mid-September through October, the pre-Christmas period, April and May) are classified as "shoulder".

Flights from the US

Alitalia, with daily flights via Rome from several North American cities, offers the best value in

return fares to Venice. Between them, British Airways, Lufthansa, Delta, Northwest/KLM and United offer daily flights from all the major cities via a variety of European hubs. Ticket prices vary according to distance and season: from New York expect to pay from around $650 in low season (roughly Nov–Feb, outside Christmas and Carnival), $800 in the shoulder periods and $1000 in high season (May–Sept). From Miami or Chicago fares are roughly $100 higher, while flights from LA cost at least $150 above those from New York. But be on the lookout for special promotional offers, which can bring fares down by up to $300 in high season.

The prices quoted above (and in the next section) are for midweek travel (add about $50 for weekend travel), exclusive of taxes (roughly $50–70). The approximate flying time to Venice from New York is 11 hours (9 hours if you can

discount agent with good prices on flights to Rome and Milan.

Encore Travel Club 4501 Forbes Blvd, Lanham, MD 20706 ☎1-800/444-9800, *www.preferredtraveller.com* Discount travel club.

Interworld Travel 800 Douglass Rd, Suite 140, Coral Gables, FL 33134 ☎1-800/468-3796, *www.interworldtravel.com* Consolidator.

Last Minute Travel Club 100 Sylvan Rd, Suite 600, Woburn, MA 01801 ☎1-800/LAST-MIN Travel club specializing in standby deals.

New Frontiers/Nouvelles Frontières Head Office: 12 E 33rd St, New York, NY 10016 ☎1-800/366-6387 or 212/779-0600 1001 Sherbrook East, Suite 720, Montréal, PQ H2L 1L3 ☎514/526-8444, *www.newfrontiers.com* French discount travel firm with summer charters to Rome. Other branches in LA, San Francisco and Québec City.

Now Voyager 74 Varick St, Suite 307, New York, NY 10013 ☎212/431-1616, *www.nowvoyagertravel.com* Courier flight broker.

STA Travel Head Office: 10 Downing St, New York, NY 10018 ☎1-800/777-0112, *www.statravel.com* Worldwide specialist in independent travel for students and under-26s only, with branches in the Los Angeles, San Francisco and Boston areas.

TFI Tours International Head Office: 34 W 32nd St, 12th Floor, New York, NY 10001 ☎1-800/745-8000, *www.tfitoursinternational.com* Consolidator; other offices in Las Vegas, San Francisco, Los Angeles.

Travac Head Office: 989 6th Ave, 16th Floor, New York, NY 10018 ☎1-877/872-8221 or 212/630-3316 2601 East Jefferson St, Orlando, FL 32803 ☎407/896-0014, *www.travac.com* Consolidator and charter broker.

Travel Avenue 10 S Riverside Plaza, Suite 1404, Chicago, IL 60606 ☎1-800/333-3335, *www.travelavenue.com* Discount travel agent.

Travel Cuts Head Office: 187 College St, Toronto, ON M5T 1P7 ☎1-800/667-2887 or 416/979-2406, *www.travelcuts.com* Canadian student travel organization with branches all over the country.

Travelers Advantage 3033 S Parker Rd, Suite 900, Aurora, CO 80014 ☎1-800/548-1116, *www.travelersadvantage.com* Discount travel club.

UniTravel 11737 Administration Drive, Suite 120, St Louis, MO 63146 ☎1-800/325-2222, *www.unitravel.com* Consolidator.

Worldtek Travel 111 Water St, New Haven, CT 06511 ☎1-800/243-1723, *www.worldtek.com* Discount travel agency.

Worldwide Discount Travel Club 11601 Biscayne Blvd, Suite 310, North Miami, FL 33181 ☎305/534-2082 Discount travel club.

---

find a direct flight), from Chicago 13 hours and from Los Angeles 15 hours 45 minutes.

Flights from Canada

If you're flying from Canada, you might have to change planes in a North American city as well as in Europe, so the waiting time between connecting flights will be more likely to figure into your choice of an airline. You should be able to find published, scheduled fares from Toronto for around CAN$850 (low season), CAN$1200 (shoulder) or CAN$1700 (high), and from Vancouver for roughly CAN$1350/1750/2000. Special promotional offers could bring the price of a high-season fare down to CAN$1300 (from Toronto) or CAN$1700 (from Vancouver).

The approximate flying time to Venice from Toronto is 11 hours 45 minutes and from Vancouver 14 hours 45 minutes.

Packages and organized tours

While there's no shortage of multi-city packages with a couple of days in Venice as part of a more extensive Italian itinerary, there's not much out there that offers Venice exclusively, apart from basic city breaks from the major airlines' vacation subsidiaries. So your best bet may be just to get a travel agent to customize one for you.

European rail passes

If you're interested in seeing more of Europe en route to Venice, it might well be worth buying a rail pass. The best-known and most flexible is the **Eurail Youthpass** (for under-26s) which costs US$388 for fifteen days, and there are also one-month and two-month versions; if you're 26 or over you'll have to buy a first-class **Eurail** pass, which costs US$522 for the fifteen-day option.

PACKAGE TOUR OPERATORS IN NORTH AMERICA

Abercrombie & Kent 1520 Kensington Rd, Oak Brook, IL 60523 ☎1-800/323-7308, *www .abercrombiekent.com* Deluxe European tours, several of which include Venice.

Delta Vacations ☎1-800/872-7786, *www .deltavacations.com* Three-night city breaks.

Elderhostel 11 Avenue de Lafayette, Boston, MA 02111-1746 ☎1-877/426-8056, *www.elderhostel .org* Not-for-profit specialists in educational and activity programs for senior travellers (companions may be younger), with a good "Arts of the Veneto: Padua and Venice" 15-night package.

Italiatour US ☎1-800/ 845-3365 Canada ☎1-888/515-5245, *www.italiatour.com* Fly-drives, escorted and individual packages all over Italy, from Alitalia.

Perillo Tours 577 Chestnut Ridge Rd, Woodcliff Lake, NJ 07675 ☎1-800/431-1515 or ☎201/307-1234 Multi-city tours of Italy including Venice.

Trafalgar Tours 11 East 26th St, New York, NY 10010 ☎1-800/854-0103 or ☎212/689-8977, *www.trafalgartours.com* Various escorted tours to Italy, some of them including Venice.

You stand a better chance of getting your money's worth out of a **Eurail Flexipass**, which is good for a certain number of travel days in a two-month period. This too comes in under-26/first-class versions: ten days in two months cost US$458 for under 26s, US$654 for over 26s. A scaled-down version of the Flexipass, the **Europass** allows travel in France, Germany, Italy, Switzerland and Spain for five days in two months

US$348, fifteen days in two months US$728; the under-26 version, the **Europass Youth**, costs about US$233 and up. These passes can be bought from the agents listed below and also from many regular travel agents, especially youth and student specialists (see listings on p.8).

Australians and Canadians can also buy Eurail passes; again they must be purchased before arrival in Europe.

RAIL CONTACTS IN NORTH AMERICA

DER Travel 9501 W Devon St, Suite 301, Rosemont, IL 60018 ☎1-800/421-2929, *www.dertravel.com* Eurail and Italian passes.

Forsyth Travel Library 226 Westchester Ave, White Plains, NY 10604 ☎1-800/367-7984, *www.forsyth.com* Eurail passes.

Italian State Railways c/o CIT Tours, 342 Madison Ave, Suite 207, New York, NY 10173 ☎1-800/223-7987 or ☎310/338-8616 in LA, *www.cit-tours.com* Eurail and Italian passes.

Rail Europe 226 Westchester Ave, White Plains, NY 10604 ☎1-800/4EURAIL or 1-800/361-RAIL in Canada, *www .raileurope.com* Official Eurail agent in North America; also sells a wide range of European regional and individual country passes.

ScanTours 3439 Wade St, Los Angeles, CA 90066 ☎1-800/223-7226, *www.scantours.com* Eurail and European country passes.

Getting to Venice from Australia and New Zealand

There are no direct flights **from Australia** to Venice, but you can easily get there via another European hub, most commonly London, Paris, Frankfurt or Amsterdam; note that flights routed via London can involve an awkward transfer between Heathrow and Gatwick airports. Another option, and a good one if you can find a flight, is to head direct to Rome or Milan and transfer there. The majority of flights refuel or stopover in Bangkok or Singapore; these can be less expensive but will often add a second touchdown to the journey, as most go via another European city anyway. Many Asian and European airlines have partner deals, so you can fly a combination of, for example, Singapore Airlines and Lufthansa (stopping over in Singapore and Frankfurt). Rock-bottom possibilities include Garuda or Aeroflot, but you might not find the savings substantial enough to compensate for the lower grade of service.

The best **fares** to Venice are to be had during the European winter (Oct–Nov is generally lowest):

AIRLINES

Alitalia Australia ☎ 02/9244 2400 or 07/3407 7278 New Zealand ☎ 09/302 1452, *www.alitalia.it* Three times weekly to Milan from Sydney and Auckland via Bangkok (refuelling) with connections to other destinations in Italy: code share with Qantas.

British Airways Australia ☎ 02/8904 8800 New Zealand ☎ 09/356 8690, *www.british-airways.com* Three flights a week to Rome from Auckland with a transfer in LA and London; and from major Australian gateways via Bangkok or Singapore and London with onward connections to other destinations in Italy.

Cathay Pacific Australia ☎ 13 1747 or ☎ 02/9931 5500 New Zealand ☎ 09/379 0861, *www.cathaypacific.com* Daily to Rome from Sydney, Melbourne, Brisbane, Cairns, Perth and Auckland, with a transfer in Hong Kong.

Garuda Australia ☎ 1300/365 330 New Zealand ☎ 09/366 1855 or 1800/128 510, *www.garuda-indonesia.com* Several flights weekly from major cities in Australia and New Zealand to Rome, with either a transfer or an overnight stop in Denpasar or Jakarta and a transfer in either Frankfurt or Amsterdam.

Japan Airlines (JAL) Australia ☎ 02/9272 1111 New Zealand ☎ 09/379 9906, *www.japanair.com* Daily flights to Rome from Brisbane and Sydney, and several flights a week from Cairns and Auckland, with either a transfer or overnight stop in Tokyo or Osaka.

Malaysian Airlines Australia ☎ 13 2627 New Zealand ☎ 09/373 2741 or 008/657 472, *www.malaysiaair.com* Three flights a week to Rome with a transfer in Kuala Lumpur.

Qantas Australia ☎ 13/1313 New Zealand ☎ 09/357 8900 or 0800/808 767, *www.qantas.com* Daily flights to Rome from major cities in Australia and New Zealand with a transfer in either Singapore or Bangkok: code share with Alitalia.

Singapore Airlines Australia ☎ 02/9350 0262 or 13 1011 New Zealand ☎ 09/303 2129 or 0800/808 909, *www.singaporeair.com* Daily flights to Rome and Milan from Brisbane, Sydney, Melbourne, Perth and Auckland with either a transfer or overnight stop in Singapore.

Sri Lankan Airlines Australia ☎ 02/9244 2234 New Zealand ☎ 09/308 3353 Three flights a week to Rome from Sydney with a transfer or overnight stop in Colombo.

Thai Airways Australia ☎ 1300/651 960 New Zealand ☎ 09/377 3886, *www.thaiair.com* Daily flights to Rome from Sydney, Melbourne, Brisbane and Auckland with a transfer in Zurich and either a transfer or overnight stop in Bangkok.

Anywhere Travel 345 Anzac Parade, Kingsford, Sydney ☎02/9663 0411, *anywhere@ozemail.com.au*

Budget Travel 16 Fort St, Auckland, plus branches around the city. ☎09/366 0061 or 0800/808 040.

CIT Travel 263 Clarence St, Sydney NSW 2000; also offices in Melbourne, Brisbane, Adelaide and Perth. ☎02/9267 1255, *www.cittravel.com.au*

Flight Centre Australia: 82 Elizabeth St, Sydney, plus branches nationwide. ☎02/9235 3522 New Zealand: 350 Queen St, Auckland, plus branches nationwide. ☎09/358 4310, *www.flightcentre.com.au*

Italia Mia 101 Bridport Rd, Melbourne VIC 3000 ☎03/9682 8098.

Northern Gateway 22 Cavenagh St, Darwin ☎08/8941 1394, *oztravel@norgate.com.au*

Rail Plus Australia: Level 3, 459 Little Collins St, Melbourne VIC 3000 ☎1300/555 003 or 03/9642 8644 New Zealand: Level 2, 6 Parnell Rd, Auckland 1 ☎09/303 2484, *info@railplus.com.au*

STA Travel Australia: 855 George St, Sydney; 256 Flinders St, Melbourne; other offices in state capitals and major universities. fastfare telesales ☎1300/360 960 New Zealand: 10 High St, Auckland, plus branches in major towns and universities. ☎09/309 0458, fastfare telesales ☎09/366 6673, *www.statravel.com.au*

Silke's Travel 263 Oxford St, Darlinghurst, Sydney ☎1800 807 860 or 02/9380 5835, *www.silkes.com.au* Tailored holidays for gay and lesbian travellers.

Student Uni Travel 92 Pitt St, Sydney, plus branches in Brisbane, Cairns, Darwin, Melbourne and Perth. ☎02/9232 8444, *sydney@backpackers.net*

Thomas Cook Australia: 175 Pitt St, Sydney ☎02/9231 2877; 257 Collins St, Melbourne ☎03/ 9282 0222; plus branches in other state capitals. Direct telesales ☎1800/801 002 New Zealand: 191 Queen St, Auckland ☎09/379 3920, *www.thomascook.com.au.*

Trailfinders 8 Spring St, Sydney ☎02/9247 7666 91 Elizabeth St, Brisbane ☎07/3229 0887 Hides Corner, Shield St, Cairns ☎07/4041 1199.

Travel.com.au 76–80 Clarence St, Sydney ☎02/9249 5444 or 1800 000 447, *www.travel.com.au*

USIT Beyond cnr Shortland St and Jean Batten Place, Auckland, plus branches in Christchurch, Dunedin, Palmerston North, Hamilton and Wellington ☎09/379 4224 or 0800/788 336, *www.usitbeyond.co.nz*

Singapore Airlines and Alitalia quote fares beginning around $1700. Peak season runs from mid-May to mid-September, with most fares fluctuating between $1800 and $2100, though British Airways and Qantas (via London) cost rather more, with a ceiling for economy fares of around $2600.

From New Zealand, you can also fly with various Asia/European airline alliances, via Bangkok or Singapore. Prices start at around NZ$2600. Alternatively, Air New Zealand fly to London via Los Angeles, with connecting British Airways flights to Venice, from NZ$3000.

Red tape and visas

British citizens can enter Italy and stay as long as they like on production of a full passport. Similarly unrestricted access is granted to all EU nationals, whereas citizens of the United States, Canada, Australia and New Zealand are limited to stays of three months, though they, too, need only a valid passport. All other nationals should consult the relevant embassies about visa requirements.

Legally, you're required to register with the police within three days of entering Italy. This will be done for you if you're staying in a hotel (this is why you have to surrender your passport on arrival), but if you're on a self-catering trip you should register at the *Questura* (HQ of the state police). It used to be the case that nobody bothered too much about this formality, but in recent years the police have begun to be more pedantic with backpacking types in Venice. So if you think you might look like the sort of person a Venetian policeman might deem undesirable, get registered (see p.289 for the address of the Venice *Questura*).

ITALIAN EMBASSIES AND CONSULATES

Australia
Getaway, Level 45, 1 Macquarie Place, Sydney, NSW 2000 ☎02/9392 7900; 509 St Kilda Rd, Melbourne, VIC 3004 ☎03/9867 5744; 12 Grey St, Deakin, ACT 2600 ☎02/6273 3333.

Britain
38 Eaton Place, London SW1X 8AN ☎020/7235 9371; 32 Melville St, Edinburgh EH3 7HA ☎0131/226 3631; 111 Piccadilly, Manchester M1 2HY ☎0161/236 9024.

Canada
275 Slater St, Ottawa, Ontario K1P 5H9 ☎613/232-2401; 3489 Drummond St, Montréal, Quebec H3G 1X6 ☎514/849-8351; 136 Beverley St, Toronto ☎416/977-1566.

Ireland
6365 Northumberland Rd, Dublin 4 ☎01/660 1744; 7 Richmond Park, Belfast ☎028/9066 8854.

New Zealand
34 Grant Rd, Thorndon, Wellington ☎04/499 4186.

USA
690 Park Ave, New York ☎212/737- 9100 or 439-8600; 12400 Wilshire Blvd, Suite 300, Los Angeles ☎310/820-0622; 1601 Fuller St NW, Washington DC ☎202/328-5500. Consulates also in Philadelphia, Houston, Detroit, Boston, New Orleans, Chicago, Atlanta, Miami and San Francisco.

Information and maps

Virtually every Veneto town has a **tourist office**, and we've given their addresses and opening hours throughout this guide (the Venice offices are listed on p.32). Their usefulness is variable: some will hand out maps, hotel lists and additional leaflets on special events, whereas others will reply to whatever questions you have but offer next to nothing in the way of printed material. As a general rule, the bigger the better, though the service in Venice itself can be somewhat cursory at busy times. Before you leave, it's worth dropping in at the nearest **Italian State Tourist Office** (ENIT) to pick up some maps and brochures. Don't overload yourself, though – not only can most of the material be picked up in Venice, but the practical information, such as accommodation prices, is often out of date in the offices outside Italy.

Web sites

Though a trawl through the search engines will bring up a lot of Venice-related sites, most of them are either out of date or so woolly as to be almost useless. You should also note that very few accommodation sites list any hotels below the three-star range.

Excite Travel
http://travel.excite.com/
A good route to a host of city listings, with links to sites for Asolo, Bassano del Grappa, Belluno, Castelfranco Veneto, Feltre, Maróstica, Padua, Venice, Verona, Vicenza and Vittorio Veneto.

Go Venice
www.govenice.com
Today's weather and events on the front page, and a huge number of links to shops, government sites, newspapers and other sites. Some pages are Italian language only.

ITALIAN STATE TOURIST OFFICES ABROAD

ENIT can be contacted at *www.enit.it*; their information portal is *www.italiantourism.com*.

Australia
Contact the consulate: Level 45, 1 Macquarie Place, Sydney 2000, NSW ☎02/9392 7900.

Canada
1 Place Ville Marie, Suite 1914, Montrèal, Québec H3B 2C3 ☎514/866-7667; 175 Bloor St East, Suite 907, South Tower, Toronto, ON M4W 3R8 ☎416/925-4882.

Ireland
47 Merrion Square, Dublin 2 ☎01/766 397.

New Zealand
Apply to the embassy: 34 Grant Rd, Thorndon, Wellington ☎04/473 5339.

UK
1 Princes St, London W1R 8AY ☎020/7408 1254.

USA
630 5th Ave, Suite 1565, New York, NY 10111 ☎212/245-5618, brochure requests ☎212/245-4822; 500 North Michigan Ave, Suite 2240, Chicago, IL 60611 ☎312/644-0996, brochure requests ☎312/644-0990; 12400 Wilshire Blvd, Suite 550, Los Angeles, CA 90025 ☎310/820-1898, brochure requests ☎310/820-0098.

MAP OUTLETS

LONDON

Daunt Books 83 Marylebone High St, London W1M 3DE ☎020/7224 2295; 193 Haverstock Hill, London NW3 4QL ☎020/7794 4006.

Italian Bookshop 7 Cecil Court, London WC2N 4EZ ☎020/7240 1634.

National Map Centre 22–24 Caxton St, London SW1H 0QU ☎020/7222 2466, *www.mapsworld.com*

Stanfords 12–14 Long Acre, London WC2E 9LP ☎020/7836 1321; At Usit CAMPUS, 52 Grosvenor Gardens, London SW1W 0AG; 156 Regent St, London W1R 5TA; 29 Corn St, Bristol BS1 1HT ☎0117/929 9966.

The Travel Bookshop 13–15 Blenheim Crescent, London W11 2EE ☎020/7229 5260, *www.thetravelbookshop.co.uk*

REST OF THE UK

Blackwell's Map and Travel Shop 53 Broad St, Oxford OX1 3BQ ☎01865/792 792.

James Thin Melven's Bookshop 29 Union St, Inverness IV1 1QA ☎01463/233500.

John Smith and Sons at Tiso Outdoor, 50 Cooper St, Glasgow G4 0DL ☎0141/552 4394.

Heffers 20 Trinity St, Cambridge CB2 1TY ☎01223/568 522.

Newcastle Map Centre 55 Grey St, Newcastle upon Tyne NE1 6EF ☎0191/261 5622, *wwwnewtraveller.com*

The Map Shop 30a Belvoir St, Leicester LE1 6QH ☎0116/247 1400.

Waterstone's 91 Deansgate, Manchester M3 2BW ☎0161/832 1992; Queens Building, 8 Royal Ave, Belfast BT1 1DA ☎02890/247355. UK-wide chain; *www.waterstones.co.uk*

IRELAND

Easons Bookshop 40 O'Connell St, Dublin 1 ☎01/873 3811.

Fred Hanna's Bookshop 1 Dawson St, Dublin 2 ☎01/677 1255.

Hodges Figgis Bookshop 56–58 Dawson St, Dublin 2 ☎01/677 4754.

Waterstones 7 Dawson St, Dublin 2 ☎01/679 1260; 69 Patrick St, Cork ☎021/276522.

USA AND CANADA

California Map & Travel Center 3312 Pico Blvd, Santa Monica, CA 90405 ☎310/396-6277, *www.mapper.com*

The Complete Traveler Bookstore 199 Madison Ave, New York, NY 10016 ☎212/685-9007; 3207 Fillmore St, San Francisco, CA 94123 ☎415/923-1511.

Curious Traveller Travel Bookstore 101 Yorkville Ave, Toronto, ON M5R 1C1 ☎1-800/268-4395.

International Travel Maps 530 W Broadway, Vancouver, BC V5Z 1E9 ☎604/879-3621, *www.itmb.com*

Phileas Foggis Books Maps and More, #87 Stanford Shopping Center, Palo Alto, CA 94304 ☎1-800/533-FOGG or ☎1-800/233-FOGG in California.

Rand McNally 24 stores across the US ☎1-800/333-0136 (ext 2111) for the location of your nearest store *www.randmcnally.com*

Sierra Club Bookstore 6014 College Ave, Oakland, CA 94618 ☎510/658-7470, *www .sierraclubbookstore.com*

Travel Books & Language Center 4437 Wisconsin Ave NW, Washington, DC 20016 ☎1-800/220-2665.

AUSTRALIA AND NEW ZEALAND

Specialty Maps 46 Albert St, Auckland ☎09/307 2217.

Worldwide Maps and Guides 187 George St, Brisbane ☎07/3221 4330.

Mapland 372 Little Bourke St, Melbourne ☎03/9670 4383.

Perth Map Centre 1/884 Hay St, Perth ☎08/9322 5733.

Italy Hotel Reservation
www.venere.it/italy_it.
Roster of 231 hotels in Venice plus numerous others in the Veneto, with links to online booking where possible.

Italy Online – Veneto
www.initaly.com/regions/veneto/veneto.htm
Good-looking Web links on a huge range of topics as diverse as Bellini and asparagus, but the quality coverage is patchy. Excellent book listings.

Budget Travel: Italy
www.budgettravel.com/italy2.htm
A misleading title, as this site gives you lots of links on far more subjects than budget accommodation – upper-bracket hotels, festivals, ski centres, hiking, caving, shopping, even flea markets.

Gay Venice
www.gay.it/arcigay/venezia
Fairly basic site, particularly the English-language pages, but offers a host of links and contacts if you can get by in Italian.

Italian Yellow Pages
www.paginegialle.it
Plan that vital shopping day.

Regione del Veneto
http://turismo.regione.veneto.it/index.phtml
The official Veneto tourist office site, replete with information on hotels, the local weather, festivals and exhibitions – even webcams from the Canal Grande.

Museum Listings
www.museionline.it
Excellent links to museums and exhibition sites, with dates of events.

Tourist Information
www.italiantourism.com
Limited site with relatively few links, but it's blessed by the state tourist office and therefore fairly reliable.

Maps

If you're going to explore Venice in depth, you might want to get hold of a map that's on a larger scale than those in this book. The most accurate map of Venice is that produced by the *Touring Club Italiano*: consisting of a large-scale foldout map, a larger-scale mini-atlas of the city and a directory of street names, it comes in a neat plastic folder and will cost you around L30,000/€15. Most of the shops listed on p.282 will stock it, but it's difficult to obtain outside Italy. TCI's 1:5000 fold-out map is a good substitute, as is the map produced by *Magnetic North*, which is on a scale of 1:3000 and uniquely marks a vast numbers of the city's restaurants, hotels, bars, shops and various other amenities. If you don't want the fuss of unfolding and refolding a large single sheet every time you inadvertently stray into a cul-de-sac, the ingeniously designed *Falkplan* is very handy, though its small scale creates a few problems.

Costs and money

There is no getting round the fact that Venice is the most expensive city in Italy. If you're on the least luxurious of expeditions – camping, walking wherever possible, cooking your own food – it would just about be possible to get by on £30/$45 a day. Assuming, though, that you share a double room in a one-star hotel, eat out in the evenings, and go to a museum each day, your minimum will be nearly twice that amount. Even in the dead of winter there are few double rooms in Venice costing less than L120,000/€62 – that's £20/$35 per person, even when the exchange rate is at its most favourable, and a strict diet of coffee and croissant (cornetto) in the mornings, a picnic at lunchtime and pizza in the evening will account for another £15/$23 at least. Add onto this the cost of the odd entrance fee and boat ticket, and you've passed the £45/$65 mark before you know it. Allowing for the occasional excursion onto the mainland and other contingencies, it's reasonable to budget for a **basic outlay of £50/$75** per person per day for a summer trip to Venice. However, if you want to enjoy the occasional special meal or do a bit of shopping without worrying that your money will run out before the end of your holiday, you should set aside about £40/$60 per day as your spending money, **not counting accommodation costs**. And don't forget that, as ever, costs are higher for the person travelling alone: for single rooms, you'd be doing well to find

anything for less than 75 percent of the cost of a double room.

Currency and banks

Italy is one of eleven European Union countries which have opted to join the European single currency, the **euro** (€). At the time of going to press, the changeover to the new currency had not been completed, though the rate of exchange between the lire and the euro had been fixed at a rate of 1936.27 lire to 1 euro. Accordingly, prices in this book are given both in lire and in euros, with an approximate equivalent being given wherever no exact euro price had yet been set. With the transition to the euro in early 2002, prices are likely to be rounded upwards.

The euro comes in coins of 1 cent, 2 cents, 5 cents, 10 cents, 20 cents, 50 cents, 1 euro (=100 cents), and 2 euro, and notes of €5, €10, €20, €50, €100, €200 and €500. Note that although most Italian words ending in -o take the plural ending -i, and the official arbiters of Italian usage have decreed that the plural of euro is euri, most people have opted to leave the plural of euro unchanged – thus it's un euro (one euro), due euro (two euros) etc.

It's an idea to have at least some cash for when you arrive, but the most painless way of dealing with your money is probably by using **credit** or **debit** cards. In conjunction with your personal identification number (PIN), these give you access to cash dispensers (Bancomat in Italian). Found even in small towns, these accept all major cards, with a minimum withdrawal of L50,000/€25.82 and a maximum of L500,000/€258.23 per day; a small fee is charged, usually of around 1.5 percent. Cards, including Visa and American Express (Mastercard comes a poor third), can also be used in most hotels, restaurants and shops.

The other option is to carry your money in the form of **travellers' cheques**, available from nearly all banks, whether or not you have an account, as well as post offices and some building societies in Britain. The most widely accepted brands are American Express, followed by Visa and Thomas Cook. The usual fee for travellers' cheque sales is 1 or 2 percent and you'll usually pay a small commission when they're cashed. However, there should be no commission for cashing euro travellers' cheques, and American Express doesn't charge for cashing its own cheques.

If you run out of money, the quickest way to get **money sent out** is to contact your bank at home and have them wire the cash to the nearest bank. Branches and agencies of *Thomas Cook*, Western Union and American Express can also wire money for a fee; often their service is virtually instantaneous.

Banking hours vary slightly, but generally banks are open Monday to Friday from 8.30am to 1.20pm and from 3 to 4pm, with major branches often opening for a couple of hours on Saturday morning. American Express and Thomas Cook offices are open longer hours, and in the largest towns you'll find exchange kiosks that stay open late, often at the train station. As a rule, though, the kiosks offer pretty bad rates – the only places where you'll get less for your money are the exchange desks of the biggest hotels.

Health and insurance

EU nationals can take advantage of Italy's health services under the same terms as the residents of the country – to obtain this benefit you'll need to present a form E111, which you can get over the counter at main post offices. However, the E111 won't cover the full cost of major treatment, and the high charges for medical treatment make travel insurance essential if you're a non-EU citizen – and the risks of theft or other unforeseen setbacks make it highly advisable even if you are. For medical treatment and drugs, keep all the

receipts and claim the money back later. If you have anything stolen (including money), register the loss immediately with the police, as without their report you won't be able to claim; the department you should go to is once again the *Questura*.

Insurance

It's always advisable to make sure that you are insured for loss, theft and illness. Bank and credit cards (particularly American Express) often have certain levels of medical or other insurance included, especially if you use them to pay for your trip. It can be quite comprehensive, anticipating anything from lost or stolen baggage and missed connections to charter companies going bankrupt; however, certain policies (notably in North America) only cover medical costs. Note also that very few insurers will arrange on-the-spot payments in the event of a major expense or loss; you will usually be reimbursed only after going home. In all case of loss or theft of goods, you will have to contact the local police to have a report made out so that your insurer can process the claim.

ROUGH GUIDES TRAVEL INSURANCE

Rough Guides now offer their own travel insurance, customized for our readers by a leading UK broker and backed by a Lloyds underwriter. It's available for anyone, of any nationality, travelling anywhere in the world, and we are convinced that this is the best-value scheme you'll find.

There are two main Rough Guide insurance plans: Essential, for effective, no-frills cover, starting at £11.75 for two weeks; and Premier – more expensive but with more generous and extensive benefits. Each offer European or Worldwide cover, and can be supplemented with a "Hazardous Activities Premium" if you

plan to indulge in sports considered dangerous, such as skiing, scuba-diving or trekking. Unlike many policies, the Rough Guides schemes are calculated by the day, so if you're travelling for 27 days rather than a month, that's all you pay for. You can alternatively take out annual multi-trip insurance, which covers you for all your travel throughout the year (with a maximum of sixty days for any one trip).

For a policy quote, call the Rough Guides Insurance Line on UK freefone ☎ 0800 015 0906, or, if you're calling from outside Britain on (☎ +44) 1243 621 046. Alternatively, get an on-line quote at *www.roughguides.com/insurance*.

British cover

Most travel agents and tour operators will offer you insurance when you book your flight or holiday, but these are often more expensive than if you shopped around. As ever, you should check the small print: if you feel the cover is inadequate, or you want to compare prices, any travel agent, insurance broker or bank should be able to help. If you have a good "all risks" home insurance policy it may well cover your possessions against loss or theft even when overseas, or you can extend cover through your household contents insurer. Many private medical schemes also cover you when abroad – make sure you know the procedure and the helpline number.

Many **credit cards** offer travel insurance if you buy your tickets using the card, but these packages rarely offer the full cover of normal travel insurance. In Britain and Ireland, travel insurance schemes are sold by almost every travel agent or bank, and by **specialist travel insurance** companies; Rough Guides now offer their own scheme too (see box above). Cover varies, but a standard policy will cover the cost of cancellation and curtailment of flights, medical expenses, travel delay, accident, missed departures, lost baggage, lost passport, personal liability and legal expenses.

Insurance for North American travellers

Before buying an insurance policy, check that you're not already covered. Canadian provincial health plans typically provide some overseas

medical coverage, although they are unlikely to pick up the full tab in the event of a mishap. Holders of official student/teacher/youth cards are entitled to accident coverage and hospital in-patient benefits – the annual membership is far less than the cost of comparable insurance. Students may also find that their student health coverage extends during the vacations and for one term beyond the date of last enrolment. Bank and credit cards (particularly American Express) often provide certain levels of medical or other insurance, and travel insurance may also be included if you use a major credit or charge card to pay for your trip. Homeowners' or renters' insurance often covers theft or loss of documents, money and valuables while overseas.

After exhausting the possibilities above, you might want to contact a **specialist travel insurance** company; your travel agent can usually recommend one, or try Rough Guides' own scheme (see box above). Travel insurance policies vary: some are comprehensive while others cover only certain risks (accidents, illnesses, delayed or lost luggage, cancelled flights, etc.). In particular, ask whether the policy pays medical costs up front or reimburses you later, and whether it provides for medical evacuation to your home country. For policies that include lost or stolen luggage, check exactly what is and isn't covered, and make sure the per-article limit will cover your most valuable possession. Note that most North American travel policies apply only to items lost, stolen or damaged while in the custody of an identifiable, responsible third party – hotel porter, airline, luggage consignment, etc. Even in these cases you will have to contact the local police within a certain time limit to have a complete report made out so that your insurer can process the claim.

Doctors and pharmacies

If you need minor treatment, go to a **doctor** (*médico*), taking your E111 with you if you're an EU citizen: this should enable you to get free treatment and prescriptions for medicines at the local rate. If you're looking for repeat medication, take any empty bottles or capsules with you to the doctor – the brand names often differ. An Italian **pharmacist** (*farmacia*) is well qualified to give you advice on minor ailments

and to dispense prescriptions; most speak good English. A rota of *Farmacie di Turno* ensures that there's always a pharmacy open all night: every *farmacia* should display the address of the nearest night pharmacy on its door – or you can ring ☎192 for information. If you get taken **seriously ill**, hunt out the nearest hospital and go to the *Pronto Soccorso* (casualty) section, or phone ☎113 and ask for *ospedale* or *ambulanza*. For the address of the Venice hospital, see p.288.

Dental treatment is expensive and is not covered by the Italian health service; private insurance is the only way to avoid getting seriously out of pocket, and even then you'll have to pay on the spot and claim later.

No vaccinations are required for entry to Italy.

Opening hours and holidays

Basic hours for most **shops and small businesses** in the Veneto are Monday to Saturday from 8 or 9am to around 1pm, and from around 4pm to 7 or 8pm, though an increasing number of offices work to a more standard European 9am to 5pm day. Everything closes on Sunday except bars and restaurants, a few shops dedicated to the tourist trade, and a handful of *pasticcerie* that stay open until lunchtime. Many food shops are closed on Wednesday afternoon.

Many **churches** open for mass in the early morning, around 7 or 8am, and close around noon, then open again at 4 or 5pm, closing at 7pm; more obscure ones will only open for early morning and evening services; some only open on Sunday and on religious holidays. Wherever possible, the opening hours of churches are given in the guide. It's impossible to generalize about the opening hours of **museums and historic sites** except to say that the largest ones tend to be open every day, most of the others are open six days a week, with Monday and Tuesday the favoured days of closure, and that winter hours are a lot shorter than summer ones; we've given opening hours of every museum covered in the guide. (For the latest opening hours of all of Venice's major museums, see

p.39). The museum **entry charges** quoted in the guide are the full adult charge – bear in mind that some museums give student discounts, and all state museums give free admission to visitors from EU countries who can prove they are aged **under 18 or over 65**, and half-price admission to young people **under 26**.

One problem you'll face is that many churches and monuments are either completely or partly **closed for restoration** (*chiuso per restauro*): at any one time dozens of projects are in progress all over Venice (see Contexts), and it's impossible to predict which buildings will be under wraps in the near future – all that can be said with any degree of certainty is that you'll find restorers at work in parts of the Basilica di San Marco and the Palazzo Ducale.

Other disrupting factors are **national holidays**. Nearly all fee-charging sights (but not bars and restaurants) will be closed on the following dates:

January 1

January 6 (Epiphany)

Good Friday

Easter Monday

April 25 (Liberation Day and St Mark's Day)

May 1 (Labour Day)
August 15 (Assumption of the Blessed Virgin Mary)
November 1 (*Ogni Santi,* "All Saints")
December 8 (Immaculate Conception of the Blessed Virgin Mary)

December 25
December 26

In addition, many shops and businesses close or work shorter hours for the local festival of the Salute on November 21 (see p.281).

Post and phones

Post offices are generally open Monday to Saturday from around 8.30am until 5pm (until around 7.30pm at main offices), but smaller towns won't have a service on a Saturday, or it will be restricted to the morning only. **Stamps** can be bought in *tabacchi,* too, as well as in some gift shops in the larger towns. **Postal rates** within Europe are L800/€0.41 for a letter or postcard (L1200/€0.62 airmail); to North America, Australia and New Zealand the rate is L1500/€0.77. The Italian postal service is one of the tardiest in Europe – if your letter is urgent, consider spending the extra L4400/€2.28 for the express service. Letters can be sent **poste restante** to any Italian town, by addressing them "Fermo Posta" followed by the name of the town. Mail will be sent to the central post office; when picking something up take your passport, and make sure they check under middle names and initials – and every other letter when all else fails – as filing is diabolical.

Public **telephones** come in various forms, usually with clear instructions in English. Most phones will only accept **telephone cards** (*carte* or *schede telefoniche*), available from *tabacchi* and newsstands for L5000/€2.58, L10,000/€5.17 or L15,000/€7.77, but there's sometimes one nearby that takes **coins** (L100, L200 and L500; you need at least L200 to start a call). Note that the perforated corner of telephone cards must be torn off before they can be used. If you can't find a phone box, bars will often have a phone you can use – look for the red phone symbol. An alternative is to find a **telephone office** run by Telecom Italia, where you make your call from a kiosk and pay afterwards.

You can make **international calls** from almost all booths, but put in at least L2000/€1 to be sure of getting through. Alternatively, use a special international phone card (*carta telefonica internazionale*) available from post offices for L12,500/€6.30, L25,000/€12.62, L50,000/€25.80 and L100,000/€51.65; all cardphones accept them, but before each call you need to dial ☎1740 and the PIN number on the back of the card. One of the cheapest ways to make international calls, however, is to get hold of a phone card from a telecom company

> For direct international calls from Italy, dial the country code (given below), the area code (minus its first 0), and finally the subscriber number.
>
> UK: 0044
>
> IRELAND: 00353
>
> US & CANADA: 001
>
> AUSTRALIA: 0061
>
> NEW ZEALAND: 0064
>
> Calling Italy from abroad, dial 00 39 then subscriber number – including the initial zero.

before you leave. Simple user instructions are supplied with the cards and the cost of the connected call is added to your domestic bill or a credit card account. You can also make international **reversed charge** or **collect calls** (*cárico al destinatario*) by dialling ☎172 followed by the country code (see box on previous page), which will connect you to an operator in your home country.

Phone **tariffs** are among the most expensive in Europe, though it's cheaper to dial internationally between 10pm and 8am Monday to Saturday, and all day on Sunday. Unusually, it's often less expensive to make calls from your hotel than to use the pricey public telephones, whether for domestic or international calls.

Telephone numbers change with amazing frequency in Italy, a practice which has resulted in numbers having anything between four and eight digits, not including the code, which is an integral part of the number. Thus, dialling Venice from within or outside the zone you have to use the full ☎041 code and moreover, when dialling from abroad you do not omit the initial zero. Throughout this guide we've given the full phone number, including the area code. Numbers beginning ☎800, ☎147 and ☎167 are free; ☎170 will get you through to an English-speaking operator, ☎176 to international directory enquiries.

Mobile phones work on the GSM European standard. You will hardly see an Italian without his or her *telefonino* but if you are going to join them make sure you have made the necessary "roaming" arrangements before you leave home – which may involve paying a hefty (refundable) deposit.

Police and trouble

Venice has a few districts where you might think twice about walking unaccompanied late at night with a wallet stuffed full of lire (over towards Sant'Elena, for example), but in comparison with most Italian cities this is a very sedate place, and attacks on tourists are virtually unknown. **Pickpockets** on crowded vaporetti are the chief threat to the visitor, followed by the city's **cat burglars**, who are renowned for their ingenuity – so don't leave the window of your hotel room open

when you're out, even if you think only Spiderman could possibly get in through it. The mainland Veneto towns are generally tamer than their southern counterparts, though the rougher zones of Verona and Padua have their practitioners of the art of scooter-propelled **bag-snatching**.

If the worst happens, you'll be forced to have some dealings with the **police**, who come in many forms. Most innocuous are the *Polizia Urbana* or town police, who are mainly concerned with directing the traffic and punishing parking offences. The *Guardia di Finanza*, often heavily armed and screaming ostentatiously through the streets (and sometimes the canals), are interested in smuggling, tax evasion and other crimes of that ilk. Most conspicuous are the **Carabinieri** and **Polizia Statale**; no one knows what distinguishes their roles, apart from the fact that the *Carabinieri* are organized along military lines, and are a branch of the armed forces. These two forces are meant to act as a check and counter-balance to each other: a fine theory, but it results in a lot of time-wasting and rivalry in practice. In the event of **theft**, you'll need to report it at the headquarters of the *Polizia Statale* (see p.289). If your passport goes astray,

EMERGENCIES

EMERGENCIES

In an emergency, dial the following national emergency telephone numbers.

☎ 112 for the police (Carabinieri).

☎ 113 for any emergency service (Soccorso Pubblico di Emergenza).

☎ 115 for the fire brigade (Vigili del Fuoco)

☎ 116 for road assistance (Soccorso Stradale).

☎ 118 for an ambulance (Ambulanza).

you'll also need to report to your nearest embassy or consulate – these are listed on p.287.

Although the streets of Venice are safer than those of any other major city in the country, **sexual harassment** can occasionally be a problem for a woman travelling on her own. The Venetian male might not be as aggressive in his attentions as some of his compatriots, but he can still be a pain in the neck. Walking alone at night at anything less than a determined pace, the odds are that you'll be approached at least once. Complete indifference is generally the most effective policy, but you may find it difficult to emulate the glacial brush-off that comes as second nature to many Italian women. A mouthful of Anglo-Saxon will often do the trick, but if he persists, *lasciátemi in pace* ("leave me alone") should see him off.

Disabled travellers

Although a few key bridges are now fitted with wheelchair lifts, Venice presents problems for anyone who is not able-bodied. The islands that make up the city are joined by bridges that are usually steeply stepped, and getting in and out of the water buses can be hazardous if the water level is low or the canals are choppy, despite the helpfulness of the conductors. Wheelchair users should avoid the smaller boats – principally the #41, 42, 51 and 52 lines (see p.36–37) – as they have just a small platform around the pilot's cabin, the main passenger area being below deck level, down steep steps. The #1 down the Canal Grande, however, is reasonably accessible. It's also important to note that many Venetian hotels, especially in the lower price ranges, occupy the upper storeys of their addresses, and that in many instances staircases provide the only access. So if mobility is at all problematic, check the layout of your hotel before making a booking.

The tourist office provides a **map of accessible Venice**, making it possible, with careful route planning, to get around the main sights in the San Marco district; it also keeps keys to the wheelchair lifts. *"Veneziapertutti"* ("Venice for All") produces another map grading the accessibility of different

islands of the city – it's on display at some of the major vaporetto stops (train station, Rialto, Accademia and San Marco) and at the information office at Piazzale Roma. Before arriving in Venice it may be worth contacting **Informa Handicap**, Via Catalani 9a, Mestre (☎041.534.1700), where they speak some English, or **ANFAS**, Frari, San Polo 3080/N (☎041.520.5724); both can give further information.

Read your travel insurance small print carefully to make sure that people with a pre-existing medical condition are not excluded. And use your travel agent to make your journey simpler: airline or bus companies can cope better if they are expecting you, with a wheelchair provided at airports and staff primed to help. A medical certificate of your fitness to travel, provided by your doctor, is also extremely useful; some airlines or insurance companies may insist on it. Make sure that you have extra supplies of drugs – carried with you if you fly – and a prescription including the generic name in case of emergency. Carry spares of any clothing or equipment that might be hard to find; if there's an association representing people with your disability, contact them early in the planning process.

CONTACTS FOR TRAVELLERS WITH DISABILITIES

WEB SITES

www.accessibleurope.com/accessibleitaly/infovene.htm

www.goeurope.about.com/travel/goeurope/library/venice/aa980202.htm

www.comune.venezia.it/handicap

UK AND IRELAND

Disability Action Group 2 Annadale Ave, Belfast BT7 3JH ☎ 028/9079 1900 Information on access for disabled travellers abroad.

Holiday Care Service 2nd Floor, Imperial Buildings, Victoria Rd, Horley, Surrey RH6 7PZ ☎ 01293/774535. Provides information on all aspects of travel.

Irish Wheelchair Association Blackheath Drive, Clontarf, Dublin 3 ☎ 01/833 8241. A national voluntary organization working with

disabled people and offering related services for holidaymakers.

RADAR 12 City Forum, 250 City Rd, London EC1V 8AS ☎ 020/7250 3222, Minicom ☎ 020/7250 4119. A good source of advice on holidays and travel abroad.

Tripscope The Courtyard, Evelyn Rd, London W4 5JL ☎ & Minicom 020/8580 7021. National telephone information service offering transport and travel advice, free of charge.

USA AND CANADA

AccessAbility Travel 186 Alewife Brook Parkway, Cambridge, MA 02138-1102 ☎ 1-800/610-5640; TTY ☎ 1-800/228-5379. A division of FPT Travel Management Travel group, with tours to Italy and travel information for disabled travelers.

Access First 45-A Pleasant St, Malden, MA 02148 ☎ 1-800/557-2047, TTY ☎ 617/397-8610. Specializes in trips to Italy.

Jewish Rehabilitation Hospital 3205 Place Alton Goldbloom, Laval, PQ H7V 1R2 ☎ 514/688-9550 ext 226. Guidebooks and travel information.

Mobility International USA PO Box 10767, Eugene, OR 97440 Voice and TDD ☎ 541/343-1284, *www.miusa.org*. Information and referral services, access guides, tours and exchange programmes. Annual membership $35 (includes quarterly newsletter).

Society for the Advancement of Travel for the Handicapped (SATH) 347 5th Ave, Suite 610, New York, NY 10016 ☎ 212/447-7284,

www.sath.org. Non-profit travel-industry referral service that passes queries on to its members as appropriate; allow plenty of time for a response.

Travel Information Service Moss Rehabilitation Hospital, 1200 West Tabor Rd, Philadelphia, PA 19141 ☎ 215/456-9600. Telephone information and referral service.

Twin Peaks Press Box 129, Vancouver, WA 98666 ☎ 360/694-2462 or 1-800/637-2256, *www.disabilitybookshop.virtualave.net* Publisher of the *Directory of Travel Agencies for the Disabled* ($19.95), listing more than 370 agencies worldwide; *Travel for the Disabled* ($19.95); the *Directory of Accessible Van Rentals* ($12.95); and *Wheelchair Vagabond* ($19.95), loaded with personal tips.

Wheels Up! P.O. Box 509, Fanwood, NJ 07023 ☎ 1-888/389-4335, *www.wheelsup.com* Provides discounted air fare, tour and cruise prices for disabled travelers, and also publishes a free monthly newsletter.

AUSTRALIA AND NEW ZEALAND

ACROD (Australian Council for Rehabilitation of the Disabled) PO Box 60, Curtin ACT 2605 ☎ 02/6282 4333; 24 Cabarita Rd, Cabarita NSW 2137 ☎ 02/ 9743 2699. Provides lists of travel agencies and tour operators for people with disabilities.

Disabled Persons Assembly 4/173–175 Victoria St, Wellington ☎ 04/801 9100. Resource centre with lists of travel agencies and tour operators for people with disabilities.

Part 2

The City

Introducing the City

The historic centre of Venice is made up of 118 islands, most of which began life as a micro-community, each with a parish church or two, and a square for public meetings. Though many Venetians maintain a strong attachment to their particular part of the city, the autonomy of these parishes has been eroded since the days when traffic between them moved by water. Some 400 bridges now tie the islands together, forming an amalgamation that's divided into six large administrative districts known as sestieri, three on each side of the Canal Grande.

The sestiere of **San Marco** is the zone where the majority of the essential sights are clustered, and is accordingly the most expensive and most crowded district of the city. On the east it's bordered by **Castello**, and on the north by **Cannaregio** – both of which become more residential, and poorer and quieter, the further you go from San Marco. On the other bank the largest of the sestieri is **Dorsoduro**, which stretches from the fashionable quarter at the tip of the Canal Grande, south of the Accademia gallery, to the docks in the west. **Santa Croce**, named after a now demolished church, roughly follows the curve of the Canal Grande from Piazzale Roma to a point just short of the Rialto, where it joins the commercially most active of the districts on this bank – **San Polo**.

To the uninitiated, the boundaries of the sestieri can seem utterly perplexing, and they are of little use as a means of structuring a guide. So, although in most instances this guide uses the name of a sestiere to indicate broadly which zone of the city we're in, the boundaries of our sections have been chosen for their practicality and do not, except in the case of San Marco, follow the city's official divisions. Most of the sestiere of Santa Croce, for example, is covered in the San Polo chapter, with the remnant covered in Dorsoduro, as the sestiere has no focal point for the visitor and very few sights.

Addresses

Within each sestiere the buildings are numbered in a sequence that makes sense solely to the functionaries of the post office – it's possible to find houses facing each other which have numbers separated by hundreds. Venetian **addresses** are conventionally written as the street name followed by the sestiere followed by the number – eg Calle Vallaresso, San Marco 1312. Sometimes, though, the sestiere is

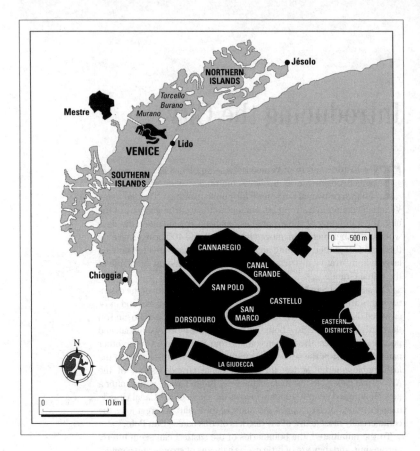

placed before the street, and sometimes the street is omitted altogether, which makes the place impossible to find. To maximize the
convenience of the guide, we've listed hotels, restaurants and bars
under headings which correspond to our chapter divisions. However,
wherever a full postal address is given in the guide, obviously the sestiere name is the one given; thus in a few instances you will find a
place listed under a heading which does not correspond to the postal
address – for example, a bar on the edge of the eccentrically defined
sestiere of Cannaregio may appear under the heading "Castello".

Names

Venetians have idiosyncratic names for features of the townscape. A
canal is a **rio**, and an alleyway that cuts through a building is a **sottoportico** or **sottoportego**, to give its dialect version. A street in
Venice is generally a **calle**, but a major street might be a **ruga** or a

salizzada, a small street may be a **ramo**, a street alongside a body of water is a **fondamenta** (or a **riva** if it's really big), and a street formed by filling in a canal is customarily a **rio terrà**. A square is usually a **campo** (there's only one Piazza), but it might be a **campiello** if it's tiny, a **piscina** if it was formed by filling in a place where boats used to turn, or a **corte** if it's more of a courtyard than a square.

The Venetian **dialect** version of **proper names** adds a further twist to the visitor's bewilderment. For example, the Italian name Giuseppe here becomes Isepo, Eustachio becomes Stae, and Giovanni becomes Zuan or Zan. Things get even worse when two names appear together – thus Giovanni e Paolo becomes Zanipolo, and Sant'Ermagora e Fortunato somehow becomes San Marcuolo. As a final refinement, the Italian name is often used alongside the dialect name, of which there may be another

---

The acqua alta

Floods – **acque alte** – have been an element of the Venetian winter for hundreds of years, but since the middle of the twentieth century there's been a relentless increase in the frequency with which the city's streets become immersed. It's now very rare indeed, between October and late February, for a week to pass without flooding, and it's not at all uncommon for flooding of some extent to occur on every day of the week – indeed, in the notoriously soggy winter of 2000 there was an *acqua alta* on thirty consecutive days. An *acqua alta* begins with water seeping up through the pavement of the Piazza and other low-lying areas, such as Campo San Polo, forming puddles that quickly merge into a shallow little lake. Soon after, you'll notice that wavelets are spilling over the quayside in front of the Palazzo Ducale. Sometimes it doesn't progress much further than this, but often it gets much worse. If you hear sirens wailing over the city it means that there's about four hours to go before the peak of a serious *acqua alta*, which is defined as a flood that rises in excess of 90cm above the mean lagoon level at the Salute. (Instruments on the side of the Campanile di San Marco display a continuous measurement of the water level and a prediction of the day's high tide – if the red light is on, a big flood is coming.)

Having lived with *acque alte* for so long, the city is well geared to dealing with the nuisance. Shopkeepers in the most badly effected areas insert steel shutters into their doorways to hold the water at bay, while teams of council workers lay jetties of duck-boards along the major thoroughfares and between the chief vaporetto stops and dry land. In extreme instances even these measures are not sufficient, and the duckboards get washed away from the Piazza, but usually the city keeps functioning through the inundation, and even on severe days there are some sectors that remain above the waves – maps at most ACTV stops show the routes of these walkways and where the high ground lies. However, Venice's pavements don't drain very efficiently, so you will find yourself splashing through water many hours after high tide. On a serious *acqua alta* day almost every Venetian is kitted out with rubber boots, and you'd be well advised to follow suit – there are plenty of shops selling them cheaply. And one other tip: if the water's high and duckboards are in place, use them – if you try to improvise a route down the back-alleys, the odds are that sooner or later you'll end up beating an ignominious retreat in the face of an unruly canal.

---

variant – thus, on the wall outside the naval museum a sign tells you that the spot on which you're standing is called Campo S. Biagio or Campo S. Blasio or Campo S. Biasio. We've generally used the standard Italian names, with the dialect version in brackets wherever it's in common use.

Arriving in Venice

Millions of visitors pour into Venice each year, most of them funnelled through a pair of airports that are not geared to deal with such heavy traffic. Arriving by train and coach is painless – but driving into Venice is unmitigated hell in summer, and just plain expensive in winter.

By air

If you are arriving by air, you'll touch down either at **Treviso**, 30km inland from Venice, or at **Marco Polo** airport, on the outskirts of Venice itself. The former is used chiefly by **charter** companies, some of which provide a bus link from the airport into Venice. An ATVO (*Azienda Trasporti Veneto Orientale*) bus service to Venice meets the twice-daily Ryanair flights as well. Otherwise, take the #6 bus from right outside the arrivals building into Treviso (30min), from where there are frequent bus and train connections to Venice. Tickets must be bought before you get onto the bus – the bar across the road sells them.

Most **scheduled** flights and some charters arrive at **Marco Polo**, around 7km north of Venice, on the edge of the lagoon. If you're on a package holiday the cost of transport to the city centre, either by land or by water, might already be covered. If it's not, the inexpensive alternatives are to take one of the hourly Alilaguna **water-buses**, which calls at Murano, the Lido, the Arsenale, and San Marco (L17,000/€8.75; journey time 1hr to San Marco), or one of the two road-going **bus services** to the terminal at Piazzale Roma: the ATVO coach, which departs every half-hour and takes around twenty minutes (L5000/€2.58), or the ACTV (*Azienda del Consorzio Trasporti Veneziano*) bus #5, which

---

Rolling Venice

If you're aged between fourteen and twenty-nine, you are eligible for a **Rolling Venice** card, which entitles you to discounts at some shops, restaurants, cinemas, museums and exhibitions, plus reductions on some transport services, all of which are detailed in a leaflet that comes with the card. The card costs L5000/€2.58, is valid for a year, and is worth buying if you're in town for at least a week and aim to make the most of every minute. The tourist offices have information on it but only the following places issue it: Agenzia Transalpino, at the train station; Assessorato alla Gioventù, Corte Contarina 1529, San Marco; Agenzia Arte e Storia, Santa Croce 659, near Campo della Lana; Associazione Italiana Alberghi per la Gioventù, Calle del Castelforte 3101, San Polo (near the Scuola di San Rocco); Agenzia Italtravel, Calle Ascensione 72b, San Marco.

---

is equally frequent, usually takes just five minutes longer (it's a local bus service, so it picks up and puts down passengers betwen the airport and Piazzale Roma), but costs just L1500/€0.78 (plus a small supplement for large pieces of luggage). The ticket office for both the water-buses and the land buses is in the arrivals hall; in addition to single tickets, you can also get ACTV passes here (see p.35) – a wise investment if you're staying more than a couple of days. Note that ACTV passes are not valid on the Alilaguna service nor on the ATVO bus, and that the airport ticket office will sell you a ticket for the ATVO rather than the ACTV bus unless you make clear your preference for *il cinque*.

The most luxurious means of getting into the city is to take a **water-taxi**, which gives you the best possible introduction to the city (the view from the taxi is far better than from the waterbus, to say nothing of the hedonistic buzz of arriving in Venice this way). The drivers tout for business in and around the arrivals hall, and will charge you in the region of L150,000/€77.47 to San Marco, for up to six people. Ordinary **car-taxis** are ranked outside the arrivals hall, and cost about L50,000/€25 to Piazzale Roma.

By road and rail

People arriving **by car** must leave their vehicle either on the main-land or try for the car parks of Venice itself – either at **Piazzale Roma** or at the ever-expanding **Tronchetto**, Europe's largest car park. Piazzale Roma is well connected with the main water-bus services (see pp.36–37), Tronchetto rather less so, though you won't have to wait more than thirty minutes for transport to the San Marco area. Prices at these two vary according to the time of year, the length of stay and the size of car, but it's never a cheap option (from about L40,000/€21 per day), and in summer the tailbacks can be horren-dous. Best to use the open-air **San Giuliano** car park at Mestre or the one at **Fusina**; both operate only in summer, at Easter and during the Carnevale, and ACTV buses connect both with central Venice.

Arriving **by train, coach or bus**, you simply get off at the end of the line. The **Piazzale Roma** bus station and **Santa Lucia** train station (not to be confused with Venezia Mestre, the last stop on the mainland) are just five minutes' walk from each other, at the top of the Canal Grande, and both are well served by vaporetto services to the core of the city. The **left-luggage** office at the train station charges L5000 per item per twelve hours; when things get frenetic, they open a separate office for larger pieces of luggage, also at the station. There are also lockers alongside platform 1, which cost L6000/€3 for six hours.

Information

The biggest **tourist office** – known as the Venice Pavilion – occupies the Palazzina del Santi, the waterfront building on the west side of the Giardinetti Reali, within a minute of the Piazza (daily 10am–6pm;

☎041.522.5150, *www.turismovenezia.it*); smaller offices operate at Calle dell'Ascension 71/c, in the corner of the Piazza's arcades (Mon–Sat: summer 9.45am–5.15pm; winter closes 3.15pm; ☎041.520.8964), the train station (daily 8am–7pm; ☎041.529.8727), in the airport arrivals area (Mon–Sat 9am–8pm), and on the Lido at Gran Viale S.M. Elisabetta 6 (May–Oct daily 9.30am–3.30pm; ☎041.526.5721). The Calle dell'Ascension 71/c office is supposed to be the city's main outlet for information on the whole Veneto, but the staff are rarely as helpful as those in the Venice Pavilion.

Venice
information is
available
online at:
www.provincia
.venezia.it/aptve

From February to October there are also tourist information booths in Campo San Felice (Cannaregio), Campo dei Frari (San Polo) and Riva dei Sette Martiri (Castello); these are all open from 10am to 1pm then from 1.30 to 5pm. The free map distributed by these offices is fine for general orientation, but not much else. Far more useful is the English–Italian magazine *Un Ospite di Venezia*, produced weekly in summer and monthly in winter, which gives up-to-date information on exhibitions, special events and vaporetto timetables – it's free from the Palazzina del Santi office, and from the receptions of the posher hotels.

City transport

Venice has two interlocking street systems – the canals and the pavements – and contrary to what you might expect, you'll be using the latter for most of the time. Apart from services #1 and the #82, which cut through the city along the Canal Grande, the water-buses skirt the city centre, connecting points on the periphery and the outer islands. In many cases the speediest way of getting around is **on foot**. Distances between major sights are sometimes tortuous but extremely short (you can cross the whole city in an hour), and once you've got your general bearings you'll find that navigation is not as daunting as it seems at first.

Water-buses

A **water-bus** is the quickest way of getting between far-flung points, and even in cases where it might be quicker to walk, a canal trip is sometimes the more pleasant way of covering the distance. The lack of clear numbering on many of the boats is confusing at first, and the ACTV map of the lagoon transport system seems at first glance to resemble the wiring diagram of a telephone exchange, but in fact the routes are pretty straightforward.

There are two basic types of boat: the **vaporetti**, which are the lumbering workhorses used on the Canal Grande stopping service and other heavily used routes, and the **motoscafi**, smaller vessels employed on routes where the volume of traffic isn't as great (at the moment this means the two 'circular routes' – #41/42 and #51/52). On both types there's a **flat-rate fare of L6000/€3.10** for any one continuous journey (unless it's a traghetto journey – see overleaf – in which case the fare is L3000/€1.65); a return ticket costs L10,000/€5.17.

Tickets are available from most landing stages, from *tabacchi*, from shops displaying the ACTV sign, at the airport, from the main tourist office, and from the two ACTV public offices – at Piazzale Roma (daily: summer 6am–midnight; winter 6am–8pm), and in Ramo dei Fuseri, close to the northwest corner of the Piazza (Mon–Fri 7.30am–6pm, Sat 7.30am–1pm). The Ramo dei Fuseri office is your best source of free up-to-date colour maps of the main routes, as the tourist offices seem to run out of them very quickly. In the remoter parts of the city, you may not be able to find anywhere to buy a ticket, particularly after working hours, when the booths at the landing stages tend to close down; tickets can be bought on board at the standard price, as long as you ask the attendant a soon as you get on board; if you delay, you could be liable for a L26,000/€13.46 spot-fine.

ACTV produces three **tourist tickets**: a **one-day** (24hr) ticket (L18,000/€9.3); a **three-day** (72hr) ticket (L35,000/€18.08), and a seven-day (168hr) ticket (L60,000/€30.99), all of which can be used on all water- and land buses within Venice. There are also 24-hour tickets for families of three, four and five (but children under the age of four can travel free), as well as a **Canal Grande**, a **Laguna Nord** (Northern Lagoon) and a **Chioggia** ticket; the last three all cost L15,000/€7.75, and allow unlimited travel along the specified routes for twelve hours.

The ACTV web
site is at
www.actv.it/

If you buy one of these tickets at the train station or Piazzale Roma it will in all likelihood be automatically **validated**, unless you specifically request a non-validated ticket; the same goes for ordinary tickets. When using a **non-validated** ticket you must validate it before embarking, by inserting it into one of the machines at the entrance to the vaporetto stop or on board the bus (the machines are painted orange); the ticket is valid from that moment, and you need to validate it just once. The **Carta Venezia**, which is advertised at many vaporetto stops and gives huge reductions on all ACTV services, is not available to non-residents.

Traghetti

There are only three bridges along the Canal Grande – at the train station, Rialto and Accademia – so the **traghetti** (gondola ferries) that cross it can be useful time-savers. Costing just L700, they are also the only cheap way of getting a ride on a gondola, albeit a stripped-down version, with none of the trimmings and no padded seats – it's *de rigueur* to stand in the traghetto gondolas. The gondola traghetti across the Canal Grande are as follows, in summer: San Marco–Salute (daily 9am–noon & 2–6pm); Santa Maria del Giglio–Salute (Mon–Sat 9am–7pm); Ca' Rezzonico–San Samuele (Mon–Sat 7.40am–1.20pm); San Tomà–Santo Stefano (Mon–Sat 7am–8.50pm; Sun 8am–7.50pm); Riva del Carbon–Riva del Vin (near Rialto; Mon–Sat 8am–2pm); Santa Sofia–Rialto (Mon–Sat 7am–8.50pm; Sun 8am–7.50pm); San Marcuola–Fondaco dei Turchi (Mon–Sat 7.30am–1.30pm); train station–San Simeone (Mon–Sat 7.45am–1.30pm). In the winter months

Water-bus Services

The **water-bus** routes operated by ACTV can seem bewilderingly complicated, and the company sometimes seems bent on maximizing confusion by altering the routes and numbers for no readily apparent reason – indeed, ACTV have been known to produce a new full-colour map of the latest network immediately prior to introducing yet more changes. As a rule, the routes displayed at each vaporetto stop are reliable, although in the outlying parishes they sometimes take a few months to get round to posting up the current map. The map handed out by the tourist offices never gives the complete picture. What follows is a run-through of the most useful services. Be warned that so many services call at San Marco, San Zaccaria, Rialto and the train station that the bus stops at these points are spread out over a long stretch of waterfront, so you might have to walk past several stops before finding the one you need. Services to San Marco will call either at plain San Marco or at the adjacent San Marco Vallaresso, which is sometimes simply referred to as Vallaresso. As a further refinement, the San Zaccaria stop, which is as close to the Basilica as the San Marco Vallaresso stop, is sometimes treated as the third San Marco stop.

At the time of going to press the waterway through the Arsenale, which has always been used by vaporetti plying the clockwise and anticlockwise routes around the centre of Venice and out as far as Murano, was closed. This closure has necessitated the diversion of the circular routes round the eastern edge of Venice, and has been in effect for so long that a new vaporetto stop – San Pietro – has been built to serve the island of that name. Or rather, it hasn't. The stop appears on ACTV maps, but after more than two years it still doesn't exist. Opinion is divided as to whether it will be completed before the work on the Arsenale, and whether the clearing of the Arsenale canal will be followed by the restoration of the routes through the Arsenale.

#1: The perversely named *accelerato* is the slowest of the water-buses, the workhorse of the system, and the one you'll use most often; it's also one of the very few routes that seems to be exempt from alterations. It starts at the Piazzale Roma, calls at every stop on the Canal Grande except San Samuele, works its way along the San Marco waterfront to Sant'Elena, then goes over to the Lido. The #1 runs every 20min between 5 and 6.30am, every 10min between 6.30am and 9.45pm, and every 20min between 9.45 and 11.45pm. For the night service, see #N.

#82: This service is the quickest means of getting from the train or bus station down the Canal Grande to San Marco, as it makes fewer stops than the #1. Its

it's common for traghetti to cease operating earlier than the times indicated above, or even to be suspended altogether.

In addition to these, some vaporetti and motoscafi operate as traghetti across the Canal Grande and over to the nearer islands: for example, if you want to go from San Zaccaria over to San Giorgio Maggiore, you need only pay the lower traghetto fare of L3000. If your journey is a short single-stop trip across a body of water, a traghetto fare almost certainly applies, even if it's not shown on the tariff list on the ticket booth.

Gondolas

*For more on
gondolas, see
p.111*

The **gondola**, once Venice's chief form of transport, has become an adjunct of the tourist industry and the city's biggest cliché. That said,

clockwise route takes it from San Zaccaria to San Giorgio Maggiore, Giudecca (Zitelle, Redentore and Palanca), Záttere, San Basilio, Sacca Fisola, Tronchetto, Piazzale Roma, the train station, then down the Canal Grande (usually calling at Rialto, Sant'Angelo, San Tomà, San Samuele and Accademia) to San Marco (Vallaresso); the anti-clockwise version calls at the same stops. The service runs every 10min from 6am to 8.30pm, then every 20min until 11pm, though the section from San Tomà to San Marco runs only every 20min through the day. Earlier in the morning (5–8am) and later in the evening (after 8.30pm) there is a more restricted service along this latter section. For the night service see #N.

#41/42: The circular service, running right round the core of Venice, with a short detour at the northern end to San Michele and Murano. The #41 travels anticlockwise, the #42 clockwise and both run every 20min from 6.30am until around 8pm, after which the service simply shuttles between Murano and Venice every 10–20min until around 11.30pm.

#51/52: Similar to the #41/42, this route also circles Venice, but heads out to the Lido (rather than Murano) at the easternmost end of the circle. The #51 runs anti-clockwise, the #52 clockwise, and both run fast through the Giudecca canal, stopping only at Záttere and Santa Marta between San Zaccaria and Piazzale Roma. Both run every 20min for most of the day.

In the early morning and late evening (4.30–6am & 8.30–11pm) the #51 doesn't do a complete lap of the city – instead it departs every 20 min from Fondamenta Nove and proceeds via the train station to the Lido, where it terminates; similarly, from 7–11pm the #52 (which starts operating at 6am) shuttles between the Lido and Fondamente Nove in the opposite direction, and from 11pm to around 1.30am goes no farther than the train station.

#12: for most of the day the #12 runs every half hour from Fondamente Nove (hourly early in the morning and evenings), calling first at Murano-Faro before heading on to Mazzorbo, Burano and Torcello (sometimes calling at Torcello before Burano).

#N: This night service (11.30pm–4.30am) is a selective fusion of the #1 and #82 routes, running from the Lido to Giardini, San Zaccaria, San Marco (Vallaresso), Canal Grande (Accademia, San Samuele, San Tomà, Rialto, Ca' d'Oro, San Stae, San Marcuola), train station, Piazzale Roma, Tronchetto, Sacca Fisola, San Basilio, Záttere, Giudecca (Palanca, Redentore and Zitelle), San Giorgio and San Zaccaria – then retracing its route. It runs along the whole of the route in both directions roughly every 30min, and along the Rialto to Tronchetto part every 20min. Another night service connects Venice with the Murano stops, running to and from Fondamente Nove every 30min between midnight and 4am.

the gondola is an astonishingly graceful craft, perfectly designed for negotiating the tortuous canals, and an hour's slow voyage through the city can give you a wholly new perspective on the place. To hire one costs L120,000/€62 per fifty minutes for up to six passengers, rising to L150,000/€77.47 between 8pm and 8am; you pay an extra L60,000/€30.99 for every additional 25 minutes, or L75,000/€38.74 from 8pm to 8am. Further hefty surcharges will be levied should you require the services of an on-board accordionist or tenor – and a surprising number of people do, despite the strangulated voices and hackneyed repertoire of most of the aquatic Carusos. Even though the tariff is set by the local authorities, it's been known for some gondoliers to try to extort even higher rates than these – if you do decide to go for a ride, establish the charge before setting off.

To minimize the chances of being ripped off by a private individual making a few million lire on the side, only take a boat from one of the following **official gondola stands**: west of the Piazza at Calle Vallaresso, Campo San Moisè or Campo Santa Maria del Giglio; immediately north of the Piazza at Bacino Orseolo; on the Molo, in front of the Palazzo Ducale; outside the *Danieli* hotel on Riva degli Schiavoni; at the train station; at Piazzale Roma; at Campo Santa Sofia, near the Ca' d'Oro; at San Tomà, to the east of the Frari; or by the Rialto Bridge on Riva Carbon. Your gondolier will assume that you'll want to be taken along the Canal Grande or across the Bacino di San Marco, but you'll probably not be making the best use of the opportunity if you opt for one of these: for one thing, these major waterways look much the same from a vaporetto as from a gondola; and for another, the gondola will tend to get bashed around by the wash from the bigger boats. Better to choose a quarter of the city that has struck you as being particularly alluring, head for the gondola stand that's nearest to it, and ask to be taken there – a gondola displaces so little water, and the gondoliers are so skilful, that there's hardly a canal in the city that they can't negotiate.

Taxis

Venice's **water-taxis** are sleek and speedy vehicles that can penetrate all but the shallowest of the city's canals. Unfortunately their use is confined to all but the owners of the deepest pockets, for they are possibly the most expensive form of taxi in western Europe: the base rate is L27,000/€14 for seven minutes, then L500/€0.24 for every extra fifteen seconds. All sorts of additional surcharges are levied as well – L3100/€1.55 for each extra person if there are more than four people in the party; L2200/€1.04 for each piece of luggage over 50cm long; L8500/€4.20 for a ride between 10pm and 7am. There are three ways of getting a taxi: go to one of the main stands (in front of the Piazzetta and at the airport), find one in the process of disgorging its passengers, or call one by phone (☎041.522.2303, 041.522.8538 or 041.523.2473). If you use the phone, the taxi will have L8000 on the clock when it arrives.

Museums and monuments

In an attempt to make sure that tourists go to see more than just the Palazzo Ducale and San Marco, the entry charges for several museums have been combined in one ticket called I **Musei di Piazza San Marco**. Costing L18,000/€9.30, the ticket allows one visit to each of the following attractions before the end of the year in which you buy the ticket: Palazzo Ducale, Museo Correr, Museo Archeologico, Biblioteca Marciana, Palazzo Mocenigo, Museo del Merletto (Burano) and Museo del Vetro (Murano). It's available at the Correr and Palazzo Ducale, each of which can be visited only with the Musei di San Marco ticket (the Museo Archeologico and Biblioteca

Marciana are now annexes of the Correr, and thus also require a combined ticket); at the other places you have the option of paying an entry charge just for that attraction.

In addition, thirteen churches that charge for entry (either to the whole structure or just part – usually the sacristy) are now part of the **Chorus Pass** scheme, whereby a L15,000/€7.75 ticket allows one visit to each of the churches over a one-year period. The individual entrance fee at each of the participating churches is L3000/€1.55, and all the churches (except for the variants given below) observe the same opening hours: Monday to Saturday 10am to 5pm, and Sunday 1 to 5pm (except in July and August, when all except the Frari are closed to tourists). The churches involved are: Santa Maria del Giglio; Santo Stefano; Santa Maria Formosa; Santa Maria dei Miracoli; the Frari (Mon–Sat 9am–6pm, Sun 1–6pm); San Polo; San Giacomo dell'Orio; San Stae; Sant'Alvise; Madonna dell'Orto; San Pietro di Castello; Redentore; and San Sebastiano (Mon–Sat 10am–5pm, Sun 3–5pm – but often closed Sun in winter).

The opening hours listed below are the latest available times of the major tourist museums and monuments, but bear in mind that they are prone to sudden, inexplicable alterations, especially in winter, when afternoon opening hours are frequently truncated.

An asterisk after the price indicates that a concessionary rate is available for students who can prove their status; under-12s are entitled to reductions at nearly all attractions, provided they are accompanied by an adult. Visitors from EU countries who can prove they are aged under 18 or over 65 are entitled to free admission at the city's state-owned museums – ie the Accademia, Ca' d'Oro, Museo Archeologico and Museo Orientale.

Accademia Mon 8.15am–2pm, Tues–Sun 8.15am–7.15pm; late opening in summer (hours are variable – usually Tues–Sat until 10pm, Sun until 8pm); L12,000/€6.20; ☎041.522.2247.

Basilica di San Marco ☎041.522.5697:

  Museo Marciano and Loggia dei Cavalli daily 9.45am–5pm (4pm in winter); L3000/€1.54.

  Pala d'Oro summer Mon–Sat 9.45am–5pm, Sun 2–5pm; winter closes 4pm; L3000/€1.54.

  Tesoro (Treasury) summer Mon–Sat 9.45am–5pm, Sun 2–5pm; winter closes 4pm; L4000/€2.07.

Ca' d'Oro Mon 8.15am–2pm, Tues–Sat 8.15am–7.15pm; L6000/€3.10; ☎041.523.8790.

Campanile di San Giorgio Maggiore daily 9.30am–noon & 2.30–6pm; L3000; ☎041.522.7827.

Campanile di San Marco daily 9am–7pm; L8000/€4.16; ☎041.522.4064.

Campanile di Torcello April–Oct daily 11am–4.30pm; L4000/€2.07; ☎041.270.2464.

Cattedrale di Torcello daily: April–Oct 10.30am–5.30pm; Nov–March 10am–4.30pm; L5000/€2.58; ☎041.270.2464.

Collezione Peggy Guggenheim 10am–6pm; April–Oct open till 10pm Sat; closed Tues; L12,000/€6.20*; ☎041.520.6288.

Convento di San Francesco del Deserto daily 9–11am & 3–5pm; donation; ☎041.528.6863.

Museums and monuments

Frari Mon–Sat 9am–6pm, Sun 1–6pm; L3000/€1.54; ☎041.522.2637.

Galleria di Palazzo Cini summer Tues–Sun 10am–1pm & 2–6pm; L5000/€2.58; ☎041.521.0755.

Monastero Mekhitarista (San Lazzaro degli Armeni) daily 3–5pm; L10,000/€5.16; ☎041.526.0104.

Museo Archeologico same hours and ticket as Museo Correr; ☎041.522.5978.

Museo Civico Correr daily: April–Oct 9am–7pm (last tickets 5.30pm); Nov–March 9am–5pm (last tickets 3.30pm) entrance with the I Musei di San Marco ticket, L18,000/€9.30*; ☎041.552.5625.

Museo d'Arte Moderna (Ca' Pésaro) Closed for restoration but previously open Tues–Sun 10am–5pm; ☎041.721.127.

Museo del Settecento Veneziano (Ca' Rezzonico) Usually open: summer 10am–5pm; winter 9am–4pm; closed Fri; L12,000/€6.20*; ☎041.520.4036.

Museo Diocesiano daily 10.30am–12.30pm; free – but donation requested; ☎041.522.9166.

Museo di Dipinti Sacri Bizantini Mon–Sat 9am–12.30pm & 1.30–4.15pm; Sun 10am– 5pm; L7000/€3.62; ☎041.522.6581.

Museo di Storia Naturale Closed for restoration but previously open Tues–Sun 9am–1pm; L5000*; ☎041.524.0885.

Museo di Torcello April–Oct Tues–Sun 10.30am–5pm, Nov–March 10am–4.30pm; L3000/€1.55*; ☎041.730.761.

Museo Ebraico 10am–5.30pm; closed Sat; L5000/€2.58; ☎041.715.359.

Museo Fortuny Closed for restoration but previously open Tues–Sun 10am–6pm; L6000; ☎041.520.0995.

Museo Goldoni Closed for restoration but previously open Mon–Thurs 8.30am–1.30pm, free; ☎041.523.6353.

Museo Orientale (Ca' Pésaro) Tues–Sun 8.15am–2pm; L4000/€2.07; ☎041.524.1173.

Museo Storico Navale Mon–Fri 8.45am–1.30pm, Sat 8.45am–1pm, plus Tues & Thurs 2.30–5pm April–Oct; L3000/€1.54; ☎041.520.0276.

Museo Vetrario (Murano) summer 10am–5pm, winter 10am–4pm; closed Wed; L8000/€4.13*; ☎041.739.586.

Oratorio dei Crociferi April–Oct Thurs–Sat 10am–1pm; L3000/€1.54; ☎041.270.2464.

Palazzo Ducale daily: April–Oct 9am–7pm (last tickets 5.30pm); Nov–March 9am–5pm; (last tickets 3.30pm) entrance is with the I Musei di San Marco ticket, L18,000/€9.30*; ☎041.522.4951.

Palazzo Mocenigo Tues–Sun: April–Oct 10am–5pm; Nov–March 10am–4pm; L3000/€1.54 or I Musei di San Marco ticket*; ☎041.721.798.

Pinacoteca Querini-Stampalia Tues–Sun 10am–1pm & 3–6pm, Fri & Sat closes 10pm; L12,000/€6.20*; ☎041.271.1411.

Scuola dei Merletti di Burano April–Oct 10am–5pm; Nov–March 10am–4pm; closed Tues; L8000/€4.13*; ☎041.730.034.

Scuola di San Giorgio degli Schiavoni Tues–Sat 9.30am–12.30pm & 3.30–6.30pm, Sun 10am–12.30pm; L5000/€2.58*; ☎041.522.8828.

Scuola Grande dei Carmini Mon–Sat 9am–noon & 3–6pm; L8000/€4.16*; ☎041.528.9420.

Scuola Grande di San Rocco daily: summer 9am–5.30pm; winter 10am–4pm; L9000/€4.62 *; ☎041.523.4864.

Chapter 1

San Marco

Enclosed by the lower loop of the Canal Grande, the sestiere of San Marco – a rectangle smaller than 1000m by 500m – has been the nucleus of Venice from the start of the city's existence. When its founders decamped from the coastal town of Malamocco to settle on the safer islands of the inner lagoon, the area now known as the **Piazza San Marco** was where the first rulers built their citadel – the **Palazzo Ducale** – and it was here that they established their most important church – the **Basilica di San Marco**. Over the succeeding centuries the Basilica evolved into the most ostentatiously rich church in Christendom, and the Palazzo Ducale grew to accommodate and celebrate a system of government that endured for longer than any other republican regime in Europe. Meanwhile, the setting for these two great edifices developed into a public space so dignified that no other square in the city was thought fit to bear the name "piazza" – all other Venetian squares are campi or campielli.

Nowadays the Piazza is what keeps the city solvent. Fifty percent of Venice's visitors make a beeline for this spot, spend a few hours and a few thousand lire here, then head for home without staying for even one night. For those who do hang around, San Marco has multitudinous ways of easing the cash from the pockets: the plushest hotels are concentrated in this sestiere; the most elegant and exorbitant cafés spill out onto the pavement from the Piazza's arcades; the most extravagantly priced seafood is served in this area's restaurants; and the swankiest shops in Venice line the Piazza and the streets radiating from it – interspersed with dozens of hugely profitable souvenir suppliers.

And yet, small though this sestiere is, it harbours plenty of refuges from the assaults of commerce. Even within the Piazza you can escape the crush, as the **Museo Correr** is rarely crowded and the excellent **archeological museum** barely sees a soul. The Renaissance church of **San Salvador** – only a few minutes' walk from the Piazza – and the Gothic **Santo Stefano** are both magnificent and comparatively neglected buildings, while **San Moisè**, **Santa Maria**

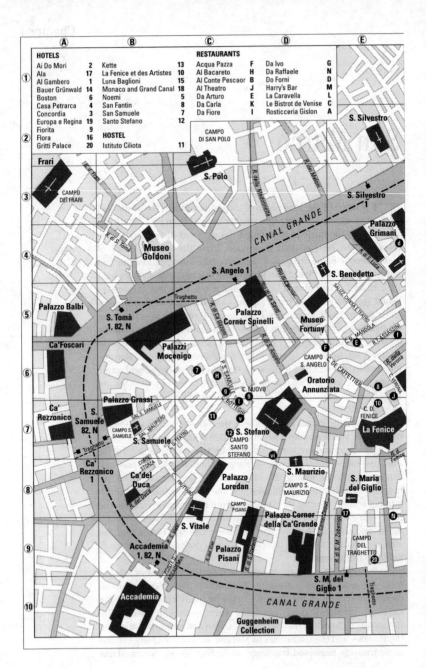

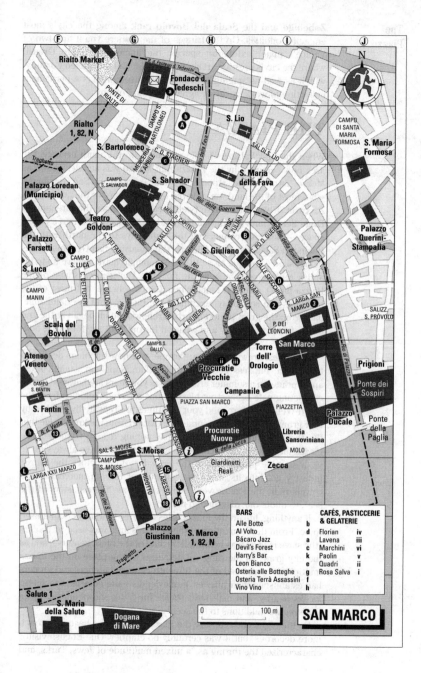

SAN MARCO

BARS

Alle Botte	b
Al Volto	d
Bácaro Jazz	a
Devil's Forest	c
Harry's Bar	k
Leon Bianco	e
Osteria alle Botteghe	g
Osteria Terrà Assassini	f
Vino Vino	h

CAFÉS, PASTICCERIE
& GELATERIE

Florian	iv
Lavena	iii
Marchini	vi
Paolin	v
Quadri	ii
Rosa Salva	i

0   100 m

Zobenigo and the **Scala del Bovolo** rank among the city's most engaging oddities. On the fringes of the sestiere you'll find two of Venice's major exhibition spaces: the immense **Palazzo Grassi**, where the city's prestige art shows are held, and the **Museo Fortuny**, which as well as staging special events also contains a permanent collection of work by the designer Mariano Fortuny.

THE PIAZZA

When the first Palazzo Ducale was built, in the ninth century, the area now occupied by the **Piazza San Marco** was an islet known as Morso. Two churches stood here – San Teodoro and San Geminiano – but most of the land was covered by the orchard of the nuns of San Zaccaria. It was in the late twelfth century, under the direction of **Doge Sebastiano Ziani**, that the land was transformed into a public space – the canal connecting the waterways to the north with the Bacino di San Marco was filled in, the canalside San Geminiano was demolished (a plaque close to the Campanile marks where it stood) and a replacement built at the far end. The general shape of the Piazza hasn't changed much since Ziani's scheme, but most of the buildings you see today, excluding the Basilica and the Campanile, date from the great period of urban renewal which began at the end of the fifteenth century and went on for much of the following hundred years.

"The finest drawing room in Europe" was how Napoleon described the Piazza, but less genteel phrases than Napoleon's might seem appropriate on a summer afternoon, as your ears are battered by the competing café orchestras blasting out selected melodies from the Lloyd-Webber oeuvre, and your sightlines are repeatedly blocked by tour groups. You can take some consolation from the knowledge that the throngs and the racket are maintaining a long tradition. The Piazza has always been crowded, and foreigners have always made up a sizeable proportion of the crowds – long before the tourist industry got into its stride, the swarms of foreign merchants and travellers in the Piazza were being cursed as "the monsters of the sea", to quote one disgruntled native.

If anything, life on the Piazza is less diverse nowadays than it used to be. From the foundation of the city, this area was used by traders (the slave market was here until the end of the ninth century), and as the city grew, so the range of activities taking place on the Piazza multiplied: by the end of the fifteenth century butchers and grocers had established their pitches, moneylenders and notaries had set up kiosks nearby, and makeshift stages for freak shows and masques were regular additions to the scene.

By the eighteenth century the Piazza might have become a touch more decorous, but it was certainly no emptier. One English visitor characterized the throng as "a mixed multitude of Jews, Turks, and

Christians; lawyers, knaves, and pick-pockets; mountebanks, old women, and physicians; women of quality, with masks; strumpets barefaced . . . a jumble of senators, citizens, gondoliers, and people of every character and condition". Jugglers, puppeteers, sweet-sellers, fortune-tellers and a host of other stallholders seem to have been almost perennial features of the landscape, while Venetian high society passed much of the day in one or other of the Piazza's dozen **coffee shops** – Europe's first *bottega del caffè* opened here in 1683, and within a few decades Goldoni had created a play in which the hero, a café owner, declared "my profession is necessary to the glory of the city". During the Austrian occupation of 1814–66 the coffee houses were drawn into the social warfare between the city's two hostile camps. Establishments used by the occupying troops were shunned by all patriotic Venetians – *Quadri* became an Austrian coffee house, whereas *Florian* remained Venetian. Certain prominent Venetians even went to the length of shunning the Piazza whenever the Austrian band was playing, a policy that entailed a thrice-weekly withdrawal from the centre of the city.

The Piazza remains the pivot of social life in Venice. Contrary to first appearances, today's customers at the tables of *Florian* and *Quadri* – the only eighteenth-century survivors – or at the equally intimidating *Lavena*, the favourite haunt of Richard Wagner, are almost as likely to be Venetians as they are to be outsiders. Wander through at midday and there'll be clusters of friends taking the air and chatting away their lunch-hour; the evening *passeggiata*

Piazza festivities

The Piazza's brightest splash of colour comes from the **Carnevale**. Though gangs of masked and wildly costumed revellers turn every quarter of the city into a week-long open-air party, all the action tends to drift towards the Piazza, and the grand finale of the whole proceedings is a huge Shrove Tuesday ball in the square, with fireworks over the Bacino di San Marco.

Mass entertainments used to be far more frequent, taking over the Piazza on feast days and whenever a plausible excuse could be found. From the twelfth century onwards pig hunts and bullfights were frequent spectacles, but from around the beginning of the seventeenth century the authorities became increasingly embarrassed by these sanguinary pursuits, and they were relegated to other squares in the city. The bloodsports were succeeded by gymnastic performances known as **Labours of Hercules**, in which teams of young men formed human pyramids and towers on platforms that were often no more than a couple of planks resting on a pair of barrels. Military victories, ducal elections and visits from heads of state were commonly celebrated with **tournaments** and pageants: a three-day tournament was held in the Piazza in 1364 after the recapture of Crete, with guest appearances by a gang of English knights on their way to create bedlam in the Holy Land, and in 1413 the election of Doge Tommaso Mocenigo was marked by a tournament that was watched by 70,000 people. Mocenigo also initiated the post-electoral ritual of carrying the new doge shoulder-high round the Piazza while he distributed coins to the populace.

The major religious festivals were the occasion for lavish celebrations, the most spectacular of which was the **Procession of Corpus Domini**, a performance meticulously recorded in a painting by Gentile Bellini in the Accademia. Regrettably, not all of Venice's holy processions achieved the solemn dignity captured in Bellini's picture – in 1513 one stately progress went wrong when a row broke out over which group had the right to enter the Piazza first, a disagreement that rapidly escalated into an almighty punch-up.

But no festivities were more extravagant than those of **Ascension Day**, and it was in the wake of Ascension that the Piazza most closely resembled the modern tourist enclave. From the twelfth century until the fall of the Republic, the day itself was marked in Venice by the ceremony of **The Marriage of Venice to the Sea**, a ritual which inaugurated a short season of feasts and sideshows in the Piazza, culminating in a trade fair called the **Fiera della Sensa** (*Sensa* being dialect for Ascension). The Fiera began in 1180, when, as a result of Pope Alexander III's proclamation that an indulgence would be granted to anyone who prayed in San Marco during the year, the city was flooded with pilgrims. Before long it became a cornucopia of luxury commodities, and by the last century of the Republic's existence it had grown into a fifteen-day fair that filled the Piazza with temporary wooden shops and arcades.

inevitably involves a circuit of the Piazza; and even at midnight you'll almost certainly see a few groups rounding off the day with a stroll across the flagstones.

A note on the ubiquitous **pigeons** – you can choose between three improbable stories about their origins: either they came here with the refugees from Attila's army; or they're the descendants of caged birds given to a doge's wife in an attempt to cheer her up; or they're the distant relatives of pigeons released by successive doges during Holy Week, in a ceremony commemorating the return of Noah's dove. Whatever their ancestry, they used to be fed daily by a council official, who was rumoured to dispense seed that had been laced with avian contraceptive; recently there have been moves to ban the selling of bird-food on the Piazza, in an attempt to reduce the health hazard presented by the disease-ridden pigeons.

The Basilica di San Marco

San Marco is the most exotic of Europe's cathedrals, and it has always provoked strong reactions. To Herman Melville it was beautiful and insubstantial – as though "the Grand Turk had pitched his pavilion here for a summer's day"; Mark Twain adored it for its "entrancing, tranquilizing, soul-satisfying ugliness"; Herbert Spencer found it "a fine sample of barbaric architecture"; and to John Ruskin it was the most gorgeous of holy places, a "treasure-heap . . . a confusion of delight".

The Basilica is certainly confusing, increasingly so as you come nearer and the details emerge, but some knowledge of the building's background helps bring a little order out of the chaos.

The history of the Basilica

All over Venice you see images of the lion of Saint Mark holding a book on which is carved the text "Pax tibi, Marce evangelista meus. Hic requiescet corpus tuum" ("Peace be with you Mark, my Evangelist. Here shall your body rest"). These supposedly are the words with which Saint Mark was greeted by an angel who appeared to him on the night he took shelter in the lagoon on his way back to Rome. This **legend of Saint Mark's annunciation** was adopted as fact in order to overcome the discrepancy between the first Venetians' notion of their spiritual pedigree – as successors of the shattered Roman Empire and as the first state to be founded as a Christian community – and the inglorious fact that the settlement of the lagoon islands had begun as a scramble to get out of the path of Attila the Hun. Having thus assured themselves of the sacred ordination of their city, the proto-Venetians duly went about fulfilling the angelic prophecy. In **828** a pair of merchants called Buono Tribuno da Malamocco and Rustico da Torcello **stole the body of Saint Mark** from its tomb in Alexandria and, having smuggled the corpse past the Muslim guards by hiding it in a consignment of pork (or so the story goes), brought it back to Venice and presented it to the doge.

Work began immediately on a shrine to house the relic; modelled on Constantinople's Church of the Twelve Apostles, it was consecrated in **832**. In 976 a riot provoked by the tyrannous Doge Pietro

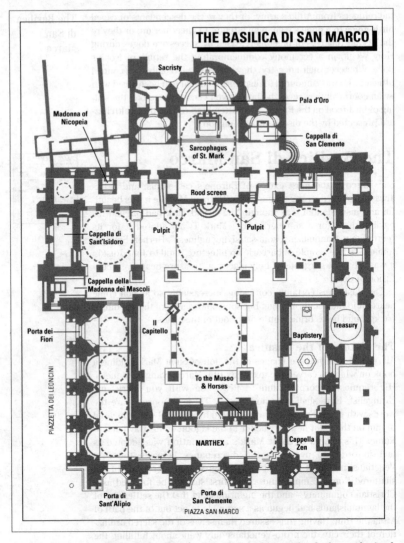

THE BASILICA DI SAN MARCO

Sacristy

Pala d'Oro

Madonna of
Nicopeia

Cappella di
San Clemente

Sarcophagus
of St. Mark

Rood screen

Cappella di
Sant'Isidoro

Pulpit

Pulpit

Cappella della
Madonna dei Mascoli

Treasury

Porta dei
Fiori

Il
Capitello

Baptistery

PIAZZETTA DEI LEONCINI

To the Museo
& Horses

Cappella
Zen

NARTHEX

Porta di
Sant'Alipio

Porta di
San Clemente

PIAZZA SAN MARCO

Candiano IV reduced the Palazzo Ducale to a pile of ashes and ruined the Basilica too; Candiano was murdered at the church's entrance. A replica was built in its place, to be in turn superseded by a **third church in 1063–94**. It is this third Basilica, embellished by the succeeding centuries, that you see now.

The combination of ancient structure and later decorations is, to a great extent, what makes San Marco so bewildering: for example, the Gothic pointed arches and carvings on the roof-line of the main

facade (mostly early fifteenth-century) are not what you'd expect to
see on top of squat, rounded Byzantine arches, and the garish sev-
enteenth- to nineteenth-century mosaics that dominate this front
must be the worst aesthetic mismatch in all Italy. But the picture is
made yet more complicated by the addition of ornaments which were
looted from abroad, are sometimes older than the building itself and
in some cases have nothing to do with the Church. Into the last category fall two of the most famous features of the exterior: the porphyry figures of the **Tetrarchs** and the **horses of San Marco**.

The reason for the presence of these seemingly profane decorations is simple: the doge was the lieutenant of Saint Mark, as the
pope was the lieutenant of Saint Peter – therefore anything that glorified Venice was also to the greater glory of the Evangelist. Every
trophy that the doge added to the Basilica was proof of Venice's secular might and so of the spiritual power of Saint Mark. Conversely,
the saint was invoked to sanctify political actions and state rituals –
the doge's investiture was consecrated in the church, and military
commanders received their commissions at its altar.

As can be imagined, the Venetians' conception of their city as the
state with the purest lineage, and the often cynical use they made of
this self-image, was not conducive to good relations with the Vatican.
"They want to appear as Christian before the world," commented
Pope Pius II, "but in reality they never think of God and, but for the
state, which they regard as a deity, they hold nothing sacred." The
Basilica is an emblem of the city's maverick position, for at no time
in the existence of the Venetian Republic was San Marco the cathedral of Venice – it was the doge's chapel, and only became the cathedral in 1807, when the French moved the Patriarch of Venice here
from San Pietro di Castello. Until the eighteenth century it was common practice for the doge to advertise his proprietorship by hanging
his coat of arms on the front of the building.

In effect, the Venetians ran a semi-autonomous branch of the
Roman Church: the Patriarch of Venice could convene a synod only
with the doge's permission, bishops were nominated by the Senate,
priests were appointed by a ballot of the parish and had to be of
Venetian birth, and the Inquisition was supervised by the Republic's
own, less draconian, doctrinal office. Inevitably, there were direct
clashes with the papacy; for the story of the most serious, the interdict of 1606, see p.159.

Although San Marco is open from 6.30am on most days, tourists are asked
not to enter before 9.30am; on most days the Basilica closes at 5.30pm.
Admission fees totalling L10,000/€5.15 are charged for certain parts of
the church. Sections of the Basilica will almost certainly be under restoration or closed off for some other reason; though restoration of the
Cappella Zen and Baptistery has at last been completed there seems little
prospect of either being reopened in the near future.

The exterior of the Basilica

Shortly after becoming the architectural custodian (*Proto Magister*) of San Marco in 1529, Jacopo Sansovino set about strengthening the building and replacing some of its deteriorating decoration, a procedure that resulted in the removal of around thirty percent of the church's mosaics. On the main facade, the only mosaic to survive this and subsequent restorations is the scene above the **Porta di Sant'Alipio** (far left) – *The Arrival of the Body of St Mark*. Made around 1260, it features the earliest known image of the Basilica. In the lunette below the mosaic are fourteenth-century bas-reliefs of the symbols of the Evangelists; the panels comprising the door's architrave are fifth-century; and the door itself dates from 1300. The next door is from the same period, and the reliefs on the arch are thirteenth-century; the mosaic of *Venice Worshipping St Mark*, however, is an eighteenth-century effort.

The worst and the best aspects of the facade are to be found above the **central entrance**: the former being the nineteenth-century mosaic of the *Last Judgement*, the latter the **Romanesque carvings** of the arches. Begun with the innermost arch in the 1220s and completed about a century later, these are among the outstanding sculptural works of their time, but about one visitor in a thousand spares them a glance, despite their recently restored sparkle. **Inner arch**: underside – animals, Earth and Ocean; outer face – fighting figures (perhaps intended as the savage antithesis of Venetian civilization). **Middle arch**: underside – the labours of the months and the signs of the zodiac; outer – Virtues and Beatitudes. **Outer arch**: under – the trades of Venice; outer – Christ and prophets. The carved panel in the lunette, *The Dream of St Mark*, is also thirteenth-century, but the door – known as the **Porta di San Clemente** – is 700 years older, and is thought to have been a gift from the Byzantine emperor Alexius Comnenus.

The fourth portal follows closely the model of the second; the mosaic of the fifth is similarly an eighteenth-century job, but the marble decoration is a mixture of eleventh- to thirteenth-century carvings, except for the architrave panel of *Christ Blessing*, a remnant of the second Basilica, built after the 976 fire.

Of the six marble panels between the entrance arches, only the Roman bas-relief of *Hercules and the Erymanthean Boar* isn't a twelfth- or thirteenth-century piece. The terrace running across the facade above them was the spot from which the doge and his guests watched the festivities in the Piazza; the mosaics on this level all date from the early seventeenth century, and the huge blank window was occupied by a Byzantine screen until a fire in 1419 destroyed everything except the four half-columns. The roof-line's encrustation of Gothic pinnacles, kiosks, figures and ornamental motifs was begun in 1385 under the direction of the **Dalle Masegne** family, the leading sculptors in Venice at that period, and was continued through the early part of the following century by various Tuscan and Lombard artists, of whom **Niccolò Lamberti** and his son **Pietro** were the most proficient.

To see the real **horses of San Marco** you have to go into the church – these are modern replicas.

The north and south facades

In the 1860s and 1870s an extensive and controversial **restoration** of the Basilica was begun, a scheme which would probably have finished with the rearrangement of the main facade. An international protest campaign, supported by Ruskin, forced the abandonment of the project soon after it had reached the Piazzetta corner of the west front, and the damage caused to that section was largely reversed in later years. The **north and south facades**, though, were altered irrevocably by the restorers, who replaced the old polychromatic marble panels with badly fitted sheets of grey stone, creating an effect described by an English stonemason in 1880 as resembling "a dirty lime wash on a white plastered wall".

The **north side** of San Marco, the last to be completed (in the first half of the thirteenth century), is studded with panels from a variety of sources – they include a seventh- or eighth-century relief showing the Apostles as twelve lambs, and a tenth-century piece illustrating Alexander the Great's mythical attempt to reach heaven by harnessing a pair of griffons to his chariot. The entrance on this side, the **Porta dei Fiori**, is thirteenth-century (the tomb of **Daniele Manin** is a bit further on); and most of the sculpture on the upper part is by the **Lamberti**.

Jutting out between the **south facade** and the entrance to the Palazzo Ducale is the wall of the treasury, thought by some to be a remnant of the **first palace of the doges** and the chamber in which the body of Saint Mark was first placed after its arrival in Venice. The screen fragments (*plutei*) set into the walls date from the ninth to the eleventh centuries.

Sometimes the heads of freshly dispatched villains were mounted on the **Pietra del Bando**, the stump of porphyry against the corner of the Basilica; a more benign service was done on the day the Campanile collapsed, when it stopped the avalanche of bricks from hitting the church. Its routine use was as one of the two stones from which the laws of the Republic were proclaimed (the other is at the Rialto). The stone was brought back from Acre in 1256, following Venice's victory over the Genoese there; the two square pillars near to it – Syrian works dating from the fifth century – were filched from Constantinople during the Fourth Crusade. High on the Basilica's facade, above the two pillars, a thirteenth-century mosaic of the Madonna is flanked by two lanterns that are kept perpetually lit, in observance of the vow of a mariner who was led to safety across the stormy waters of the lagoon by a light burning on the Piazzetta.

A number of tales centre on the group of porphyry figures set into the angle of the treasury. Thomas Coryat tells a version in which four Albanian brothers plotted against each other for possession of the cargo their ship was carrying, and ended up poisoning each other. But the most popular version turns them into a gang of Saracens who raided the Treasury and then contrived to murder each other in a squabble over the spoils – hence, like the figures on the Torre dell'Orologio, they're often nicknamed "The Moors". More properly they're known as the **Tetrarchs**, as in all likelihood they're a fourth-century Egyptian work depicting Diocletian and the three colleagues with whom he ruled the unravelling Roman Empire – peculiar adornments for a church, bearing in mind Diocletian's notoriety as a persecutor of Christians.

The narthex

*Given the
enormous
complexity of
the Basilica's
mosaics, this
account is
necessarily
sketchy; if you
want a more
thorough but
portable guide,
go for* The
Mosaics of St
Mark's *in the
Electa Artistic
Guides series –
recommended
bookshops are
listed on
p.282.*

From the Piazza you pass into a vestibule called the **narthex**, which once, before the partitioning of the baptistery and the Cappella Zen, bracketed the entire west end of the church. The intricately patterned stonework of the narthex **floor** is mostly eleventh- and twelfth-century, and one fragment of it is especially significant: the small white lozenge set into the floor in front of the main entrance is said to mark the spot on which Emperor Frederick Barbarossa knelt before Pope Alexander III on August 23, 1177. Prior to this, the empire and the papacy had been at each other's throats, and this symbolic reconciliation in the portal of San Marco clinched one of Venice's greatest diplomatic triumphs.

Most of the **mosaics** on the domes and arches constitute a series of **Old Testament scenes** which complements the New Testament iconography in the main body of the church. Predominantly thirteenth-century, the mosaics were begun in the dome on the far right, with scenes from Genesis (c.1230 but much restored, as indicated by the inset red lines), and executed in a continuous series right round the narthex. The Genesis dome is followed by: **first arch** – *Noah and the Flood* (note the preferential treatment handed out to the lion); in the **bay in front of main door** – double tier of niches containing the **oldest mosaics in San Marco**, a group showing *The Madonna with Apostles and Evangelists* (c.1065); **second arch** – end of *Life of Noah*, and a strikingly vivid *Tower of Babel*; **second dome** – *Story of Abraham* and four tondi of *Prophets*; **third arch** – *SS. Alipio and Simon Stylites* and tondo of *Justice*; **third, fourth and fifth domes** – *Story of Joseph*; **sixth dome** – *Story of Moses*.

Three doges and one dogaressa have tombs in the narthex. That of **Vitale Falier**, the doge who consecrated the Basilica in 1094, two years before his death, is the **oldest funerary monument in Venice** – it's at the base of the first arch. The others are of Felicità, wife of Doge Vitale Michiel (1101; second arch), Doge Bartolomeo Gradenigo (1342; northwest corner of narthex, beyond third dome) and Doge

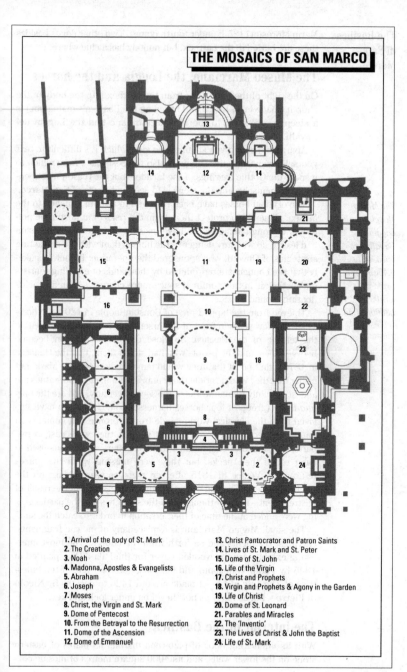

THE MOSAICS OF SAN MARCO

1. Arrival of the body of St. Mark
2. The Creation
3. Noah
4. Madonna, Apostles & Evangelists
5. Abraham
6. Joseph
7. Moses
8. Christ, the Virgin and St. Mark
9. Dome of Pentecost
10. From the Betrayal to the Resurrection
11. Dome of the Ascension
12. Dome of Emmanuel
13. Christ Pantocrator and Patron Saints
14. Lives of St. Mark and St. Peter
15. Dome of St. John
16. Life of the Virgin
17. Christ and Prophets
18. Virgin and Prophets & Agony in the Garden
19. Life of Christ
20. Dome of St. Leonard
21. Parables and Miracles
22. The 'Inventio'
23. The Lives of Christ & John the Baptist
24. Life of St. Mark

Marin Morosini (1253; under fourth dome). Two other doges besides these are buried in the narthex, but nobody has a clue where.

The Museo Marciano, the Loggia and the horses

On the right of the main door from the narthex into the body of the church (made in 1113–18 and based on the Basilica's main door) is a steep staircase up to the **Museo Marciano** and the **Loggia dei Cavalli**.

Apart from giving you an all-round view which it's difficult to tear yourself away from, the Loggia is also the best place from which to inspect the Gothic carvings of the facade – but the reason most people haul themselves up the steps is to see the **horses of San Marco**.

The Museo Marciano and Loggia dei Cavalli are open daily 9.45am–5pm (4pm in winter); L3000/€1.54.

The original horses have been removed to a room attached to the Museo, allegedly to protect them from the risks of atmospheric pollution, although some cynics have insisted that the rescue mission had less to do with any danger to the horses than with the marketing strategies of Olivetti, who sponsored the operation. In fact, it's likely that the condensation produced by thousands of exhaling tourists makes the air in this confined space more corrosive than any acids floating around outside.

Thieved from the hippodrome of Constantinople in 1204, the horses spent a few years in front of the Arsenale before being installed on the terrace of the Basilica. So close did the association become between them and the people who had stolen them, that the Genoese in 1378 didn't boast that they would tame the lion of Saint Mark, but rather that they would "bridle those unbridled horses". The statues are almost certainly Roman works of the second century, and are the only *quadriga* (group of four horses harnessed to a chariot) to have survived from the classical world. Made from a bronze that contains an unprecedentedly high percentage of copper, they were cast in two parts, the junction being masked by their collars; medallions used to hang round their necks, but they were missing when the horses returned to Venice in 1815 after an eighteen-year sojourn on the Champs Élysées. The marks on the horses' skins are not the result of mistreatment – it's now thought that the scratches and the partial gilding were added at the time of their creation in order to catch the sun.

The small **Museo Marciano** is a miscellany of mosaic fragments, carvings, vestments and so forth from the church. The most interesting exhibits are the wooden cover for the Pala d'Oro, painted in 1345 by **Paolo Veneziano** and his sons, and the cycle of ten tapestries of *The Life of Christ* made around 1420 to designs by **Nicolò di Pietro** – but as likely as not they'll be under lock and key.

The interior of the Basilica

With its undulating floor of patterned marble, its plates of eastern stone on the lower walls, and its 4000 square metres of mosaic cov-

ering every other inch of wall and vaulting, the golden **interior** of San
Marco achieves a hypnotic effect. Whether you look down or up,
some decorative detail will catch your eye, drawing you into the narratives of its mosaics, or the geometric complexities of its pavements.
One visit is not enough: there's too much to take in at one go, and the
shifting light reveals some parts and hides others as the day progresses – at noon you might have to peer through the murk to see a
patch of wall that two hours later could be as bright as a projected picture. The only way to do it justice is to call in for at least half an hour
at the beginning and end of a couple of days. Be warned, however,
that for virtually the whole year a system of barriers is used to channel visitors in one direction round the interior of the basilica, that
there is nowhere to sit down inside the church, and that at peak times
– which is almost the entire day between May and September – the
congestion makes it impossible to stop for a long look at anything.

The mosaics

The majority of the **mosaics** were in position by the middle of the
thirteenth century, but scenes were added right down to the eighteenth century, most of the later work being carried out to replace
damaged early sections. An adequate guide to them would take
volumes: this is only a key to the highlights. The mosaics in the
nave, transepts and presbytery are dealt with first; the mosaics in
the chapels come into the entries on those chapels. The complex
shape of the Basilica makes it most convenient to locate the various features by points of the compass, with the high altar marking
the east.

On the **west wall**, **above the door** – *Christ between the Virgin
and St Mark* (thirteenth-century, restored). **West dome** –
Pentecost (early twelfth-century); the paired figures between the
windows represent the diverse nations in whose languages the
Apostles spread the Word after Pentecost. **Arch between west and
central domes** – *Betrayal of Christ, Crucifixion, Marys at the
Tomb, Descent into Limbo, Incredulity of Thomas* (all late
twelfth-century except the *Marys*, which is a fifteenth-century
copy); these are among the most inventive of all the ancient
mosaics, both in terms of their richness of colour and their presentation of the intense drama of the events.

The **central dome**, a dynamic composition of concentric circles,
depicts the *Ascension, Virgin with Angels and Apostles, Virtues
and Beatitudes, Evangelists, Four Allegories of the Holy Rivers*
(late twelfth-century except *St Mark* and *St Matthew*, which are
mid-nineteenth-century); the four allegorical figures shown watering
the earth are almost certainly a coded reference to the Christian des-
tiny of the city built on water.

East dome – *Religion of Christ Foretold by the Prophets* (early
to mid-twelfth-century; tondo of Christ restored c.1500). A *Christ*

Pantocrator (1506, based on twelfth-century figure) blesses the congregation from the position in the **east apse** traditionally occupied by such figures in Byzantine churches; between the windows below stand the *Four Patron Saints of Venice*, created around 1100 and thus among the earliest works in San Marco. **Arches above north and south singing galleries** (ie linking chancel to side chapels) – *Acts from the Lives of St Peter and St Mark* (early twelfth-century, altered in the nineteenth-century); this sequence, mingled with *Scenes from the Life of St Clement*, is continued on the end walls, but is obscured by the organs.

North transept: dome – *Acts of St John the Evangelist* (early to mid-twelfth-century); **arch to west of dome** (continued on upper part of adjacent wall) – *Life of the Virgin, Life of the Infant Christ* (late twelfth- to early thirteenth-century); **arch at north end of transept** (above Cappella di Sant'Isidoro) – *Miracles of Christ* (late twelfth- to early thirteenth-century). On **wall of north aisle** – five mosaic tablets of *Christ with the Prophets Hosea, Joel, Micah and Jeremiah* (c.1210–30). This series is continued on the **wall of the south aisle** with figures of *The Virgin, Isaiah, David, Solomon* and *Ezekiel*; above these five is the large and complex *Agony in the Garden* (early thirteenth-century); Mark's Gospel tells us that Christ fell on the ground in the Garden of Gethsemane, Matthew describes him falling on his face, and Luke writes that he simply knelt down – the mosaic thus shows Christ in three different positions. On the wall above and on the arch overhead are *Scenes from the Lives of the Apostles* (late twelfth- to early thirteenth-century).

South transept: dome (the *Dome of St Leonard*) – *SS. Nicholas, Clement, Blaise and Leonard* (early thirteenth-century), with *St Dorothea* (thirteenth-century), *St Erasma* (fifteenth-century), *St Euphamia* (fifteenth-century) and *St Thecla* (1512) in the **spandrels**. The formality of the mosaics in the **arch between dome and nave** – *Scenes from the Life of Christ* (early twelfth-century) – makes a striking contrast with the slightly later scenes on the church's central arch; the depiction of Christ's temptation is especially beautiful, showing the protagonists suspended in a field of pure gold. **Arch above Altar of the Sacrament** – *Parables and Miracles of Christ* (late twelfth- or early thirteenth-century); **arch in front of Gothic window** – *SS. Anthony Abbot, Bernardino of Siena, Vincent Ferrer and Paul the Hermit* (1458); **west wall of transept** – *Rediscovery of the Body of St Mark* (second half of thirteenth century).

This last picture refers to a miraculous incident known as the *Inventio* (or "Rediscovery"). In 1094 the body of Saint Mark, having been so well hidden during the rebuilding of the Basilica in 1063 that nobody could find it again, interrupted the service of consecration by breaking through the pillar in which it had been buried. The actual pillar is to your right as you enter the sanctuary, and the very place at which the Evangelist's arm appeared is marked by a marble and mosaic panel.

The sanctuary and the Pala d'Oro

Steps lead from the south transept up to the **sanctuary**, via the **Cappella di San Clemente**, where most of the sculpture is by the **Dalle Masegne** family.

On the fronts of the singing galleries next to the rood screen are eight **bronze panels** of *Scenes from the Life of St Mark* by **Sansovino** (1537), who also executed the figures of *The Evangelists* on the balustrade of the high altar. The other four figures, *The Doctors of the Church*, are seventeenth-century pieces.

Officially the remains of Saint Mark lie in the sarcophagus underneath the altar, but it's quite likely that the body was actually destroyed in the fire of 976. The altar **baldachin** is supported by four creamy **alabaster columns** carved with mostly indecipherable scenes from the lives of Christ and His Mother; the date of the columns is a matter of intense argument – estimates fluctuate between the fifth and the thirteenth centuries.

Behind the altar, and usually enveloped by a scrum, is the most precious of San Marco's treasures, the astonishing **Pala d'Oro** – the "golden altar screen". Commissioned in 976 in Constantinople, the *Pala* was enlarged, enriched and rearranged by Byzantine goldsmiths in 1105, then by Venetians in 1209 to incorporate some of the less cumbersome loot from the Fourth Crusade, and again (finally) in 1345. The completed screen, teeming with jewels and minuscule figures, holds 83 enamel plaques, 74 enamelled roundels, 38 chiselled figures, 300 sapphires, 300 emeralds, 400 garnets, 15 rubies, 1300 pearls and a couple of hundred other stones. Such is the delicacy of the work that most of the subjects depicted on the screen are impossible to make out if you don't have 40/20 vision, and you'd need an encyclopedic knowledge of medieval iconography to decipher every episode and figure, but the rough scheme is easy enough to follow.

In the top section there's the Archangel Michael surrounded by medallions of saints, with *The Entry into Jerusalem*, *The Crucifixion*, *The Resurrection*, *Ascension*, *Pentecost* and *The Death of the Virgin* to the sides. Below, *Christ Pantocrator* is enclosed by the four Evangelists, to the side of whom are ranked a host of angels, prophets and saints; these ranks are framed on three sides by scenes from the life of Christ (the horizontal band) and the life of Saint Mark (the vertical bands). The outer frame of the entire *Pala d'Oro* is adorned with small circular enamels, some of which (in the lower part of the frame) represent hunting scenes; most of these enamels survive from the first *Pala* and are thus its oldest components.

Before leaving the sanctuary, take a look at **Sansovino**'s door to the sacristy (invariably shut) – it incorporates portraits of Titian (top left) and Sansovino himself (under Titian's head).

The sanctuary is open: summer Mon–Sat 9.45am–5pm, Sun 2–5pm; winter closes 4pm; L3000/€1.54.

*The treasury
is open: sum-
mer Mon–Sat
9.45am–5pm,
Sun 2–5pm;
winter closes
4pm;
L4000/€2.07.*

The treasury

Tucked into the corner of the south transept is the door of the **treasury**, installed in a thick-walled chamber which is perhaps a vestige of the first Palazzo Ducale. This dazzling warehouse of chalices, icons, reliquaries, candelabra and other ecclesiastical appurtenances is an unsurpassed collection of Byzantine silver and gold work. Particularly splendid are a twelfth-century Byzantine incense burner in the shape of a domed church, and a gilded silver Gospel cover from Aquileia, also made in the twelfth century.

Much of the treasury's stock owes its presence here to the great Constantinople robbery of 1204, and there'd be a lot more of the same on display if the French occupation force of 1797 hadn't given Venice a taste of its own medicine by helping itself to a few cartloads. To be fair to the Venetians, they at least gave the stuff a good home – the French melted down their haul, to produce a yield of 55 gold and silver ingots.

The sanctuary attached to the treasury, in which are stored over a hundred reliquaries, is hardly ever open to the public.

The baptistery and the Cappella Zen

The **baptistery**, entered from the south aisle (but in recent years very rarely open), was altered to its present form by **Doge Andrea Dandolo** (d. 1354), whose tomb (facing the door) was Ruskin's favourite monumental sculpture in the city. It was Dandolo who ordered the creation of the baptistery **mosaics** of *Scenes from the Lives of Christ and John the Baptist*, works in which the formality of Byzantine art is blended with the anecdotal observation of the Gothic. "The most beautiful symbolic design of the Baptist's death that I know in Italy," wrote Ruskin. The tomb of Dandolo's predecessor, Doge Giovanni Soranzo (d. 1328) is on the right as you come in, and **Jacopo Sansovino** – who designed the enormous font – lies beneath a slab at the eastern end. The huge granite block at the altar is said to have been brought back from Tyre in 1126; more imaginatively, it's also claimed as the stone from which Christ delivered the Sermon on the Mount.

In the **Cappella Zen**, adjoining the baptistery, there's an object of similar mythical potency – a bas-relief of the Virgin that is supposed to have been carved from the rock from which Moses struck water. As its rich decoration indicates, the portal from the chapel into the narthex used to be the entrance from the Piazzetta; this portico was closed in 1504, when work began on the tomb of Cardinal Giambattista Zen, whose estate was left to the city on condition that he was buried within San Marco. The two **mosaic angels** alongside the Virgin on top of the doorway are twelfth-century; the mosaics below are early fourteenth-century and the small statues between them date from the thirteenth. The mosaics on the **vault** show *Scenes from the Life of St Mark* (late thirteenth-century, but restored). The Cappella Zen is sometimes known as the Chapel of the Madonna of the Shoe, taking its name from the *Virgin and Child* by **Antonio Lombardo** (1506) on the high altar.

Stonework, carvings and icons

Back in the main body of the Basilica, make sure you give the **pavement** a good look – laid out in the twelfth and thirteenth centuries, it's a constantly intriguing patchwork of abstract shapes and religious symbols. Of the church's other marvels, the next three paragraphs are but a partial list.

The **rood screen** is surmounted by a silver and bronze **cross** (1394) and marble figures of *The Virgin, St Mark and the Apostles* (also 1394) by **Jacobello and Pietro Paolo Dalle Masegne**. The **pulpits** on each side of the screen were assembled in the early fourteenth century from assorted panels, some of them taken from Constantinople; the new doge was presented to the people of Venice from the right-hand one.

Venice's most revered religious image is the tenth-century **Icon of the Madonna of Nicopeia**, in the chapel on the east side of the north transept; until 1204 it was one of the most revered in Constantinople, where it used to be ceremonially carried at the head of the emperor's army. At the north end of this transept is the **Cappella di Sant'Isidoro**: the mosaics, which have scarcely been touched since their creation in the mid-fourteenth century, depict scenes from the life of the saint, whose remains were grabbed from Chios by Doge Domenico Michiel in 1125. A beautiful mid-fifteenth-century mosaic cycle of *Scenes from the Life of the Virgin*, one of the earliest Renaissance works in Venice, is to be seen in the adjacent **Cappella della Madonna dei Mascoli**, which takes its name from the male confraternity that took it over in the seventeenth century. (The Sant'Isidoro chapel is nearly always closed or reserved for prayer, and you may find the entire north transept roped off to prevent incursions from sightseers.)

Against the west face of the end pillar on the north side of the nave stands **Il Capitello**, a tiny chapel fabricated from a variety of rare marbles to house the *Crucifix* on the altar; the painting arrived in Venice the year after the Nicopeia icon (and came from the same source), and in 1290 achieved its exalted status by spouting blood after an assault on it. Finally, the **galleries** merit a perusal from below (visitors are rarely allowed to walk round them): the parapets facing the aisle consist of reliefs dating from between the sixth and the eleventh century, some of them Venetian, some Byzantine. They weren't designed as catwalks, as they now appear: this is what was left when the women's galleries over the aisles were demolished in the late twelfth century to let more light into the building, after some windows had been bricked over to make more surfaces for mosaics. Apart from this, no major structural change has been made to the interior of San Marco since its consecration in 1094.

PIAZZA SAN MARCO

The Palazzo Ducale

Architecturally, the **Palazzo Ducale** is a unique mixture: the style of its exterior, with its geometrically patterned stonework and continuous tracery walls, can only be called Islamicized Gothic, whereas the courtyards and much of the interior are based on Classical forms – a blending of influences that led Ruskin to declare it "the central building of the world". Unquestionably, it is the finest secular building of its era in Europe, and the central building of Venice. The Palazzo Ducale was far more than the residence of the doge – it was the home of all of Venice's governing councils, its law courts, a sizeable number of its civil servants and even its prisons. All power in the Venetian Republic and its domains was controlled within this one building.

For a list of all the doges, see p.402

The Government of Venice

Virtually from the beginning, the **government of Venice** was dominated by the merchant class, despite the existence, in the early years, of nominally democratic assemblies in which the general male populace was represented. The principal governing council evolved into a self-electing body, and in 1297 the exclusion of the public was institutionalized by an act known as the **Serrata del Maggior Consiglio** (Closure of the Great Council). From then onwards, any man not belonging to one of the patrician families on the list compiled for the *Serrata* was ineligible to participate in the running of the city. After a while, this list was succeeded by a register of patrician births and marriages called the Libro d'Oro, upon which every patrician's claim to membership of the elite was based (in times of economic emergency, some *arrivistes* were allowed to buy their way into the book). By the second decade of the fourteenth century, the constitution of Venice had reached a form that was to endure until the coming of Napoleon; its civil and criminal code, defined in the early thirteenth century, was equally resistant to change.

What made the political system stable was its web of counterbalancing councils and committees, and its exclusion of any youthful element. Most patricians entered the Maggior Consiglio at 25 (although a group of younger high-fliers was admitted annually) and could not expect a middle-ranking post before 45; from the middle ranks to the top was another long haul – the average age of the doge from 1400 to 1600 was 72. As promotion was dependent upon a network of supporters in the elderly and conservative upper ranks, a situation was created in which, as Marin Sanudo wrote in the sixteenth century, "anyone who wishes to dissent must be mad".

However, although Venice's domestic history can seem placid to the point of tedium, backstage politics were as sordid a business as anywhere else. Cabals of the **Case Grandi** (Great Houses) for centuries had a stranglehold on most influential positions, corruption in various guises was endemic, and voting conspiracies were constantly being hatched and thwarted. Even within the *Case Grandi* there were vicious struggles for influence, the battle lines being drawn between the **Longhi**, the families who claimed descent from the city's founders, and the **Curti**, whose genealogical tables ran a bit

The exterior of the Palazzo Ducale

Like San Marco, the Palazzo Ducale has been rebuilt many times. The original fortress, founded at the start of the ninth century, was razed by the fire of 976, and fire destroyed much of its replacement in 1106. The third palace was habitable within ten years, and was extended and altered frequently over the next couple of centuries. But it was with the construction of a new hall, parallel to the waterfront, for the Maggior Consiglio, that the Palazzo began to take on its present shape. Work began in 1340, and the hall was inaugurated in 1419; then, three years later, it was decided to extend the new building along the Piazzetta, and to carry on in the same style. One feature of the exterior gives away the fact that its apparent unity is the product of two distinct phases of building: if you look at the Piazzetta side, you'll notice that the

---

short. An outside observer, exposed to the machinations of Venice's rulers, noted – "They kill not with blood but with ballots".

The seeming compliance of the 98 percent of the population that was shut out from active politics is largely explained by the economic cohesion of the city: its governors were also its businessmen and its chief employers, so were unlikely to adopt policies damaging to the financial interests of themselves and their workforce. The paternalism of the Venetian system helped keep things quiet too – the public health measures and emergency plans for bad harvest years were admired throughout Europe. And when, on the odd occasion, the bosses did contemplate measures that would have been unpopular outside the council chambers, there is plenty of evidence that "the murmuring in the city" quickly put them right. In 1510, for example, a massive demonstration in the Piazza persuaded the government that they should imprison the defeated general whose arrest the people were demanding.

The doge

Regarding the **doge**, it's a common misunderstanding that he was a mere figurehead, confined to his palace under a sort of luxurious house arrest. It's true that there were numerous restrictions on his activities – all his letters were read by censors, for example, and he couldn't receive foreign delegations alone – but these were steps taken to reduce the possibility that an ambitious leader might exploit his office, and they didn't always succeed. Whereas his colleagues were elected for terms as brief as a month, the doge was **elected for life** and sat on all the major councils of state, which at the very least made him extremely influential in the formation of policy. The dogeship was the monopoly of old men not solely because of the celebrated Venetian respect for the wisdom of the aged, but also because a man in his seventies would have fewer opportunities to abuse the unrivalled powers of the dogeship. So it was that in 1618 a certain Agostino Nani, at 63 the youngest candidate for the dogeship, feigned a life-threatening decrepitude to enhance his chances of getting the job. A neat summary of the doge's position was made by **Girolamo Priuli**, an exact contemporary of Sanudo – "It is true that if a doge does anything against the Republic, he won't be tolerated; but in everything else, even in minor matters, he does as he pleases."

1. Porta della Carta
2. Porta del Frumento
3. Bookshop
4. Ticket office
5. Museo dell'Opera
6. Arco Fóscari
7. Scala dei Giganti
8. Cafeteria
9. Cloakroom
10. Pozzi
11. Scala dei Censori

12. Scala d'Oro
13. Ponte dei Sospiri
14. Prigioni
15. Censori
16. Avogaria
17. Sala dello Scrigno
18. Milizia da Mar
19. Bookshop
20. Administration offices

Ground Floor

First Floor

seventh column is fatter than the rest and has a tondo of *Justice* above it – that's where the two stages meet. (Incidentally, folklore has it that the two reddish columns on the upper arcade on this side were crimsoned by the blood of traitors, whose tortured corpses were hung here for public edification; certainly this is the spot where Filippo Calendario, one of the Palazzo Ducale's architects, was quartered for abetting the conspiracy of Marin Falier – see p.167 for more.)

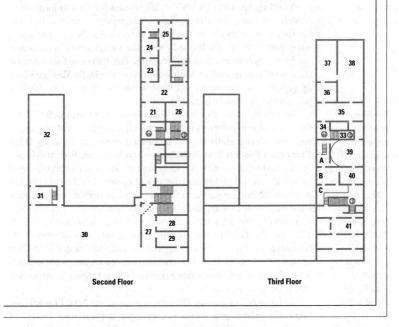

21. Sala degli Scarlatti
22. Sala dello Scudo
23. Sala Grimani
24. Sala Erizzo
25. Sala dei Filosofi
26. Sala degli Scudieri
27. Liagò del Maggior Consiglio
28. Sala della Quarantia Civil Vecchia
29. Sala dell'Armamento or del Guariento
30. Sala del Maggior Consiglio
31. Sala della Quarantia Civil Nuova
    (Bookshop)
32. Sala dello Scrutinio

33. Scala d'Oro
34. Atrio Quadrato
35. Sala delle Quattro Porte
36. Sala dell'Anticollegio
37. Sala del Collegio
38. Sala del Senato
39. Sala del Consiglio dei Dieci
40. Sala della Bussola
41. Armoury

[Itinerari Segreti]
A Sala dei Tre Capi
B Sala degli Inquisitori
C Passage to the Piombi and Torture Chamber

Second Floor

Third Floor

A huge restoration project in the 1870s entailed the replacement or repair of every external column of the palace, the opening up of the arcade on the waterfront side (partly blocked up since the 1574 fire – see p.67) and the repositioning of some of the columns there, and the substitution of copies for fifteen of the fourteenth- and fifteenth-century **capitals** of the lower portico. (It's fairly obvious which are the copies; many of the originals have been restored, and are on display in the Palazzo's Museo dell'Opera.) Ruskin is at his most fanciful when writing about these carvings, which for him exemplified the transition from the purity of the Gothic (see the heads of children on the fourth capital from the *Drunkenness of Noah*) to the vulgar decadence of the Renaissance (compare the fifteenth-century children, second from the Porta della Carta – "capable of becoming nothing but perfumed coxcombs"); if you've got a copy of *The Stones of Venice*, take it with you to the Palazzo Ducale – for all its dottiness, it's still the best guide to the sculpture.

The interventions of restorers are less obtrusive on the late fourteenth-century to early fifteenth-century **corner sculptures**: by the Ponte della Paglia – *Archangel Raphael* and *Drunkenness of Noah*; Piazzetta corner – *Archangel Michael* and *Adam and Eve*; Basilica corner – *Archangel Gabriel* and *Judgement of Solomon*. Some see these pieces as a cogent sequence, illustrating justice (Solomon) and the counterbalancing qualities of severity (expulsion of Adam and Eve) and compassion (Noah's sons) needed for its administration; Ruskin, naturally, saw things slightly differently – whereas the humble Gothic mind dwells on the frailty of humanity (Noah's intemperance, Adam and Eve's disobedience), the vainglorious Renaissance celebrates Solomon's God-like wisdom. The **balconied window** on the lagoon side is another contribution from the **Dalle Masegne** family (1404); the corresponding window on the Piazzetta facade is a mid-sixteenth-century imitation.

*The Palazzo
Ducale is open
daily:
April–Oct
9am–7pm (last
tickets
5.30pm);
Nov–March
9am–5pm;
(last tickets
3.30pm)
entrance is
with the I
Musei di San
Marco ticket,
costing
L18,000/€9.30.*

The principal entrance to the Palazzo was the **Porta della Carta**, the name of which derives perhaps from the archives kept nearby, or from the clerks' stalls around it. Commissioned in 1438 by **Doge Francesco Fóscari** from **Bartolomeo and Giovanni Bon**, this is one of the most ornate Gothic works in the city. Many of its carvings used to be painted and gilded, and the lack of colour isn't the only respect in which the Porta della Carta differs nowadays from its original state – the figures of Fóscari and his attendant lion are nineteenth-century replicas. The fifteenth-century pieces were smashed to bits in 1797 by the head of the stonemasons' guild, who offered to do Napoleon a favour by removing from his sight all images of the lion of Saint Mark. Luckily, his iconoclastic career seems to have ended soon after it began. The solitary remnant of the original is on display inside the Palazzo Ducale.

The passageway into the Palazzo ends under the **Arco Fóscari** (see opposite), which you can see only after getting your ticket, as tourists are nowadays directed into the building through the Porta del Frumento, under the arcades on the lagoon side.

The interior

Several sections of the Palazzo Ducale can be dealt with fairly briskly. The building is clad with paintings by the hectare, but a lot of them are just wearying exercises in self-aggrandizement (no city in Italy can match Venice for the narcissism of its art), and if you take away the paintings, there's not much left to some of the rooms. But it seems perverse not to visit so integral a part of the city, and there are parts you will not want to rush. For this reason a visit needs to be timed carefully. In high season scores of tour groups are being propelled round the place by multilingual guides for much of the day. If you want any control over what you get a look at, buy your ticket within half an hour of opening, or a couple of hours before closing.

A word of warning. As with San Marco, restoration work is always taking place somewhere in the Palazzo Ducale, and there is rarely any indication before you go in as to how much of the building is under wraps, so prepare to be disappointed – you are almost certain to come across scaffolding and plywood barriers at some point.

The courtyard, Museo dell'Opera and Arco Fóscari

From the ticket office you're directed straight into the **Museo dell'Opera**, where the originals of more than forty of the capitals from the lower and upper loggias are well displayed and explicated. In the last room look out for the stone head of Doge Francesco Fóscari, the only item salvaged from the great sculpture on the Porta della Carta.

On the far side of the courtyard, opposite the entrance, stands the Arco Fóscari, which like the Porta della Carta was commissioned from the Bons by Doge Fóscari, but it was finished a few years after his death by **Antonio Rizzo** and **Antonio Bregno**. Rizzo's *Adam* and *Eve* (c.1470), the best of the Arco Fóscari sculptures, have been replaced by copies – the originals, along with the original of Bandini's late sixteenth-century statue of Francesco Maria I della Rovere (on the courtyard side), are on show inside. In 1483 yet another fire demolished most of the wing in front of you (the east), and led to more work for Rizzo – he designed the enormous, over-ornamented staircase called the **Scala dei Giganti**, and much of the new wing. Underneath the lion at the top of the staircase is the spot where the new doge was crowned with the jewel-encrusted cap called the *zogia*; the ungainly figures of *Neptune* and *Mars* were sculpted in 1566 by **Sansovino**. Reconstruction of the east wing continued under **Pietro Lombardo**, **Spavento** and **Scarpagnino** (who created the **Senators' Courtyard** to the left of the staircase), and finally (c.1600) **Bartolomeo Monopola**, who finished the facade overlooking the Rio di Palazzo and completed the main courtyard by extending the arcades along the other two sides.

The Scala d'Oro and the Doge's Apartments

From ground level the traffic is directed up the Scala dei Censori to the upper arcade and thence up Sansovino's gilded **Scala d'Oro**, the main internal staircase of the Palazzo Ducale, with its stuccoes by Vittoria (c.1558). A subsidiary staircase on the right leads to the

Doge's Apartments, in which the head of the republic was obliged to live after his election. All the furniture and much of the decoration have been stripped from this floor, but some of the rooms have ornate ceilings and fireplaces, several of which were installed when the Lombardo family were in charge of rebuilding this part of the palace. The first room is one of the finest. Named the **Sala degli Scarlatti**, probably after the scarlet robes of the officers who attended the corpse of the doge as it lay in state in the adjacent **Sala dello Scudo** (they wore red rather than funereal black to signify that the decease of an individual doge did not diminish the government), it has a fireplace by **Antonio and Tullio Lombardo**, a bas-relief by **Pietro Lombardo** over the door and a gilded ceiling from 1505. The Sala dello Scudo, the largest room of the apartments, is where the doge would receive those to whom he had granted a private audience. The fire of 1483 reduced to ashes the maps that had been painted on the walls, depicting the extent of Venice's domains and the lands visited by the Polo family. Replacements were soon created and were later augmented; the ones you see now date from 1762, and similarly celebrate the explorations of great Venetians and the wide reach of the city's control.

*For the story
of Doge
Francesco
Fóscari, see
p.138.*

The **Sala Grimani**, which marks the beginning of the doge's private accommodation, now houses four large paintings of the Lion of St Mark, including the most famous such image, the one by Carpaccio, in which the heraldic lion stands on an imaginary wild island in the lagoon, with the Palazzo Ducale behind him. Next door, the **Sala Erizzo** has another spectacular fireplace and is decorated with gold and scarlet wall hangings of the sort that would once have adorned many of the building's rooms. Beyond here lies a stucco-laden room from which the doge could enter the patriarchal palace (the door remains but the connecting passageway has gone), which in turn connects with the **Sala dei Filosofi**, a corridor-like extension of the Sala dello Scudo. On one side of this long room a doorway opens onto a staircase; above the door, on the other side, is **Titian**'s *St Christopher*, a fresco in which the artist conflates the Venice cityscape with the mountains of his native Cadore. On the other side of the corridor, the final sequence of rooms contains a picture showing the mayhem of the annual Ponte dei Pugni brawls (see p.116) and a poor Giovanni Bellini (*Dead Christ*), and culminates with the **Sala dei Scudieri**, the room through which the doge's visitors would have entered his apartments.

The Atrio Quadrato and Sala delle Quattro Porte

The Scala d'Oro continues up to the **secondo piano nobile**, ending in the **Atrio Quadrato**, which has a ceiling painting of *Justice* by Tintoretto. This small anteroom opens into the first of the great public spaces, the **Sala delle Quattro Porte**. Before 1574 this room was the meeting place of the Collegio (see opposite), but in that year a

fire gutted this portion of the building, necessitating a major programme of reorganization and decoration. (Three years later an even
worse blaze destroyed the hall of the Maggior Consiglio and other
rooms around it – this is why the Palazzo Ducale contains so few
paintings that predate the 1570s.) After the repairs the Sala delle
Quattro Porte was where ambassadors awaited their summons to
address the doge and his councillors. **Tintoretto**'s ceiling frescoes,
most of which are allegories of the Veneto cities subservient to the
Republic, are in a generally dilapidated condition. The painting
opposite the entrance is a reasonably accurate record of the show
put on to welcome Henry III of France when he arrived in the city a
few weeks before the fire of 1574 – by all accounts the young king
never quite got over this week of overwhelming Venetian hospitality.
The easel painting at the far end of the room – *Venus Receiving the
Homage of Neptune* by **Giambattista Tiepolo** – can be seen at closer range when the itinerary doubles back through here.

The Anticollegio

As regards the quality of its decorations, the next room – the
Anticollegio (the inner waiting room) – is one of the richest in the
Palazzo Ducale. It has looked like this only since the early eighteenth
century, though – after the 1574 fire it was decked out with tapestries and gilded leather, a Venetian speciality. Four pictures by
Tintoretto hang on the door walls: *Vulcan's Forge, Mercury and
the Graces, Bacchus and Ariadne* and *Minerva Dismissing Mars*
(all c.1578); it almost goes without saying that these pictures were
open to a propagandist reading – eg Ariadne = Venice, Bacchus =
the Adriatic. Facing the window wall is **Veronese**'s characteristically
benign *Rape of Europa* – "the brightest vision that ever descended
upon the soul of a painter," sighed Henry James. The ensemble is
completed by Jacopo Bassano's *Jacob's Return to Canaan*, and by
Paolo Veronese's badly deteriorated ceiling fresco of *Venice
Distributing Honours*.

The Sala del Collegio

Thoroughly humbled by now, the emissaries to Venice were ultimately admitted to the **Sala del Collegio**. Presiding over the Senate
and deciding the agenda it would discuss, the full Collegio was the
cabinet of Venetian politics, and consisted of the doge, six ducal
councillors, the three heads of the judiciary, and sixteen *Savi* (senators with special responsibility for maritime, military and govern-
mental affairs). The **Signoria**, Venice's highest executive body, was
the inner council of this inner council, comprising the Collegio minus
the *Savi*. In Ruskin's opinion, in no other part of the palace could
you "enter so deeply into the heart of Venice" as in the Sala del
Collegio, but his observation referred not to the mechanics of
Venetian power but to the luscious cycle of ceiling paintings by

For more on
Doge Gritti,
see p.190.

Veronese. Outstanding is *Venice Triumphant*, the central panel above the throne.

Veronese also produced the picture on the wall over the throne – *Doge Sebastiano Venier Offering Thanks to Christ for the Victory of Lépanto*, in which, as is so often the case in Venetian state-sponsored art, the Son of God is obliged to share top billing. Other doges get similarly immodest treatment in the adjoining paintings: *Doge Alvise Mocenigo Adoring Christ*, *Doge Niccolò da Ponte Invoking the Protection of the Virgin*, *The Mystic Marriage of St Catherine*, *with Doge Francesco Donato* (all by Tintoretto and his workshop) and, over the door to the Anticollegio, *Doge Andrea Gritti before the Virgin* (Tintoretto).

The Sala del Senato

The room next door – the **Sala del Senato** – was where most major policies, both domestic and foreign, were determined. It was also where the ambassadors of Venice delivered their reports on the countries in which they had served. These *relazioni* were essential to the formation of foreign policy, and a Venetian nobleman did his career prospects no harm by turning in a detailed document; few, however, equalled the conscientiousness of the sixteenth-century ambassador to France whose speech to the Senate kept them in their seats for two whole days. The Senate originally comprised sixty councillors invited to take the higher office by the doge (hence the alternative name Sala dei Pregadi, from *pregati*, meaning "prayed" or "beseeched") but eventually grew to contain almost three hundred officials under the doge's chairmanship.

A motley collection of late sixteenth-century artists, Tintoretto and his pupils prominent among them, produced the mechanically bombastic decoration of the walls and ceiling. Tintoretto's personal touch is most evident in the picture above the throne: *Descent from the Cross*, *with doges Pietro Lando and Marcantonio Trevisan*. For sheer shamelessness, however, nothing can match the centrepiece of the ceiling, Tintoretto's *Venice Exalted Among the Gods*. (On rare occasions the doors to the side of the throne are open – they lead to the doge's chapel and its anteroom; only the marble *Virgin and Child* by Sansovino, in the former, is of interest.)

The Sala del Consiglio dei Dieci and Sala della Bussola

After recrossing the Sala delle Quattro Porte you enter the **Sala del Consiglio dei Dieci**, the room in which all matters relating to state security were discussed. The Council of Ten was established in 1310 in response to the revolt of disaffected nobles led by Bajamonte Tiepolo – and the secrecy and speed of its deliberations, and the fact that it allowed no defence counsel, soon made it the most feared of the Republic's institutions. Its members held office for one year and their number was supplemented by the doge and the ducal councillors – which meant, confusingly, that the Ten were never fewer than seventeen.

In the sixteenth century the Ten became even stronger, as an indirect result of the War of the League of Cambrai. What happened was that places on the Senate were taken by a bunch of social climbers as reward for the loans they'd made for the war effort. The men of the *Case Grandi* (see p.60) retaliated by increasing the power of the bodies they could still control – the Collegio and the Ten. Only in the seventeenth century, when the power of the old families was weakened by the sale of places on the Maggior Consiglio, did the Senate revert to being the nucleus of the Venetian state.

Of the paintings here, the finest are a couple of **Veronese** panels on the ceiling, painted at the age of 25 – *Juno Offering Gifts to Venice* and *Old Man in Oriental Costume with Young Woman*. The central panel is a copy of a Veronese original that was packed off to the Louvre by Napoleon's army and has never made it back.

The unfortunates who were summoned before the Ten had to await their grilling in the next room, the **Sala della Bussola**; in the wall is a *Bocca di Leone* (Lion's Mouth), one of the boxes into which citizens could drop denunciations for the attention of the Ten and other state bodies. Nobody could be convicted without corroborating evidence, and all anonymous accusations were rejected (or at least were technically illegal), but nonetheless the legend spread throughout Europe that one word to the Ten was tantamount to a death sentence. The door in the corner leads to the office of the Three Heads of the Council of Ten, which in turn leads to the State Inquisitors' room, then on to the torture chamber and finally the prisons – a doleful route that can be followed on the *Itinerari Segreti* (see p.72). As for the decoration, the last sentence of the previous paragraph applies.

The armoury and the Andito del Maggior Consiglio

From the landing, steps lead up to the **armoury**, consisting in part of weapons assembled for the defence of the Palazzo Ducale, and in part of specially commissioned pieces and gifts from foreign rulers. Amid the horrifying but sometimes exquisitely manufactured metalwork you'll find immense two-handed swords, an ancient twenty-barrelled gun, early sixteenth-century firearms that could be used as maces or axes when there was no time for reloading, and two outstanding pieces of armour: a unique sixteenth-century beaked helmet, and a suit of white armour given to Henry IV of France in 1603 (both in room 2). There's also a bust of Marcantonio Bragadin, whose gruesome demise has kept his name alive (for the story, see p.172), and one grotesque piece of non-military hardware – a pronged chastity belt.

The **Scala dei Censori** takes you back to the second floor; here you go along the **Liagò** (or Andito) **del Maggior Consiglio** (Lobby of the Great Council), past the **Sala della Quarantia Civil Vecchia**, the seat of the civil court, and the **Sala del Guariento**, the old ammunition store, containing the remnants of a fourteenth-century fresco of Paradise by Guariento that used to be in Sala del Maggior Consiglio, where it was covered by Tintoretto's massive image of the same subject. The veranda at the end now houses the sculptures by **Rizzo** and Bandini from the Arco Fóscari; allegedly, the Duke of Mantua offered to buy Rizzo's *Eve* for her weight in gold, but for once the Venetians found it within themselves to resist the lure of huge sums of money.

The Sala del Maggior Consiglio

Now comes the stupendous **Sala del Maggior Consiglio**, the assembly hall of all the Venetian patricians eligible to participate in the running of the city. By the mid-sixteenth century 2500 men were entitled to sit here, but frequently as few as half that number were present. This was the forum of the so-called *giovani*, the younger men on the bottom rung, and it was here that the voice of the populace filtered into the system. Technically, the Maggior Consiglio had little direct impact on government as it voted directly only on administrative legislation, and for much of the time the *giovani* kept fairly quiet in order to stay on the right side of the power-brokers. But if the bosses did something that alienated the majority of the underlings, the Maggior Consiglio was able to make things awkward, because the electoral process for nearly all state officials, including the doge, began here. Its last political act was on May 12, 1797, when it put an end to Venice's independence by voting to accept Napoleon's constitution.

The disastrous fire of December 1577 destroyed the paintings by Bellini, Titian, Carpaccio, Veronese and others that had lined this room; most of the replacements have the sole merit of covering a lot of space. There are, of course, notable exceptions. The immense *Paradiso*, begun at the age of 77 by **Tintoretto** and completed by his son Domenico, is an amazing feat of pictorial organization and a perfect work for its setting; the cast of five hundred figures is arrayed in the ranks ordained by Dante in Canto XXX of his *Paradiso*. Two of the **ceiling panels** are well worth a crick in the neck – *The Apotheosis of Venice*, a late work by Veronese (large oval above tribune), and *Venice Welcoming the Conquered Nations* by Palma il Giovane (large oval at opposite end).

Tintoretto was commissioned to replace the room's **frieze of portraits** of the first 76 doges (the series continues in the Sala dello Scrutinio), but in the event his son (with assistants) did the work. On the Piazzetta side the sequence is interrupted by a painted black veil, marking the place where **Marin Falier** would have been honoured had he not conspired against the state in 1355 and (as the lettering on the veil says) been beheaded for his crime. After two years spent in the city, Byron wrote that Falier's black veil was for him the city's most memorable image.

*For more on
the treason of
Marin Falier,
see p.167.*

Falier remains the most celebrated of Venice's errant leaders, but he is far from being alone in the ranks of the disgraced – by the end of the twelfth century about half the doges had been killed, exiled or simply run out of office. Nor is he the only eminent Venetian to be posthumously vilified in such a manner: for instance, under the arcade of the Palazzo Ducale you'll find a plaque perpetuating the dishonour of Girolamo Loredan and Giovanni Contarini, exiled for abandoning a fort to the Turks. In the Venetian Republic, where staunch service to the state was regarded as a duty, the backsliders were the ones singled out for special treatment, and the city is almost devoid of public monuments to its great statesmen.

The Sala della Quarantia Civil Nuova and Sala dello Scrutinio

The door at the far end opens into the **Sala della Quarantia Civil Nuova**, where civil cases involving Venetian citizens outside the city were heard; it retains some rare examples of Venetian gilt leather-work (downstairs you'll see another room decorated with it), though nothing really grabs the attention. From here you pass into the **Sala dello Scrutinio**, the room in which votes by the Maggior Consiglio were counted and certain electoral committees met. The system for **electing the doge** was the most complex of these procedures. In a nutshell: 30 men were selected by lot from the Maggior Consiglio; they reduced themselves by lot to 9 members; they elected 40, who reduced themselves to 12, who elected 25, who reduced themselves to 9, who elected 45, who reduced themselves to 11, who elected 41, who finally elected the doge – 25 votes was the winning number. This rigmarole could last quite a while, you might think, and you'd be right – it took a minimum of five days, and in the record-breaking 1615 election the last stage alone went to 104 ballots and lasted 24 days. And this intricately democratic machinery was in fact extreme-ly undemocratic – everyone had an equal chance of getting through the first lottery, but only those with a lot of friends and hangers-on could expect to be nominated to the decisive committees.

Perhaps to ensure that the electoral colleges kept their minds on the job, the decoration of the room is stunningly dreary; among the celebrations of great moments in Venetian military history there is just one decent picture – *The Conquest of Zara*, a late **Tintoretto** painting (first on right). The frieze of the last 42 doges was begun by assistants of Tintoretto and continued by contemporaries of each of the doges.

The prisons and beyond

Sometimes visits are directed down the staircase from the Sala dello Scrutinio, but more often the route backtracks through the Sala del Maggior Consiglio and then goes into the **Quarantia Criminale**, the office of the appeal court. This is followed by the **Magistrato alle**

Leggi, in which three works by **Hieronymus Bosch** are displayed: *Heaven and Hell*, the *Triptych of the Hermits* and the *Martyrdom of St Liberata*. They were left to the Palazzo Ducale in the will of Cardinal Domenico Grimani, a connoisseur whose art collection also provided the foundations of the city's archeological museum (see p.78).

The Scala dei Censori descends from here to the **Ponte dei Sospiri** (Bridge of Sighs) and the **Prigioni** (Prisons). The bridge was built in 1600 by Antonio Contino, and takes its popular name from the sighs of the prisoners who shuffled through its corridor. In reality, though, anyone passing this way had been let off pretty lightly, and would soon be at liberty again. Before the construction of these cells in the early seventeenth century, prisoners were kept either in the sweltering **Piombi** (the Leads), under the roof of the Palazzo Ducale, or in the damp, stygian gloom of the **Pozzi** (the Wells) in the bottom two storeys. This new block was occupied mainly by petty criminals – political prisoners were still incarcerated in the *Piombi*, and a few hard cases went to the *Pozzi*.

After recrossing the bridge, you pass through the offices of the **Censori**, a two-man institution set up in 1517 to maintain standards of political behaviour at a time when corruption was getting out of hand, and then the **Avogaria**, the officers who prepared the documents for the courts from the sixteenth century onwards, and also maintained the records of patrician marriages. Marriage certificates were filed in the adjoining **Sala dello Scrigno**, which connects with the office of the **Milizia da Mar**, the functionaries who from 1541 were put in charge of naval recruitment. Leaving this room you emerge at the bookshop, from where you can either go on into the cafeteria, or step outside to the top of the Scala dei Giganti, from where the exit signs take you past the original statue of St Theodore and his dragon from the Piazzetta (see p.81).

The Itinerari Segreti

If you want to see the rooms in which the day-to-day administration of Venice took place, take the **Itinerari Segreti del Palazzo Ducale**, a fascinating ninety-minute guided tour through the warren of offices and passageways that interlocks with the public rooms of the building.

The myriad councils and committees of Venice required a vast civil service, which was staffed by men drawn from the social class immediately below the patriciate – the *cittadini originarii*. (To be accepted into this class of full citizens one had to have lived in Venice for 25 years and never engaged in manual labour.) Roaming through the shadow-palace in which these functionaries carried out their duties, you begin to understand why, for all the Palazzo Ducale's extravagant show of democratic rectitude, the Venetian Republic aroused in many people the sort of dread a police state inspires.

The Itinerari Segreti begin daily at 10am & 11.30am (in English), and cost L24,000/ €12.40; tickets must be booked at least two days in advance, by phoning ☎041.522.4951 or by calling at the Palazzo Ducale administration office, which is close to the bookshop on the upper loggia.

The tour begins with the chambers of the **Chancellery**, the tiny rooms in which all acts of state were drafted and tabulated, then passes through the eighteenth-century Hall of the Chancellery, lined with cabinets for filing state documents. From here it's onward into the belly of the beast, through the judiciary's suites and into a high-ceilinged den where a rope hangs between two tiny wooden cells – the idea being that their two occupants, hearing the screams of the suspended victim, would need no further encouragement to talk. Paintings by Veronese and Tintoretto provide a civilizing gloss in the **Sala dei Tre Capi** – for the Heads of the Council of Ten – and the **Sala degli Inquisitori** – for the officers who investigated charges of treason.

After these, you're led up into the roof to see the timber-lined **Piombi**. By the standards of the day they are not too grim, but the climate up here could be unbearable, and there's a typically Venetian touch of refined malevolence – the doors have a superfluity of locks, just so that the noise of turning keys and slamming bolts would impress upon the inmate the finality of his incarceration. A few recalcitrant cases were not deterred – you're shown the cell from which Casanova escaped in 1775, with the assistance of a fellow prisoner called Father Balbi. (Displaying typical *sang-froid*, Casanova made his way to the Scala d'Oro, where the doors were unlocked for him by a guard who mistook him for a civil servant, then stopped on the Piazza for a quick coffee before heading for the frontier.) Under the rafters there's a museum of Venetian history that deserves more time than is allotted for it, but you do have time to be stunned by the views from the portholes in the roof. And if you wondered, when you were in the Sala del Maggior Consiglio, how the ceiling stays up with no visible means of support, all is revealed near the end.

The Campanile and the Clock Tower

The **Campanile** began life as a combined lighthouse and belltower in the early tenth century, when what's now the Piazzetta was the city's harbour. Modifications were made continually up to 1515, the year in which Bartolomeo Bon the Younger's rebuilding was rounded off with the positioning of a golden angel on the summit. Each of its five bells had a distinct function: the *Marangona*, the largest, tolled the beginning and end of the working day; the *Trottiera* was a signal for members of the Maggior Consiglio to hurry to the council chamber; the *Nona* rang midday; the *Mezza Terza* announced a session of the Senate; and the smallest, the *Renghiera* or *Maleficio*, gave notice of an execution.

The Campanile is open daily 9am–7pm; L8000/€4.16.

The Campanile played another part in the Venetian penal system – "persons of scandalous behaviour" ran the risk of being subjected to

The Campanile and the Clock Tower

the *Supplizio della Cheba* (Torture of the Cage), which involved being stuck in a crate which was then hoisted up the south face of the tower; if you were lucky you'd get away with a few days swinging in the breeze, but in some cases the view from the Campanile was the last thing the sinner saw. A more cheerful diversion was provided by the *Volo dell'Anzolo* (or *del Turco* – Flight of the Angel or Turk), a stunt which used to be performed each year at the end of the Carnevale, in which an intrepid volunteer from the Arsenale would slide on a rope from the top of the Campanile to the first-floor loggia of the Palazzo Ducale, there to present a bouquet to the doge.

But the Campanile's most dramatic contribution to the history of the city was made on July 14, 1902, the day on which, at 9.52am, the tower succumbed to the weaknesses caused by recent structural changes, and fell down. (At some postcard stalls you can buy faked photos of the very instant of disaster.) The collapse was anticipated and the area cleared, so there were no human casualties; the only life lost was that of an incautious cat called Mélampyge (named after Casanova's dog). What's more, the bricks fell so neatly that San Marco was barely scratched and the Libreria lost just its end wall. The town councillors decided that evening that the Campanile should be rebuilt "dov'era e com'era" (where it was and how it was), and a decade later, on St Mark's Day 1912, the new tower was opened, in all but minor details a replica of the original.

At 99m, the Campanile is the tallest structure in the city, and from the top you can make out virtually every building, but not a single canal – which is almost as surprising as the view of the Dolomites, which on clear days seem to be in Venice's back yard. Among the many who have marvelled at the panorama are Galileo, who demonstrated his telescope from here; Goethe, who had never before seen the sea; and the Emperor Frederick III, whose climb to the top was achieved with a certain panache – he rode his horse up the tower's internal ramp. The ready access granted to the tourist is a modern privilege: the Venetian state used to permit foreigners to ascend only at high tide, when they would be unable to see the elusive channels through the lagoon, which were crucial to the city's defence.

The collapse of the Campanile of course pulverized the **Loggetta** at its base, but somehow it was pieced together again, mainly using material retrieved from the wreckage. **Sansovino**'s design was for a building that would completely enclose the foot of the Campanile, but only one quarter of the plan was executed (in 1537–49). Intended as a meeting place for the city's nobility, it was soon converted into a guardhouse for the *Arsenalotti* (workers from the Arsenale) who patrolled the area when the Maggior Consiglio was sitting, and in the last years of the Republic served as the room in which the state lottery was drawn. The bronze figures in niches are also by Sansovino (Pallas, Apollo, Mercury and Peace), as is the terracotta group inside (although the figure of St John is a modern facsimile); the three marble reliefs on the attic are, as ever, allegories of the power and beneficence of the *Serenissima* (the Most Serene Republic): Justice = Venice, Jupiter = Crete, Venus = Cyprus.

The Torre dell'Orologio and Piazzetta dei Leoncini

The other tower in the Piazza, the **Torre dell'Orologio** (Clock Tower), was built between 1496 and 1506, the central portion being by **Mauro Codussi** and the wings possibly by Pietro Lombardo. (The three ornate **flagstaff bases** between the Campanile and the Torre were made at the same time – 1505 – by **Leopardi**, the sculptor who finished the Colleoni monument.) A gruesome popular tale relates that the makers of the clock's elaborate mechanism, Paolo and Carlo Rainieri, slaved away for three years at their project, only to have their eyes put out so that they couldn't repeat their engineering marvel for other patrons. In fact the Venetians were suitably grateful and gave the pair a generous pension – presumably too dull an outcome for the city's folklorists.

The tower's roof terrace supports the two bronze wild men known as "The Moors", because of their dark patina; they were cast in the Arsenale in 1497. Until the mid-1980s it was possible to climb the internal stairs past the innards of the clock, but it seems unlikely that the authorities will ever again risk exposing the delicate structure to the depredations of mass tourism. Anyway, the view from the top couldn't compete with the Campanile's, and you can watch the Moors strike the hour perfectly well from the ground. If you're in Venice on Epiphany or during Ascension week, you'll witness the clock's star turn – on the hour the Magi, led by an angel, troop out and bow to the figure of the Madonna.

To your right as you face the Torre is the **Piazzetta Giovanni XXIII**, familiarly known as **dei Leoncini**, after the two eighteenth-century marble lions – if you can't see them immediately, it's because they're smothered in children. Facing San Marco's flank is **San Basso**, a deconsecrated church now used for exhibitions, and at the far end is the nineteenth-century **Palazzo Patriarcale**, home of the Patriarch of Venice. The Palazzo contains the banqueting hall in which the doge used to entertain official guests and, once a year, the *Arsenalotti*; a corridor, now demolished, ran from the hall, through San Marco and into the Palazzo Ducale.

The Procuratie

Away to the left, from the Torre dell'Orologio, stretches the **Procuratie Vecchie**, once the home of the **Procurators of San Marco**, whose responsibilities included the upkeep of San Marco and the administration of the other government-owned properties. Never numbering more than nine, the procurators were second in position only to the doge, who himself was generally drawn from their ranks. With the doge and the Grand Chancellor – the head of the civil service – they shared the distinction of being the only state officials elected for life.

From the time of Doge Ziani, the procurators and their attendant bureaucracies were installed on this side of the Piazza, but the present building was begun around 1500 by **Codussi**, continued after a fire in 1512 by **Bartolomeo Bon the Younger** and completed around 1532 by **Sansovino**. Much of the block earned rents for the city coffers, the upper floors housing some of the choicest apartments in town and the ground floor being leased to shopkeepers and craftsmen.

Within a century or so, the procurators were moved across the Piazza to new premises. Sansovino, who had only recently completed the old offices, proposed a development that involved knocking down a pilgrims' hospice, along with the unsightly shacks around it.

The **Procuratie Nuove** were eventually built between 1582 and 1640, first to designs by **Scamozzi**, and then under Longhena's control. Napoleon's stepson Eugène Beauharnais, the Viceroy of Italy, appropriated the quarters for use as a royal palace, and then discovered that the accommodation lacked a ballroom. His solution had the true, gossamer-light Napoleonic touch to it: he demolished Sansovino's church of San Geminiano, which had taken up part of the third side of the Piazza, and connected the Procuratie Nuove and Vecchie with a wing containing the essential facility. Generally known as the **Ala Napoleonica**, the building is topped by a gallery of Roman emperors – there are no prizes for guessing whose effigy was meant to fill the gap in the middle.

The Correr and archeological museums

Many of the rooms in the Ala Napoleonica and Procuratie Nuove have been occupied since 1923 by the **Museo Correr**, the civic museum of Venice. In the late 1990s the authorities combined the Correr's entry ticket with that for the Palazzo Ducale in an attempt to siphon tourists into this neglected museum, and at the same time they gave the Correr something of a facelift. At the start of the new millennium the Correr's attractiveness was further enhanced by making the archeological museum and Sansovino's library accessible only through the galleries of the Correr. So far the strategy has only limited success, for the Correr is now given the whistlestop treatment by sightseers who just want to feel that they've got their money's worth. Nobody could make out that this immense collection is consistently fascinating, but it incorporates a picture gallery that more than makes up for the duller stretches, and its sections on Venetian society contain some eye-opening exhibits.

The Museo Correr is open daily: April–Oct 9am–7pm (last tickets 5.30pm); Nov–March 9am–5pm (last tickets 3.30pm) entrance is with the I Musei di San Marco ticket.

The first floor starts off with a gallery of Homeric reliefs by **Canova**, whose large self-portrait faces you as you enter. In the small room at the end of the gallery, beyond the marble bowls of fruit that the young Canova made as a bravura exercise in stone carving, are displayed his model for the tomb of Titian (which became his own tomb – see p.139), and his figure of *Paris*. Sculpted in gypsum, the latter was in effect Canova's final draft before moving on to the marble: the pins that cover the hero's skin were placed there to enable his assistants to map the co-ordinates on the block of marble. (Canova's working methods are fully revealed at his birthplace museum in Possagno – see p.381.) The next room, the Throne Room, contains Canova's *Daedalus and Icarus*, the group that made his name at the age of twenty-one; in the adjacent Dining Room you'll find his faux-modest *Venus Italica* and some of the rough clay models he created as first drafts for his classically poised sculptures. After that you're into the **historical collection**, which might be intermittently enlightening if your Italian is good and you already have a pretty wide knowledge of Venetian history. A beautiful reconstructed seventeenth-century library and a few rooms devoted to ducal edicts, Venetian elections, coinage, ceremonials, bureaucracy and the Arsenale precede the one astonishing item in this section: **Jacopo de'Barbari**'s aerial view of Venice, engraved in 1500. A print of de'Barbari's masterpiece is displayed alongside the original wooden blocks, a dumbfoundingly accurate mirror-image of the city. (Sometimes both the print and the block are inexplicably removed to a room upstairs, thereby removing the focal point of the downstairs room, the subject of which is the topography of the city.) After that you pass through an armoury (look out for the key that fired poisoned darts) and a celebration of Doge Francesco Morosini's exploits in the Morea, and then comes an exhibition of small bronze sculptures from Padua and Venice, featuring tabletop gods, nymphs and suchlike by Vittoria, Campagna and Roccatagliata.

The Museo Archeologico

From the first of the rooms devoted to small bronzes you can turn into the recently relocated **Museo Archeologico**. The core of the museum is formed by two collections of Greek and Roman sculpture that had been assembled by members of the Grimani family: Cardinal Domenico Grimani, whose bequest passed to the city in 1523 and proved immensely influential on Venice's artists; and his nephew Giovanni Grimani, whose donation of classical statuary, made in 1587, was so substantial that Scamozzi was commissioned to turn the vestibule of Sansovino's library into a public gallery for its display. Augmented by various other gifts over the intervening centuries, the Museo Archeologico is now a somewhat scrappy museum, with cases of Roman coins and gems, fragments of sarcophagi and inscriptions, miscellaneous headless statues and bodiless heads interspersed with the odd Bronze Age, Egyptian or Assyrian relic, generally presented in a manner that isn't very inspiring. Yet the drearier exhibits are punctuated by some interesting pieces from the Grimani collections, with the bulk of the finest pieces being concentrated towards the end of the itinerary: look out for an assertive head of Athena from the fourth century BC, a trio of wounded Gallic warriors (Roman copies of Hellenistic originals) and busts of a phalanx of Roman emperors, including Domitian, Vitellius, Hadrian, Trajan, Tiberius, Marcus Aurelius, Septimius Severus, and the demented Caracalla.

At the furthest point of the archeological museum a door opens into the hall of Sansovino's library, which is covered on p.81.

The Quadreria and the rest of the Correr

Back in the Correr, a staircase beyond the sculpture section leads to the **Quadreria**, which may be no rival for the Accademia's collection but nonetheless sets out clearly the evolution of painting in Venice from the thirteenth century to around 1500, and does contain some gems. In the early rooms the outstanding Venetian figure is **Paolo Veneziano**, who in the second half of the fourteenth century began to blend the city's Byzantine pictorial conventions with the more supple styles of Padua, Bologna and other mainland centres. The influence of other artistic schools – especially those of the Low Countries, a region with strong mercantile links to Venice – is a dominant theme in the succeeding rooms, where there are remarkable pieces by **Cosmè Tura** (an angular *Pietà*) and **Antonello da Messina** (a defaced but nonetheless powerful *Pietà*), the latter artist being a conduit through which the compositional techniques of the Tuscan Renaissance came to Venice. The delicate colouring and stillness of Flemish painting are central to the cultural genealogy of the **Bellini** family, to whom the Correr devotes a whole room, featuring a *Crucifixion* that's probably by Jacopo and a few pictures that are definitely by his sons: Gentile's touching portrait of Doge Giovanni Mocenigo, and Giovanni's *Transfiguration, Madonna and Child, Crucifixion* and *Christ Supported by Angels* (the last sporting a fake Dürer monogram, which once fooled the experts).

After the Bellini section you'll pass Alvise Vivarini's portrait of a fine-boned Saint Anthony of Padua, before coming to the museum's best-known possession, the **Carpaccio** painting of two terminally bored women. Once known as *The Courtesans*, it in fact depicts a couple of late fifteenth-century bourgeois ladies dressed in a style at which none of their contemporaries would have raised an eyebrow. Their perilous platform shoes (*ciapine*), placed beside the balustrade, served a twin function: they kept the silks and satins out of the mud, and they enabled the wearer to circumvent the sumptuary laws, which naively attempted to limit the volume of expensive materials used in dresses by forbidding trailing hems. In the room beyond there's another much-reproduced image, the *Portrait of a Young Man in a Red Hat*, once attributed to Carpaccio, now given to an anonymous painter from Ferrara or Bologna. A roomful of fine ivory carvings comes next, then a cubicle of pictures from Venice's community of **Greek artists**, some of whom continued to paint in pre-Renaissance style well into the seventeenth century; this immensely conservative community was the nursery of the painter who later became known as El Greco – there's a picture by him here which you'd walk straight past if it weren't for the label. At room 42 the Quadreria turns into a display of Renaissance ceramics, most of them hideous to modern eyes; beyond it lies the last section on this floor, the library from the Palazzo Manin, which contains **Alessandro Vittoria**'s bust of Tomasso Rangone – his full-length portrait of the same subject is on the facade of a nearby church (see p.85).

From the Quadreria you're directed to the **Museo del Risorgimento**, which resumes the history of the city with its fall to Napoleon, and takes it through to the career of Daniele Manin (see p.89), the anti-Austrian revolt of 1848 and the eventual birth of a united Italy. Although there are some mildly amusing contemporary cartoons on display, and some strange memorabilia (a bottle in the form of Garibaldi's head, portraits of Risorgimento heroes painted on tiny buttons), extensive prior knowledge is again immensely helpful.

Back downstairs, the itinerary passes through a section on Venetian festivals and then a sequence devoted to Venetian crafts, trades and everyday life, where the frivolous items are what catch the eye, especially a pair of eighteen-inch stacked shoes (as worn by the women in the Carpaccio painting), and an eighteenth-century portable hair-care kit that's the size of a suitcase. After a miscellany of restored stonework you'll encounter various exhibits relating to Venetian games and sports, with some remarkable prints of the alarming displays of strength known as the Labours of Hercules (see p.46). Finally you're steered down a corridor containing **Canova**'s reliefs of scenes from the life of Socrates and his immense bust of Pope Clement XIII (the Rezzonico pope – see p.118), and then into the ballroom, where again Canova takes pride of place: the floor is left to his *Orpheus and Eurydice*, created in 1777, when the sculptor was still in his teens.

The Piazzetta and the Molo

For much of the Republic's existence, the **Piazzetta** – the open space between San Marco and the waterfront – was the area where the councillors of Venice would gather to scheme and curry favour. Way back in the earliest days of the city, this patch of land was the garden – or *broglio* – of the San Zaccaria convent: this is the probable source of the English word "imbroglio". But as well as being a sort of open-air clubhouse, the Piazzetta played a crucial part in the penal system of Venice.

Those found guilty of serious crime by Venice's courts were often done away with in the privacy of their cells; for public executions the usual site was the pavement between the **two granite columns** on the **Molo**, as this stretch of the waterfront is called. Straightforward hanging or decapitation were the customary techniques, but refinements were available for certain offenders, such as the three traitors who, in 1405, were buried alive, head down. Even this was mild by comparison with an execution that goes some way to explaining the reputation for barbarity that the Venetian system had abroad: the victim was taken to a raft over in the west of the city, where he was mutilated and burned until almost dead, then tied to a horse and hauled through the streets to the columns, where he was at last given the *coup de grâce*. The last person to be executed here was one Domenico Storti, condemned to death in 1752 for the murder of his brother. Superstitious Venetians avoid passing between the columns.

The columns should have a companion, but the third one fell off the barge on which they were being transported and has remained sub-

merged somewhere off the Piazzetta since around 1170. The co
themselves were purloined from the Levant, whereas the fig
perched on top are bizarre hybrids. The statue of **St Theodore** – t
patron saint of Venice when it was dependent on Byzantium – is a
modern copy; the original, now on show in a corner of one of the
Palazzo Ducale's courtyards, was a compilation of a Roman torso, a
head of Mithridates the Great (first century BC) and miscellaneous
bits and pieces carved in Venice in the fourteenth century (the dragon included). The **winged lion** on the other column is an ancient
3000-kilo bronze beast that was converted into a lion of Saint Mark by
jamming a Bible under its paws. When this was done is not clear, but
the lion is documented as having been restored in Venice as far back
as 1293. Of numerous later repairs the most drastic was in 1815,
when its wings, paws, tail and back were recast, to rectify damage
done by the French engineers who, in the course of arranging its
return from Paris, broke it into twenty pieces. Scientific analysis for
its most recent restoration revealed that the lion is composed of a
patchwork of ancient metal plates, but its exact provenance remains
a mystery – the currently favoured theory is that it was originally part
of a Middle Eastern monument made around 300 BC.

The Libreria Sansoviniana

The Piazzetta is framed by two outstanding buildings – the Palazzo
Ducale on one side and the **Libreria Sansoviniana** or **Biblioteca
Marciana** on the other. Sansovino's contemporaries regarded the
Libreria as one of the supreme designs of the era: Palladio remarked
that it was "perhaps the richest and most ornate building to be created since the times of ancient Greece and Rome". Venice had an
opportunity to establish a state library in the fourteenth century,
when Petrarch left his priceless collection to the city – but the bene-
ficiaries somehow mislaid the legacy, which gives you some idea of
the importance of literature in Venetian culture. In the end, the impetus to build the library came from the bequest of Cardinal Bessarion,
who left his celebrated hoard of classical texts to the Republic in
1468. Bessarion's books and manuscripts were housed in San Marco
and then the Palazzo Ducale, but finally it was decided that a special
building was needed.

Sansovino got the job, and in 1537 the site was cleared of its hostels, slaughterhouse and bakery, thus turning the Campanile into a
freestanding tower. Construction was well advanced when, in
December 1545, the project suffered a major setback: frost got into
the vaulted ceiling of the main hall and brought it crashing down.
Charged with incompetence, Sansovino was thrown into prison, and
it took some determined pleading by his cronies – Titian among them
– to get him out. Upon being allowed back on the job he belatedly
took notice of conventional wisdom, which argued that vaults really
weren't a terrific idea in a place where the land keeps shifting, and

stuck a flat ceiling in its place, with a wooden vault attached, to keep up appearances. The library was finished in 1591, two decades after Sansovino's death.

Entering the library from the archeological museum (see p.78), you come straight into the **main hall**, one of the most beautiful rooms in the city. Paintings by **Veronese**, **Tintoretto**, **Andrea Schiavone** and others cover the walls and ceiling: five of the *Philosophers* are by Tintoretto, while the pair that flank the entrance door, and three of the ceiling medallions, are by Veronese, whose work in the library earned him a gold chain from the procurators in charge of the project, acting on Titian's recommendation. Special exhibitions of precious items from the library, such as the *Grimani Breviary* of 1500 or Fra' Mauro's 1459 map of the world, are sometimes held here; at other times, reproductions are on show. **Titian**'s *Allegory of Wisdom* occupies the central panel of the ceiling of the **anteroom**, which has been restored to the appearance it had from the end of the sixteenth century, when the Giovanni Grimani collection was first put on show here, until 1812, when Napoleon turned the library into an annexe to the viceroy's palace and shifted its contents over to the Palazzo Ducale. Beyond lies the intended approach to the library, a magnificent staircase encrusted with stucco work by Vittoria.

The Zecca and the Giardinetti Reali

Attached to the Libreria, with its main facade to the lagoon, is Sansovino's first major building in Venice, the **Zecca** or Mint. Constructed in stone and iron to make it fireproof (most stonework in Venice is just skin-deep), it was built between 1537 and 1545 on the site occupied by the mint since the thirteenth century, when it was moved from a factory near the Rialto bridge. Some of the finance for the project was raised on the Venetian colony of Cyprus, by selling the island's slaves their liberty. By the beginning of the fifteenth century the city's prosperity was such that the Venetian gold ducat was in use in every European exchange, and Doge Tommaso Mocenigo could look forward to the day when the city would be "the mistress of all the gold in Christendom". In later years the ducat became known as the *zecchino*, source of the word "sequin". The rooms of the Mint are now part of the library, but are not open to tourists.

Beyond the Zecca, and behind a barricade of postcard and toy gondola sellers, is a small public garden – the **Giardinetti Reali** – created by Eugène Beauharnais on the site of the state granaries as part of his improvement scheme for the Procuratie Nuove. It's the nearest place to the centre where you'll find a bench and the shade of a tree, but in summer it's about as peaceful as a school playground. On the far side of the gardens is that rare thing in Venice – a public toilet. The spruced-up building at the foot of the nearby bridge is the Casino da Caffè, another legacy of the Napoleonic era, now the city's main tourist office.

OUT FROM THE PIAZZA

From the Piazza the bulk of the pedestrian traffic flows **north to the
Rialto** along the **Mercerie**, the most aggressive shopping mall in
Venice and the part of the city which comes closest to being devoid
of magic. Apart from the church of **San Giuliano** – one of Venice's
lesser eccentricities – only the stately **San Salvador** provides a diversion from the spotlights and price tags until you come to the **Campo
San Bartolomeo**, the forecourt of the Rialto bridge and the locals'
favoured spot for an after-work drink and chat. Another square that's
lively at the end of the day is the **Campo San Luca**, within a minute's
stroll of the bar at *Al Volto*, the best-stocked *enoteca* in town.
Secreted in the folds of the alleyways are the old Armenian quarter
and the spiralling **Scala del Bovolo** – featured on a thousand postcards, but actually seen by a minority of visitors. And slotted away in
a tiny square close to the Canal Grande you'll find the most delicate
of Venice's museum buildings – the Palazzo Pésaro degli Orfei, home
of the **Museo Fortuny**.

Leaving the Piazza **by the west side**, through the colonnade of the
Ala Napoleonica, you enter another major shopping district, but one
that presents a contrast to the frenetic Mercerie: here the clientele is
drawn predominantly from the city's well-heeled or from the four-
star tourists staying in the hotels that overlook the end of the Canal
Grande – though in recent years it's also become a favourite pitch for
African street traders, whose presence has not been entirely welcomed by local shop-owners. To a high proportion of visitors, this
part of the city is just **the route to the Accademia** – many pass
through with their noses buried in their maps, and hardly break step
before they reach the bridge over the Canal Grande. It's true that
none of the first-division attractions is here and that much of the
northern part of the area offers little but the pleasure of wandering
through its alleyways, but there are things to see apart from the latest creations from Milan and Paris – the extraordinary Baroque
facades of **Santa Maria del Giglio** and **San Moisè**, for instance, or
the graceful **Santo Stefano**, which rises at the end of one of the
largest and most attractive squares in Venice. Two of the city's great
artistic venues lie within this district: **La Fenice**, at the moment a
building site in the wake of the fire that wrecked the opera house in
1996; and the **Palazzo Grassi**, an exhibition centre with the highest
production values in Italy.

North of the Piazza

The **Mercerie**, a chain of streets that starts under the Torre
dell'Orologio and finishes at the Campo San Bartolomeo, is the most
direct route between the Rialto and San Marco and has always been

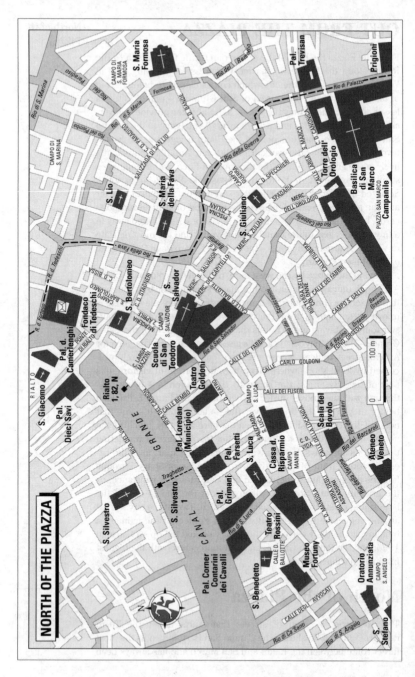

NORTH OF THE PIAZZA

S. Maria Formosa

Pal. Trevisan

Prigioni

CAMPO DI S. MARIA FORMOSA

Rio del Paradiso

Rio del Mondo

Rio di S. Marina

CAMPO DI S. MARINA

Rio di S. Maria

Formosa

Rio del Remedio

Rio di Palazzo

Torre dell' Orologio

S. Maria della Fava

S. Lio

SALIZZADA DI SAN LIO

C. D. PARADISO

Rio della Guerra

CAMPO GUERRA

C. D. SPECCHIERI

S. MARCO

CALLE LARGA S. MARCO

C. D. CANONICA

Basilica di San Marco

Campanile

SPADARIA

PISCINA S. ZULIAN

S. Giuliano

MERC. S. ZULIAN

MERC. DELL'OROLOGIO

PIAZZA SAN MARCO

Rio del Cappello

S. Bartolomeo

CAMPO S. BARTOLOMEO

C. D. STAGNERI

MERCERIA 2 APRILE

S. Salvador

MERC. S. SALVADOR

MERC. DEL CAPITELLO

CALLE BALLOTTE

CALLE FIUBERA

CALLE DEI FABBRI

R. d. Tedeschi

R. D. BISSA

Fondaco dei Tedeschi

PONTE DI RIALTO

Pal. d. Camerlenghi

RIALTO

R. d. Fontego

Rio di San Salvador

CAMPO S. SALVADOR

CALLE DEI FABBRI

Bacino Orseolo

R. d. Bacino Orseolo

FOND. ORSEOLO

CAMPO S. GALLO

RIO TERRA DELLE COLONNE

S. Giacomo

Pal. Dieci Savi

RIVA DEL FERRO

C. LARGA MAZZINI

Scuola di San Teodoro

Teatro Goldoni

CALLE DEL TEATRO

Rialto 1, 82, N

RIVA DEL CARBON

CALLE BEMBO

CANAL GRANDE

Pal. Loredan (Municipio)

CALLE CARLO GOLDONI

CALLE DEI FUSERI

CAMPO S. LUCA

C. D. FORNO

Scala del Bovolo

C. D. LOCANDE

Rio dei Barcaroli

Ateneo Veneto

Traghetto

Pal. Farsetti

S. Luca

SALIZZADA S. LUCA

Cassa di Risparmio

CAMPO MANIN

CALLE DELLA VIDA

C. D. MANDOLA

RIO TERRA DEGLI ASSASSINI

RIO DI S. LUCA

S. Silvestro

Pal. Grimani

Rio di S. Luca

Teatro Rossini

CALLE D. BALLOTTE

Museo Fortuny

CAMPO S. ANGELO

Oratorio Annunziata

S. Benedetto

Pal. Corner Contarini dei Cavalli

CALLE DEGLI AVVOCATI

Rio di Ca Santi

Rio di S. Angelo

S. Stefano

N

0   100 m

a prime site for Venice's shopkeepers. (Each of the five links in the chain is a *merceria*: Merceria dell'Orologio, di San Zulian, del Capitello, di San Salvador and 2 Aprile.) A wide-eyed inventory of the Mercerie in the sixteenth century noted "tapestry, brocades and hangings of every design, carpets of all sorts, camlets of every colour and texture, silks of every variety; and so many warehouses full of spices, groceries and drugs, and so much beautiful white wax!" Nowadays it's both slick and tacky: the empire of kitsch has a firm base here, sharing the territory with the likes of MaxMara, Gucci and Cartier. The mixture ensnares more window-shoppers and buyers than any other part of Venice, and even in the off-season a stroll along the Mercerie is akin to a slalom run. In summer things get so bad that the police often have to enforce a pedestrian one-way system.

For those immune to the charms of consumerism there are only a couple of things to stop for between the San Marco end of the Mercerie and the church of San Salvador. Over the Sottoportego del Cappello (first left after the Torre) is a relief known as **La Vecia del Morter** – the Old Woman of the Mortar. The event it commemorates happened on the night of June 15, 1310, when the occupant of this house, an old woman named Giustina Rossi, looked out of her window and saw a contingent of Bajamonte Tiepolo's rebel army passing below. Possibly by accident, she knocked a stone mortar from her sill, and the missile landed on the skull of the standard-bearer, killing him outright. Seeing their flag go down, Tiepolo's troops panicked and fled back towards the Rialto. (Scores of other rebels were killed in the Piazza – those ringleaders who survived the carnage were punished with execution or exile.) Asked what she would like as her reward for her patriotic intervention, Giustina requested permission to hang the Venetian flag from her window on feast days, and a guarantee that her rent would never be raised; both requests were granted.

Further on is the church of **San Giuliano** (or San Zulian), rebuilt in the mid-sixteenth century with the generous aid of the physician **Tommaso Rangone**. His munificence and intellectual brilliance (but not his Christian faith) are attested by the Greek and Hebrew inscriptions on the facade and by **Alessandro Vittoria**'s portrait statue above the door, for which Rangone paid almost as much as he paid for the church's stonework. (He originally wished to be commemorated by an effigy on the facade of his parish church, San Geminiano, which used to stand facing the Basilica di San Marco, but the city's governors vetoed this excessively vainglorious proposal.) Inside, the central panel of the ceiling, *St Julian in Glory* by **Palma il Giovane** and assistants, is a cut above the man's general standard; over the first altar on the right is a late work by **Veronese** – *Pietà with SS. Roch, Jerome and Mark*; and in the chapel to the left of the chancel there are ceiling stuccoes by **Vittoria**, and three pieces by

North of the
Piazza

For more on
the Armenians
of Venice, see
p.242.

Campagna – terracotta figures of *The Virgin* and *The Magdalen*, and a marble altar panel (all from c.1583).

Obscure corners are to be discovered even in the vicinity of this main avenue. Very close to San Giuliano is the heart of the old **Armenian quarter**: take Merceria di San Zulian, which comes into the Campo San Zulian opposite the church, then cross the bridge into Calle Fiubera, and then take the first right – Calle degli Armeni. Under the sottoportego is the door to the best-hidden church in Venice, **Santa Croce degli Armeni**, which was founded as an oratory in 1496 and rebuilt as the community's church in 1688. Nowadays the congregation is small (the church has just one Mass each week, at 11am on Sunday) and the most visible Armenian community is the one on the island of San Lazzaro.

San Salvador and its campo

San Salvador
is open to
tourists
Mon–Sat
9am–noon &
3–6pm.

At its far end, the Mercerie veers right at the church of **San Salvador** (Salvatore), which was consecrated in 1177 by Pope Alexander III, on the occasion of his reconciliation with Emperor Barbarossa (see p.52). The facade of the present structure, applied in 1663, is less interesting than the interior, which was begun around 1508 by Spavento and continued by Tullio Lombardo and Sansovino. It's cleverly designed in the form of three domed Greek crosses placed end to end, thus creating the longitudinal layout required by the religious orders while paying homage to the centrally planned churches of Byzantium and, of course, to the Basilica di San Marco. One major defect marred this elegant conceit, however – which was that it didn't let enough light into the church. Scamozzi rectified the situation in the 1560s by inserting a lantern into each of San Salvatore's domes.

In the middle of the right-hand wall stands the **tomb of Doge Francesco Venier**, designed by Sansovino, who also sculpted the figures of *Charity* and *Hope*; these were possibly his last sculptures. To the left hangs **Titian's** *Annunciation* (1566), signed *"Fecit, fecit"*, supposedly to emphasize the wonder of his continued creativity in extreme old age; its cumbersome angel is often held to be the responsibility of assistants. A scrap of paper on the rail in front of the picture records the death of the artist on August 25, 1576. The end of the

For more on
Caterina
Cornaro, see
p.384.

right transept is filled by the **tomb of Caterina Cornaro**, one of the saddest figures in Venetian history. Born into one of Venice's pre-eminent families, she became Queen of Cyprus by marriage, and after her husband's death was forced to surrender the strategically crucial island to the doge. On her return to Venice she was led in triumph up the Canal Grande, as though her abdication had been entirely voluntary, and then was presented with possession of the town of Ásolo as a token of the city's gratitude. She died in 1510 and was given a heroine's funeral in the Apostoli church, her body being removed to San Salvador, and this tomb erected, at the end of the century.

The **altarpiece**, a *Transfiguration* by **Titian** (c.1560), covers a fourteenth-century silver reredos that is exposed to view at Easter, on other special occasions, and if the sacristan is in a particularly good mood. In front of the main altar, a glass disc set into the pavement allows you to see a recently unearthed merchant's tomb, with badly damaged decoration by Titian's brother Francesco, who also painted the doors of the church organ (on the left side of the church) and frescoed a delightful fantasy of bird-filled vegetation high on the walls of the sacristy (the sacristan will let you in, and probably expect a donation). The lustrous *Supper at Emmaus* to the left of the altar is possibly from the workshop of Giovanni Bellini, but the attribution seems to change with the seasons – it's sometimes implausibly labelled as a Carpaccio. Finally, the third altar of the left aisle, the altar of the sausage-makers' guild, was designed by Vittoria, who sculpted its figures of *St Roch* and *St Sebastian*.

Next door to the church is the former monastery, now the local headquarters of the phone company; the person at the desk might allow you a look at the beautiful **cloisters**, attributed to Sansovino. Overlooking the campo is the home of the last of the major scuole to be established, the **Scuola di San Teodoro**, which was founded in 1530; the facade was designed in 1655 by Sardi, the architect responsible for the front of San Salvatore. After several years as a cinema, it's now a general purpose exhibition hall, but the shows hardly ever live up to their setting. The column in the centre of the campo is a memorial to the revolt of 1848–49, and was placed here on the fiftieth anniversary of the insurrection.

Campo San Bartolomeo

Campo San Bartolomeo, terminus of the Mercerie, is at its best in the evening, when it's as packed as any bar in town – the hum of voices can be picked up from a hundred metres away. To show off their new wardrobe the Venetians take themselves off to the Piazza, but Campo San Bartolomeo is the spot to just meet friends and talk. For a crash course in the Venetian character, hang around the statue of the playwright Goldoni at about 7pm. A handful of functional bars are scattered about, but it's really the atmosphere you come for – unless, that is, you want to join the kids in *McDonald's*, a controversial arrival in Venice. The burger giant has got a foothold here, in Calle Larga San Marco and in a couple of other places in the city, an invasion seen by many Venetians as marking the final capitulation to the tourist dollar.

The restoration of the **church of San Bartolomeo** has at last been completed after many years, but access seems to be at the whim of the musicians who use the building for their recitals, just like at the Pietà (see p.183). For the foreseeable future, anyway, its best paintings – organ panels by Sebastiano del Piombo – will remain in the Accademia; its most famous picture, the altarpiece painted by Dürer

*For more on
the Fondaco
dei Tedeschi,
see p.206.*

in 1505 at the request of the German merchant Christopher Fugger, long ago migrated to Prague. In the sixteenth century this area would have been swarming with men like Dürer's patron, as the base for the German traders was the **Fondaco dei Tedeschi**, now the main post office, at the far end of the campo.

Campo San Luca and around

If the crush of San Bartolomeo is too much for you, you can retire to **Campo San Luca** (past the front of San Salvatore and straight on), another open-air social centre, where market traders set up their stalls from time to time, temporarily shifting the campo's centre of gravity away from the fast-food outlets. From Campo San Luca, Calle Goldoni is a direct route back to the Piazza, via the Bacino Orseolo – the city's major gondola depot, and one of the few places where you can admire the streamlining and balance of the boats without being hassled by their owners. Calle dei Fuseri leads down to the smart Frezzeria (its name derived from the arrow-makers who worked there), which takes you in one direction to La Fenice and in the other to the area just west of the Piazza.

*The workshop
of Aldus
Manutius once
stood on the
site of the
Cassa di
Risparmio
building – for
more, see
p.131.*

Unusually, the church of **San Luca** is not on the campo named after it, but on a campiello some way off, down Salizzada San Luca, then right and then left. Somewhere in the church is buried a writer whose name would have been known to all Venetians in the mid-sixteenth century – **Pietro Aretino**. Nicknamed "The Scourge of Princes", Aretino milked a hefty income from the rulers of a dozen states, who coughed up either in response to his flattery or out of terror at the damage that his vicious tongue could do. So adept was he at juggling his various sponsors that he managed simultaneously to be on the payroll of Emperor Charles V and his enemy King Francis I of France. With Sansovino and Titian (who painted his portrait several times and used him as a model for Pontius Pilate) he formed a clique that dominated artistic circles in the city and made life intolerable for anyone they didn't like – both Lorenzo Lotto and Pordenone suffered at their hands. Aretino's notoriety rested as much on his dubious morals as on his scurrilous poetry and brilliant letters (which were a Venetian bestseller); some idea of the man is given by the story that his death was brought about by his uncontrollable laughter at a filthy story about his own sister. Today there's not even a tombstone left to mark his existence. The church itself is a drab nineteenth-century reconstruction, and its one picture of any importance – *The Virgin and St Luke* by **Veronese** (on the high altar) – is in a ruinous state.

Campo Manin and the Scala del Bovolo

Campo Manin – where unusually the most conspicuous building is a modern one, Pier Luigi Nervi's **Cassa di Risparmio di Venezia** – was enlarged in 1871 to make room for the monument to **Daniele Manin**, the lawyer who led the revolt of 1848–49; his statue looks towards his house, alongside the left-hand bridge (as you look west). Under Manin's control the provisional government of Venice was run with exemplary efficiency – a legislative assembly was set up, a new currency printed, and a newspaper was even circulated. In the course of the Austrian blockade Venice became the first city ever to be bombarded from the air, when explosives attached to balloons were floated over the city. The damage caused by this ploy was not too substantial, but inevitably the resistance was short-lived, and on August 23, 1849, weakened by hunger and disease, the Venetians surrendered. Manin and the other leaders of the uprising died in exile.

On the wall of the alley on the south side of Campo Manin, a sign directs you to the staircase known as the **Scala del Bovolo** (a *bovolo* is a snail shell in Venetian dialect). External staircases, developed originally as a way of saving space inside the building, were a common feature of Venetian houses into the sixteenth century, but this specimen, dating from around 1500, is the most flamboyant variation on the theme. You can pay to go up the staircase, but the view of it is rather more striking than the view from it.

The Scala del Bovolo is open: March–Oct daily 10am –5.30pm; Nov–April Sat & Sun 10am –4pm; L4000/ €2.07.

The Museo Fortuny and San Benedetto

The fifteenth-century Palazzo Pésaro degli Orfei, now the **Museo Fortuny**, is close at hand, hidden away in a campo you'd never accidentally pass – take either of the bridges out of the Campo Manin, turn first right, and keep going.

Born in Catalonia, **Mariano Fortuny** (1871–1949) is famous chiefly for the body-clinging silk dresses he created, which were so finely pleated that they could be threaded through a wedding ring, it was claimed. However, Fortuny was also a painter, architect, engraver, photographer, theatre designer and sculptor, and the contents of this rickety and atmospheric palazzo reflect his versatility, with ranks of exotic landscapes, symbolist scenes, come-hither nudes, terracotta portrait busts, stage machinery and so forth. The Fortuny museum has been undergoing restoration work for many years, but should you find it open you'll probably come out thinking that he's best known for what he was best at, and lamenting the fact that the museum doesn't contain any of the sexy frocks. The top floor houses a collection of paintings by Virgilio Guidi (1892–1983), about which the kindest comment would be that they are generally no worse than Fortuny's. Design and photography exhibitions are often held here, and as a rule are more interesting than the permanent displays – if the show's good, you'll have to queue, as the building is so fragile that only 75 people are allowed in at a time.

When it reopens the Museo Fortuny will probably be open Tues–Sun 10am–6pm.

The church of **San Benedetto** (San Beneto in dialect) – founded in the eleventh century, rebuilt in 1685 – gangs up with Fortuny's house to overwhelm the little square. It has a few good pictures: *St*

Sebastian by Strozzi (second altar on right); two paintings of *St Benedict* by Mazzoni (over the doors to the side of the high altar); and *St Francis of Paola* by Giambattista Tiepolo (first altar on left). Finding this church open is a matter of pot-luck – late afternoon is normally a good bet.

West of the Piazza

Heading west from the Piazza, on the most direct road to the Accademia, you soon pass on the left the **Calle del Ridotto**, named after the most notorious of Venice's gambling dens, which operated from 1638 to 1774 in the Palazzo Dandolo (no. 1332). Gamblers of all social classes were welcome at the Ridotto's tables – as long as they wore masks – but most of the clients came from the nobility. The consequent damage to the financial resources of the Venetian upper class became so great that the government was finally forced to close the joint. There was, though, no shortage of alternative houses in which to squander the family fortune – in 1797 some 136 gambling establishments were operating in the city. The modern visitor to Venice can experience the frisson of self-induced bankruptcy by nipping into *Harry's Bar*, right by the San Marco Vallaresso landing stage in nearby Calle Vallaresso, and ordering a *Bellini* (prosecco and fruit juice) and one of Harry's fabled sandwiches. Hemingway did some celebrated boozing here, but only the wealthiest of inebriates should contemplate emulating him.

San Moisè and Calle Larga XXII Marzo

San Moisè is open daily 3.30–7pm, plus Sun 9am–noon.

The first church you come across on this route is **San Moisè**, runaway winner of any poll for the ugliest church in Venice. (Its neighbour, the *Hotel Bauer-Grünwald*, would corner several votes for the Worst Building in All Categories.)

The church's name means "Saint Moses", the Venetians here following the Byzantine custom of canonizing Old Testament figures, while simultaneously honouring Moisè Venier, who paid for a rebuilding way back in the ninth century. Its facade sculpture, featuring a species of camel unknown to zoology, was created in 1668 by **Heinrich Meyring**, known locally as Enrico or Arrigo; and if you think this bloated display of fauna and flora is in questionable taste, wait till you see the miniature mountain he carved as the main altarpiece, representing *Mount Sinai with Moses Receiving the Tablets*. In the sacristy you'll find a fine example of comparatively restrained proto-Baroque – a bronze altar panel of the *Deposition* by Niccolò and Sebastiano Roccatagliata.

If you're looking for an escritoire for your drawing room, an oriental carpet for the reception area, a humble Dutch landscape or a new designer suit, then you'll probably find what you're after on or

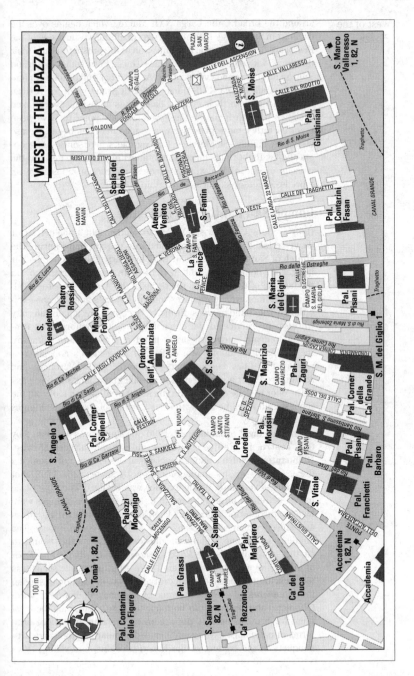

around the broad **Calle Larga XXII Marzo**, which begins over the canal from San Moisè. Many of the streets off the western side of the Piazza are dedicated to the beautification of the prosperous and their dwellings, with names such as Versace, Gucci, Ferragamo, Prada and Vuitton lurking round every corner. At the other end of the economic scale, Calle Larga XXII Marzo is also a prime pitch for African street-traders with their ersatz Chanel bags and similar well-faked designer portables; so far these new arrivals seem to have been received rather more generously in Venice than has been the case elsewhere in Italy – in Florence, for example, where some shopkeepers and far-Right thugs formed an intimidating alliance. Perhaps the citizens of one of the world's greatest mercantile cities have an inbred respect for skilful salesmanship.

Campo San Fantin and La Fenice

Halfway along Calle Larga XXII Marzo, on the right, Calle del Sartor da Veste takes you over a canal and into **Campo San Fantin**. The church of **San Fantin**, begun in 1507 by Scarpagnino, is notable for its graceful domed apse, built in 1549–63 to plans by Sansovino. On the far side of the campo is the home of the **Ateneo Veneto**, a cultural institution which organizes some of Venice's more arcane exhibitions. The building was formerly occupied by a confraternity whose main service to the community was to comfort those sentenced to death – hence the name by which it was generally known: the Scuola della Buona Morte. Part of the scuola's collection of works of art has been dispersed, but pieces by Veronese and Alessandro Vittoria, among others, are still in the building; if you ask at the door in Calle della Verona you might be allowed a look, but the request could well be met with a brisk reminder that the building is private property.

Until the night of January 29, 1996, the square was dominated by the **Teatro la Fenice**, Venice's oldest and largest theatre. **Giannantonio Selva**'s gaunt Neoclassical design was not deemed a great success on its inauguration on December 26, 1792, but nonetheless very little of the exterior was changed when the place had to be rebuilt after a fire in 1836. More extensive changes were made to the interior, a luxuriant late-Empire confection of gilt, plush and stucco which will be replicated in the re-reborn Fenice. The building saw some significant musical events in the twentieth century – Stravinsky's *The Rake's Progress* and Britten's *The Turn of the Screw* were both premiered here – but the music scene was more exciting in the nineteenth century, when, in addition to staging the premieres of several operas by Rossini, Bellini and Verdi (*Rigoletto* and *La Traviata* both opened here), it became the focal point for protests against the occupying Austrian army. Favourite forms of nationalist expression included bombarding the stage with bouquets in the colours of the Italian tricolour, and yelling "Viva

Verdi!" at strategic points in the performance – the composer's name being the acronym for *Vittorio Emanuele, Re d'Italia* (Vittorio Emanuele, King of Italy).

La Fenice was perhaps the world's finest opera house. Seating just 900 people, it had an intimate atmosphere that brought out the best in performers, and its acoustics were superb, thanks largely to the fact that the interior structure was entirely wooden. It was this last characteristic that made the 1996 fire disastrous – though the fire brigade was at the site within twenty minutes of the alarm being raised, it was all they could do to prevent the blaze spreading to the surrounding houses, which would similarly have burned rapidly, owing to the prevalence of combustible timber. Unable to get right up to the building because the flanking canals had been drained for dredging (in order eventually to allow the emergency services easier access), the firefighters had to pump water from the Canal Grande and scoop it out of the lagoon by helicopter to contain the damage. La Fenice itself was quickly reduced to its external walls, as the flames spread unstoppably.

A picture taken from a nearby apartment seemed to show that the fire sprang from two different places in the top storey – the only explanation for which would be that the fire was started deliberately. Investigations soon focused on the contractors who were at work on the opera house at the time, and had fallen behind schedule on a major refurbishment project. Very quickly a conspiracy theory was in circulation and gaining wide acceptance: the contractors were controlled by organized crime, the argument ran, and their bosses had decided to torch the opera house either to avoid paying the penalties for failing to meet their deadlines, or because they fancied their chances of getting the lucrative contracts to rebuild the theatre. It was pointed out that the mafia had turned out to be behind the destruction by fire of the Bari opera house in 1991, and that suspicions of foul play were strengthened by the fact that, though by law a caretaker and two firefighters should have been on duty at La Fenice on the fateful night, there was just one doorman inside the building to operate its fire extinguishers, and the smoke detectors were turned off. On the other hand, some sceptics countered that it was common knowledge that fire precautions and security at La Fenice had been lax for years (the doorman had complained that he was routinely left in sole charge, and that the management had disabled the fire alarms), and it was not impossible that the fire was an accident, as long as one accepted that the extraordinarily rapid spread of the flames was due to the extreme combustibility of the old building, and that the incriminating photographs show a slightly later phase of the fire than was at first thought. Eventually, however, prosecutions were brought and in March 2001 two electricians were imprisoned for arson. Many Venetians are convinced that the real instigators of the Fenice fire have yet to be punished.

Straight after the disaster it was rashly claimed that the new Fenice would open before the end of 1998, but no sooner had reconstruction begun than it ran into litigation. A Fiat-controlled company originally won the contract on the basis of a plan drawn up by Gae Aulenti, designer of the revamped Palazzo Grassi, but the firm that came second in the competition for the work promptly objected that Aulenti's scheme failed to meet the specified brief. The committee administering the contract agreed with the complaint, legal action ensued, and in the end the former runners-up – a German-Italian consortium headed by the practice of the late Aldo Rossi, one of Europe's greatest modern architects – were told they could start building their state-of-the-art replica of La Fenice, a process that should be aided by the recent discovery of the plans that were used to rebuild the opera house after the 1836 fire. Progress has still been shamefully slow, however. More than five years after the blaze, some very impressive scaffolding encases La Fenice, but the husk of the building looks much as it did when the flames died out. The revised opening date is the spring of 2003; nobody seriously believes it will happen. In the interim, opera and ballet performances are being held over on Tronchetto, in a vast tent called the Palafenice (see p.276).

Santa Maria del Giglio and San Maurizio

Santa Maria del Giglio is open Mon–Sat 10am–5pm, Sun 1–5pm (closed Sun in July & Aug); L3000/€1.54.

Back on the route to the Accademia, another extremely odd church awaits – **Santa Maria del Giglio** (Mary of the Lily), more commonly known as Santa Maria Zobenigo, an alternative title derived from the name of the Jubanico family, who founded it in the ninth century. You can stare at the front of this church for as long as you like, but you still you won't find a single unequivocally Christian image. The main statues are of the five **Barbaro** brothers, who financed the rebuilding of the church in 1678; Virtue, Honour, Fame and Wisdom hover at a respectful distance; and relief maps at eye level depict the towns distinguished with the brothers' presence in the course of their military and diplomatic careers. Antonio Barbaro – the central figure and chief benefactor of the church – was not rated by his superiors quite as highly as he was by himself: he was in fact dismissed from Francesco Morosini's fleet for incompetence. The interior, full to bursting with devotional pictures and sculptures, overcompensates for the impiety of the exterior. A *Madonna and Child* in the sacristy is implausibly attributed to Rubens, but the eighteenth-century *Stations of the Cross* by various artists in the body of the church have a better claim on your attention, as do the *Evangelists* by **Tintoretto** behind the altar. The detached one-storey shop right by the church occupies the stump of the campanile, pruned to its present dimensions in 1774.

The tilting campanile of Santo Stefano (see opposite) soon looms into view over the vapid and deconsecrated church of **San Maurizio**, a collaboration between Giannantonio Selva and Antonio Diedo, secretary of the Accademia. The inside of the church is sometimes used as an exhibition space, and the exterior is overshadowed by the fifteenth-century **Palazzo Zaguri**, on the campo's east side. This district is the antiques centre of Venice, and from time to time the Campo San Maurizio is taken over by an antiques and bric-a-brac fair. The antiques business has a permanent representative on the campo in the form of *V. Trois*, the city's only outlet for genuine Fortuny fabrics.

If you wander off the campo down Calle del Dose you'll come to a short fondamenta on the Canal Grande, with fabulous views of its lower reach. Continuing along the Accademia route, at the beginning of Calle del Piovan stands a diminutive building that was once the **Scuola degli Albanesi**; it was established in 1497 and the reliefs on the facade date from shortly after that. In 1504 Carpaccio produced a cycle of *Scenes from the Life of the Virgin* for the scuola, and the pictures remained here even after the declining Albanian community led to the disbanding of the confraternity in the late eighteenth century; it wasn't until 1808, when the baker's guild that had moved into the building was itself scrapped, that the series was broken up. The bits that remained in Venice are now in the Correr collection and the Ca' d'Oro.

Stop for a second on the bridge just after the Scuola, and look down the canal to your right – you'll see that it runs right under the east end of Santo Stefano, the only church in Venice to have quite so intimate a relationship with the city's waterways.

Campo Santo Stefano

The church of Santo Stefano closes one end of the next square – **Campo Santo Stefano**. Large enough to hold several clusters of tourists, a few dozen café tables plus a kids' football match or two, the campo is always lively but never feels crowded; provided you're willing to do battle against the rapacious pigeons, a picnic can be spread around the well-head or the base of the statue of Risorgimento ideologue Nicolò Tommaseo – and there's an additional inducement to sit down for a while in the form of *Paolin*, purveyors of the city's ultimate pistachio ice cream. One of the city's sunniest spots (it opens to the west), this used to be one of its bloodiest – it was a popular bullfighting arena until 1802, when the collapse of a bank of seats killed a number of spectators and provoked an absolute ban on such events.

The campo has an alias – Campo Francesco Morosini – that comes from a former inhabitant of the palazzo at no. 2802, at the Canal Grande end of the square. The last doge to serve as military commander of the Republic (1688–94), **Francesco Morosini** became a Venetian hero with his victories in the Peloponnese, as is attested by the triumphal arch built in his honour in the Palazzo Ducale's Sala dello Scrutinio, and the exhaustive documentation of his career in the Museo Correr. But to those few non-Venetians to whom his name means anything at all, he's known as the goon who lobbed a missile through the roof of the Parthenon, detonating the Turkish gunpowder barrels that had been stored there. He then made matters even worse by trying to prise some of the decoration off the half-wrecked temple, shattering great chunks of statuary in the process. Morosini and Venice didn't come back from that campaign empty-handed though – the Arsenale gate is guarded by two of his trophies.

San Vitale and the Palazzo Pisani

Right at the end of the campo, past the elongated **Palazzo Loredan** (originally fifteenth-century but rebuilt around 1540; facade towards Santo Stefano added in 1618), stands the deconsecrated church of **San Vitale** (or Vidal). It's now a private art gallery, but has somehow hung onto a painting by **Carpaccio** of *San Vitale and other Saints*, which you can just about see over the screens erected for the usually terrible exhibitions. If the facade of the church seems strangely familiar, that's because it's a slavish replica of San Giorgio Maggiore's.

Campiello Pisani, at the back of Morosini's house, is effectively a forecourt to the **Palazzo Pisani**, one of the biggest houses in the city, and now the Conservatory of Music. Work began on it in the early seventeenth century, continued for over a century, and was at last brought to a halt by the government, who decided that the Pisani, among the city's richest banking families, were getting ideas above their station. Had the Pisani got their way, they wouldn't have stopped building until they reached the Canal Grande.

The church of Santo Stefano

Santo Stefano is open Mon–Sat 10am–5pm, Sun 1–5pm (closed Sun in July & Aug).

As a building, the church of **Santo Stefano** – founded in the thirteenth century, rebuilt in the fourteenth and altered again in the first half of the fifteenth – is notable for its Gothic doorway and beautiful **ship's keel roof**, both of which belong to the last phase of building. The airy and calm interior is one of the most pleasant places in Venice to just sit and think, but it also contains some major works of art. The **tomb of Giacomo Surian**, on the entrance wall, was designed and carved in the final decade of the fifteenth century by Pietro Lombardo and his sons. Less easily overlooked is the **tomb of Francesco Morosini**: it's the oversized bronze badge in the centre of the nave. A more discreet funerary monument – Canova's stele for Giovanni Falier (1808) – is in the baptistery (door off left aisle), but this part of the church is usually locked. The major **paintings** are in the picture-packed sacristy (L3000/€1.54): a *St Lawrence* and a *St Nicholas of Bari* by Bartolomeo Vivarini, a Crucifix by Paolo Veneziano, and a trio of late works by Tintoretto – *The Agony in the Garden*, *The Last Supper* and *The Washing of the Disciples' Feet*.

You can walk round the **cloister** (far door in left aisle), even though it's been appropriated by government offices, to see the **tomb of Doge Andrea Contarini**, head of state when the Venetians took on the Genoese at Chioggia. The weather long ago wiped out the frescoes by Pordenone that used to cover much of the walls – a few scraps are preserved in the Ca' d'Oro. Pordenone was for a while Titian's main rival in the city, and such was his fear of the great man and his cronies that he invariably turned up to work here with daggers and swords hanging from his belt. No assault actually occurred, but there has been plenty of bloodshed within the church precincts – so much, in fact, that the place has had to be reconsecrated half a dozen times.

Premature death on a terrible scale accounts for the peculiar raised pavement of nearby **Campo Novo**, off Calle del Pestrin: formerly the churchyard of Santo Stefano, it was used as a burial pit during the catastrophic plague of 1630, and such was the volume of corpses interred here that for health reasons the site remained closed to the public from then until 1838.

Campo Sant'Angelo

A door leads from the cloister of Santo Stefano into the **Campo Sant'Angelo** (or Anzolo), a square almost as capacious as Campo Santo Stefano, but which usually feels more like a crossroads than a meeting place. It's bounded by some fine buildings, however, including two magnificent fifteenth-century palaces: the **Palazzo Gritti** and, facing it, the **Palazzo Duodo**, home of the composer Cimarosa, who died there in 1801. The minuscule **Oratorio dell'Annunziata** – founded in the tenth century, rebuilt in the twelfth and once the home of the Scuola dei Sotti ("of the Lame") – contains a sixteenth-century crucifix and an *Annunciation* by the omnipresent Palma il Giovane. Nothing remains of Sant'Angelo church, which was demolished in 1837 but is still remembered as a leading player in one of Venice's great architectural cock-ups. By 1445 the lean of the church's campanile had become so severe that urgent measures were deemed necessary to right it. It was discovered that there was a builder in Bologna who had made such problems his speciality, and so he was brought onto the case. The expert fixed it so the tower was as straight as a pine tree; the scaffolding was taken down; a banquet was held to honour the engineering genius; and the next morning the whole thing keeled over.

San Samuele and the Palazzo Grassi

From opposite the entrance to Santo Stefano church, Calle delle Botteghe and Crosera lead up to Salizzada San Samuele, a route that's lined with private galleries, arty shops and generally good places to eat; a left turn along Salizzada San Samuele takes you past

the house in which **Paolo Veronese** lived his final years, and on to
Campo San Samuele. Built in the late twelfth century and not much
altered since, the **campanile** of the church is one of the oldest in the
city. The church itself was founded in the previous century but was
largely reconstructed in the late seventeenth century; there are fifteenth-century frescoes by Paduan artists in the apse, but the building is generally more absorbing when there's a show on at the
Palazzo Grassi, at which times it becomes an annexe for showing
videos and slides.

San Samuele is dwarfed by the glitzy **Palazzo Grassi**, which in
1984 was bought by Fiat and converted into a cultural centre. No
expense was spared in realizing the plans drawn up by Gae Aulenti,
the fashionable architect of Paris's Musée d'Orsay, and the refurbished palace now stages the flashiest exhibitions you'll ever see.
Blockbuster overviews of entire cultures is the Grassi's speciality,
and no expense is spared when it comes to presentation: for *I Fenici*
(The Phoenicians) the glazed courtyard was filled with an artificial
sand dune, almost every wall was painted with illustrative maps and
diagrams, and a full-colour catalogue as heavy as a paving stone was
printed. Subsequent shows on subjects such as the Celts and the
Etruscans (the 2001 extravaganza) maintained the reputation for
unbeatable production values, and attracted thousands of visitors
from all over the continent, turning the campo outside the Grassi
into one of the city's most crowded spots.

From San Samuele a fairly straightforward chain of alleys leads
back to Campo Santo Stefano (follow the trail of "Palazzo Grassi"
signs). On the corner of the first of these – Calle Malipiero – is a
plaque marking the birthplace of one of the paltry band of world-
famous native Venetians: **Giovanni Giacomo Casanova**. Both his
parents were actors, and the family lived within a stone's throw of
one of Venice's main theatres, the San Samuele, which until its demolition in the nineteenth century stood in the adjoining Calle del
Teatro.

Chapter 2

Dorsoduro

There were not many places among the lagoon's mudbanks where Venice's early settlers could be confident that their dwellings wouldn't slither down into the water, but with Dorsoduro they were on relatively solid ground: the sestiere's name translates as "hard back", and its buildings occupy the largest area of firm silt in the centre of the city. Some of the finest minor domestic architecture in Venice is concentrated here, and in recent years many of the area's best houses have been bought up by industrialists and financiers from elsewhere in northern Italy, investing in permanent homes or merely weekend havens from their places of work. The top-bracket colony is, however, pretty well confined to a triangle defined by the Accademia, the Punta della Dogana and the Gesuati. Stroll up to the area around Campo Santa Margherita and the atmosphere is quite different, in part because of the proximity of the university.

During the day at least, it's the paintings of Dorsoduro's art galleries and religious institutions that draw most visitors across the Ponte dell' Accademia. The **Gallerie dell'Accademia**, replete with masterpieces from each phase in the history of Venetian painting up to the eighteenth century, is the area's essential port of call, and figures on most itineraries as the place to make for when the Piazza's sights have been done. The huge church of **Santa Maria della Salute**, the grandest gesture of Venetian Baroque and a prime landmark when looking across the water from the Molo, is architecturally the major religious building of the district – but in terms of artistic contents it takes second place to **San Sebastiano**, the parish church of **Paolo Veronese**, whose paintings clad much of its interior. **Giambattista Tiepolo**, the master colourist of a later era, is well represented at the **Scuola Grande dei Carmini**, and for an overall view of Tiepolo's cultural milieu there's the **Ca' Rezzonico**, home of Venice's museum of eighteenth-century art and artefacts. Unusually for Venice, art of the twentieth century is also in evidence – at the **Guggenheim Collection**, which is small yet markedly superior to the city's (frequently closed) public collection of modern art in the Ca' Pésaro. And yet despite all these attractions the district as a whole is

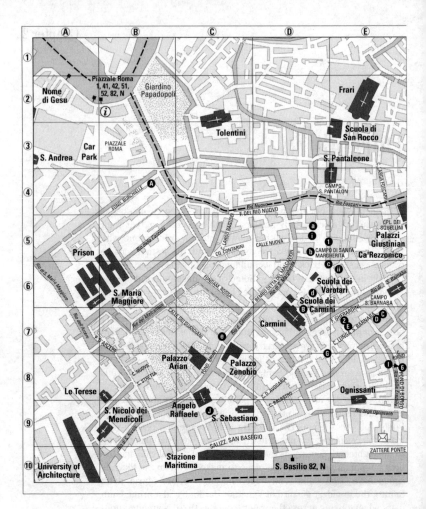

remarkably quiet – most tourists step across the Accademia bridge, whirl through the gallery, then cross back over the Canal Grande again.

As with San Polo, the area designated by the chapter title is slightly more extensive than the sestiere of the same name, since in order to simplify the scheme of the city it incorporates a portion of the Santa Croce sestiere – for the visitor, the most arbitrary and confusing of Venice's divisions. For our purposes Dorsoduro stretches from the Punta della Dogana and the Salute west to the docks of the Stazione Maríttima, and north to Piazzale Roma (which is technically in Santa Croce).

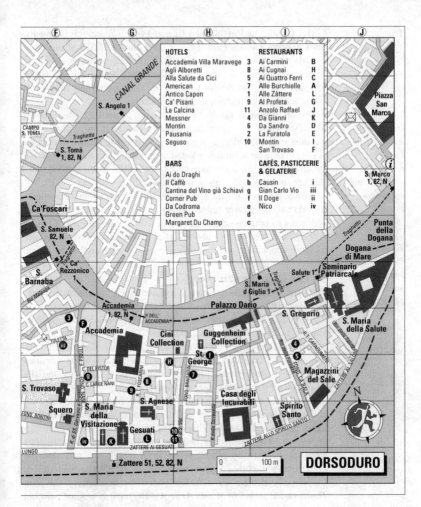

HOTELS		RESTAURANTS	
Accademia Villa Maravege	3	Ai Carmini	B
Agli Alboretti	8	Ai Cugnai	H
Alla Salute da Cici	5	Ai Quattro Ferri	C
American	7	Alle Burchielle	A
Antico Capon	1	Alle Zàttere	L
Ca' Pisani	9	Al Profeta	G
La Calcina	11	Anzolo Raffael	J
Messner	4	Da Gianni	K
Montin	6	Da Sandro	D
Pausania	2	La Furatola	E
Seguso	10	Montin	I
		San Trovaso	F

BARS		CAFÉS, PASTICCERIE	
		& GELATERIE	
Ai do Draghi	a	Causin	i
Il Caffè	b	Gian Carlo Vio	iii
Cantina del Vino già Schiavi	g	Il Doge	ii
Corner Pub	f	Nico	iv
Da Codroma	e		
Green Pub	d		
Margaret Du Champ	c		

DORSODURO

The Accademia

The fame of Venice's school of art, the **Accademia di Belle Arti**, nowadays has nothing to do with the reputation of its staff or pupils – it's been going steadily downhill since the lively days of 1968 – and everything to do with the attached **Gallerie dell'Accademia**, one of Europe's finest specialized art collections. A Napoleonic decree of 1807 moved the Accademia to its present site and instituted its galleries of Venetian paintings, a stock drawn largely from the city's suppressed churches and convents. Parts of the premises themselves were formerly religious buildings: the church of **Santa Maria della**

The Accademia

The Accademia is open Mon 8.15am–2pm, Tues–Sun 8.15am –7.15pm; late opening in summer (hours are variable – usually Tues–Sat until 10pm, Sun until 8pm); L12,000/€6.20.

Carità (rebuilt by **Bartolomeo Bon** in 1441–52) and the **Convento dei Canonici Lateranensi** (built by **Palladio** in 1561 but not completed) were both suppressed in 1807. The third component of the Accademia used to be the **Scuola della Carità**, founded in 1260 and the oldest of the six Scuole Grande; the Gothic building dates from 1343, but has an eighteenth-century facade.

The art school is gradually transferring to another site, a move which will allow the gallery to display the paintings currently gathering dust in the Quadreria, a collection consisting mostly of uncompelling efforts by second-tier Venetian artists; if you want to visit the Quadreria, you can book yourself a place on one of the guided tours that are given occasionally at weekends.

With San Marco and the Palazzo Ducale, the Accademia completes the triad of obligatory tourist sights in Venice, but admissions are restricted to batches of 300 people at a time. Accordingly, if you're visiting in high summer and don't want to wait, get there well before the doors open or at about 1pm, when most people are having lunch.

To the early Renaissance

The **first room** of the Accademia's generally chronological arrangement is the fifteenth-century former chapterhouse of the scuola (with its original gilded ceiling), now filled with pieces by the earliest-known individual Venetian painters. The icon-like Byzantine-influenced figures of **Paolo Veneziano** (first half of the fourteenth century) are succeeded by the Gothic forms of his follower **Lorenzo Veneziano** – look at the swaying stances of his figures and the emphasis on the sinuous lines of the drapery.

Room 2 is given over to large altarpieces from the late fifteenth and early sixteenth centuries, including works by **Giovanni Bellini**, **Cima da Conegliano** and **Vittore Carpaccio**. All of these paintings appear to have slightly warped perspectives: this is because they were intended to be placed above head height – a fact that the Accademia's picture-hangers have not taken into consideration. Carpaccio's strange *Crucifixion and Glorification of the Ten Thousand Martyrs of Mount Ararat* is the most gruesome painting in the room, and the most charming is by him too: *The Presentation of Jesus in the Temple*, with its pretty, wingless, lute-playing angel.

The beginnings of the Venetian obsession with the way in which forms are defined by light (as differentiated from the Florentines' more geometrical notions of form) and the emergence of the characteristically soft and rich Venetian palette are seen in **rooms 3, 4 and 5**, the last two of which are a high point of the Accademia. Almost all of the small paintings here would alone be worth a detour, but outstanding are an exquisite *St George* by **Mantegna** (c.1466), a series of *Madonnas* and a *Pietà* by **Giovanni Bellini**, and two pieces by the most mysterious of Italian painters, **Giorgione** – his *Portrait of an Old Woman* and the so-called *Tempest* (c.1500). The former is an urgent and compassionate study of mortality (the inscription means "with time"), while the latter resists all attempts to deduce its meaning – the first known painting to have no historical, religious, mythological or factual basis, it seems to have been as perplexing to Giorgione's contemporaries as it is to us.

Tintoretto, Titian and Veronese

Rooms 6 to 8 mark the entry of the heavyweights of the Venetian High Renaissance, the period in which the cult of the artist really took hold, with painters cultivating their reputations and writers boosting their favourites while damning their rivals. These works would be the prize of many other collections, but here they are just appetizers for what's to come. In **room 6**, Jacopo Robusti, alias **Tintoretto**, is represented by a *Creation of the Animals* that features a few species that must have followed the unicorn into extinction; Tiziano Vecellio, alias **Titian**, comes in with *John the Baptist*; and Paolo Caliari, better known as **Paolo Veronese** (he came to Venice from Verona), is represented by a series of ceiling panels. In the parallel suite, **rooms 7 and 8**, the most compelling picture is the *Young Man in his Study* by **Lorenzo Lotto** (c.1528), a portrait in which the subject's gaze manages to be simultaneously sharp and evasive. Lotto was eventually driven from Venice by the vindictiveness of Titian and his entourage; the beguiling *Tobias and the Angel* nearby has recently, after being cleaned, been identified as a Titian.

Room 6 is in effect the anteroom to the large **room 10**, one whole wall of which is needed for *Christ in the House of Levi* by **Paolo Veronese**. Originally called *The Last Supper* – being a replacement for a Titian painting of the same subject that was destroyed by a fire in the refectory of San Zanipolo – this picture brought down on Veronese the wrath of the Inquisition, who objected to the inclusion of "buffoons, drunkards, Germans, dwarfs, and similar indecencies" in the sacred scene. (What really raised their hackles was the German contingent, who were perceived by the Holy Office as the incarnation of the Reformation menace.) Veronese's insouciant response was simply to change the title, an emendation that apparently satisfied his critics.

Among the works by **Tintoretto** is the painting that made his reputation: *St Mark Freeing a Slave* (1548), showing Saint Mark's intervention at the execution of a slave who had defied his master by travelling to the Evangelist's shrine. Comparison with Gentile Bellini and Carpaccio's unruffled depictions of miraculous events in rooms 20–21 (see p.105) makes it easy to understand the sensation caused by Tintoretto's whirling, brashly coloured scene. The legend of Venice's patron saint is further elaborated by his dreamlike *The Translation of the Body of St Mark* (see p.47 for the story of the "translation" – ie theft) and *St Mark Saving a Saracen* (both from the 1560s), and *The Dream of St Mark* (1570), which is largely by his son **Domenico**. Tintoretto's love of physical and psychological drama, the energy of his brush-strokes, and the sometimes uncomfortable originality of his colours and poses, are all displayed in this group. (And all over Venice you can see how his concentration on dramatic highlights and his use of gesture spawned a shoal of imitators, whose clichéd contortions of pose and expression covered oceans of canvas.) Opposite is **Titian**'s highly charged *Pietà* (1576), painted for his own tomb in the Frari; the immediacy of death is expressed in the handling of the paint, here scratched, scraped and dolloped onto the canvas not just with brushes but with the artist's bare hands. It was completed after Titian's death by Palma il Giovane, as the inscription explains.

The eighteenth century

In the first half of **room 11** there's more from **Tintoretto**, including the sumptuous *Madonna dei Tesorieri* (1566), showing the city's treasurers hobnobbing with the Mother of Our Saviour. Halfway down the room a major shift into the eighteenth century occurs, with pieces by **Giambattista Tiepolo** that survived the destruction of the Scalzi's ceiling in 1915, and the long frieze of *The Miracle of the Bronze Serpent*, which sustained some damage when it was rolled up for storage in the nineteenth century, at a time when the artist was out of fashion. The long corridor of **room 12** marks the beginning of a rather dull section of the gallery. Although some of the side rooms contain a few decent sixteenth- and seventeenth-century pieces, in particular works by **Jacopo Bassano**, and **Tintoretto**'s portraits of officials of the republic, the chief interest is provided by eighteenth-century painters. **Giambattista Piazzetta**'s extraordinary *The Fortune-Teller* (1740), in **room 16a**, is also known as *The Enigma*, although the woman is offering the least enigmatic sexual invitation you'll ever see on canvas; some interpreters see it as a satirical allegory, showing how once-glorious Venice now behaved towards the rest of the world. In **room 17** there is a trio of small Canalettos, accompanied by **Guardi**'s impressionistic views of Venice, **Pietro Longhi**'s documentary interiors and a series of portraits by **Rosalba Carriera**, one of the very few women shown in the collection. Carriera's work established the use of pastel as a medium in its own right, rather than as a preparation for oil paint, and her moving *Self-Portrait in Old Age*, done at a time when her sight was beginning to fail, is a high point of her work.

To the Miracles of the Relic of the Cross

The top part of the Carità church now forms **room 23**, which houses works mainly from the fifteenth and early sixteenth centuries, the era of two of Venice's most significant artistic dynasties, the **Vivarini** and **Bellini** families. Of the pieces by the Vivarini – **Antonio**, his brother **Bartolomeo** and his son **Alvise** – the most striking is Alvise's

Santa Chiara (1485–90). **Giovanni Bellini** is represented by four workshop-assisted triptychs (painted for this church in the 1460s), and his brother **Gentile** by the intense portrait of *The Blessed Lorenzo Giustinian* (1445). One of the oldest surviving Venetian canvases and Gentile's earliest signed work, it was possibly used as a standard in processions, which would account for its tatty state.

There's more from Gentile over in **room 20**, which is entirely filled by the cycle of *The Miracles of the Relic of the Cross*. The work was produced by various artists between 1494 and 1501, and was commissioned by the Scuola Grande di San Giovanni Evangelista to extol the holy fragment it had held since 1369. Gentile's *Procession in Piazza San Marco* (1496), executed the year the Torre dell'Orologio was started (and with artistic licence shifting the Campanile to the right), is perhaps the best-known image of the group; the devotional moment is easily missed – the bare-headed man in a red cloak kneeling as the relic passes him is one Jacopo de' Salis, praying for his son's recovery from a fractured skull. In *The Miracle of the True Cross at the Bridge of San Lorenzo* (1500) Gentile shows Andrea Vendramin, Grand Guardian of the Scuola, retrieving the relic from the spot where it had floated after being knocked into the water during a procession; the fourth figure from the left in the group of donors in the right foreground is alleged to be a self-portrait, and Caterina Cornaro is portrayed on the far left.

A wealth of anecdotal detail adds historical veracity to **Carpaccio**'s *Miracle of the True Cross at the Rialto Bridge* (1494). Set by the Rialto (and showing one of the wooden precursors of the present bridge), its cast of characters includes turbanned Turks and Arabs, Armenian (or Greek) gentlemen in tall brimmed hats, an African gondolier, a woman beating carpets on an *altana* and a man repairing a roof; the miracle – the cure of a lunatic – is happening on the first floor of the building on the left. **Giovanni Mansueti**'s *Miracle of the Relic in Campo San Lio* (1494) shows what happened at the funeral of a dissolute and impious member of the confraternity: the relic refused to allow itself to be carried into the church for his service. Each window has a woman or child in it, witnessing the shame of the old reprobate. The reason for all these anecdotal details and the marginalizing of the miracles was not a lack of piety but quite the reverse: the miracle was authenticated by being depicted in the documentary context of teeming everyday life.

Carpaccio's St Ursula paintings – and Titian's Presentation

Another remarkable cycle fills **room 21** – Carpaccio's *Story of St Ursula*, painted for the Scuola di Sant'Orsola at San Zanipolo in 1490–94. A superlative exercise in pictorial narrative, the paintings are especially fascinating to the modern viewer as a meticulous record of domestic architecture, costume, the decorative arts, and even ship design in Venice at the close of the fifteenth century – and a scrupulous recent renovation has further increased their lustre. The legend is that a British prince named Hereus proposed marriage to Ursula, a Breton princess, who accepted on two conditions: that Hereus convert to Christianity, and that he should wait for three years, during which time he should escort Ursula and her company of 11,000 virgins on a pilgrimage to Rome. The conditions were accepted, and the eventual consequence was that Ursula and her troop were massacred by the Huns near Cologne – as she had been forewarned by an angel in a dream.

After this room, you leave the Accademia through the former *albergo* of the scuola; **Titian**'s *Presentation of the Virgin* (1539) occupies the wall over the door, the place for which it was painted – and the triptych by **Antonio Vivarini** and **Giovanni d'Alemagna** (1446) similarly hangs where it always has.

Eastern Dorsoduro

Along the east flank of the Accademia runs the wide Rio Terrà Foscarini, named after **Senator Antonio Foscarini**, victim of the Venetian judicial system's most notorious gaffe; he lived at no. 180–181, but the house was radically altered in the nineteenth century.

For the story of Antonio Foscarini, see p.208.

The street cuts down almost as far as the Záttere, but for the direct route to the mouth of the Canal Grande you turn left along Calle Nuova a Sant'Agnese, one of the district's main shopping streets.

The Cini and Guggenheim collections

The Cini collection is open summer Tues–Sun 10am–1pm & 2–6pm; L5000/€2.58.

Just before the Rio San Vio you pass the Palazzo Cini (no. 864), once the home of the industrialist Vittorio Cini (founder of the Fondazione Cini on San Giorgio Maggiore) and now occupied by the **Galleria di Palazzo Cini**. Although Cini's private collection contains a miscellany of valuable manuscripts, porcelain and other artefacts, the substance of the museum is its gathering of Tuscan paintings, including pieces by Bernardo Daddi, Filippo Lippi, Piero di Cosimo and Pontormo. It also occasionally hosts special exhibitions – keep an eye out for posters.

Over the water lies the **Campo San Vio**, a fine platform from which to watch the traffic on the Canal Grande. The reason this little square opens out onto the water is that the houses on that side were demolished in order to make it easier for the doge and his entourage to disembark for the annual thanksgiving service in the church of saints Vito and Modesto (contracted to Vio in Venetian); held on the saints' joint feast day, June 15, the service commemorated the defeat of the Bajamonte Tiepolo revolt (see p.85), which occurred on June 15, 1310. The church itself was demolished in 1813; the walls of the small chapel that took its place are encrusted with stone fragments taken from the Tiepolo palazzo, which was destroyed in punishment for their treason.

From here you just follow your nose for the **Peggy Guggenheim Collection**, installed in the peculiarly modernistic fragment of the quarter-built Palazzo Venier dei Leoni, a bit farther down the Canal Grande.

In the early years of this century the leading lights of the Futurist movement came here for the parties thrown by the dotty Marchesa Casati, who was fond of stunts like setting wild cats and apes loose in the palazzo garden, among plants sprayed lilac for the occasion. Peggy Guggenheim, a considerably more discerning patron of the arts, moved into the palace in 1949; since her death in 1979 the Guggenheim Foundation has looked after the administration of the place, and has turned her private collection into one of the city's glossiest museums – and the second most popular after the Accademia. It's a small but generally top-quality assembly of twentieth-century art, touching on most of the major modern movements, and the Guggenheim is also a prime venue for touring shows, which usually make the entrance fee seem less inflated. In the permanent collection the core pieces include Brancusi's *Bird in Space* and *Maestra*, De Chirico's *Red Tower* and *Nostalgia of the Poet*, Max Ernst's *Robing of the Bride* (Guggenheim was married to Ernst in the 1940s), some of Joseph Cornell's boxes, sculpture by Laurens and Lipchitz, and works by Malevich and Schwitters; other artists include Picasso, Braque, Chagall, Pollock, Duchamp, Giacometti, Picabia and Magritte. Marino Marini's *Angel of the Citadel*, out on the terrace, flaunts his erection at the passing canal traffic; more decorous pieces by Giacometti, Moore, Paolozzi and others are planted in the garden, surrounding Peggy Guggenheim's burial place.

The Salute and around

After the wrought iron and greenery of the tiny **Campo Barbaro** (from where you can see the Gothic back half of the Palazzo Dario – see p.214) you'll come to the Gothic church of San Gregorio (now a restoration centre). The flank of the Salute is visible at the other end, but this preview doesn't quite prepare you for the mountain of white stone that confronts you when you emerge from the tunnel.

In 1630–31 Venice was devastated by a plague that exterminated nearly 95,000 of the lagoon's population – one person in three. In October 1630 the Senate decreed that a new church would be dedicated to Mary if the city were saved, and the result was the **Salute** (*salute* meaning "health" and "salvation"), or Santa Maria della Salute, to use its full title.

Resting on a platform of more than 100,000 wooden piles, the Salute took half a century to build; its architect, **Baldassare**

Eastern Dorsoduro

The Guggenheim collection is open 10am–6pm; April–Oct open till 10pm Sat; closed Tues; L12,000/€6.20. For more on the Palazzo Venier, see p.213.

The Salute is open daily 9am–noon & 3–5.30pm.

Longhena, was only 26 years old when his proposal was accepted. He lived just long enough to see it finished – he died in 1682, one year after completion.

Each year on November 21 (the feast of the Presentation of the Virgin) the Signoria processed from San Marco to the Salute for a service of thanksgiving, crossing the Canal Grande on a pontoon bridge laid from Santa Maria del Giglio. The Festa della Madonna della Salute is still a major event in the Venetian calendar, with thousands of people making their way over the water in the course of the day to pray for, or give thanks for, their health.

The form of the Salute owes much to the plan of Palladio's Redentore – the obvious model for a dramatically sited votive church – and to the repertoire of Marian symbolism. The octagonal plan and eight facades allude to the eight-pointed Marian star, for example, while the huge dome represents Mary's crown and the centralized plan is a conventional symbol of the Virgin's womb. Its decorative details are saturated with coded references: the inscription in the centre of the mosaic floor, "Unde Origo, Inde Salus" (From the Origins came Salvation), refers to the coincidence of Mary's feast day and the legendary date of Venice's foundation – March 25, 421; the Marian rosary is evoked by the encircling roses.

Less arcane symbolism is at work on the **high altar**, where the Virgin and Child rescue Venice (kneeling woman) from the plague (old woman); in attendance are Saint Mark and Saint Lorenzo Giustiniani, first Patriarch of Venice. The Byzantine painting, a little uneasy in this Baroque opulence, was brought to Venice in 1672 by Francesco Morosini, never a man to resist the opportunity for a bit of state-sanctioned theft.

For more on Francesco Morosini, see p.95.

The most notable paintings in the Salute are the **Titian** pieces brought from the suppressed church of Santo Spirito in 1656, and now displayed in the sacristy (L2000/€1.03): an early altarpiece of *St Mark Enthroned with SS. Cosmas, Damian, Sebastian and Roch* (the plague saints), three violent ceiling paintings of *David and Goliath*, *Abraham and Isaac* and *Cain and Abel* (1540s), and eight late tondi of the Doctors of the Church (Jerome, Augustine, Gregory and Ambrose) and the Evangelists. Tintoretto has included himself in the dramatis personae of his *Marriage at Cana* (1561) – he's the first Apostle on the left. Nearby is a fine *Madonna* by Palma il Vecchio, one of the sixteenth century's more placid souls.

The Manfrediana and the Dogana di Mare

Longhena was also the architect of the **Seminario Patriarcale**, within which lurks one of the city's more ramshackle museums. The collection of tombstones and sculptural pieces around the cloister, many of them trawled from suppressed religious foundations, was thrown together in the early years of the nineteenth century; it was augmented soon after by the **Pinacoteca Manfrediana**, a motley collection of artworks incorporating items as diverse as paintings by Antonio Vivarini and Paolo Veronese, and portrait busts by Vittoria, Bernini and Canova. It's many years since the museum was last opened to the public on a regular basis, but if you give them a call (☎041.520.8565) it should be possible to arrange a visit.

On the point where the Canal Grande and the Giudecca canal merge stands the **Dogana di Mare** (Customs House), another late seventeenth-century building, which may one day be converted into a gallery of contemporary art. The figure which swivels in the wind on top of the Dogana's gold ball is said by most to represent Fortune, though others identify it as Justice. From the tip of Dorsoduro, the Punta della Dogana, you're treated to one of the city's great panoramas.

Along the Záttere

Known collectively as the **Záttere**, the sequence of waterfront pavements between the Punta della Dogana and the Stazione Maríttima are now a popular place for a stroll or an al fresco pizza, but were formerly the place where most of the bulky goods coming into Venice were unloaded onto floating rafts called *záttere*. A fair quantity of cargo was carted into the state-run and highly lucrative **Magazzini del Sale** (Salt Warehouses), the vast low structure near the Punta della Dogana. In the tenth century the Venetians established a regional monopoly in salt production by destroying the rival town of Comacchio, near the Po delta; some 44,000 tons of salt, most of it made in salt pans near Chioggia, could be stored in this one building, a stockpile that represented at its peak nearly ten percent of the state's income. Part of it is now a boathouse, part is used as exhibition space during the Biennale and occasionally at other times.

The Gesuati to San Trovaso

There's an appealing mix of architectural exteriors on the eastern reaches of the Záttere: the fifteenth-century facade of **Spirito Santo** church, the pink **Casa degli Incurabili** (once one of Venice's four main hospitals, now a children's home), and the Veneto-Byzantine church of **Sant'Agnese**, begun in the twelfth century but much remodelled since then. However, the first building to break your stride for is the church of the **Gesuati** or Santa Maria del Rosario.

The Gesuati is open Mon–Sat 9am–6pm, Sun 1–6pm; L2000/€1.03.

Rebuilt in 1726–43, about half a century after the church was taken over from the order of the Gesuati by the Dominicans, this was the first church designed by **Giorgio Massari**, an architect whose work combines Rococo preciousness with a more robust classicism – here his creation forms a sort of counterpoint to the Redentore, over the water. He often worked with **Giambattista Tiepolo**, who painted the first altarpiece on the right, *The Virgin with SS.*

Catherine of Siena, Rose and Agnes (c.1740), and the three magnificent ceiling panels of Scenes from the Life of St Dominic
(1737–39), which are seen to best effect in the afternoon, when the
natural light comes from the same direction as the artificial light in
the paintings. The third altar on this side of the church is adorned
with a painting of SS. Vincent Ferrer, Giacinto and Luigi Beltran
by Tiepolo's principal forerunner, Giambattista Piazzetta; opposite,
the first altar has Sebastiano Ricci's Pius V with SS. Thomas and
Peter Martyr (1739), completing the church's array of Rococo propaganda on behalf of the exalted figures of Dominican orthodoxy,
followed by a tragically intense Crucifixion by Tintoretto (c.1555)
on the third altar.

Santa Maria
della
Visitazione is
open daily
8am–noon &
3–7.

Santa Maria della Visitazione, a couple of doors down, has an
attractive Lombardesque facade, but the only notable aspect of the
interior is its sixteenth-century **ceiling**, with panels painted by
Umbrian artists. The lion's-mouth letter box to the right of the facade
was for the use of residents with complaints relating to health and
sanitation; a complaint sent to the authorities in 1498 resulted in
punishment for the tradesmen who had sold oil that was full of
"immonditie e sporchezi" (filth and dirt) – syphilitic patients had
been immersed in it as a cure.

San Trovaso is
open to
tourists
Mon–Sat
3–6pm.

Don't bother consulting your dictionary of saints for the dedicatee
of **San Trovaso** church – the name's a baffling dialect version of
Santi Gervasio e Protasio. Since its tenth-century foundation the
church has had a chequered history, falling down once, and twice
being destroyed by fire; this is the fourth incarnation, built in
1584–1657.

Venetian folklore has it that this church was the only neutral
ground between the Nicolotti and the Castellani, the two factions in
to which the working-class citizens of the city were divided – the former, coming from the west and north of the city, were named after
the church of San Nicolò dei Mendicoli (see p.113), the latter, from
the sestieri of Dorsoduro, San Marco and Castello, took their name
from San Pietro di Castello. The rivals celebrated inter-marriages
and other services here, but are said to have entered and departed by
separate doors: the Nicolotti by the door at the traditional "west"
end, the Castellani by the door on the "south" side.

For more on
the Nicolotti
and the
Castellani see
p.116.

One of Venice's
few remaining
gondola yards
is next to San
Trovaso; for
more on gon-
dolas, see the
box opposite.

Inside, San Trovaso is spacious and somewhat characterless, but
it does boast a pair of fine paintings by **Tintoretto**: The Temptation
of St Anthony and The Last Supper. The former is in the chapel to
the left of the high altar, with St Crysogonus on Horseback by
Michele Giambono (c.1450), Venice's main practitioner of the
International Gothic style; the latter is in the chapel at ninety
degrees to the first one. The two large pictures on each side of the
choir, The Adoration of the Magi and The Expulsion from the
Temple, were begun by Tintoretto at the very end of his life, but so
much of the finished work is by his son and other assistants that

they are now attributed to Domenico. Finally, in the chapel next to the south door you'll find a marble altar-front carved with angels – dated around 1470, it's one of the first Renaissance low reliefs produced in Venice.

Gondolas

Ten thousand gondolas operated on the canals of sixteenth-century Venice, when they were the standard form of transport around the city; nowadays the tourist trade is pretty well all that sustains the city's fleet of around five hundred gondolas, which provide steady employment for a few **squeri**, as the gondola yards are called. A display in the Museo Storico Navale (see p.196) takes you through the construction of a gondola, but no abstract demonstration can equal the fascination of a working yard, and the most public one in Venice is the **squero di San Trovaso**, on the Záttere side of San Trovaso church. The San Trovaso is the oldest squero still functioning – established in the seventeenth century, it looks rather like an alpine farmhouse, a reflection of the architecture of the Dolomite villages from which many of Venice's gondola-builders once came. Another squero is tucked away on the Rio dell'Avogaria, a short distance west of here, beyond the former Benedictine convent of Ognissanti (now a hospital).

The earliest mention of a gondola is in a decree of 1094, but the vessel of that period bore little resemblance to today's streamlined thoroughbred. As late as the thirteenth century the gondola was a twelve-oared beast with an iron beak – an adornment that evolved into the saw-toothed projection, called the **ferro**, which fronts the modern gondola. (The precise significance of the ferro's shape is unclear – tradition has it that the six main prongs symbolize the six sestieri, with the backward-facing prong representing La Giudecca.) Over the next two centuries the gondola shrank to something near its present dimensions, developed multicoloured coverings and sprouted the little chair on carved legs that it still carries. The gondola's distinctive oarlock, an elaborately convoluted lump of walnut or cherry wood known as a **forcola**, which permits the long oar to be used in eight different positions, reached its definitive form at this time too.

By the sixteenth century the gondola had become a mode of social ostentation, with gilded prows, fantastically upholstered **felzi** (cabins), cushions of satin and silk, and hulls decked out with a profusion of embroidery, carvings and flowers. Sumptuary laws were introduced to quash this aquatic one-upmanship, and though some of them had little effect, one of them changed the gondola's appearance for good – since an edict of 1562 gondolas have been uniformly black, a livery which prompted Shelley to liken them to "moths of which a coffin might have been the chrysalis".

There's been little alteration in the gondola's dimensions and construction since the end of the seventeenth century: the only significant changes have been adjustments of the gondola's asymmetric line to compensate for the weight of the gondolier – a characteristic that's particularly noticeable when you see the things out of water. All gondolas are 10.87 metres long and 1.42 metres wide at their broadest point, and are assembled from nearly three hundred pieces of seasoned mahogany, elm, oak, lime, walnut, fir, cherry and larch. Plenty of gondolas pass through, under repair, but each squero turns out only about four new gondolas a year, at a cost of around forty million lire.

San Sebastiano and beyond

At the end of the Záttere the barred gates of the Stazione Maríttima deflect you away from the waterfront and towards the church of **San Sebastiano**. The parish church of **Paolo Veronese**, it contains a group of resplendent paintings by him that gives it a place in his career comparable to that of San Rocco in the career of Tintoretto, but in contrast to San Rocco, this church is frequently overlooked, despite recent bursts of restoration work.

San Sebastiano is open Mon–Sat 10am–5pm, Sun 3–5pm – but often closed Sun in winter; L3000/€1.54.

Veronese was still in his twenties when, thanks largely to his contacts with the Verona-born prior of San Samuele, he was asked to paint the ceiling of the **sacristy** with a *Coronation of the Virgin* and the *Four Evangelists* (1555); once that commission had been carried out, he decorated the **nave ceiling** with *Scenes from the Life of St Esther*. His next project, the dome of the chancel, was later destroyed, but the sequence he and his brother Benedetto then painted on the walls of the church and the nun's choir at the end of the 1550s has survived in pretty good shape. (Current restoration work has closed access to the choir and necessitated the removal of the *Coronation of the Virgin* and the *Four Evangelists* to the Accademia.) In the following decade he executed the last of the pictures, those on the **organ shutters** and around the **high altar** – on the left, *St Sebastian Leads SS. Mark and Marcellian to Martyrdom*, and on the right *The Second Martyrdom of St Sebastian* (the customarily depicted torture by arrows didn't kill him). Other riches include a late **Titian** of *St Nicholas* (on the left wall of the first chapel on the right), and the early sixteenth-century majolica pavement in the chapel to the left of the chancel – in front of which is Veronese's tomb slab.

Angelo Raffaele

Angelo Raffaele is open daily 8am–noon & 4–6pm.

Across the campo, the seventeenth-century church of **Angelo Raffaele** is instantly recognisable by the two huge war memorials blazoned on the canal façade. Inside, the organ loft above the entrance on the canal side is decorated with *Scenes from the Life of St Tobias* (accompanied, as ever, by his little dog), painted by one or other of the **Guardi** brothers (nobody's sure which). Although small in scale, the free brushwork and imaginative composition make the panels among the most charming examples of Venetian Rococo, a fascinating counterpoint to the grander visions of Giambattista Tiepolo, the Guardis' brother-in-law.

In the campo behind the church is a well-head built from the bequest of Marco Arian, who died of the Black Death in 1348, an outbreak which he blamed on contaminated water. The **Palazzo Arian**, on the opposite bank of the canal, was built in the second half of that century and is adorned by one of the finest and earliest Gothic windows in Venice. It's the only window in the city that replicates the distinctive pattern of the Palazzo Ducale's stonework.

San Nicolò dei Mendicoli

Although it's located on the edge of the city, the church of San
Nicolò dei Mendicoli is one of Venice's oldest – said to have been
founded in the seventh century, San Nicolò is traditionally predated
only by San Giacomo di Rialto. Its long history was reflected in the
fact that it gave its name to the **Nicolotti** faction, whose titular head,
the so-called *Gastaldo* or the *Doge dei Nicolotti*, was elected by the
parishioners and then honoured by a ceremonial greeting from the
Republic's doge.

*San Nicolò dei
Mendicoli is
open daily
10am–noon &
4–6pm.*

The church has been rebuilt and altered at various times, and was
last restored by Venice in Peril in the 1970s, when Nic Roeg used it
as a setting for *Don't Look Now*. In essence, however, its shape is
still that of the Veneto-Byzantine structure raised here in the twelfth
century, the date of its rugged campanile. The other conspicuous feature of the exterior is the fifteenth-century porch, a type of construction once common in Venice, and often used here as makeshift
accommodation for penurious nuns. (The only other example left
standing is at San Giacomo di Rialto.) The interior is a miscellany of
periods and styles. Parts of the apse and the columns of the nave go
back to the twelfth century, but the capitals were replaced in the
fourteenth – the penultimate one on the left side bears an inscription
dating it January 25, 1366. Above, the darkened gilded woodwork
that gives the interior its rather overcast appearance was installed
late in the sixteenth century, as were most of the paintings – most of
those above the right colonnade come from the workshop of Paolo
Veronese, whose son painted the organ gallery. Occupying the high
altar is a large wooden statue of Saint Nicholas, a mid-fifteenth-century piece, possibly from the workshop of Bartolomeo Bon.

The convent and church of **Le Terese**, on the other side of the
canal, are due to be restored as student accommodation and a university auditorium (the church has famously fine acoustics), but for
the time being there's no reason to set foot on the island on which it
stands, as it's a zone of docks, new housing developments and warehouses, one of which has been converted into the city's University of
Architecture.

Northern Dorsoduro

The vast, elongated **Campo Santa Margherita**, ringed by houses that
date back as far as the fourteenth century, is the social heart of
Dorsoduro, many of whose inhabitants come here daily to stock up at
the market stalls. Students from the nearby university hang out in the
campo's bars, and the place as a whole – with its herbalist, wholefood
store and wooden sculpture shop – has a vaguely alternative feel. The
church that gives the campo its name was closed in 1810, for a while
functioned as a cinema, and is now a university auditorium; the drag-
ons that feature so prominently in the decorative stonework on and

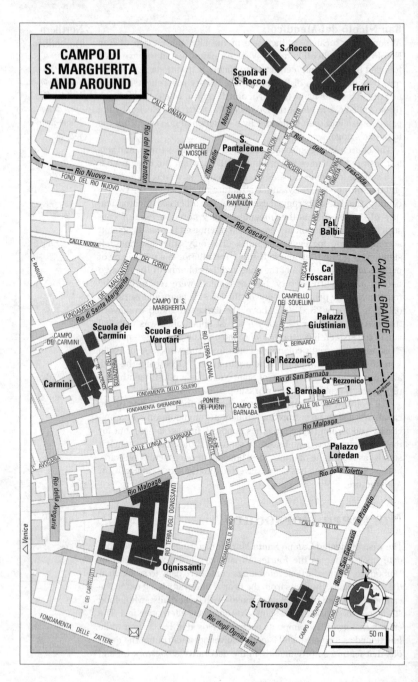

CAMPO DI S. MARGHERITA AND AROUND

S. Rocco

Scuola di S. Rocco

Frari

CALLE VINANTI

Rio delle Mosche

C. DEL SCALATER

Rio della Frescada

C. DONNA ONESTA

CAMPIELLO D. MOSCHE

S. Pantaleone

CALLE S. PANTALON

CROSERA

CALLE LARGA FOSCARI

Rio Nuovo

FOND. DEL RIO NUOVO

CAMPO S. PANTALON

Rio Foscari

Pal. Balbi

CALLE NUOVA

C. DEL FORNO

C. Foscari

CANAL GRANDE

C. RAGUSEI

FONDAMENTA DEL MALCANTON

Rio di Santa Margherita

CAMPO DI S. MARGHERITA

CALLE SAGNER

CAMPIELLO DEI SQUELLINI

Palazzi Giustinian

CAMPO DEI CARMINI

Scuola dei Carmini

Scuola dei Varotari

RIO TERRA CANAL

CALLE DELLA VIDA

C. CAPPELER

C. BERNARDO

Ca' Rezzonico

Carmini

CALLE DELLA SCOAZZERA

FONDAMENTA DELLO SQUERO

Rio di San Barnaba

Ca' Rezzonico

Traghetto

S. Barnaba

FONDAMENTA GHERARDINI

PONTE DEL PUGNI

CAMPO S. BARNABA

CALLE DEL TRAGHETTO

Rio Malpaga

C. AVOGARIA

CALLE LUNGA S. BARNABA

C. DE LUGHETTI

Palazzo Loredan

Rio della Toletta

Rio della Avogaria

Rio Malpaga

RIO TERRA DEGLI OGNISSANTI

FONDAMENTA D. BORGO

CALLE D. TOLETTA

a Priaroso

Rio di San Gervasio

FOND. NANI

Venice

Ognissanti

C. DEI CARTELLOTTI

S. Trovaso

CAMPO S. TROVASO

FOND. NANI

N

FONDAMENTA DELLE ZATTERE

Rio degli Ognissanti

0   50 m

around the church relate to the legend of Saint Margaret, who emerged unscathed after the dragon that had swallowed her exploded. Isolated at the fish-stall end of the campo stands the **Scuola dei Varotari** (tanners' guild), bearing an eroded relief of the Madonna with members of the scuola.

The Carmini and around

Just off Campo Santa Margherita's southwest tip is the **Scuola Grande dei Carmini**, once the Venetian base of the Carmelites. Originating in Palestine towards the close of the twelfth century, the Carmelites blossomed during the Counter-Reformation, when they became the shock-troops through whom the cult of the Virgin could be disseminated, as a response to the inroads of Protestantism. As happened elsewhere in Europe, the Venetian Carmelites became immensely wealthy, and in the 1660s they called in an architect – probably Longhena – to re-design the property they had acquired. The core of this complex, which in 1767 was raised to the status of a Scuola Grande, is now effectively a showcase for the art of **Giambattista Tiepolo**, who in the 1740s painted the ceiling of the upstairs hall.

The Scuola Grande dei Carmini is open Mon–Sat 9am–noon & 3–6pm; L8000/€4.16.

The central panel, framed by four *Virtues* in the corners of the ceiling, was recently restored after the cords that suspended it rotted away, causing it to crash from the ceiling. Depicting *Simon Stock Receiving the Scapular*, it is not the most immediately comprehensible image in Venetian art. The Carmelite order was in some disarray by the mid-thirteenth century, but it acquired a new edge when the English-born Simon Stock was elected prior general in 1247; under his control, the Carmelites were transformed into a well-organized mendicant order, with houses in the main university cities of Europe – Cambridge, Oxford, Paris and Bologna. Some time after his death the tradition grew that he had experienced a vision of the Virgin, who presented him with a scapular (two pieces of cloth joined by cords) bearing her image: as the scapular was the badge of the Carmelites, its gift was evidently a sign that Simon should undertake the development of the order. Tiepolo has translated this crucial episode from the place where it allegedly happened (Cambridge) to his customary floating world of blue skies and spiralling perspectives (a world seen at its most vertiginous in the painting of an angel rescuing a falling mason). The painting was such a hit with Tiepolo's clients that he was instantly granted membership of the scuola, a more generous reward than you might think – a papal bull had ordained that all those who wore the scapular would, through the intercession of the Virgin, be released from the pains of Purgatory on the first Saturday after the wearer's decease, "or as soon as possible" (sic). The edict was probably a forgery, but the Carmelites believed it, and from the passion of his work here, it would seem that Tiepolo did too.

*The Carmini
church is open
Mon–Sat
3–6pm.*

The **Carmini** church (or Santa Maria del Carmelo) is a collage of architectural styles, with a sixteenth-century facade, a Gothic side doorway which preserves several Byzantine fragments, and a fourteenth-century basilican interior. A dull series of Baroque paintings illustrating the history of the Carmelite order covers a lot of space inside (the same subject is covered by the gilded carvings of the nave), but the second altar on the right has a *Nativity* by Cima da Conegliano (before 1510), and Lorenzo Lotto's *St Nicholas of Bari* (1529) – featuring what Bernard Berenson ranked as one of the most beautiful landscapes in all Italian art – hangs on the opposite side of the nave.

The most imposing building on Fondamenta del Soccorso (leading from Campo dei Carmini towards Angelo Raffaele) is the **Palazzo Zenobio**, built in the late seventeenth century when the Zenobio family were among the richest in Venice. It's been an Armenian college since 1850, but visitors are sometimes allowed to see the ballroom: one of the city's richest eighteenth-century interiors, it was painted by Luca Carlevaris, whose trompe l'oeil decor provided a model for the decoration of the slightly later Ca' Rezzonico. In the late sixteenth century a home for prostitutes who wanted to get off the game was set up at no. 2590 – the chapel of Santa Maria del Soccorso – by **Veronica Franco**, a renowned ex-courtesan who was as famous for her poetry and her artistic salon as she was for her sexual allure; both Michel de Montaigne and King Henry III of France were grateful recipients of samples of her literary output.

Between here and Piazzale Roma lies a predominantly residential area that constitutes the largest completely uninteresting sector of central Venice. Santa Maria Maggiore, the only church before you reach the bus station, is now part of the city **prison**. The fifteenth-century church of **Sant'Andrea della Zirada**, in the lee of the Piazzale's multistorey car park, is rarely open and only has its Baroque altar to recommend it anyway; and the diminutive Neoclassical **Nome di Gesù**, cringing underneath the flyover, has absolutely nothing going for it.

San Barnaba

Cutting down the side of the Carmini church takes you over the Rio di San Barnaba, along which a fondamenta runs to the church of San Barnaba. Just before the end of the fondamenta you pass the **Ponte dei Pugni**, the main link between San Barnaba and Santa Margherita, and one of several bridges with this name. Originally built without parapets, they were the sites of ritual battles between the Castellani and Nicolotti (see p.110); this one is inset with marble footprints marking the starting positions. These massed brawls took place between September and Christmas, and obeyed a well-defined etiquette, with prescribed ways of issuing challenges and deploying the antagonists prior to the outbreak of hostilities, the aim of which was to gain possession of the bridge. The fights themselves, however, were sheer bedlam, and fatalities were commonplace, as the armies slugged it out with bare knuckles and steel-tipped lances made from hardened rushes. The lethal weaponry was outlawed in 1574, after a particularly bloody engagement which was arranged for the visit of Henry III of France, and in 1705 the punch-ups were finally banned, and less dangerous forms of competition, such as regattas, were encouraged instead. Pugilists have now been replaced by tourists taking shots of the photogenic San Barnaba grocery barge moored at the foot of the bridge.

The huge, damp-ridden and deconsecrated **San Barnaba** church, built in 1749, has a trompe l'oeil ceiling painting of *St Barnabas in Glory* by Constantino Cedini, a follower of Tiepolo. Despite recent restoration, the ceiling is being restored again because of moisture damage.

San Barnaba is open daily 7.30am–noon & 3–7pm; opening times may vary during exhibitions.

At the time of the church's construction the parish was swarming with so-called *Barnabotti*, impoverished noble families who had moved into the area's cheap lodgings to eke out their meagre incomes. Forbidden as members of the aristocracy to practise a craft or run a shop, some of the *Barnabotti* supported themselves by selling their votes to the mightier families in the Maggior Consiglio, while others resigned themselves to subsistence on a paltry state dole. Visitors to the city often remarked on the incongruous sight of its silk-clad beggars – the nobility of Venice were obliged to wear silk, regardless of their ability to pay for such finery.

The Ca' Rezzonico

The eighteenth century, the period of Venice's political senility and moral degeneration, was also the period of its last grand flourish in the visual and decorative arts, so it's entirely appropriate that the **Museo del Settecento Veneziano** (The Museum of the Venetian Eighteenth Century) should be an ambivalent place. Culled from dozens of different buildings, the collection spreads through most of the enormous **Ca' Rezzonico**, which the city authorities bought in 1934 specifically as a home for the museum. It's a spectacular building and deserves to be a more popular attraction than it is; perhaps the ambitious restoration that's now in progress will rectify this situation, but at the moment it's in something of a state of flux, with only the first floor open to the public. Some of the rooms on this floor have been filled out with the highlights of the second and third floors (eg the **Canalettos**, the Giandomenico **Tiepolo** frescoes, and the Longhi portraits), which will be refurbished whenever sufficient funding can be found. This could take some time, and it's impossible to say for certain what will be on show at any one time; the following account more or less describes the Ca' Rezzonico as it used to be arranged, and as it will in all likelihood be arranged when the work is finished.

The Ca' Rezzonico is usually open: summer 10am–5pm; winter 9am–4pm; closed Fri; L12,000/€6.20.

Most of the decorations and furnishings in the Ca' Rezzonico are genuine items, and where originals weren't available the eighteenth-century ambience has been preserved by using almost indistinguishable modern reproductions. Sumptuary laws in Venice restricted the quantities of silk, brocade and tapestry that could be draped around a house, so legions of painters, stuccoists, cabinet-makers and other such applied artists were employed to fanfare the wealth of their patrons to the world. The work they produced is certainly not to everyone's taste, but even if you find most of the museum's contents frivolous or grotesque, the frescoes by the Tiepolo family and Pietro Longhi's affectionate Venetian scenes should justify the entrance fee.

A man in constant demand in the early part of the century was the Belluno sculptor-cum-woodcarver **Andrea Brustolon**, much of whose output consisted of wildly elaborate pieces of furniture. A few of his pieces are displayed in the chandeliered ballroom at the top of the entrance staircase, and elsewhere on this floor there's an entire roomful of them, including the *Allegory of Strength* console. Featuring Hercules underneath, two river gods holding four vases and a fifth vase held up by three black slaves in chains, this is a creation that makes you marvel at the craftsmanship and wince at the ends to which it was used.

The less fervid imaginations of **Giambattista Tiepolo** and his son **Giandomenico** are introduced in room 2 (off the far right-hand corner of the ballroom) with the ceiling fresco celebrating Ludovico Rezzonico's marriage into the hugely powerful Savorgnan family in 1758. This was quite a year for the Rezzonico clan, as it also brought the election of Carlo Rezzonico as Pope Clement XIII; the son of the man who bought the uncompleted palace and finished its construction, Carlo the pontiff was notorious both for his rampant nepotism and for his prudery – he insisted that the Vatican's antique nude statuary be made more modest by the judicious application of fig leaves. Beyond room 4, with its array of pastels by **Rosalba Carriera**, you come to two other Tiepolo ceilings, enlivening the rooms overlooking the Canal Grande on each side of the main portego – an *Allegory of Merit* by Giambattista and Giandomenico, and *Nobility and Virtue Triumphing over Perfidy*, a solo effort by the father.

In the portego of the second floor are the only two canal views by **Canaletto** on show in public galleries in Venice. Off to the right, room 18 boasts a full suite of green and gold lacquer pieces, one of the finest surviving examples of Venetian chinoiserie, and from there you enter the room devoted to **Pietro Longhi**, whose scenes of life in eighteenth-century Venice – including a version of the famous *Rhinoceros* – have more than enough curiosity value to make up for their shortcomings in execution. Visitors at Carnevale time will recognize several of the festival's components in the Longhi room: the beak-like *volto* masks, for example, and the little doughnuts called *frittelle*, an essential part of the Carnevale scene. Next come

Francesco Guardi's technically more adroit scenes of high society in the parlour of San Zaccaria's convent and the gambling rooms of the Ridotto, but you have to wait until the last suite of rooms on the second floor to see the museum's most engaging paintings – Giandomenico Tiepolo's sequence of **frescoes from the Villa Zianigo** near Mestre, the Tiepolo family home. With the exception of the pieces from the villa's chapel, which date from 1749, the frescoes were painted towards the end of the century, at a time when their satirical playfulness was going out of fashion. *The New World* shows a crowd turned out in its best attire to watch a Sunday peepshow; another room is devoted to the antics of *Pulchinello*, the ancestor of our Mr Punch; and typically good-humoured centaurs and satyrs lark around on nearby walls.

The low-ceilinged rooms of the third floor contain yet more Longhi paintings, but the main point of clambering upstairs (apart from the tremendous view across the rooftops) is to see the **pharmacy** and **puppet theatre**. A sequence of wood-panelled rooms full of the appropriate furniture, ceramic jars and glass bottles, the pharmacy has to be viewed through windows, rather like peering into the set of a Longhi picture. The puppets are fairly unremarkable specimens, each about one foot high, but their very ordinariness makes their survival remarkable in itself.

From the Ca' Rezzonico, the quickest route up to the Rialto takes you across the herringbone-patterned pavement of the Campiello dei Squellini, past the entrance to the main university building and over the Rio Fóscari – whereupon you're in the *San Polo* section. Just to the right of the Ponte dei Fóscari, on the north side, is the central station of Venice's **fire brigade**. One of the few Fascist-era constructions in Venice, it is easily recognizable by the red launches moored under the arches.

For the background to the university building – the Ca' Fóscari – and the neighbouring Palazzi Giustinian, see p.212.

Chapter 3

San Polo

Bounded on one side by the Rio Nuovo–Rio di Ca' Fóscari (the waterways dug under Mussolini's instructions from Piazzale Roma to the Volta del Canal) and on the others by the upper loop of the Canal Grande, the area covered by this chapter is composed of the entire San Polo sestiere, the greater part of the sestiere of Santa Croce and a couple of slivers of Dorsoduro. This jigsaw is not as baffling as it at first appears. There are two main routes through the district, each following approximately the curve of the Canal Grande – one runs between the Rialto and the Scalzi bridge, the other takes you in the opposite direction from the Rialto, down towards the Accademia. Virtually all the essential sights lie on, or just off, one of these two routes, and once you've become familiar with these the exploration of the streets and squares between them can be attempted with only a minimal risk of feeling that you'll never see friends and family again. Wherever you are in this area, you cannot be more than a couple of minutes' well-navigated walk from one of the two roads to the Rialto.

As far as the day-to-day life of Venice is concerned, the focal points of the district are the sociable open space of **Campo San Polo** and the **Rialto** area, once the commercial heart of the Republic and still the home of a **market** that's famous far beyond the boundaries of the city. The bustle of the stalls and the unspoilt bars used by the porters are a good antidote to cultural overload. Nobody, however, should miss the extraordinary pair of buildings in the southern part of San Polo: the colossal Gothic church of the **Frari**, embellished with three of Venice's finest altarpieces, and the **Scuola Grande di San Rocco**, decorated with an unforgettable cycle of paintings by Tintoretto.

In the northern part of the district, Venice's erratically open **modern art, oriental and natural history museums** are clustered together on the bank of the Canal Grande: the first two collections occupy one of the city's most magnificent palaces, while the third is installed in the former headquarters of the Turkish merchants. As ever, numerous treasures are also scattered among the minor churches – for example in **San Cassiano**, **San Simeone Grande** and **San**

Pantaleone. Lastly, if you're in search of a spot in which to sit for an hour and just watch the world go by, head for the **Campo San Giacomo dell'Orio**, one of Venice's better-kept secrets.

From the Rialto to San Simeone Piccolo

Relatively stable building land and a good defensive position drew some of the earliest lagoon settlers to the high bank (*rivo alto*) that was to develop into the **Rialto** district. By 810, when the capital of the lagoon confederation was moved – in the wake of Pepin's invasion – from Malamocco to the more secure islands around here, the inhabited zone had grown well beyond the Rialto itself. While the political centre of the new city was consolidated around San Marco, the Rialto became the commercial area. In the twelfth century Europe's first state bank was opened here, and the financiers of this quarter were to be the heavyweights of the international currency exchanges for the next three hundred years and more. The state departments that oversaw all maritime business were here as well, and in the early sixteenth century the offices of the exchequer were installed in the new **Palazzo dei Camerlenghi**, at the foot of the Rialto bridge.

The connection between wealth and moral turpitude was exemplified by the Rialto, which was almost as famous for its fleshpots as for its cashboxes. A sixteenth-century survey showed that there were about 3000 patrician women in the city, but well over 11,000 prostitutes, the majority of them based in the banking quarter. One Rialto brothel, the *Casteletto*, was especially esteemed for the literary, musical and sexual talents of its staff, and a perennial Venetian bestseller was the *Catalogue of the Chief and Most Renowned Courtesans of Venice*, a directory that told you everything you needed to know, right down to prices. If Thomas Coryat's report of 1608 is anything to go by, the courtesans were seen in some quarters as the city's main attraction – "So infinite are the allurements of these amorous Calypsoes that the fame of them hath drawn many to Venice from some of the remotest parts of Christendome."

The Market

It was through the **markets of the Rialto** that Venice earned its reputation as the bazaar of Europe. Virtually anything could be bought or sold here: Italian fabrics, precious stones, silver plate and gold jewellery, spices and dyes from the Orient. Trading had been going on here for over four hundred years when, in the winter of 1514, a fire destroyed everything in the area except the church. (Most of the wells and canals were frozen solid, so the blaze burned virtually unchecked for a whole day.) The possibility of relocating the

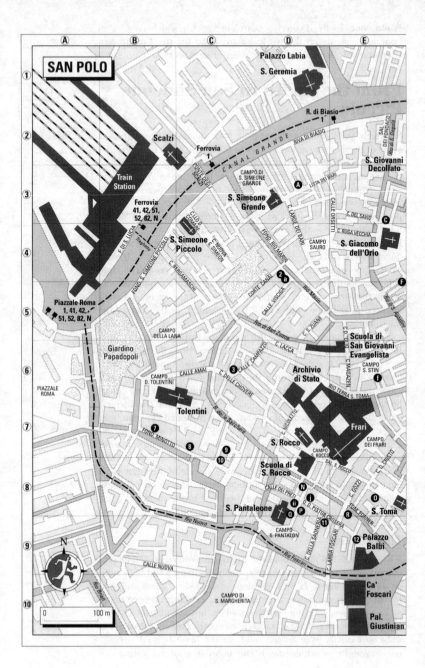

SAN POLO

Palazzo Labia
S. Geremia

R. di Biasio
1

Scalzi
Ferrovia
1

CANAL GRANDE
RIVA DI BIASIO

SAL. DEL FONDACO
Rio di S. Gegola

Train
Station

Ferrovia
41, 42, 51,
52, 82, N

CAMPO D.
S. SIMEONE
GRANDE

LISTA DEI BARI

S. Giovanni
Decollato

S. Simeone
Grande

C. LARGA DEI BARI

CALLE ONSETTI

C. DEL SAVIO

C. RUGA VECCHIA

C

F. DI S. LUCIA

C. LIO D.
COMARE

S. Simeone
Piccolo

C. NUOVA
DI S. SIMEON

FOND. RIO MARIN

CAMPO
SAURO

S. Giacomo
dell'Orio

F

FONDA. S. SIMEONE PICCOLO

C. BERGAMASCHI

CORTE CANAL

2
a

Rio Marin

Rio de S. Agostin

Piazzale Roma
1, 41, 42,
51, 52, 82, N

CALLE VISCIGA

Rio di Sant'Zuane

C. S. ZUANE

CAMPO
DELLA LANA

C. LACCA

PIAZZALE
ROMA

Giardino
Papadopoli

CAMPO
D. TOLENTINI

CALLE AMAI

3 CALLE CAMPAZZO

C. DELLE CHOVERE

Scuola di
San Giovanni
Evangelista

Archivio
di Stato

C. MAGAZEN

CAMPO
S. STIN

i

RIO TERRA S. TOMA

Tolentini

Fo. della Stùcchere

Frari

FOND. MINOTTO

7

8

9

10

C. NICOLETTO

S. Rocco

CAMPO
S. ROCCO

SAL. S. ROCCO

CAMPO
DEI FRARI

C. D. CRISTO

Scuola di
S. Rocco

N

CALLE DEI PRETI

C. GOZZI

FUM. FORNER

S. Tomà

O

Rio Nuovo

S. Pantaleone

ii

C. D. PISTOR CROSERA

R

CAMPO
S. PANTALON

O
P

11

12

CALLE NUOVA

Rio Foscari

C. LARGA FOSCARI

C. DELLA SAONERIA

Palazzo
Balbi

Rio Brieti

CAMPO DI
S. MARGHERITA

Ca'
Foscari

Pal.
Giustinian

0   100 m

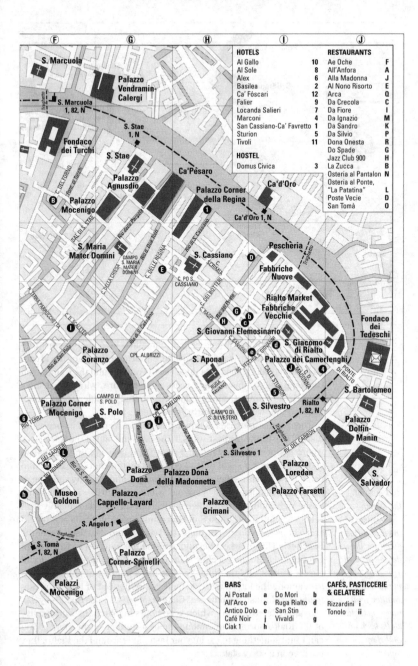

HOTELS		RESTAURANTS	
Al Gallo	10	Ae Oche	F
Al Sole	8	All'Anfora	A
Alex	6	Alla Madonna	J
Basilea	2	Al Nono Risorto	E
Ca' Fóscari	12	Arca	Q
Falier	9	Da Crecola	I
Locanda Salieri	7	Da Fiore	C
Marconi	4	Da Ignazio	M
San Cassiano-Ca' Favretto	1	Da Sandro	K
Sturion	5	Da Silvio	P
Tivoli	11	Dona Onesta	R
		Do Spade	G
HOSTEL		Jazz Club 900	H
Domus Civica	3	La Zucca	B
		Osteria al Pantalon	N
		Osteria al Ponte, "La Patatina"	L
		Poste Vecie	D
		San Tomà	O

BARS		CAFÉS, PASTICCERIE & GELATERIE	
Ai Postali	a	Do Mori	b
All'Arco	c	Ruga Rialto	d
Antico Dolo	e	San Stin	f
Café Noir	j	Vivaldi	g
Ciak 1	h		
		Rizzardini	i
		Tonolo	ii

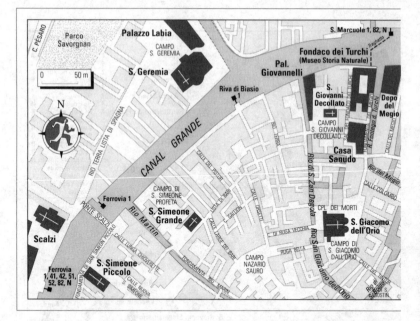

business centre was discussed but found little favour, so reconstruction began almost straight away: the **Fabbriche Vecchie** (the arcaded buildings along the Ruga degli Orefici and around the Campo San Giacomo) were finished five years after the fire, with Sansovino's **Fabbriche Nuove** (running along the Canal Grande from Campo Battisti) following about thirty years later.

Today's Rialto market is tamer than that of Venice at its peak, but it's still one of the liveliest spots in the city, and one of the few places where it's possible to stand in a crowd and hear nothing but Italian spoken. There's a shoal of trinket sellers by the church, gathered to catch the tourists as they spill off the bridge, and a strong showing of glass junk, handbags and "Venezia" sweatshirts further on, but swing to the right and you're in the true heart of the market – mainly fruit sellers around the **Campo San Giacomo**, vegetable stalls and butcher's shops as you go through to the **Campo Battisti**, then the **Pescheria** (fish market) beyond. Around the junction of **Ruga degli Orefici** and **Ruga Vecchia San Giovanni** you'll find wonderful cheese kiosks, and the Ruga Vecchia has a number of good *alimentari* among the kitsch merchants. If you're in need of liquid refreshment, the old-fashioned bars of Calle do Mori–Calle do Spade (by San Giovanni Elemosinario), which keep hours to match the working day of the Rialto porters, are among the best in the city. In short, if you can't find something to excite your taste buds around the Rialto, they must be in a sorry state.

The Pescheria and most of the larger wholesalers at the Rialto close down for the day at around 1pm, but many of the smaller fruit and vegetable stalls keep normal shop hours.

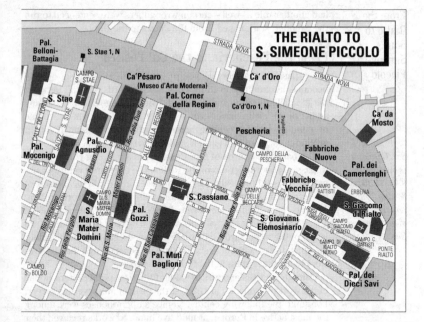

THE RIALTO TO
S. SIMEONE PICCOLO

San Giacomo – and the Gobbo di Rialto

A popular Venetian legend asserts that the city was founded at noon on Friday, March 25, 421; from the same legend derives the claim that the church of **San Giacomo di Rialto** was consecrated in that year, and is thus **the oldest church in Venice**. It might actually be the oldest, though it was rebuilt in 1071, about the same time as San Marco's reconstruction.

San Giacomo is supposed to be open daily from 10am to noon, and sometimes is.

Parts of the present structure date from this period – the interior's six columns of ancient Greek marble have eleventh-century Veneto-Byzantine capitals – and it seems likely that the reconstruction of the church prompted the establishment of the market here. On the outside of the apse a twelfth-century inscription addresses the merchants of the Rialto – "Around this temple let the merchant's law be just, his weights true, and his promises faithful." Early Venetian churches often had lean-to porticoes like that of San Giacomo, but this is one of only two examples left in the city (the other being San Nicolò dei Mendicoli). The inaccuracy of the clock above – a fifteenth-century addition, like the portico – has been a standing joke in Venice since the day it was installed.

On the opposite side of the campo from the church crouches a stone figure known as the **Gobbo di Rialto** or the Rialto hunchback. It was carved in the sixteenth century and supports a granite platform from which state proclamations were read simultaneously with their announcement from the Pietra del Bando, beside San Marco; it had another role as well – certain wrongdoers were sentenced to run the gauntlet, stark naked, from the Piazza to the Gobbo.

From the Pescheria to the Ca' Pésaro

Once past the Pescheria, you're into a district which quickly becomes labyrinthine even by Venetian standards. A stroll between the Rio delle Beccarie and the Rio di San Zan Degolà will satisfy any addict of the picturesque – you cannot walk for more than a couple of minutes without coming across a workshop crammed into a ground-floor room or a garden spilling over a canalside wall.

San Cassiano is open daily 9.45–11.30am & 4.30–7pm; no tourists allowed on Sun.

The barn-like church of **San Cassiano** is a building you're bound to pass as you wander out of the Rialto. The thirteenth-century campanile is the only appealing aspect of the exterior, and the interest of the interior lies mainly with its three paintings by **Tintoretto**: *The Resurrection*, *The Descent into Limbo* and *The Crucifixion* (all 1565–68). The first two have been mauled by restorers, but the third is one of the most startling pictures in Venice – centred on the ladder on which the executioners stand, it's painted as though the observer were lying in the grass at the foot of the Cross.

Campo San Cassiano was the site of the **first public opera house** in the world – it opened in 1636, at the peak of Monteverdi's career. Long into the following century Venice's opera houses were among the most active in Europe; around five hundred works received their first performances here in the first half of the eighteenth century.

A sign directs you from the campo over the right-hand bridge towards the Ca' Pésaro, home of the modern art and oriental collections, but before you reach it you'll pass the back of the **Palazzo Corner della Regina**, home of the Biennale archive. Currently it's closed for restoration, but when it eventually reopens it may have a small selection of works from past shows on display, as it used to do.

Santa Maria Mater Domini is open Mon–Sat 10am–noon.

A diversion down Corte Tiossi from Calle Tiossi brings you to **Santa Maria Mater Domini**, an early sixteenth-century church of disputed authorship – Mauro Codussi and Giovanni Buora are the leading candidates. The rescue of this building is one of Venice in Peril's proudest achievements; now protected by a totally reconstructed roof, the crisp white and grey interior boasts an endearing *Martyrdom of St Christina* by **Vincenzo Catena** (second altar on the right), showing a flight of angels plucking the saint from a carpet-like Lago di Bolsena, into which she had been hurled with a millstone for an anchor. Few works by the elusive Catena have survived, and it is not even certain what he did for a living. He seems to have been a successful spice trader, and thus may have been a businessman who painted for recreation; alternatively, he may have been an artist who subsidized himself through commercial dealings – he is mentioned on the reverse of one of Giorgione's paintings as a "colleague". On the opposite side of the church you'll find one of the city's numerous Tintoretto paintings, a *Discovery of the Cross*.

The small **Campo Santa Maria Mater Domini** would have to be included in any anthology of the hidden delights of Venice; it's a typically Venetian miscellany – a thirteenth-century house (the Casa Zane), a few ramshackle Gothic houses, an assortment of stone reliefs of indeterminate age, a fourteenth-century well-head in the centre, a couple of bars, and an ironsmith's workshop tucked into one corner.

Back at the end of Calle Tiossi, in front of you on the other side of the bridge as you turn right for the Ca' Pésaro, is the late fourteenth-century **Palazzo Agnusdio**, which takes its name not from the family that lived there but from the *patera* of the mystic lamb over the watergate.

The **Ca' Pésaro** was bequeathed to the city at the end of the last century by the Duchessa Felicità Bevilacqua La Masa, who stipulated in her will that it should provide studio and exhibition space for impoverished young artists. Subsequent machinations put paid to the Duchess's enlightened plans, and in place of the intended living arts centre the city acquired the **Museo d'Arte Moderna**. Most of the stuff in this collection is modern only in the chronological sense of the term: pieces bought from the Biennale formed the foundation of the collection, and in its early years the Biennale was a celebration of all that was most conservative in European art. Hence the prevalence of bucolic landscapes and cosy portraits by predominantly Italian artists of limited familiarity. There is a smattering of more challenging work – the likes of Klimt, Kandinsky, Matisse, Klee, Nolde, Ernst and Miró are here, albeit with rarely more than one item – and from time to time there's a good solo retrospective on show here, but all in all this is one of the city's weaker museums. The same goes for the **Museo Orientale**, on the palace's top floor. Built round the hoard of artefacts amassed by the Conte di Bardi during a long Far Eastern voyage in the last century, the jumble of lacquer work, armour, screens, weaponry and so forth is likely to perplex and tire all but the initiated.

From the
Rialto to San
Simeone
Piccolo

*The Museo
d'Arte Moderna
is usually open
Tues–Sun
10am–5pm,
but recently
has often been
closed for
restoration.*

*The Museo
Orientale is
open Tues–Sun
8.15am–2pm;
L4000/€2.07.*

From San Stae to the Museo di Storia Naturale

Continuing along the line of the Canal Grande from the Ca' Pésaro, Calle Pésaro takes you over the Rio della Rioda, and so to the seventeenth-century church of **San Stae** (a contraction of San Eustachio); its Baroque facade, enlivened by precarious statues, was added around 1710. Repairs to the *marmorino* (pulverized marble) surfaces of the interior have made San Stae as bright as an operating theatre. In the chancel there's a series of paintings from the beginning of the eighteenth century, the pick of which are *The Martyrdom of St James the Great* by Piazzetta (low on the left), *The Liberation of St Peter* by Sebastiano Ricci (same row) and *The Martyrdom of St Bartholomew* by Giambattista Tiepolo (opposite). In the first chapel on the left side there's a bust of Antonio Foscarini (see p.208), wrongly executed for treason, as the inscription explains. Exhibitions and

*San Stae is
open Mon–Sat
10am–5pm,
Sun 1–5pm
(closed Sun in
July & Aug);
L3000/€1.54.*

*The Palazzo
Mocenigo is
open
Tues–Sun:
April–Oct
10am–5pm;
Nov–March
10am–4pm;
L3000/€1.54 or
I Musei di San
Marco ticket.*

*San Giovanni
Decollato is
open Mon–Sat
10am–noon.*

*The Museo di
Storia
Naturale is
under restora-
tion, but was
previously
open Tues–Sun
9am–1pm;
L5000/€2.58.*

*San Giacomo
dell'Orio is
open Mon–Sat
10am–5pm,
Sun 1–5pm
(closed Sun in
July & Aug);
L3000/€1.54.*

concerts are often held in San Stae, and exhibitions are also held from time to time in the diminutive building alongside, the early seventeenth-century **Scuola dei Battioro e Tiraoro** (goldsmiths' guild).

Halfway down the salizzada flanking San Stae is the early seventeenth-century **Palazzo Mocenigo**, now the home of the *Centro Studi di Storia del Tessuto e del Costume*. The library and archive of the study centre occupy part of the building, but a substantial portion of the *piano nobile* is open to the public, and there are few Venetian interiors of this date that have been so meticulously preserved. The main room is decorated with workaday portraits of various Mocenigo men, while the rooms to the side are full of miscellaneous pictures, antique furniture, Murano chandeliers and display cases of dandified clothing and cobweb-fine lacework. The curtains are kept closed to protect such delicate items as floral silk stockings, silvery padded waistcoats, and an extraordinarily embroidered outfit once worn by what must have been the best-dressed five-year-old in town.

The signposted route to the train station passes the deconsecrated and almost permanently shut church of **San Giovanni Decollato**, or San Zan Degolà in dialect – it means "St John the Beheaded". Established in the opening years of the eleventh century, it has retained its basilican layout through several alterations; the columns and capitals of the nave date from the first century of its existence, and parts of its fragmentary frescoes (at the east end) could be of the same age. Some of the paintings are certainly thirteenth century, and no other church in Venice has frescoes that predate them. The church also boasts one of the city's characteristic ship's-keel ceilings.

The **Museo di Storia Naturale** is right by the church, in the **Fondaco dei Turchi**. Top-billing exhibits are the remains of a 37-foot-long ancestor of the crocodile and an Ouranosaurus, both dug up in the Sahara in 1973; of stricter relevance to Venetian life is the display relating to the lagoon's marine life, and a pre-Roman boat dredged from the silt. However, in recent years the building has been undergoing a major restoration, which shows little sign of drawing to a close soon; for an entry on the building itself, see p.210.

From San Giacomo dell'Orio to San Simeone Piccolo

Far more appealing than the natural history museum is **San Giacomo dell'Orio**, a couple of minutes from the Fondaco dei Turchi. Standing in a shaded campo which, despite its size, you could easily miss if you weren't looking for it, the church perhaps takes its enigmatic name from a laurel (*lauro*) that once grew here, or might once have been called San Giacomo dal Rio (St James of the River), or once have stood on a *luprio*, the term for a tract of dried swampland.

The fascinating **interior** is an agglomeration of materials and styles from the thirteenth century to the sixteenth. Founded in the ninth century and rebuilt in 1225 – the approximate date of the campanile

– San Giacomo was remodelled on numerous subsequent occasions. Its **ship's-keel roof** dates from the fourteenth century; the massive columns, made stockier by frequent raisings of the pavement, are a couple of hundred years older. Two of the columns – behind the pulpit and in the right transept – were brought to Venice by the fleet returning from the Fourth Crusade; the latter, an extraordinary chunk of *verde antico*, was compared by the excitable Gabriele d'Annunzio to "the fossilized compression of an immense verdant forest". The shape of the main apse betrays its Byzantine origins, but the inlaid marbles were placed there in the sixteenth century. The main altarpiece, *Madonna and Four Saints*, was painted by Lorenzo Lotto in 1546, shortly before he left the city complaining that the Venetians had not treated him fairly; the Crucifix that hangs in the air in front of it is attributed to Paolo Veneziano. In the left transept there's an altarpiece by Paolo Veronese, and there's a fine set of pictures from Veronese's workshop on the ceiling of the **new sacristy**: *Faith* and *The Doctors of the Church*. Also in the new sacristy you'll see Francesco Bassano's *Madonna in Glory* and *St John the Baptist Preaching* – Bassano's family provide the Baptist's audience, while the spectator on the far left, in the red hat, is Titian. The **old sacristy** is a showcase for the art of Palma il Giovane, whose cycle in celebration of the Eucharist covers the walls and part of the ceiling.

San Giacomo dell'Orio is plumb in the middle of an extensive residential district, much of which is as close to bland as you can get in Venice. Don't, though, leave out the church of **San Simeone Profeta** (or Grande) – remarkable for its reclining **effigy of Saint Simeon** (to the left of the chancel), a luxuriantly bearded, larger than lifesize figure, whose half-open mouth disturbingly creates the impression of the moment of death. According to its inscription, it was sculpted in 1317 by **Marco Romano**, but some experts doubt that the sculpture can be that old, as nothing else of that date bears comparison with it. On the left immediately inside the door, there's a run-of-the-mill *Last Supper* by **Tintoretto**. Originating in the tenth century, the church has often been rebuilt – most extensively in the eighteenth century, when the city sanitation experts, anxious about the condition of the plague victims who had been buried under the flagstones in the 1630 epidemic, ordered the whole floor to be relaid. Close by the church, the **Riva di Biasio** allows a short walk on the bank of the Canal Grande, with a view across the water of San Geremia. This stretch of paving allegedly takes its name from a butcher named Biasio who was decapitated between the columns of the Piazzetta after it was discovered that his prime pork cuts were in fact lumps of human flesh.

San Simeone Profeta is the last stop before the Scalzi bridge. Immediately after the bridge rises the green dome of the early eighteenth-century **San Simeone Piccolo**, where for many years Venice's only Latin Mass has been conducted, despite the church's notorious state of dilapidation; it is now at last receiving a facelift.

*San Simeone
Profeta is open
to tourists
Mon–Sat
9am–noon &
4–6pm.*

From the Rialto to San Tomà

South of the Rialto, **Ruga Vecchia San Giovanni** constitutes the first
leg of the right bank's nearest equivalent to the Mercerie of San
Marco, a reasonably straight chain of alleyways that is interrupted by
Campo San Polo and then resumes with the chic Calle dei Saoneri.
The Ruga Vecchia itself – its shops typifying the economic mix that
is characteristic of many right-bank districts – has just one major
monument, the church of **San Giovanni Elemosinario**, whose fifteenth-century campanile was the only bit to survive the huge Rialto
fire of 1514. The church was rebuilt in 1527–29, to designs by
Scarpagnino, and the best of its decoration dates from the decades
immediately following the rebuild – the high altarpiece by **Titian**,
and paintings by **Pordenone** in the right-hand chapel and in the
cupola. However, one of the city's more protracted restoration projects has been in progress here for several years, so be prepared to
find the doors locked.

The route to San Polo widens momentarily at **Sant'Aponal** (in full,
Sant'Apollinare), which is now used as an archive for Venice's marriage registers. Its most interesting feature is on the outside, anyway
– the *Crucifixion and Scenes from the Life of Christ* (1294), in the
tabernacle over the door. Venetian legend has it that Pope Alexander
III, on the run in 1177 from the troops of Emperor Frederick
Barbarossa, found refuge close to Sant'Aponal; over the entrance to
the Sottoportego della Madonna (to your left and slightly behind you
as you face the church facade), a plaque records his plight and
promises a perpetual plenary indulgence to anyone saying a Pater
Noster and Ave Maria on the spot.

Slip down Calle Sbianchesini from Sant'Aponal (towards the Canal
Grande), and you come to the nondescript church of **San Silvestro**.
It deserves a visit for Tintoretto's *Baptism of Christ*, one of his sim-
plest paintings. Across from the church, at no. 1022, is the Palazzo
Valier, where Giorgione died in 1510.

If you wander in the opposite direction from Sant'Aponal you'll
find yourself in one of the district's most seductive backwater town-
scapes. Leave Campo Sant'Aponal by Calle Ponte Storto, which leads
to the crook-backed Ponte Storto; the gorgeous building on your
right, as you cross the water, is the palace where Bianca Cappello
was living when she met Pietro Bonaventuri (see p.180 for the
story). At the foot of the bridge go left onto Fondamenta Banco
Salviati, then halfway along the colonnade turn right into Calle
Stretta, the narrowest alley in the whole city. Calle Stretta emerges
on Campiello Albrizzi, which is dominated by the huge late seventeenth-century **Palazzo Albrizzi**, the interior of which remains virtually unchanged since the time of its construction (but at the moment
you can admire it only in picture books). Cross the campiello and go
down Calle Albrizzi; turn left at the end and you'll come to the water

at Fondamenta delle Tette. Stand on the little bridge here – **Ponte delle Tette** – and to the north you have a view of a ravine of palaces leading off towards the Canal Grande, while to the south you'll see the side of the Palazzo Albrizzi, with the foliage of a neighbouring garden spilling over towards it across the canal. If you're wondering about the name of the delle Tette bridge and canalside, it means exactly what you suspect it means: the bridge marks the edge of the zone within which the Rialto prostitutes were allowed to solicit, and one of their advertising ploys was to air their breasts on the balconies of their houses.

Campo San Polo

The largest square in Venice after the Piazza, the **Campo San Polo** is the best place in the area to sit down and tuck into a bagful of supplies from the Rialto market. Most of the traffic passes down the church side, leaving a huge area of the campo free for those in no hurry to get a bit of sun, and for any budding Paolo Maldini of the parish to practise his ball skills. In earlier times it was the site of

---

Aldus Manutius

Except for the scurrilous hack Pietro Aretino and the altogether more proper Cardinal Bembo (whose Ciceronian prose spawned an imitative style known as Bembismo), Renaissance Venice produced virtually no writers of any importance – and yet it was the greatest printing centre in Italy. By the second half of the sixteenth century there were over one hundred presses in Venice, and their output was more than three times greater than that of Rome, Florence and Milan added together. The doyen of Venetian printers was **Aldus Manutius** (Aldo Manuzio), creator of italic typeface and publisher of the first pocket editions of the classics, whose workshop stood close to Campo San Polo. Founded in 1490, the Aldine Press employed teams of printers, die-cutters, proof-readers and compositors, but was always on the lookout for casual labour, as the sign over the door made clear – "Whoever you are, Aldus earnestly begs you to state your business in the fewest words possible and begone, unless, like Hercules to weary Atlas, you would lend a helping hand. There will always be enough work for you and all who pass this way." Erasmus once grudgingly did a stint here, when the Aldine workshop was producing an edition of his *Proverbs*.

If you leave Campo San Polo at its northeast corner, walk along Calle Bernardo (past the florid Gothic Palazzo Bernardo), cross the canal to Calle del Scaleter and then follow that alley to its end, you'll come to Rio Terrà Seconda, where a plaque at no. 2311 identifies a small Gothic house as the site of the workshop of Manutius. However, documentary evidence makes it clear that the Manutius shop was located "by the Santo Agostino baker"; off Campo San Agostin, which lies at the south end of Rio Terrà Seconda, you'll find a Calle del Pistor ("Baker's Alley"), where a bakery is still in operation. So in all likelihood it was here rather than at no. 2311 that Manutius was based until the last years of his life, when he moved over the Canal Grande to what is now Campo Manin.

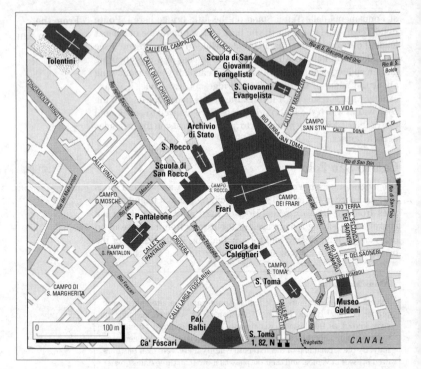

weekly markets and occasional fairs, as well as being used as a parade ground and bullfighting arena. And on one notorious occasion Campo San Polo was the scene of a bloody act of political retribution. On February 26, 1548, Lorenzaccio de'Medici, having fled Florence after murdering the deranged duke Alessandro (a distant relative and former friend), emerged from San Polo church to come face to face with the emissaries of Duke Cosimo I, Alessandro's successor. A contemporary account records that a struggle ensued, at the end of which Lorenzaccio was left "with a great cut across his head, which split in two pieces", and his uncle, Alessandro Soderini, lay dead beside him. The assassins took refuge in the Spanish embassy, but the Venetian government, with customary pragmatism, decided that the internal squabbles of Florence were of no concern to Venice, and let the matter rest.

Several palaces overlook the campo, the most impressive of which is the double **Palazzo Soranzo**, built between the late fourteenth and mid-fifteenth centuries, across the square from the church. This might seem an exception to the rule that the main palace facade should look onto the water, but in fact a canal used to run across the campo just in front of the Soranzo house. Casanova gained his intro-

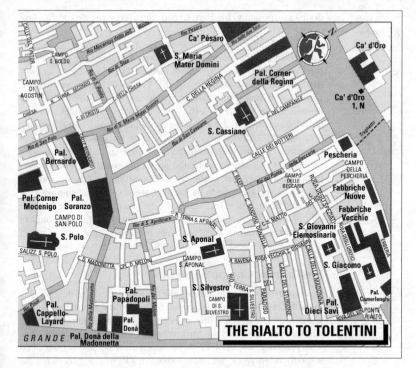

THE RIALTO TO TOLENTINI

duction to the Venetian upper classes through a senator who lived in this palace; he was hired to work as a musician in the house and so impressed the old man that he was adopted as his son.

On the same side of Campo San Polo as the church, but in the opposite corner, is the **Palazzo Corner Mocenigo**, designed around 1550 by Sanmicheli – the main facade is visible from the bridge beyond the church. In 1909 **Frederick Rolfe** (Baron Corvo) became a tenant here, an arrangement that came to an abrupt end the following year when his hosts discovered that the manuscript he was working on – *The Desire and Pursuit of the Whole* – was a vitriolic satire directed at them and their acquaintances. Rolfe was given the alternative of abandoning the libellous novel or moving out; he moved out, contracted pneumonia as a result of sleeping rough and became so ill he was given the last rites – but he managed to pull through, and lived for a further three disreputable years.

San Polo is open Mon–Sat 10am–5pm, Sun 1–5pm (closed Sun in July & Aug); L3000/€1.54.

San Polo church

Restoration carried out in the early nineteenth century made a thorough mess of the fifteenth-century Gothic of **San Polo** church, which was established as far back as the ninth century. The beautiful main

doorway, possibly by Bartolomeo Bon, survives from the first church.

The bleak interior is worth a visit for a superior *Last Supper* by **Tintoretto** (on the left as you enter) and a cycle of the *Stations of the Cross* (*Via Crucis*) by **Giandomenico Tiepolo** in the Oratory of the Crucifix (entrance under organ). This powerful series, painted when the artist was only twenty, may persuade you to amend a few preconceptions about the customarily frivolous-seeming Giandomenico, even if some of the scenes do feature some lustrously attired sophisticates who seem to have drifted into the action from the salons of eighteenth-century Venice. A couple of Tiepolo ceiling panels and two other easel paintings supplement the *Via Crucis*; back in the main part of the church, paintings by Giandomenico's father and Veronese are to be found on the second altar opposite the door and in the chapel on the left of the chancel respectively, but neither shows the artist at his best. The detached campanile, built in 1362, has a couple of twelfth-century lions at its base, one of which is playing with a snake, the other with a severed human head.

South from Campo San Polo

If you turn right halfway down Calle dei Saoneri, you're on your way to the Frari (see opposite); carry on to the end and then turn left, and you'll soon come to the fifteenth-century **Palazzo Centani**, in Calle dei Nomboli. This was the birthplace of **Carlo Goldoni** (1707–93), who practised law until 1748, by which time he had accumulated some fourteen years' part-time experience in writing pieces for the indigenous *commedia dell'arte*. Like all *commedia* pieces, the scripts written during that period were in essence little more than vehicles for the semi-improvised clowning of the actors impersonating the genre's stock characters – tricky Harlequin, doddering Pantalon, capricious Colombine, and so on. Goldoni set about reforming the *commedia* from within, turning it eventually into a medium for sharp political observation – indeed, his arch-rival Carlo Gozzi accused Goldoni of creating an "instrument of social subversion". Despite his enormous success, in 1762 he left Venice to work for the Comédie Italienne in Paris, where he also taught Italian in the court of Louis XVI, and received a royal pension until the outbreak of the Revolution. Goldoni's plays are still the staple of theatrical life in Venice, and there's no risk of running out of material – allegedly, he once bet a friend that he could produce one play a week for a whole year, and won. Goldoni's home now houses the *Istituto di Studi Teatrali* and the **Museo Goldoni**, a small collection of first editions, autograph papers and theatrical paraphernalia; for the lay person the museum is less diverting than the building itself, which has one of Venice's finest Gothic courtyards and a beautiful well-head.

The Museo Goldoni is being restored; its opening hours used to be Mon–Thurs 8.30am–1.30pm, admission free.

The parish of San Tomà, the base of many of Venice's best silver- and goldsmiths, is focused on **San Tomà** church, a few yards past

Goldoni's house. For many years a sad, broken-backed structure encased in scaffolding, San Tomà has been gleamingly restored, but is hardly ever open. In the days when the Venetians were known as the sharpest religious relic-hunters around, San Tomà was the city's bumper depository, claiming to possess some 10,000 sacred bits and pieces, and a dozen intact holy corpses. At the other end of the campo stands the **Scuola dei Calegheri** – the shoemakers' guild, as advertised by the footwear carved into the lintel, below the relief by Pietro Lombardo (1478) that shows Saint Mark healing the cobbler Ananias. The building is now used as a library and exhibition space.

Vaporetto and traghetto stages – two of the transport system's most useful time-savers – are at the back of the church, midway between the Rialto and Accademia bridges; go down the left side of the church for the gondola traghetto, go right for the vaporetto.

The Frari district

For a rapid survey of the summit of Venetian painting in its golden age, your first stop after the Accademia should be the constellation of buildings a few alleys west of San Polo – the **Frari**, the **Scuola Grande di San Rocco** and **San Rocco** church. The genesis of Ruskin's obsession with Venice was a visit to the Scuola, where a pictorial interpretation of the life of Christ by **Tintoretto** flows through the entire building; and if you can take yet more after the intensity of the Scuola's cycle, the church next door contains further works by him. A trio of magnificent altarpieces by **Bellini** and **Titian** are the principal treasures of the Frari, but even if these don't strike a chord, there's bound to be something among the church's assembly of paintings, sculptures and monuments that'll get it onto your list of Venetian highlights.

Santa Maria Gloriosa dei Frari

San Zanipolo and **Santa Maria Gloriosa dei Frari** – abbreviated to the Frari – are the twin Gothic giants of Venice: from the campanile of San Marco they can be seen jutting above the rooftops on opposite sides of the Canal Grande, like a pair of destroyers amid a flotilla of yachts.

The Frari is open Mon–Sat 9am–6pm, Sun 1–6pm; L3000/€1.54.

The Franciscans were granted a plot of land here around 1250, not long after the death of their founder, but almost no sooner was the first church completed (in 1338) than work began on a vast replacement – a project which took well over a hundred years. The campanile, one of the city's landmarks and the tallest after San Marco's, was finished in 1396.

Admirers of northern Gothic are unlikely to fall in love at first sight with this mountain of brick. Only a few pieces of sculpture relieve the monotony of the exterior: on the **west front**, there's a figure of *The Risen Christ* by **Vittoria**, and a *Virgin* and *St Francis* from the workshop of **Bartolomeo Bon**; an impressive early fifteenth-century Tuscan

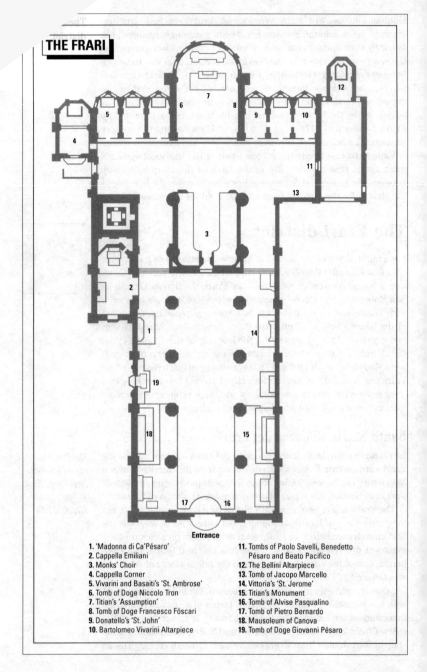

THE FRARI

1. 'Madonna di Ca'Pésaro'
2. Cappella Emiliani
3. Monks' Choir
4. Cappella Corner
5. Vivarini and Basaiti's 'St. Ambrose'
6. Tomb of Doge Niccolo Tron
7. Titian's 'Assumption'
8. Tomb of Doge Francesco Fóscari
9. Donatello's 'St. John'
10. Bartolomeo Vivarini Altarpiece

11. Tombs of Paolo Savelli, Benedetto Pésaro and Beato Pacifico
12. The Bellini Altarpiece
13. Tomb of Jacopo Marcello
14. Vittoria's 'St. Jerome'
15. Titian's Monument
16. Tomb of Alvise Pasqualino
17. Tomb of Pietro Bernardo
18. Mausoleum of Canova
19. Tomb of Doge Giovanni Pésaro

Entrance

relief of the *Madonna and Child with Angels* is set into the side of the left transept. As is so often the case in Venice, though, the outside of the church is a misleadingly dull prelude to a remarkable interior.

Titian's altarpieces

Paradoxically, Venice is under-endowed with paintings by **Titian**, its most illustrious artist: apart from the Accademia and the Salute, the Frari is the only building in Venice with more than a single first-rate work by him. One of these – the **Assumption** – you see immediately as you look towards the high altar through the monks' choir. (The choir itself was built in the late fifteenth century, with a marble screen by Bartolomeo Bon and Pietro Lombardo; it's the only one left in Venice that occupies a site in the nave.)

A piece of compositional and colouristic bravura for which there was no precedent in Venetian art – for one thing, no previous altarpiece had emphasized the vertical axis over the horizontal – the *Assumption* nevertheless fits its surroundings perfectly. The spiralling motion of the Apostles and the Virgin complements the vertical movement of the surrounding architecture, an integration that is strengthened by the coincidence between the division of the painting's two major groupings and the division of the windows in the chancel. It seems to have disconcerted the friars for whom it was painted, but nonetheless was instantly recognized as a major work. **Marin Sanudo**, whose *Diaries* are an essential source for historians of the Republic, somehow wrote 58 volumes containing scarcely a mention of any Venetian artist – yet even he refers to the ceremony on May 19, 1518, at which the picture was unveiled.

The other Titian masterpiece here, the **Madonna di Ca' Pésaro** (on the left wall, between the third and fourth columns), was completed eight years after the *Assumption* and was equally innovative in its displacement of the figure of the Virgin from the centre of the picture. The altarpiece was commissioned by Bishop Jacopo Pésaro, who managed to combine his episcopal duties with a military career; in 1502 he had led a successful naval campaign against the Turks – hence the prisoners being dragged in, behind the kneeling figure of Pésaro himself, to meet the Redeemer and His Mother. Pésaro's tomb, with an effigy, is to the right of the picture (c.1547).

The chapels, chancel and sacristy

A doorway next to the Pésaro monument leads into the **Cappella Emiliani**, which has a fifteenth-century marble altarpiece by followers of Jacobello Dalle Masegne. The **Cappella Corner**, at the end of left transept, contains a superbly vibrant painting by Bartolomeo Vivarini, *St Mark Enthroned* (1474), and, on the font, a damaged figure of St John the Baptist by Sansovino (1554).

St Ambrose and other Saints, the last painting by **Alvise Vivarini**, the nephew of Bartolomeo, stands in the adjoining chapel.

Overpopulated with meticulously drawn but emotionally inert fig-ures, like a roomful of mannequins, it was finished around 1503 by a pupil, Marco Basaiti. A plaque in the floor marks the **grave of Monteverdi**, for thirty years the choirmaster of San Marco.

Two monuments illustrating the emergence in Venice of Renaissance sculptural style flank the Titian *Assumption*: on the left the proto-Renaissance **tomb of Doge Niccolò Tron**, by Antonio Rizzo and assistants (1476); on the right, the more archaic and chaotic **tomb of Doge Francesco Fóscari**, carved shortly after Fóscari's death in 1457 (after 34 years as doge) by **Antonio and Paolo Bregno**. The story of Fóscari's last days is one of the most poignant in Venice's history. Already in ill health and constantly harried by political ene-mies, Fóscari went into a rapid decline when his son, Jacopo, was found guilty of treason and exiled for life. Within half a year Jacopo was dead, and Doge Fóscari sank further into a depression which his opponents lost no time in exploiting. After several months of pres-sure, they forced him into resignation; a week later he died. It was reported that when the senators and new doge were told of his death, during Mass in the Basilica, they looked guiltily at each other, "know-ing well that it was they who had shortened his life".

The wooden statue of *St John the Baptist*, in the next chapel, was commissioned from **Donatello** in 1438 by Florentine merchants in Padua; recent work has restored the luridly naturalistic appearance of what seems to be the sculptor's first work in the Veneto. In the last of the chapels stands a Bartolomeo Vivarini altarpiece, *Madonna and Child with Saints*; painted in 1482, it reminds you of the con-servatism of most Venetian *quattrocento* art in comparison to that being created at the same time in Donatello's native Tuscany.

Above the door to the sacristy most of the space is occupied by three very different tombs. The one on the left is the **tomb of Paolo Savelli** (c.1406), the first equestrian monument in Venice; next along is **Lorenzo Bregno**'s tomb of another Pésaro – Benedetto, head of the Venetian army, who died in Corfu in 1503. The flamboyant Gothic work on the other side of the door is the terracotta **tomb of Beato Pacifico**, who is traditionally credited with beginning the present church; he was placed here in 1437, nearly a century after his death.

Giovanni Bellini's *Madonna and Child with SS. Nicholas of Bari, Peter, Mark and Benedict* was painted in 1488 for the altar of the **sacristy**. It's still there, in its original frame, and alone would justify a long visit to the Frari. Gazing at this picture is like looking into a room that's soaked in a warm dawn light; in the words of Henry James – "it is as solemn as it is gorgeous and as simple as it is deep". From the sacristy there's occasional access to the **chapter house**, with its tomb of Doge Francesco Dandolo (c.1340); the paint-ing above it by **Paolo Veneziano** (which is sometimes displayed in the sacristy) contains what is probably the first portrait of a doge ever painted from life.

The rest of the church

Back in the right transept, on the west wall, there's the very odd
tomb of **Jacopo Marcello**, supported by small stooping figures
(c.1485, probably by Giovanni Buora). High on the wall round the
corner is something far less florid but equally strange – a plain black
coffin which is said to have been meant for the body of the *condottiere* **Carmagnola**, who, having shown a suspicious reluctance to
earn his money against the Milanese (his former employers), was
executed after a dodgy treason trial in 1432. Carmagnola is now in
Milan, and another tenant occupies the coffin.

Facing the Pésaro altarpiece stands one of **Alessandro
Vittoria**'s best marble figures – *St Jerome*, for which Titian was
reputedly the model. The house-sized tomb further along is the
bombastic **monument to Titian**, built in the mid-nineteenth century on the supposed place of his burial. He died in 1576, in
around his ninetieth year, a casualty of the plague; such was the
esteem in which Titian was held, he was the only victim to be
allowed a church burial in the course of the outbreak, one of the
most terrible in the city's history.

The delicate statuettes on the water stoups against the last
columns, facing each other across the nave, are *St Anthony of
Padua* and *St Agnes* by Campagna (1609). The **tomb of Procurator
Alvise Pasqualino**, to the left of the door, is attributed to Lorenzo
Bregno, whose death in 1523 preceded his client's by five years.
Ordering your tomb in advance was not an unusual practice: **Pietro
Bernardo** (died 1538), whose tomb (possibly by Tullio Lombardo,
who died in 1532) is on the other side of the door, did the same thing
– although the finished article was rather more humble than he had
intended. In his will he specified, among other provisions, that his
epitaph should be cut in letters legible from 25 paces, and should be
accompanied by an epic poem of 800 stanzas, extolling the Bernardo
family. His executors seem to have wriggled out of these clauses, and
out of another that ordered that a monastic choir should sing psalms
in front of his tomb on the first Sunday of every month until
Judgement Day.

The marble pyramid with the troop of mourners is the **Mausoleum
of Canova**, erected in 1827 by pupils of the sculptor, following a
design he himself had made for the tombs of Titian and Maria
Christina of Austria. Only the artist's heart is actually entombed here
– most of the body was interred at his birthplace, Possagno, but his
right hand is somewhere in the Accademia. Finally, moving along
from the Canova monument, you'll be stopped in your tracks by what
is surely the most grotesque monument in the city; this is the tomb
of yet another Pésaro – **Doge Giovanni Pésaro** (1669). The architecture is usually attributed to Longhena; for the gigantic ragged-
trousered Moors and decomposing corpses, a German sculptor
called Melchiorre Barthel must take the blame.

*For more on
Canova, see
p.381.*

The state archive

At the fall of the Republic the Franciscan monastery attached to the church was taken over for use as the **Archivio di Stato** (State Archive). Its documents, cramming more than three hundred rooms, relate to the Council of Ten, the courts, the embassies, the Arsenale, the scuole – to every aspect of Venetian public life – and go back as far as the ninth century. From time to time the archive puts on an exhibition of material dredged from the shelves; the shows habitually sound unenthralling, but if you're at all interested in the city's past you should get something from them.

The Scuola Grande di San Rocco

Venice may not tell you much about Titian's work that you didn't already know, but in the case of **Tintoretto** the situation is reversed – until you've been to Venice, and in particular the **Scuola Grande di San Rocco**, you haven't really seen him.

"As regards the pictures which it contains, it is one of the three most precious buildings in Italy," wrote Ruskin, and although the claim's open to argument, it's not difficult to understand why he resorted to such hyperbole. (His other votes were for the Sistine Chapel and the Campo Santo at Pisa – the latter was virtually ruined in World War II.) The unremitting concentration and restlessness of Tintoretto's paintings won't inspire unqualified enthusiasm in everyone: Henry James, though an admirer, found the atmosphere of San Rocco "difficult to breathe". But even those who prefer their art at a lower voltage will find this an overwhelming experience.

From its foundation in 1478, the special concern of this particular scuola was the relief of the sick – a continuation of the Christian mission of its patron saint, Saint Roch (Rocco) of Montpellier, who in 1315 left his home town to work among plague victims in Italy, then returned home only to be spurned by his wealthy family and die in prison, aged just thirty-two. The Scuola had been going for seven years when the body of the saint was brought to Venice from Germany, and the consequent boom in donations was so great that in 1489 it acquired the status of *scuola grande*.

The intervention of Saint Roch was held to be especially efficacious in cases of bubonic plague, an illness from which he himself had been saved by the ministrations of a divinely inspired dog, which brought him bread and licked his wounds clean (which is why the churches of Venice are littered with paintings of the saint pointing to a sore on his thigh, usually with a dog in attendance). When, in 1527, the city was hit by an outbreak of plague, the Scuola's revenue rocketed to record levels as gifts poured in from people hoping to secure Saint Roch's protection against the disease. In 1515 the Scuola, previously based in a room within the Frari, had commissioned a prestigious new headquarters from **Bartolomeo Bon the Younger**, but for

The Scuola Grande di San Rocco is open daily: summer 9am–5.30pm; winter 10am–4pm; L9000/€4.62 – including rental of a very good audio guide.

The Scuole

The Venetian institutions known as the **scuole** seem to have originated in the thirteenth century, with the formation of the flagellant orders, whose public scourgings were intended to purge the sins of the world. The inter-action between these societies of flagellants and the lay brotherhoods established by the city's branches of the mendicant orders (the Franciscans and the Dominicans) gave rise in 1260 to the formation of the confraternity called **Scuola di Santa Maria della Carità**, the first of the so-called **Scuole Grande**. By the middle of the sixteenth century there were five more of these major confraternities – **San Giovanni Evangelista**, **San Marco**, **Santa Maria della Misericordia**, **San Rocco** and **San Teodoro** – plus scores of smaller bodies known as the Scuole Minore, of which at one time there were as many as four hundred.

The Scuole Grande, drawing much of their membership from the wealthiest professional and mercantile groups, and with rosters of up to six hundred men, received subscriptions that allowed them to fund lavish architectural and artistic projects, of which the Scuola Grande di San Rocco is the most spectacular example. The Scuole Minore, united by membership of certain guilds (eg goldsmiths at the Scuola dei Battioro e Tiraori, shoe-makers at the Scuola dei Calerghi), or by common nationality (as with San Giorgo degli Schiavoni, the Slavs' scuola), generally operated from far more modest bases. Yet all scuole had the same basic functions – to provide assistance for their members (eg dowries and medical aid), to offer a place of communal worship, and to distribute alms and services in emergencies (anything from plague relief to the provision of troops). It was a frequently expressed complaint, however, that the Scuole Grande were prone to lose sight of their original aims in their rush to outdo each other; a piece of dog-gerel written in 1541 lays this accusation against the Misericordia:

> *These men have caused ruin, it's easy to see,*
> *Merely to satisfy whims on condition*
> *Of giving San Rocco some stiff competition.*

To an extent, the scuole also acted as a kind of political safety valve. The councils of state were the unique preserve of the city's self-designat-ed patrician class, but the scuole were administered by traders, doctors, lawyers, artisans and civil servants. Technically they had no real power, but a wealthy private club like the Scuola Grande di San Rocco could, if it chose, act as an effective pressure group. Like all other Venetian institu-tions, the scuole came to an end with the coming of Napoleon, who dis-banded them in 1806. Most of their possessions were scattered, and their headquarters were in time put to new uses – thus the Scuola Grande di San Marco became the city hospital, the Scuola Grande di Santa Maria della Carità became the galleries of the Accademia, the Scuola Grande di Maria della Misericordia has become a sports hall. Two of the scuole, however, were revived in the middle of the nineteenth century and continue to func-tion as charitable bodies in the magnificently decorated buildings they commissioned centuries ago – they are the Scuola di San Giorgo degli Schiavoni and Scuola Grande di San Rocco.

various reasons the work had ground to a halt within a decade; the fattened coffers prompted another phase of building, and from 1527 to 1549 the scheme was taken over by **Scarpagnino**.

When the scaffolding came down in 1560, the end product was somewhat incoherent and lopsided. Not that the members of the Scuola would have been bothered for long: within a few years the decoration of the interior was under way, and it was this decoration – **Tintoretto**'s cycle of more than fifty major paintings – that secured the confraternity's social standing. An opportunistic little trick won the first contract for Tintoretto. In 1564 the Scuola held a competition to decide who should paint the inaugural picture for the recently completed building. The subject was to be *The Glorification of St Roch*, and four artists were approached for proposals: Salviati, Zuccari, Veronese and Tintoretto, who had already painted a number of pictures for the neighbouring church of San Rocco. On the day for submissions the first three duly presented their sketches; Tintoretto, though, had painted a finished panel and persuaded a sidekick to rig it up, hidden by a veil, in the very place in which the winning picture was to be installed – the centre of the ceiling in the Sala dell'Albergo. A rope was pulled, the picture revealed, and the commission, despite the opposition's fury, was given to Tintoretto. Further commissions duly ensued.

The paintings

The narrative sequence of the cycle begins with the first picture in the lower room – the *Annunciation*. But to appreciate Tintoretto's development you have to begin in the smaller room on the upper storey – the **Sala dell'Albergo**. This is dominated by the stupendous *Crucifixion* (1565), the most compendious image of the event ever painted. Henry James made even greater claims for it: "Surely no single picture in the world contains more of human life; there is everything in it." Ruskin was reduced to a state of dumbfounded wonder – his loquacious commentary on the San Rocco cycle concludes with the entry: "I must leave this picture to work its will on the spectator; for it is beyond all analysis, and above all praise." Tintoretto's other works in this room – aside from the contract-winning *Glorification of St Roch* in the middle of the celing – are on the entrance wall: *The Way to Calvary*, *Christ Crowned with Thorns* and *Christ before Pilate*.

Tintoretto finished his contribution to the Sala dell'Albergo in 1567. Eight years later, when the Scuola decided to proceed with the embellishment of the main upper hall – the **chapter house** – he undertook to do the work in return for nothing more than his expenses. In the event he was awarded a lifetime annuity, and then commenced the three large panels of the **ceiling**, beginning with *The Miracle of the Bronze Serpent*. With their references to the alleviation of physical suffering, this colossal picture and its companions – *Moses Striking Water from the Rock* and *The Miraculous Fall of Manna* – constitute a coded declaration of the Scuola's charitable programme, and the Scuola's governors were so satisfied with Tintoretto's conception that he was given the task of completing the decoration of the entire interior. It was a project to which he would

give precedence over all his other commissions in the city: thereafter, on every St Roch's day until 1581, Tintoretto presented the
Scuola with three new pictures, a sequence that extended at a slow-
er rate of production until 1588, when he painted the altarpiece of
the chapter house, with the help of his son, Domenico.

The New Testament scenes around the **walls** defy every convention
of perspective, lighting, colour and even anatomy, an amazing feat of
sustained inventiveness from a mind that was never content with
inherited ideas, and rarely content with its own. On the **left wall** (as
you face the altar) – *The Nativity, The Baptism, The Resurrection,
The Agony in the Garden, The Last Supper*; on the **right wall** – *The
Temptation of Christ, The Miracle at the Pool of Bethesda, The
Ascension, The Raising of Lazarus, The Miracle of the Loaves and
Fishes*; on the **end wall** by the Sala dell'Albergo – *St Roch* and *St
Sebastian*; on the **altar** – *The Vision of St Roch*. On easels to the side
of the altar are displayed an *Annunciation* by **Titian**, a *Visitation*
and a portrait by **Tintoretto** that's often wrongly called a self-portrait,
and *Christ Carrying the Cross*, an early Titian (though it's attributed
to Giorgione by some) that from about 1510 until 1955 was displayed
in the church of San Rocco, where it was revered as a miraculous
image. At the other end of the hall, beside the door into the Sala
dell'Albergo, you'll find *Hagar, Ishmael and an Angel* and
Abraham and an Angel, both by **Giambattista Tiepolo**.

The **carvings** underneath the paintings – a gallery of vices, virtues
and other allegorical figures, plus an amazing trompe l'oeil library –
were created in the late seventeenth century by **Francesco Pianta**.
Not far from the altar, opposite the stairs, you'll find the allegory of
painting: a caricature of the irascible Tintoretto, with a jarful of
brushes. The painter's short temper was notorious: for instance,
when a group of senators, seeing him at work on the *Paradiso* in the
Palazzo Ducale, observed that some of his rivals painted more slowly and more carefully, he's said to have replied that this was possibly
because they didn't have to contend with such stupid onlookers.

The **lower hall** – connected to the chapter house by a stairway that's
lined with pictures recording the plague that struck Venice in the 1630s
– was painted between 1583 and 1587, when Tintoretto was in his late
sixties. The tempestuous *Annunciation*, with the Archangel crashing
into the room through Joseph's shambolic workshop, trailing a tornado
of cherubim, is followed by *The Adoration of the Magi, The Flight into
Egypt, The Massacre of the Innocents, St Mary Magdalen, St Mary
of Egypt, The Circumcision* and *The Assumption*. The landscapes in
the *Flight into Egypt* and the meditative depictions of the two saints
are among the finest Tintoretto ever painted.

The church of San Rocco

Yet more Tintorettos are to be found in the neighbouring **church of
San Rocco**, built in 1489–1508 to designs by **Bartolomeo Bon the**

*The church of
San Rocco is
open daily
8am–12.30pm
& 3–5pm.*

Younger, but altered extensively in the eighteenth century. On the right wall of the nave you'll find *St Roch Taken to Prison*, and below it *The Pool of Bethesda*; only the latter is definitely by Tintoretto. Between the altars on the other side are a couple of good pictures by **Pordenone** – *St Christopher* and *St Martin*. Four large paintings by Tintoretto hang in the chancel, often either lost in the gloom or glazed with sunlight: the best (both painted in 1549) are *St Roch Curing the Plague Victims* (lower right) and *St Roch in Prison* (lower left). The two higher pictures are *St Roch in Solitude* and *St Roch Healing the Animals* – the second is a doubtful attribution.

San Pantaleone

The canal behind the Scuola di San Rocco provides an especially attractive waterscape, with a promontory of pavement jutting out into an unusually wide confluence. Cross this canal (there's a bridge at the back of the Scuola; another connects with the sottoportego facing the back of the Frari) and you'll hit the teeming Crosera San Pantalon, where the atmosphere in the shops, cafés and bars has a lot to do with the proximity of the university. Between this street and the Rio di Ca' Fóscari stands the church of **San Pantaleone**, which possesses a picture by **Antonio Vivarini and Giovanni d'Alemagna** (*Coronation of the Virgin*, in the Chapel of the Holy Nail, to the left of the chancel) and **Veronese's** last painting, *St Pantaleone Healing a Boy* (second chapel on right). San Pantaleone was credited with medicinal capabilities only slightly less awesome than San Rocco's, and Veronese's scene emphasizes the miraculous nature of his power (he spurns the offered box of potions) and the impotence of non-Christian treatment (symbolized by the limbless figure of Asclepius, the classical god of medicine).

San Pantaleone is open Mon–Sat 4–6pm.

The church can also boast of having the most melodramatic **ceiling** in the city: *The Martyrdom and Apotheosis of St Pantaleone*. Painted on sixty panels, some of which actually jut out over the nave, it kept **Gian Antonio Fumiani** busy from 1680 to 1704. Sadly, he never got the chance to bask in the glory of his labours – he died in a fall from the scaffolding from which he'd been working.

San Giovanni Evangelista to the Tolentini

Another of the Scuole Grandi nestles in a line of drab buildings very near to the Frari – the **Scuola di San Giovanni Evangelista**, founded in 1261 by one of the many flagellant confraternities that sprang up at that time. The quickest way to get to it is to take the bridge facing the Frari's facade, turn left and then left again, then second right into Calle del Magazzen – the Scuola is halfway down on the left.

This institution's finest hour came in 1369, when it was presented with a **relic of the True Cross**, an item that can be seen to this day in the first-floor **Oratorio della Croce**. The miracles effected by the relic were commemorated in the Oratory by a series of paintings by Carpaccio, Gentile Bellini and others, now transplanted to the Accademia.

Nowadays the delights of the Scuola are architectural. The **courtyards** are something of a composite: the mid-fifteenth-century facade of the Scuola incorporates two mid-fourteenth-century reliefs, and the **screen** of the outer courtyard was built in 1481 by **Pietro Lombardo**. The latter is one of Venice's pleasantest surprises – approached from the train station direction it just looks like any old brick wall, but round the other side it reveals itself to be as delicate a piece of marble carving as any church interior could show. Inside, a grand **double staircase** built by **Codussi** in 1498 rises to the main hall and the Oratorio; the climb is more enjoyable than its culmination, as the hall is clad with lifeless paintings, many showing scenes from the life of Saint John, most of them by Domenico Tintoretto. The Scuola is open Monday to Friday 9.30am to 12.30pm; ring for admission – they might balk at letting you into the Oratorio, but there shouldn't be any problem about getting a look at the Codussi bits, unless one of the Scuola's frequent conferences is in progress.

The church of San Giovanni Evangelista is one of the select band of religious buildings in Venice that are of no interest whatsoever.

The Tolentini and the Giardino Papadopoli

Calle della Lacca–Fondamenta Sacchere–Calle Amai is a dullish but uncomplicated route from San Giovanni Evangelista to the portentous church of San Nicolò da Tolentino – alias the **Tolentini**. Venetian home of the Theatine Order, which found refuge in Venice after the Sack of Rome by the army of Charles V in 1527, it was begun in 1590 by Palladio's follower Scamozzi, and finished in 1714 by the addition of a freestanding portico – the first in Venice – designed by Andrea Tirali. Among the scores of seventeenth-century paintings, just two stand out. The first is a *St Jerome* by Johann Lys, on the wall outside the chancel, to the left; it was painted in 1628, just two years before German-born Lys died of the plague, aged thirty-three. The other is *St Lawrence Giving Alms* by Bernardo Strozzi, round the corner from the Lys painting. Up the left wall of the chancel swirls the best Baroque monument in Venice: the **monument to Francesco Morosini**, created in 1678 by a Genoese sculptor, Filippo Parodi. That's Francesco Morosini, Patriarch of Venice, on no account to be confused with Francesco Morosini, Doge of Venice 1688–94, buried in Santo Stefano – though that Francesco Morosini did present the Tolentini with the banner of the Turkish general whom he had trounced in the Morea in 1685.

If fatigue is setting in and you need a pit-stop, the **Giardino Papadopoli**, formerly one of Venice's biggest private gardens but now owned by the city, is just over the Rio dei Tolentini. In winter you may have to make do with the pavement, since the park's often shut then.

*The Tolentini
is open daily
8am–noon &
4.30–7pm.*

Chapter 4

Cannaregio

Within the northernmost section of Venice, Cannaregio, you pass from one urban extreme to another in a matter of minutes, the time it takes to escape the hubbub of the train station and the hustle of the Lista di Spagna – the tawdriest street in Venice – and into the backwaters away from the Canal Grande. There may no longer be any signs of the bamboo clumps that were probably the source of the sestiere's name (canna means "reed"), but in all of Venice you won't find as many village-like parishes as you'll see in Cannaregio, and in few parts of the city are you more likely to get well away from the tourist crowds.

Imprisoned in the very centre of Cannaregio is the **Ghetto**, the first area in the world to bear that name, and one of Venice's most evocative areas. The pleasures of the rest of Cannaregio are generally more a matter of atmosphere than of specific sights, but there are some special buildings to visit too: **Madonna dell'Orto**, with its astonishing Tintoretto paintings; **Sant'Alvise** and the **Palazzo Labia**, the first remarkable for canvases by Giambattista Tiepolo, the second for the same artist's frescoes; the **Ca' d'Oro**, a gorgeous Canal Grande palace housing a fine collection of paintings and carving; and the **Gesuiti**, a Baroque creation in the northeastern part of the district which boasts perhaps the weirdest interior in the city.

From the train station to San Giobbe

The area around Venice's train station is one in which nearly every visitor sets foot but very few actually investigate. Nobody could pretend that it's one of the city's enticing spots, but it does repay a saunter. The station building itself is a gracefully functional 1950s effort, but the rail link to the mainland was opened in 1846; within a few years the expansion of traffic had made it necessary to demolish Palladio's church of Santa Lucia, the building from which the station's name is taken.

The Scalzi

From the train station to San Giobbe

Right by the station stands the **Scalzi** (formally Santa Maria di Nazaretta), which was begun in 1672 for the barefoot ("scalzi") order of Carmelites, but is anything but barefoot itself. Giuseppe Sardi's facade – now finally restored after years of being fenced off to protect mortals from falling angels – is fairly undemonstrative compared with **Baldassare Longhena**'s opulent interior, where the walls are plated with dark, multicoloured marble and overgrown with Baroque statuary. Ruskin condemned it as "a perfect type of the vulgar abuse of marble in every possible way, by men who had no eye for colour, and no understanding of any merit in a work of art but that which rises from costliness of material, and such powers of imitation as are devoted in England to the manufacture of peaches and eggs out of Derbyshire spar".

The Scalzi is open daily 7–11.50am & 4–6.50pm.

Before an Austrian bomb plummeted through the roof in 1915 there was a splendid **Giambattista Tiepolo** ceiling to introduce a bit of good taste into the proceedings; a couple of scraps are preserved in the Accademia, and some wan frescoes by the man survive in the first chapel on the left and the second on the right. The second chapel on the left is the resting place of **Lodovico Manin** (d.1802), Venice's last doge. The bare inscription set into the floor – "Manini Cineres" (the ashes of Manin) – is a fair reflection of the low esteem in which he was held. His chief rival for the dogeship wailed "a Friulian as doge! The Republic is dead!" when Manin was elected, and although Lodovico can't take the blame for the death of independent Venice, he did on occasion display a certain lack of backbone. In response to French demands he meekly surrendered his insignia of office to be burned on a bonfire in the Piazza, and when later called upon to swear an oath of allegiance to Austria, he fell down in a dead faint.

The Lista di Spagna, San Geremia and Palazzo Labia

Foreign embassies used to be corralled into this area to make life a little easier for the Republic's spies, and the **Lista di Spagna** takes its name from the Spanish embassy which used to be at no. 168. (*Lista* indicates a street leading to an embassy.) It's now completely given over to the tourist trade, with shops and stalls, bars, restaurants and hotels all plying for the same desperate trade – people who are spending one day "doing Venice", or those who have arrived too late and too tired to look any farther. Whether you're hunting for a trinket, a meal or a bed, you'll find better elsewhere, and usually cheaper.

The church of **San Geremia**, at the end of the Lista, is where the travels of **Saint Lucy** eventually terminated – martyred in Syracuse in 304, she was stolen from Constantinople by Venetian Crusaders in 1204, then ousted from her own church in Venice by the railway

San Geremia is open Mon–Sat 8am–noon & 3–7pm; Sun 9.15am– 12.15pm & 3–7pm.

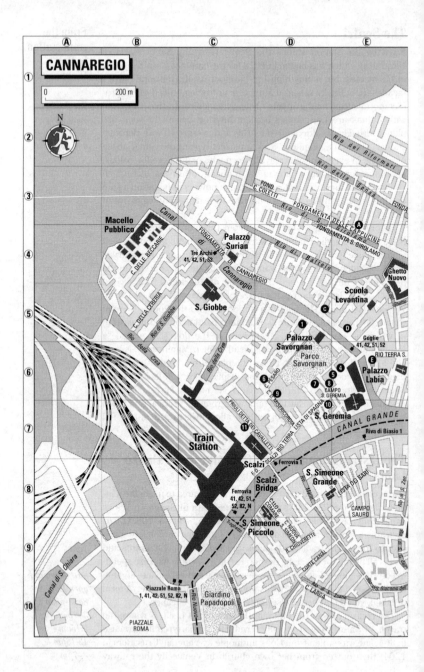

CANNAREGIO

0   200 m

N

Macello Pubblico

Canal

C. DELLE BECCARIE

FONDAMENTA di CANNAREGIO

Palazzo Surian

C. DELLA CERERIA

Tre Archi
41, 42, 51, 52

DI CANNAREGIO

Rio di S. Giobbe

S. Giobbe

Rio della Crea

Rio dell'Crea

FOND.
C. COLETTI

FONDAMENTA DELLE CAPPUCINE

Rio dei S.

FONDAMENTA S. GIROLAMO

Rio del Battello

Rio della Sensa

Rio dei Riformati

FONDA

FONDA

Ⓐ

Scuola Levantina

Ⓒ

Ⓓ

Ghetto Nuovo

Ghetto

Guglie
41, 42, 51, 52

RIO TERRA S.

Palazzo Savorgnan

❶

Parco Savorgnan

Ⓔ

C. CESARO

❻

❾

C. MISERICORDIA

❼

❹

CAMPO
S. GEREMIA

❽

❺

Palazzo Labia

❿

❷

S. Geremia

C. PRIULI DETTA DEI CAVALLETTI

SCALZI

RIO TERRA LISTA DI SPAGNA

CANAL GRANDE

Riva di Biasio 1

Train Station

Scalzi

F.O.

Ferrovia 1

Scalzi Bridge

Ferrovia
41, 42, 51,
52, 82, N

Traghetto

C. FORNER

C. NUOVA

R. CHIOVERETTE

F.D. CHIOVERE

S. Simeone Piccolo

S. Simeone Grande

LISTA DEI BARI

CAMPO SAURO

Rio di S. Chiara

Canal di S. Chiara

Piazzale Roma
1, 41, 42, 51, 52, 82, N

Rio Nuovo

Giardino Papadopoli

CORTE CANAL

Rio di S. Giacomo dell'

C. LARGA

S. Zuane

PIAZZALE ROMA

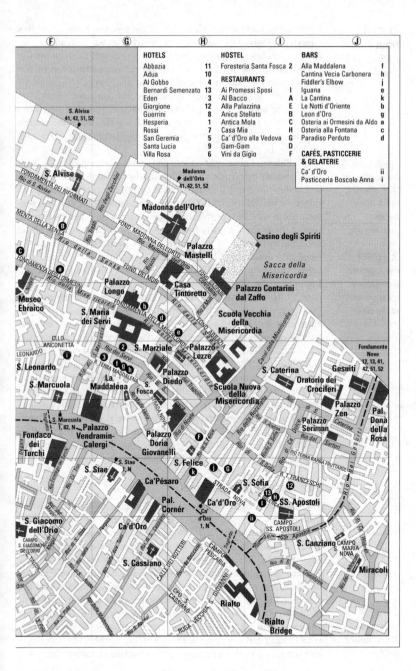

HOTELS

Abbazia	11
Adua	10
Al Gobbo	4
Bernardi Semenzato	13
Eden	3
Giorgione	12
Guerrini	8
Hesperia	1
Rossi	7
San Geremia	5
Santa Lucia	9
Villa Rosa	6

HOSTEL

Foresteria Santa Fosca	2

RESTAURANTS

Ai Promessi Sposi	I
Al Bacco	A
Alla Palazzina	E
Anice Stellato	B
Antica Mola	C
Casa Mia	H
Ca' d'Oro alla Vedova	G
Gam-Gam	D
Vini da Gigio	F

BARS

Alla Maddalena	f
Cantina Vecia Carbonera	h
Fiddler's Elbow	j
Iguana	e
La Cantina	k
Le Notti d'Oriente	b
Leon d'Oro	g
Osteria ai Ormesini da Aldo	a
Osteria alla Fontana	c
Paradiso Perduto	d

CAFÉS, PASTICCERIE & GELATERIE

Ca' d'Oro	ii
Pasticceria Boscolo Anna	i

board in the mid-nineteenth century. (She was also stolen from this church in 1994, but was soon returned.) Lucy's response to an unwanted suitor who praised her beautiful eyes was to pluck out the offending organs, a display of otherworldliness which led to her adoption as the patron saint of eyesight and, logically enough, of artists. Her dessicated body, wearing a lustrous silver mask, lies behind the altar, reclining above a donations box that bears the prayer "Saint Lucy, protect my eyes". Nothing else about the church is of interest, except the twelfth-century **campanile**, one of the oldest left in the city.

The Palazzo Labia is open Wed, Thurs & Fri 3–4pm; for an appointment ring ☎041.524. 2812, though admission is often granted at the door; free.

The **Palazzo Labia**, next door to San Geremia, was built in 1720–50 for a famously extravagant Spanish family by the name of Lasbias, who had bought their way into the *Libro d'Oro* (the register of the nobility) for the obligatory 100,000 ducats in the middle of the previous century. Their taste for conspicuous expenditure wasn't lessened by the cost of the house – a party here once finished with a member of the Labia family hurling the gold dinner service from the window into the canal and declaiming the memorable Venetian pun: "L'abia o non l'abia, sarò sempre Labia" (Whether I have it or whether I have it not, I will always be a Labia). The impact of the gesture is somewhat lessened by the rumour that fishing nets had been placed in the canal so that the service could be retrieved under cover of darkness.

No cost was spared on decoration either, and no sooner was the interior completed than **Giambattista Tiepolo** was hired to cover the walls of the ballroom with **frescoes** depicting the story of Anthony and Cleopatra. (The architectural trompe l'oeil work is by another artist – Gerolamo Mengozzi Colonna.) Restored to something approaching their original freshness after years of neglect and some damage in the last war, this is the only sequence of Tiepolo paintings in Venice that is comparable to his narrative masterpieces in such mainland villas as the Villa Valmarana near Vicenza (see p.343). RAI, the Italian state broadcasting company, now owns the palace, but they allow visitors in for a few hours each week.

The San Giobbe district

The Palazzo Labia's longest facade overlooks the **Canale di Cannaregio**, the main entrance to Venice before the rail and road links were constructed; if you turn left along its fondamenta rather than going with the flow over the Ponte delle Guglie, you'll be virtually alone by the time you're past the late seventeenth-century **Palazzo Savorgnan**. This was the home of one of Venice's richest families – indeed, so great was the Savorgnans' social clout that the Rezzonico family marked their intermarriage by getting Tiepolo to paint a fresco celebrating the event in the Ca' Rezzonico. Beyond the palazzo, swing left at the Ponte dei Tre Archi (Venice's only multiple-span bridge) and you're at the church of **San Giobbe**, like San Moisè an example of Venice's habit of canonizing Old Testament figures.

San Giobbe is open Mon–Sat 10am–noon & 4–6pm.

"So went Satan forth from the presence of the Lord and smote Job with sore boils from the sole of his foot unto his crown," records the Bible. Job's physical sufferings – sanctioned by the Almighty in order to test his faith – greatly endeared him to the Venetians, who were regularly afflicted with malaria, plague and a plethora of water-related diseases, and in the fourteenth century an oratory and hospice dedicated to him was founded here. In 1428 the complex was taken over by the Observant Franciscans, and in 1443 the order's greatest preacher, Bernardine of Siena, was a guest here, in what turned out to be the last year of his life. Bernardine's canonization followed in 1450, an event commemorated here by the construction of a new church, a Gothic structure commenced by Antonio Gambello soon after the canonization. However, the specially interesting parts of the building are its exquisitely carved early Renaissance doorway and chancel – begun in 1471, they were the first Venetian projects of **Pietro Lombardo**.

After the Lombardo carvings, the most appealing elements of the interior are the roundels and tiles from the Florentine **della Robbia** workshop, in the Cappella Martini (second chapel on left); the presence of these Tuscan features is explained by the fact that the chapel was funded by a family of Lucca-born silk weavers. The tomb slab in the centre of the chancel floor is that of **Doge Cristoforo Moro**, the donor of the new building; a satirical leaflet about Moro may have been a source for Shakespeare's *Othello*, even though – as the portrait in the sacristy shows – Moro bore no racial similarity to the Moor of Venice. San Giobbe's great altarpieces by Bellini and Carpaccio have been removed to the damp-free environment of the Accademia (the original marble frame for the Bellini now encloses a dull *Vision of Job*); the parishioners might not weep if someone removed the ludicrous lions on the tomb of the magnificently named **Renato de Voyer de Palmy Signore d'Argeson**, who served as the French ambassador to Venice and died here in 1651. At the end of the nave, a doorway leads into a room that was once part of the original oratory, which in turn connects with the **sacristy**, where there's a fine triptych by Antonio Vivarini, a fifteenth-century terracotta bust of Saint Bernardine and a *Marriage of St. Catherine* attributed to Andrea Previtali.

North of San Giobbe
At the top of the fondamenta to the north of San Giobbe, looking over the lagoon to the mainland, is the **Macello Pubblico** (municipal slaughterhouse), built by the hygiene-conscious Austrians in 1843 and adorned with ox-skulls. It is now used by the university, following many years of discussion – Le Corbusier designed a hospital for the site in 1964, but the plan was shelved in the face of local opposition to the demolition of the building, opposition with which the architect himself sympathized.

...site side of the Canale di Cannaregio, immediately ...e Ponte dei Tre Archi, stands the **Palazzo Surian**, once the ...ch embassy. **Jean-Jacques Rousseau** lived here in 1743–44 as secretary to an indolent boss: "The French who lived in Venice would never have known that there was a French ambassador resident in the city, had it not been for me," he wrote. His *Confessions* record the political bickerings of his time here, and a number of discreditable sexual adventures. At the far northern end of this fondamenta you'll find one of the few new building projects in central Venice – a new **housing development** which elegantly combines modern architectural techniques with elements of Venetian vernacular style, such as the characteristic flowerpot chimneys.

The Ghetto

The name of the Venetian **Ghetto** – a name bequeathed to all other such enclaves of deprivation – is probably derived from the Venetian dialect *geto*, foundry, which is what this area was until 1390. The city's **Jewish population** at that time was small and dispersed, and had only just achieved any degree of legal recognition: a decree of 1381 gave them the right to settle in Venice, and permitted them to lend money and to trade in second-hand items. Before the decade's end the Jews of Venice had become subject to legislation which restricted their residency to periods of no more than fifteen consecutive days, and forced them to wear distinguishing badges. Such punitive measures remained their lot for much of the succeeding century.

The creation of the Ghetto was a consequence of the War of the League of Cambrai, when hundreds of Jews fled the mainland in fear of the Imperial army. Gaining safe haven in Venice, many of the *terrafirma* Jews donated funds for the defence of the city, and were rewarded with permanent protection – at a price. In 1516 the **Ghetto Nuovo** became Venice's Jewish quarter, when all the city's Jews were forced to move onto this small island in the north of Cannaregio. At night the Ghetto was sealed by gates (marks left by their hinges can still be seen in the Sottoportego Ghetto Nuovo) and guarded by Christian watchmen, whose wages were levied from the Jews. In the daytime their movement wasn't restricted, but they were still obliged to wear distinctively coloured badges or caps. Regarded warily because of their mercantile and financial astuteness, yet exploited for these very qualities, the Jews were barred from certain professions but allowed to pursue others: they could trade in used cloth, lend money (you'll find the inscription *Banco Rosso* on no. 2911 in the campo) and also practise medicine – doctors were the only people allowed out of the Ghetto at night. In addition, the Jews' property rights were limited and they were subjected to a range of financial penalties. Changing faith was not a way to escape the shackles, as converts were forbidden "to enter or to practise any activity under any pretext whatsoever in this city . . . on pain of hanging, imprisonment, whipping or pillory". (This statute is carved in stone a little way down Calle di Ghetto Vecchio.)

Yet the fact remains that Venice was one of the few states to tolerate the Jewish religion, and the Ghetto's population was often swelled by refugees from more oppressive societies. Jews expelled from Spain and Portugal in the 1490s came here, as did Jews later displaced from the Veneto by the Habsburg army during the War of the League of Cambrai, and from the eastern Mediterranean by the Ottoman Turks. Venice's burdensome protection was entirely pragmatic, however, as is shown by two conflicting responses to Church interference: when criticized by the Inquisition for not burning enough Jews as heretics, Venetian leaders replied that non-Christians logically could not commit heresy; yet when Pope Julius II ordered the destruction of the Talmud in 1553, the Signoria obligingly arranged a bonfire of Jewish books in the Piazza.

Parts of the Ghetto look quite different from the rest of Venice, as a result of the overcrowding that remained a problem even after the Jewish population was allowed to spread into the **Ghetto Vecchio** (1541) and the **Ghetto Nuovissimo** (1633). As buildings in the Ghetto were not allowed to be more than one-third higher than in the rest of Venice, storeys were made as low as possible in order to fit in the maximum number of floors; seven is the usual number. The gates of the Ghetto were finally torn down by Napoleon in 1797, but it wasn't until the city's unification with the Kingdom of Italy in 1866 that Jews achieved equal status with their fellow citizens.

Present-day Venice's Jewish population of around six hundred (compared to the Ghetto's peak of around five thousand) is spread all over the city, but the Ghetto is still the centre of the community, with offices and a library in Calle Ghetto Vecchio, a nursery, an old people's home, an excellent kosher restaurant (see p.266), and a baker of unleavened bread. Recent years have seen an influx of young Italians and North Americans belonging to the Lubavitch (Hasidic) sect. There are currently around thirty students at the small school on the campo, and on Saturdays the normally serene atmosphere of the Ghetto gives way to something of a party spirit.

The scole and the campo

Each wave of Jewish immigrants, while enriching the overall cultural environment of the city (Venetians of all religions frequented the Ghetto's salons), also maintained their own synagogues with their distinctive rites: the **Scola Tedesca** (for German Jews) was founded in 1528, the **Scola al Canton** (probably Jews from Provence) in 1531–32, the **Scola Levantina** (eastern Mediterranean) in 1538, the **Scola Spagnola** (Spanish) at an uncertain date in the later sixteenth

*The Museo
Ebraico is
open
10am–5.30pm;
closed Sat;
L5000/€2.58,
or
L12,000/€6.20
with guided
tour; tours in
English hourly
from 10.30am
to 4.30pm.*

century, and the **Scola Italiana** in 1575. Since the Jews were disqualified from the profession of architect and forbidden to use marble in their buildings, the *scole* tend to have oddly Christian interiors, thickly adorned with gilt and stucco. Funded by particularly prosperous trading communities, the Scola Levantina and the Scola Spagnola are the most lavish of the synagogues (the latter, redesigned by Longhena, greatly influenced the look of the others), and are the only two still used on a daily basis – the Levantina in summer and the Spagnola in winter, as there is only one rabbi. Depending on the season, one of the above can be viewed, along with the Scola al Canton and the Scola Italiana, in an informative English-language guided tour that begins in the **Museo Ebraico**, above the Scola Tedesca in Campo del Ghetto Nuovo. The museum's collection consists mainly of silverware, sacred objects, textiles and furniture.

In the northern corner of the campo is a reminder of the ultimate suffering of the Jewish people: a series of seven reliefs by **Arbit Blatas**, with a poem by André Tranc, commemorating the 200 Venetian Jews deported to the death camps in 1943 and 1944.

Northern Cannaregio

Land reclamation and the consolidation of the lagoon's mudbanks has been a continuous process in Venice since the time of the first settlers, but the contours of the city have been modified with particular rapidity in the last hundred years or so. As its long straight canals and right-angled alleyways suggest, much of northern Cannaregio has come into existence comparatively recently: the Sacca (inlet) di San Girolamo, for example, was reclaimed in the first half of this century to provide working-class housing of a higher standard than in much of the rest of the city.

In the area **northwest from the Ghetto**, inland from the Sacca, there's nothing to ferret out: the tiny seventeenth-century church of the Cappuccine (open for services) faces the equally dull but bigger and uglier (and closed) San Girolamo, a church once used by the Austrians as a steam-powered flour mill, with the campanile converted to a chimney. **Northeast of the Ghetto**, though, is one of the most attractive domestic quarters of Venice, and some of the city's best restaurants and bars are dotted along its lengthy fondamente. The colourful juxtapositions of walls, shutters, water and boats compose a scene like Henry James's evocation of the essence of Venice – "a narrow canal in the heart of the city – a patch of green water and a surface of pink wall . . . a great shabby facade of Gothic windows and balconies – balconies on which dirty clothes are hung and under which a cavernous-looking doorway opens from a low flight of slimy water-steps".

Sant'Alvise to Campo dei Mori

Northern
Cannaregio

For all the apparent rationality of the city's layout in this district, the church of **Sant'Alvise** is fairly tricky to get to, standing as it does on an island with no eastward land connection with the rest of the city. Dedicated to Saint Louis of Toulouse (Alvise being the Venetian version of Louis/Luigi), the church was commissioned in the 1380s by Antonia Venier, daughter of Doge Antonio Venier, after the saint appeared to her in a vision. Despite having recently undergone major restoration work, Sant'Alvise is still suffering from severe damp, and more restoration is now under way – paintings may be moved around as work progresses. Still in its original position is the chancel's immense *Road to Calvary* by **Giambattista Tiepolo**, which was restored last time round. His *Crown of Thorns* and *Flagellation*, slightly earlier works, hang on the right-hand wall of the nave. Under the nuns' choir you'll find eight small tempera paintings, familiarly known as "The Baby Carpaccios" since Ruskin assigned them to the painter's precocious childhood; they're not actually by Carpaccio, but were produced around 1470, when he would indeed have been just an infant. The likeliest candidate for their authorship is an unknown pupil of Lazzaro Bastiani, Carpaccio's master. The extraordinary seventeenth-century trompe l'oeil **ceiling** is a collaboration between Antonio Torri (the architectural work) and Paolo Ricchi (the religious scenes).

*Sant'Alvise is
open Mon–Sat
10am–5pm &
Sun 1–5pm;
L3000/€1.55.*

To get from Sant'Alvise to Madonna dell'Orto you can either take a one-stop vaporetto trip, or cross over the canal to the Fondamenta della Sensa, the main street immediately to the south. One bridge after the early fifteenth-century **Palazzo Michiel** (the French embassy at the time of Henry III's visit), the fondamenta opens out at the **Campo dei Mori**, a square whose name possibly comes from the proximity of the now extinct Fondaco degli Arabi (Arabs' warehouse). There is another explanation: the four thirteenth-century **statues** around the campo are popularly associated with a family of twelfth-century merchants called the Mastelli brothers, who used to live in the palace into which two of the figures are embedded – they hailed from the Morea (the Peloponnese), and hence were known as *Mori*. Venice's more malicious citizens used to leave denunciations at the feet of "Sior Antonio Rioba" (the statue with the rusty nose), and circulate vindictive verses signed with his name.

*For more on
the Mastelli
brothers'
house, see
p.157.*

Just beyond the campo is the elegant fifteenth-century house where **Tintoretto** lived for the last two decades of his life (1574–94), accompanied by one of his daughters, **Marietta**. Supremely skilled as a painter, and a fine musician and singer too, Marietta was married off to a man who preferred his wife to produce portraits of his colleagues and his friends instead of painting more ambitious works. She died aged 34, four years before her father, her career having epitomized the restriction of women's talents to genres compatible with a life of domestic conformity. None of her paintings is on public show in Venice, though scholars have detected her touch in some of her father's large-scale works.

Madonna dell'Orto

Madonna
dell'Orto is
open Mon–Sat
10am–5pm &
Sun 1–5pm;
L3000/€1.55.

Marietta, her father, and her brother Domenico are all buried in **Madonna dell'Orto**, the family's parish church and arguably the superlative example of ecclesiastical Gothic in Venice. The church was founded in the name of Saint Christopher some time around 1350; ferrymen for the northern islands used to operate from the quays near here, and it's popularly believed that the church received its dedication because Christopher was their patron saint, though there's a stronger connection with the merchants' guild, who funded much of the building and who also regarded Christopher as their patron.

It was popularly renamed after a large stone *Madonna* by **Giovanni de'Santi**, found in a nearby vegetable garden (*orto*), began working miracles; brought into the church in 1377, the heavily restored figure now sits in the Cappella di San Mauro. (The chapel is through the door at the end of the right aisle, next to the chapel containing Tintoretto's tomb; it's set aside for prayer, but access is allowed if no one's using it.)

The main figure on the **facade** is a *St Christopher* by the Florentine **Nicolò di Giovanni**; commissioned by the merchants' guild in the mid-fifteenth century, it became the first major sculptural project in the restoration programmes that began after the 1966 flood. **Bartolomeo Bon the Elder**, formerly credited with the *St Christopher*, designed the portal in 1460, shortly before his death. The **campanile**, finished in 1503, is one of the most notable landmarks when approaching Venice from the northern lagoon.

Restoration work in the 1860s made a right mess of the **interior**, ripping up memorial stones from the floor, for instance, and destroying the organ, once described as the best in Europe. Partial reversal of the damage was achieved in the 1930s, when some over-painting was removed from the Greek marble columns, the fresco work and elsewhere, and in 1968–69 the whole building was given a massive overhaul.

An amusing if implausible tale explains the large number of **Tintoretto** paintings here. Having added cuckold's horns to a portrait of a doge that had been rejected by its subject, Tintoretto allegedly took refuge from his furious ex-client in Madonna dell'Orto; the doge then offered to forget the insult if Tintoretto agreed to decorate the church, figuring it would keep him quiet for a few years. Famously rapid even under normal circumstances, the painter was in fact out and about again within six months, most of which time must have been spent on the epic numbers on each side of the choir: *The Last Judgement*, described by Ruskin as the only painting ever to grasp the event "in its Verity . . . as they may see it who shall not sleep, but be changed", and *The Making of the Golden Calf*, in which the carriers of the calf have been speculatively identified as portraits of Giorgione, Titian, Veronese and the artist himself (fourth from the left), with Aaron (pointing on the right) identified as Sansovino.

There could hardly be a sharper shift of mood than that from the apocalyptic temper of *The Last Judgement* to the reverential tenderness of *The Presentation of the Virgin* (end of right aisle), which makes a fascinating comparison with Titian's Accademia version of the incident. It's by a long way the best of the smaller Tintorettos, but most of the others are interesting: *The Vision of the Cross to St Peter* and *The Beheading of St Paul* flank an *Annunciation* by Palma il Giovane in the chancel; four *Virtues* (the central one is ascribed to Sebastiano Ricci) are installed in the vault above; and *St Agnes Reviving Licinius* stands in the fourth chapel on the left. A major figure of the early Venetian Renaissance – **Cima da Conegliano** – is represented by a *St John the Baptist and Other Saints*, on the first altar on the right; a *Madonna and Child* by Cima's great contemporary, Giovanni Bellini, used to occupy the first chapel on the left, but thieves made off with it in 1993.

To the Scuole della Misericordia

Looking across the canal to the southeast of the church stands the **Palazzo Mastelli**, former home of the mercantile family of the same name. The facade of the much-altered palazzo is a sort of architectural scrap-album, featuring a Gothic top-floor balcony, thirteenth-century Byzantine fragments set into sixteenth-century work below, a bit of a Roman altar set into a column by the corner, and a quaint little relief of a man leading a laden camel – hence its alternative title, Palazzo del Cammello.

On the canal's north side stand the seventeenth-century **Palazzo Minelli Spada** and the sixteenth-century **Palazzo Contarini dal Zaffo**, one of the many palaces owned by the vast Contarini clan. Numerous though they once were, the last male of the Contarini line died in 1836, thus adding their name to the roll-call of patrician dynasties that vanished in the nineteenth century. Lack of money almost certainly accounts for their extinction – already impoverished by loans made to the dying Republic and by the endless round of parties, many of the Venetian aristocracy were bankrupted during the Napoleonic and Austrian occupations, and so, no longer having money for dowries and other related expenses, they simply chose not to marry.

Crossing the canal at the Sacca della Misericordia, you quickly come to the fondamenta leading to the defunct **Abbazia della Misericordia** and the **Scuola Vecchia della Misericordia**; neither is particularly lovely, and the latter's proudest adornment – Bartolomeo Bon's relief of the *Madonna della Misericordia* – is exiled in

The Casino degli Spiriti, in the garden of the Palazzo Contarini dal Zaffo, is covered on p.163, as it can only be seen from the far side of the Sacca della Misericordia.

London's Victoria and Albert Museum. The complex is now used as a restoration centre. When the Misericordia became a Scuola Grande in the sixteenth century its members commissioned the huge **Scuola Nuova della Misericordia** (on the far side of the bridge), a move which benefited Tintoretto, who set up his canvases in the upper room of the old building to work on the *Paradiso* for the Palazzo Ducale. Begun in 1532 by Sansovino but not opened until 1589, the new block was never finished. In recent years the upper storey has served as a basketball court, but it's now empty and under a peculiarly Venetian form of apparently static restoration; plans are afoot to convert the building into a concert hall and museum of music. Its neighbour is the **Palazzo Lezze**, another project by Longhena.

Southern Cannaregio

If you follow the main route east from the station, crossing the Canale di Cannaregio by the Guglie bridge, you come onto the shopping street of **Rio Terrà San Leonardo**. Like the Lista di Spagna, this thoroughfare follows the line of a former canal, filled in during the 1870s by the Austrians as part of a scheme to rationalize movement round the north bend of the Canal Grande. (The name "Rio Terrà", prefixed to many alleyways in Venice, signifies a pavement that was once a waterway.) The continuation of the route to the Rialto bridge – the Strada Nova – was by contrast created by simply ploughing a line straight through the houses that used to stand there.

Rio Terrà Cristo, on the south of Rio Terrà San Leonardo, just before the market stalls of the Campiello dell'Anconetta, runs down to Giorgio Massari's church of **San Marcuola** (1728–36), whose unfinished brick front is as clear a landmark on the Canal Grande as the facade of the Palazzo Vendramin-Calergi, which stands a little to the east of it. The tiered ledges and sockets of the exterior, intended for marble cladding but now crammed with pigeons, are a more diverting sight than the inside, where statues of the church's two patron saints by Gian Maria Morleiter, and an early *Last Supper* by Tintoretto (left wall of the chancel) are the only things to seek out. Those apart, the church's main interest is in a story about one of its priests. He was once foolish enough to announce from the pulpit that he didn't believe in ghosts, and that "where the dead are, there they stay"; that night all the corpses buried in the church rose from their graves, dragged him from his bed and beat him up. Incidentally, the church's name is perhaps the most baffling of all the Venetian diminutives – it's somehow derived from Santi Ermagora e Fortunato.

San Marcuola is open daily 8am–noon & 4–6.30pm.

The Maddalena district

For more on the Palazzo Vendramin-Calergi, see p.204.

Take the angled bridge that's visible from the northern flank of San Marcuola and you'll come to the land entrance of the **Palazzo**

Vendramin-Calergi, where a plaque records the death of Richard Wagner here in 1883; the surprisingly tatty entrance is as far as you'll get unless your wallet's full and your attire smart, because it's now the winter home of the casino (see p.278). Cut straight up from here and you're back on the main route between the train station and the centre of town, a street here named Rio Terrà della Maddalena, after the little Neoclassical church of **La Maddalena** (1760), which is set back on its own small campo. Its designer, the unprolific **Tomasso Temanza**, was more noted as a theoretician than as an architect, and his *Lives of the Most Famous Venetian Architects and Sculptors* (modelled on Vasari's *Lives of the Artists*) remains the classic text for those interested in the subject.

If you follow the main drag eastward, the next sight is the nineteenth-century monument of **Paolo Sarpi** (see box below) that fronts

---

Paolo Sarpi and the Excommunication of Venice

Unswerving moral rectitude and fierce intellectual rigour are not qualities that come first to mind when considering most of the public men of Venetian history, but both were exemplified by the Servite priest **Fra' Paolo Sarpi**, one of Venice's titanic figures. Author of a magisterial history of the Council of Trent, discoverer of the mechanics of the iris of the eye and a partner in Galileo's optical researches, Sarpi was described by Sir Henry Wotton, the English ambassador to Venice, as 'the most deep and general scholar of the world'. Sarpi is best known, however, as the adviser to the Venetian state in its row with the Vatican at the start of the seventeenth century.

Although Venice's toleration of non-Christians was a cause of recurrent friction with the Vatican, the area of greatest discord was the Republic's insistence on separating the sovereignty of the Church and that of the State – "The Church must obey the State in things temporal and the latter the former in things spiritual, each maintaining its proper rights", to quote Sarpi himself. Matters came to a head when Venice restricted the amount of money that monasteries on the mainland could return to Rome from their rents and commerce, and then imprisoned two priests found guilty in secular courts of secular crimes. Pope Paul V's demand for the return of the priests and the repeal of the monastic legislation was firmly rebuffed, and the upshot was a **papal interdict** in April 1606, forbidding all religious services in Venice. Excommunication for the entire city then followed. In retaliation, Venice booted out the Jesuits and threatened with exile or death any priests who didn't ignore the interdict – a priest in Padua who insisted that the Holy Spirit had moved him to obey the pope was informed by the Council of Ten that the Holy Spirit had already moved them to hang any who disagreed with them. Sarpi and Doge Leonardo Donà maintained their closely argued defiance of Rome until French mediation brought about a resolution which in fact required no compromises from the Venetians. The moral authority of Rome was diminished forever. Six months later, Sarpi was walking home past Santa Fosca when he was set upon by three men and left for dead with a dagger in his face. 'I recognise the style of the Holy See,' the dauntless Sarpi quipped, punning on the word 'stiletto'. He eventually died naturally on January 15, 1623.

---

the church of **Santa Fosca**, an architecturally unmemorable building, containing nothing of interest to the casual visitor apart from a Byzantine *Pietà* at the facade end of the north aisle. Across the Strada Nova, the *Farmacia Ponci* has the oldest surviving shop interior in Venice, a wonderful display of seventeenth-century heavy-duty woodwork in walnut, kitted out with eighteenth-century majolica vases.

The western part of the island immediately north of Santa Fosca is occupied by the **Palazzo Diedo**, scene of a peculiar incident in 1606. An astrologer named Benedetto Altavilla rushed in to tell its owner that the stars had revealed to him that a quantity of gun-powder had been stacked feloniously under the Sala del Maggior Consiglio. The Council of Ten duly found the explosives, but suspected, not unreasonably, that Altavilla had put them there. Shaved and shorn, in case his hair gave him occult strength, the astrologer was tortured to unconsciousness and then hanged, protesting throughout his ordeal that the stars had told him everything. On the little island to the north of Palazzo Diedo stands **San Marziale**, where, if you nip inside just before or after daily Mass (at 6.30pm), you'll see **Sebastiano Ricci's** ceiling paintings, a set of works that made his reputation in the city. Those who haven't acquired the taste will get more of a buzz from the dotty Baroque high altar, depicting Saint Jerome at lunch with a couple of associates – Faith and Charity.

Most of the island to the west of San Marziale is occupied by the remnants of the church and ex-convent of **Santa Maria dei Servi**. When the church was demolished in 1812, some of its monuments were thrown away and others were shuffled around Venice – such as Doge Andrea Vendramin's tomb, now in Santi Giovanni e Paolo; the ruins themselves were offered to Ruskin, who turned the deal down.

Along the Strada Nova

Continuing east from Santa Fosca, you pass the church of **San Felice** – rebuilt in the 1530s, savagely renovated in the last century, it's a thriving place of worship rather than a major monument. One local curiosity: at the far end of the fondamenta going up behind the church is the only parapet-less bridge left in the main part of Venice. It leads to a private door. Once over the canal that's crossed by this oddity, you're on the **Strada Nova**, a brisk, broad and basic shopping street where you can buy anything from delicious home-made cakes to surgical trusses.

The Ca' d'Oro is open Mon 8.15am–2pm, Tues–Sat 8.15am–7.15pm; L6000/€3.10.

The Ca' d'Oro

Nearly halfway along the Strada an inconspicuous calle leads down to the **Ca' d'Oro** (House of Gold), the showpiece of domestic Gothic architecture in Venice and home of one of the city's most patchy art collections, the **Galleria Giorgio Franchetti**. Built for procurator Marino Contarini between 1425 and 1440, the palace takes its name from its Canal Grande **facade**: incorporating parts of the thirteenth-century palace that used to stand here, it was highlighted in gold leaf, ultramarine and vermilion – materials which, as the three most expensive pigments of the day, spectacularly publicized the wealth of its owner. The house's cosmetics have now worn off, but the facade has at least survived unaltered, whereas the rest of the Ca' d'Oro was badly abused by later owners.

After the dancer Maria Taglioni had finished her home improvements, Ruskin lamented that it was "now destroyed by restorations", and today, despite the subsequent structural repairs, the interior of the Ca' d'Oro is no longer recognizable as that of a Gothic building. The staircase in the **courtyard** is an original feature, though – ripped out by Taglioni, it was reacquired and reconstructed by Franchetti, who likewise put back the well-head by Bartolomeo Bon (1427).

The gallery's main attraction is undoubtedly the *St Sebastian* painted by **Mantegna** shortly before his death in 1506, now installed in a chapel-like alcove on the first floor. Many of the big names of Venetian art are found on the second floor, but the canvases by Titian and Tintoretto are not among their best, and Pordenone's fragmentary frescoes from Santo Stefano require a considerable feat of imaginative reconstruction, as do the remains of Giorgione and Titian's work from the exterior of the Fondaco dei Tedeschi. You'll get more out of pieces from less elevated artists – **Tullio Lombardo**'s beautifully carved *Young Couple* shows him on top form, and Biagio d'Antonio da Firenze's *The Story of Lucrezia* reminds us that for a long time suicide was one of the few "honourable" responses a woman could have to rape. **Andrea di Bartolo**'s fine *Coronation of the Virgin* shows one way in which the impossible female ideal was maintained. Keep an eye out also for an anonymous *Madonna and Child* in the midst of the Flemish collection, a sixteenth-century English alabaster polyptych of *Scenes from the Life of St Catherine*, and a case of Renaissance medals containing fine specimens by **Gentile Bellini** and **Pisanello**, to name just two.

Santa Sofia and Santi Apostoli

A little further down the Strada Nova, opposite a campo bordering the Canal Grande but camouflaged by house fronts, is the entrance to the small church of **Santa Sofia**, which contains sculptures of four saints by followers of Antonio Rizzo. At the eastern end of the Strada you come to the Campo dei Santi Apostoli, an elbow on the road from the Rialto to the train station, with the church of **Santi Apostoli**, a dark and frequently renovated building last altered substantially in the eighteenth century.

The **campanile** was finished in 1672 – and soon afterwards, according to James (Jan) Morris, "an old and simple-minded sacristan" fell from it, "but was miraculously caught by the minute hand

Santi Apostoli is open daily 7.30–11.30am & 5–7pm.

of the clock, which, slowly revolving to six o'clock, deposited him safely on a parapet".

The **Cappella Corner**, off the right side, is the most interesting part of the interior – attributed to Mauro Codussi, its altarpiece (under restoration at the time of writing) is the *Communion of St Lucy* by Giambattista Tiepolo (1748). One of the inscriptions in the chapel is to Caterina Cornaro, who was buried here before being moved to San Salvatore; the tomb of her father Marco (on the right) is probably by Tullio Lombardo, who also carved the peculiar plaque of Saint Sebastian in the chapel to the right of the chancel, which makes him look as if he has a tree growing out of his head.

The Gesuiti district

The Gesuiti is open daily: summer 10am–noon & 5–7pm; winter 10am–noon & 4–6pm.

The major monument in the northeastern corner of Cannaregio is **Santa Maria Assunta**, commonly known simply as the **Gesuiti**. Built for the Jesuits in 1714–29, six decades after the foundation here of their first monastery in Venice, the church was clearly planned to make an impression on a city that was habitually mistrustful of the order's close relationship with the papacy.

Although the disproportionately huge facade clearly wasn't the work of a weekend, most of the effort went into the stupefying **interior**, where green and white marble covers every wall and stone is carved to resemble swags of damask. The result is jaw-dropping, and also very heavy – a factor in the subsidence which is a constant problem with the Gesuiti. Unless you're a devotee of Palma il Giovane (in which case make for the sacristy, where the walls and ceiling are covered with paintings by him), the only painting to seek out is the *Martyrdom of St Lawrence* on the first altar on the left; painted by **Titian** in 1558, it's a night scene made doubly difficult to see by the lighting arrangements.

The Oratorio dei Crociferi is open April–Oct Thurs–Sat 10am–1pm; L3000/€1.54.

Almost opposite the church is the **Oratorio dei Crociferi**, the remnant of a convent complex founded in the twelfth century by the crusading religious order known as the *Crociferi* or The Bearers of the Cross. After a fire in 1514 the buildings were enlarged, and towards the end of the century **Palma il Giovane** was commissioned to paint a cycle of *Scenes from the History of the Order of the Crociferi* (1583–91). Restored in the 1980s, the paintings show Palma's technique at its subtlest, and the richness of the colours is a good advertisement for modern cleaning techniques.

There's not much else to look at in the immediate vicinity. Titian used to live in Calle Larga dei Botteri (no. 5179–83), across the Rio dei Gesuiti – but the house has been rebuilt and the construction of the Fondamente Nove (see opposite) did away with the waterside garden where he entertained such exalted clients as Henry III of France. A short distance to the west, past the huge sixteenth-century Palazzi Zen, the church of **Santa Caterina** comes into view. The fourteenth-century ship's-keel ceiling, destroyed by fire in 1978, has now been rebuilt, but the building belongs to a school and is thus out of bounds.

The Fondamente Nove

The long waterfront to the north of the Gesuiti, the **Fondamente Nove** (or Nuove), is the point at which the vaporetti leave the city for San Michele, Murano and the northern lagoon. On a clear day you can follow their course as far as the distant island of Burano, and you might even be treated to the startling sight of the snowy Dolomite peaks, apparently hanging in the sky over the Veneto. Being relatively new, this waterfront isn't solidly lined by buildings like its counterpart in the south of the city, the Záttere. The one house of interest is the **Palazzo Donà delle Rose** on the corner of the Rio dei Gesuiti. Architecturally the palace is an oddity, as the main axis of its interior runs parallel to the water instead of at ninety degrees; the cornerstone was laid in 1610 by **Doge Leonardo Donà** (Paolo Sarpi's boss), who died two years later from apoplexy after an argument with his brother about the house's layout. It's one of the very few Venetian residences still owned by the family for whom it was built.

From the northern tip of the Fondamente the sixteenth-century **Casinò degli Spiriti** can be seen across the inlet known as the Sacca della Misericordia. A *casinò* (little house) – a suite set aside for private entertainments – was a feature of many Venetian palaces, and a few were set up in separate pavilions in the grounds. This is one of only two surviving examples of the latter, yet it's best known not for its architectural rarity but for the ghost story that's sometimes said to be the source of its name. A certain noblewoman took her husband's best friend as a lover, and this is where they would meet. At her paramour's sudden death she began to pine away, and shut herself in the *casinò* to die. No sooner had she exhaled her last breath than the ghost of her lover came in, raised her from the bed and, pushing the nursemaid to one side, made off with her. Whether they turned up in another city under assumed names is not recorded.

Chapter 5

Castello

Bordering San Marco on one side and spreading across the city from Cannaregio in the west to the housing estates of Sant'Elena in the east, Castello is the most amorphous of the sestieri. So unwieldy is this district that somewhat altered boundaries have been used in laying out our guide. In the west, this chapter starts off from the waterway that cuts round the back of Santi Apostoli to the northern lagoon, rather than following the zigzagging border of the sestiere. In the east we've stopped at a line drawn north from the landmark Pietà church; the atmospherically distinct area beyond this boundary is covered in the next chapter.

The points of interest in the area covered by this chapter are evenly distributed, but in terms of its importance and its geographical location, Castello's central building is the immense Gothic church of **Santi Giovanni e Paolo** (or **Zanipolo**), the pantheon of Venice's doges. A couple of minutes away stands the much-loved **Santa Maria dei Miracoli**, the city's most refined architectural miniature, which in turn is close to the often overlooked **San Giovanni Crisostomo**. The museums covered in this chapter lie in the southern zone – the **Querini-Stampalia** picture collection, the museum at **San Giorgio dei Greci**, and the **Museo Diocesano**'s sacred art collection. This southern area's dominant building is the majestic **San Zaccaria**, a church that has played a significant part in the history of the city – as has nearby **Santa Maria Formosa**, on the liveliest and friendliest square in Castello. Busier still is the southern waterfront, the **Riva degli Schiavoni**, Venice's main promenade.

San Giovanni Crisostomo to the Miracoli

On the western edge of Castello, a couple of minutes' walk north of the post office, stands **San Giovanni Crisostomo** (John the Golden-Mouthed), named after the eloquent Archbishop of Constantinople. An intimate church with a compact Greek-cross plan, it was possibly

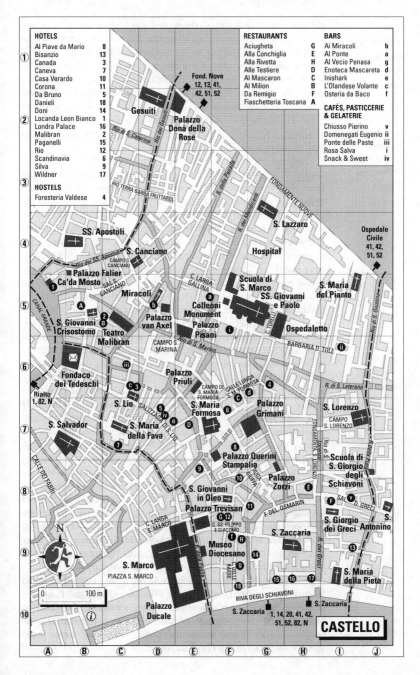

HOTELS

Al Piave da Mario	8
Bisanzio	13
Canada	3
Caneva	7
Casa Verardo	10
Corona	11
Da Bruno	5
Danieli	18
Doni	14
Locanda Leon Bianco	1
Londra Palace	16
Malibran	2
Paganelli	15
Rio	12
Scandinavia	6
Silva	9
Wildner	17

HOSTELS

Foresteria Valdese	4

RESTAURANTS

Aciugheta	G
Alla Conchiglia	E
Alla Rivetta	H
Alle Testiere	D
Al Mascaron	C
Al Milion	B
Da Remigio	F
Fiaschetteria Toscana	A

BARS

Ai Miracoli	b
Al Ponte	a
Al Vecio Penasa	g
Enoteca Mascareta	d
Inishark	e
L'Olandese Volante	c
Osteria da Baco	f

CAFÉS, PASTICCERIE & GELATERIE

Chiusso Pierino	v
Domenegati Eugenio	ii
Ponte delle Paste	iii
Rosa Salva	i
Snack & Sweet	iv

Fond. Nove
12, 13, 41,
42, 51, 52

Gesuiti

Palazzo Donà della Rose

S. Lazzaro

Hospital

Ospedale Civile
41, 42,
51, 52

SS. Apostoli

S. Canciano

CAMPO S. CANCIANO

Palazzo Falier

Ca'da Mosto

Miracoli

Scuola di S. Marco

SS. Giovanni e Paolo

S. Maria del Pianto

S. Giovanni Crisostomo

Teatro Malibran

Palazzo van Axel

Colleoni Monument

Palazzo Pisani

Ospedaletto

BARBARIA D. TOLE

Fondaco dei Tedeschi

Palazzo Priuli

Rialto
1, 82, N

S. Lio

CAMPO DI S. MARIA FORMOSA

S. Maria Formosa

Palazzo Grimani

S. Lorenzo

CAMPO S. LORENZO

S. Salvador

S. Maria della Fava

Palazzo Querini Stampalia

Scuola di S. Giorgio degli Schiavoni

Palazzo Zorzi

S. Giovanni in Oleo

Palazzo Trevisan

S. Giorgio dei Greci

S. Antonino

Museo Diocesano

S. Zaccaria

S. Marco

PIAZZA S. MARCO

S. Maria della Pieta

0   100 m

RIVA DEGLI SCHIAVONI

Palazzo Ducale

S. Zaccaria

S. Zaccaria

1, 14, 20, 41, 42,
51, 52, 82, N

CASTELLO

San Giovanni Crisostomo to the Miracoli

San Giovanni Crisostomo is open Mon–Sat 8.15am– 12.15pm & 3–7pm, Sun 3–7pm.

the last project of Mauro Codussi, and was built between 1497 and 1504. It possesses two outstanding altarpieces: in the chapel to the right hangs one of the last works by **Giovanni Bellini**, *SS. Jerome, Christopher and Louis of Toulouse*, painted in 1513 when the artist was in his eighties; and on the high altar, **Sebastiano del Piombo**'s gracefully heavy *St John Chrysostom with SS. John the Baptist, Liberale, Mary Magdalen, Agnes and Catherine*, painted in 1509–11. On the left side is a marble panel of the *Coronation of the Virgin* by Tullio Lombardo, a severe contrast with his more playful stuff in the nearby Miracoli (see opposite).

Calle del Scaleter, virtually opposite the church, leads to a secluded campiello flanked by the partly thirteenth-century **Palazzo Lion-Morosini**, whose external staircase is guarded by a little lion apparently suffering from indigestion; the campiello opens onto the Canal Grande, and if you're lucky you'll be able to enjoy the view on your own. Behind the church is the **Teatro Malibran**, which opened in the seventeenth century, was rebuilt in the 1790s, and soon after renamed in honour of the great soprano Maria Malibran (1808–36), who saved the theatre from bankruptcy by giving a fund-raising recital here, then topping the proceeds by donating the fee she had just been paid for singing at the Fenice. Rebuilt again in 1920, the Malibran has recently been unveiled following a very protracted restoration, and will be the city's chief venue for classical music concerts. The Byzantine arches on the facade of the theatre are said to have once been part of the house of **Marco Polo**'s family, who probably lived in the heavily restored place overlooking the canal at the back of the Malibran, visible from the Ponte Marco Polo (see below).

Polo's tales of his experiences in the empire of Kublai Khan were treated with incredulity when he returned to Venice in 1295, after seventeen years of trading with his father and uncle in the Far East. His habit of talking in terms of superlatives and vast numbers earned him the nickname *Il Milione*, the title he gave to the memoir he dictated in 1298 while he was a prisoner of the Genoese. It was the first account of Asian life to appear in the West, and for centuries was the most reliable description available in Europe – and yet on his deathbed Polo was implored by his friends to recant at least some of his tales, for "there are many strange things in that book which are reckoned past all credence". Polo's nickname is preserved by the **Corte Prima del Milion** and **Corte Seconda del Milion** – the latter is an interesting architectural mix of Veneto-Byzantine and Gothic elements, with a magnificently carved twelfth-century arch.

From here Ponte Marco Polo leads off to the Campo di Santa Marina. The bridge heading north from the square, the Ponte del Cristo, offers a view of the seventeenth-century facade of the Palazzo Marcello-Pindemonte-Papadopoli (attributed to Longhena) and the Gothic Palazzo Pisani across the water. Otherwise, keep going straight for Santa Maria Formosa (see p.177).

Palazzo Falier and the Ca' da Mosto

Two of the oldest houses in Venice are to be found on the small patch between San Giovanni Crisostomo and the Rio dei Santi Apostoli. At the foot of the bridge arching over to Campo Santi Apostoli there's the **Palazzo Falier**, parts of which date back to the second half of the thirteenth century. Traditionally this was the home of the ill-fated **Doge Marin Falier**, a branch of whose family was certainly in possession at the time of his dogeship (1354–55). A man noted for his unswerving rectitude, Falier was greatly offended by the licence routinely allowed to the unruly nobles of Venice; when a lenient punishment was given to a young nobleman who had insulted Falier, his wife and her ladies, he finally went right off the rails and hatched a conspiracy to install himself as the city's benevolent despot – a plot into which he conscripted the overseer of the Arsenale and Filippo Calendario, one of the architects of the Palazzo Ducale. Their plan was discovered and Falier, admitting the conspiracy, was beheaded on the very spot on which he had earlier been invested as doge.

Interlocking with the Falier house is the equally ancient **Ca' da Mosto**, reached through the passage going towards the Canal Grande – though the best view of it is from the deck of a vaporetto. This was the birthplace of **Alvise da Mosto** (1432–88), a Venetian merchant-explorer who threw in his lot with Portugal's Henry the Navigator and went on to discover the Cape Verde Islands. The ruinous state of the building, and the trash littering the grand staircase makes it hard to imagine the days when it housed the popular *Albergo del Leon Bianco*; among its guests were J.M.W. Turner, who had himself rowed up and down the Canal Grande while he scribbled in his notebook, and two German officers who in 1716 fought a duel in the courtyard and contrived to skewer each other to death.

Santa Maria dei Miracoli

Inland from these palaces, beyond the dull San Canziano, stands the church which Ruskin paired with the Scuola di San Marco as "the two most refined buildings in Venice" – **Santa Maria dei Miracoli**, usually known simply by the last word of its name.

It was built in 1481–89 to house an image of the Madonna that was painted in 1409 then began working miracles seventy years later – it was credited with the revival of a man who'd spent half an hour at the bottom of the Giudecca canal and of a woman left for dead after being stabbed. Financed by gifts left at the painting's nearby shrine, the church was most likely designed by **Pietro Lombardo**; certainly he and his two sons **Tullio** and **Antonio** oversaw the construction, and the three of them executed much of the carving. Richness of effect takes precedence over classical correctness on the **exterior**: pilasters are placed close together along the sides to create the

San
Giovanni
Crisostomo
to the
Miracoli

There's an unusual memorial to Marin Falier in the Palazzo Ducale – see p.70.

Santa Maria dei Miracoli is open Mon–Sat 10am–5pm & Sun 1–5pm; L3000/€1.55.

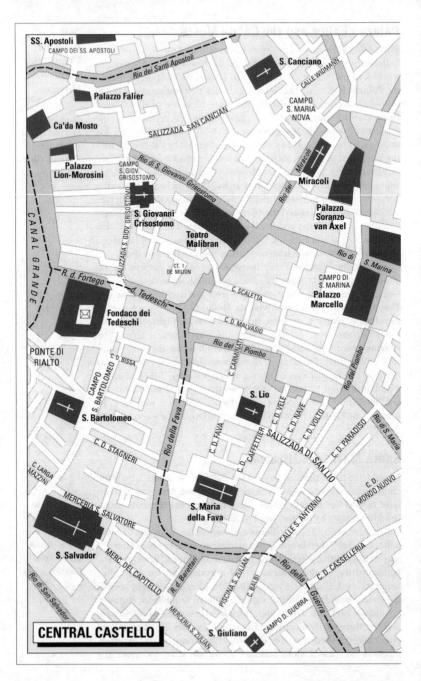

CENTRAL CASTELLO

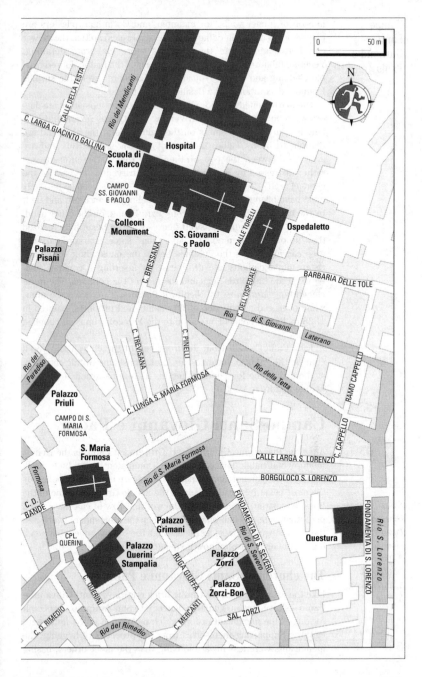

illusion of longer walls, for example, and Corinthian pilasters are placed below Ionic (in defiance of classical rules) so that the viewer can better appreciate the former's more elaborate detailing. Venetian folklore has it that the materials for the multicoloured marble cladding and inlays, typical of the Lombardi, were the surplus from the decoration of the Basilica di San Marco.

The marble-lined **interior** contains some of the most intricate decorative sculpture to be seen in Venice. The *Annunciation* and half-length figures of two saints on the balustrade at the altar end are thought to be by Tullio; the rest of the carvings at this end are arguable between the two brothers and their father. Ruskin was rather distressed by the children's heads carved at the base of the chancel arch – "the man who could carve a child's head so perfectly must have been wanting in all human feeling, to cut it off, and tie it by the hair to a vine leaf," he wrote; Ezra Pound, on the other hand, declared that the adjacent siren figures were so beautifully realized that "no one has been able to carve them" since. Extraordinary filigree carving covers the columns below the nuns' choir – the sacristan might demonstrate its finesse by inserting a cocktail stick between the tiny birds' legs and the face of the columns. The miracle-working *Madonna* by Nicolò di Pietro still occupies the altar, while overhead a sequence of fifty saints and prophets, painted in 1528 by Pier Pennacchi, are set into the Miracoli's unusual panelled ceiling.

Take Calle Castelli from the front end of the church and you'll come to the **Palazzo Soranzo-van Axel**, whose fine Gothic entrance, at the end of the fondamenta, retains its original wooden door – a unique feature in Venice.

*Santi
Giovanni e
Paolo is open
Mon–Sat
7.30am–
12.30pm &
3.30–7pm, Sun
3–6pm.*

Campo Santi Giovanni e Paolo

After the Piazza, the **Campo Santi Giovanni e Paolo** is the richest monumental public space in Venice. Dominated by the huge brick church from which it gets its name, the square is also overlooked by the most beautiful facade of any of the Scuole Grandi and one of the finest equestrian monuments in the world. A row of café-bars and a perpetual gaggle of ball-playing kids keep the atmosphere lively, and there's a constant flow of traffic through the square, much of it heading for the civic hospital now installed in the scuola.

The church of Santi Giovanni e Paolo

Like the Frari, the massive Gothic brick edifice of **Santi Giovanni e Paolo** – slurred by the Venetian dialect into **San Zanipolo** – was built for one of the mendicant orders which burgeoned in the fourteenth century. Supporting themselves from the proceeds of begging, the mendicants were less inward-looking than the older orders, basing themselves in large urban settlements and working to relieve the sick and the poor. Reflecting this social mission, mendicant churches contain a vast area for the public congregation, and this requirement for space meant that the mendicants typically built on the edges of city centres. In Venice the various mendicant orders are scattered outside the San Marco sestiere: the **Dominicans** here, the Franciscans at the Frari and San Francesco della Vigna, the Carmelites at the Carmini and the Servites at Santa Maria dei Servi. (The dedicatees of the church, by the way, are not the apostles John and Paul, but instead a pair of probably fictional saints whose story seems to be derived from that of saints Juventinus and Maximinius, who were martyred during the reign of Julian the Apostate, in the fourth century.)

The first church built on this site was begun in 1246 after **Doge Giacomo Tiepolo** was inspired by a dream to donate the land to the Dominicans – he dreamed that a flock of white doves, each marked on its forehead with the sign of the Cross, had flown over the swampland where the church now stands, as a celestial voice intoned "I have chosen this place for my ministry" (the scene is depicted in the sacristy). That initial version was soon demolished to make way for this larger building, begun in 1333, though not consecrated until 1430. Tiepolo's simple sarcophagus is outside, on the left of the door, next to that of his son **Doge Lorenzo Tiepolo** (d.1275); both tombs were altered after the Bajamonte Tiepolo revolt of 1310 (see p.405), when the family was no longer allowed to display its old crest and had to devise a replacement. The **doorway**, flanked by Byzantine reliefs, is thought to be by **Bartolomeo Bon**, and is one of the major transitional Gothic-Renaissance works in the city; apart from that, the most arresting architectural feature of the exterior is the complex brickwork of the **apse**. The **Cappella di Sant'Orsola** (closed), between the door to the right transept and the apse, is where the two **Bellini** brothers are buried; it used to house the Scuola di Sant'Orsola, the confraternity which commissioned from Carpaccio the *St Ursula* cycle now installed in the Accademia.

The simplicity of the cavernous **interior** – approximately 90 metres long, 38 metres wide at the transepts, 33 metres high in the centre – is offset by Zanipolo's profusion of tombs and monuments, including those of some twenty-five doges.

The Mocenigo tombs and south aisle

The only part of the entrance wall that isn't given over to the glorification of the Mocenigo family is the monument to the poet Bartolomeo Bragadin, which happened to be there first. It is now engulfed by the **monument to Doge Alvise Mocenigo and his wife** (1577) which wraps itself round the doorway; on the right is Tullio Lombardo's **monument to Doge Giovanni Mocenigo** (d.1485); and on the left is the superb **monument to Doge Pietro Mocenigo** (d.1476), by Pietro

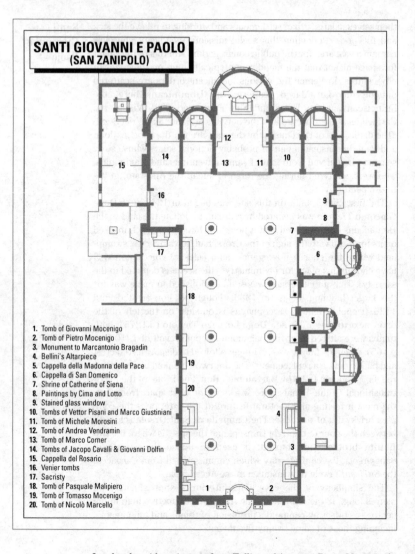

SANTI GIOVANNI E PAOLO
(SAN ZANIPOLO)

1. Tomb of Giovanni Mocenigo
2. Tomb of Pietro Mocenigo
3. Monument to Marcantonio Bragadin
4. Bellini's Altarpiece
5. Cappella della Madonna della Pace
6. Cappella di San Domenico
7. Shrine of Catherine of Siena
8. Paintings by Cima and Lotto
9. Stained glass window
10. Tombs of Vettor Pisani and Marco Giustiniani
11. Tomb of Michele Morosini
12. Tomb of Andrea Vendramin
13. Tomb of Marco Corner
14. Tombs of Jacopo Cavalli & Giovanni Dolfin
15. Cappella del Rosario
16. Venier tombs
17. Sacristy
18. Tomb of Pasquale Malipiero
19. Tomb of Tomasso Mocenigo
20. Tomb of Nicolò Marcello

For more on Caterina Cornaro, see p.384.

Lombardo, with assistance from Tullio and Antonio. Pietro Mocenigo's sarcophagus, supported by warriors representing the three Ages of Man, is embellished with a Latin inscription (*Ex Hostium Manibus*) pointing out that his enemies paid for the tomb, and a couple of reliefs showing his valorous deeds, including the handing of the keys of Famagusta to the doomed Caterina Cornaro.

To the left of the first altar of the right aisle is the **monument to Marcantonio Bragadin**, the central figure in one of the grisliest episodes in Venice's history. The commander of the Venetian garrison at Famagusta during the Turkish siege of 1571, Bragadin marshalled a resistance which lasted eleven months until, with his force reduced from 7000 men to 700, he was forced to sue for peace. Given guarantees of safety, the Venetian officers entered the enemy camp, whereupon most were dragged away and cut to pieces, whilst Bragadin himself had his ears cut off in an assault that proved to be a foretaste of days of torture. His eventual execution was appalling – chained to a stake on the public scaffold, he was slowly flayed alive in front of the Pasha. His skin, stuffed with straw, was then mounted on a cow and paraded through the streets, prior to being hung from the bowsprit of the admiral's galley for the return voyage to Constantinople. Later the skin was brought back to Venice, and today it sits in that urn high up on the wall.

Giovanni Bellini's painting for the first altar went up in smoke some years ago, but his marvellous polyptych of *SS. Vincent Ferrer, Christopher and Sebastian* (on the second altar) has come through the centuries in magnificent fettle, although it has lost the image of God the Father that used to be in the lunette. The oozing effigy reclining below is of Tommaso Caraffini, confessor and biographer of Saint Catherine of Siena.

The next chapel but one, the **Cappella della Madonna della Pace**, is named after its Byzantine Madonna, brought to Venice in 1349 and attributed with amazing powers. Above the chapel entrance the figures of Doge Bertucci Valier (d.1658), Doge Silvestro Valier (d.1700) and Silvestro's wife, Dogaressa Elizabetta Querini (d.1708), are poised like actors taking a bow.

St Dominic in Glory, the only ceiling panel in Venice by Giambattista Piazzetta, Giambattista Tiepolo's tutor, covers the vault of the neighbouring **Cappella di San Domenico**, alongside which is a tiny shrine containing a relic of **Saint Catherine of Siena**. Born in 1347 as the youngest of 25 children, Catherine manifested early signs of uninhibited piety – wearing hair shirts, sleeping on bare boards, and crashing up and down stairs on her knees, saying a Hail Mary on each step. She died in 1380 and her body promptly entered the relic market – most of it is in Rome, but her head is in Siena, one foot is here, and other lesser relics are scattered about Italy.

The south transept and the chancel

San Zanipolo's best paintings are clustered in the **south transept**: a *Coronation of the Virgin* attributed to Cima da Conegliano and Giovanni Martini da Udine, and Lorenzo Lotto's *St Antonine* (1542). As payment for his work Lotto asked only for his expenses and permission to be buried in the church; presumably the first part of the deal went through all right, but Lotto soon afterwards quit the backbiting of Venice's artistic circles, and eventually died in Loreto, where he was buried. Dominating the end wall of the transept is a

*For more on
Vettor Pisani,
see p.241.*

superb fifteenth-century **stained-glass window**, which depicts a sacred hierarchy that rises from the four Dominican saints on the lowest row to God the Father at the summit. Thought to be the work of one Giannantonio Licino da Lodi, a Murano craftsman, this is an extremely rare instance of stained glass in Venice, where the instability of the buildings makes ambitious glazing a somewhat hazardous enterprise.

Much of the right wall of the second apsidal chapel – the **Cappella della Maddalena** – is taken up with a twentieth-century reconstruction of the **monument to Admiral Vettor Pisani**. Pisani's role in the victory over the Genoese at Chioggia in 1380 – a campaign in which he was mortally wounded – is neatly summed up by John Julius Norwich: "it would perhaps be an exaggeration to say that he saved Venice single-handed; the fact remains that she would not have survived without him." The tomb supported by what look like the heads of giant elves is of another sea captain, Marco Giustiniani (d.1346).

The **chancel** is one of the high points of funerary art in Venice. **Doge Michele Morosini**, who ruled for four months before dying of plague in 1382, is buried in the tomb at the front on the right, a work which in Ruskin's eyes marked a fault-line in European civilization, showing as it does "not only the exactly intermediate condition in style between the pure Gothic and its final Renaissance corruption, but, at the same time, the exactly intermediate condition of feeling between the pure calmness of early Christianity, and the boastful pomp of the Renaissance faithlessness". The fallen Renaissance world is represented by the tomb of **Doge Andrea Vendramin** (d.1478), diagonally opposite from Morosini's, which was moved here in 1818 from the church of the Servi. The sculptor (probably Tullio Lombardo) carved only the half of the figure that could be seen from below, an act which Ruskin condemned as being of "such utter coldness of feeling as could only consist with an extreme of intellectual and moral degradation". Next to it is the Gothic tomb of **Doge Marco Corner** (d.1368), which was hacked about to make way for its neighbour.

The north transept and north aisle
Of the **tomb of Jacopo Cavalli** (d.1384), on the right of the final chapel in the north transept, Ruskin scornfully remarked: "I find no especial reason for the images of the Virtues, especially that of Charity, appearing at his tomb, unless it be this: that at the siege of Feltre, in the war against Leopold of Austria, he refused to assault the city because the senate would not grant his soldiers the pillage of the town." As if in response, the Virtues are no longer in place; the frescoes around the tomb are by Titian's nephew, Lorenzo Vecellio. On the left is the tomb of **Doge Giovanni Dolfin** (d.1361), who was besieged by the Hungarians in Trieste when elected in 1356, and had to charge through enemy lines under cover of darkness in order to take up the post.

The tombs of three members of the **Venier** family adorn the end wall of the transept: the figure of Doge Sebastiano Venier, victor over the Turkish fleet at the battle of Lépanto, is a twentieth-century creation; the monuments to the left were carved in the early fifteenth century by the Dalle Masegnes – the one above the door is the tomb of Doge Antonio Venier (d.1400), with his wife and daughter, Agnese and Orsola, alongside. The **Cappella del Rosario**, at the end of the north transept, was built in 1582 and dedicated to the victory at Lépanto, which happened on the feast day of the Madonna of the Rosary, October 7, 1571. In 1867 a fire destroyed its paintings by Tintoretto, Palma il Giovane and others, as well as Giovanni Bellini's *Madonna* and Titian's *Martyrdom of St Peter*, San Zanipolo's two most celebrated paintings, which were in here for restoration; arson by anti-Catholics was suspected, but nothing was ever proved. A lengthy twentieth-century restoration made use of surviving fragments and installed other pieces such as **Veronese**'s ceiling panels of *The Annunciation, The Assumption* and *The Adoration of the Shepherds*, and another *Adoration* by him on the left of the door.

In the north aisle, Bartolomeo Vivarini's *Three Saints* (1473), a portion of a dismantled polyptych, is the first thing to grab your eye. Busts of Titian, Palma il Vecchio and Palma il Giovane look down from over the sacristy door, forming the monument which the last of the three designed for himself. The chief draws in the **sacristy** are Alvise Vivarini's luminescent *Christ Carrying the Cross* (1474) and the wood panelling by Andre Brustolon, though there is some historical interest in Andrea Vicentino's painting of Doge Giacomo Tiepolo donating the land for the site of present church. Most of the other paintings depict scenes from the life of St Dominic or major events in the history of the Dominican order.

After the sacristy the rest of the aisle is stacked with monuments, the first of which is that of **Doge Pasquale Malipiero** (d.1462) – created by **Pietro Lombardo**, it's one of the earliest in Renaissance style in Venice. After the equestrian monument of the *condottiere* **Pompeo Giustiniani** (aka *Braccio di Ferro* – Iron Arm) comes the **tomb of Doge Tommaso Mocenigo** (d.1423) by Pietro di Nicolò Lamberti and Giovanni di Martino, followed by another Pietro Lombardo monument, for **Doge Nicolò Marcello** (d.1474), just before the altar with the copy of Titian's *Martyrdom of St Peter*. Three eminent Venetians of a more recent time – the Risorgimento heroes Attilio and Emilio Bandiera and Domenico Moro – are commemorated alongside; they're also honoured by having a square named after them (see p.192). On the last altar is a somewhat overdramatic figure of *St Jerome* by Alessandro Vittoria (1576).

Around the church

The *condottiere* **Bartolomeo Colleoni**, celebrated by the great **equestrian statue** outside Santi Giovanni e Paolo, began his wayward career in Venice's army in 1429, after a spell in the pay of Naples, and for a while took orders from Gattamelata, who's commemorated in Padua by Donatello's superb monument. In the succeeding years Colleoni defected to Milan, was imprisoned there, escaped, re-enlisted for Venice, fled once again, and finally joined the Republic's ranks for good in 1455 – whereupon Venice suffered an outbreak of peace which resulted in his being called upon to fight on just one occasion during the last twenty years of his life. Resisting several lucrative offers from France and Rome, he settled into a life of prosperous leisure, and when he died in 1475 he left a legacy of some 700,000 ducats to the Venetian state. But there was a snag to this bequest: the Signoria could have the money only if an equestrian monument to him were erected in the square before San Marco – an unthinkable proposition to Venice's rulers, with their cult of anonymity. The problem was circumvented with a fine piece of disingenuousness, by which Colleoni's will was taken to allow the state to claim his money if his statue were raised before the Scuola di San Marco, rather than the Basilica.

Andrea Verrocchio won the commission for the monument in 1481, and difficulties cropped up in this stage of the proceedings, too. Verrocchio was preparing the figure of the horse for casting when he heard that another artist was being approached to sculpt the rider. Insulted, he smashed up his work and returned to Florence in a rage, to be followed by a decree forbidding him on pain of death to return to Venice. Eventually he was invited back, and was working again on the piece when he died in June 1488. The Signoria then hired **Alessandro Leopardi** to finish the work and produce the plinth for it, which he gladly did – even signing his own name on the horse's girth, and taking the self-bestowed title *del Cavallo*. According to Marin Sanudo, when the monument was finally unveiled in 1496 all of Venice came to marvel at it. Don't run away with the notion that Colleoni was a dead ringer for Klaus Kinski – this isn't a portrait (Verrocchio never met his subject), but rather an idealized image of steely masculinity. And talking of masculinity, Thomas Coryat noted that Colleoni "had his name from having three stones, for the Italian word Coglione doth signify a testicle".

An entirely different spirit of that age is manifested by Colleoni's backdrop, the **Scuola Grande di San Marco,** which since its suppression in the early nineteenth century has provided a sumptuous facade and foyer for Venice's hospital. The **facade**, currently under wraps and undergoing restoration, was started by Pietro Lombardo and Giovanni Buora in 1487, half a century after the scuola moved here from its original home over in the Santa Croce sestiere, and finished in 1495 by Mauro Codussi. Taken as a whole, the perspectival panels by **Tullio** and **Antonio Lombardo** might not quite create the intended illusion, but they are nonetheless among the most charming sculptural pieces in Venice. The **interior** was radically altered by the

Austrians in 1819 but partly reconstructed using some original bits. The second doorway to the right, past the reception desk, leads up to the **library** (mornings only; ring bell for entry), which preserves a glorious gilt carved ceiling from the early sixteenth century. In the depths of the hospital, the church of **San Lazzaro dei Mendicanti** contains a Veronese and an early Tintoretto – but it's rarely open outside Mass hours and bear in mind that this is a hospital like any other, so be discreet.

Another hospital block is attached to Longhena's church of the **Ospedaletto** (or Santa Maria dei Derelitti), beyond the east end of the church. The leering giants' heads and over-ripe decorations of its facade drew Ruskin's wrathful attention – "it is almost worth devoting an hour to the successive examination of five buildings as illustrative of the last degradation of the Renaissance. San Moisè is the most clumsy, Santa Maria Zobenigo the most impious, San Eustachio the most ridiculous, the Ospedaletto the most monstrous, and the head at Santa Maria Formosa the most foul." The much less extravagant interior, recently restored, has a series of eighteenth-century paintings high on the walls above the arches, one of which – *The Sacrifice of Isaac* – is an early **Giambattista Tiepolo** (fourth on the right). The adjoining **music room**, frescoed in the eighteenth century and recently restored, is still used for concerts, many of them free.

Campo
Santa Maria
Formosa
and around

*The
Ospedaletto
and music
room are open
April–Sept
Thurs–Sat
4–7pm;
Oct–March
same days
3–6pm; entry
to the church is
free,
L2500/€1.29
for the music
room.*

Campo Santa Maria Formosa and around

The spacious **Campo di Santa Maria Formosa**, virtually equidistant from the Piazza, San Zanipolo and the Ponte di Rialto, is a major confluence of routes on the east side of the Canal Grande, and one of the most attractive and atmospheric squares in the city. Its fruit and vegetable stalls may be less numerous than those of the Rialto, but they're very nearly as fertile, and their owners are generally readier to pass the time of day with you. It's also an occasional pitch for sellers of antiquarian bits and pieces, their tables laden with the harvest of a few attic clearances. A number of elegant buildings border the square, the most enigmatic of which is the sixteenth-century **Palazzo Priuli**, which has been closed up for a very long time, pending the resolution of a Dickensian dispute between warring heirs.

The church of Santa Maria Formosa

The uniquely named **Santa Maria Formosa** was founded in the seventh century by San Magno, Bishop of Oderzo, who was guided by a dream in which he saw the Madonna *formosa* – a word which most closely translates as buxom and beautiful.

In 944 it gained a place in the ceremonials of Venice when a group of its parishioners rescued some young women who had been

*Santa Maria
Formosa is
open Mon–Sat
10am–5pm &
Sun 1–5pm;
L3000/€1.55.*

abducted from San Pietro di Castello (see p.198); as a reward, the doge thereafter visited the church each year, when he would be presented with a straw hat to keep the rain off and wine to slake his thirst. The hat given to the last doge can be seen in the Museo Correr.

Mauro Codussi, who rebuilt the church in 1492, followed quite closely the original Greek-cross plan, both as an evocation of Venice's Byzantine past and as a continuation of the tradition by which Marian churches were centrally organized to symbolize the womb. A dome was frequently employed as a reference to Mary's crown; this one was rebuilt in 1922 after an Austrian bomb had destroyed its predecessor in World War I.

There are two **facades** to the church. The one on the west side, close to the canal, was built in 1542 in honour of the military leader Vincenzo Cappello (d.1541); Ruskin, decrying the lack of religious imagery on this facade, identified Santa Maria Formosa as the forerunner of those churches "built to the glory of man, instead of the glory of God". The decoration of the other facade, constructed in 1604, is a bit less presumptuous, as at least there's a figure of the Virgin to accompany the three portrait busts of other members of the Cappello clan. Ruskin reserved a special dose of vitriol for the **mask** at the base of the Baroque campanile: "huge, inhuman and monstrous – leering in bestial degradation, too foul to be either pictured or described . . . in that head is embodied the type of the evil spirit to which Venice was abandoned." Pompeo Molmenti, the most assiduous chronicler of Venice's socio-cultural history, insists that the head is both a talisman against the evil eye and a piece of clinical realism, portraying a man with the same rare congenital disorder as disfigured the so-called Elephant Man.

The church contains two good paintings. Entering from the west side, the first one you'll see is **Bartolomeo Vivarini**'s triptych of *The Madonna of the Misericordia* (1473), once the church's high altarpiece, but now in a nave chapel on the right-hand side of the church. It was paid for by the congregation of the church, and some of the figures under the Madonna's cloak are believed to be portraits of the parishioners. Such images of the merciful Madonna, one of the warmest in Catholic iconography, can be seen in various forms throughout the city – there's another example a few minutes' walk away, on the route to the Rialto bridge.

Nearby, closer to the main altar, is **Palma il Vecchio**'s *St Barbara* (1522–24), praised by George Eliot as "an almost unique presentation of a hero-woman, standing in calm preparation for martyrdom, without the slightest air of pietism, yet with the expression of a mind filled with serious conviction". Having added a third window to her two-windowed bathroom to symbolize the Trinity and generally displayed an intolerable Christian recalcitrance, Barbara was hauled up a mountain by her exasperated father and there executed. On his way down, the man was struck down by lightning, a fate which turned

Barbara into the patron saint of artillery-men, the terrestrial agents of violent, sudden death. This is why Palma's painting stands in the former chapel of the Scuola dei Bombardieri, and shows her treading on a cannon. (Her brief was later widened to include all those in danger of sudden death – including miners.)

Santa Maria Formosa to the Rialto

Either of the two bridges on the canal side of Santa Maria Formosa will take you onto the busy Salizzada di San Lio, a direct route to the Rialto that has a good *pasticceria* (*Snack & Sweet*) and a handy supermarket. Calle del Paradiso, off to the right as you head towards the Rialto, is a pocket of almost untouched Gothic Venice, overlooked at one end by an early fifteenth-century arch showing the *Madonna della Misericordia*, sheltering two people within her cloak. The coats of arms on the arch are those of the Fóscari and Mocenigo families, who owned the adjoining buildings.

The church of **San Lio** – dedicated in 1054 to Pope Leo IX, an ally of Venice – is notable for its ceiling panel of the *The Apotheosis of St Leo* by **Giandomenico Tiepolo**, and for the chapel to the right of the high altar, which was designed by the Lombardi and contains a *Pietà* possibly by Tullio Lombardo; there's also a low-grade late Titian on the first altar on the left.

San Lio is open daily 9am–noon.

A diversion south from San Lio down Calle della Fava brings you to the church of **Santa Maria della Fava** (or Santa Maria della Consolazione), whose peculiar name derives from a sweet cake called a *fava* (bean), once an All Souls' Day speciality of a local baker and still a seasonal treat. Canova's tutor Giuseppe Bernardi (known as Torretto) carved the statues in niches along the nave. On the first altar on the right stands Giambattista Tiepolo's early *Education of the Virgin* (1732) in which the open Bible appears to be emanating a substantial cloud of Holy Spirit, with fleshy angels appearing in the miasma and Joachim, the father of Mary, apparently warming his hands on the blessed effluvium. On the other side of the church there's *The Madonna and St Philip Neri*, painted five years earlier by Giambattista Piazzetta, the most influential painter in early eighteenth-century Venice.

Santa Maria della Fava is open daily 8.30am–noon & 4.30– 7.30pm.

The Querini-Stampalia and Museo Diocesano

Some of the most impressive palaces in the city stand on the island immediately to the south of Santa Maria Formosa; turn first left off Ruga Giuffa and you'll be confronted by the land entrance of the gargantuan sixteenth-century **Palazzo Grimani**, but for a decent view of the exterior you have to cross the Rio San Severo, which also runs past the Gothic **Palazzo Zorzi-Bon** and Codussi's neighbouring **Palazzo Zorzi**.

On the south side of Campo Santa Maria Formosa, a footbridge over a narrow canal leads into the Renaissance **Palazzo Querini-**

*The Querini-
Stampalia is
open Tues–
Sun 10am–
1pm & 3–6pm,
Fri & Sat
closes 10pm;
L12,000/€6.20.*

*The Museo
Diocesano is
open daily
10.30am–
12.30pm; free
– but donation
requested.*

Stampalia. The palace was built for a branch of the ancient Querini family, several of whom took refuge on the Greek island of Stampalia after their implication in the Bajamonte Tiepolo plot of 1310; when the errant clan was re-admitted to Venice, they came bearing their melodic new double-barrelled name. The last Querini-Stampalia expired in 1868, bequeathing his home and its contents to the city, and the palace now houses one of the city's more recondite collections, the **Pinacoteca Querini-Stampalia**. Although there is a batch of Renaissance pieces – such as Palma il Vecchio's marriage portraits of Francesco Querini and Paola Priuli Querini (for whom the palace was built), and Giovanni **Bellini**'s *Presentation in the Temple* – the general tone of the collection is set by the culture of eighteenth-century Venice, a period to which much of the palace's decor belongs. The winningly inept pieces by **Gabriel Bella** form a comprehensive record of Venetian social life in that century, and genre paintings by **Pietro and Alessandro Longhi**, a few rungs up the aesthetic ladder, feature prominently as well. All in all, unless you've a voracious appetite for Venice's twilight decades, the Querini-Stampalia isn't going to thrill you, but it does offer a diversion on a Friday or Saturday evening, when concerts by the Scuola di Musica Antica di Venezia (at 5pm and 8.30pm) are included in the price of the entrance ticket. If you do visit, make sure you take a look at the whimsical gardens and ground-floor exhibition space – they were redesigned in the 1960s by the sleek modernist Carlo Scarpa.

South of the Querini-Stampalia lies the crumbly, deconsecrated church of **San Giovanni in Oleo**, standing empty again after the Museo Guidi (a gallery of donations from contemporary Venetian artists) proved too costly to run. Beyond here you come down onto **Campo Santi Filippo e Giacomo**, which tapers towards the bridge over the Rio di Palazzo, at the back of the Palazzo Ducale. Just before the bridge, a short fondamenta on the left leads to the early fourteenth-century cloister of **Sant'Apollonia**, the only Romanesque cloister in the city. Fragments from the Basilica di San Marco dating back to the ninth century are displayed here, and a miscellany of sculptural pieces from other churches are on show in the adjoining **Museo Diocesano d'Arte Sacra**, where the permanent collection consists chiefly of a range of religious artefacts and paintings gathered from churches that have closed down or entrusted their possessions to the safety of the museum. In addition, freshly restored works from other collections or churches sometimes pass through here, giving the museum an edge of unpredictability.

The sixteenth-century **Palazzo Trevisan-Cappello**, opposite the Fondamenta della Canonica (beyond the bridge), was once the home of Bianca Cappello, who was sentenced to death in her absence for eloping with Pietro Bonaventuri, a humble bank clerk at the local branch of the Salviati bank, a Florentine institution. All was forgiven when she later dumped her hapless swain for Francesco de'Medici,

Grand Duke of Tuscany, who she eventually married, having endured banishment from Florence by the Grand Duke's first wife. The pair bought this palazzo together, and died together in 1587. They were probably killed by a virulent fever, but there was a strong suspicion that they had been poisoned by another Medici, which rather embarrassed the Venetians, who couldn't publicly mourn their "daughter of the Republic" for fear of offending the couple's unknown but probably influential murderer. These days the bridge which leads into the palazzo is the entrance to lace and glass showrooms.

San Zaccaria to San Giorgio dei Greci

The Salizzada di San Provolo, leading east out of Campo Santi Filippo e Giacomo, runs straight to the elegant **Campo San Zaccaria**, a spot with a chequered past. The convent attached to the church was notorious for its libidinous goings-on – a state of affairs not so surprising if you bear in mind that many of the nuns were incarcerated here either because they were too strong-willed for their families or because their fathers couldn't afford a dowry. On one occasion officials sent to put a stop to the nuns' amorous liaisons were pelted with bricks by the residents, but behaviour was customarily more discreet: Venice's upper classes supplied the convent with several of its novices, and the nuns' parlour became one of the city's most fashionable salons, as recorded by a Guardi painting in the Ca' Rezzonico (see p.117).

There's a gory side to the area's history as well. In 864 **Doge Pietro Tradonico** was murdered in the campo as he returned from vespers, and in 1172 **Doge Vitale Michiel II**, having not only blundered in peace negotiations with the Byzantine empire but also brought the plague back with him from Constantinople, was murdered as he fled for the sanctuary of San Zaccaria. Michiel's assassins disappeared into Calle delle Rasse, between the Palazzo Ducale and San Zaccaria, and it was later decreed that only wooden buildings should be built there, to make it easier to flatten the hideout of any future doge-assassin. The decree wasn't contravened until 1948, with the construction of the annexe of the *Danieli* hotel.

The church of San Zaccaria

Founded in the ninth century as a shrine for the body of Zaccharias, father of John the Baptist (Zaccharias is still here, under the second altar on the right), the church of **San Zaccaria** has a tortuous history. A Romanesque version was raised a century after the foundation, this in turn was overhauled in the 1170s (when the present campanile was constructed), a Gothic church followed in the fourteenth century, and finally in 1444 **Antonio Gambello** embarked on a

*San Zaccaria
is open daily
10am–noon &
4–6pm.*

massive rebuilding project that was concluded some seventy years later by **Mauro Codussi**, who took over the **facade** from the first storey upwards – hence its resemblance to San Michele (see p.216). The end result is a harmonious and distinctively Venetian mixture of Gothic and Renaissance styles.

The interior's notable architectural feature is its **ambulatory**: unique in Venice, it might have been built to accommodate the procession of the doges' Easter Sunday visit, a ritual that began back in the twelfth century after the convent had sold to the state the land that was to become the Piazza. Nearly every inch of wall surface is hung with seventeenth- and eighteenth-century paintings, all of them outshone by **Giovanni Bellini**'s large *Madonna and Four Saints* (1505), on the second altar on the left; you might think that the natural light is enough, but drop a coin into the light-box and you'll see what you were missing. The continuation of the architectural frame (possibly by Pietro Lombardo) into the canvas reveals that the painting hangs in its original spot – although it sojourned briefly in the Louvre, a period in which the top arched segment was removed. Further up the left aisle, by the sacristy door, is the tomb of **Alessandro Vittoria** (d.1608), including a self-portrait bust; he also carved the *St Zaccharias* and *St John the Baptist* for the two holy water stoups, and the now faceless *St Zaccharias* on the facade above the door.

The L2000/€1.03 fee payable to enter the **Cappella di Sant'Atanasio** and **Cappella di San Tarasio** (off the right aisle) is well worth it. The former was rebuilt at the end of the sixteenth century, and contains **Tintoretto**'s early *The Birth of St John the Baptist*, some fifteenth-century stalls, and a painting by Palma il Vecchio that stood in for the Bellini altarpiece during the years the Bellini was on show in Paris, along with other Napoleonic loot. Only in the latter chapel does it become obvious that the chapels occupy much of the site of the Gothic church that preceded the present one. Three wonderful *anconas* (composite altarpieces) by **Antonio Vivarini and Giovanni d'Alemagna** (all 1443) are the highlight: the one on the left is dedicated to Saint Sabine, whose tomb is below it; the main altarpiece has recently been restored, a process that has revealed a seven-panelled predella now attributed to Paolo Veneziano, the earliest celebrated Venetian artist (d. c.1358). You can also make out the decayed frescoes by Andrea del Castagno and Francesco da Faenza in the vault (painted a year before the Vivarinis), while the floor has been cut away in places to reveal mosaics from the twelfth-century San Zaccaria. Downstairs is the spooky and perpetually waterlogged ninth-century crypt, the burial place of eight early doges.

The Riva degli Schiavoni

The broad **Riva degli Schiavoni**, stretching from the edge of the Palazzo Ducale to the canal just before the Arsenale entrance, is con-

stantly thronged during the day, with an unceasing flow of prome-
nading tourists and passengers hurrying to and from its vaporetto
stops, threading through the souvenir stalls and past the wares of the
African street vendors. The Riva is at its best in the evening, when the
crowds have dwindled and the sun goes down over the Salute. The
name is a vestige of an ignominious side of the Venetian economy, as
schiavoni denotes both slaves and the Slavs who in the early days of
Venice provided most of the human merchandise. By the early
eleventh century Christianity was making extensive inroads among
the Slavs, who thus came to be regarded as too civilized for such
treatment; in succeeding centuries the slave trade turned to Greece,
Russia and Central Asia for its supplies, until the fall of
Constantinople in 1453 forced a switch of attention to the black pop-
ulations of Africa.

Now colonized by the aristocracy of the hotel trade, the Riva has
long been one of Venice's smart addresses. **Petrarch** and his daughter lived at no. 4145 in 1362–67, and **Henry James** stayed at no.
4161, battling against the constant distractions outside to finish *The
Portrait of a Lady*. George Sand, Charles Dickens, Proust, Wagner
and the ever-present Ruskin all checked in at the **Hotel Danieli** (the
former Palazzo Dandolo), which nowadays is outside the reach of
those with less than stratospheric income levels; Monteverdi's
Proserpina Rapita was first performed here – one of the earliest
opera productions. The *Danieli*'s nondescript extension, built in
1948, was the first transgression of the 1172 ban on stone buildings
on this spot (see p.181).

The Pietà

Looking east from the Molo, the main eyecatcher – rising between
the equestrian monument to King Vittorio Emanuele II and the tug-
boats berthed in the distance – is the white facade of **Santa Maria
della Visitazione**, known less cumbersomely as **La Pietà**. **Vivaldi**
wrote many of his finest pieces for the orphanage attached to the
church, where he worked as violin-master (1704–18) and later as
choirmaster (1735–38). Such a success did the orchestra and choir
of the Pietà become that some unscrupulous parents tried to get their
progeny into its famous ranks by foisting them off as orphans.

During Vivaldi's second term **Giorgio Massari** won a competition
to rebuild the church, and it's probable that the composer advised
him on acoustic refinements such as the positioning of the double
choir on the entrance wall and the two along the side walls. He may
also have suggested adding the vestibule to the front of the church,
as insulation against the background noise of the city. Building eventually began in 1745 (after Vivaldi's death), and when the interior
was completed in 1760 (the facade didn't go on until 1906) it was
regarded more as a concert hall than a church. You get some idea of
the showiness of eighteenth-century Venice from the fact that

whereas this section of the Riva was widened to give a grander approach to the building, Massari's plans for the orphanage were shelved owing to lack of funds.

The newly restored white and gold interior, looking like a wedding cake turned inside out, is crowned by a superb ceiling painting of *The Glory of Paradise* by **Giambattista Tiepolo**, who also painted the ceiling above the high altar. Unfortunately the Pietà is still one of Venice's busiest music venues, mostly for second-rate renditions of Vivaldi favourites, and just about the only time you can get a peek inside is when the box office is open; even then the entrance is barred by a rope – and usually, in a display of extreme bloody-mindedness, the custodians of the box office pull a heavy curtain across, to stop anyone taking a free look.

The Greek quarter

*San Giorgio
dei Greci is
open Mon–Sat
9.30am–1pm
& 3.30–
5.30pm, Sun
9am–1pm.*

A couple of minutes' walk north of La Pietà the campanile of **San Giorgio dei Greci** lurches spectacularly canalwards. The **Greek** presence in Venice was strong from the eleventh century, and became stronger still after the Turkish seizure of Constantinople. This mid-fifteenth-century influx of Greek speakers provided a resource which was exploited by the city's numerous scholarly publishing houses, and greatly enriched the general culture of Renaissance Venice: the daughter of the *condottiere* Gianfrancesco Gonzaga, for example, is known to have written perfect Greek at the age of ten. At its peak, the Greek community numbered around 4000, some of whom were immensely rich: a Greek merchant murdered in Venice in 1756 left 4,000,000 ducats to his daughters, a legacy that was said to have made them the richest heiresses in Europe.

The church was built in 1539–61 to a Sansovino-influenced design by **Sante Lombardo**; the cupola and campanile came later in the century. Inside, the Orthodox architectural elements include a *matroneo* (women's gallery) above the main entrance and an iconostasis (or rood screen) that completely cuts off the high altar. The icons on the screen are a mixture of works by a sixteenth-century Cretan artist called **Michael Danaskinàs** and a few Byzantine pieces dating back as far as the twelfth century.

*The Museo di
Dipinti Sacri
Bizantini is
open Mon–Sat
9am–12.30pm
&
1.30–4.15pm;
Sun 10am–
5pm;
L7000/€3.62.*

Permission to found an Orthodox church was given at the end of the fifteenth century, and a Greek college (the Collegio Flangini) and scuola were approved at the same time. The college, redesigned in 1678 by **Longhena**, is now home to the Hellenic Centre for Byzantine and Post-Byzantine Studies, custodian of Venice's Greek archives. Longhena also redesigned the Scuola di San Nicolò dei Greci, to the left of the church, which now houses the **Museo di Dipinti Sacri Bizantini**, a collection of predominantly fifteenth- to eighteenth-century icons, many of them by the *Madoneri*, the school of Greek and Cretan artists working in Venice in that period.

Although many of the most beautiful of these works maintain the compositional and symbolic conventions of icon painting, it's fascinating to observe the impact of Western influences – one or two of the artists achieve a synthesis, while others clearly struggle to harmonize the two worlds.

The area to the north of San Giorgio dei Greci is more interesting for its associations than its sights. The unfinished and hangar-like **San Lorenzo** – undergoing a glacially slow restoration – was where Marco Polo was buried, but his sarcophagus went astray during sixteenth-century rebuilding. Gentile Bellini's *Miracle of the Relic of the Cross*, now in the Accademia, depicts an extraordinary incident that once occurred in the Rio di San Lorenzo (see p.105).

Chapter 6

The Eastern Districts

For all that most visitors see of Venice's eastern districts (the remotest section of the Castello sestiere), the city may as well peter out a few metres to the east of the Palazzo Ducale, and at first glance the map of the city would seem to justify this neglect. Certainly the sights are thinly spread, and a huge bite is taken out of the area by the pools of the Arsenale, for a long time the largest manufacturing site in Europe, but now little more than a decoratively framed blank space.

Yet the slab of the city immediately to the west of the Arsenale contains places that shouldn't be ignored – the Renaissance **San Francesco della Vigna**, for example, and the **Scuola di San Giorgio degli Schiavoni**, with its endearing cycle of paintings by **Carpaccio**. And although the mainly residential area beyond the Arsenale has little to offer in the way of cultural monuments other than the ex-cathedral of **San Pietro di Castello** and the church of **Sant'Elena**, it would be a mistake to leave the easternmost zone unexplored. Except in the summer of odd-numbered years, when the **Biennale** sets up shop in the specially built pavilions behind the **Giardini Pubblici** and elsewhere in the neighbourhood, few visitors stray into this latter area – and there lies one of its principal attractions. And the whole length of the waterfront gives spectacular panoramas of the city, with the best coming last: from near the Sant'Elena landing stage you get a view that takes in the Palazzo Ducale, the back of San Giorgio Maggiore and La Giudecca, the tiny islands of La Grazia, San Clemente, Santo Spirito, San Servolo and San Lazzaro degli Armeni, and finally the Lido. A picnic here, having stocked up at the shops and stalls of Via Garibaldi, is guaranteed to recharge the batteries.

San Francesco della Vigna to the waterfront

The area that lies to the **east of San Zanipolo** is not, at first sight, an attractive district. The church of Santa Maria del Pianto, so prominent on the city's maps, turns out to be an abandoned hulk, and is barely visible over its surrounding wall. Cross the Rio di Santa Giustina and you're confronted by the shabby, graffiti-plastered church of the same name; it's now part of a school. Round the back of Santa Giustina stand the rusting remains of the local gasworks. But it's not all decay and dereliction – carry on east for just a minute more (turn left in front of Santa Giustina then first right) and a striking Renaissance facade blocks your way.

San Francesco della Vigna

The ground occupied by **San Francesco della Vigna** has a hallowed place in the mythology of Venice, as according to tradition it was around here that the angel appeared to Saint Mark to tell him that the lagoon islands were to be his final resting place. (The angel's words – "Pax tibi" and so forth – remained unchanged on the book held by Venice's symbolic lion until Napoleon substituted the rubric "To the Rights of Men and Citizens" on official proclamations; "at last he's turned the page," remarked an anonymous wag.) Some time after the alleged annunciation the area was cultivated as a vineyard, and when the land was given to the Franciscans in 1253 as a site for a new church, the vines were immortalized in their church's name.

San Francesco della Vigna is open daily 8am–12.30pm & 3–7pm.

Begun in 1534, to a design by **Sansovino**, the present building was much modified in the course of its construction. **Palladio** was brought in to provide the **facade** (1568–72), a feature that looks like something of an afterthought from the side, but which must have been quite stunning at the time, when the only other white Istrian stone facade in Venice would have been that of San Michele. The **interior** was altered by a humanist scholar monk, **Fra' Francesco Zorzi**, who rearranged the proportions along philosophically approved lines and generally amended its acoustic and decorative design. The calculated Renaissance improvements and cold colouring make the church less welcoming than the two great mendicant churches of San Zanipolo and the Frari, despite its less belittling dimensions; however, there are some fine works of art here, for whose essential light-boxes you should take a pocketful of coins.

Some of Venice's wealthiest families contributed to the cost of building San Francesco by paying for family chapels: the third on the right belonged to the **Contarini**, and contains memorials to a pair of seventeenth-century Contarini doges; the next is the **Badoer** chapel (with a *Resurrection* attributed to Veronese); and after that comes the chapel of the **Barbaro** family. The Barbaro ancestral device – a red circle on a white field – was granted in the twelfth century after a particularly revolting act by the Admiral Marco Barbaro: in the thick of battle he cut off a Moor's hand and used the bleeding stump to draw a circle on the man's turban, which he then flew as a pennant from the mast-head. Around the corner in the right transept is a large *Madonna and Child Enthroned* by **Antonio da Negroponte** (c.1450), a picture full of meticulously detailed and glowingly colourful birds and plants.

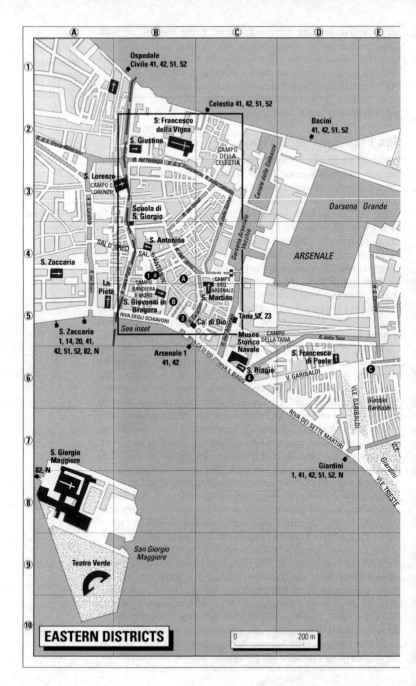

EASTERN DISTRICTS

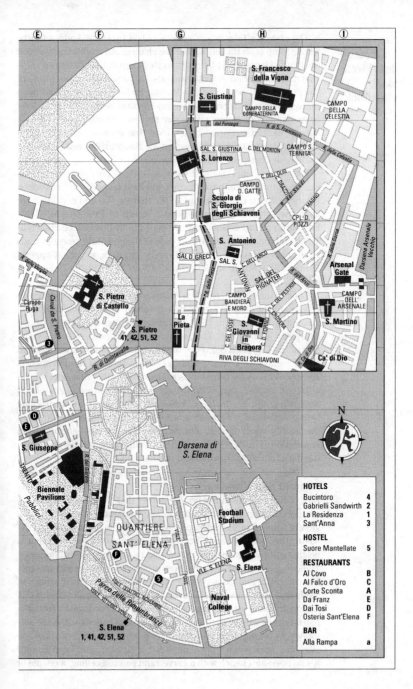

HOTELS

Bucintoro	**4**
Gabrielli Sandwirth	**2**
La Residenza	**1**
Sant'Anna	**3**

HOSTEL

| Suore Mantellate | **5** |

RESTAURANTS

Al Covo	**B**
Al Falco d'Oro	**C**
Corte Sconta	**A**
Da Franz	**E**
Dai Tosi	**D**
Osteria Sant'Elena	**F**

BAR

| Alla Rampa | **a** |

The church's foundation stone was laid by **Doge Andrea Gritti**, whose tomb is on the left wall of the chancel. An intellectually versatile man – he spoke six languages other than Italian and was a close friend of Sansovino – Gritti was also a formidable womanizer, of whom one rival remarked "we cannot make a doge of a man with three bastards in Turkey". After his election he carried on making bastards, including one with a nun named Celestina, but it was his equally Rabelaisian appetite for food that proved his undoing: he died on Christmas Eve after eating too many grilled eels. It's still a traditional Christmas dish in Venice.

Left of the chancel is the **Giustiniani** chapel, lined with marvellous sculpture by the **Lombardo** family and their helpers. Commissioned for the previous church by one of the Badoer clan and installed here after the rebuilding, they include a group of Prophets by Pietro Lombardo and assistants and reliefs of the Evangelists attributed to Tullio and Antonio Lombardo. A door at the end of the transept leads to a pair of tranquil fifteenth-century cloisters, via the **Cappella Santa**, which has a *Madonna and Child* by Giovanni Bellini and assistants.

Back in the church, the first chapel after the cloister door (another Giustiniani chapel) contains a gorgeous *Sacra Conversazione* painted by **Veronese** in 1562, following the model of Titian's Pésaro altarpiece in the Frari. The predominantly monochromatic decoration of the **Cappella Sagredo**, the next chapel but one, was created in the eighteenth century, and features frescoes of the Evangelists and two Virtues by Giambattista Tiepolo. On the altarpiece of the adjacent chapel you'll find figures of *St Anthony Abbot*, *St Sebastian* and *St Roch* by **Alessandro Vittoria**, who also made bronze figures of *St Francis* and *John the Baptist* that should be on the nearby water stoups, but only the former has returned from restoration. Finally, on the entrance wall, to the left as you leave, there's a fine triptych attributed to Antonio Vivarini.

Around San Francesco

East of San Francesco is a remote corner that can be summarized as a vaporetto stop (*Celestia*), a scummy backwater of a canal, and a view of the wall of the oldest part of the Arsenale. Immediately to the south (the route to San Giorgio degli Schiavoni) lies an area that is destitute of monuments but could stand as the epitome of domestic Venice – densely textured, in places grotty and in others picturesque. The Salizzada and Campo delle Gatte ("paved street and square of the female cats") are typical of the district; the peculiar name of this unexceptionally catty avenue is a corruption of "de legate", from the papal legates who used to stay here. An oddity to seek out is the sottoportego on the corner of Calle Zorzi and Corte Nuova (take the alley that goes south from Campo Santa Giustina and keep going): it's an open-air chapel, with a carved and painted ceiling, a couple of shrines dedicated to the dead of various wars, and four paintings so flaked and grimy that they could depict anything.

San Giorgio degli Schiavoni

Venice has two brilliant cycles of pictures by **Vittore Carpaccio**, the most disarming of Venetian artists – one is in the Accademia, the other is in the **Scuola di San Giorgio degli Schiavoni**. Venice's relations with the Slavs (*schiavoni*) were not always untroubled – the city's slave markets were originally stocked with captured Slavs, and in later centuries the settlements of the Dalmatian coast were a harassment to Venetian shipping.

By the mid-fifteenth century, though, Venice's Slavic inhabitants – many of them sailors and merchants – were sufficiently established for a scuola to be set up in order to protect their interests. After several years of meeting in the church of San Giovanni di Malta, the scuola built itself a new headquarters on the church's doorstep at the start of the sixteenth century, and summoned Carpaccio to brighten up the first-storey hall. Painted from 1502 to 1508, after the Accademia's *St Ursula* cycle, Carpaccio's pictures were moved downstairs when the building was rearranged in 1551, and the interior has scarcely changed since.

The cycle illustrates mainly the lives of the Dalmatian patron saints – George, Tryphone and Jerome. As always with Carpaccio, what holds your attention is not so much the main event as the incidental details with which he packs the scene, and the incidentals in this cycle feature some of the most arresting images in Venetian painting, from the limb-strewn feeding-ground of Saint George's dragon in the first scene of the cycle, to the endearing little white dog in the final one. The scenes depicted are: *St George and the Dragon*; *The Triumph of St George*; *St George Baptizing the Gentiles* (George had rescued the princess Selene, daughter of the royal couple being baptized); *The Miracle of St Tryphone* (the dainty little basilisk is a demon just exorcized from the daughter of the Roman emperor Gordianus); *The Agony in the Garden*; *The Calling of Matthew*; *St Jerome Leading the Lion to the Monastery*; *The Funeral of St Jerome*; and *The Vision of St Augustine* (he was writing to Saint Jerome when a vision told him of Jerome's death).

The *Madonna and Child* altarpiece is by **Benedetto Carpaccio**, Vittore's son, while the panelled upstairs hall is decorated with mundane early seventeenth-century paintings in honour of various brethren of the scuola, which is still functioning today.

From Sant'Antonino to the waterfront

The frequently closed church of **Sant'Antonino**, the next stop south along the fondamenta from San Giorgio, is an unenticing seventeenth-century effort housing nothing except a picture by Carpaccio's not

San Francesco della Vigna to the waterfront

The Scuola di San Giorgio degli Schiavoni is open Tues–Sat 9.30am–12.30pm & 3.30–6.30pm, Sun 10am–12.30pm; L5000/€2.58.

over-talented teacher, but has some good stories attached to it. It enshrined the body of a certain Saint Sabus from the mid-thirteenth century until 1965, when Pope Paul VI returned the relic to the monastery in Istanbul whence it had been stolen by a future doge; for all that time the Turkish monks had been meeting disconsolately every night at their saint's empty sarcophagus. The emblems of Saint Anthony Abbot are a pig and a bell, and this church once kept a sty of belled and notoriously unruly pigs – though it's not clear if this was some sort of tribute to their patron. The bell-ringing swine were allowed to roam the parish unfettered, but eventually they so annoyed the locals that in 1409 their freedom was curtailed by a sumptuary edict. "Saint Anthony loved a pig" is still a Venetian saying, used to express a lack of surprise at a supposedly odd occurrence. And finally, in 1819 an elephant escaped from a visiting menagerie and took refuge in Sant'Antonino; having cornered the hapless beast, its pursuers shot it.

San Giovanni in Brágora

Salizzada Sant'Antonin curves down to the quiet **Campo Bandiera e Moro**, named after the Venetians Attilio and Emilio Bandiera and Domenico Moro, who in 1844 were executed for leading an abortive revolt against the Bourbons. The Bandiera brothers were born at no. 3610, and all three are buried together in Santi Giovanni e Paolo. Across the alley from the Bandiera house stands the campo's handsomest building, the fifteenth-century Palazzo Gritti Badoer; a complete ruin a hundred years ago, it has been renovated as a hotel.

San Giovanni in Brágora is open Mon–Sat 3.30–5.30pm.

Across the square stands **San Giovanni in Brágora**, probably best known to Venetians as the baptismal church of Antonio Vivaldi. The church is dedicated to the Baptist, and some people think that its strange suffix is a reference to a region from which some relics of the saint were once brought; others link the name to the old dialect words for mud (*brago*) and backwater (*gora*), or to the verb *bragolare* (to fish), or even to the Greek word for the main public square, *agora*. The origins of the church itself are equally disputed – folklore insists that this is one of the city's oldest, dating back to the early eighth century, but there's no documentary proof of its existence prior to 1090.

The present structure was begun in 1475, about the same time that San Michele was finished and only six years before the Miracoli was started, although the simple Gothic building shows no sign of the arrival of Renaissance architecture in Venice. However, you can trace the development of a Renaissance aesthetic in its best paintings, all of which were created within a quarter-century of the rebuilding: a triptych by **Bartolomeo Vivarini**, on the wall between the first and second chapels on the right (1478); a *Resurrection* by **Alvise Vivarini**, to the left of the sacristy door (1498); and two paintings by **Cima da Conegliano** – a *SS. Helen and Constantine*, to the right of the sacristy door (1501), and a *Baptism* on the high altar (1494). The remains of Saint John the Almsgiver, stolen from Alexandria in 1247, lie in the second chapel on the right, though the Venetian church dedicated to him – San Giovanni Elemosinario – is over in the Rialto. Set into an alcove at the west end of the left aisle is the font in which Vivaldi was baptised for the second time, having been given an emergency baptism at home because he seemed unlikely to survive more than a few hours.

San Martino to the waterfront

A group of Paduan refugees are said to have founded a church on the site of the nearby **San Martino** in 593, which would give it one of Venice's longest pedigrees; Sansovino designed the present Greek-cross building in around 1540. To get a decent perusal of **Domenico Bruni**'s distortedly perspectival ceiling painting (seventeenth-century) you have to lie on your back in the very middle of the church, more or less where most of **Doge Francesco Erizzo** (d.1646) is buried; his heart is in the Basilica di San Marco.

San Martino is open Mon–Sat 11am–noon & 5–6.30pm, Sun 10.30am– 12.30pm.

Across the canal that runs down the side of San Martino – the Rio Ca' di Dio – is the *Spazio Legno* workshop, where *forcole* (rowlocks for gondolas) are crafted. Follow the fondamenta south and then turn right into Calle de la Pegola and you'll emerge on the main waterfront, with the **Ca' di Dio** to your right. Founded in the thirteenth century as a hospice for pilgrims and Crusaders, the Ca' di Dio was extended in 1545 by Sansovino – his new wing, with its profusion of chimneys, is visible from the bridge. The building on the other side of Calle de la Pegola, decorated with a second-storey frieze of little stone peaks, is the **Forni Pubblici** (1473), the bakery which supplied the vessels leaving the Arsenale with ship's biscuit, the last stage in the preparations for sailing (see overleaf for more).

The Arsenale

A corruption of the Arabic *darsin'a* (house of industry), the very name of the **Arsenale** is indicative of the strength of Venice's links with the eastern Mediterranean, and the workers of these dockyards and factories were the foundations upon which the city's maritime supremacy rested. Visiting dignitaries were often as astonished by the industriousness of the Arsenale as by the opulence of the Canal Grande. At the beginning of the fourteenth century Dante came to Venice twice (once as ambassador from Ravenna), and was so impressed by what he saw on his first mission that he evoked the sight in a famous passage of the *Inferno*, in which those guilty of selling public offices are tortured in a lake of boiling pitch like the caulkers' vats in the Arsenale.

The development of the Arsenale seems to have commenced in the early years of the twelfth century, when the maintenance of galleys became the main industry in this part of the city; by the third decade of the fourteenth century a massive expansion was under way, as the Arsenale established a state monopoly in the construction of galleys and large merchant vessels. By the 1420s it had become the base for some 300 shipping companies, operating around 3000 vessels of 200 tons or more; at the Arsenale's zenith, around the middle of the sixteenth century, its wet and dry docks, its rope and sail factories, its ordnance depots and gunpowder mills employed a total of 16,000 men – equal to the population of a major town of the period.

In *The City in History*, Lewis Mumford credits the Venetians with the invention of "a new type of city, based on the differentiation and zoning of urban functions, separated by traffic ways and open spaces", and cites the island of Murano and the Arsenale as Europe's first examples of industrial planning. Of these two, the Arsenale most closely resembled a modern factory complex. Construction techniques in the Arsenale were the most sophisticated of their time: by the fifteenth century the Venetians had perfected a production-line process for equipping their warships, in which the vessels were towed past a succession of windows, to collect ropes, sails, armaments, oars and all their other supplies (ending with barrels of hard biscuits), so that by the time they reached the lagoon the vessels were fully prepared for battle. The productivity of the wharves was legendary: at the height of the conflict with the Turks in the sixteenth century, one ship a day was being added to the Venetian fleet. On the occasion of the visit of Henry III of France in 1574, the Arsenale workers put on a bravura performance – in the time it took the king and his hosts to work their way through a state banquet in the Palazzo Ducale, the *Arsenalotti* assembled and made sea-worthy a ship sturdy enough to bear a crew plus a cannon weighing 16,000 pounds.

To an extent, the governors of the city acknowledged their debt to the workers of the Arsenale. They were a privileged group within the Venetian proletariat, acting as watchmen at the Palazzo Ducale whenever the Maggior Consiglio was in session, carrying the doge in triumph round the Piazza after his inauguration, and serving as pallbearers at ducal funerals. By the standards of other manual workers they were not badly paid either, although the 50 ducats that was the typical wage of a master shipwright in the early sixteenth century should be set against the 40,000 ducats spent by Alvise Pisani, one of the most powerful politicians of the period, on the weddings of his five daughters. The *Arsenalotti* were also less docile than most of their fellow artisans, and were responsible for a number of strikes and disturbances. A dramatic protest took place in 1569, when a gang of 300 *Arsenalotti* armed with axes smashed their way into the hall of the Collegio to present their grievances to the doge in person.

The growth and decline of the Arsenale

Expansion of the Arsenale was particularly rapid in the fourteenth century and continued into the sixteenth – **Sanmicheli**'s covered dock for the state barge (the *Bucintoro*) was built in 1544–47, for example, and **da Ponte**'s gigantic rope factory – the *Corderia* or **Tana** – in 1579. (The greater part of the *Tana* runs along the Rio della Tana; a single room 316m long – not far off twice the length of the Piazza – it provides an extraordinary exhibition space for the *Aperto* section of the Biennale.) By that time, though, the maritime strength of Venice was past its peak: Vasco da Gama had rounded the Cape of Good Hope in 1497, thus opening a direct sea route to the East; the New World routes were growing; and there was the perpetual threat of the ever stronger Turkish empire. The shrinkage of the Venetian mercantile fleet was drastic – between 1560 and 1600 the volume of shipping registered at the Arsenale was halved. Militarily as well, despite the conspicuous success at Lépanto (1571), Venice was on the wane, and the reconquest of the Morea (Peloponnese) at the end of the seventeenth century was little more than a glorious interlude in a long story of decline. When **Napoleon** took over the city in 1797 he burned down the docks, sank the last *Bucintoro* and confiscated the remnant of the Venetian navy, sailing off with it to attempt the invasion of Ireland. After the failure of that expedition the fleet was taken back to the Mediterranean, only to be destroyed by Nelson at the battle of Aboukir.

Under Austrian occupation the Arsenale was reconstructed, and it stayed in continuous operation until the end of 1917 when, having produced a number of ships for the Italian navy in World War I, the dockyards were dismantled to prevent them being of use to the enemy forces that seemed likely to invade the lagoon. Since then it has been used by the navy for storage and repairs, and as a venue for part of the Biennale, but plans exist to extend the Museo Storico Navale into the Arsenale buildings and to convert other parts into sports halls, accommodation for the University of Architecture and premises for ACTV.

The Arsenale buildings

There is no public access to the Arsenale. You can get a look at part of it, however, from the bridge connecting the Campo Arsenale and the Fondamenta dell'Arsenale; a better view can be had from one of the vaporetti that cut through the oldest part of the complex, taking you past Sanmicheli's *Bucintoro* building, alongside which is the mouth of the Darsena Grande. (At the time of going to press, the vaporetto routes through the Arsenale were suspended while work was being done inside the complex; once that work is completed, it's likely that the routes will be restored.)

The main **gateway** to the Arsenale was the first structure in Venice to employ the classical vocabulary of Renaissance architecture. Built by **Antonio Gambello** in 1460 (but incorporating, at ground level, Veneto-Byzantine capitals from the twelfth century), it consists of a triumphal arch topped by a less precisely classical storey – a design that was possibly intended to create the illusion that the entrance to the Arsenale was an amalgam of a genuine Roman edifice and more modern Venetian building. You'll notice that the book being held by the Lion of St Mark, unlike any other in the city, doesn't reveal the traditional inscription, perhaps because "Pax tibi . . ." was thought to be too pacific for this context; the statue above his head, *Santa Justina* by **Campagna**, was put there in 1578.

The **four lions** outside the gateway feature in coffee-table books on Venice almost as frequently as the San Marco horses, and, like the horses, they are stolen goods. Exactly when the two furthest on the right were grabbed isn't known, but they probably came from the Lion Terrace at Delos, and date from around the sixth century BC; the left-hand one of the pair (with the prosthetic head) was positioned here to mark the recapture of Corfu in 1716 – the other was in place slightly earlier.

*For more on
Doge
Francesco
Morosini, see
p.95.*

The larger pair aren't as enigmatic: they were swiped from Piraeus in 1687 by Francesco Morosini, after the reconquest of the Morea. The blurred and incomprehensible inscription on the shoulder and side of the lion on the left of the gate (which started life as an ancient Greek fountain) is a piece of runic graffiti, the handiwork of a Norse mercenary serving with the army hired by the Byzantine emperor in the eleventh century to suppress a rebellion of his Greek subjects.

The Museo Storico Navale and San Biagio

*The Museo
Storico Navale
is open
Mon–Fri
8.45am–
1.30pm, Sat
8.45am–1pm,
plus Tues &
Thurs
2.30–5pm
April–Oct;
L3000/€1.54.*

Nearby, on the other side of the Rio dell'Arsenale, is the **Museo Storico Navale**, most of which is housed in a former granary. Documenting every conceivable facet of Venice's naval history, the museum is another loose baggy monster like the Correr, but a selective tour is an essential supplement to a walk round the Arsenale district – and it's laid out far better than the Correr, with bilingual captions on many of the exhibits. Improbable though it sounds, the models of Venetian craft – from the gondola to the 224-oar fighting galley and the last *Bucintoro* – will justify the entrance fee for most people. It was common practice in the Venetian shipyards to build their boats not from scale drawings but from models, and the most meticulous pieces in the collection (on the first floor) are the functional models retrieved from the yards after Napoleon's arsonists had done their work.

At ground level there's a room dedicated to Angelo Emo, the last admiral of the Republic, the focal point being Canova's monument to him. A miscellany of armaments occupies the rest of the space, with the most remarkable invention being a manned torpedo; a caption explains how the captain of the *HMS Valiant*, which was crippled by one of these contraptions, came to award a military honour to the

Italian lieutenant who had carried out the attack. Models of modern warships take up much of the second floor; the third has a display about the vessels of the lagoon, a section on the evolution of the gondola and a roomful of models of Far Eastern vessels. The top storey's installation, illustrating the part played by Sweden in the maritime history of Italy, reveals more connections than you might think, but is nonetheless likely to fascinate maritime historians only; it's difficult to imagine who might be fascinated by the final room, with its hundreds of highly polished, unlabelled seashells, arrayed in cabinets that look like they've come from a liquidated jeweller's store. About 250 metres along the fondamenta is the second section of the museum, the **Padiglioni delle Navi**, a vast shed full of craft with Venetian connections.

The church of **San Biagio**, alongside the main museum block, was the Greek community's church before San Giorgio dei Greci, and took on its present municipal office appearance after an eighteenth-century refit. It's now the naval chapel and is rarely open, though you can normally look through the inner wrought-iron door at the interior, where **Giovanni Ferrari**'s reclining statue of Admiral Angelo Emo (1792) is the main point of interest. Tucked behind the church is the concrete bunker known as Palasport (or Palazzetto dello Sport), the city's main indoor sports hall, used for handball and basketball matches.

Beyond the Arsenale

The Riva San Biagio is the only land route into the districts to the east of the Arsenale, but once over the wide bridge that traverses the Rio della Tana you have to make a choice. By following the waterfront you'll pass the main public gardens of Venice before finally reaching the ramshackle football stadium and the isolated church of Sant'Elena. Opt for the less picturesque Via Garibaldi, and you're on your way to the church of San Pietro di Castello, the major monument of this part of the city.

To San Pietro di Castello

In 1808 the greater part of the canal connecting the Bacino di San Marco to the broad northeastern inlet of the Canale di San Pietro was filled in to form what is now **Via Garibaldi**, the widest street in the city and the busiest commercial area in the eastern district. (The pattern of the pavement shows clearly the course of the former canal.) The bars, *pasticcerie* and *alimentari* of Via Garibaldi are as good as most of those in the more comfortable areas of the city, and are far less likely to treat you as a tedious occupational hazard. Roaming through the alleyways and squares of the vicinity, it's possible to forget for a while that you're in the most commercialized city in the country.

Beyond the Arsenale

There's just a couple of spots of cultural or historical significance along Via Garibaldi. The first house on the right was for a time the home of the navigators **John and Sebastian Cabot**, explorers of Newfoundland (together) and Paraguay (just Sebastian) in the late fifteenth and early sixteenth century. The church of **San Francesco di Paola**, opposite the entrance to the tree-lined alley that glories in the name Giardini Garibaldi, has a painting by Giandomenico Tiepolo on its cornice. A far more impressive sight awaits if you walk beyond the market stalls on the right-hand side of the street, which becomes the Fondamenta di Sant'Anna: this takes you onto the Ponte di Quintavalle, and so to the island of San Pietro.

The island of San Pietro di Castello

Originally named **Castello**, after a castle that used to stand here (built by either the Romans or the first "Venetian" settlers), the island of **San Pietro** was one of the very first parts of central Venice to be occupied. Nowadays this is a run-down district where the repairing of boats is the main occupation, yet it was once the ecclesiastical centre of Venice. By 775 the settlement here had grown sufficiently to be granted the foundation of a bishopric under the authority of the Patriarch of Grado. Within the next half-century Castello joined the immediately surrounding islands to form Rivoalto, the embryonic city of Venice. From the beginning, the political and economic power was concentrated in the distant Rialto and San Marco districts, and the relationship between the Church and the geographically remote rulers of the city was never to be close. In 1451 the first **Patriarch of Venice** was invested, but still his seat remained at Castello, and succeeding generations of councillors and senators showed no inclination to draw the father of the Venetian Church into the centre of power. San Pietro di Castello remained the cathedral of Venice, emblematically marooned on the periphery of the city, until 1807, when the patriarch was at last permitted to install himself in San Marco – ten years after the Republic had ceased to exist.

One of the major Venetian festivals – the Festival of the Marys – had its origin in an incident that occurred here in the tenth century. A multiple marriage in the church was interrupted by a posse of Slav pirates, who carried away the brides and their substantial dowries. Men from the parish of Santa Maria Formosa led the pursuit, which succeeded in retrieving the women. To celebrate their safe return, every year two girls were chosen from each sestiere to be married in a single ceremony at San Pietro, the weddings being followed by an eight-day junket that culminated at Santa Maria Formosa on the Day of the Purification of Mary – the day on which the brides had been kidnapped.

As with the Arsenale, the history of San Pietro is somewhat more interesting than what you can see. A church was raised here as early as the seventh century, but the present **San Pietro di Castello** was

San Pietro di Castello is open Mon–Sat 10am–5pm, Sun 1–5pm (closed Sun in July & Aug); L3000/€1.54.

built nearly a millennium later. A new facade was designed in the mid-sixteenth century by **Palladio**, but the work was not carried out until the end of the century, and the executed project was a feeble version of the original scheme. Similarly, the interior is an early seventeenth-century derivation from a plan by Palladio, and is unlikely to convince any Ruskinite that classicism has something to it after all. Nor will the paintings put a skip in your stride: best of the bunch are *SS. John the Evangelist, Peter and Paul*, a late work by Veronese (left aisle), and the altarpiece by Luca Giordano in the Cappella Vendramin (left transept). The Vendramin chapel and the high altar were both designed by Longhena; take a look as well at the Cappella Lando (left aisle), which has a fifth-century mosaic fragment and a bust of San Lorenzo Giustiniani, the first Patriarch of Venice, by a follower of Antonio Rizzo. The most unusual feature of the church is the so-called **Throne of St Peter** (right aisle), a marble seat made in the thirteenth century from an Arabic funeral stone cut with texts from the Koran.

The **campanile**, one of the most precarious in the city, was rebuilt by Mauro Codussi in the 1480s, and was the first tower in Venice to be clad in Istrian stone. Its original cupola was replaced with the present one in 1670.

The public gardens, the Biennale site and Sant'Elena

Stretching from Via Garibaldi to the Rio di Sant'Elena, the arc of green spaces formed by the **Giardini Garibaldi, Giardini Pubblici** and **Parco delle Rimembranze** can usually be relied on to provide a remedy for the claustrophobia that overtakes most visitors to Venice at some point. The first of the three is really little more than a short cut from Via Garibaldi to the Giardini Pubblici, which Eugène Beauharnais created by draining a swamp and demolishing a batch of monastic buildings.

Largely obscured by the trees are the rather more extensive grounds belonging to the **Biennale**, an entirely dormant zone except when the arts shindig is in progress, in the summer of odd-numbered years. Various countries have built permanent pavilions for their Biennale representatives, forming a unique colony that features work by some of the great names of modern architecture and design: the Austrian pavilion was built by the Secession architect Josef Hoffman in the 1930s; the Finnish pavilion was created by Alvar Aalto in the 1950s; the Netherlands pavilion was designed by archmodernist Gerrit Thomas Rietveld, also in the 1950s; and the Venezuelan pavilion, completed in 1954, is by Carlo Scarpa. Naturally enough, the biggest pavilion is the Italian one – five times larger than the next largest, it was refurbished in 1989, giving it a glossier finish than most of its neighbours. On the approach to the Italian pavilion stands one of the newest additions to the ensemble,

Beyond the Arsenale

For more on the Biennale, see p.278.

James Stirling's hull-like pavilion for the Biennale's book exhibition; built in 1991, it is funded by Electa, Italy's leading art-book publisher, hence the company logo on the "funnel". Before long it should have several younger neighbours, as there are plans for the construction of as many as ten new national pavilions.

If you want to squeeze every last drop from the eastern districts, call in at the church of **San Giuseppe di Castello** (or San Isepo), to the north of the Giardini Pubblici – a gateway from the gardens opens onto a street just yards from the church. It houses Alessandro Vittoria's monument to Procurator G. Grimani (in the chancel), and a vast **monument to Doge Marino Grimani**, designed in the late sixteenth century by Vincenzo Scamozzi, with reliefs and figures by Campagna (left side).

The island of **Sant'Elena**, the city's eastern limit, was greatly enlarged during the Austrian administration, partly to furnish accommodation and exercise grounds for the occupying troops. Much of the island used to be covered by a meadow, a favourite recreation area in the last century, but the strip of park along the waterfront is all that's left of it, houses having been built on the rest. Still, the walk out here is the nearest you'll get to country pleasures in central Venice, and the **church of Sant'Elena**, approached between the walls of the naval college and the ramshackle home of Venice's second-division football team, is worth a visit.

A church was erected here in the thirteenth century, following the acquisition of the body of Saint Helena, Constantine's mother. It was rebuilt in 1435 but from 1807 to 1928 it was abandoned, except for a spell as an iron foundry. The spartan Gothic interior has recently been restored, as have the cloister and campanile – the latter so zealously that it now looks like a chimney, which is exactly what it was used as when the church did service as a factory. The main attraction is the **doorway** to the church, an ensemble created in the 1470s (probably by **Antonio Rizzo**) and incorporating the **monument to Vittore Cappello**, showing him kneeling before St Helena. Cappello was captain-general of the republic's navy in the 1460s, a period in which the Turks were beginning to loosen Venice's grip on the Aegean; so dejected was he by the signs of decline in the Venetian empire that he was reputed to have gone for five months without once smiling, before dying of a broken heart.

Chapter 7

The Canal Grande

Known to the locals as the Canalazzo, the Canal Grande is Venice's high street, and divides the city in half, with three sestieri to the west and three to the east. Pending the construction of the much-discussed bridge to link the bus and train stations, only three bridges cross the waterway – at the station, Rialto and Accademia – but a number of gondola traghetti provide additional crossing points at regular intervals, as does the #1 vaporetto, which slaloms from one bank to the other along its entire length. The Canal Grande is almost four kilometres long and varies in width between thirty and seventy metres; it is, however, surprisingly shallow, at no point much exceeding five metres. In the fourteenth century an earthquake pulled the plug out and the entire contents drained away – for the best part of a fortnight Venice's finest waterway was an avenue of slime.

The section that follows is principally a guide to the Canal Grande palaces – the churches and other public buildings that you can see from the vaporetto are covered in the appropriate geographical sections. You'd need an amazing reading speed and a rubber neck to do justice to the Canal Grande in one run, though; even these edited highlights cover around fifty buildings (less than a third of the total). Try to allow for several trips, and don't miss the experience of a nocturnal boat ride – the romance of Venice at night survives even the din of a vaporetto.

See p.36–37 and colour map 2 for details of the #1 vaporetto and other water-bus services.

The Left Bank

If you come into Venice by train, your first sight of the Canal Grande will be from the upper stretch of its left bank, with the vaporetto landing stages directly in front. To the left is the northernmost of the Canal Grande's three bridges, the **Ponte degli Scalzi**, successor of an iron structure put up by the Austrians in 1858–60; like the one at the Accademia, it was replaced in the early 1930s to give the new steamboats sufficient clearance.

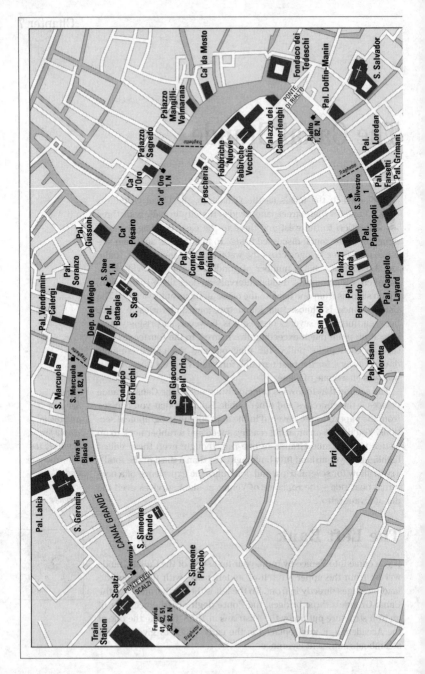

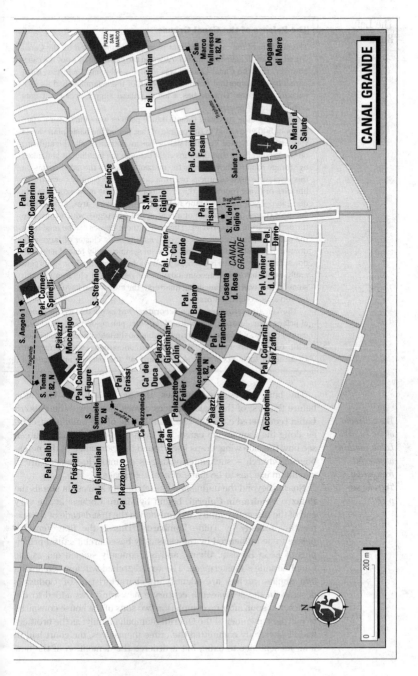

CANAL GRANDE

PIAZZA SAN MARCO

Pal. Giustinian

Pal. Contarini dei Cavalli

Pal. Benzon

Pal. Corner-Spinelli

S. Angelo 1

La Fenice

S.M. del Giglio

Pal. Corner d. Ca' Grande

Pal. Pisani

San Marco Vallaresso 1, 82, N

Pal. Contarini-Fasan

Salute 1

Traghetto

S.M. del Giglio 1

Traghetto

S. Stefano

Palazzi Mocenigo

Pal. Contarini d. Figure

Pal. Grassi

Ca' del Duca

Palazzo Giustinian-Lolin

Palazzetto Falier

Accademia 1, 82, N

Pal. Barbaro

Pal. Franchetti

Casetta d. Rose

CANAL GRANDE

Pal. Venier d. Leoni

Pal. Dario

Pal. Contarini dal Zaffo

S. Toma 1, 82, N

Traghetto

S. Samuele 82, N

Traghetto

Ca' Rezzonico 1

Pal. Loredan

Palazzi Contarini

Accademia

Pal. Balbi

Ca' Foscari

Pal. Giustinian

Ca' Rezzonico

S. Maria d. Salute

Dogana di Mare

200 m

N

0

The Left Bank

The ballroom of the Palazzo Labia contains wonderful frescoes by Tiepolo; see p.150.

The boat passes two churches, the **Scalzi** and **San Geremia**, before the first of the major palaces comes into view – the **Palazzo Labia** (completed c.1750). The main facade of the building stretches along the Cannaregio canal, but from the Canal Grande you can see how the side wing wraps itself round the campanile of the neighbouring church – such interlocking is common in Venice, where maximum use has to be made of available space.

Not far beyond the unfinished church of **San Marcuola** stands the **Palazzo Vendramin-Calergi**, begun by Mauro Codussi at the very end of the fifteenth century and finished in the first decade of the sixteenth, probably by Tullio Lombardo. This is the first Venetian palace to be influenced by the classically based architectural principles of Leon Battista Alberti, and is frequently singled out as the Canal Grande's masterpiece. The round-arched windows enclosing two similar arches are identifying characteristics of Codussi's designs. In the seventeenth century a new wing was added to the palace, but soon after its completion two sons of the house conspired to murder a member of the Querini-Stampalia family; as the brothers hadn't physically committed the crime themselves, the court had to limit its sentence to exile, but it ordered the demolition of the new

brick, which is cheaper, lighter and easier to obtain in the Veneto than building stone. Obviously mudbanks are not the stablest of bases, so the builders' usual procedure was to drive oak piling into the mud as a foundation, and then consolidate this with a superstructure of planks and cement. Between this "raft" and the brickwork, they often placed a damp-course of highly resistant Istrian stone.

A couple of features of the Venetian skyline call for explanation. The bizarre **chimneys** were designed to function as spark-traps – fire being a constant hazard in a city where the scarcity of land inevitably resulted in a high density of housing. (The development of Venice has been punctuated by terrible fires – notably at the Rialto, San Marco and, at least four times, the Palazzo Ducale.) The **roof-level platforms (altane)** you'll see here and there had a variety of uses, drying laundry and bleaching hair being two of the most common. For the latter operation, the women of Renaissance Venice wore wide-brimmed crownless straw hats, which allowed them to get the sun on their hair while keeping it off their complexions.

The frequency with which the same **family names** recur can be confusing. More than ten palaces bear the Contarini name, for example, and at one time there were around thirty. Intermarriage between families is one reason for this – dynastic marriages were often marked by grafting the new relatives' surname onto the house's original name. The other main explanation is the fact that under Venetian law the eldest son was not the sole heir – the sons of wealthy patricians would often, upon receiving their shares of the father's estate, set up their own branches of the family in houses in other parts of the city. This did not always involve commissioning a new building; palaces were regularly bought and sold within the patriciate, and the transaction often resulted in another double-barrelled palace name.

block for good measure. The palazzo's most famous subsequent resident was Richard Wagner, who died here in February 1883; the size of the palace can be gauged from the fact that his rented suite of fifteen rooms occupied just a part of the mezzanine level.

The **Palazzo Soranzo**, a bit further along, dates from the same period as the Vendramin-Calergi, and the contrast between the two gives you an idea of the originality of Codussi's design. The **Palazzo Gussoni-Grimani della Vida**, on the near side of the Rio di Noale, was rebuilt to Sanmicheli's designs in the middle of the sixteenth century. From 1614 to 1618 it was occupied by the English consul Sir Henry Wotton, at the time of whose residence the facade of the palace was covered with frescoes by Tintoretto – they have long since faded. Wotton spent much of his time running a sort of import–export business: when he wasn't buying paintings to ship back to England he was arranging for Protestant texts to be brought into Venice, a city he thought ripe for conversion. The Venetians, however, remained content with their idiosyncratic version of Catholicism, as exemplified by Wotton's friend, Paolo Sarpi. In Britain, Wotton is best remembered for his rueful definition of an ambassador – "an honest man sent to lie abroad for the good of his country".

*For more on
Paolo Sarpi,
see p.159.*

*For more on
the Ca' d'Oro,
see p.160.*

From the Ca' d'Oro to the Rialto

The next palace of interest is the most beguiling on the canal – the
Ca' d'Oro. (*Ca'* is an abbreviation of *Casa* – house. It was only after
the fall of the Republic that the title *Casa* was dropped in favour of
Palazzo.) Incorporating fragments of a thirteenth-century palace
that once stood on the site, the Ca' d'Oro was built in the 1420s and
1430s, and acquired its nickname – "The Golden House" – from the
gilding that used to accentuate much of its carving.

The facade of the **Palazzo Sagredo**, on the near side of the Campo
Santa Sofia, is an overlay of different periods, and a good demonstration of the Venetian custom of adapting old buildings to current
needs and principles. The tracery of the *piano nobile* is fourteenth-
century, and clearly later than the storeys below; the right wing, however, seems to belong to the fifteenth century.

On the near corner of the Rio dei Santi Apostoli stands the **Palazzo
Mangilli-Valmarana**, built in the eighteenth century for the English
consul Joseph Smith, who was one of the chief patrons of Canaletto.
More interesting is the **Ca' da Mosto**, close to the Rio's opposite
bank. The arches of the first floor and the carved panels above them
are remnants of a thirteenth-century Veneto-Byzantine building, and
are thus among the oldest structures to be seen on the Canal Grande.
Alvise da Mosto, discoverer of the Cape Verde Islands, was born here
in 1432; by the end of that century the palazzo had become the
Albergo del Lion Bianco, and from then until the last century it was
one of Venice's most popular hotels.

As the canal turns, the **Ponte di Rialto** comes into view. The huge
building before it is the **Fondaco dei Tedeschi**, once headquarters of
the city's German merchants. On the ground floor their cargoes were
weighed, packaged and stored; the upper storeys contained a refectory and around sixty bedrooms, many of which were rented on an
annual basis by the biggest firms. The German traders were the most
powerful foreign grouping in the city, and as early as 1228 they were
leased a building on this central site. In 1505 the Fondaco burned
down, and was rebuilt by Spavento and Scarpagnino; Giorgione and
Titian, who had helped the firefighters on the night of the blaze, were
then commissioned to paint the exterior walls. The remains of their
contribution are now in the Ca' d'Oro. The Fondaco has been renovated several times since the sixteenth century, and is now the main
post office.

The famous **bridge** superseded a succession of wooden and sometimes unreliable structures – in 1444 a forerunner collapsed under
the weight of the crowd gathered to watch the wedding procession of
the Marquis of Ferrara; and one of Carpaccio's *Miracles of the True
Cross*, in the Accademia, shows you what the next drawbridge
looked like. The decision to construct a stone bridge was taken in
1524, and over the following sixty years proposals by Michelangelo,
Vignola, Sansovino and Palladio were considered and rejected.

Eventually the job was awarded to the aptly named **Antonio da Ponte**, whose top-heavy design was described by Edward Gibbon as "a fine bridge, spoilt by two rows of houses upon it". Until 1854, when the first Accademia bridge was built, this was the only point at which the Canal Grande could be crossed on foot.

From the Rialto to the Volta del Canal

Immediately before the next rio is Sansovino's first palace in Venice, the **Palazzo Dolfin-Manin**. It dates from the late 1530s, a period when other projects by Sansovino – the Libreria, the Zecca and the Loggetta – were transforming the centre of the city. The public passageway (sottoportego) running under the facade is a feature common to many Venetian houses. Lodovico Manin, the last doge of Venice, lived here – he had the interior rebuilt, so the facade is the only bit entirely by Sansovino.

The **Palazzo Loredan** and the **Palazzo Farsetti**, standing side by side at the end of the Fondamenta del Carbon, are heavily restored Veneto-Byzantine palaces of the thirteenth century. The former was the home of **Elena Corner Piscopia**, who in 1678 graduated from Padua University, so becoming the first woman ever to hold a university degree. The two buildings are now occupied by the town hall.

Work began on the **Palazzo Grimani** (on the near side of the Rio di San Luca) in 1559, to designs by Sanmicheli, but was not completed until 1575, sixteen years after his death. Ruskin, normally no fan of Renaissance architecture, made an exception for this colossal palace, calling it "simple, delicate, and sublime". A Venetian folk tale attributes the scale of the palace to a thwarted passion: it's said that the young man who built it was in love with a woman from the Coccina-Tiepolo palace over the way, but was turned away by her father who wanted someone wealthier for his offspring. The suitor's revenge was to humiliate the father by building a palace which had windows bigger than the main doorway at the Coccina-Tiepolo.

The **Palazzo Corner Contarini dei Cavalli**, on the other side of the rio, was built around 1445; the "cavalli" part of the name comes from the horses on the crest of the facade's coat of arms. The pink **Palazzo Benzon**, just before the next canal, was where the most fashionable salon of early nineteenth-century Venice used to meet – regular guests included Byron, Thomas Moore, Ugo Foscolo and Canova. Their hostess, Contessa Querini-Benzon, was celebrated in a song that still occupies a place in the gondoliers' repertoire – "La Biondina in Gondoleta" (The Blonde in a Gondola). The **Palazzo Corner-Spinelli**, on the far side of the Rio di Ca' Santi, is another work by Codussi; it dates from 1490–1510, so preceding his more monumental Palazzo Vendramin-Calergi.

Four houses that once all belonged to the Mocenigo family stand side by side on the **Volta del Canal**, as the Canal Grande's sharpest turn is known: the **Palazzo Mocenigo-Nero**, a late sixteenth-century

building; the double **Palazzo Mocenigo**, built in the eighteenth century as an extension to the Nero house; and the **Palazzo Mocenigo
Vecchio**, a Gothic palace remodelled in the seventeenth century.

One of the great Venetian scandals centres on the first of the four.
In 1621 Lady Arundel, wife of one of King James's most powerful
courtiers, became its tenant; before long it was rumoured that the
house was being visited by **Antonio Foscarini**, a former ambassador from Venice to England, whose term in London had ended
with an abrupt recall home and a three-year stay in prison under
suspicion of treason. On that occasion Foscarini had finally been
cleared, but now there were renewed allegations of treacherous
behaviour, and the Council of Ten quickly shifted into top gear.
Foscarini was arrested, interrogated and, twelve days later, executed. Lady Arundel instantly demanded an audience with the doge, the
result of which was a public declaration that she had not been
involved in any plot; and within a few months the Council of Ten had
conclusive evidence that Foscarini had been framed. The men who
had accused him were put to death, and Foscarini's body was
exhumed and given a state funeral.

Byron and his menagerie – a dog, a fox, a wolf and a monkey –
lived in the Mocenigo-Nero palace for a couple of years. Much of his
time was taken up with a local baker's wife called Margarita Cogni,
the most tempestuous of his mistresses – her reaction to being rejected by him was to attack him with a table knife and then, having been
shown the door, hurl herself into the Canal Grande. The Palazzo
Mocenigo Vecchio is supposed to be haunted by the ghost of the
philosopher-alchemist Giordano Bruno, whose betrayal to the
Vatican by his former host, Giovanni Mocenigo, led ultimately to his
torture and execution in 1600.

The neighbouring building is the early sixteenth-century **Palazzo
Contarini delle Figure** – the *figure* are the almost invisible figures
above the water entrance. It was begun by Spavento and completed
by Scarpagnino, a combination previously employed on the Fondaco
dei Tedeschi and the Palazzo Ducale.

To the Palazzo Giustinian

*For more on
the Palazzo
Grassi, see
p.98.*

The vast and pristine palace round the *Volta* is the **Palazzo Grassi**,
built in 1748–72 by Massari, who supervised the completion of the
Ca' Rezzonico on the opposite bank. Its first owners were accepted
into the ranks of the nobility in return for a hefty contribution to the
war effort against the Turks in 1718. Nowadays it's owned by Fiat –
hence the sparkling renovation – and is used as an exhibition and
conference centre.

On the edge of the first canal after the campo of San Samuele
stands the **Ca' del Duca**. Commissioned in the mid-fifteenth century
from Bartolomeo Bon, it was left unfinished in 1461 when the Corner
family sold it to Francesco Sforza, Duke of Milan (from whom it takes

its name) – the wedge of rusticated masonry gives some idea of the sort of fortified look the Corners had in mind. In 1514 Titian had a studio here. Across the rio there's the tiny **Palazzetto Falier**, a reworked Gothic house of the fifteenth century, chiefly remarkable for its two roofed terraces. Although they used to be quite common, very few examples of this feature (called a *liagò*) have survived. Next door is one of Longhena's earliest projects, the **Palazzo Giustinian-Lolin** (1623).

As the larger vaporetti couldn't get under the iron **Ponte dell' Accademia** built by the Austrians in 1854, it was replaced in 1932 by a wooden one – a temporary measure that became permanent with the addition of a reinforcing steel substructure. At the foot of the bridge, on the far side, is the huge fifteenth-century **Palazzo Franchetti**; repaired and enlarged at the end of the nineteenth century, it's often cited as one of the city's most heavy-handed pieces of restoration work.

On the opposite side of the Rio dell'Orso are the twinned **Palazzi Barbaro**; the house on the left is early fifteenth-century, the other late seventeenth-century. Henry James, Monet, Whistler, Browning and John Singer Sargent were among the luminaries who stayed in the older Barbaro house as guests of the Curtis family in the late nineteenth century. James finished *The Aspern Papers* here, and used it as a setting for *The Wings of a Dove* (as did the makers of the film of the book); so attached was he to the place that when given the opportunity of buying a home in Venice at a very reasonable price, he decided he would rather go on living here as a lodger.

Soon after the short fondamenta comes the tiny **Casetta delle Rose**, where Canova once had his studio and D'Annunzio lived during World War I. The Casetta lies in the shadow of one of the Canal Grande's most imposing buildings – Sansovino's **Palazzo Corner della Ca' Grande**. The palace that used to stand here was destroyed when a fire lit to dry out a stock of sugar in the attic ran out of control, an incident that illustrates the dual commercial-residential function of many palaces in Renaissance Venice. Sansovino's replacement, commissioned by the nephew of Caterina Cornaro, was built from 1545 onwards. The rustication of the lower storey – a distinctive aspect of many Roman and Tuscan buildings of the High Renaissance – makes it a prototype for Longhena's Ca' Pésaro and Ca' Rezzonico.

The heavily restored fifteenth-century **Palazzo Pisani**, now the *Gritti Hotel*, looms over the Santa Maria del Giglio landing stage – John and Effie Ruskin stayed here in 1851, the year *The Stones of Venice* began to appear in print. Squeezed into the line of buildings that follows is the narrow **Palazzo Contarini-Fasan**, a mid-fifteenth-century palace with unique wheel tracery on the balconies. It's popularly known as "the house of Desdemona", but although the model for Shakespeare's heroine did live in Venice, her association with this house is purely sentimental. The last major building before the Giardinetti Reali is the fifteenth-century **Palazzo Giustinian**; now the HQ of the Biennale offices and the tourist board, in the last century it was one of the plushest hotels in town, its registers signed by the likes of Verdi, Ruskin and Proust.

The Right Bank

Arriving in Venice by road, you come in on the right bank of the Canal Grande at Piazzale Roma, opposite the train station. Orientation is initially difficult, with canals heading off in various directions and no immediate landmark; it's not until the vaporetto swings round by the train station that it becomes obvious that this is the city's main waterway.

Having passed the green-domed church of **San Simeone Piccolo**, the end of the elongated campo of **San Simeone Grande** and a procession of nondescript buildings, you come to the **Fondaco dei Turchi** (opposite San Marcuola). A private house from the early thirteenth century until 1621 (including spells when it was used as a guesthouse for VIPs), the building was then turned over to the Turkish traders in the city, who stayed here until 1838. By the 1850s it was in such a terrible state that a campaign for its restoration was started, with Ruskin at the helm; the city undertook the repair, but the result was judged nearly as bad an eyesore as the ruin had been, and has had few admirers since. There's hardly an original brick left in the building, but whatever the shortcomings of the work, the building's towers and long water-level arcade give a reasonably precise, if schematic, picture of what a Veneto-Byzantine palace would have looked like. One of the sarcophagi underneath the portico belongs to the family of the disgraced Marin Falier. The Fondaco housed the Correr collection from 1880 to 1922, and now contains the natural history museum.

For more on Marin Falier see p.167; for the natural history museum, see p.128.

The crenellated structure next along from the Fondaco is the fifteenth-century **Depositi del Megio** (public granary); its neighbour is another palace by Longhena – the **Palazzo Belloni-Battagia** (1647–63). Longhena's client experienced severe cash-flow problems not long after the house was finished, a consequence of simultaneously building the house and buying his way into the pages of the *Libro d'Oro* (the register of the nobility), and so was obliged to rent the place out rather than live in it himself.

The Ca' Pésaro contains the Galleria d'Arte Moderna and the Museo Orientale – see p.127.

A short distance down the canal, after the church of **San Stae**, stands a far more impressive Longhena building – the thickly ornamented **Ca' Pésaro**, bristling with diamond-shaped spikes and grotesque heads. Three houses had to be demolished to make room for this palace and its construction lasted half a century – work started in 1652 and finished in 1703, long after Longhena's death. Unusually, the Ca' Pésaro has a stone-clad side facade: most houses in Venice have plain brick sides, either because of the cost of stone, or because of the possibility that a later building might be attached.

The next large building is the **Palazzo Corner della Regina**, built in 1724 on the site of the home of Caterina Cornaro, Queen of Cyprus, from whom the palace takes its name. The base of the Biennale archives, it was formerly the *Monte di Pietà* (municipal pawnshop).

Beyond, there's nothing especially engrossing until you reach the **Rialto markets**, which begin with the neo-Gothic fish market, the **Pescheria**, built in 1907; there's been a fish market here since the fourteenth century. The older buildings that follow it, the **Fabbriche Nuove di Rialto** and (set back from the water) the **Fabbriche Vecchie di Rialto**, are by Sansovino (c.1550) and Scarpagnino (c.1520) respectively.

*For more on
the Rialto
markets, see
p.121.*

The large building at the base of the Rialto bridge is the **Palazzo dei Camerlenghi** (c.1525), the former chambers of the Venetian exchequer. Debtors could find themselves in the cells of the building's bottom storey – hence the name *Fondamenta delle Prigioni* for this part of the canalside. At the foot of the Rialto bridge, on the other side, were the offices of the state finance ministers, in Scarpagnino's **Palazzo dei Dieci Savi**.

From the Rialto to the Volta del Canal

From the Rialto down to the *Volta del Canal* the right bank is of more sporadic interest. The **Palazzo Papadopoli** (aka **Palazzo Coccina-Tiepolo**), on the far side of Rio dei Meloni, was built in the 1560s; the Venetian mercantile class rarely wanted adventurous designs for their houses, and the conservative Papadopoli palace, with its emphasis on blank wall spaces broken up with applied decoration, was to prove extremely influential. (Contrast it with the contemporaneous Grimani palace, on the opposite side of the Canal Grande.) The adjacent **Palazzo Donà** and **Palazzo Donà della Madonnetta** (named after the fifteenth-century relief on the facade) date from the twelfth and thirteenth centuries; they have been frequently altered, but some original features survive, notably the main windows.

The tracery of the mid-fifteenth-century **Palazzo Bernardo** (across the Rio della Madonnetta), among the most beautiful on the Canal Grande, is copied from the loggia of the Palazzo Ducale – you'll find echoes of the pattern all over the city. The sixteenth-century **Palazzo Cappello-Layard**, on the edge of the wide Rio San Polo, was the home of the English ambassador Sir Henry Layard, whose astuteness assured that the British public profited from the destitution of Venice in the last century. His collection of nineteen major Venetian paintings, picked up for a song, was left to the National Gallery in London. Another of the National's masterpieces – Veronese's *The Clemency of Alexander* – was bought in 1857 from the **Palazzo Pisani della Moretta** (mid-fifteenth-century), second along on the other side of the rio.

The cluster of palaces at the *Volta* constitutes one of the city's architectural glories. The **Palazzo Balbi**, on the near side of the Rio di Ca' Fóscari, is the youngest of the group, a proto-Baroque design executed in the 1580s to plans by Alessandro Vittoria, whose sculpture is to be found in many Venetian churches. Nicolò Balbi is reputed to have been so keen to see his palace finished that he moored a boat alongside the building site so that he could watch the work progressing – and died of a chill caught by sleeping in it. Had Frank Lloyd Wright got his way, the Palazzo Balbi would have acquired a new neighbour in the 1950s, but local opposition, orchestrated from the Balbi palace, scuppered the scheme.

*For more on
Doge Fóscari,
see p.138.*

On the opposite bank stands the **Ca' Fóscari** (c.1435), which Ruskin thought "the noblest example in Venice" of late Gothic architecture. The largest private house in Venice at the time of its construction, it was the home of one of the more colourful figures of Venetian history, Doge Francesco Fóscari, whose extraordinarily long term of office (34 years) came to an end with his forced resignation. When Henry III of France passed through Venice on the way to his coronation in 1574, it was at the Ca' Fóscari that he was lodged. After a banquet for which all sumptuary laws had been suspended and at which the tables had been laid with utensils and decorative figures made from sugar to Sansovino's designs, Henry reeled back here to find his rooms decked out with silks and cloth of gold, and lined with paintings by Bellini, Titian, Veronese and Tintoretto. Venice's university now owns the building, which has been undergoing major restoration for several years.

Adjoining it are the **Palazzi Giustinian**, a pair of palaces built in the mid-fifteenth century for two brothers who wanted attached but self-contained houses. In the twelfth century the Giustinian family was in danger of dying out, and such was the panic induced in Venice by the thought of losing one of its most illustrious dynasties (it traced its descent from the Emperor Justinian), that papal permission was sought for the young monk who was the one surviving male of the clan to be released from his vows in order to start a family. The pope gave his consent, a bride was found, and twelve Giustinians were propagated; his duty done, the father returned to his monastery, and his wife went off to found a convent on one of the remoter islands of the lagoon. For a while one of the Palazzi Giustinian was **Wagner**'s home. Finding the rooms inimical to the creative process he made a few improvements, such as hanging the walls with red cloth and importing his own bed and grand piano from Zurich. Having made the place comfortable, he settled down, flirted with the idea of suicide, and wrote the second act of *Tristan und Isolde*, inspired in part by a nocturnal gondola ride, as he recorded in his autobiography. At the sight of the moon rising over the city, the composer's gondolier "uttered a cry like a wild creature, a kind of deep groan that rose in crescendo to a prolonged 'Oh' and ended with the simple exclamation 'Venezia!' . . . The sensations I experienced at that moment did not leave me throughout my sojourn in Venice."

From the Ca' Rezzonico to the Dogana di Mare

A little farther on comes Longhena's **Ca' Rezzonico**, as gargantuan as his Ca' Pésaro, but less aggressive. It was begun in 1667 as a commission from the Bon family, but their ambition exceeded their financial resources, and not long after hiring Giorgio Massari to complete the upper part they were obliged to sell the still unfinished palace to the Rezzonico family, who were Genoese bankers. Despite having lashed out 100,000 ducats to buy their way into the *Libro d'Oro* (at a time when 1000 ducats per annum was a comfortable income for a noble), the new owners could afford to keep Massari employed on the completion of the top floor, and then to tack a ballroom and staircase onto the back. Among its subsequent owners was Pen Browning, whose father Robert died here in 1889; and both Whistler and Cole Porter stayed here briefly.

*The Ca'
Rezzonico
houses the
Museo del
Settecento
Veneziano –
see p.117.*

After a couple of canals you pass the **Palazzo Loredan dell' Ambasciatore**, opposite the Ca' del Duca. Taking its name from the Austrian embassy that used to be here, it was built in the fifteenth century, and is notable mainly for the figures in niches on the facade, which possibly came from the workshop of Antonio Rizzo. On the far side of the next canal, the Rio di San Trovaso, stand the **Palazzo Contarini-Corfu** and the **Palazzo Contarini degli Scrigni**. The "Corfu" bit of the first name derives either from the fact that a Contarini was once a military commander on that island, or from the name of a family that lived in the parish before the Contarini crew. The two palaces form a single unit: the Scrigni was built in 1609 as an extension to the Corfu, a fifteenth-century Gothic house. A similar operation was carried out at the Palazzi Barbaro (opposite, just after the Accademia bridge), with less jarring results.

Yet another Contarini palace stands a few yards past the Accademia bridge – the **Palazzo Contarini-Polignac**. This branch of the Contarini family made itself rich through landholdings around Jaffa, and the dialect version of that place-name is the source of the alternative name for the palace: Contarini dal Zaffo. The facade, which was applied to the Gothic building in the late fifteenth century, represents a transitional phase between the highly decorative style associated with the Lombardi and their imitators (see the Palazzo Dario, overleaf) and the classicizing work of Codussi.

The Venier family, another of Venice's great dynasties (they produced three doges, including the commander of the Christian fleet at Lépanto), had their main base just beyond the Campo San Vio. In 1759 the Veniers began rebuilding their home, but the **Palazzo Venier dei Leoni**, which would have been the largest palace on the

For an entry on the Guggenheim collection, see p.107.

canal, never progressed further than the first storey – hence its alternative name, **Palazzo Nonfinito**. (The "dei Leoni" part of the full name comes from the pet lion that the Veniers kept chained in the courtyard.) Its abandonment was almost certainly due to the ruinous cost, but there's a tradition which says the project was stopped by the objections of the Corner family across the water, who didn't want their sunlight blocked by a house that was bigger than theirs. The stump of the building and the platform on which it is raised (itself an extravagant and novel feature) are occupied by the Guggenheim collection of modern art.

The one domestic building of interest between here and the end of the canal is the miniature **Palazzo Dario**, the next building but one after the Palazzo dei Leoni. Compared by Henry James to "a house of cards that hold together by a tenure it would be fatal to touch", the palace was built in the late 1480s not for a patrician family but for a member of the middle ("citizen") class – a chancery secretary named Giovanni Dario, who had distinguished himself on diplomatic missions to the Turkish court. The multicoloured marbles of the facade are characteristic of the work of the Lombardo family, and the design may actually be by the founder of that dynasty, Pietro Lombardo. Several of the Palazzo Dario's occupants have come to a sticky end, giving the place a certain notoriety in Venetian folklore: the English scholar Rawdon Lubbock Brown committed suicide in the house after sinking a fortune into its renovation in the mid-nineteenth century; Kit Lambert, manager of The Who, was murdered soon after moving out; in 1979 Count Filippo Giordano delle Lanze had his brains smashed with a candlestick wielded by his lover; a Venetian businessman named Fabrizio Ferrari went bust and then his sister was murdered; and in 1993 the industrialist and yachtsman Raul Gardini, who had bought the house in 1985, was found dead in Milan, apparently having shot himself.

Two doors down, the technicolour **Palazzo Salviati** was built in 1924 by the glassmakers of the same name, and vacated by them seventy years later; the most garish building on the canal, its brash decoration is a foretaste of what awaits you in many of the glass showrooms of Murano.

For the entries on the Salute and the Dogana di Mare, see p.107.

The focal point of this last stretch of the canal is Longhena's masterpiece, **Santa Maria della Salute** – it's dealt with in the Dorsoduro chapter, as is the **Dogana di Mare** (Customs House), the Canal Grande's full stop.

Chapter 8

The Northern Islands

The main islands lying to the north of Venice – **San Michele**, **Murano**, **Burano** and **Torcello** – used to be good places to visit when the throng of tourists in the main part of Venice became too oppressive. Nowadays the throngs are almost everywhere for most of the year, but a northwards excursion is still a restorative when the stone pavements and endless brick walls become wearying – out here the horizons are distant and the bleak swathes of *barèna* (marshland) give a taste of what conditions were like for Venice's first settlers. A day trip through this part of the lagoon will reveal the origins of the glass and lace work touted in so many of the city's shops, and give you a glimpse of the origins of Venice itself, embodied in Torcello's magnificent cathedral of Santa Maria dell'Assunta. Those intent on an exhaustive exploration of the lagoon could plan a visit to the islets of San Francesco del Deserto and Lazzaretto Nuovo – the former a Franciscan retreat, the latter a charismatic wasteland.

If you're setting off for a day in the northern islands and don't fancy taking a picnic, you should plan on spending lunchtime on Burano. Although Thomas Coryat declared of Murano "here did I eat the best oysters that ever I did in all my life", food on the glass-blowers' island today is nothing special, while on Torcello there's just a couple of mediocre trattorias and an exorbitant restaurant.

To get to the northern islands, the main **vaporetto stop** is **Fondamente Nove** (or Nuove), as most of the island services start here or call here. (You can hop on elsewhere in the city, of course – but make sure that the boat is going towards the islands, not away from them.) For **San Michele and Murano only** the circular #41 and #42 vaporetti both run every twenty minutes from Fondamente Nove, circling Murano before heading back towards Venice; the #41 follows an anticlockwise route around the city, the #42 a clockwise route. For **Murano, Burano and Torcello** the #12 leaves every half hour from Fondamente Nove (hourly early in the morning and evenings), calling first at Murano-Faro before heading on to Mazzorbo, Burano and Torcello, from where it proceeds, via Treporti, to Punta Sabbioni,

where it links up with the #14, which links Punta Sabbioni to San Marco (San Zaccaria stop), via the Lido. Note that some services, particularly on Saturdays and Sundays, call at Torcello before Burano, and that the #12 does not stop at San Michele.

San Michele

A church was founded on **San Michele**, the innermost of the northern islands, in the tenth century, and a monastery was established in the thirteenth. Its best-known resident was Fra Mauro (d.1459), whose map of the world – the most accurate of its time – is now one of the most precious possessions of the Libreria Sansoviniana. The monastery was suppressed in the early nineteenth century, but in 1829, after a spell as an Austrian prison for political offenders, it was handed back to the Franciscans, who look after the church and the cemetery to this day.

The high brick wall around the island gives way by the landing stage to the elegant white facade of **San Michele in Isola**, designed by **Mauro Codussi** in 1469. With this building Codussi quietly revolutionized the architecture of Venice, advancing the principles of Renaissance design in the city and introducing the use of Istrian stone as a material for facades. Easy to carve yet resistant to water, Istrian stone had long been used for damp courses, but never before had anyone clad the entire front of a building in it; after the construction of San Michele, most major buildings in Venice were given an Istrian veneer.

The **interior** of the church has the air of being well and constantly used, with a scent which is a mixture of fresh flowers, incense and a little hint of cypress trees. Attached on the left is the dainty hexagonal **Cappella Emiliana**, built around 1530 by **Guglielmo dei Grigi** and completely marble-lined. Ruskin was impervious to its charm: "It is more like a German summer-house, or angle-turret, than a chapel, and may be briefly described as a bee-hive set on a low hexagonal tower, with dashes of stonework about its windows like the flourishes of an idle penman." In front of the main entrance a floor plaque marks the final resting place of **Fra Paolo Sarpi** (d.1623), Venice's principal ideologist during the tussle with the papacy at the start of the seventeenth century; buried first in his Servite monastery, Sarpi's remains were removed here when that order was suppressed in 1828.

For more on Paolo Sarpi, see p.159.

The cemetery

The main part of the island, through the cloisters, is covered by the **cemetery** of Venice, established here by a Napoleonic decree which forbade further burials in the centre of the city. Space is at a premium, and most of the Catholic dead of Venice lie here in cramped conditions for just ten years or so, when their bones are dug up and removed to an ossuary, and the vacated plot is recycled. Protestants are permitted to stay in their sector indefinitely, as each year's new arrivals are never numerous, but otherwise only those whose descendants can afford to lease a resting place get to stay longer than a decade. (There is a separate Jewish cemetery over on the Lido.)

The cemetery is open daily: summer 7.30am–6pm; winter 7.30am–4pm.

Even with this grave-rotation system in operation, however, the island is reaching full capacity, so in 1998 a competition was held for the redevelopment of San Michele. The winning entry, from English architect David Chipperfield, places a sequence of formal courtyards lined with wall tombs on the presently unkempt parts of the island, alongside a new funerary chapel and crematorium (the Church's line on space-saving cremation having become more flexible of late). On the eastern side of San Michele two footbridges will connect with a rectangular expanse of reclaimed land, site of a trio of tomb buildings overlooking two tiers of waterside gardens, which in turn will overlook central Venice. Making much use of Istrian stone and earthenware plasterwork, Chipperfield's creation promises to be an austerely beautiful addition to the cityscape – and there's a certain appropriateness to the fact that Venice's first great architectural project of the twenty-first century will be a cross between a necropolis and a philosopher's retreat.

At the entrance to the cemetery you can pick up a small plan of the various sections. Most dilapidated at the moment is the **Protestant** section (no. XV), where **Ezra Pound's grave** is marked by a crude slab with his name on it. Adjoining is the **Greek and Russian Orthodox** area (no. XIV), including the simple gravestones of **Igor and Vera Stravinsky** – Stravinsky was given a funeral service in San Zanipolo, the highest funeral honour the city can bestow – and the more elaborate tomb for **Serge Diaghilev**. Fans of **Frederick Rolfe** (Baron Corvo) can reach his disconsolate memorial by going through the gap in the wall-graves to the right of sections M and N, then doubling back behind section M: he's up on the top row of block 13. The most poignant section is C, for **infants**, behind which are piled the discarded crosses of dug-up graves, many still hung with dead flowers.

Murano

Murano

In 1276 the island of **Murano** became a self-governed enclave within the Republic, with its own judiciary, its own administration and a *Libro d'Oro* to register its nobility. By the early sixteenth century Murano had thirty thousand inhabitants, and was a favourite summer retreat for Venice's upper classes, who could lay out gardens here that were far more extensive than those in the cramped centre of the city. The Mocenigo family had a house here, and Caterina Cornaro often stayed at her family's palace. The intellectual life of the island was especially healthy in the seventeenth century, when literature, philosophy, the occult and the sciences were discussed in the numerous small *accademie* that flourished here. In the same century the mint on Murano was granted the privilege of forging the tribute medals known as *oselle*. But Murano nowadays owes its fame entirely to its **glass-blowing industry**, and its main fondamente are crowded with shops selling the fruit of the furnaces, some of it fine, most of it repulsive and some of it laughably pretentious. You'll see little in the showrooms to equal the remarkable work on display in the Murano glass museum, and even that takes second place to the island's beautiful main church.

Around the island

San Pietro
Martire is
open daily
9am–noon &
3–6pm.

From the *Colonna* vaporetto stop (the first after San Michele) you step onto the Fondamenta dei Vetrai, traditionally the core of the glass industry (as the name suggests) and now the principal tourist trap. Towards the far end is the Dominican church of **San Pietro Martire**, one of only two churches still in service on the island (compared with seventeen when the Republic fell in 1797). Begun in 1363

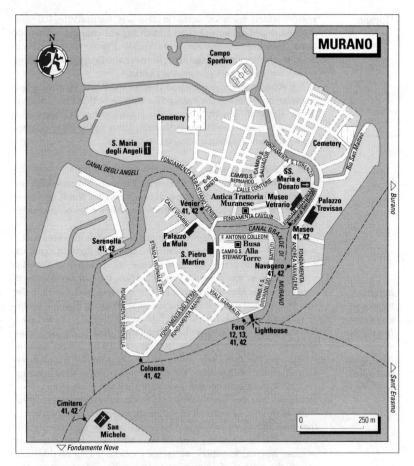

but largely rebuilt after a fire in 1474, its main interest lies with its paintings, which are lit by an annoying system that entails either a lot of running about with coins or, if the machines are broken (they often are), cajoling the sacristan. Save most of your change for a pair of paintings by **Giovanni Bellini** hanging on the right wall: on the left is the large and elegant *Madonna and Child with St Mark, St Augustine and Doge Barbarigo*, on the right an *Assumption*, recently returned to its home after many years of restoration. On the opposite side of the church are two slight pieces by **Veronese** – *St Agatha in Prison* and *St Jerome in the Desert*. The Cappella del Sacramento, to the left of the main altar, was originally dedicated to the angels and contains four paintings of personable representatives of the heavenly host. The **sacristy**, with its modest museum (L3000/€1.55), is only worth seeing for the wood carving in the vestry, which includes some grotesquely naturalistic Baroque atlantes depicting historical and mythological characters such as Nero, Socrates, Pythagoras and Pontius Pilate, with the Four Seasons on either side of the altar. Between the figures, panels show scenes from the career of John the Baptist.

Just round the corner is the main bridge, the **Ponte Vivarini**, a few yards beyond which is the **Palazzo da Mula**, a Gothic palace altered in the sixteenth century, one of the few surviving examples of a Venetian summer residence on Murano. Many of the other palaces were demolished during the nineteenth century.

The Museo Vetrario

A left turn on the far side of the bridge comes to a dead end at the church of **Santa Maria degli Angeli** (open only for Mass), in whose convent Casanova had an amorous experience involving many changes of costume.

Turn right along Fondamenta Cavour and you'll soon come to the seventeenth-century Palazzo Giustinian, facing the sixteenth-century Palazzo Trevisan across the canal. Home of the Bishop of Torcello until his diocese was joined to Venice in 1805, the Palazzo Giustinian now houses the **Museo Vetrario**. Featuring pieces dating back to the first century and examples of Murano glass from the fifteenth century onwards, the museum exerts a fascination even if you can't read the Italian labels. Perhaps the finest single item is the dark blue Barovier marriage cup, dating from around 1470; it's on show in room 1 on the first floor, along with some splendid Renaissance enamelled and painted glass. But every room contains some amazing creations: glass beakers that look as if they are made from veined stone; jars that look like bubbles of blue water; a chalice with a spiral stem as slender as a strand of spaghetti; sixteenth-century platters that look like discs of cracked ice; stupendously ugly nineteenth-century decorative pieces, with fat little birds enmeshed in trellises of glass. A separate display, with some captions in English this time, covers the history of Murano glass techniques – look out for the extraordinary *Murine in Canna*, the method of placing different coloured rods together to form an image in cross-section.

The **Modern and Contemporary Glass Museum,** which used to be in a separate building opposite, is in the process of being moved over to the Palazzo Giustinian. Currently some of the glass from this modern section is on display in the main room on the first floor, including a carafe designed by Carlo Scarpa and a few pieces by Seguso and Tagliapietra. When the restoration is finished, the rest of the collection will move over.

The Museo Vetrario is open summer 10am–5pm, winter 10am–4pm; closed Wed; L8000/€4.13.

Santi Maria e Donato

The other Murano church, and the main reason for visiting the island today, is **Santi Maria e Donato**. It was founded in the seventh cen-

Santi Maria e Donato is open daily 8am–noon & 4–7pm.

Venetian Glass

Because of the risk of fire, Venice's glass furnaces were moved to Murano from central Venice in 1291, and thenceforth all possible steps were taken to keep the secrets of the trade locked up on the island. Although Muranese workers had by the seventeenth century gained some freedom of movement, for centuries prior to that any glass-maker who left Murano was proclaimed a traitor, and a few were even hunted down. Various privileges reduced the temptation to rove – unlike other artisans, the glass-blowers were allowed to wear swords, and from 1376 the offspring of a marriage between a Venetian nobleman and the daughter of a glass-worker were allowed to be entered into the *Libro d'Oro*, unlike the children of other inter-class matches. Normal principles of justice were sometimes waived for the glass-blowers. On one occasion a man who had committed a murder and then fled Murano was accepted back without punishment once his father had hinted to the city's governors that his son might set up a furnace in Mantua.

A fifteenth-century visitor judged that "in the whole world there are no such craftsmen of glass as here", and the Muranese were masters of every aspect of their craft. They were producing spectacles by the start of the fourteenth century, monopolized the European manufacture of mirrors for a long time (and continued making larger mirrors than anyone else even after the monopoly had gone), and in the early seventeenth century became so proficient at making coloured crystal that a decree was issued forbidding the manufacture of false gems out of glass, as many were being passed off as authentic stones. Understatement has rarely been a characteristic of Murano produce: in 1756 Lady Mary Wortley Montague was wonderstruck by a set of furniture made entirely out of glass, and earlier this century the less favourably impressed H.V. Morton longed "to see something simple and beautiful", adding that sixteenth-century customers felt the same way "when, looking around for something to take home, they were repelled by drinking-glasses in the shape of ships, whales, lions and birds". Murano kitsch extends to all price categories, from the mass-produced nicknacks sold for a couple of thousand lire, through to monstrosities such as Peggy Guggenheim's pieces based on figures from the works of Picasso – specially commissioned by her, they are on show in that bastion of modernist art, the Guggenheim Collection.

The traditional style of Murano glass, typified by the multi-coloured floral chandeliers sold in showrooms on Murano and round the Piazza, is still very much in demand. However, in recent years there's been turmoil in the glass industry, due to an inundation of cheap Murano-style tableware and ornaments from Asia and eastern Europe. Many Murano factories have been unable to compete, and at least one company has marketed imported glass under the Murano label. There's talk of a Murano "copyright" to protect the island's reputation and of a school to promote local talent, but meanwhile the only concrete response to the crisis has come from a few companies who are following the example of Paolo Venini, the Milanese lawyer and entrepreneur who in the 1920s pulled Murano from the doldrums by commissioning work from designers outside the rarefied world of glass. It's a strategy that has been tried a few times, and luminaries such as Carlo Scarpa, Gio Ponti and Gianni Versace have previously made their mark on Murano. Now there's more at stake for Murano's 250 glass companies, few of which remain in Venetian hands – the long-established firm of Salviati is French-owned, and even Venini has been bought out, by the Royal Copenhagen company.

tury but rebuilt in the twelfth, and is one of the lagoon's best examples of Veneto-Byzantine architecture – the ornate **rear apse** being particularly fine. Originally dedicated to the Virgin, the church was rededicated in 1125 when the relics of Saint Donatus were brought here from Cephalonia by **Doge Domenico Michiel**, who also picked up the remains of Saint Isidore and the stone on which Jesus stood to preach to the men of Tyre – both of which are now in the Basilica di San Marco. Saint Donatus once slew a dragon simply by spitting at it – the four splendid bones hanging behind the altar are allegedly from the unfortunate beast.

The glory of the interior is its **mosaic floor** (dated 1141 in the nave), a beautiful weave of abstract patterns and figures – an eagle carries off a deer; two roosters carry off a fox, slung from a pole (symbols of the triumph of Christianity over paganism). The floor was extensively restored and completely relaid in the 1970s, a process illustrated by photos on display in the right aisle. Apart from the arresting twelfth-century **mosaic of the Madonna** in the apse, a variant (without *bambino*) of the contemporaneous mosaic at Torcello, the features that invite perusal are the fifteenth-century ship's-keel roof, the sixth-century pulpit, the Veneto-Byzantine capitals, and the lunette painting halfway down the left aisle, Lazzaro Bastiani's *Madonna and Child with Saints and Donor* (1484).

Burano and San Francesco del Deserto

After Murano, the next stop for the #12 boat is at the small island of **Mazzorbo**, a densely populated town a couple of centuries ago, before it became a place of exile for disgraced noblemen, whereupon the undisgraced citizens decamped for homes elsewhere in the lagoon. Nowadays Mazzorbo doesn't amount to much more than a few scattered villas, a lot of grassy space, a handsome new housing development and the unremarkable church of Santa Caterina. You can either get off the boat here, and walk round Mazzorbo to the sixty-metre footbridge to Burano (which offers beautifully framed views of distant Venice), or continue on the boat to the main Burano stop (bear in mind that some boats go via Torcello).

After the peeling plaster and eroded stonework of the other lagoon settlements, the small, brightly painted houses of **Burano** come as something of a surprise. Local tradition says that the colours once enabled each fisherman to identify his house from out at sea, but now the colours are used simply for pleasant effect. A resident called Bepe is the most fearless exterior decorator on the island – his house, covered in a constantly changing arrangement of painted diamonds, triangles and bars, is in a courtyard off the alley opposite the *Galuppi* restaurant in Via Baldassare Galuppi, the main street.

(Galuppi was an eighteenth-century Buranese composer, known to his admirers as *Il Buranello*; the main piazza is named after him, too, and further commemorates him with an awkward half-length bronze statue and a plaque at no. 24.)

Burano was settled in the seventh century by mainland refugees who named their new home Boreana, perhaps after the *bora*, as the north-easterly winter wind is known. Safely removed from the malarial

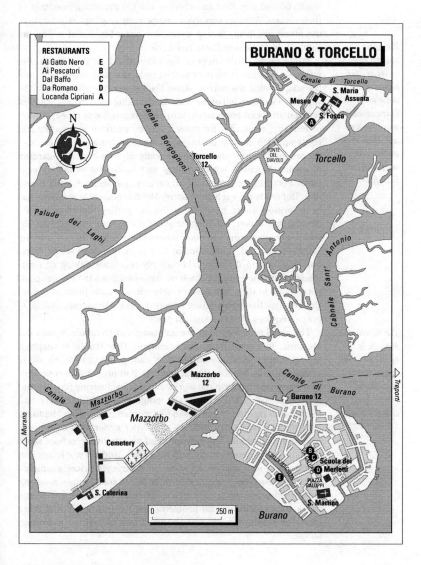

Burano and San Francesco del Deserto

swamps that did so much to ruin neighbouring Torcello, Burano became a prosperous fishing village, and is still largely a fishing community – you can't walk far along the shores of the island without seeing a fishing boat beached for repair, or nets laid out to dry or be mended, or a jumble of crab boxes. It's a solitary way of life under any circumstances, but a couple of fishermen have scavenged wood and other materials to build vulnerable-looking houses out on the higher mudflats, and now lead an existence not too dissimilar from that of their earliest Venetian ancestors – perpetually tending to the fabric of the house and boat, fishing among the water-birds, and selling the catch at the Burano or Rialto *pescherie*.

Burano's seafood restaurants are far better than those on Murano, and more reasonable than those on Torcello; see p.268 for listings.

While many of the men of Burano depend on the lagoon, the women's lives are given over to the production and sale of **lace**, and the shops lining the narrow street leading into the village from the vaporetto stop are full of the stuff. Lacemaking used to be a skill that crossed all social boundaries: for noblewomen it was an expression of feminine creativity; for nuns it was an exercise in humility and contemplation; and for the poorest it was simply a source of income. Its production was once geographically diverse, too – **Dogaressa Morosina Morosini** set up a large and successful workshop near Santa Fosca in the late sixteenth century, for instance – but nowadays Burano is the exclusive centre. Much sentimental nonsense has been written about how "every Burano cottage doorway has its demure lace-maker, stitching away in the sunshine, eyes screwed up and fingers flickering", to quote James (Jan) Morris. In fact, making Burano-point and Venetian-point lace is extremely exacting work, both highly skilled and mind-bendingly repetitive, taking an enormous toll on the eyesight. Each woman specializes in one particular stitch, and as there are seven stitches in all, each piece is passed from woman to woman during its construction. An average-size table centre requires about a month of work.

The Scuola dei Merletti is open April–Oct 10am–5pm; Nov–March 10am–4pm; closed Tues; L8000/€4.13.

The skills of lacemaking are still taught at Burano's **Scuola dei Merletti**, in Piazza Baldassare Galuppi. This scuola is simply a school rather than a confraternity-cum-guild (unlike all other craftspeople in Venice, the lacemakers had no guild to represent them, perhaps because the workforce was exclusively female) and it was opened in 1872, when the indigenous crafting of lace had declined so far that it was left to one woman, Francesca Memo, to transmit the necessary skills to a younger generation of women. Although the scuola has not operated as a full-time school since the late 1960s, courses are still held here, and on weekdays you might see local women at work on their cylindrical cushions. Pieces produced here are displayed in the attached museum, along with specimens dating back to the sixteenth century; after even a quick tour you'll have no problems distinguishing the real thing from the machine-made and imported lace that fills the Burano shops.

Opposite the lace school stands the church of **San Martino**, with its drunken campanile; inside, on the second altar on the left, you'll find a fine *Crucifixion* by Giambattista Tiepolo, painted in 1725.

San Francesco del Deserto

While on Burano, try to get across to the island of **San Francesco del Deserto**. Unfortunately, the only form of public transport is a taxi, but depending on the number of passengers, the length of the visit and the time of year, the price may be open to negotiation. There's a taxi-rank next to the vaporetto stop, with a free telephone booth for use if no taxi is waiting. You could also try asking around at the harbour, but it's not very likely that you'll find a boat-owner prepared to make a deal.

Saint Francis ran aground here in 1220 and decided to build a chapel and cell on the island. Jacopo Michiel, the owner of the island, gave it to the Franciscans soon after the saint's death, and apart from deserting it for a while in the fifteenth century because of malaria, and being pushed out in the nineteenth century by the military, they have been here ever since.

The present chapel was built over the original one in the fifteenth century, and was lovingly and simply restored in 1962, uncovering some of the original floor and foundations. Seven friars live here, some in retreat, and a few young men stay for a year before becoming Franciscan novices. With its birdsong, its profusion of plants and its cypress-scented air, the monastery is the most tranquil place in the lagoon.

Torcello

Torcello has now come full circle. Settled by the very first refugees from the mainland in the fifth century, it became the seat of the Bishop of Altinum in 638 and in the following year its cathedral – the oldest building in the lagoon – was founded. By the fourteenth century its population had peaked at around twenty thousand, but Torcello's canals were now silting up, malaria was rife, and the ascendancy of Venice was imminent. By the end of the fifteenth century Torcello was largely deserted – even the bishop lived in Murano – and today only about thirty people remain in residence, their numbers swelled by thousands of tourists, and by the ever-increasing ranks of stallholders eager to sell lace and glass to the summer boatloads.

Santa Maria dell'Assunta

The main reason for a visit is to see Venice's first cathedral and the serenest building in the lagoon – the **Cattedrale di Santa Maria dell'Assunta**.

Torcello

San Martino is open daily 8am–noon & 3–7pm.

Visitors are shown round the island and convent of San Francesco del Deserto daily 9–11am & 3–5pm; a few thousand lire should be left as a donation.

Santa Maria dell'Assunta is open daily: April–Oct 10.30am– 5.30pm; Nov–March 10am–4.30pm; L5000/€2.58, including audio-guide.

A Veneto-Byzantine building dating substantially from 1008, the cathedral has evolved from a church founded in the seventh century, of which the crypt and the circular foundations in front of the **facade** have survived. The first major transformation of the church occurred in the 860s, the period to which the **facade and portico** belong (though they were altered in later centuries). For the most unusual features of the exterior, go down the right-hand side of the cathedral, where the windows have eleventh-century **stone shutters**. Ruskin described the view from the campanile as "one of the most notable scenes in this wide world", a verdict you can test for yourself, as the campanile has now been reinforced, cleaned and reopened, after thirty years' service as a pigeon-coop.

The Campanile is open April–Oct daily 11am–4.30pm; L4000/ €2.07.

The dominant tones of the **interior** come from pink brick, gold-based mosaics and the watery green-grey marble of its columns and panelling, which together cast a cool light on the richly patterned eleventh-century **mosaic floor**. (Between the fifth and sixth columns on both sides are glazed panels revealing a portion of the church's first mosaic floor.) On the semi-dome of the apse a stunning twelfth-century **mosaic of the Madonna and Child**, the figures isolated in a vast field of gold, looks down from above a **frieze of the Apostles**, dating from the middle of the previous century. Below the window, at the Madonna's feet, is a much restored image of **Saint Heliodorus**, the first Bishop of Altinum, whose remains were brought here by the earliest settlers. It makes an interesting comparison with the gold-plated face mask on his sarcophagus in front of the high altar, another seventh-century vestige. His original Roman sarcophagus is placed below and to the left of the altar. Just above, set into the wall, is the foundation stone of the cathedral, which was laid in 639, the same year as the fall of Oderzo, the Byzantine provincial capital on the mainland. Named on the stone are the fleeing leaders of that town, both temporal (the the *magister militum*) and spiritual (the Exarch), as well as Bishop Mauro of Altinum, the first to transfer his see to Torcello.

Mosaic work from the ninth and eleventh centuries adorns the chapel to the right of the high altar, while the other end of the cathedral is dominated by the tumultuous **mosaic of the Apotheosis of Christ and the Last Judgement** – created in the twelfth century, but renovated in the nineteenth. Have a good look, too, at the **rood screen**, where paintings of *The Virgin and Apostles* are supported by eleventh-century columns connected by finely carved marble panels. Alongside the chapel to the left of the altar the waterlogged ancient crypt is visible.

Santa Fosca is open the same hours as Santa Maria.

Santa Fosca and the Museo dell'Estuario

Torcello's other church, **Santa Fosca**, was built in the eleventh and twelfth centuries for the body of the martyred Saint Fosca, brought to Torcello from Libya some time before 1011 and now resting under the altar. A dome was planned to cap the martyrium but was never built, perhaps because of the desertion of the Greek builders who alone possessed the secret of constructing a self-supporting dome. Though much restored, the church retains the Greek-cross form and a fine exterior apse; the bare interior, with beautiful marble columns and elegant brick arches, exudes a calmness which no number of visitors can quite destroy.

In the square outside sits the curious **chair of Attila**, perhaps once the throne of Torcello's judges in its earliest days; local folklore has it that if you sit in it, you will be wed within a year. Behind it, the well laid-out **Museo di Torcello** includes thirteenth-century beaten gold figures, jewellery, mosaic fragments (including pieces from the cathedral's *Last Judgement*, in which the hands of several artists can be distinguished) and a mish-mash of pieces relating to the history of the area.

A major archeological survey of the island was carried out by a Polish team in the 1960s, but once in a while someone finds a pot shard while wandering off to look for a picnic spot. And anything more ambitious than a picnic is really not on – there are a couple of **bars** near the parapet-less Ponte del Diavolo, but the restaurants are overpriced – especially the one owned by the *Cipriani*.

Lazzaretto Nuovo

Once a bustling quarantine encampment, sixteenth-century Venice's equivalent of Ellis Island, the island of **Lazzaretto Nuovo** now preserves only a huge abandoned warehouse and an unusually peaceful atmosphere. Getting there is simple enough, as the vaporetto #13 to Sant' Erasmo stops at the jetty on request.

In 1468, fear of plague led the Senate to augment the existing plague hospital (now known as Lazzaretto Vecchio) with a dedicated quarantine island, and huge warehouses were erected to store merchandise arriving in Venice from suspect areas, with merchants and sailors quartered alongside. The largest of these warehouses, the **Tezon Grande**, still stands in the centre of the island, and while it's little more than an empty shed, the sixteenth-century graffiti on the far interior wall conjure something of a more cosmopolitan past – picked out in red are lists of cargoes and voyages made to the further corners of the Mediterranean. Much of the island is still encircled by brick fortifications which date from the occupations of Napoleon and the Austrians, when it formed part of Venice's system of defences. There's little else to see other than a small museum of archeological finds, but the view from the walls across the bleak marshes is impressive, with little egrets and grey herons fishing among the rushes.

Chapter 9

The Southern Islands

The section of the lagoon to the south of the city, enclosed by the long islands of the **Lido** and **Pellestrina**, has far fewer outcrops of solid land than the northern half. Once past **San Giorgio Maggiore** and **La Giudecca**, and clear of the smaller islands beyond, you could look in the direction of the mainland and think you were out in the open sea – an illusion strengthened by the sight of tankers making their way across the lagoon to the port of Marghera. On the other hand, the shallowness of most of the lagoon is brought home to you with a jolt when you happen upon a fisherman standing on a barely submerged sandbank a long way from the shore – a spectacle that initially makes you doubt the evidence of your senses.

The nearer islands are the more interesting: the Palladian churches of San Giorgio and La Giudecca are among Venice's most significant Renaissance monuments, while the alleyways of the island are full of reminders of the city's manufacturing past. The Venetian tourist industry began with the development of the Lido, which has now been eclipsed by the city itself as a holiday destination, yet still draws thousands of people to its beaches each year, many of them Italians. A visit to the Armenian island, **San Lazzaro degli Armeni**, makes an absorbing afternoon's round trip, and if you've a bit more time to spare you could undertake an expedition to the fishing town of **Chioggia**, at the southern extremity of the lagoon. The fartherflung settlements along the route to Chioggia may have seen more glorious days, but the voyage out from the city is a pleasure in itself.

S. Giorgio
Maggiore

San Giorgio Maggiore

Palladio's church of **San Giorgio Maggiore**, facing the Palazzo Ducale across the Bacino di San Marco, is one of the most prominent and familiar of all Venetian landmarks. It is a startling building, whose isolation almost forces you to have an opinion as to its architectural merits. Ruskin didn't much care for it: "It is impossible to conceive a

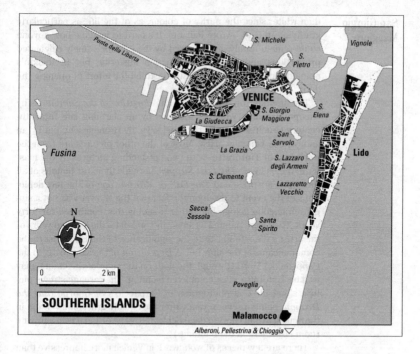

San Giorgio Maggiore is open daily 10am– 12.30pm & 2.30–5pm.

design more gross, more barbarous, more childish in conception, more servile in plagiarism, more insipid in result, more contemptible under every point of rational regard." Goethe, on the other hand, sick of the Gothic art that was to Ruskin the touchstone of spiritual health, gave thanks to Palladio for purging his mind of medieval clutter.

Designed in 1565 and completed forty-five years later, San Giorgio Maggiore was a greatly influential solution to the chief problem of Renaissance church design: how to use classical forms in a structure that, with its high central nave and lower aisles, had no precedent in classical culture. Palladio's answer was to superimpose two temple fronts: the nave being defined by an upper pediment supported by gigantic Composite columns, and the aisles by lower half-pediments resting on Corinthian pilasters. Inside, the relationship between the major Composite order and the minor Corinthian is maintained, so unifying the facade of the church and its interior. The scale of Palladio's forms and his use of shadow-casting surfaces ensure that the design of the facade retains its clarity across the water.

The interior

The Venetians were the first to cover church interiors with white stucco, and the technique is used to dazzling effect in San Giorgio Maggiore – "Of all the colours, none is more proper for churches than white; since the purity of colour, as of the life, is particularly gratifying to God," wrote Palladio. It's hard to imagine how anyone could remain totally unimpressed by the interior's finely calculated proportions and Counter-Reformation austerity, but in Ruskin's opinion, only the paintings inside justified the effort of opening the door.

The first altar on the right has an *Adoration of the Shepherds* by **Jacopo Bassano**, which is followed by an alarming late fifteenth-century Crucifix – not, as the label says, by Brunelleschi, but by an anonymous Venetian artist. Most of the other pictures are from the workshop of **Tintoretto**, with two outstanding pictures by the master in the chancel: *The Last Supper*, perhaps the most famous of all Tintoretto's works, and *The Fall of Manna*, one of the few depictions of the event to dwell on the fact that the shower was not a single miraculous deluge but rather a supply that continued for forty years. They were painted as a pair in 1592–94 – the last two years of the artist's life – to illustrate the significance of the Eucharist to the communicants at the altar rail. A *Deposition* of the same date, in the Cappella dei Morti (through the door on the right of the choir), may well be Tintoretto's last completed painting. The carnage-strewn picture alongside is a photograph of Carpaccio's *St George and the Dragon*, painted several years after the equally gruesome version in the Scuola di San Giorgio degli Schiavoni. (The original is in a private room elsewhere in the building.)

There are few pieces of woodwork in Venice more impressive than the **choir stalls** of San Giorgio Maggiore. Decorated with scenes from the life of St Benedict, they were carved in the late 1590s, as the church was being completed; the bronze figures of *St George* and *St Stephen* on the balustrade are by **Niccolò Roccatagliata** (1593), who also made the florid candlesticks at the entrance to the chancel. Apart from Roccatagliata's pieces, the best sculptures in the church are the *Evangelists* by **Vittoria**, flanking the **tomb of Doge Leonardo Donà**, on the west wall. A close friend of Paolo Sarpi and Galileo, the scholarly Donà was the redoubtable leader of Venice at the time of the Interdict of 1602. The Papal Nuncio was sent packing by him with the lofty dismissal – "We ignore your excommunication: it is nothing to us. Now think where our resolution would lead, were our example to be followed by others."

The door on the left of the choir leads to the **campanile** (L3000/€1.54), via a corridor that houses the charred original version of the angel that stands on the church's summit; the angel was replaced by a copy after being charred and half-melted by a lightning strike in 1993. Rebuilt in 1791 after the collapse of its predecessor, the San Giorgio campanile surpasses that of San Marco as the best vantage point in Venice, because it has the advantage of being slightly detached from the main part of the city, giving you a view that includes many of the canals (all of which are hidden from the San

Marco tower) and, of course, the spectacular San Marco campanile itself.

The monastery – and the harbour

Since the early ninth century there's been a church on this island, and at the end of the tenth century the lagoon's most important Benedictine monastery was established here. Both church and monastery were destroyed by an earthquake in 1223, but were rebuilt straight away, and subsequently renovated and altered several times. Cosimo de' Medici stayed at the monastery in 1433, during his exile from Florence, and it was with his assistance that the monastic library was set up; by the end of the century the Benedictines of San Giorgio Maggiore had become renowned for their erudition. With the upheavals of the early nineteenth century things changed rapidly. When the conclave that elected Pope Pius VII met here in 1800, having been turfed out of Rome by Napoleon, the confiscation of the monastery's property had already begun, and six years later the order was suppressed. By the mid-nineteenth century the monastery had been converted into workshops and offices for the Austrian artillery, and the decline of the complex continued for another hundred years until, in 1951, it was acquired by Count Vittorio Cini and converted into the home of the **Fondazione Giorgio Cini** (named after Cini's son), an organization that now runs an arts research institute, a naval college and a craft school on the island.

The restored monastery is one of the architectural wonders of the city. Two adjoining cloisters form the heart of the complex: the **Cloister of the Bay Trees**, planned by Giovanni Buora and built by his son Andrea in the two decades up to 1540; and the **Cloister of the Cypresses**, designed in 1579 by Palladio. Inside, there's a 128-metre-long **dormitory** by Giovanni Buora (c.1494), a **double staircase** (1641–43) and **library** (1641–53) by Longhena and, approached by an ascent through two anterooms, a magnificent **refectory** by Palladio (1560–62) – for which Veronese's *Marriage at Cana*, now in the Louvre, was painted. Exhibitions are regularly held at the Fondazione (often solemn and bookish affairs), and the open-air Teatro Verde is occasionally used for plays and concerts. It's always possible to visit the monastery at other times by ringing for an appointment (☎041.528.9900); if you just turn up unannounced, a word with the custodian could do the trick if he's not feeling harassed or if you can convince him of an unquenchable interest in Palladian architecture.

The little **harbour** on the other side of the church was expanded during the second French occupation of 1806–15, when Napoleon decided to accord the island the status of a free port, in emulation of the tariff-free port of Trieste. A professor of architecture at the Accademia designed the two diminutive lighthouses in 1813.

Giudecca

La Giudecca

In the earliest records of Venice the chain of islets now called **La Giudecca** was known as Spina Longa, a name clearly derived from its shape. The modern name might refer to the Jews (*Giudei*) who lived here from the late thirteenth century until their removal to the Ghetto, but is most likely to originate with the two disruptive noble families who in the ninth century were shoved into this district to keep them out of mischief (*giudicati* means "judged"). Before the Brenta River became the prestigious site for summer abodes, La Giudecca was where the wealthiest aristocrats of early Renaissance Venice built their villas. Michelangelo, self-exiled from Florence in 1529, consoled himself in the gardens of this island, traces of which remain on its south side. The most extensive of La Giudecca's surviving private gardens, the so-called Garden of Eden (at the end of the Rio della Croce), is bigger than any other in Venice – larger even than the public Giardini Papadopoli, at the head of the Canal Grande. Its name refers not to its paradisical properties but to a certain Mr Eden, the English gardener who planted it.

Giudecca was also the city's **industrial** inner suburb: Venice's public transport boats used to be made here; an asphalt factory and a distillery were once neighbours on the western end; and the matting industry, originating in the nineteenth century, kept going until 1950. However, the present-day island is a potent emblem of Venice's loss of economic self-sufficiency in the twentieth century.

LA GIUDECCA & SAN GIORGIO MAGGIORE

In the mid-1990s the clock and watch firm Junghans, one of the city's major employers for half a century, closed its huge factory between Rio del Ponte Lungo and Rio del Ponte Piccolo, adding another ruin to the array of abandoned workshops and roofless sheds that shared the southern side of the island with the boatyards and fishing quays. While the *Cipriani*, one of the city's most expensive hotels, occupies the eastern extremity of La Giudecca, the western edge has for years been dominated by the derelict neo-Gothic fortress of the Mulino Stucky flour mill, the largest industrial wreck in Venice (see p.235). Swathes of La Giudecca are now purely residential areas, but in this respect things are looking up, with a spate of housing developments and ancillary social facilities being funded in recent years, while artists, theatre co-operatives and other creative groups have moved into a number of the redundant buildings. And at the start of the new century there's been an acceleration in the process of La Giudecca's rejuvenation. Under the aegis of the Judecanova consortium a variety of substantial projects are under way: a nautical centre is being constructed within one of the deserted factories on the main waterfront, for example, and a residential block for students has risen on the site of the Junghans factory, next door to a beautiful old school building that is due to be converted into an annexe of the university. In no other part of Venice are you as likely to see a site occupied by cranes and bulldozers, and the chances are about even that they'll be putting something up rather than pulling it down.

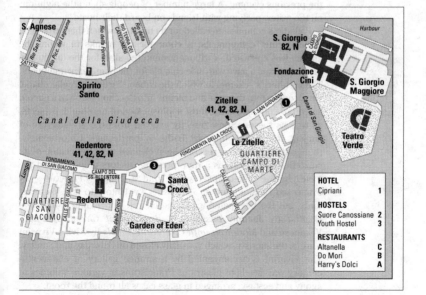

La Giudecca

The Zitelle and the Redentore

The Zitelle is
open for Mass
Sun
10am–noon.

The first vaporetto stop after San Giorgio Maggiore is close to the tiny church of the **Zitelle**, which was built in 1582–86 from plans worked out some years earlier by Palladio, albeit for a different site. In the eighteenth century the convent attached to the church was renowned for the delicacy of the lace produced by the young girls who lived in its hostel. The **Casa de Maria**, to the right of the Zitelle, is an inventive reworking of Venetian Gothic, built as a studio by the painter Mario de Maria in 1910–13. Its diaper-pattern brickwork, derived from that of the Palazzo Ducale, is the only example of its kind in Venetian domestic building. The neigbouring building is somewhat less inventive but very welcome nonetheless – it's a new housing development, one of several such schemes to revitalize the island.

The Redentore
is open
Mon–Sat
10am–5pm,
Sun 1–5pm
(closed Sun in
July & Aug);
L3000/€1.54.

La Giudecca's main monument, beyond the tug-boats' mooring and the youth hostel (once a granary), is the Franciscan church of Il **Redentore**, designed by **Palladio** in 1577. In 1575–76 Venice suffered an outbreak of plague which killed nearly fifty thousand people – virtually a third of the city's population. The Redentore was built by the Senate in thanks for Venice's deliverance, and every year until the downfall of the Republic the doge and his senators attended a Mass here to renew their declaration of gratitude, walking to the church over a pontoon bridge from the Záttere. The *Festa del Redentore* has remained a major event on the Venetian calendar – celebrated on the third Sunday of July, it's marked by a general procession over the temporary bridge and a huge fireworks display on the previous evening. A large number of people spend the night out on the water, partying with friends on board their boats.

Palladio's commission called for a church to which there would be three distinct components: a choir for the monks to whom the church was entrusted, a tribune around the altar for the dignitaries of the city, and a nave with side chapels for the humbler worshippers. The architect's scheme, in which the tribune forms a circular chapel which opens into the nave and blends into the choir through a curved screen of columns, is the most sophisticated of his church projects, as well as the one most directly evolved from the architecture of ancient Rome (the Imperial baths in particular). Unfortunately, though the interior has recently been cleaned, an appreciation of its subtleties is difficult, as a rope prevents visitors going beyond the nave. In the side-chapels you'll find a couple of pictures by Francesco Bassano and an *Ascension* by Tintoretto and his assistants, but the best paintings in the church – including a *John the Baptist* by **Jacopo Bassano**, a *Baptism of Christ* by **Paolo Veronese** and *Madonna with Child and Angels* by **Alvise Vivarini** – are in the sacristy, which is usually closed on Saturday and Sunday. The Vivarini is accompanied by a strange gallery of eighteenth-century wax heads of illustrious Franciscans in various attitudes of agony and ecstasy, arranged in glass cases all round the room.

Sant'Eufemia and the interior of La Giudecca

Founded in the ninth century and often rebuilt, the church of **Sant'Eufemia** is one of Venice's most engaging stylistic discords: late sixteenth-century portico, nave and aisles still laid out as in the original basilica (with some eleventh-century columns and capitals), stucco work and painted decoration in eighteenth-century boudoir mode. It has one good painting, immediately on your right as you go in: *St Roch and an Angel* (with lunette of *Madonna and Child*), the central panel of a triptych painted in 1480 by **Bartolomeo Vivarini**.

Sant'Eufemia is open Mon–Sat 9am–noon & 6–7pm, Sun 7am–12.30pm.

Beyond Sant'Eufemia, on Fondamenta San Biagio, stands the HQ of the **Fortuny** company, which still makes some of the fabrics designed by the founder. Towering over it is the gargantuan **Mulino Stucky**, which got to look the way it does in 1895–96, after Giovanni Stucky brought in a German architect, Ernst Wullekopf, to convert and expand the premises of his flour mill. Planning permission for the brick bastion that Wullekopf came up with was obtained by the simple expedient of threatening to sack all the workers if the OK were withheld by the council. By the beginning of this century Stucky had become one of the richest men in the city, and in 1908 he bought one of the Canal Grande's less discreet houses, the Palazzo Grassi. He didn't enjoy his occupancy for long, though – in 1910 one of his employees murdered him at the entrance to the train station. With the development of the industrial sector at Marghera after World War I, the Mulino Stucky went into a nose dive, and in 1954 it closed. Since then its future has been a perennially contentious issue – it was planned to convert it into housing but it's now being restored for use as a convention centre and hotel.

There's not much point in going past the Stucky building: **Sacca Fisola**, the next island along, is all modern apartments, bordered on one side by boatyards and on the other by the site at which waste is mixed with silt to form the basic material of land reclamation in the lagoon.

For a taste of the economic past and present of La Giudecca, double back along the waterfront and then turn down the Fondamenta del Rio di Sant'Eufemia; a circuitous stroll from the run-down Campo di San Cosma (where the church of SS Cosma e Damiano, having undergone a flurry of restoration, has now once again been left to crumble) to the Rio Ponte Lungo will take you through the core of Giudecca's former manufacturing district. The interior of the island on the other side of the Rio Ponte Lungo is not so densely built up, with a fair amount of open space (even vegetable gardens) around the Redentore and the hulk of Santa Croce church (built c.1510 and long ago deconsecrated). Frustratingly, hardly any of La Giudecca's alleyways lead down to the lagoon on the south side; if you want a view across the water in that direction, it's best to take Calle

Michelangelo, which comes onto the main fondamenta between the Zitelle and the youth hostel.

The Lido

The shores of the **Lido** have seen some action in their time: in 1202 a huge French army, assembled for the Fourth Crusade, cooled its heels on the beaches while its leaders haggled with the Venetians over the terms for transport to the East; Henry III of France was welcomed here in 1574 with fanfares and triumphal monuments made in his honour; and every year, for about eight centuries, there was the hullaballoo of Venice's **Marriage to the Sea**.

This ritual, the most operatic of Venice's state ceremonials, began as a way of commemorating the exploits of Doge Pietro Orseolo II, who on Ascension Day of the year 1000 set sail to subjugate the pirates of the Dalmatian coast. (Orseolo's standard, by the way, featured possibly the first representation of what was to become the emblem of Venice – the Lion of Saint Mark with its paw on an open book.) According to legend, the ritual reached its definitive form after the Venetians had brought about the reconciliation of Pope Alexander III and Frederick Barbarossa in 1177; the grateful

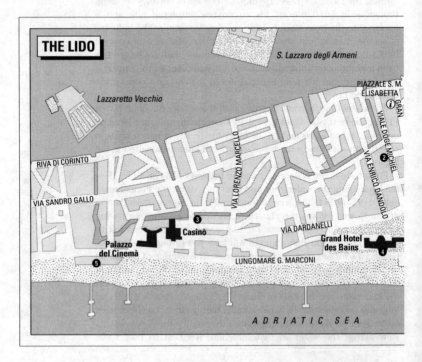

Alexander is supposed to have given the doge the first of the gold rings with which Venice was married to the Adriatic. It's more likely that the essential components of the ritual – the voyage out to the Porto di Lido in the *Bucintoro* with an escort of garlanded vessels, the dropping of the ring into the brine "In sign of our true and perpetual dominion", and the disembarkation for a solemn Mass at the church of San Nicolò al Lido – were all fixed by the middle of the twelfth century. Unless you steadfastly shun all the public collections in Venice, you're bound to see at least one painting of the ceremony during your stay. Nowadays the mayor, patriarch and a gaggle of other VIPs annually enact a sad facsimile of the grand occasion. And in case you're thinking of launching a salvage operation for all those gold rings, a fifteenth-century traveller recorded – "After the ceremony, many strip and dive to the bottom to seek the ring. He who finds it keeps it for his own, and, what's more, lives for that year free from all the burdens to which dwellers in that republic are subject."

In the twelfth century the Lido was an unspoilt strip of land, and it remained so into the last century. Byron used to gallop his horses across the fields of the Lido every day, and as late as 1869 Henry James could describe the island as "a very natural place". Before the nineteenth century was out, however, it had become the smartest **bathing resort** in Italy, and although it's no longer as chic as it was

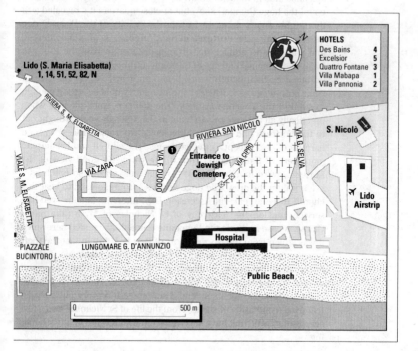

when Thomas Mann installed von Aschenbach, the central figure of *Death in Venice*, as a guest at the Lido's *Grand Hotel des Bains*, there's less room on its beaches now than ever before. But unless you're staying at one of the flashy hotels that stand shoulder to shoulder along the seafront, or are prepared to pay a ludicrous fee to rent one of their beach hutches for the day, you won't be allowed to get the choicest Lido sand between your toes.

If you're the sort of person who regards access to the sea as a God-given right, then you'll have to content yourself with the ungroomed **public beaches** at the northern and southern ends of the island – though if you're tempted by the thought of a dip, bear in mind that this stretch of the Adriatic isn't one of the cleanest. (The traffic, incidentally, is the other health hazard of the Lido. Just as the Venetians were once regarded as the worst riders in Italy, they are now ranked as its most inept drivers.) The northern beach is twenty minutes' walk from the vaporetto stop at Piazzale Santa Maria Elisabetta; the southern one, right by the municipal golf course, necessitates a bus journey from the Piazzale, and is consequently less of a crush.

The monuments of the Lido

The green-domed Santa Maria della Vittoria might be the most conspicuous Lido monument on the lagoon side of the island (unless you count the huge Campari sign) but at close quarters it's revealed as a thoroughly abject thing. In fact, in the vicinity of the Piazzale one building alone – the **Fortezza di Sant'Andrea** – is of much interest, and you have to admire that from a distance, across the Porto di Lido. The principal defence of the main entrance to the lagoon, it was designed by **Sanmicheli**; work began on it in 1543, in the face of some scepticism as to whether the structure would be strong enough to support the Venetian artillery. The doubters were silenced when practically all the cannons to hand in the Arsenale were brought out to the Fortezza and fired simultaneously from its terraces, with no harmful effects except to the eardrums. The church and Franciscan monastery of **San Nicolò**, from where you get a good view of the Fortezza, were founded in 1044, when there wasn't so much as a brick wall in the area. The doge and his entourage used to visit this church twice a year: on Ascension Day, after the aquatic wedding service, and on the feast day of St Nicholas of Myra (aka Santa Claus), whose body, so the Venetians claimed, had rested here since it was stolen from the Norman port of Bari in 1099. In fact the theft never happened – the Venetian raid on Bari was a classic piece of disinformation, devised to score points off the Normans, and the grand display on the saint's day was a propagandist sham. The present church is notable for its splendid seventeenth-century choir stalls, featuring a multitude of scenes from the life of St Nicholas, and a few scraps of mosaic that have survived from the eleventh century building.

A stroll along the nearby Via Cipro (facing the San Nicolò vaporetto stop) will bring you to the entrance to Venice's **Jewish cemetery**, which was founded in 1386 and in places has fallen into atmospheric decay. Adjoining is a Catholic burial ground, in a corner of which have been stacked the stones from the old Protestant cemetery, ploughed over in the 1930s to make more room for the Lido's airstrip.

Towards the southern end of the seafront road are two buildings which, with the fire station on the Rio di Ca' Fóscari, constitute Venice's main examples of Fascist architecture – the **Palazzo del Cinema** and the **Casinò**. In late August and early September the **Venice Film Festival** occupies the former, while the latter is in use only in the summer – in winter the action shifts to the Palazzo Vendramin-Calergi, on the Canal Grande.

From the
Lido to
Chioggia

*The Jewish
cemetery is
open Sun–Fri:
April–Sept
9.30am–
12.30pm &
3–6.30pm;
Oct–March
9.30am–
2.30pm.*

From the Lido to Chioggia

The trip across the lagoon to **Chioggia** is a more protracted business than simply taking the land bus from Piazzale Roma, but it will give you a curative dose of salt air and a good knowledge of the lagoon. From Gran Viale Santa Maria Elisabetta – the main street from the Lido landing stage to the sea front – the more or less hourly #11 bus goes down to **Alberoni**, where it drives onto a ferry for the five-minute hop to Pellestrina; the 10km to the southern tip of Pellestrina are covered by road, and then you switch from the bus to a steamer for the 25-minute crossing to Chioggia. The entire journey takes about eighty minutes, and costs L7000/€3.62 for a through-ticket, including the cost of the hop from San Zaccaria to the Lido – but be sure to check the timetable carefully at Gran Viale Santa Maria Elisabetta – not every #11 goes all the way to Chioggia. The quickest way **back to Venice** is by bus from the Duomo or Sottomarina to Piazzale Roma, but it's a dispiriting drive, is only about twenty minutes quicker than the island-hop route, and ACTV passes are not valid, as this is an extra-urban bus service. All in all, your best plan is to get an ACTV tourist ticket, or buy the special Chioggia ticket (L15,000/€7.75), which gives unlimited travel along the Chioggia route for twelve hours.

Lido to
Chioggia

Malamocco and Pellestrina

The fishing village of **Malamocco**, about 5km into the expedition, is the successor of the ancient settlement called Metamauco, which in the eighth century was the capital of the lagoon confederation. In 810 the town was taken by **Pepin**, son of Charlemagne, and there followed one of the crucial battles in Venice's history, when Pepin's fleet, endeavouring to reach the islands of Rivoalto (forerunner of Venice), became jammed in the mudbanks and was swiftly pounced

*The vaporetto
to San Lazzaro
– see p.242 –
passes along a
section of the
Canal Orfano.*

upon. After the battle the capital was promptly transferred to the safer islands of Rivoalto, and in 1107 the old town was destroyed by a tidal wave. The new town has a place in the bloodier footnotes of later Venetian history – the **Canal Orfano**, off the Malamocco shore, was the spot where some of those condemned by the Council of Ten were bound, gagged, weighted and thrown overboard by the executioner. Rebuilt Malamocco's most appealing building – the church's scaled-down replica of the Campanile of San Marco – can be seen without getting off the bus.

The most ferocious defenders of the lagoon in the war against Pepin came from the small island of **Poveglia**, just off Malamocco. Once populous enough to have a practically independent administration, it suffered greatly in the war against Genoa (see below) and went into a steep decline immediately after, becoming little more than a fort. For much of this century it was a hospital island, but since the closure of the hospital in the late 1960s it has been abandoned.

Fishing and the production of fine pillow-lace are the mainstays of life in the village of **Pellestrina**, which is strung out along nearly a third of the ten kilometres of the next island. There's one remarkable structure here, but you get the best view of it as the boat crosses to Chioggia. This is the **Murazzi**, the colossal walls of Istrian boulders, 4km long and 14m thick at the base, which were constructed at the sides of the Porto di Chioggia to protect Venice from the battering of the sea. The maintenance of the water level in the lagoon has always been a preoccupation of Venetian life: very early in the city's development, for example, the five gaps in the *lidi* (the Lido–Chioggia sandbars) were reduced to the present three to strengthen the barrier against the Adriatic and to increase the dredging action of the tides through the three remaining *porti*. In time a special state official, the *Magistrato alle Acque*, was appointed to supervise the management of the lagoon, and the Murazzi were the last major project undertaken by the *Magistrato*'s department. Devised as a response to the increased flooding of the early eighteenth century, the Murazzi took 38 years to build, and remained unbreached from 1782, the year of their completion, until the flood of November 1966. The latest flood-prevention scheme on Pellestrina involves the widening and raising of its beaches, to take the force out of the action of the sea; by the year 2000 some 9km of new beach had been created here, and similar projects are under way at various other points along the shore between the Lido and Chioggia.

Chioggia

Once a Roman port, then in the eleventh and twelfth centuries a major producer of salt, **Chioggia** secured its place in the annals of Venetian history in 1379, when it became the scene of the most serious threat to Venice since Pepin's invasion, as the Genoese, after copious shedding of blood on both sides, took possession of the town. Venice at this time had two outstanding admirals: the first, **Vettor Pisani**, was in prison on a charge of military negligence; the second, **Carlo Zeno**, was somewhere off in the East. So serious was the threat to the city that Pisani was promptly released, and then put in command of the fleet that set out in December – with the doge himself on board – to blockade the enemy. Zeno and his contingent sailed over the horizon on the first day of the new year and there followed months of siege warfare, in the course of which the Venetian navy employed shipboard cannons for the first time. (Casualties from cannonballs were as high on the Venetian side as on the Genoese, and some crews refused to operate these suicidal weapons more than once a day.) In June 1380, with medieval Chioggia in ruins, the enemy surrendered, and from then until the arrival of Napoleon's ships the Venetian lagoon remained impregnable.

Modern Chioggia is the second largest settlement in the lagoon after Venice, and one of Italy's busiest fishing ports. Lorenzetti describes the *Chioggiotti* as "extremely individual types and among the most expert and intrepid sailors of the Adriatic", but those with insufficient time to plumb the depths of the local character will probably find Chioggia one of the less charming towns of the region. With the exception of a single church, you can see everything worth seeing in an hour's walk along the **Corso del Popolo**, the principal street in Chioggia's grid-iron layout (probably a Roman inheritance). The exception is the church of **San Domenico**, which houses Carpaccio's *St Paul*, his last known painting, plus a couple of pictures by **Leandro Bassano**; you get to it by taking the bridge to the left of the Chioggia landing stage and going straight on until you can't go any further.

The boat sets you down at the **Piazzetta Vigo**, at the head of the Corso. The locals are reputedly touchy about the excuse for a lion that sits on top of the column here, a beast known to the condescending Venetians as the Cat of St Mark. Only the thirteenth-century campanile of the church of **San Andrea** (rebuilt in 1743) is likely to catch your eye before the street widens at the **Granaio**, a grain warehouse built in 1322 but got at by nineteenth-century restorers; the facade relief of the *Madonna and Child* is by Sansovino. Behind the Granaio is the **fish market**; open for business every morning except Monday, it's a treat for gourmet and marine biologist alike – make sure you don't arrive too late to see it.

In the Piazzetta Venti Settembre, immediately after the town hall, there's the church of the **Santissima Trinità**, radically altered in 1703 by Andrea Tirali and almost perpetually shut – the Oratory, behind the main altar, has an impressive ceiling set with paintings by followers of Tintoretto. **San Giacomo Apostolo**, a bit further on, has a sub-Tiepolo ceiling by local boy Il Chiozzotto, and a much venerated fifteenth-century Venetian painting known as the *Madonna della*

Navicella. Soon you pass a house once occupied by the family of Rosalba Carriera and later by Goldoni, and then, on the opposite side of the road, just before the duomo, the **Tempio di San Martino**, built immediately after the war of 1380. It's rarely open except for temporary exhibitions.

The **Duomo** was the first major commission for **Longhena**, who was called in to design a new church after the previous cathedral was burned down in 1623; the detached fourteenth-century campanile survived the blaze. The chapel to the left of the chancel contains half a dozen good eighteenth-century paintings, including one attributed to Tiepolo; except in freakish weather conditions they're all but invisible, a drawback that the over-sensitive might regard as a blessing in view of the subjects depicted – *The Torture of Boiling Oil, The Torture of the Razors, The Beheading of Two Martyrs*, and so on.

Buses run from the duomo to **Sottomarina**, Chioggia's down-market answer to Venice's Lido. On the beaches of Sottomarina you're a fraction closer to nature than you would be on the Lido, and the resort does have one big plus – after your dip you can go back to the Corso and have a fresh seafood meal that's cheaper than any you'd find in Venice's restaurants and better than most.

San Lazzaro degli Armeni and the minor islands

S. Lazzaro & minor islands

No foreign community has a longer pedigree in Venice than the Armenians. Their position in the economy of the city, primarily as tradesmen and moneylenders, was secure by the end of the thirteenth century, and for around five hundred years they have had their own church within a few yards of the Piazza, in the narrow Calle degli Armeni (see p.86). The Armenians are far less numerous now than formerly, and the most conspicuous sign of their presence is the Armenian island by the Lido, **San Lazzaro degli Armeni**, identifiable from the city by the onion-shaped summit of its campanile.

Visitors are received at San Lazzaro daily 3–5pm; L10,000/€5.16; take the #20 vaporetto from San Zaccaria – you have to catch one just before 3pm.

From the late twelfth century to the beginning of the seventeenth the island was a leper colony – hence *Lazzaro*, Lazarus being the patron saint of lepers – but the land was disused when in 1717 an Armenian monastery was founded here by one Manug di Pietro. Known as **Mekhitar** ("The Consoler"), he had been driven by the Turks from the religious foundation he had established with Venetian aid in the Morea. Within a few years the monks of San Lazzaro earned a wide reputation as scholars and linguists, a reputation that has persisted to the present. Today, Vienna has the only community outside Armenia that can compare to Venice's as a centre of Armenian culture. (If you're wondering how the Armenians escaped suppression by the French, it's allegedly got something to do with the presence of an indispensible Armenian official in Napoleon's secretariat.)

Tours are conducted by one of the thirty or so priests who currently live in the monastery, and you can expect him to be trilingual, at the very least. The tour begins in the turquoise-ceilinged church, in which you'll be given a brief introduction to the culture of Armenia in general and the San Lazzaro Armenians in particular – whereas the Armenian Church is Orthodox, San Lazzaro is an Armenian Catholic foundation, which means it follows the Roman liturgy but is not subject to the authority of the pope. Reflecting the encyclopedic interests of its occupants, the monastery is in places like a whimsically arranged museum: at one end of the old **library**, for example, a mummified Egyptian body is laid out near the sarcophagus in which it was found (the sarcophagus was made for a different occupant), while at the other is a teak and ivory throne that once seated the governor of Delhi, and a Sanskrit Buddhist manuscipt. The monastery's collection of precious manuscripts and books – the former going back to the fifth century – is another highlight of the visit, occupying a modern rotunda in the heart of the complex.

Elsewhere you'll see antique metalwork, extraordinarily intricate Chinese ivory carvings, pieces of Roman pottery, a gallery of paintings by Armenian painters, a ceiling panel by the young Giambattista Tiepolo, and Canova's figure of Napoleon's infant son, which sits in a corner of the book-lined chamber in which Byron studied while lending a hand with the preparation of an Armenian–English dictionary – it took him just six months to get a working knowledge of the language, it's said. The tour might also take you into a small museum dedicated to Mekhitar (featuring the scourging chain found on his body after his death), but will certainly end at the monastery's shop. A polyglot press was founded on San Lazzaro in 1789 and an Armenian press is still administered from here, although since 1992 the printing – of everything from books to wine labels – has been done out at Punta Sabbioni. If you're looking for an unusual present to take home, you could buy something here: the old maps and prints of Venice are a bargain.

The "Hospital Islands"

San Lazzaro is the only minor island of the southern lagoon that's of interest to tourists. The boat out to San Lazzaro calls at **La Grazia**, successively a pilgrims' hostel, a monastery and now a hospital, and **San Servolo**, once one of the most important Benedictine monasteries in the region (founded in the ninth century), then a hospital for the insane, then the home of the Council of Europe's School of Craftsmanship, and now the base of Venice International University, a study centre administered by universities in Italy, Japan, Germany and the US. **San Clemente**, to the south of La Grazia, was another hospital island until 1992, when it was closed down; a scheme for an upmarket hotel complex on the island has been approved, but at the moment it serves as a refuge for Venice's stray cats, which are

Listings

Chapter 10

Accommodation

The virtually limitless demand for **accommodation** in Venice has pushed prices to such a level that it's possible to pay in excess of L200,000/€105 for a double room in a one-star hotel in high season. What's more, the **high season** here is longer than anywhere else in the country – it is officially classified as running from March 15 to November 15 and then from December 21 to January 6, but many places don't recognize the existence of a low season any more. If you intend to stay in Venice at any time during the official high season it's wisest to book your place at least three months in advance, whether it's a hostel bed or a five-star suite, and for June, July and August it's virtually obligatory to reserve half a year ahead. Should you bowl into town unannounced in high summer, the booking offices (see below) may be able to dig out something in the hotels of mainland Mestre or way out in the lagoon at the unlovely neighbouring

resorts of Jesolo and Cavallino (a half-hour boat ride). During the winter it may be possible to bargain for a reduced-rate room, but some hotels – especially the cheaper ones and the hotels on the Lido – close down from November to February or even March (reopening briefly for Christmas and New Year in many cases), so you might have to put in a bit of leg-work before finding somewhere.

If you arrive with nowhere to stay and find that there is no space in any of the places listed in the following sections, try one of the following **booking offices**: at the **train station** (daily: summer 8am–9pm; winter 8am–7pm); on the **Tronchetto** (9am–8pm); in the multi-storey car park at **Piazzale Roma** (9am–9pm); at **Marco Polo airport** (summer 9am–7pm; winter noon–7pm); at the **autostrada's Venice exit** (8am–8pm). They only deal with hotels (not hostels) and take a deposit that's deductible from your first night's bill.

Hotels in this guide are classified into nine price categories, indicating the **minimum** you can expect to pay for **a double room in high season**, including the cost of breakfast. For many Veneto hotels, high season is now an all-year phenomenon, but in those places that do reduce their prices for the quieter months of the winter, you can expect prices to be around ten percent lower on average.

① Under L100,000/€51.65.
② L100,000–150,000/€51.65–77.47.
③ L150,000–200,000/€77.47–103.29.
④ L200,000–250,000/€103.29–129.11.
⑤ L250,000–300,000/€129.11–154.94.

⑥ L300,000–400,000/€154.94–206.58.
⑦ L400,000–500,000/€206.58–258.23.
⑧ L500,000–600,000/€258.23–309.87.
⑨ Over L600,000/€309.87.

Accommodation

Hotels

Venice has around two hundred hotels, ranging from spartan one-star joints to five-star establishments charging a million lire a night, and what follows is a rundown on the best choices in all categories. Though there are some typical anomalies, the star system is a broadly reliable indicator of quality, but always bear in mind that you pay through the nose for your proximity to the Piazza. So if you want maximum comfort for your money, decide how much you can afford then look for a place outside the San Marco sestiere – after all, it's not far to walk, wherever you're staying.

Breakfast is nearly always included in the room rate; if it isn't, you should anticipate a charge of at least L10,000/€5 for a jug of coffee and a croissant. By law, the price of a room must be displayed on the back of its door; if it's not, or if the price doesn't correspond to what you're being charged, complain first to the management and then to the *Questura* (see p.289).

The subheadings used below correspond to the chapter areas in which the hotels are to be found, while the addresses given are the full postal addresses. For the explanation as to how a place can be in the Castello district but not in the Castello chapter, see p.29. In the listings for hotels in central Venice, the phone number is followed by a grid reference to make it easy to locate the hotel; the note following the area heading tells you which map to consult.

San Marco

The grid references at the end of each address relate to the map on p.42.

Ai Do Mori, Calle Larga S. Marzo, S. Marco 658 ☎041.520.4817; fax 041.520.5328; I5. Very friendly, and situated a few paces off the Piazza, this recently refitted hotel is one of Venice's most attractive (and expensive) one-stars. The top-floor room has a private terrace looking over the roofs of the Basilica and the Torre dell'Orologio. ④.

Ala, Campo S. Maria del Giglio, S. Marco 2494 ☎041.520.8333; fax 041.520.6390; *www.hotelala.it*; E8. If you want to stay in the city's aristocratic accommodation zone but can't stretch to the prices of the Bauer Grünwald and its coevals, the three-star Ala is a logical choice. There are more welcoming places in Venice, but the rooms are spacious and the Ala has a perfect location, on a square that opens out onto the mouth of the Canal Grande. ⑥.

Al Gambero, Calle dei Fabbri, S. Marco 4687 ☎041.522.4384; fax 041.520.0431; *hotgamb@tin.it*; G5. Large and recently refurbished one-star hotel in an excellent position a short distance off the north side of the Piazza; the rooms are well maintained, and many of them overlook a canal that's on the standard gondola route from the Bacino Orseolo. Has more single rooms than many Venice hotels. There's a boisterous Franco-Italian bistro on the ground floor. ③.

Bauer Grünwald, Campo S. Moisè, S. Marco 1459 ☎041.520.7022; fax 041.520.7557; *www.bauervenezia.com*; G8. This is one of the city's top-notch hotels, and if you take the best room you'll pay a couple of million lire per night. It does have doubles for as little as L350,000/€180.76, but that's in the dead months of the year, and in the unbeguiling boxy modern part of the hotel. If you're going to blow your cash here, you have to do it in style, and book into the thirteenth-century building, on the Canal Grande. ⑨.

Boston, Calle dei Fabbri, S. Marco 848 ☎041.528.7665; fax 041.522.6628; G5. Large and efficient three-star hotel on one of the main shopping streets. Closed from mid-Nov to mid-Feb. ⑤.

Casa Petrarca, Calle delle Colonne, S. Marco 4394 ☎041.520.0430; G5. One of the cheapest hotels within a stone's throw of the Piazza – but phone first, as it only has seven rooms. ③.

Concordia, Calle Larga S. Marzo, S. Marco 367 ☎041.520.6866; fax

041.520.6775; *www.hotelconcordia.it;*
I5. This sixty-room four-star is the only
hotel that actually looks onto the
Piazza, which enables it to charge more
than its rather characterless furnishings
might justify. The cheapest double in
low season is around
L330,000/€170.43; in high season
you'll be lucky to get away with anything under double that. ⑨.

Europa e Regina, Corte Barozzi, S. Marco
2159 ☎041.520.0477; fax 041.523.1533;
www.luxurycollection.com/europa&regina;
F8. Four-star establishment run by the
Ciga chain, which also owns the *Danieli,*
the *Gritti* and the *Excelsior* over on the
Lido. As grotesquely expensive as its sib-
lings (no doubles under L600,000/€310
per night; best rooms around one and a
half million), it commands stunning views
from the mouth of the Canal Grande, and
its terraces must be the most spectacular
places to eat in the city. ⑨.

Fiorita, Campiello Nuovo, S. Marco 3457
☎041.523.4754; fax 041.522.8043;
locandafior@tin.it; C6. One-star with just
nine rooms, so again it's crucial to book
well in advance. Welcoming management, and there's a nearby traghetto
across the Canal Grande. ③.

Flora, Calle Larga XXII Marzo, S. Marco
2283/a ☎041.520.5844; fax
041.522.8217; *www.hotelflora.it;* F8.
Some of the rooms are too cramped, but
this large three-star is very close to the
Piazza and has a peaceful little garden,
too. ⑥.

Gritti Palace, S. Maria del Giglio, S.
Marco 2467 ☎041.794.611; fax
041.520.0942; *www.luxurycollection*
.com/grittipalace; E9. One of Venice's
most prestigious addresses,
reeking of old regime opulence.
No doubles under L650,000/
€335.70 per night, and the plushest
suite will set you back
L1,700,000/€977.98. ⑨.

Kette, Piscina S. Moisè, S. Marco 2053
☎041.520.7766; fax 041.522.8964;
www.hotelkette.com; F7. A favourite
with the upper-bracket tour companies,

mainly on account of its quiet location,
in an alleyway parallel to Calle Larga
XXII Marzo. In season there's nothing
under L450,000/€232.41, but out of
season prices tumble by more than forty
percent. ⑦.

La Fenice et des Artistes, Campiello
Fenice, S. Marco 1936 ☎041.523.2333;
fax 041.520.3721;
fenice@fenicehotels.it; E7. This large
three-star was always a favoured hang-
out of the opera crowd, performers and
audience alike. With La Fenice turned
into a building site, it might have more
vacancies than it used to. Unusually for
a three-star, it has some rooms without
private bathrooms. ⑤.

Luna Baglioni, Calle Vallaresso, S. Marco
1243 ☎041.528.9840; fax
041.528.7160; *www.baglionihotels.com;*
G7. Established in the late fifteenth century, this four-star claims to be the oldest
hotel in the city, but much of it has been
modernized almost to death. No doubles
under L600,000/€310 at any time of
year; the best rooms cost fifty percent
more than that. ⑨.

Monaco and Grand Canal, Calle
Vallaresso, S. Marco 1325
☎041.520.0211; fax 041.520.0501;
mailbox@hotelmonaco.it; G7. Very stylish
four-star hotel – try to get one of the
ground-floor rooms, which look over to
the Salute. Has a few rooms around
L350,000/€181 in summer, but most are
more than double that. ⑨.

Noemi, Calle dei Fabbri, San Marco
909 ☎041.523.8144;
hotelnoemi@tin.it; G5. The rooms are
basic (only two of the 15 have bathrooms) and the decor is rather dowdy,
but the one-star Noemi is right in the
thick of the action, just a minute's
walk north of the Piazza, and its prices
are lower than most rival one-stars –
which is remarkable, given its unbeatable location. ②.

San Fantin, Campiello Fenice, S. Marco
1930/a ☎ & fax 041.523.1401; E7. Bland
little two-star hotel, but it's in a prime site,
right next to the opera house. ④.

Accommodation

San Samuele, Piscina S. Samuele, S. Marco 3358 ☎ & fax 041.522.8045; B7. A friendly one-star place close to the Palazzo Grassi, with rooms distinctly less shabby than some at this end of the market, if not exactly plush. ②.

Santo Stefano, Campo Santo Stefano, S. Marco 2957 ☎041.520.0166; fax 041.522.4460; C7. Well-maintained eleven-room three-star hotel on one of the city's largest squares. As is so often the case in Venice, the rooms aren't exactly capacious, but the prices are good for this grade and location. ⑥.

Dorsoduro

The grid references at the end of each address relate to the map on p.100.

Accademia Villa Maravege, Fondamenta Bollani, Dorsoduro 1058 ☎041.521.0578; fax 041.523.9152; *pensioneaccademia@flashnet.it*; F7. Once the Russian embassy, this three-star seventeenth-century villa has a devoted following, not least on account of its garden, which occupies a promontory at the convergence of two canals, with a view of a small section of the Canal Grande. To be sure of a room, get your booking in at least three months ahead. ⑥.

Agli Alboretti, Rio Terrà Foscarini, Dorsoduro 884 ☎041.523.0058; fax 041.521.0158; *www.cash.it//alboretti*; G8. Good two-star very close to the Accademia. Avoid the murky room 19 and you can't go wrong. ⑤.

Alla Salute da Cici, Fondamenta Ca' Balà, Dorsoduro 222/8 ☎041.523.5404; fax 041.522.2271; *www .hotelsalutedacici.com*; I7. This two-star's pleasant canalside locale close to the Salute compensates for the slightly brisk atmosphere. Closed Dec & Jan. ③.

American, Fondamenta Bragadin, Dorsoduro 628 ☎041.520.4733; fax 041.520.4048. *www.hotelamerican.com*; H8. Nicely located and well-refurbished three-star, with some rooms overlooking the Rio di San Vio, a couple of minutes' stroll from the Accademia. Especially good value in winter. ⑥.

Antico Capon, Campo S. Margherita, Dorsoduro 3004/b ☎ & fax 041.528.5292; D5. Seven rooms above a pizzeria-restaurant on an atmospheric square in the heart of the student district. ③.

Ca' Pisani, Rio Terà Foscarini, Dorsoduro 979a ☎041.240.1411; *www.capisanihotel.it*; G8. This very glamorous 29-room four-star, just a few metres from the Accademia, created quite a stir when it opened in 2000, partly because of its location, on the opposite side of the Canal Grande from its top-echelon peers, but chiefly because of its high-class retro look. Taking its cue from the style of the 1930s and '40s, the Ca' Pisani makes heavy use of dark wood and chrome, a refreshing break from the Renaissance and Rococo tones that tend to prevail in Venice's upmarket establishments. Very highly recommended. ⑧.

La Calcina, Zàttere ai Gesuati, Dorsoduro 780 ☎041.520.6466; fax 041.522.7045; *lacalcina@iol.it*; G9. Unpretentious and charismatic three-star hotel in the house where Ruskin wrote much of *The Stones of Venice*. From some of the rooms you can gaze across to the Redentore, a church that gave him apoplexy. ⑤.

Messner, Rio Terrà dei Catacumeni, Dorsoduro 216 ☎041.522.7443; fax 041.522.7266; *messner@doge.it*; I7. Nicely refurbished hotel close to the Salute vaporetto stop. The one-star annexe has doubles without private bathroom for around half the price of the doubles in the smaller and more appealing two-star main building. ④.

Montin, Fondamenta di Borgo, Dorsoduro 1147 ☎041.522.7151; fax 041.520.0255; E8. The Montin is known principally for its upmarket and once-fashionable restaurant; few people realise that it offers some of Venice's best budget accommodation. Only eleven rooms (no singles), three of them without private bathroom. ④.

Pausania, Fondamenta Gherardini, Dorsoduro 3942 ☎041.522.2083; fax 041.522.2989; E7. This quiet, comfortable and friendly three-star offers good value for money, especially in the off-season, when you can pick up a double for under L150,000/€78. Its location is excellent too – very close to San Barnaba church, just five minutes from the Accademia. ⑥.

Seguso, Záttere ai Gesuati, Dorsoduro 779 ☎041.528.6858; fax 041.522.2340; H9. This long-established old-fashioned two-star is always booked months ahead, but its reputation exceeds reality nowadays, as the rooms have become rather dowdy, and the owners usually insist on half-board terms – an overpriced offer you should decline. The location is terrific, but the neighbouring *Calcina* is definitely a better deal. Closed Dec–Feb. ⑥.

San Polo

The grid references at the end of each address relate to the map on p.122.

Al Gallo, Calle del Forno, S. Croce 88 ☎ & fax 041.523.6761; C6. A few basic rooms not far from the Frari; a good bet for cost-cutters. Closed Jan. ③.

Al Sole, Fondamenta Minotto, S. Croce 136 ☎041.523.2144; fax 041.719.061; *www.corihotels.it*; B7. Huge three-star hotel in a gorgeous Gothic palazzo on a tiny canal. A wonderful place to stay. ⑥.

Alex, Rio Terrà Frari, S. Polo 2606 ☎ & fax 041.523.1341; F7. A longstanding budget travellers' favourite, this one-star hotel is decorated in 1960s style, but bearably so. The supermarket in front is useful for picnic preparations. ②.

Basilea, Fondamenta Rio Marin, S. Croce 817 ☎ 041.718.477; fax 041.720.851; D4. Situated on a quiet canal between the train station and the Frari district, this 30-room three-star has been run by the same family for almost half a century, and is one of the most welcoming hotels you'll find in Venice. Rooms in the two-star annexe, which don't have private bathrooms, are about 25 percent cheaper. ⑤.

Ca' Fóscari, Calle della Frescada, Dorsoduro 3888 ☎ & fax 041.522.5817;

valtersc@tin.it; E9. Quiet, well decorated and relaxed one-star, tucked away in a micro-alley near S. Tomà. Just eleven rooms (most without bathroom), so it's quickly booked out. ②.

Falier, Salizzada S. Pantalon, S. Croce 130 ☎041.522.8882; fax 041.520.6554; *falier@tin.it*; C8. Neat, sprucely renovated little two-star, very close to San Rocco and the Frari. ⑤.

Locanda Salieri, Fondamenta Minotto, S. Croce 160 ☎041.710.035; fax 041.721.246; B7. Slightly tatty but exceptionally friendly one-star hotel, on a very picturesque canalside. ②.

Marconi, Riva del Vin, San Polo 729 ☎041.522.2068; *www.hotelmarconi.it*; I7. Converted from an inn in the 1930s, this three-star hotel is situated just a few metres south of the Rialto Bridge, and offers a fine view of the Canal Grande from some of its 26 rooms, all of which in the 1990s were refurbished in a manner that retains the charisma of the old building. Once one of the city's more exclusive establishments, it's now one of its most attractive mid-range hotels. ⑦.

San Cassiano-Ca' Favretto, Calle della Rosa, S. Croce 2232 ☎041.524.1768; fax 041.721.033; *www.sancassiano.it*; H3. Beautiful three-star run by the same management team as the Marconi, with some rooms looking across the Canal Grande towards the Ca' d'Oro. Expensive in summer, but in the quiet months you can get a double for as little as L150,000/€78. ⑦.

Sturion, Calle del Sturion, S. Polo 679 ☎041.523.6243; fax 041.522.8378; *www.locandasturion.com*; I6. This immaculate 11-room three-star has a very long pedigree – the sign of the sturgeon (*sturion*) appears in Carpaccio's *Miracle of the True Cross at the Rialto Bridge* (in the Accademia). It's on a wonderful site a few yards from the Canal Grande, close to the Rialto, and is run by an exceptionally welcoming management. Visitors with mobility difficulties should look elsewhere, however, as the hotel is at the top of three flights of stairs and has no lift. ⑥.

Accommodation

Accommodation

Tivoli, Crosera S. Pantalon, Dorsoduro 3638 ☎041.524.2460; fax 041.522.2656; D8. With 22 rooms, this two-star is the biggest moderately priced hotel in the immediate vicinity of the Frari and S. Rocco, so it often has space when the rest are full. ④.

Cannaregio

The grid references at the end of each address relate to the map on p.148.

Abbazia, Calle Priuli, Cannaregio 66 ☎041.717.333; fax 041.717.949; *www.veneziaalberghi.com*; C7. Walking away from the train station, turn left immediately after the Scalzi church and you'll arrive at Cannaregio's most restful hotel. Occupying a former Franciscan monastery (the monks attached to the Scalzi still live in a building adjoining the hotel), the light-filled Abbazia provides three-star amenities without losing its air of quasi-monastic austerity. ⑥.

Adua, Lista di Spagna, Cannaregio 233/a ☎041.716.184; fax 041.244.0162; D7. Eleven-room, third-floor one-star; recently brightened up by redecoration, it has friendly management and benign prices. Most of the rooms do not have a private bathroom. ②.

Al Gobbo, Campo S. Geremia, Cannaregio 312 ☎041.715.001; D6. Rather more genteel than most of its fellow one-stars on the adjacent Lista di Spagna; the better rooms overlook an attractive small garden. ②.

Bernardi Semenzato, Calle dell'Oca, Cannaregio 4363/6 ☎041.522.7257; fax 041.522.2424; *mtfepoli@tin.it*; I8. The big advantages of this recently upgraded two-star are its prime location (in a tiny alleyway close to Campo S. Apostoli) and its owners, who speak good English and are immensely helpful. ③.

Eden, Rio Terrà della Maddalena, Cannaregio 2357 ☎041.524.4003; fax 041.720.228; *hotel.eden@libero.it*; G6. Very pleasant three-star located in a characterful area about midway between the Rialto bridge and the train station; has just eight rooms, so book ahead. ⑤.

Giorgione, Calle Larga dei Proverbi, Cannaregio 4587 ☎041.522.5810; fax 041.523.9092; *www.hotelgiorgione.it*; I9. Modern, high-class hotel, on a lively square not far from the Rialto bridge. With off-peak doubles from just L230,000/€119, this is the most reasonable four-star in town. ⑥.

Guerrini, Calle delle Procuratie, Cannaregio 265 ☎041.715.333; fax 041.715.114; D7. This two-star is just about as enjoyable a hotel as you can find on the Lista itself. ④.

Hesperia, Calle Riello, Cannaregio 459 ☎041.715.251; fax 041.715.112; *hesperia@shineline.it*; D6. Sixteen-room two-star in a secluded alleyway just beyond the Palazzo Savorgnan, close to the Cannaregio canal. Rooms are small but very homely, and come complete with Murano glass fittings (not the garish variety). ⑤.

Rossi, Calle delle Procuratie, Cannaregio 262 ☎041.715.164; fax 041.717.784; D6. In a quiet back-street off the Lista; rather functional one-star, but as pleasant as you could expect in this price range. ②.

San Geremia, Campo S. Geremia, Cannaregio 290 ☎041.716.245; fax 041.524.2342; D6. This two-star is one to try if you're on your own, as it has a larger than average quotient of single rooms. ③.

Santa Lucia, Calle della Misericordia, Cannaregio 358 ☎ & fax 041.715.180; D7. Clean, moderately sized one-star secreted in a narrow alley off the Lista di Spagna, well away from the hubbub; has a garden, which is something of a rarity in this price range. ③.

Villa Rosa, Calle della Misericordia, Cannaregio 389 ☎041.718.976; fax 041.716.569; *villarosa@ve.nettuno.it*; D7. Close neighbour of the Santa Lucia, this is a similarly recommendable one-star. ③.

Castello

The grid references at the end of each address relate to the map on p.165.

Al Piave da Mario, Ruga Giuffa, Castello 4838 ☎041.528.5174; fax 041.523.8512; *hotelalpiave@iol.it*; G8. This eight-roomed two-star is not the most picturesque of hotels, but it's frequented mainly by Italians, which must mean something. ④.

Bisanzio, Calle della Pietà, Castello 3651 ☎041.520.3100; fax 041.520.4114; *wwwbisanzio.com*; I9. Very quiet and unshowy big three-star hotel, right by Vivaldi's church. Good value for this location. ⑥.

Canada, Campo S. Lio, Castello 5659 ☎041.522.9912; fax 041.523.5852; C7. Pristine two-star, with more single rooms than most. Book well in advance for the double room with a roof terrace. ④.

Caneva, Corte Rubbi, Castello 5515 ☎041.522.8118; fax 041.520.8676; C7. Close to the church of Santa Maria della Fava, on the approach to the busy Campo S. Bartolomeo, yet very peaceful; has a private inner courtyard and overlooks the Rio della Fava. Well-appointed for a one-star, but not the most genial proprietors in town. ③.

Casa Verardo, Calle della Chiesa, Castello 4765 ☎041.528.6127; fax 041.523.2765; G8. One of the best one-stars in Venice (but also the most expensive), this small hotel is just off Campo Santi Filippo e Giacomo, a couple of minutes from San Marco and similarly close to Campo Santa Maria Formosa. Most of the nine rooms have a bath or shower. ③.

Corona, Calle Corona, Castello 4464 ☎ & fax 041.522.9174; G8. Charmless rooms – and you have to climb a lot of stairs to get to them – but the price is a real bargain, and it's run by very friendly people. Only two of the eleven rooms have a private bathroom. ②.

Da Bruno, Salizzada S. Lio, Castello 5726 ☎041.523.0452; fax 041.522.1157; D7. Rooms in this two-star are not the biggest you'll get for the money, but the location – on one of the principal routes to the Rialto – is excellent, and with 32 rooms (most with private bathroom) it often has space. ⑤.

Danieli, Riva degli Schiavoni, Castello 4196 ☎041.522.6480; fax 041.520.0208; *www.sheraton.com*; F10. No longer the most expensive hotel in Venice (the *Cipriani* and the *Bauer* share that title), but no other place can compete with the glamour of the *Danieli*. Balzac stayed here, as did George Sand, Wagner and Dickens. This magnificent Gothic palazzo affords just about the most sybaritic hotel experience on the continent – provided you book a room in the old part of the building, not the modern extension. Most double rooms cost around a million lire (€520), though the best suites come in at fifty percent more. ⑨.

Doni, Fondamenta del Vin, Castello 4656 ☎ & fax 041.522.4267; G9. A cosy one-star, with wooden floors instead of the usual stone. It's near San Zaccaria, and most of the thirteen rooms look over the Rio del Vin or over a courtyard. Only six of the rooms have a private bathroom. ②.

Locanda Leon Bianco, Corte Leon Bianco, Castello 5629 ☎ 041.523.3572; *leonebi@tin.it*; A5. This new three-star has a superb location not far from the Rialto Bridge, tucked away beside the decaying Ca' da Mosto. Only eight rooms, but three of them overlook the Canal Grande and four of the others are spacious and tastefully furnished in eighteenth-century style – one even has a huge fresco in the mode of Giambattista Tiepolo. A gem of a place. ⑤.

Londra Palace, Riva degli Schiavoni, Castello 4171 ☎041.520.0533; fax 041.522.5032; *www.hotelondra.it*; H10. The entrance area creates an aura of grandeur that some of the rooms in this 53-room four-star don't live up to (the ones at the back are dismal, and the uppermost storey is cramped), but the majority of guests get a glorious view for a bill that often won't give you any change from L1,000,000/€516. ⑨.

Malibran, Corte Milion, Cannaregio 5864 ☎041.522.8028; fax 041.523.9243; *www.veneziavision.it/malibran*; C5. Very

Accommodation

Accommodation

comfortable, antiques-furnished three-star in an atmospheric cubby-hole of a square where Marco Polo used to live. ⑥.

Paganelli, Riva degli Schiavoni, Castello 4182 ☎041.522.4324; fax 041.523.9267; hotelpag@tin.it; G10. This two-star is a great place to stay, as long as you get one of the rooms on the lagoon side – the ones in the annexe look onto S. Zaccaria, which is a nice enough view, but not really in the same league. ⑤.

Rio, Campo SS. Filippo e Giacomo, Castello 4356 ☎041.523.4810; fax 041.520.8222; F9. A couple of minutes' walk from the Piazza, so this two-star is something of a bargain in the circumstances. ④.

Scandinavia, Campo S. Maria Formosa, Castello 5240 ☎041.522.3507; fax 041.523.5232; www.scandinaviahotel.com; F7. Sizeable and comfortable three-star hotel on one of the city's most lively and spacious squares. Decorated mainly in eighteenth-century style (ie lots of Murano glass and floral motifs), it has an unusually wide range of rooms, so you might pick up a bargain (off-peak doubles at around L100,000/€51.65) or be told that there's nothing left under L600,000/€310. ⑥.

Silva, Fondamenta del Rimedio, Castello 4423 ☎041.522.7643; fax 041.528.6817; E8. Sizeable one-star overlooking a quiet canal to the north of San Marco. ③.

Wildner, Riva degli Schiavoni, Castello 4161 ☎041.522.7463; fax 041.526.5615; wildner@hotels.it; G10. Modestly attractive little hotel that offers gorgeous views over to San Giorgio Maggiore – which is why it charges more than almost every other two-star in Venice. ⑦.

Eastern districts

The grid references at the end of each address relate to the map on p.188.

Bucintoro, Riva San Biagio, Castello 2135 ☎041.522.3240; fax 041.523.5224; C6.

Almost completely characterless, despite its great age, the two-star Bucintoro nonetheless has one trump card – virtually all 28 of its rooms look out over the water towards San Giorgio Maggiore and the Lido, a view for which you pay an enormous premium at other quayside hotels. ⑤.

Gabrielli Sandwirth, Riva degli Schiavoni, Castello 4110 ☎041.523.1580; fax 041.520.9455; B5. A converted Gothic palace, with a lovely courtyard. *Danieli*-style views across the Bacino di San Marco, for a fraction of the price. Four-star doubles start at L270,000/€139.44 (as against L600,000/€310 at the *Danieli*), with the best rooms costing around L700,000/€361. ⑨.

La Residenza, Campo Bandiera e Moro, Castello 3608 ☎041.528.5315; fax 041.523.8859; B4. Even though the rooms are somewhat bare, this four-teenth-century palazzo is a mid-budget gem (in Venetian terms), occupying much of one side of a tranquil square just off the main waterfront. It was once a tad pricier than the average two-star, but the rest of the pack have raised their tariffs more in recent years, making *La Residenza* a top choice. ⑤.

Sant'Anna, Corte del Bianco, Castello 269 ☎ & fax 041.528.6466; E5. Good for families with children, as it has rooms for three or four people and is fairly near the Giardini Pubblici. Although it's in one of the remotest parts of the city, beyond the far end of Via Garibaldi, this one-star has been discovered in recent years – so book well in advance. ③.

Northern islands

Raspo de Ua, Piazza Galuppi 560, Burano ☎ & fax 041.730.095. The occupants of the other six rooms in this family one-star hotel will probably be the only non-locals you'll see around here, once the daily rush has gone back to the city. Only two of the rooms have a private bathroom, but that's a minor inconvenience, given the atmosphere of the place. ②.

Southern islands

Cipriani, Giudecca 10 ☎041.520.7744; fax 041.520.3930; *www.orient-expresshotels.com*. The priciest and most decadent retreat in Venice – perks include butler service, jacuzzis in every suite, and Olympic-size swimming pool. Though guests can avail themselves of limitless complimentary motorboat rides over to the city, it's not unknown for people to stay within the confines of the *Cipriani* for their entire visit. With prices starting at L950,000/€490 per night and rising to double that, it's not surprising they want to get every lira's worth. ⑨.

Des Bains, Lungomare Marconi 17, Lido ☎041.526.5921; fax 041.526.0113; *www.sheraton.com/DesBains*. Thomas Mann stayed here, rubbing shoulders with the continent's vacationing aristocracy as he crafted *Death in Venice*. Set in its own park, this four-star Art Deco extravaganza has almost 200 rooms (doubles from around L550,000/€284, up to L1,100,000/€568) and, of course, exclusive rights to a slab of the Lido beach. ⑨.

Excelsior, Lungomare Marconi 41, Lido ☎041.526.0201; fax 041.526.7276; *www.luxurycollection.com /excelsiorvenicelido*. Built in the 1900s as the world's top resort hotel, the de luxe five-star *Excelsior* is like something devised by Cecil B. de Mille, and is a favourite with film festival glitterati. Its private beach huts are so well appointed that your average visitor would be perfectly content with one of them as holiday accommodation. From L650,000/ €335 to around L1,250,000/€645. ⑨.

Quattro Fontane, Via delle Quattro Fontane 16, Lido ☎041.526.0227; fax 041.526.0726; *quafonve@tin.it*. By Lido standards, this four-star is quite a humble establishment – the guests have to use public transport to get into the city, for example, rather than being able to summon a flunky in a private boat. But many people for whom L550,000/€284 per night is no problem prefer this quiet, antiques-furnished villa to the more ostentatious competition. ⑧.

Villa Mabapa, Riviera San Nicolò 16, Lido ☎041.526.0590; fax 041.526.9441; *www.villamabapa.com*. Set in its own garden, this sixty-room four-star hotel offers a relatively inexpensive way of sampling the indolent Lido experience. The better rooms (around L450,000/€232) are in the main building, rather than in the modern annexe, the Villa Morea, where you can pick up a room for as little as L200,000/€103. ⑦.

Villa Pannonia, Via Doge Michiel 48, Lido ☎041.526.0162; fax 041.526.5277. This three-star commands the loyalty of numerous Italian families, so book your room months in advance. ⑤.

Accommodation

Self-catering apartments

The very high cost of hotel rooms in Venice makes self-catering an attractive option – for the price of a week in a cramped double-room in a three-star hotel you could book yourself a two-bedroomed apartment right in the centre of the city. Many package holiday companies have a few Venetian apartments in their brochures, and the tourist office in Venice has a couple of landlords on its books, but you'll get a far better selection if you go to a company that specializes in short-let self-catering accommodation. The two listed below are recommended.

Italian Breaks, 16–18 Pampisford Road, Purley, Surrey CR8 2NE ☎020/8660 0082; *www.italianbreaks.com*. This company has a selection of a couple of dozen apartments in Venice, ranging from a two-bed place by the Arsenale (approx. £500–700 per week) to a huge five-bedroomed apartment on the Canale Grande (approx. £1300).

Venetian Apartments, 408 Parkway House, Sheen Lane, London SW14 8LS ☎020/8878 1130; *www.venice -rentals.com*. The leader in the field, Venetian Apartments manages holiday accommodation in Rome, Florence and Siena as well as Venice, but Venice is at the heart of an operation that offers more than seventy apartments in the

Accommodation

city, ranging from studios at around £450 per week through 1- 2- 3- and 4-bedroomed apartments to extraordinarily sumptuous palazzi on the Canal Grande that will set you back around £1000 per day. The properties are immaculately maintained, and the agency provides very friendly back-up in Venice itself. It also has an exemplary Web site, with detailed maps showing the location of each apartment, photographs of virtually every room in each property, ground plans and full rental details.

Hostels and institutions

Venice's hostels, most of which are run by religious foundations, are generally comfortable, well-run and inexpensive by Venetian standards – moreover, even in the high season they might well have a place or two to spare. The tourist office regularly produces a simple typed list of all hostel accommodation in the city; if the places listed below are full up, ask for a copy of it at the train station or San Marco branch.

Domus Civica, Calle Campazzo, S. Polo 3082 ☎041.721.103; map on p.122, D6. A student house in winter, open to travellers July–Oct. A little awkward to find: it's off Calle della Lacca, to the west of San Giovanni Evangelista. Most rooms are double with running water; showers free; no breakfast; 11.30pm curfew. Single L42,000/€21.70, double L70,000/€36.15, with 20 percent reduction for ISIC card holders.

Foresteria Santa Fosca, S. Maria dei Servi, Cannaregio 2372 ☎041.715.775; map on p.148, G5. Student-run hostel in the former Servite convent, with dorm beds and double rooms. Check-in 4–7pm; 11.30pm curfew. Open all year. L30,000/€15.49 for a dorm bed, L40,000/€20.66 in a double.

Foresteria Valdese, S. Maria Formosa, Castello 5170 ☎041.528.6797; map on p.165, G6. Installed in a palazzo at the end of Calle Lunga S. Maria Formosa, with flaking frescoes and a large salon. Run by Waldensians, it's principally a

hostel for grown-ups, with occasional school groups. Three large dorms, and a couple of rooms for two to four people. It also has a couple of self-catering flats for four and five people. Bookings for groups only. Open for registration 9am–1pm and 6–8pm. Open all year. L28,000–L40,000 (€14.50–20.66) per person.

Istituto Ciliota, Calle delle Muneghe, S. Marco 2976 ☎041.520.4888; fax 041.521.2730; map on p.42, C7. Welcoming but expensive mixed hostel-style accommodation, close to Campo S. Stefano. Open mid-June to mid-Sept. Singles with bathroom L85,000/€43.90, without L65,000/€33.57; doubles with bathroom L125,000/€64.56, without bathroom L105,000/€54.22.

Ostello Venezia, Fondamenta delle Zitelle, Giudecca 86 ☎041.523.8211; fax 041.523.5689. The city's HI hostel occupies a superb location looking over to San Marco, but it's run with a certain briskness – notices demand "perfect sobriety and cleanliness". Registration opens at 1.30pm in summer and 4pm in winter. Curfew at 11pm, chucking-out time 9.30am. Gets so busy in July and August that written reservations must be made by April. If it's full, they use a local school with camp-beds as an annexe. Breakfast and sheets included in the price – but remember to add the expense of the boat over to Giudecca (the nearest stop is Zitelle). No kitchen, but full (and excellent) meals for L14,000/€7.23. Luggage can't be left here after you've checked out. L27,000/€14 per bed; HI card necessary, but you can join on the spot for L30,000/€15.49.

Suore Canossiane, Fondamenta del Ponte Piccolo, Giudecca 428 ☎041.522.2157. Women-only hostel near the Palanca vaporetto stop. Open 8am–noon & 2–10pm; no pre-booking. L20,000/€10.33 per night.

Suore Mantellate, Calle Buccari, Castello 10 ☎041.522.0829; fax 041.277 0486; map on p.188; G9. Convent-run hostel in a quiet part of the lagoon, near Sant'Elena vaporetto stop. Rooms of 2–6 beds. Essential to book ahead, as it gets booked up by groups. Closed Aug. L55,000/€28.41 per bed, including breakfast.

Camping

If you're coming from the airport and want to pitch your tent promptly, you could settle for one of the two large sites nearby, which at least have the benefit of frequent bus connections to Piazzale Roma: the one-star *Marco Polo*, Via Triestina 167 (open Feb15–Nov 15; ☎041.541.6033; from L14,000/€7.23 per tent plus L7000/€3.62 per person per night) which is within walking distance of the airport; and the friendlier four-star *Alba d'Oro*, Via Triestina 214/b (open April–Sept; ☎041.541.5102; from L14,000/€7.23 per tent plus L9000/€4.65 per person per night, or L65,000/€33.57 per night for a bungalow that sleeps four) just beyond the airport (take bus #15 to Cánoghera, the fourth stop after the airport). More attractive sites are to be found on the outer edge of the lagoon on the **Litorale del Cavallino**, which stretches from the Punta Sabbioni to Jésolo and has a total of around 60,000 pitches, many of them quite luxuriously appointed. Vaporetto #14, from the Riva degli Schiavoni to the Punta, stops close to the two-star *Miramare*, Lungomare Dante Alighieri 29 (April–Nov; ☎041.966.150;

web.tin.it/camping_miramare; from L7000/€3.10 per tent plus L7000/€3.10 per person per night); a bit further away there's the more luxurious four-star *Marina di Venezia*, Via Montello 6 (April–Sept; ☎041.966.146; *www.cavallino.net/marinave*; from L30,000/€15.70 per tent plus L11,000/€5.68 per person per night). Price can be a problem here – when you've added on the fare for the forty-minute boat trip into the city you're not left with a particularly economical proposition.

Alternatively, back on the mainland there's a site at **Fusina**, Via Moranzani 79 (open all year; ☎041.547.0064); it has 650 places, and charges from L15,000/€7.75 per tent plus L10,000/€5.16 per person. A *LineafusinA* waterbus links Fusina to central Venice (ACTV tickets not valid), taking twenty-five minutes, with an hourly service until around 11pm from late May to the end of September, and till around 8pm in April, most of May and all of October; the rest of the year there's a skeleton two-hourly service that stops around 7pm. Alternatively, you can get a bus to Mestre and change there for the #1 bus or a train.

There are also several sites at **Sottomarina**, the resort attached to Chioggia, at the southern end of the lagoon (see p.242), but getting between there and the centre of Venice involves, at best, a fifty-minute bus journey each way.

Accommodation

Chapter 11

Eating and drinking

Not long ago the reliable judges of the Accademia della Cucina ventured that it was "a rare privilege" to eat well in Venice, and there's more than an element of truth to Venice's reputation as a place where mass tourism has produced homogenized menus and slapdash standards. Venice has fewer good moderately priced **restaurants** than any other major Italian city, it has more really bad restaurants than any other, and in some of the expensive establishments you're paying not for a fine culinary experience but for the event of dining in a posh Venetian restaurant. However, things have been getting better, an improvement due in part to the efforts of the Ristorante della Buona Accoglienza, an association of restaurateurs determined to present the best of genuine Venetian cuisine at sensible prices. In the Venetian context, "sensible" means in the region of L50,000/€25 per person, but even in the lower price ranges there are plenty of acceptable little places hidden away in the city's quieter quarters – and some are rather more than merely acceptable. And of course, **pizza** is a reliable standby if you're watching your budget, though – as with all restaurants in Venice – the general rule is that places within two hundred metres of the Piazza get so much tourist traffic that they don't have much incentive to make an effort.

More than anywhere else in Italy, the division between **bars** and restaurants is often difficult to draw. A distinctive aspect of the Venetian social scene is the *bácaro*, which is essentially a bar but also serves a range of snacks called *cicheti* (some times spelled *ciccheti*); the array will typically include *polpette* (small beef and garlic meatballs), *carciofini* (artichoke hearts), hard-boiled eggs, anchovies, *polipi* (baby octopus or squid), and sun-dried tomatoes, peppers and courgettes cooked in oil. Some *bácari* also produce one or two more substantial dishes each day, such as risotto or seafood pasta. Most bars of this type are long-established places, but in recent years there's been something of a *bácaro* revival, and you're more likely to find a seating area in these newer establishments; in the older ones it's more usual to eat standing up, or seated on stools at a ledge. Virtually all bars will have a selection of plump *tramezzini* (sandwiches) at lunch time.

Many of the places listed below under "Restaurants" have a bar area on the street side of the dining room, while some of the "Bars" serve food at tables that's a touch more ambitious than a plate of sandwiches. We've classified our bars and restaurants according to which aspect of the business draws most of the customers, but if you're looking for a simple meal in a particular area of the city, be sure to check both sets of listings – both are sub-categorized into areas that match the chapters of this guide.

As enticing as the city's bars are its **cafés** and **pasticcerie** (most of which also serve alcohol), where a variety of waistline-threatening delicacies are on offer, and there aren't too many nicer things you can do to your taste buds than hit them with a coneful of **ice cream** from *Paolin* or *Nico*. Stocking up for an alfresco lunch, you'll be spoiled for choice at the stalls of the Rialto and the smaller **markets** pitched in a number of Venice's campi, whilst there's a host of tempting *alimentari* to supplement supplies.

As elsewhere in Italy, take-away **pizza** is all over the place, but most of it is pretty miserable fare in Venice – you'd be better advised to sit down in a pizzeria or have a snack in a bar. The widest range of take-out pizza slices (*pizza al taglio*) and pies is offered by *Cip Ciap*, across the canal from the west side of Santa Maria Formosa, at Calle Mondo Nuovo 5799 (9am–9pm; closed Tues) – their spinach and ricotta pie is especially tasty and filling. Next best choice is the simple take-away place over on the other side of the Canal Grande at Calle della Madonetta 1463, a few metres north of Campo San Polo.

VENETIAN FOOD AND DRINK

Venetian cuisine bears little trace of the city's past as Europe's trading crossroads, when spices from the East were among the most lucrative commodities sold in Venice's markets. Nowadays Venetian food is known for its simplicity, with plain pepper and salt as the principal means of gingering up a meal. **Fish and seafood** dominate the restaurant menus, the former being netted in the Adriatic and the rivers and lakes of the mainland, the latter coming from the lagoon and open sea. Prawns, squid and octopus are typical Venetian *antipasti* (usually served with a plain dressing of olive oil and lemon), as are Murano crabs and *sarde in saor* (marinated sardines). Dishes like eel cooked in Marsala wine, *baccalà* (salt cod) and *seppioline nere* (baby cuttlefish cooked in its own ink) are other Venetian staples, but the quin-

tessential dish is the **risotto**, made with rice grown along the Po valley. Apart from the seafood variety (*risotto bianco, risotto di mare* or *risotto dei pescatori*), you'll come across risottos that incorporate some of the great range of vegetables grown in the Veneto, and others that draw on such diverse ingredients as snails, tripe, quails and sausages.

Venetian **soups** are as versatile as their risottos, with *brodetto* (mixed fish) and *pasta e fasioi* (pasta and beans) being the most popular kinds. **Polenta** is another recurrent feature of Venetian meals; made by slowly stirring maize flour into boiling salted water, it's served as an accompaniment to a number of dishes, in particular liver (*fegato*), a special favourite in Venice.

Pastries and sweets are also an area of Venetian expertise. Look out for the thin oval biscuits called *baicoli*, the ring-shaped cinnamon-flavoured *bussolai* (a speciality of Burano), and *mandolato* – a cross between nougat and toffee, made with almonds. The Austrian occupation has left its mark in the form of the ubiquitous *strudel* and the cream- or jam-filled *krapfen* (doughnuts).

Particular foods are traditional to certain **feast days**. During Carnevale you can buy small doughnuts known as *frittelle*, which come plain, *con frutta* (with fruit), *con crema* (confectioner's cream) or *con zabaglione* (which is made out of egg yolks and Marsala). During Lent there's an even greater emphasis on fish, and also on omelettes (*frittata*), often made with shrimps and wild asparagus; lamb is popular at Easter. On Ascension Day it's customary to have pig's trotter, either plain or stuffed, while for the feast of the Redentore (third Sunday in July) *sarde in saor* or roast duck are in order. Tiny biscuits called *fave* ("beans") fill the *pasticcerie* around All Saints' Day and All Souls' Day (November 1 & 2); on the feast of Saint Martin (November 11) you get biscuits or heavy quince jelly cut into the shape of the saint on his horse; and on the feast of the Madonna della Salute (November 21) it's traditional to have *castradina*

Eating and drinking

Eating and drinking

(salted smoked mutton). On Christmas Eve many Venetians eat eel, usually grilled, though with variations from island to island; on Christmas Day the traditional dishes are roast turkey, veal, duck or capon.

Many of the **wines** of the Veneto will already be familiar, especially **Valpolicella** (red), **Bardolino** (red) and **Soave** (white) – the Veneto produces more DOC (*Denominazione di origine controllata*) wine than any other region, and this trio of Veronese wines comprises the bulk of exported quality Italian wine. Far more rarely exported is **Prosecco**, light, champagne-like wine from the area around Conegliano – don't miss a chance to sample Prosecco Rosé and the delicious **Cartizze**, the finest type of Prosecco. Wines from neighbouring Friuli are well worth exploring too: the most common reds are Pinot Nero, Refosco, Raboso, Merlot and Cabernet, with Tocai, Pinot Bianco and Sauvignon the most common whites. **Grappa** is the local fire-water – associated particularly with the town of Bassano del Grappa, it's made from grapes, juniper berries or plums, and will take your head off if you don't exercise a degree of caution.

Apart from coffee in its manifold varieties, **non-alcoholic drinks** include: *frullati*, a milk shake made with fruit; freshly squeezed fruit juice (*spremuta*), which is usually *d'arancia* (orange), *pompelmo* (grapefruit), *limone* (lemon) or *mele* (apple); and *granita*, which is crushed ice with syrup (often coffee-flavoured).

Restaurants

Virtually every budget restaurant in Venice advertises a set-price **menù turistico**, which at its best will offer a choice of three or four dishes for each course. This can be a cheap way of sampling Venetian specialities, but the quality and certainly the quantity won't be up to the mark of an **à la carte** meal, and frequently won't even be acceptable. As a general rule, value for money tends to increase with the distance from San Marco; plenty of restaurants within a

short radius of the Piazza offer menus that seem to be reasonable, but you'll probably find the food unappetizing, the portions tiny and the service abrupt.

In the following listings, the term "inexpensive" means that you should be able to get a two-course meal with a drink for under L35,000/€17.50, including service and *coperto* (cover charge); "moderate" means L35,000–70,000/€17.50–35; "expensive" means L70,000–100,000/€35–50; and "very expensive" covers the rest. We've supplied the phone numbers for those places where **booking** is advisable in high season. Wherever possible, we've also supplied the day of the week on which each restaurant is closed, but bear in mind that many restaurateurs take their annual holiday in August, and that quite a few places close down on unscheduled days in the dead weeks of winter. You should also be aware that Venetians tend to eat early and that restaurateurs routinely close early if trade is slack, so if you're in town at a quiet time, don't turn up much later than 8.30pm.

San Marco

The grid references at the end of each address relate to the map on p.42.

Al Bacareto, Calle Crosera San Samuele 3447; C6. Dishes such as the excellent *risotto alla pescatore* (fisherman's risotto) can be eaten either in the dining room or standing at the bar area (the cheaper option). Handy for the Palazzo Grassi. Closed Sun. Inexpensive to moderate.

Al Conte Pescaor, Piscina S. Zulian 544 ☎041.522.1483; H3. Fine little fish restaurant that draws its custom mainly from the locals. Closed all Sun & Mon lunchtime. Expensive.

Al Theatro, Campo S. Fantin 1916 ☎041.522.1052; E6. This long-established bar-restaurant used to do a roaring trade before and after the performances at the Fenice but has become far less frenzied since the fire. Has outside tables in summer. Closed Mon. Moderate to expensive.

Acqua Pazza, Campo Sant'Angelo 3808, ☎041.277.0688; D6. Classy new self-styled Mediterranean restaurant, serving good seafood and Neapolitan pizzas in an airy, spacious environment. Moderate to expensive. Closed Mon.

Da Arturo, Calle degli Assassini 3656 ☎041.528.6974; E6. Celebrated as the only top-notch restaurant in Venice that doesn't serve fish. Closed Sun. Expensive.

Da Carla, Sottoportego Corte Contarina 1535a; G7. Tiny bar-trattoria hidden down a sottoportego off the west side of Frezzeria, a few paces from the Piazza. The battered old sign – reading "Pietro Panizollo" – is a fair indication of the character of this place, which at lunctimes is packed with workers dropping in for simple pasta dishes and salads at L10,000/€5.16 a plate. Closed Sun. Inexpensive.

Da Fiore, Calle delle Botteghe 3461; C7. Established in the mid-1990s, this popular restaurant offers genuine Venetian cuisine in a classy trattoria-style setting. The anteroom is a nice small bar that does very good *cicheti*. Open until midnight. Closed Tues. Moderate to expensive.

Da Ivo, Ramo dei Fuseri 1809 ☎041.528.004; F5. As with 95 percent of Venice's restaurants, fish features at Ivo's, but its reputation rests on its *bistecca* and other Tuscan dishes. Closed Sun. Expensive.

Da Raffaele, Fondamenta delle Ostreghe 2347 ☎041.523.2317; E9. Menu varies according to what's in season, so seafood gives way to meat in the autumn (most seafood restaurants just resort to frozen fish out of season). Eat on the terrace rather than in the large Merrie Italie dining room. Closed Thurs. Expensive.

Do Forni, Calle dei Specchieri 468 ☎041.523.2148; I5. Famous Venetian restaurant with two dining rooms – one like an Orient Express cabin, the other in "farmhouse" style. Quality and prices are high in both. Closed Thurs. Very expensive.

Harry's Bar, Calle Vallaresso 1323 ☎041.528.5777; G8. Often described as the most reliable of the city's gourmet restaurants, though there are sceptics who think the place's reputation has more to do with glamour than cuisine – when the Film Festival is on, it's wall-to-wall starlets and paunchy producers. Closed Mon. Very expensive.

La Caravella, Calle Larga XXII Marzo 2396 ☎041.520.8901; F8. One of two restaurants inside the *Saturnia* hotel, the *Caravella* has an ambitious *nouvelle* pan-European menu, rated by many as the best food in the city. Closed Wed. Very expensive.

Le Bistrot de Venise, Calle dei Fabbri 4685; G5. This place is done up as a facsimile of a wood-panelled French bistrot, but the menu is based on old-style Venetian recipes, both for full meals and *cicheti*. The food is generally OK, but the atmosphere is the main attraction, as *Le Bistrot* has become something of a community arts centre: from September to June there's music on Tuesday nights, cabaret on Mondays and poetry on Fridays, and the management also co-sponsors an annual art competition, with the shortlisted artists being displayed here. The bar opens daily at 9am, the kitchen at noon, and food is served until 15min before closing, at 1am. Inexpensive to moderate.

Rosticceria Gislon, Calle della Bissa 5423; H2. Downstairs it's a sort of glorified snack-bar, serving pizzas and set meals starting at around L15,000/€7.50 – the trick is to first grab a place at the long tables along the windows, then order from the counter. Good if you need to refuel quickly and cheaply, but can't face another pizza. There's a less rudimentary restaurant upstairs, where prices are a bit higher for no real increase in quality. Closed Mon. Inexpensive.

Dorsoduro

The grid references relate to the map on p.100.

Ai Carmini, Calle delle Pazienze 2894; D6. A menu at L20,000/€10.35 attracts tourists rather than locals but for once

Eating and drinking

Eating and drinking

the deal is good value, and the friendly service makes up for a lack of ambience. Just off the west end of Campo S. Margherita. Closed Sun. Inexpensive to moderate.

Ai Cugnai, Piscina del Forner 857; G8. A few yards to the east of the Accademia, but remarkably unspoilt considering how close it is to one of the city's biggest tourist draws, this is a very popular and very welcoming little trattoria, run by a family of gregarious Venetian senior citizens. Orders are memorized rather than written down, and can become scrambled between table and kitchen, but that's part of the fun. Supposed to close at 9pm, but keeps going if the mood takes them. This used to be Alberto Moravia's local when he was living in the Salute district. Closed Mon. Moderate.

Ai Quattro Ferri, Calle Lunga S. Barnaba; E7. Basic, easy-going osteria with delicious *cicheti* and a menu that changes daily. Just off Campo S. Barnaba. Closed Sun. Inexpensive.

Alle Burchielle, Fondamenta Burchielle; B4. Well-known trattoria facing the southern corner of Piazzale Roma across the canal, and relatively unspoilt for the location. Just ask for the day's special. Closed Mon. Moderate.

Alle Záttere, Fondamenta Záttere ai Gesuati 794; G9. This place does trattoria basics, but go for the pizzas – *Primavera*, with vegetables, is recommended. Closed Tues. Inexpensive to moderate.

Al Profeta, Calle Lunga S. Barnaba 2671; E7. Popular pizzeria and trattoria with a garden at the back. Closed Wed. Moderate.

Anzolo Raffael, Campo Angelo Raffaele 1722; C8. Unpretentious parish restaurant tucked in a corner of the *sestiere* where few tourists venture. First-class fish dishes. Closed Tues. Inexpensive to moderate.

Da Gianni, Fondamenta Záttere 918a; G9. Nicely sited restaurant-pizzeria, right by the Záttere vaporetto stop and slightly better than the nearby *Alle Záttere*. Closed Wed. Inexpensive to moderate.

Da Sandro, Calle Lunga S. Barnaba 2753a; E7. Traditional osteria with a short but well-chosen menu of Venetian specialities. Tiny dining room and garden tucked away behind an *enoteca* that has a brief but discerning wine list. Closed Sun & Mon. Moderate.

La Furatola, Calle Lunga S. Barnaba 2870a ☎041.520.8594; E7. Classy seafood restaurant, popular with the local philosophy faculty. Small, so booking is advisable. Closed Thurs. Expensive.

Montin, Fondamenta di Borgo 1147 ☎041.522.7151; E8. Still very highly rated by some people, but the quality is far more erratic than you'd expect for the money; you'll pay in the region of L60,000/€30 here for what would cost L40,000/€20 in some places. It's always been a place for the literary/artistic set – Pound, Hemingway, Peggy Guggenheim and Visconti, for example – and the restaurant doubles as a commercial art gallery. Closed Tues & Wed. Expensive.

San Trovaso, Fondamenta Priuli 1016; F7. An efficient two-storey restaurant-pizzeria which is packed most nights with a mix of tourists and locals. Straightforward food in robust portions. Closed Mon. Inexpensive to moderate.

San Polo

The grid references at the end of each address relate to the map on p.122.

Ae Oche, Calle del Tentor 1459; F4. Excellent pizzeria on an alley that leads into the south side of Campo S. Giacomo dell'Orio. Has about fifty varieties to choose from, so if this doesn't do you, nothing will; on summer evenings if you're not there by 8pm you may have to queue on the pavement. Open daily noon–3pm & 7pm–midnight (1am Fri & Sat). Inexpensive.

All'Anfora, Lista Vecchia dei Bari; D3. An unpretentious local restaurant that's open for breakfast coffee and still going late at night. Has a pizza list, but the trattoria food is not expensive: the seafood risotto is good, as is the *spaghetti del doge*. Closed Fri. Moderate.

Alla Madonna, Calle della Madonna 594 ☎041.522.3824; I6. Roomy, bustling seafood restaurant that's been going strong for four decades. Little finesse but good value for money, and many locals rate its kitchen as one of the city's best, though it has to be said that standards are far from consistent. Closed Wed. Moderate.

Al Nono Risorto, Sottoportego de Siora Bettina 2338; H4. Busy pizzeria-restaurant just off Campo S. Cassiano; has a pleasant garden, and a predominantly twenty-something following. Often has live jazz and blues. Open noon–2pm & 7pm–midnight; closed Wed. Inexpensive to moderate.

Arca, Calle S. Pantalon 3760; D8. This pizzeria-trattoria is one of the favourites with the university students. Superb pizzas and a good range of *cicheti*. Closed Sun. Inexpensive to moderate.

Da Crecola, Campiello del Piovan; E4. Nudging the church of San Giacomo dell'Orio, this little place is high on atmosphere, and serves good pizzas and basic trattoria fare. Closed Wed. Moderate.

Da Fiore, Calle del Scaleter 2202a ☎041.731.308; F5. Small restaurant off Campo San Polo; prides itself on its seafood, regional cheeses, desserts and homemade bread. Definitely well above average – indeed, some rank it among the very best in Venice. Has a bar in the front room. Closed Sun & Mon. Expensive.

Da Ignazio, Calle Saoneri 2749 ☎041.523.4852; F7. Situated between the Frari and San Polo, this place has a good name as a genuine Venetian trattoria – it does a small range of dishes, and does them well, at reasonable cost. Foreigners might find, however, that the staff have an attitude that crosses the line between insouciance and superciliousness. Closed Sat. Moderate.

Da Sandro, Campiello dei Meloni; H6. Split-site pizzeria-trattoria, with rooms on both sides of the campiello and tables on the pavement. Often frenetic, though not aggressively so. The pizzas are the best thing they do. Open until 12.30am. Closed Fri. Inexpensive to moderate.

Da Silvio, Calle S. Pantalon 3748; D8. Sizeable pizzeria-trattoria, with a reputation for its *tortellini*. Has a nice courtyard for open-air dining. Sometimes too busy for the staff to manage comfortably (and they aren't the city's greatest charmers at the best of times), but the buzzing atmosphere makes a pleasant break from the staidness of many Venetian restaurants. Closed Sun. Inexpensive to moderate.

Dona Onesta, Calle della Madonna Onesta 3922; E8. Once a simple little seafood trattoria, the *Dona Onesta* is going increasingly for the tourist market, with a corresponding drop in quality and rise in prices. Still better than many, though. Closed Sun. Moderate.

Do Spade, Sottoportego delle Do Spade 860; I5. This was once the city's nearest rival to the nearby *Do Mori* bar, but it now emphasizes its food rather than its drink, and it stays open rather later in order to catch a tourist clientele. Something of its old character remains, but not much. Almost impossible to locate from a map – walk past the *Do Mori* and keep going as straight as possible. Open Sept–June 9am–2pm & 5–11pm; closes 8pm July & Aug; closed Thurs afternoon & all Sun.

Jazz Club 900, Campiello del Sansoni 900; H5. Just off Ruga Vecchia S. Giovanni, by the Rialto Bridge, *Novecento* serves some of the best pizzas in the city, accompanied by non-stop jazz (live on Thursdays only). Open till midnight. Closed Mon.

La Zucca, Ponte del Megio 1762 ☎041.524.1570; F3. Long a well-respected restaurant, *La Zucca* was once a vegetarian establishment (its name means "pumpkin") but now goes against

Eating and drinking

Eating and drinking

the Venetian grain by featuring a lot of meat – chicken, lamb, goose, turkey. The quality remains high, and the canalside setting is nice, though the service is not always as pleasant as it might be. Mon–Sat 12.30–2.30pm & 7–10.30pm. Moderate.

Osteria al Pantalon, Sottoportego San Rocco 3958; D8. Located on an alley-way connecting Crosera to Campo S. Rocco, this is a good-value eatery that attracts a lot of custom from the university. Inexpensive to moderate. Closed Sun.

Osteria al Ponte, "La Patatina", 2741a Calle dei Saoneri; F7. Bustling osteria, serving excellent *cicheti* and other Ventian specialities, with set menus that change regularly. Closed Sun. Inexpensive to moderate.

Poste Vecie, Pescheria 1608 ☎041.721.822; I4. As you'd expect by the location next to the fish market, this excellent restaurant – run by the owners of the *Regina* – is another place for connoisseurs of maritime dishes. Closed Tues evening & all Wed. Expensive.

San Tomà, Campo S. Tomà 2864; E8. Much of the menu is slightly overpriced, but the pizzas are good, and so is the *paëlla*, the unusual house speciality; with tables on the campo and under a pergola out the back, this is one of the best places to regather your strength after a session at San Rocco and the Frari. Closed Tues. Inexpensive.

Cannaregio

The grid references relate to the map on p.148.

Ai Promessi Sposi, Calle dell'Oca 4367; I8. Bar-trattoria specializing in *baccalà* and other basic traditional fish recipes. Excellent range of *cicheti* at the bar. Closed Wed. Inexpensive to moderate.

Al Bacco, Fondamenta delle Cappuccine 3054 ☎041.717.493; F4. Like the *Antica Mola*, further east along the canal, *Al Bacco* started life as a humble neighbourhood stop-off, but has grown

into a fully fledged restaurant, with prices to match. It retains a rough-and-ready feel, but the food is distinctly classy. Closed Mon. Moderate.

Alla Palazzina, Rio Terrà San Leonardo 1509; E6. Cosy, romantic setting by one of the city's best-looking bridges, the Ponte delle Guglie, which spans the Cannaregio canal. Venetian cuisine as good as you'll find anywhere near the station, and excellent pizzas too. Has a garden overlooking the canal. Closed Wed & Mon–Thurs lunchtime. Moderate.

Anice Stellato, Fondamenta della Sensa 3272 ☎041.720.744; F4. Hugely popular with Venetians for the superb, reason-ably priced meals and unfussy atmos-phere. Situated by one of the northern-most Cannaregio canals, it's rather too remote for most tourists. If you can't get a table – it's frequently booked solid – at least drop by for the excellent *cicheti* at the bar. Closed Mon.

Antica Mola, Fondamenta degli Ormesini 2800; F4. This family-run trattoria, near the Ghetto, is very popular (nowadays mainly with tourists), but the food is good value, and there's a nice garden at the back. Closed Wed. Inexpensive to moderate.

Casa Mia, Calle dell'Oca 4430; I8. Always heaving with locals, who usually go for the pizza list rather than the menu, though the standard dishes are reliable enough. Closed Tues. Inexpensive.

Ca' d'Oro alla Vedova, Calle del Pistor 3912; I8. Located in an alley directly opposite the one leading to the Ca' d'Oro, this long-established little restau-rant is fronted by a bar offering a mouth-watering selection of *cicheti* (the *polpette* are famous) and a good range of wines. Closed Thurs & Sun lunch. Inexpensive to moderate.

Gam-Gam, Fondamenta di Cannaregio 122; E5. Refreshing change from every-thing *a la Venexiana*, with an intriguing menu of Israeli and Venetian cuisine – all kosher. The *cholent* (chick pea stew) and *latkas* (potato balls) are particularly good. Excellent for vegetarians. Closed Fri evening and Sat lunch. Inexpensive to moderate.

Vini da Gigio, Fondamenta S. Felice 3628a; H7. Family-run wine bar-trattoria. Until a couple of years ago most of the customers were locals; it's now on the tourist map yet it retains its authenticity and is still, by Venetian standards, excellent value. Closed Mon. Moderate.

Castello

The grid references relate to the map on p.165.

Aciugheta, Campo SS. Filippo e Giacomo 4357; F9. A bar with a sizeable pizzeria-trattoria attached. The closest spot to San Marco to eat without paying through the nose. Good bar food to nibble or have as a meal. The name translates as "the little anchovy" and there are portraits of anchovies on the wall. Closed Wed. Inexpensive to moderate.

Alla Conchiglia, Fondamenta S. Lorenzo 4990; H8. The food at this pizzeria-trattoria is nothing out of the ordinary, but the canalside tables give you a great view of the precarious campanile of San Giorgio dei Greci. Stick to the pizza. Closed Wed. Moderate.

Alla Rivetta, Ponte S. Provolo 4625; F9. For a fish dinner close to the Piazza, you won't find many places to beat this one, near Campo SS. Filippo e Giacomo. Very friendly as well: the management has been known to dispense free prosecco to people queueing for a table. Closed Mon. Inexpensive to moderate.

Alle Testiere, Calle Mondo Nuovo 5801 ☎041.522.7220; E7. Very small seafood restaurant in the alley on the other side of the canal from the front of Santa Maria Formosa, with excellent daily specials. Closed Sun. Moderate to expensive.

Al Mascaron, Calle Lunga S. Maria Formosa 5225 ☎041.522.5995; F7. Restaurant with an arty feel and interesting *cicheti* at the bar, but definitely two types of clientele – Italians and non-

Italians – with service to match. Has a good reputation among the locals, though, and gets very busy, so book if you can. Closed Sun. Moderate.

Al Milion, Corte del Milion 5841; C5. Trattoria with bar that serves snacks. Vine-covered outside seating area in a small courtyard. Wide selection of Veneto wines. Closed Wed. Moderate.

Da Remigio, Salizzada dei Greci 3416 ☎041.523.0089; I8. Brilliant trattoria, serving gorgeous homemade *gnocchi*. Be sure to book – the locals pack this place every night, and it's gathering a wider reputation. Closed Mon evening & all Tues. Moderate to expensive.

Fiaschetteria Toscana, Salizzada S. Giovanni Crisostomo 5719 ☎041.528.5281; B5. The name means "Tuscan Wine Shop", but the menu is quintessentially Venetian. Highly rated for its food, the *fiaschetteria* also has an excellent wine list. Closed Mon lunch, Tues, a few days after Carnevale and mid July–mid Aug. Expensive.

Eastern districts

The grid references at the end of each address relate to the map on p.188.

Al Covo, Campiello della Pescaria ☎041.533.3812; B5. Located in a backwater to the east of Campo Bandiera e Moro, the innovative *Covo* opened in the mid-1980s, and its stock has been rising steadily since. Closed Tues & Wed. Moderate.

Al Falco d'Oro, Via Garibaldi 1252 ☎041.523.1179; D6. No frills, slightly shabby decor, but genuine home cooking at this small trattoria, which perfectly encapsulates the atmosphere of this robust quarter of the city. Closed Thurs. Moderate.

Corte Sconta, Calle del Pestrin 3886 ☎041.522.7024; B5. Secreted in a lane to the east of San Giovanni in Brágora, on the route to San Martino, this restaurant is a candidate for the title of Venice's finest. The *menù degustazione*, costing L90,000/€46 (without wine), gives you a chance to sample all their

Eating and drinking

Eating and drinking

specialities in one gourmet experience, and is probably the best meal that sum will get you in the entire city. However, the exceptionally pleasant staff tend to make it difficult to resist ordering the day's specials, which will result in a bill not far short of double that price. If expenditure is an issue, check the menu in the window carefully before going in (often the waiters will simply recite what's on offer rather than give you anything printed); but if one restaurant in Venice justifies a no-holds-barred night out, this is it. Booking essential for most of the year. Closed Sun & Mon. Expensive to very expensive.

Da Franz, Fondamenta S. Isepo 754 ☎041.522.7505; E7. Lurking in an extremely unfashionable area to the north of the Giardini Pubblici, this is one of the choicest seafood kitchens in the city. Closed Mon. Expensive.

Dai Tosi, Calle Secco Marina 738 ☎041.523.7102; E7. Terrific pizzeria-trattoria, with excellent homemade pasta as well as delicious pizzas. There's a bar in front of the small dining room, where they mix the house aperitif, a delicious mingling of vodka, peach juice and prosecco. A really buzzing and gritty place, with a devoted local clientele – you'd be well advised to book at the weekend. Open 9.30am–11.30pm; closed Wed (and sometimes closed Mon, Tues and/or Thurs in winter). Inexpensive to moderate.

Osteria Sant'Elena, Calle Chinotto 24; F9. Known to the locals as *Dal Pampo*, in honour of the boss, this utterly genuine nieghbourhood restaurant is the preserve of the residents of Sant'Elena except when the Biennale is in full swing. The menu is simple, the cooking good. There's a bar serving *cicheti* at the front; outside tables add to the appeal. The quickest way there is to follow the path that leads straight ahead from the bridge after the Biennale grounds – this takes you across the Parco delle Rimembranze to Calle Chinotto. Open till midnight; closed Thurs. Inexpensive to moderate.

Northern islands

Ai Pescatori, Via Galuppi 373, Burano ☎041.730.650. One of the top choices on Burano. Risotto and other fish dishes predominate. Closed Wed. Moderate.

Al Gatto Nero, Fondamenta Giudecca 88, Burano. Plain local trattoria, just a few minutes' walk from the busy Via Galuppi, opposite the Pescheria. Tends to be a favourite with tour groups. Closed Mon. Inexpensive to moderate.

Antica Trattoria Muranese, Riva Longa Cavour 20, Murano ☎041.739.610. If you fancy a meal on Murano but the *Busa alla Torre* is closed or too busy, this is the place to go for. Closed Sat. Moderate.

Busa alla Torre, Campo S. Stefano 3, Murano ☎041.739.662. In the opinion of many, this place serves the best fish on Murano. Closed Mon. Moderate to expensive.

Dal Baffo, Via Galuppi 359, Burano. A good choice for a simple, inexpensive *fritto misto* – if there's room at one of the four tables. Closed Wed.

Da Romano, Via Galuppi 221, Burano ☎041.730.030. Huge old Burano restaurant with no lack of local devotees. Like the *Gatto Nero* it's popular with groups, but usually a few tables are kept free for smaller parties. Closed Tues. Moderate.

Locanda Cipriani, Torcello ☎041.730.757. Desperately modish and desperately overpriced offspring of *Harry's Bar*, though some may think the money well spent for the Torcello setting alone. Closed Tues. Expensive.

Southern islands

Altanella, Calle delle Erbe 270, Giudecca ☎041.522.7780. Run by the same family for three generations, this restaurant is highly recommended for its fish dishes, welcoming staff and the terrace overlooking the island's central canal. No credit cards. Closed Mon & Tues. Moderate.

Bella Venezia, Calle Corona 51, Chioggia ☎ 041.400.500. A lot of people think that Chioggia's market sells better quality fish and seafood than Venice's, and this is one of the best places to check out the truth of the claim. Closed Thurs. Moderate.

Do Mori, Fondamenta Sant'Eufemia 588, Giudecca ☎ 041.522.5452. Run by the former chef at Harry's Bar. Serves humble pizzas as well as classier fare, and everything is more democratically priced than at any of the other establishments bearing the "Harry" tag. Closed Sun. Moderate to expensive.

El Gato, Corso del Popolo 653, Chioggia ☎ 041.401.806. Another fine Chioggia fish restaurant, and less crowded than the Bella Venezia. Closed Mon. Moderate.

Harry's Dolci, Fondamenta S. Biagio 773, Giudecca ☎ 041.522.4844. Despite the name, sweets aren't the only things on offer here – the kitchen of this off-shoot of Harry's Bar is rated by many as the equal of its ancestor. It's less expensive than Harry's Bar, but you're nonetheless talking about a place where the cheapest set menu will cost you around L100,000/€50 a head, drink excluded. Still, if you want to experience Venetian culinary refinement at its most exquisite, this is it. Closed Tues. Very expensive.

Bars and snacks

One of the most appealing aspects of Venetian social life is encapsulated in the phrase "andemo a ombra", which translates literally as an invitation to go into the shade, but is in fact an invitation for a drink – more specifically, a small glass of wine (an *ombra*), customarily downed in one. (The phrase is a vestige of the time when wines were unloaded on the Riva degli Schiavoni and then sold at a shaded kiosk at the base of the Campanile; the kiosk was shifted as the sun moved round, so as to stay in the shade.) Stand at a bar any time of the day and you won't

have to wait long before a customer drops by for a reviving mouthful. Occasionally you'll come across a group doing a *giro de ombre*, the highly refined Venetian version of the pub-crawl; on a serious *giro* it's almost obligatory to stop at an *enoteca* – a bar where priority is given to the range and quality of the wines (for example, Al Volto).

Most bars serve some kind of **food**, their counters usually bearing trays of the characteristically Venetian fat little crustless sandwiches called *tramezzini*. Stuffed with delicious fillings – eggs and mushrooms, eggs and anchovies, Parma ham and artichokes – they cost from L1500/€0.75 up to about L3000/€1.50. Some bars will have a selection of *cicheti* as well, and even a choice of one or two more substantial dishes each day.

San Marco
The grid references at the end of each address relate to the map on p.42.

Alle Botte, Calle della Bissa 5482; H2. Well-hidden little *ôsteria*, just off Campo San Bartolomeo, offering an excellent spread of *cicheti*. Calle della Bissa is one of the most confusing alleyways in Venice – to find All Botte, take either of the alleys labelled Calle della Bissa (on the east side of the campo), turn first left and go as straight as you can. Closed Wed evening and all Thurs.

Al Volto, Calle Cavalli 4081; E4. This dark little bar is an *enoteca* in the true sense of the word – 1300 wines from Italy and elsewhere, some cheap, many not; good snacks, too. Closed Sun.

Bácaro Jazz, Salizzada Fondaco Dei Tedeschi, G1. A jazz-themed bar that's proving a big hit with cool Venetian kids, despite the indifferent quality of its food. Open 4pm–2am; closed Wed.

Devil's Forest, Calle Stagneri; H2. The liveliest bar in the vicinity of Campo San Bartolomeo, and a convincing facsimile

Eating and drinking

Eating and drinking

of a British pub, with a good range of beers and a dartboard – though the food is a lot better than you'd find in most real pubs. Open Mon–Sat 8am–1am.

Harry's Bar, Calle Vallaresso 1323; G8. Most glamorous bar in town since time immemorial; famed in equal measure for its cocktails, its sandwiches and its celebrity league prices. Open 3pm–1am; closed Mon.

Leon Bianco, Salizzada San Luca 4153; F4. Wood-panelled bar between Campo San Luca and Campo Manin. Good range of sandwiches, and a decent selection of more substantial fare, for consumption at the tables in the back room. Mon–Sat 8am–8pm.

Osteria alle Botteghe, Calle delle Botteghe 3454; C7. Sumptuous sandwiches and snacks; most lunchtimes you need a shoehorn to get in the place. Closed Sun.

Osteria Terrà Assassini, Rio Terrà degli Assassini; E6. Very good range of wines and small selection of choice snacks and small meals. Closed Mon.

Vino Vino, Ponte delle Veste 2007; F7. Very close to the Fenice opera house, this wine bar stocks more than 100 wines. It also serves relatively inexpensive meals as well, but the food isn't great. Open 10am–midnight; closed Tues.

Dorsoduro

The grid references relate to the map on p.100.

Ai do Draghi, Campo S. Margherita 3665; D5. Tiny, friendly café-bar with a good range of wines. The tiny back room exhibits the work of local photographers. Open 8am–11pm.

Il Caffè, Campo S. Margherita 2963; D5. Known as *Caffè Rosso* for its big red sign, this inviting, old-fashioned café-bar is one of the student favourites, with chairs out on the square and great music. Open till 1am. Closed Sun.

Cantina del Vino già Schiavi, Fondamenta Nani 992; F8. Great bar and wine shop opposite San Trovaso – do some sampling before you buy. Open till 8.30pm. Closed Sun.

Late-night drinking

The following places all stay open after 11pm, and most keep going until midnight at least. Except where indicated otherwise, you'll find them reviewed in the "Bars" listings. In addition to these, you'll always find one of the cafés on the Piazza open late, but bear in mind that prices at *Florian*, *Quadri* and their kin are around four or five times higher than the Venetian average.

Ai Postali, San Polo.

Cafè Noir, San Polo.

Cantina Vecia Carbonera, Cannaregio.

Ciak 1, San Polo.

Corner Pub, Dorsoduro.

Da Codroma, Dorsoduro.

Da Fiore, San Marco (see "Restaurants").

Devil's Forest, San Marco.

Enoteca Mascareta, Castello.

Green Pub, Dorsoduro.

Harry's Bar, San Marco.

Fiddler's Elbow, Cannaregio.

Il Caffè, Dorsoduro.

Il Doge, Dorsoduro (see "Cafés, pasticcerie and gelaterie").

Le Bistrot de Venise, San Marco (see "Restaurants").

Le Notti d'Oriente, Cannaregio.

Leon d'Oro, Cannaregio.

L'Olandese Volante, Castello.

Margaret Du Champ, Dorsoduro.

Osteria da Baco, Castello.

Paradiso Perduto, Cannaregio.

Vino Vino, San Marco.

Vivaldi, San Polo.

Corner Pub, Calle della Chiesa 684; H8. Very close to the Guggenheim, this place usually has a few arty foreigners in attendance, but they are always outnumbered by the locals. Open till 12.30am, and often later. Closed Mon.

Da Codroma, Fondamenta Briati 2540; C7. The kind of place where you could sit for an hour or two with a beer and a book and feel comfortable. Popular with students from the nearby University of Archiecture, it shows work by local artists, and is a venue for poetry readings and live music on Tuesday nights. Open till 1am or later, depending on demand. Closed Sat.

Green Pub, Campo S. Margherita 3053a; D6. Despite the name, this is a Venetian bar much like any other, except that it stays open till around 1am if there are customers. Seating on the campo is another plus. Closed Thurs.

Margaret Du Champ, Campo S. Margherita 3019; D6. Much the classiest of the campo's late bars, with a showy ambience and less overwhelmingly student-oriented. Open till 2am. Closed Wed.

San Polo

The grid references at the end of each address relate to the map on p.122.

Ai Postali, Fondamenta Rio Marin 821; D4. You can eat crêpes and various other light meals here, but the wine and the ambience are what draws the customers to this backwater bar. Open 10am–2pm & 6pm–2am; closed Tuesday.

All'Arco, Calle del'Ochialer 436; I5. Good no-nonsense Rialto bar, tucked under the end of a sottoportego just a few metres from *Do Mori* (see below). Closed Wed.

Antico Dolo, Ruga Vecchia S. Giovanni 778; I5. Excellent *osteria*-style establishment, a good source of wine and snacks near the Rialto. Closed Sun.

Café Noir, Crosera San Pantalon 3805; D8. A candidate for the title of absolute

favourite student bar, with a trendy all-day crowd chatting over *spritz* or dabbling on the Internet in the small room at the back. Open Mon–Sat 7am–2am, Sun 9am–2am.

Ciak 1, Campiello S. Tomà, F8. Glossy, brightly lit, predominantly young bar, on the north side of San Tomà church. Open until 12.30am. Closed Sun night.

Do Mori, Calle Do Mori 429; I5. Hidden just off Ruga Vecchia S. Giovanni, this is the most authentic old-style Venetian bar in the market area – some would say in the entire city. It's a single narrow room, with no seating, packed every evening with home-bound shopworkers, Rialto porters, and locals just out for a stroll. Delicious snacks, great range of wines, terrific atmosphere. Open 9am–1pm & 5–9pm; closed Wed afternoon & all Sun.

Ruga Rialto, Ruga Vecchia S. Giovanni 692; I6. Spartan bar near Rialto, popular with young Venetians and students. Good *cicheti* at the bar, and fuller meals are served in the back rooms. Closed Mon.

San Stin, Campo San Stin 2532; E6. This nice little *paninoteca* is the place to go if you want a quick sandwich and a glass of wine after doing the Frari or San Rocco. It has a few tables on the campo. Mon–Sat 6.30am–8pm.

Vivaldi, Calle della Madonetta 1457; G7. Busy parish bar just to the north of Campo San Polo; far more authentic than you'd think from the name and decor, it serves excellent snacks in the front part, and inexpensive full meals at the tables in the back. Mon–Sat 10am–3pm & 6pm–midnight.

Cannaregio

The grid references relate to the map on p.148.

Alla Maddalena, Rio Terrà della Maddalena 2348; G6. This bar-trattoria has good sandwiches and basic pasta dishes, though the food tends to run out some way in advance of the 9pm closing time. Closed Sun.

Eating and drinking

Eating and drinking

Cantina Vecia Carbonera, Rio Terrà della Maddalena 2329; G6. Old-style *bácaro* atmosphere attracts a young, stylish clientele. Good wine and plenty of space to sit down. Live jazz on Thurs and Sun. Tues–Thurs 5pm–1.30am, Fri–Sun 10am–2.30pm & 5pm–1.30am.

Fiddler's Elbow, Corte dei Pali 3847; H8. Self-styled "Irish pub"; usually has a few Venetian lads trying to act rowdily, and a smattering of Brits showing them how it's really done, but most of the kids are content with sipping a small glass of Guinness for an hour. Open 5pm–12.30am.

Iguana, Fondamenta della Misericordia 2517; H5. A somewhat uncomfortable cross between a *bácaro* and a Mexican cantina, this bar serves reasonably priced Tex-Mex fare to a young crowd. Live Latin and jazz Tues. Open till 1am; happy hour 6–7.30pm. Closed Mon.

La Cantina, Strada Nuova 3689; H8. Handily placed *enoteca* with a good range of wines. Watch out for their ingenious corkscrews – the owner's design (and for sale). Closed Sun.

Le Notti d'Oriente, Fondamenta delle Misericordia 2578; G5. Serves Middle Eastern food, should the Venetian diet pall, but recommended mostly for its late bar and trendy World music – live performances sometimes include a belly dance on Fridays. Closed Tues.

Leon d'Oro, Rio Terrà della Maddalena 2343; G6. A pleasant family-run place, a couple of doors down from *Alla Maddalena*. Excellent thick hot chocolate; good range of sandwiches, with *osteria* food at the back. Open until 12.30am. Closed Fri.

Osteria ai Ormesini da Aldo, Fondamenta degli Ormesini 2710; F4. One of a number of bars beside this long canal, and a particularly pleasant spot for a lunchtime snack in the sun. Closed Sun.

Osteria alla Fontana, Fondamenta di Cannaregio 1102; C4. Small local bar with an impressive kitchen. One, inexpensive, main dish which changes daily. Tends to shut early. Closed Sun afternoon & all Mon.

Paradiso Perduto, Fondamenta della Misericordia 2540; G5. Lashings of simple (but not always inexpensive) Venetian food are served at the refectory-like tables of *Paradiso Perduto*, but essentially this place is Venice's leading boho bar, attracting students, arty types and the gay community. The bar opens around 7.30pm, the kitchen gets going at 8pm, and the doors close at midnight or later, depending on how things are going. Bar prices are higher when live music is playing – usually Sun. Closed Wed.

Castello

The grid references relate to the map on p.165.

Ai Miracoli, Campiello Miracoli 6075; D5. Somewhat eccentric "classical music lovers' club", though it's not necessary to join for the first few visits. Loud operatic and symphonic selections in a posh drawing room, with locals and tourists playing chess and chatting over drinks. Closed Sun.

Al Ponte, Calle Larga G. Gallina 6378; F5. Typical *osteria* just off Campo Santi Giovanni e Paolo. Good for a glass of wine and a snack. Open till 8.30pm. Closed Sun.

Al Vecio Penasa, Calle delle Rasse 4587; F10. Possibly the best bar to sit down for a reviving measure after a tour of the Piazza – it's a few minutes' stroll from the Palazzo Ducale, off the Riva degli Schiavoni. Excellent sandwiches and friendly staff. Closed Wed.

Enoteca Mascareta, Calle Lunga Santa Maria Formosa 5183; F7. Popular wine bar that serves snacks but nothing grander. Open 6pm–1am. Closed Sun.

Inishark, Calle del Mondo Novo, 5787; E7. Yet another "Irish pub" with the requisite beers and whiskies, and the odd whiff of a more Venetian style. Open till 2am. Closed Mon.

L'Olandese Volante, Campo San Lio; C7. Busy brasserie-style pub with plenty of outdoor tables. Open until 1am. Closed Sun morning.

Osteria da Baco, Calle delle Rasse 4620; F9. Traditional-style *osteria*, with a wide selection of sandwiches. Open until midnight or later if the custom's there. Open daily.

Eastern Districts

The grid reference at the end of the address relates to the map on p.188.

Alla Rampa, Salizzada S. Antonin 3607; B4. Slightly rough and utterly traditional bar, which has been run for decades by the no-nonsense Signora Leli. Great for an inexpensive *ombra*, if you don't mind being the only customer who isn't a Venetian male. Closed Sun.

Cafés, pasticcerie and gelaterie

When **coffee** first appeared in Venice in 1640, imported by the Republic from the Levant, it was treated as a medicine; today it's a drug of which all Venetians need a fix several times a day. (Tea-drinkers will be horrified by the Venetian notion of their favoured beverage – often a jug of hot water with a tea-bag lying on the saucer.) High-quality outlets range from the *Rosa Salva* chain, whose businesslike ambience might not tempt you to hang around for longer than it takes to slug the coffee back, to the decadent old coffee houses of the Piazza, whose prices will prompt you to linger just so you can feel you've had your money's worth.

As with bars, if you **sit in a café** you will be charged more, and if you **sit outside** the bill will be even higher. Nearly all **pasticcerie** also serve coffee and alcohol, but will have at most a few barstools; they're all right for a swift caffeination before the next round of church-visiting, but not for a session of postcard writing or a longer recuperative stop. Elbow-room in the city's *pasticcerie* is especially restricted first thing in the

morning, as the citizens pile in for a coffee and *cornetto* (croissant). You can also stop for a coffee at most of Venice's **gelaterie**, where the ice cream comes in forms that you won't have experienced before, unless you're a seasoned traveller in Italy.

General areas to find good cafés include **Campo Santa Margherita**, **Crosera San Pantalon** (running just south of San Rocco), **Campiello Meloni** (between S. Polo and S. Aponal), **Calle della Bissa** (behind Campo S. Bartolomeo), **Salizzada San Giovanni Crisostomo**, the **Strada Nova** and its continuations towards the train station, and **Via Garibaldi**. In one way or another, the following specific places stand out from the rest.

San Marco

The grid references at the end of each address relate to the map on p.42.

Florian, Piazza S. Marco 56–59; H7. Opened in 1720 by Florian Francesconi, and frescoed and mirrored in a passable pastiche of that period, this has long been the café to be seen in. A simple *cappuccino* will set you back around L15,000/€7.70 (more, if you're outside and the band's performing), and you'll have to take out a mortgage for a cocktail. Closed Wed in winter.

Lavena, Piazza S. Marco 133–134; H6. Wagner's favourite café (there's a commemorative plaque inside) is the third member of the Piazza's top-bracket trio. For privacy you can take a table in the narrow little gallery overlooking the bar. Closed Tues in winter.

Marchini, Ponte S. Maurizio 2769; D8. The most delicious and most expensive of Venetian *pasticciere*, where people come on Sunday morning to buy family treats. Indulge at least once.

Paolin, Campo S. Stefano 2962; C7. Thought by many to be the makers of the best ice cream in Venice, but many would argue that it's lost ground to *Causin* (see overleaf). Good nonetheless,

Eating and drinking

Eating and drinking

and the outside tables have one of the finest settings in the city. Closed Fri.

Quadri, Piazza S. Marco 120–124; H6. In the same price league as *Florian*, but not quite as pretty. Austrian officers patronized it during the occupation, while the natives stuck with *Florian*, and it still has something of the air of being a runner-up in the society stakes. Closed Mon in winter.

Rosa Salva, Campo S. Luca (F4), Merceria S. Salvador (G3) and Campo Santi Giovanni e Paolo (Castello – F5). Venice's premier catering chain: excellent coffee, very good pastries, pretty good ice creams, but slightly surgical ambience.

Dorsoduro

The grid references relate to the map on p.100.

Causin, Campo S. Margherita 2996; D5. Excellent homemade ice cream at this long-established café, which has seating on the campo. Closed Sun.

Gian Carlo Vio, Rio Terrà Toletta 1192; F7. Great cakes – one to make for after the Accademia.

Il Doge, Campo S. Margherita 3058; D5. Well-established gelateria. Open daily till midnight. Closed Oct.

Nico, Záttere ai Gesuati 922; G9. A high-point of a wander in the area, celebrated for an artery-clogging creation called a *gianduiotto* – ask for one *da passeggio* (to take out) and you'll be given a paper cup with a block of praline ice cream drowned in whipped cream. Closed Thurs.

San Polo

The grid references at the end of each address relate to the map on p.122.

Rizzardini, Calle della Madonetta 1415; G7. Founded in 1742, *Rizzardini* is one of the best outlets for the less florid varieties of Venetian pastries. Closed Mon.

Tonolo, Crosera S. Pantalon 3764; D8. One of the busiest cafés on one of the busiest streets of the student district; especially

hectic on Sunday mornings, when the fancy *Tonolo* cakes are in high demand for the day's main meal. Closed Mon.

Cannaregio

The grid references relate to the map on p.148.

Ca' d'Oro, Strada Nova 3843a; H8. Belt-loosening cakes. Closed Mon.

Pasticceria Boscolo Anna, Campiello dell'Anconetta; F6. One of a chain of "Antichi pasticceri Venexiani", established in the 1930s and still going strong. Closed Mon.

Castello

The grid references relate to the map on p.165.

Chiusso Pierino, Salizzada dei Greci 3306; I8. Another of the reliable "Antichi pasticceri Venexiani" group. Closed Wed.

Domenegati Eugenio, Calle Caffettier 6645; I6. Belongs to the same organization as *Chiusso Pierino*, and does equally fine cakes. Closed Mon.

Ponte delle Paste, Ponte delle Paste 5991; C6. Excellent *pasticceria* with a small "tea room", though it also serves alcoholic drinks. Closed Mon.

Rosa Salva see "San Marco" section, above.

Snack & Sweet, Salizzada S. Lio 5689; D7. *Pasticceria* and bar with a glorious spread of cakes and sandwiches; does delicious *spremute*. Closed Sat.

Food markets and shops

The campi, parks and canalside steps make picnicking a particularly pleasant alternative in Venice, and if you're venturing off to the outer islands it's often the only way of fuelling yourself. Supplies are always sold by weight (even bread): order by the *chilo, mezzo chilo* (kilo, half-kilo) or the *etto* (100g). Bear in mind that food shops are generally open 8.30am–1pm and 4–7pm or thereabouts, and that the great majority are closed on Wednesday afternoons and all day Sunday (though some supermarkets stay open all day Wednesday). And don't try to picnic in the Piazza – the by-laws against it are strictly enforced.

Markets

Open-air **markets** for fruit and vegetables are held in various squares every day except Sunday: check out the stalls on **Campo Santa Maria Formosa**, **Campo Santa Margherita**, **Campiello dell'Anconetta** and **Rio Terrà San Leonardo** (these two often flow into each other), and the barges moored by **Campo San Barnaba** and at the top end of **Via Garibaldi**. The market of markets, however, is the one at the **Rialto**, where you can buy everything you need for an impromptu feast – wine, cheese (the best stalls in the city are here), fruit, salami, vegetables, and bread from nearby bakers or *alimentari* (delicatessens). The stalls of the Rialto **Erberia** (fruit and vegetables), arranged with wonderful colour sense, are laden at different times of the year with peaches, peppers, apples, artichokes, fresh herbs and salad leaves nameless in English – look out for the produce labelled "Sant'Erasmo", which is grown on the island of that name and is held by many locals to be the best quality. The Rialto market is open Monday to Saturday 8am–1pm, with a few stalls opening again in the late afternoon; the **Pescheria** (fish market) – of no practical interest to picnickers but a sight not to be missed – is closed on Monday as well.

Food shops and supermarkets

Virtually every parish has its *alimentari* and most of them are good; one to single out, though, is *Aliani Gastronomia* in Ruga Vecchia San Giovanni (San Polo) –

scores of cheeses, meats and salads that'll have you drooling as soon as you're through the door. As you'd expect, the cheaper *alimentari* are those farthest from San Marco – such as the ones along Via Garibaldi, out beyond the Arsenale.

Alternatively, you could get everything from one of Venice's well-hidden **supermarkets**, the most central of which is *Su.Ve.*, on the corner of Salizzada San Lio and Calle Mondo Nuovo (Castello). Others are as follows: tucked between houses 3019 and 3112 on Campo Santa Margherita (Dorsoduro); on Rio Terrà Frari and on Campo San Giacomo dell'Orio (both San Polo); at Fondamenta San Giacomo 203a (Giudecca); Billa on Záttere Ponte Lungo, by the San Basilio vaporetto stop (Dorsoduro); Full on Via Garibaldi (Eastern Districts); and the main Standa store at Strada Nova 3659, near San Felice (Cannaregio). Billa is open daily 8.30am–8pm; the rest have similar hours – approximately 8.30am–12.30pm and 3–7.30pm, closed Sunday.

Wine

For **local wines**, Venice has four branches of a wine merchant called La Nave d'Oro, at Campo S. Margherita 3664 (Dorsoduro), Calle del Mondo Novo 5786 (Castello), Rio Terrà S. Leonardo 1370 (Cannaregio), and Via Lépanto 241 (Lido); these shops sell not just bottles but also draught Veneto wine to take out. Many ordinary bars also offer wine on draught – look for the sign *vino sfuso*, or for the tell-tale shelf of wine vats with siphon attachments. In addition, the wine bars *Al Volto*, *Cantina del Vino già Schiavi* and *Do Mori* (see pp.269–273) boast comprehensive cellars, and many *alimentari* have an impressive choice of bottles.

Chapter 12

Nightlife, the arts and festivals

As recently as just one generation ago Venice was a night city, where the residents of each parish set out tables on the street at the flimsiest excuse. Nowadays, with the pavements overrun by outsiders, the social life of the Venetians is more of an indoor business – a restaurant meal or a drink with friends might feature in most people's diary for the week, and a conversational stroll is certainly a favourite Venetian pastime, but home entertainment takes up most time and energy. That said, Venice's calendar of special events is pretty impressive, with the Carnevale, the Film Festival and the Biennale ranking among the continent's hottest dates. To find out what's on in the way of concerts and films, check **Un Ospite di Venezia**, a free bilingual magazine available from the tourist office and some of the more expensive hotels – it's produced weekly in peak season, monthly in winter. Information and listings for bars, events, festivals can also be found at *www.govenice.com*.

Music and theatre

Music in Venice, to all intents and purposes, means classical music – rock bands rarely come nearer than Padua, and big names stop at Verona. The top-bracket **music venues** are La Fenice (temporarily rehoused on Tronchetto)

and the Teatro Goldoni in Calle Goldoni, in the San Marco sestiere.

Prior to the fire of 1996, **La Fenice** was the third-ranking Italian opera house after Milan's La Scala and Naples' San Carlo. While the building is being reconstructed, performances are held in a vast marquee called **Palafenice**, over on Tronchetto; a special water-bus transports ticket-holders from San Marco to the tent. **Tickets** for Palafenice can be bought from the temporary box office in the Cassa di Risparmio building on Campo S. Luca (Mon–Fri 8.30am–1.30pm; ☎041.521.0161; fax 041.786.580; *www.tin.it/fenice*), or at Palafenice itself, where the box office is open from two hours before the start of the night's show. Tickets usually start at around L30,000/€16, though prices are higher for the more glamorous productions, and you'll pay twice as much for the opening night of a production as you would for the same seat later in the run. The opera season runs from late November to the end of June, punctuated by ballet performances.

The city's major venue for classical music concerts used to be the Sale Apollinee in La Fenice. When La Fenice is at last rebuilt it may reclaim that position, but for now the principal concert hall is the **Teatro Malibran** (by the church of San Giovanni Crisostomo), which will soon re-open after years of dereliction. At the time of going to press, box-office details were not available – the tourist offices should be able to supply programmes.

Music performances at the **Goldoni** (box office 9.30am–12.30pm & 4–6pm; ☎041.520.5422) are somewhat less frequent than at La Fenice and the Malibran; the repertoire here tends to be more populist, with a jazz series cropping up every now and then. For most of the year the Goldoni specializes in the works of the eponymous writer.

Classical concerts, with a strong bias towards the eighteenth century, are also performed at the **Palazzo Prigione Vecchie**, the **Scuola Grande di San Giovanni Evangelista**, the **Scuola Grande di San Rocco**, **Palazzo Mocenigo** (San Stae) and the churches of **Santo Stefano**, the **Frari**, **San Stae**, **San Samuele**, **San Bartolomeo**, **Zitelle**, **San Barnaba**, the **Ospedaletto** and the **Pietà** (the most regularly used – it specializes in Vivaldi in particular). The average ticket price for these concerts is around L30,000 (often with a L10,000 reduction for students and children), which is expensive for performances more often distinguished by enthusiasm than professionalism – for the same price you can get to hear real stars at La Fenice. The state radio service sometimes records concerts at the **Palazzo Labia**, to which the public are admitted free of charge, as long as seats are reserved in advance (☎041.716.666). In summer the Italian-German Cultural Association presents free chamber music concerts every Saturday at 5.30pm in the **Palazzo Albrizzi**, Fondamenta S. Andrea, Cannaregio.

Up beat and down market from the theatre and classical concerts, some **bars** have live music: the main ones are *Paradiso Perduto* in Cannaregio and *Da Codroma* in Dorsoduro (see p.272 & p.271 for addresses). They don't charge for entrance, but a mark-up on the drinks pays for the bands.

Cinema

English-language films are the basic fare for Venice's moviegoers, and virtually every screening is dubbed rather than subtitled. From around mid-July to the end of August, however, an open-air cinema in Campo S. Polo shows dubbed or Italian-language films to a high-spirited local audience. Films start each night at around 9pm, and it's worth an evening of anyone's holiday, if only for the atmosphere. (For information ring ☎041.524.1320; *circuitocinema @commun.venezia*.) A big new media and cinema centre is planned for Calle Vallaresso, but for the meantime the main cinemas are as follows:

Accademia, Calle Corfù, Dorsoduro 1019 ☎041.528.7706. By the Accademia; mixture of general release and art-house films.

Giorgione, Rio Terrà dei Franceschi 4612a ☎041.522.6298. Two small screens, occasionally showing independent films.

Ritz, Calle dei Segretaria, San Marco 617 ☎041.520.4429. By S. Zulian; general release.

Rossini, Calle delle Muneghe, San Marco 4000 ☎041.523.0322. The biggest screen in the city. Facing the church of S. Luca; general release.

The Film Festival

The **Venice Film Festival**, founded in 1932 as a propaganda showcase for Mussolini's "progressive" Italy, is the world's oldest and the most important in Europe after Cannes. Originally the festival had no competitive element, but with the creation of the Leon d'Oro (the Golden Lion) in 1949, the organizers created a focal point for the rivalries that beset this narcissistic business. Spike Lee is far from being the only director to feel slighted by a biased jury. In the student-orchestrated turmoil of 1968 the Leon d'Oro was deemed to be an insult to the workers of Venice, and it was only in 1980 that the trophy was reinstated. Now every Festival is beset with rows

Nightlife, the arts and festivals

Nightlife, the arts and festivals

between directors of differing political persuasions and vehement disputes over the programming.

The eleven-day Film Festival takes place on the Lido every year in **late August and/or early September**. Posters advertising the Festival's schedule appear weeks in advance, and the tourist office will have the festival programme a fair time before the event, as will the two cinemas where the films are shown – the **Palazzo del Cinemà** on Lungomare G. Marconi and the neighbouring **PalaGalileo**. Tickets are available to the general public, but you have to go along and queue for them at the PalaGalileo on the day before the performance. Any remaining tickets are sold off at PalaGalileo one hour before the screening, but nearly all shows are sold out well before then.

Discos and clubs

Venice is notorious for its lack of decent nightlife, relying mostly on the handful of late bars dotted around the city (see box on p.270). The most buzzing area, particularly in winter, is along the Fondamenta della Misericordia, in Cannaregio, where *Iguana*, *Le Notti d'Oriente* and *Paradiso Perduto* (see listings under "Bars and snacks") stay open late and have occasional DJs or live music. Dorsoduro, on and around the studenty Campo S. Margherita, is another good bet, particularly in the warmer months: try *Margaret DuChamp*, *Il Caffè* or *Green Pub*, all of which stay open late. To really get down, however, there's only one recommendable option, *Casanova* (☎041.534.7479, *www.casanova.it*), on the Lista di Spagna. As a huge, old-fashioned disco-club it would be half empty anywhere else, but in Venice it stays fairly busy from Thursday to Saturday. The current regime is salsa (Wed), student/Indie (Thurs), classic dance (Fri) and House (Sat), but don't even think about arriving before around 2am.

There's a tiny disco over on the Lido, *Nuova Acropolis*, Lungomare Marconi 22, and Mestre has several identikit clubs

which are listed in the local press. The real action is further away, out in the northern reaches of the lagoon at **Jesolo**. Every Friday and Saturday evening, this sedate resort transforms itself into a ravers' haven, as a swarm of clubs kick into life. Just stroll into town after 11pm and you'll find the hot spots. The problem is that though there are plenty of buses out to Jesolo, there's no way of getting back except to get a lift with someone – and Jesolo is notorious not so much for its weekend bacchannals as for what happens afterwards, when hundreds of inebriated young Italians go blasting back home. The Jesolo–Venice road has just about the highest death toll of any strip of tarmac in the country.

The Casinò

Only one aspect of Venice's nightlife attracts the kids from the mainland, and that's the **Casinò**, one of only half a dozen in the entire country. The Saturday night migration is a strange sight – the vaporetto pulls in at the dismal Tronchetto stop, and on board step the well-groomed young gamblers, having parked their Alfa Romeos in the Tronchetto's multistorey. Minimum age is 18, and the dress code is not as strict as you'd think – even jeans are acceptable in the rooms given over to slot machines (L5000/€2.58 admission), though jacket and tie are obligatory for the "French" games (L10,000/€5.16), such as roulette and chemin de fer. From mid-September to mid-June the Casinò occupies the magnificent Palazzo Vendramin-Calergi (Cannaregio) on the Canal Grande; in high summer it migrates to the Lido's Palazzo del Casinò on Lungomare Marconi. At both sites it operates from 4pm until 2.30am (3.30am on Saturday).

Special exhibitions – and the Biennale

As if the profusion of galleries, museums and picture-stuffed churches weren't enough, Venice boasts a phalanx of venues for **special exhibitions**. Listed below are the places where you'll find the first-rank shows, with an indication of the themes favoured by each venue – look in *Un Ospite di Venezia* for details of fringe events, and take note of advertising posters and banners.

Archivio di Stato (San Polo): Venetian history.

Ca' Pésaro (San Polo): modern art.

Fondazione Cini, on San Giorgio Maggiore: art history.

Guggenheim (Dorsoduro): modern art.

Museo Correr (San Marco): exhibitions usually related to Venetian history or art.

Museo Fortuny (San Marco): design and photography.

Palazzo Ducale (San Marco): art history, ethnology and archeology.

Palazzo Grassi (San Marco): major art and cultural shows, on subjects as diverse as Celtic civilization and Futurism.

Querini-Stampalia (Castello): art history.

Scuola Grande di San Giovanni Evangelista (San Polo): photography, video, technology as applied to the arts.

Scuola Grande di San Teodoro (San Marco): modern and applied art – often tacky.

Contemporary private galleries in Venice are generally timorous affairs, most of them functioning more as shops for arty artefacts than as exhibition spaces; again, look in *Un Ospite* for their latest offerings. A handful stand out against a background of dross, all of them in the sestiere of San Marco:
Arte Moderna Contini, Calle Spezier, off Campo S. Stefano.
Bugno & Samueli, Campo San Fantin.
Santo Stefano, Campo S. Stefano.
Traghetto, Campo S. Maria del Giglio.

The Biennale

The **Venice Biennale**, Europe's most glamorous international forum for contemporary art, was first held in 1895 as the city's contribution to the celebrations for the silver wedding anniversary of King Umberto I and Margherita of Savoy. In the early years the exhibits were dominated by standard academic painting, despite the presence of such artists as Ensor, Klimt and Whistler. (In 1910, furious at the bourgeois stolidity of the Biennale, Marinetti and his Futurist gang bombarded the Piazza with pamphlets launched from the clock tower, demanding, among other things, that the city's canals be asphalted into decent modern roadways.) Since World War II, however, the Biennale has become a self-consciously avant-garde event, a transformation symbolized by the award of the major Biennale prize in 1964 to Robert Rauschenberg, the enfant terrible of the American art scene. The French contingent campaigned vigorously against the nomination of this New World upstart, and virtually every Biennale since then has been characterized by the sort of controversy that is now endemic in the publicity-addicted art circuit.

After years of occurring in even-numbered years, the Biennale shifted back to being held **every odd-numbered year from June to September**, so that the centenary show could be held in 1995. The main site is in the Giardini Pubblici, where there are permanent pavilions for about forty countries plus space for a thematic international exhibition. This central part of the Biennale is usually supplemented by the *Aperto* ("Open"), a mixed exhibition showing the work of younger or less established artists – though the 1995 *Aperto* somehow got cancelled. When it's on, the *Aperto* takes over spaces all over the city: the salt warehouses on the Záttere, for instance, or the colossal Corderie in the Arsenale. In addition, various sites throughout the city host fringe exhibitions, installations and performances, particularly in the opening weeks. There are also plans to utilize the pavilions in non-Biennale years by instituting an independent Biennale for **architecture**, a discipline whose practitioners have played an increasingly active role in the main Biennale – Aldo Rossi's floating *Teatro del Mondo*, for example, was the showstopper of the 1980 festival.

Nightlife, the arts and festivals

Nightlife, the arts and festivals

Exhibits from earlier years, plus a fabulous collection of magazines and catalogues from all over the world, are kept in the **archive** in the Palazzo Corner della Regina (close to Ca' Pésaro); entrance is free to visitors who can prove a more than casual interest. The general public can get information on the Biennale at *www.labiennale.org*.

Festivals

Venice celebrates enthusiastically a number of special days either not observed elsewhere in Italy, or, like the Carnevale, celebrated to a lesser extent. Although they have gone through various degrees of decline and revival, the form they take now is still related very strongly to their traditional character.

Carnevale

John Evelyn wrote of the 1646 Carnevale: "all the world was in Venice to see the folly and madness . . . the women, men and persons of all conditions disguising themselves in antique dresses, & extravagant Musique & a thousand gambols." Not much is different in today's Carnevale, for which people arrive in such numbers that the causeway from the mainland has sometimes had to be closed because the city has been too packed.

The origins of the Carnevale can be traced in the word itself: *carne vale*, a "farewell to meat" before the rigours of Lent – the same origin as the tamer British custom of eating pancakes on Shrove Tuesday. The medieval European carnival developed into a period when the world could be turned over – a time of licence for those normally constrained by rank, and a means of quelling discontent by a ritualized relinquishing of power. Venice's Carnevale can be related to the surrender of power on a wider scale, as the festival's heyday – the eighteenth century – coincided with the terminal decline of the Republic. The eighteenth-century Carnevale officially began on December 26, lasting for nearly two months until Shrove Tuesday;

aspects of it, such as the wearing of masks, stretched into the rest of the year, until Carnevale unofficially continued for six months.

Today's Carnevale is limited to the **ten days leading up to Lent**, finishing on Shrove Tuesday with a masked ball for the glitterati, and dancing in the Piazza for the plebs. It was revived in 1979 by a group of non-Venetians, and soon gained support from the canny city authorities, who now organize various pageants and performances. (Details from the San Marco tourist office.) Apart from these events, Carnevale is very much a case of see and be seen. During the day people don costumes and go down to the Piazza to be photographed; parents dress up their kids; businessmen can be seen doing their shopping in the classic white mask, black cloak and tricorne hat. In the evening some congregate in the remoter squares, while those who have spent literally hundreds of pounds on their costumes install themselves in the windows of *Florian*'s and pose for a while before making an exit with an adoring entourage. But you don't need to spend money or try to be "traditional" in your disguise: a simple black outfit and a painted face is enough to transform you from a spectator into a participant.

Masks are on sale throughout the year in Venice, but new mask and costume shops suddenly appear during Carnevale, when Campo San Maurizio sprouts a marquee with mask-making demonstrations and a variety of designs for sale. For the best stockists, see p.285.

La Sensa and Vogalonga

The feast of **La Sensa** happens in May on the **Sunday after Ascension Day** – the latter being the day on which the doge enacted the wedding of Venice to the sea (see p.236). The ritual has recently been revived – a distinctly feeble procession which ends with the mayor and a gang of other dignitaries getting into a present-day approximation of the *Bucintoro* (the state barge) and sailing off to the Lido. A gondola regatta follows the ceremony, but far more spectacular is the **Vogalonga** (long row), which is held on the same day. Established in 1974 as a protest against the excessive number of motorboats on the canals, the *Vogalonga* is now open to any crew in any class of rowing boat, and covers a 32-kilometre course from the Bacino di San Marco out to Burano and back; the competitors set off at 8.30am and arrive at the bottom of the Canal Grande anywhere between about 11am and 3pm.

Festa di San Pietro

Held in the week of Saint Peter's saint's day (June 29), the **Festa di San Pietro** is a small-scale festival of concerts, open-air shows and food stalls, held around the church of San Pietro di Castello. Entirely untouched by tourism, it's an authentic antithesis to Carnevale.

Festa del Redentore

The **Festa del Redentore** is one of Venice's plague-related festivals, marking the end of the epidemic of 1576. Celebrated on the **third Sunday in July**, the day is centred on Palladio's church of the Redentore, which was built by way of thanksgiving for the city's escape. A bridge of boats is strung across the Giudecca canal to allow the faithful to walk over to the church, and on the Saturday night hundreds of people row out for a picnic on the water. The night ends with a grand fireworks display, after

which it's traditional to row to the Lido for the sunrise.

The Regata Storica

Held on the **first Sunday in September**, the **Regata Storica** is the annual trial of strength and skill for the city's gondoliers and other expert rowers. It starts with a procession of richly decorated historic craft along the Canal Grande course, their crews all decked out in period dress. Bystanders are expected to join in the support for the contestants in the main event, and may even be issued with appropriate colours. Other *regate* are held throughout the year in various parts of the lagoon, the main ones being the **Regata di San Zanipolo** (June), the **Regata di Murano** (July), the **Regata di Pellestrina** (Aug) and the **Regata di Burano** (Sept).

La Salute

Named after the church of the Salute, the **Festa della Salute** is a reminder of the plague of 1630–31, which killed one third of the population of the lagoon. The church was built in thanks for deliverance from the outbreak, and every **November 21** since then the Venetians have processed over a pontoon bridge across the Canal Grande to give thanks for their good health, or to pray for sick friends and relatives. It offers the only chance to see the church as it was designed to be seen – with its main doors open and hundreds of people milling up the steps.

Nightlife,
the arts and
festivals

Chapter 13

Shopping

The torpor of Venice after dark is inversely proportional to the hustle of its shopping streets in the daytime, when vast sums are trawled daily from the tourists' pockets. It's easy to get the impression that Venice's shops are polarized at two extremes – geared either to the trinket trade or to expense-account fashion and accessories. The middle ground does exist, however, and it doesn't take too much ferreting around to find it: small workshops all over the city produce a range of reasonably priced items such as bags, masks and decorative papers; unusual prints and books are on sale in a number of shops; and there's even the odd bargain to be picked up amid the antique stalls.

Food shops and markets are covered in Chapter 11.

Antiques

Although the antiques shops around **San Maurizio** and **Santa Maria Zobenigo** cater for the wealthier collectors, bargain hunters should be able to pick something up at the **antiques fairs** that crop up throughout the year in Campo San Maurizio, where the stalls groan under the weight of old books, prints, silverware and general bric-a-brac. (The tourist office will be able to tell you if one is due.) The traders in the **San Barnaba** district are also slightly downmarket, running the kind of places where you could find a faded wooden cherub or an old picture frame.

Art materials

Should you want to add your own contribution to the stockpile of visual images of Venice, all the necessary materials can be bought in the city. The best-known supplier is Testolino on Fondamenta Orseolo, north of the Piazza, though Seguso, in nearby Calle dei Fabbri, is almost as good. Three other general suppliers are in Campiello di Ca' Zen on the north side of the Rio dei Frari (San Polo), at Crosera S. Pantalon 3954 (San Polo), and at Campo S. Margherita 2928 (Dorsoduro).

Books

Alberto Bertoni, Rio Terrà degli Assassini 3637/b, San Marco. For remaindered and secondhand books, including a number of art-book bargains.

Ca' Foscarina, Campiello Squellini 3243, Dorsoduro. Good range of non-Italian titles amid a wide stock of generally academic books (the university is almost next door).

Cluva, Campo dei Tolentini 197, Santa Croce (San Polo chapter). Situated next to the university's architecture department, this unsurprisingly is the most comprehensive stockist of books on architecture.

Fantoni, Salizzada S. Luca 4121, San Marco. For the glossiest, weightiest and most expensive art books.

Filippi Editore Venezia, Caselleria 5284

and Calle del Paradiso 5762, both Castello. The family-run Filippi business produces a vast range of Venice-related facsimile editions, including Francesco Sansovino's sixteenth-century guide to the city (the first city guide ever published) and sells an amazing stock of books about Venice in its two shops.

Goldoni, Calle dei Fabbri 4742, San Marco. The best general bookshop in the city; also keeps an array of maps and posters.

Libreria della Toletta, Sacca della Toletta 1214, Dorsoduro. Sells reduced-price books, mainly in Italian, but some dual language and translations. Bargains on Electa art books.

Libreria Emiliana, Calle Goldoni 4487a, San Marco. A small shop, but well-stocked with books relating to Venice, and a selection of English-language titles.

Sangiorgio, Calle Larga XXII Marzo 2087, San Marco. A small but well-stocked art bookshop.

Sansovino, Bacino Orseolo 84, San Marco. Second only to Fantoni for books on art.

Clothes

As you'd expect, many of the top-flight Italian designers and fashion houses – Versace, Missoni, Krizia, MaxMara, Trussardi, Gucci, Armani, Prada, Valentino and Dolce e Gabbana (the only ones with a local connection) – are represented in Venice, most of their outlets being clustered within a street or two of the Piazza. For those with wallets as deep as oil wells, the **Mercerie**, **Frezzeria**, **Calle Goldoni**, **Calle Vallaresso** and **Calle Larga XXII Marzo** are the most fruitful zones. The best shops for a range of high fashion are La Coupole (Frezzeria and Calle Larga XXII Marzo), Elysée (Frezzeria and Calle Goldoni), Al Duca d'Aosta (Merceria del Capitello), and La Fenice (Calle Larga XXII Marzo).

For more moderately priced clothes, there's the inevitable Benetton, Sisley and Stefanel (all with branches in the Mercerie), and Coin, a national department store based in Venice. Coin's home branch specializes in clothing, and is located between the Rialto and San Giovanni Crisostomo. The area **between Campo San Bartolomeo and Santi Apostoli** is well supplied with shops aimed at a young clientele, as is the line of streets running from **Ruga Vecchia San Giovanni** to **San Polo**, on the other side of the Canal Grande. None really stands out from the crowd, though.

The Venetian taste in clothes is pretty conservative, but more idiosyncratic stuff is sold at Fiorella, on Campo S. Stefano (San Marco), where the wacky jackets are beautifully made and wittily displayed – the mannequins have female bodies but their faces are modelled on portraits of the doges.

Venezia Studium – in Calle XXII Marzo 2425 (San Marco), Merceria S. Zulian 723 (San Marco) and Campo dei Frari 3006 (San Polo) – sells lamps, bags and scarves in Fortuny-style pleated velour and crepe. For real Fortuny fabrics, go to V. Trois, Campo S. Maurizio 2666, where they sell the luscious stuff manufactured over on La Giudecca, at L420,000 (€217) per metre.

Glass

As with lace, for Venetian **glass** you're better off going to the main source of production, in this case **Murano**. The Piazza and its environs are prowled by well-groomed young characters offering free boat trips to the island – on no account accept, as you'll be subjected to a relentless hard sell on arrival. If you are in the market, just take the vaporetto to the Colonna stop and follow your eyes: the most expensive and most pretentious shops are to the fore, the rest stretch out beyond. Pseudo-artistic ornaments, extortionately expensive tableware and ranks of eye-bruising kitsch – a life-size bush with a cast of glass parrots – make up the bulk of the stock, but there are some more tasteful pieces on sale in the showrooms listed

Shopping

For more on Murano glass, see p.231.

Shopping

For more on Burano lace, see p.224.

below. Unless stated otherwise, they are on Murano.

Barovier, Salizzada San Samuele 3216 (San Marco). Art gallery dealing in work from glass-blowers from all over the world. This place displays what is perhaps the most inventive and beautiful glass in Venice, and – contrary to appearances – the stuff is for sale, albeit at very high prices.

Barovier & Tosio, Fondamenta Vetrai 28. Not to be confused with the gallery listed above, this is a family-run firm which can trace its roots back to the fourteenth century. Predominantly traditional designs.

Berengo Fine Arts, Fondamenta Vetrai 109a, Fondamenta Manin 68 and Salizzada San Samuele 3337 (San Marco). This firm has pioneered a new approach to Venetian glass manufacture, with foreign artists' designs being vitrified by Murano glass-blowers.

Domus Vetri d'Arte, Fondamenta Vetrai 82. Stocks work by the major postwar Venetian glass designers, artists such as Barbini, Lino Tagliapietra, Ercole Moretti and Carlo Moretti.

L'Isola, Salizzada S. Moisè 1468, San Marco. Chiefly a showcase for work by Carlo Moretti, the doyen of modernist Venetian glass artists.

Murano Collezioni, Fondamenta Manin 1c. Outlet for work from the Venini, Moretti and Barovier & Toso factories.

Penso Davide, Fondamenta Cavour 48. The jewellery sold here is both manufactured and designed by the firm, which specializes in giving a new slant to traditional Murano styles.

Seguso, Piazza San Marco 143 and San Marco Frezzeria 1230–6. Traditional style and quality Murano glass, much of it created by proprietor Archimede Seguso, who is now in his eighties.

Venini, Fondamenta Vetrai 50 (Murano) and Piazzetta dei Leoncini 314 (San Marco). One of the more adventurous producers, Venini often employs designers from other fields of the applied arts.

Jewellery

Anticlea Antiquariato, Calle San Provolo 4719a, Castello. Specialising in the glass beads known as *perle veneziane*, with ready-made jewellery, or drawers of beads to choose from.

Codognato, Calle Secondo dell'Ascensione 1295, San Marco. One of the city's most expensive outlets, selling everything from antique pieces through to Art Deco brooches and modern designs.

Costantini, Calle Zaguri 2627, San Marco. Good array of *perle veneziane* sold individually, made into jewellery, or by the bag, plus various (and surprisingly cheap) antique African currency beads.

Laberintho, Calle Scalater 2236, San Polo. Tiny workshop specializing in inlaid earrings, necklaces and rings.

Missiaglia, Piazza San Marco 125, San Marco. Peerless, expensive gold and silver work from a firm that has a good claim to be Venice's classiest.

Nardi, Piazza San Marco 69–71, San Marco. Coral, tortoiseshell, ebony and other environment-abusing materials are the keynote of Nardi's production. Also makes some less objectionable if similarly overwrought gold objects.

Paolo Scarpa, Merceria S. Salvador 4850, San Marco. Gallery-like shop specializing in "primitive" jewellery from all corners of the planet.

Totem, Campo Carità 878b, Dorsoduro. As well as exhibiting and marketing 'tribal' art, Totem sells an intriguing range of jewellery made from ordinary materials, most of it inspired by African artefacts.

Lace

It's cheaper to buy **lace** on **Burano** than in the centre of Venice, but be warned that the cheapest stuff is machine-made and not from Burano either. The hand-made work sold at the island's Scuola dei Merletti is expensive, though not to a degree that's disproportionate to the hours and labour that go into making it. If you want an inexpensive example of the work, a little butterfly goes for about L15,000. In **Venice** itself, the most impressive shop is Jesurum at Merceria San Salvador 4857, San Marco, and also at Piazza San Marco 60–61; if that's out of your price range, try the vast Kerer showroom, installed in the Palazzo Trevisan-Cappello over the bridge at the rear of the Basilica di San Marco – it sells a wide range of lace, both affordable and exclusive.

Masks

Many of the Venetian **masks** on sale today are derived from the Carnevale of old: the ones representing characters from the *Commedia dell'Arte* (Pierrot, Harlequin, Columbine) for example, and the classic white half-mask called a *volto*, with a kind of beak over the mouth so the wearer could eat and drink. Although masks are worn only during the ten days of Carnevale, they are on sale all year round; most designs are conveyor-belt stuff, which you'll soon recognize – for genuinely crafted examples, go to one of the following.

Bottega dei Mascareri, Calle del Cristo 2919 (San Polo). Run for many years by the brothers Sergio and Massimo Boldrin, the Bottega dei Mascareri sells some wonderfully inventive masks, such as faces taken from Tiepolo paintings or Donald Sutherland in Fellini's *Casanova*.

Ca' Macana, Calle delle Botteghe 3172 (Dorsoduro). Huge mask shop, with perhaps the biggest stock in the city; has another branch on the other side of Campo San Barnaba, at Barbaria delle Tole 1169.

MondoNovo, Rio Terrà Canal 3063, Dorsoduro. This workshop, located just off Campo S. Margherita, is perhaps the most imaginative in the city, producing everything from ancient Greek tragic masks to portraits of Richard Wagner.

Tragicomica, Calle dei Nomboli 2800, San Polo. A good range and some nice eighteenth-century styles, as you might expect from a shop that's opposite Goldoni's house.

Prints, postcards, paper and stationery

Postcards are on sale everywhere, though the fund of images isn't as imaginative as it could be. Just inside the Basilica di San Marco there's a stall selling a vast spread of good quality cards of the church and its mosaics, and many of the city's other churches offer a small range of good cards. Venice's museums are a letdown, usually offering a choice of a bare half-dozen – the stalls outside the Accademia have a better selection of the gallery's paintings than you'll find in the gallery itself. For something a little more unusual, such as mug-shots of famous doges or ancient views of the city, try Filippi Editore (see "Books"). For reprints of old topographical engravings of Venice at very moderate prices, visit the Armenian island of **San Lazzaro** (see p.242).

Most of the decorative **paper** on sale in Venice comes from Florence or is affiliated to or inspired by Florentine producers, but is none the worse for that. Shops selling these marbled papers, notebooks and so forth are all over the city; more idiosyncratic stuff is sold at the following places.

Alberto Valese, Calle del Teatro 1920, San Marco. Valese not only produces the most luscious marbled papers in Venice, but also transfers the designs onto silk scarves and a variety of ornaments; the marbling technique he uses is a Turkish process called *ebrû* – hence the alternative name of his shop.

Legatoria Piazzesi, Campiello della Feltrina 2511, San Marco. Located near S. Maria Zobenigo, this long-established paper-producer uses the old wooden-block method of printing; stunning hand-printed papers and cards, and a nice line in pocket diaries, too.

Linda Gonzalez, corner of Campiello San Fantin and Calle Fruttarol. Beautiful leather-bound notebooks and albums.

Paolo Olbi, Calle della Mandola 3653, San Marco. The founder of this shop was largely responsible for the revival of

Shopping

Shopping

paper marbling; today it sells a whole range of marbled stationery. The nearby Il Prato, at no. 3633, sells a very similar line of goods.

Il Pavone, Salizzada San Samuele 3287. Nice wooden-block printed papers, folders and so on, plus an interesting line in personalized rubber stamps and *Ex Libris* bookplates.

Polliero, Campo dei Frari 2995, San Polo. A bookbinding workshop that sells patterned paper as well as heavy, leather-bound albums of handmade plain paper.

Shoes, bags and leather

As far as chic shoes, bags and wallets go, the shops around the **Mercerie**, **Frezzeria** and **Calle Goldoni** are not as expensive as they might first appear, and sales are a regular occurrence in the Mercerie. If you can afford the very best, on the other hand, you should take a look at Rolando Segalin, Calle dei Fuseri 4365 (San Marco) – established in 1932, this workshop produces wonderful handmade shoes, from sturdy brogues to whimsical Carnival footwear, such as leather shoes with toes. Delicate silk and velvet shoes, bags, hats and gloves are a speciality of Valeria Bellinaso, Campo Sant'Aponal (San Polo).

If money is no object, go browsing around **Calle Vallaresso and** Calle Larga XXII Marzo, where names such as Vogini and Bottega Veneta uphold the city's reputation as a market for immaculately produced leather goods. In Merceria dell'Orologio you'll find a big branch of Mandarina Duck, whose stylish and

durable bags, often manufactured from rubber and heavy-gauge nylon, have become classic accessories all over Italy. For something unique to Venice, call in at Francis Model, Ruga Rialto 773a (San Polo), a father and son workshop that produces high-quality handbags and briefcases.

Miscellaneous

All manner of small **handmade gifts** in wood, tapestry and various other materials can be found at Toti Campizi in Calle Marcello, off Campo S. Marina (Castello). Jigsaw-like wooden objects – musical instruments, palace facades – are sold by Signor Blum at Campo S. Barnaba (Dorsoduro). Somewhat stranger wooden creations are on sale from the workshops of Livio de Marchi, in Salizzada S. Samuele (San Marco), and Loris Murazzi, on Campo S. Margherita (Dorsoduro): life-sized battered shoes and hanging items of underwear are among the more portable items, and if you have the transport you could take back a gigantic bundle of wooden paintbrushes. Models, model kits and elegantly drawn plans for **Venetian boats** are sold at La Scialuppa, Gilberto Penzo's shop at Calle Seconda Saoneri (San Polo).

Lastly, aficionados of souvenir **kitsch** can have a field day around the main tourist traps, especially the Lista di Spagna (Cannaregio): plastic gondolas set against blurred photos and fixed in illuminated plastic frames; gondolas that play *O Sole Mio*, gondola cigarette-lighters . . . the list is endless.

Chapter 14

Directory

ACTV ENQUIRIES Piazzale Roma, daily 7.30am–8pm ☎041.528.7886.

AIRLINES Alitalia, Salizzada S. Moisè, San Marco 1463 ☎041.520.0355; British Airways, Riva degli Schiavoni, Castello 4191 ☎041.528.5026.

AIRPORT ENQUIRIES Marco Polo airport, ☎041.260.9260.

AMERICAN EXPRESS The American Express office is in Salizzada S. Moisè, a couple of minutes' walk west of the Piazza; Mon–Fri 9am–5.30pm, Sat 9am–12.30pm; emergency number ☎041.1678.72.000 (toll-free).

BANKS Banks in Venice are concentrated on Calle Larga XXII Marzo (west of the Piazza), and along the chain of squares and alleyways between Campo S. Bartolomeo and Campo Manin (in the north of the San Marco sestiere). There's not much to choose between them in terms of commission and exchange rates, and their hours are generally Mon–Fri 8.30am–1.30pm and 2.30–3.30pm. The main ones are as follows:

Banca Commerciale Italiana, Calle Larga XXII Marzo, San Marco 2188.

Banca d'Italia, Campo S. Bartolomeo, San Marco 4799.

Banca Credito Italiano, Campo S. Salvador, San Marco.

Banco Ambrosiano Veneto, Calle Goldoni, San Marco 4481.

Banco di Roma, Mercerie dell'Orologio, San Marco 191.

Banco San Marco, Calle Larga XXII Marzo, San Marco 383.

BEACHES The Lido has two public beaches, at the northern and southern extremities of the island. The southern is the less crowded; better still, go down to Sottomarina, in the south of the lagoon (see p.242).

CAR RENTAL

At Marco Polo airport:
Avis ☎041.541.5030
Europcar ☎041.541.5654
Hertz ☎041.541.6075
Maggiore Budget ☎041.541.5040

At Piazzale Roma:
Avis ☎041.522.5825
Europcar ☎041.523.8616
Hertz ☎041.528.3524
Mattiazzo ☎041.522.0884

CONSULATES AND EMBASSIES The British consulate is in the Palazzo Querini, Dorsoduro 1051 ☎041.522.7207 (by the Accademia); this office is staffed by an honorary consul – the closest full consulate is in Milan, at Via San Paolo 7 ☎02.723.001. The nearest US consulate is also in Milan, at Largo Donegani 1 ☎02.290.351. Travellers from Ireland, Australia, New Zealand and Canada should contact their Rome embassies: Irish Embassy, Via Largo Nazareno 3 ☎06.678.2541; Australian Embassy, Via Alessandria 215 ☎041.06/832.721; New Zealand Embassy, Via Zara 28 ☎06.440.2928; Canadian Embassy, Via G. B. de Rossi 27 ☎041.06/841.5341.

Directory

ELECTRICITY The supply is 220 volts AC, but anything requiring 240V will work. Most plugs are two round pins: a travel plug is useful.

EMERGENCIES For all emergency services ring ☎113. Alternatively, dialling ☎112 puts you straight through to the *Carabinieri* (police) and ☎115 goes straight to the *Vigili del Fuoco* (fire brigade).

EXCHANGE There are clusters of exchange bureaux (*cambios*) where most tourists gather – near San Marco, the Rialto and the train station. Open late every day of the week, they can be useful in emergencies, but their rates of commission and exchange tend to be steep. The best rates are at American Express and the main banks.

FOOTBALL Venice's football team, which recently has yo-yo'ed between Serie A and Serie B, plays in the Pierluigi Penzo stadium, the most ramshackle ground in top-flight Italian football. Tickets can be bought from the Banca Antoniana Popolare Veneta: there are branches on Campo San Bartolomeo and Strada Nova.

HOSPITAL Ospedale Civile, Campo SS. Giovanni e Paolo; casualty dept ☎041.529.4517, ambulance service ☎041.523.0000

INTERNET ACCESS A number of dedicated Internet points have opened in the last couple of years, most charging around L10,000/€5.16 per half-hour, though rates usually drop the longer you stay online.

San Marco: *The Net House*, Campo S. Stefano 2967 (24hr).

Dorsoduro: *Omniservice*, Fondamenta dei Tolentini; *Internet Point*, Campo S. Margherita.

San Polo: *Café Noir*, Crosera S. Pantalon (see p.271); *CreArte*, Calle del Luganegher 1085 (daily 10am–8pm); *Gibo Bar*, Ponte della Donna Onesta (Tues–Sat 7.30pm–midnight); *Horus Explorer*, Fondamenta dei Tolentini 220 (Mon–Fri 8.30–1pm & 3–7pm); *Internet Point*, Calle S.Pantalon; *The Netgate*, Crosera

S.Pantalon 3812a (Mon–Sat 11.15am–8pm, Sun 2.15–8pm).

Cannaregio: *Planet Internet*, Ponte delle Guglie 1519 (daily; 9am–11pm); *Virtualia*, Rio Terrà dei Franceschi 4563 (9.45am–1pm & 4–8pm).

Castello: *Play the Game*, Calle Lunga S. Maria Formosa 6187 (daily 9.30am–1pm & 3.30–7.30pm); *Venetian Navigator*, Casselleria 5300 (summer 10am–10pm; winter 10am–7.30pm), with another branch nearby on Calle delle Bande 5269 (same hours); Fondazione Querini Stampalia (Mon–Sat 4pm–midnight; free).

Eastern Districts: *Internet Point*, Via Garibaldi 1592; *Internet Service*, Corte dei Preti 3546a (daily 10am–1pm, 3–6pm & 9–11pm).

LAUNDRIES There are no self-service laundries in Venice any more, but every parish has a dry cleaners.

LEFT LUGGAGE The desk at the end of platform 14, in the train station, charges L5,000/€2.58 per item per 12 hours. For a shorter stay it makes sense to use the lockers alongside platform 1, which cost L3000/€1.55 per 6 hours. Both open 24hr.

LOST PROPERTY If you lose anything on the train or at the station, call ☎041.785.238; at the airport call ☎041.260.6436; on the vaporetti call ☎041.780.310; and anywhere in the city itself call the town hall on ☎041.520.8844.

NEWSPAPERS You'll find the main national newspapers on any newsstand: *La Repubblica* is middle-to-left with a lot of cultural coverage; *Il Corriere della Sera* is authoritative and rather right-wing; *L'Unità* is the Communist Party organ; and *Il Manifesto* a more radical left-wing daily. Venice's local papers are the *Gazzettino* and *Nuova Venezia* (good for listings). More widely read than any, however, is the pink *Gazzettino dello Sport*, essential for the serious sports fan. English and American newspapers can be found at the train station, by the Calle dell'Ascensione post office and at various stands throughout the city – usually a day or two late.

POLICE To notify police of a theft, report to the *Questura* on Fondamenta S. Lorenzo (☎041.528.4666); in the event of a lost passport, notify the *Questura* and then your consulate or embassy; in emergencies, ring ☎113.

PORTERS Porters tout for trade at Piazzale Roma and the train station, and at places in the city where luxury hotels are concentrated – such as Riva degli Schiavoni and Calle Larga XXII Marzo. Their charges begin at L20,000/€10.35 for carrying one piece of luggage between any two points in the centre of the city, with a L10,000/€5.17 supplement for each additional item.

POST OFFICES Venice's main post office is in the Fondaco dei Tedeschi, near the Rialto bridge. Any poste restante should be addressed to Fermo Posta, Fondaco dei Tedeschi, 80100 Venezia; it can be collected Mon–Sat 8.15am–6.45pm – take your passport with you. Stamps are on sale Mon–Sat 8.15am–7pm; the telegram service operates round the clock. The principal branch post offices are in Calle dell'Ascensione (Mon–Sat 8.10am–6pm) and at Záttere 1406 (same hours). Stamps can also be bought in *tabacchi*, as well as in some gift shops.

PUBLIC TOILETS The lack of public toilets in Venice used to be a common complaint from tourists, but *AmaV* (*Azienda multiservizi ambientale Veneziana*) has now installed facilities on or very near to most of the main squares, and all over the city you'll see green, blue and white *AmaV* signs high on the walls, directing you to the nearest toilet. Costing L1000 (you'll need coins for the turnstiles), the main facilities are at the train station, at Piazzale Roma, on the west side of the Accademia bridge, by the main tourist office at the Giardinetti Reali, off the west side of the Piazza, off Campo S. Bartolomeo, on Campo S. Polo, Campo Rialto Nuovo, Campo S. Leonardo, Campo San'Angelo and on Campo S. Margherita. Toilets are to be found in most of the city's bars as well – it's diplomatic, to say the least, to buy a drink before availing yourself.

TELEPHONES All Venice's public call-boxes accept phone cards (the vast majority accept nothing but cards), which can be bought from *tabacchi* and some other shops (look for the *Telecom Italia* sticker); the less expensive type of cards can be bought from machines by the *Telecom Italia* phone booths in Strada Nova (near S. Felice), Calle S. Luca, Piazzale Roma and adjoining the main post office building near the Rialto Bridge. (See p.21 for more on phone cards.) You're never far from a pay phone – every sizeable campo has at least one, and there are phones by every vaporetto stop. For lengthy long-distance calls, however, it might be best to go to one of the two main *Telecom Italia* offices, where you can dial direct and be charged afterwards: the office at Piazzale Roma is open daily 8am–9.30pm, and the one at the main post office is open Mon–Fri 8.30am–12.30pm & 4–7pm.

TIME Italy is one hour ahead of Britain, six hours ahead of Eastern Standard Time and nine hours ahead of Pacific Standard Time.

TRAIN ENQUIRIES ☎1478.88.088.

Directory

The Veneto

The Veneto:
an introduction

Taking its name – as does Venice itself – from the pre-Roman people known as the Veneti, the present-day region of the Veneto essentially covers the area that became the core of the Republic's mainland empire. Everywhere in the Veneto you'll find the imprint of Venetian rule. In Belluno, right under the crags of the Dolomites, the style of the buildings declares the town's former allegiance. A few kilometres away, the lion of Saint Mark looks over the central square of the hill town of **Feltre**, as it does over the market square of **Verona**, on the Veneto's western edge. On the flatlands of the Po basin (the southern border of the region) and on farming estates all over the Veneto, the elegant villas of the Venetian nobility are still standing.

Yet the Veneto is as diverse culturally as it is geographically. The aspects of Verona's urban landscape that make the city so attractive were created long before the expansion of Venice's *terra firma* empire, and in **Padua** – a university seat since the thirteenth century – the civilization of the Renaissance displays a character quite distinct from that which evolved in Venice. Even in **Vicenza**, which reached its present form mainly during its long period of subservience, the very appearance of the streets is proof of a fundamental independence.

This is Italy's wealthiest region, and there's plenty of support here for the sharp-suited mediacrats of Silvio Berlusconi's Forza Italia party, and for the raging separatists of the Lega Nord, who like to depict the north as the underwriter of the parasitic south. But the economics of the Veneto have undergone a reversal over the last century or so. Venice, formerly the great power, is now the region's biggest headache, tourist-choked and physically fragile. The one-time provinces are now dominant: Verona, Padua, Vicenza and **Treviso** are all major industrial and commercial centres, while intensive dairies, fruit farms and vineyards (around **Conegliano** and Verona especially) have made the Veneto a leading agricultural

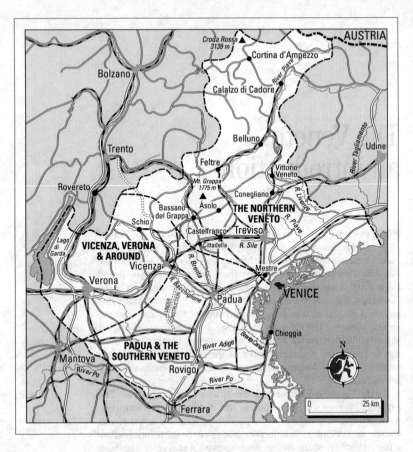

producer as well. The Veneto's income is boosted by the industrial complex of **Mestre** and **Marghera**, the grim conurbation through which all road and rail lines from Venice pass before spreading out over the mainland. It's less a city than an economic life-support system for Venice, and the negative impression you get on your way through is entirely justified. Some people trim their holiday expenses by staying in Mestre's less expensive hotels (Venice's tourist offices will supply addresses), but venturing further inland is a more pleasurable cost-cutting exercise. Padua and Vicenza are your best bets for good-value accommodation; Treviso's hotels are predominantly for commercial travellers, and Verona is just a bit too far from Venice to make daily commuting a sensible proposition.

The administrative region of the Veneto actually extends right to the Austrian border, taking in the portion of the **Dolomites** known as the Cadore, the main town of which is Pieve di Cadore – Titian's birthplace. Further north still is Cortina d'Ampezzo, the swishest ski resort of the eastern Dolomites since it hosted the Winter Olympics in 1956. This whole area offers some of Italy's most sublime landscapes, but the mountains are quite distinct from Venice's immediate hinterland, and cannot really be visited on an excursion from the city. As the purpose of this section of the guide is to reveal the mainland sights and towns that can be seen on a day's excursion from Venice, its northern limit is Belluno.

Getting around the Veneto

The Veneto's public transport system will easily get you to almost all the places covered in the following chapters, at generally low cost. In nearly all cases a day-trip from Venice is feasible, though obviously the larger towns need more than a day to do them justice.

By train

Trains run by the Italian State Railways (*Ferrovie dello Stato* or *FS*) are an inexpensive form of public transport in the Veneto – as a rule of thumb, for journeys within the Veneto you'll pay L100 per kilometre (eg a second-class ticket from Venice to Vicenza, a trip of 68km, costs L6800/€3.60. The trains are very convenient as well, with all the major towns interconnected: one main line runs from Venice through Treviso and northwards, another through Castelfranco up to Bassano, and a third through Padua, Vicenza and Verona. Frequencies of services are given in the box overleaf and in the text, but bear in mind that comments such as "every half-hour" are approximations – as with all Italian train services, there are occasional gaps in the schedule, typically occurring just after the morning rush hour, when the gap between trains may be twice as long as normal.

There are now six types of train in Italy. Top of the range is the **ETR 450 "Pendolino"**, an exclusively first-class inter-city service on which your ticket includes seat reservation, newspapers and a meal. **Eurocity** trains connect the major Italian cities with centres such as Paris, Vienna, Hamburg and Barcelona, while **Intercity** trains link the Italian centres with each other; reservations are obligatory on both of these services, and a supplement in the region of 30 percent of the ordinary fare is payable. (Make sure you pay your supplement before getting on board – you'll have to cough up a far bigger surcharge to the conductor.) **Interregionale** trains are the common-or-garden long-distance expresses, calling only at larger stations; then come the **Regionale** trains, stopping at most stations; and lastly there are the **Locale** services, which stop at every place with a population higher than zero.

The main routes (*Interregionale* and upwards) are covered by *FS*'s national pocket book, *Principali Treni*, issued twice yearly

MAIN VENETO TRAIN SERVICES

Belluno to: Calalzo (10 daily; 1hr); Conegliano (15 daily; 1hr–1hr 30min); Vittorio Veneto (15 daily; 30min).

Castelfranco Veneto to: Belluno (12 daily; 1hr 20min); Feltre (12 daily; 50min); Padua (12 daily; 35min); Treviso (hourly; 25min); Venice (at least every 2hr; 50min); Vicenza (hourly; 40min).

Conegliano to: Belluno (15 daily; 1hr–1hr 30min); Udine (30 daily; 1hr 15min); Venice (34 daily; 1hr); Vittorio Veneto (15 daily; 25min).

Monsélice to: Venice (6 daily; 50min); Padua (9 daily; 20min); Montagnana (9 daily; 25min); Este (9 daily; 10min).

Padua to: Bassano (10 daily; 1hr 5min); Belluno (12 daily; 2hr); Feltre (12 daily; 1hr 30min); Milan (25 daily; 2hr 30min); Monsélice (9 daily; 25min); Rovigo (hourly; 40min); Venice (every 30min; 35min); Verona (25 daily; 55min); Vicenza (25 daily; 20min).

Rovigo to: Venice (22 daily; 90min); Padua (22 daily; 40min).

Treviso to: Castelfranco Veneto (hourly; 25min); Cittadella (hourly; 35min); Conegliano (hourly; 30min); Venice (30 daily; 30min); Vicenza (hourly; 1hr).

Venice to: Bassano (14 daily; 1hr); Belluno (1 daily; 2hr); Castelfranco Veneto (at least every 2hr; 50min); Conegliano (34 daily; 1hr); Milan (25 daily; 2hr 50min–3hr 50min); Monsélice (6 daily; 50min); Padua (every 30min; 35min); Rovigo (19 daily; 1hr–1hr 30min); Treviso (30 daily; 30min); Trieste (14 daily; 2hr 10min); Udine (hourly; 2hr); Verona (at least 25 daily; 1hr 30min); Vicenza (25 daily; 55min); Vittorio Veneto (4 daily; 1–2hr).

Verona to: Milan (30 daily; 1hr 40min); Padua (25 daily; 50min); Venice (25 daily; 90min); Vicenza (30 daily; 30min).

Vicenza to: Castelfranco Veneto (hourly; 40min); Cittadella (hourly; 30min); Milan (30 daily; 1hr 40min); Padua (25 daily; 20min); Thiene (hourly; 25min); Treviso (hourly; 1hr); Venice (25 daily; 55min); Verona (30 daily; 30min).

and free from most train stations, but if you're travelling extensively by train you should pick up the free *FS* leaflets detailing individual lines (readily available from the larger stations). Pay attention to the timetable notes, which may specify the dates between which some services run (*Si effetua dal . . . al . . .*), or whether a service is seasonal (*periódico*). On routes to or from smaller towns, you should also look carefully for a little bus symbol in the margin of the timetable: this indicates that the train service is replaced by a bus (*autocorsa*), which will generally depart from outside the station.

A last word of warning. All train stations have now installed machines in which passengers have to stamp their ticket before embarking. Look out for them in ticket halls and on platforms – they are inconspicuous yellow boxes mounted at waist height. If you realise that you've forgotten to validate your ticket at the station, find the train guard (he or she is nearly always in the first carriage) and present your ticket for clipping – that way you'll be spared a spot-fine of at least L30,000/€15.50.

By bus

Buses offer frequent connections between the main towns: they generally cost more or less the same as the equivalent train journey, and in some instances are actually quicker than the trains. For visits to smaller towns, there is sometimes no alternative unless you have a car – Ásolo, for instance, has no train connection, and you'll need to take a bus for the great Villa Barbaro at Masèr. Usually the bus station (*Autostazione*) is close to the train station, and even when the terminus is elsewhere, many services call at the train station along their route. Tickets have to be bought before getting on board, either from the bus company's office at the station, or from the nearest agent – their name and address is always shown on the timetable at the bus stop. If you're setting off for a remote place, it's always a good idea to buy your ticket for the return leg at the point of departure, as some villages have just a single outlet which might well be closed when you need it. Services are drastically reduced, or nonexistent, on Sunday, and note that lots of departures are linked to school requirements – which sometimes means no services during school holidays.

City buses usually charge a flat fare of around L2000/€1, and again tickets should be bought before getting on – either from offices at bus terminals and stops, or from *tabacchi* and other shops displaying the company's logo and ticket emblem. Stamp your ticket in the machine on the bus – inspectors get on board quite regularly.

By car

Although public transport is adequate for most occasions, there are instances when a **car** is a great convenience. In Venice the **car rental** companies are clustered around Piazzale Roma (for phone numbers, see p.287); you might find slightly better deals in large towns such as Verona, Padua, Vicenza and Treviso, where the car rental offices congregate around the train station – if you see anything for under L500,000/€260 per week (with unlimited mileage), you've found a bargain. The cheapest plan is to arrange the rental in conjunction with your flight or holiday.

For **documentation** you need a valid driving licence and – if you're taking your own car – an international green card of insurance. It's compulsory to carry your car documents and passport while you're driving, and you'll be required to present them if you're stopped by the police. **Rules of the road** are straightforward: drive on the right; at junctions, where there's any ambiguity, give precedence to vehicles coming from the right; observe the speed limits (50kph in built-up areas, 110kph on country roads and on motorways during the week, 130kph on motorways at weekends); and don't drink and drive. If you **break down**, dial ☎116 at the nearest phone and tell the operator where you are, the type of

car and your registration number: the nearest office of the
Automobile Club d'Italia (ACI), an AA/RAC/AAA equivalent, will be
informed and they'll send someone to help, though it's not a free
service. If you need towing anywhere, you can count on it costing
a fairly substantial amount, and it might be worth joining ACI to
qualify for their discounted repairs scheme; write to ACI, Via
Marsala 8, 00185 Rome.

Chapter 15

Padua and the southern Veneto

Summer in Venice used to be the season for people to leave the city in great numbers, rather than pour into it as they do today. When the temperature rose, the gentry would make for their country retreats along the **Brenta**, which flows into the lagoon at the nearest point on the mainland to the city. Many of these houses still stand, and the finest of them can be visited easily by taking one of the buses that run along the Brenta from Venice to Padua.

Situated a little under forty kilometres west of Venice, the ancient university city of **Padua** is the obvious place to seek a room if the hotels of Venice are reaching capacity. It's only half-an-hour's train journey away, accommodation is comparatively inexpensive, and the city's student population guarantees a lively social scene. Moreover, Padua itself has plenty of sights to fill a protracted stay, notably the **Cappella degli Scrovegni**, with its astonishing fresco cycle by Giotto, the **Basilica di Sant'Antonio**, a pilgrimage church which contains some of the finest sculpture in the Veneto, and the vast

---

Hotels in this guide are classified into nine price categories, indicating the **minimum** you can expect to pay for **a double room in high season**, including the cost of breakfast. For many Veneto hotels, high season is now an all-year phenomenon, but in those places that do reduce their prices for the quieter months of the winter, you can expect prices to be around ten percent lower on average.

① Under L100,000/€51.65.
② L100,000–150,000/€51.65–77.47.
③ L150,000–200,000/€77.47–103.29.
④ L200,000–250,000/€103.29–129.11.
⑤ L250,000–300,000/€129.11–154.94.
⑥ L300,000–400,000/€154.94–206.58.
⑦ L400,000–500,000/€206.58–258.23.
⑧ L500,000–600,000/€258.23–309.87.
⑨ Over L600,000/€309.87.

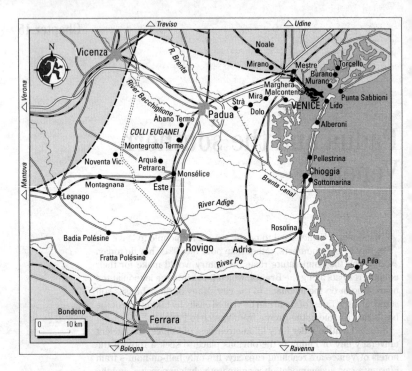

Palazzo della Ragione, the frescoed medieval hall that overlooks Padua's twin market squares.

Of the small towns to the **south of Padua** the most enticing are **Monsélice**, which has a superbly restored castle, and **Montagnana**, whose medieval town walls have survived in almost pristine form. And if you need a rest from urban pursuits, the green **Colli Euganei** (Euganean Hills) offer a pleasant excursion, while the **Po delta**'s nature reserves and beaches are the quietest stretches of coastline in the area.

The Brenta

The southernmost of the three main rivers that empty into the Venetian lagoon (the other two are the Sile and Piave), the **Brenta** caused no end of trouble to the earliest settlers on both the mainland and the islands: on the one hand, its frequent flooding made agriculture difficult, and on the other, the silt it dumped into the lagoon played havoc with Venice's water channels. Land reclamation schemes were carried out from the eleventh century, but it was in the fourteenth century that Venice began the large-scale canalization of the Brenta, an intervention which both reinforced the banks of the river and controlled the deposition of its contents in the lagoon. The largest of the artificial channels, La Cunetta, which runs from Stra to Chioggia, was finished as recently as 1896, but by the sixteenth century the management of the Brenta was sufficiently advanced for the land along its lower course, from Padua to the river-mouth at Fusina, to become a favoured building site for the Venetian aristocracy.

Some of these Venetian **villas** were built as a combination of summer residence and farmhouse – most, however, were intended solely for the former function. From the sixteenth century to the eighteenth, the period from mid-June to mid-November was the season of the *villeggiatura*, when the patrician families of Venice would load their best furniture onto barges and set off for the relative coolness of the Brenta. Around one hundred villas are left standing: some are derelict, a large number are still inhabited and a handful are open to the public. Of this last category, two are outstanding – the Villa Fóscari and the Villa Pisani.

Getting to the Brenta villas

During the eighteenth century, the mode of transport the gentry used for the *villeggiatura* was a capacious and well-padded vessel known as the *Burchiello*. The modern *Burchiello*, a tub that looks like a river-going shoebox, is one of a small flotilla of pleasure craft that shuttles tourists along the river, making a few brief stops at selected villas, pausing rather longer for lunch, and finally unloading them at Padua or Venice to catch the bus or train back to where they started. Day-trips on the *Burchiello* and its cousins cost around L120,000/€62 (excluding lunch and bus ticket), and you can get tickets from many of Venice's travel agents – all those near the Piazza sell them.

Hoi polloi can get to **Malcontenta** for L1400/€0.72 on the half-hourly Padua ACTV **bus** from Piazzale Roma – the trip takes twenty minutes (not all of the Padua buses go via Malcontenta so check before you get on). On your way back, if the first bus that comes along isn't going to Venice, take it as far as Corso del Popolo in Mestre, then cross the road for a #4 to Piazzale Roma – you can do it on the one ticket, which is valid for an hour.

The same Padua-bound bus goes onto **Stra** (another twenty minutes from Malcontenta; L4000/€2.07 from Venice), goes right past the door and gives you a good view of dozens of villas on the way. They are particularly thick on the ground from **Oriago** onwards (16km out of Venice), the most attractive stretch being centred on the elongated town of **Mira**, shortly after Oriago. The Villa dei Contarini in Mira was one of Henry III of France's ports of call on his visit of 1574, and Byron wrote part of *Childe Harold* in the Palazzo Fóscarini (now the post office), where he lived in 1817–19.

The Brenta

For more information on villas in the Veneto, check out www.ville.inews.it/eintro.htm, *a well presented and informative Web site, with good links and some beautiful photos.*

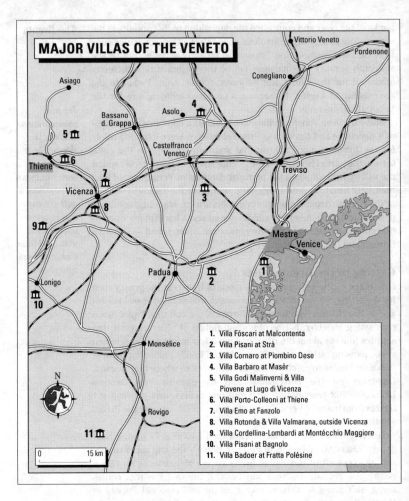

MAJOR VILLAS OF THE VENETO

1. Villa Fóscari at Malcontenta
2. Villa Pisani at Strà
3. Villa Cornaro at Piombino Dese
4. Villa Barbaro at Masèr
5. Villa Godi Malinverni & Villa
   Piovene at Lugo di Vicenza
6. Villa Porto-Colleoni at Thiene
7. Villa Emo at Fanzolo
8. Villa Rotonda & Villa Valmarana, outside Vicenza
9. Villa Cordellina-Lombardi at Montécchio Maggiore
10. Villa Pisani at Bagnolo
11. Villa Badoer at Fratta Polésine

The Brenta tourist office produces a comprehensive bilingual booklet on the villas and hotels of the Brenta, *Riviera del Brenta*, which can be picked up at their office in the Villa Wildmann Fóscari or in Venice, at the Calle dell'Ascension tourist office.

The Villa Fóscari

The Villa Fóscari is open May to mid-Nov Tues & Sat 9am–noon; L12,000/€6.20.

Sometimes known as the Villa Malcontenta (or Villa Fóscari La Malcontenta di Mira), the **Villa Fóscari** at **MALCONTENTA** was designed in 1559 for the brothers Alvise and Niccolò Fóscari by **Palladio**, and is the nearest of his villas to Venice. None of Palladio's villas more powerfully evokes the architecture of ancient Rome: the heavily rusticated exterior suggests the masonry of Roman public buildings; the massive Ionic portico alludes to classical temple fronts (which Palladio believed to be derived from domestic architecture); and the two-storey main hall was inspired by the bath complexes of imperial Rome, as was the three-sectioned arched window (a feature known as a thermal window, from the Roman *thermae*). Palladio was practical as well as erudite: to keep the living quarters well clear of the swampy land, he raised them on a high podium, and to keep building costs down he used the cheapest materials that would do the job – look closely at the columns and you'll see that they're made out of hundreds of bricks in the shape of cake slices.

The main hall and the rooms leading off it (only some of which are open to the public) were frescoed as soon as the walls were up, by **Battista Franco** and **Giovanni Battista Zelotti**, a colleague of Veronese; their work includes what is said to be a portrait of a woman of the Fóscari family who was exiled to the house as punishment for an amorous escapade, and whose consequent misery, according to legend, was the source of the name *Malcontenta*. The reality is more prosaic – the area was known by that name long before the Fóscari arrived, either because of some local discontent over the development of the land, or because of the political *malcontenti* who used to hide out in the nearby salt marshes.

Only two things detract from the pleasure of a trip to the Villa Fóscari – the proximity of the chimneys of Marghera, and the entry fee, which is a bit steep in view of the very limited section of the house that's open.

The Pisani, Widmann Fóscari and Barchessa Valmarana villas

At **STRA**, virtually on the outskirts of Padua, stands the **Villa Pisani** (or **Nazionale**), an immense country palace that looks more like a product of the *ancien régime* than a house for the Venetian gentry. The branch of the Pisani family for whom this place was built was an astronomically wealthy dynasty of bankers, based in Venice in the similarly excessive Palazzo Pisani at Santo Stefano. When Alvise Pisani was elected doge of Venice in 1735, the family celebrated by commissioning the villa from the Paduan architect **Girolamo Frigimelica**; later on the work was taken over by **F.M. Preti** (see the Castelfranco account, p.371, for more specimens of his work). By 1760 it was finished – the biggest such residence to be built in Venetian territory during the century. It has appealed to megalomaniacs ever since: Napoleon bought it off the Pisani in 1807 and handed it over to Eugène Beauharnais, his stepson and Viceroy of Italy; and in 1934 it was the place chosen for the first meeting of Mussolini and Hitler.

The house has been stripped of nearly all its original furnishings, and it's as hard to thrill to the eighteenth-century frescoes of smiling nymphs and smirking satyrs that decorate some of the rooms as to

The Villa Pisani and its grounds are open daily: April–Sept 9am–6pm; Oct–March 9am–4pm; L10,000/€5.16.

the almost blank walls elsewhere. But then there's the **ballroom**, its ceiling covered with a fresco of *The Apotheosis of the Pisani Family*, the last major piece painted by **Giambattista Tiepolo** before his departure for Spain in 1762, at the age of 66. It's a dazzling performance, as full of blue space as it could possibly be without falling apart; and if you're trying to puzzle out what's going on – the Pisani family, accompanied by Venice, are being courted by the Arts, Sciences and Spirits of Peace, while Fame plays a fanfare in praise of the Pisani and the Madonna looks on with appropriate pride. The monochrome frescoes on Roman themes around the musicians' gallery are by Giambattista's son, Giandomenico.

In the **grounds**, the long fish-pond ends in front of a stable-block which from a distance might be mistaken for another grand house. Off to the right (as you look away from the villa) is a peculiar belvedere, resembling a chapel with its dome lopped off; and close by there's an impressive maze – unless a blizzard is blowing, it'll be packed with half a dozen coachloads of Italian schoolkids.

The Villa Widmann Fóscari is open Tues–Fri 10am–6pm, Sat & Sun 10am–7pm; L8000/ €4.13.

The Villa Barchessa Valmarana is open Tues–Sun 9.30am–noon & 2–5.30pm; L8000/ €4.13.

Two other villas often feature on suggested itineraries of the Brenta. The **Villa Widmann Fóscari** at Mira Porte, just after Oriago, was built in the early eighteenth century and redecorated fifty years or so later. It's probably a delight for admirers of French Rococo style, but for most people it will only demonstrate by contrast how inventive Tiepolo was. The **Villa Barchessa Valmarana**, just across the canal, was built in the seventeenth century but the main accommodation block was destroyed by the Valmarana family at the end of the nineteenth to avoid paying luxury taxes. Today, the only part of the villa which can be visited is one of the wings that flanked the house; originally built as boat and agricultural storage space, it was soon after converted into guest quarters. The furniture on display was brought over from the main house when it was demolished, and the dining room has a ceiling fresco glorifying the Valmarana family, but the main interest of this villa is as a symbol of the demise of the Venetian aristocracy.

Padua

Extensively reconstructed after the damage caused by World War II bombing, and hemmed in by the sprawl which has accompanied its development into the most important economic centre of the Veneto, **PADUA** (Padova) is not at first sight as alluring as many of the region's towns. It was, however, one of the most important cultural centres of northern Italy, and retains plentiful evidence of its impressive lineage in its churches, museums and frescoed interiors. In recent years, civic efforts to polish and pedestrianize the city centre – even to the extent of mapping out the medieval street plan in marble flagstones – have made it easier to conjure up the context of Padua's many historic buildings.

Legend has it that Padua was founded in 1185 BC by Antenor of Troy – a story propagated first by the Roman historian Livy, who was

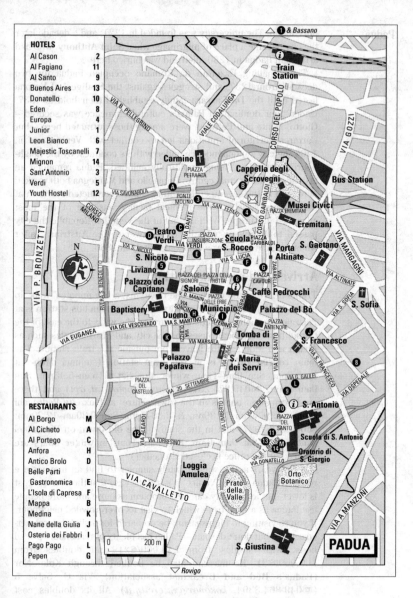

HOTELS

Al Cason	2
Al Fagiano	11
Al Santo	9
Buenos Aires	13
Donatello	10
Eden	8
Europa	4
Junior	1
Leon Bianco	6
Majestic Toscanelli	7
Mignon	14
Sant'Antonio	3
Verdi	5
Youth Hostel	12

RESTAURANTS

Al Borgo	M
Al Cicheto	A
Al Portego	C
Anfora	H
Antico Brolo	D
Belle Parti Gastronomica	E
L'Isola di Capresa	F
Mappa	B
Medina	K
Nane della Giulia	J
Osteria dei Fabbri	I
Pago Pago	L
Pepen	G

PADUA

born in a nearby village and spent much of his life here. A Roman *municipium* from 45 BC, the city thrived until the barbarian onslaughts and the subsequent Lombard invasion at the start of the seventh century. Recovery was slow, but by the middle of the twelfth century, when it became a free commune, Padua was prosperous once again. The university was founded in 1221, and a decade later the city became a place of pilgrimage when **Saint Anthony**, who had arrived in Padua in 1230, died and was buried here.

The appalling **Ezzelino da Romano** occupied Padua for two decades from 1237, and struggles against the **Scaligeri** of Verona lasted until the **Da Carrara** family established their hold in 1337. Under their domination Padua's cultural eminence was secured – Giotto, Dante and Petrarch were among those attracted here – but Carraresi territorial ambitions led to conflict with Venice, and in 1405 the city's independence ended with its conquest by the neighbouring republic. Though politically nullified, Padua remained an artistic and intellectual centre: Donatello and Mantegna both worked here, and in the seventeenth century Galileo conducted research at the university, where the medical faculty was one of the most advanced in Europe. With the fall of the Venetian Republic the city passed to Napoleon, who handed it over to the **Austrians**, after whose regime Padua was annexed to Italy in 1866.

Arrival and accommodation

Trains arrive in the north of the town, just a few minutes' walk up Corso del Popolo from the old city walls. The main **bus station** is at Piazzale Boschetti, immediately north of the walls to the east of the Corso; however, **local buses** for the city and nearby towns such as Ábano and Montegrotto leave from outside the train station. The main **tourist office** is at the train station (summer Mon–Sat 9am–7pm, Sun 9am–1pm; winter Mon–Sat 9.15am–5.45pm, Sun 9am–noon; ☎049.875.2077, *www.padovanet.it/apt*) and there are information booths in the town centre, at Piazzetta Pedrocchi (Mon–Sat 9.30am–12.30pm & 3.30–7pm, Sun 9.30am–12.30pm; ☎049.876.7927) and in the south of the old town, on Piazza del Santo (Mon–Sat 9am–6pm, Sun 9am–1pm; in winter hours are reduced or the office is closed altogether).

A few years ago it was infinitely simpler to find an inexpensive room in Padua than in Venice; it's still the case that the average cost is lower, but availability can be a problem as more and more people use Padua as a base from which to visit its overcrowded neighbour. If you're visiting in high season, be prepared for a slightly protracted search, but don't despair – Padua has plenty of reasonably priced beds, with singles from L40,000/€21 and doubles from L60,000/€31. Rooms can also be booked through Koko Nor (Padua's **Bed and Breakfast** association), Via G. Selva 5 (☎049.864.3394, *kokonor@intercity.it*). All its doubles cost L90,000/€46.49, singles L50,000/€25.82.

Hotels

Al Cason, Via Fra Paolo Sarpi 40 ☎049.662.636 fax 049.875.4217, *hotelcason @icl.it*. Large and efficiently run two-star, a few minutes from the station. ③.

Al Fagiano, Via Locatelli 45 ☎049.875.3396. Good two-star near the Basilica. ②.

Al Santo, Via del Santo 147 ☎049.875.2131. One-star, slightly lacking in atmosphere, but near the Basilica. Needs a refit, but the rooms are clean and bright and all doubles have a bathroom. ①.

Buenos Aires, Via L. Belludi 37 ☎049.665.633 fax 049.658.685. Decent two-star off the Piazza del Santo; bright, airy rooms with or without private bathroom. There is also a car park round the back (L10,000/€5.16 per day). ③.

Donatello, Via del Santo 102–4 ☎049.875.0634 fax 049.875.0829, *www.hoteldonatello.net*. A big, if bland, four-star hotel just north of the Basilica, with some rooms looking onto the piazza – one of only two smart hotels in the historic centre. Private parking at L28,000/€14.46 per day. ⑤.

Eden, Via C. Battisti 255 ☎049.650.484. A cut above other one-stars, though offers something of a mixed bag of rooms. All doubles have showers, but avoid the coffin-like singles. Situated in a good location near Piazza del Santo, in the university quarter. ②.

Europa, Largo Europa 9 ☎049.661.200 fax 049.661.508. A big, modernish three-star situated in a busy and potentially noisy area just west of Piazza Eremitani. ⑤.

Junior, Via L. Faggin 2 ☎049.611.756. Acceptable one-star, close to the station. Just seven rooms and two shared bathrooms. ②.

Leon Bianco, Piazzetta Pedrocchi 12 ☎049.875.0814 fax 049.875.6184, *leonbianco@toscanelli.com*. Situated close to Piazza della Frutta, this is the best-located of Padua's mid-range three-star hotels. ③.

Majestic Toscanelli, Via dell'Arco 2 ☎049.663.244 fax 049.876.0025, *majestic@toscanelli.com*. Padua's other central four-star (with the *Donatello*), and probably the hotel of choice if you want to stay in style; it's located just south of Piazza delle Erbe, off Via SS. Martino e Solferino. ⑤.

Mignon, Via L.Belludi 22 ☎049.661.722. Comfortable two-star between Prato delle Valle and the Basilica. They also have rooms that sleep three and four. ③.

Sant'Antonio, Via San Fermo 118 ☎049.875.1393 fax 049.875.2508. Pleasant, larger-than-average two-star in the northern part of central Padua. Rooms have slightly faded modern interiors but the better ones (those at the back) have views over the canal and the lovely Ponte Molino. ②.

Verdi, Via Dondi dell'Orologio 7 ☎049.875.5774. Centrally located and inexpensive one-star, with just three bathrooms between fifteen rooms. ①.

Hostels and campsites

Ostello Città di Padova, Via A. Aleardi 30 ☎049.875.2219 fax 049.654.210. Padua's HI hostel is a good 30min walk from the train station. Alternatively, take bus #8, #12 or #18 (#32 on Sundays) to Prato della Valle, from where it's a short walk northwest. Very quiet and friendly, but has an 11pm curfew. L21,000/€10.85 per person, including breakfast. Open for depositing luggage and booking a bed Mon–Fri 8–9.30am & 2.30–11pm, Sat & Sun 8–9.30am & 4–11pm.

Montegrotto Terme, Strada Romana Aponense 104 ☎049.793.400 fax 049.807.0266. This is the nearest campsite to Padua – 15km south from the city centre, but frequent trains take around 15min; a very upmarket site, it boasts not merely a swimming pool but thermal baths too. L28,000/€14.46 per person per night. Open March–Nov.

Padua

The City

The Musei Civici degli Eremitani and Cappella degli Scrovegni are open Tues–Sun: Feb–Oct 9am–7pm; Nov–Jan 9am–6pm; L10,000/€5.16 for joint ticket. The Cappella alone is open on Mon. Booking esssential: ☎049.820.4550.

From the train station, the drab Corso del Popolo and Corso Garibaldi lead south through a gap in the Renaissance city walls towards the centre of the city, passing after a short distance some public gardens and the **Cappella degli Scrovegni**. The **Giotto frescoes** in the Scrovegni chapel constitute one of the key works in the development of European art, and draw thousands of people to the city every year – so many people, indeed, that drastic steps have had to be taken to reverse the damage caused to the frescoes by the high levels of humidity created by the breath and perspiration of the massed tourists. Entrance to the chapel is through a sophisticated airlock: at the time printed on your ticket, the glass door to the waiting room slides open to allow the next set of visitors in, and almost immediately shuts again, obliging anyone left outside to pay for another slot. Once inside, a high-tech system lowers the humidity of the waiting room to that of the chapel, and filters away any stray spores and pollutants. Fourteen minutes later another door leading to the chapel itself opens and you have exactly a quarter of an hour to take in the frescoes before being ejected through a third glass door back into the grounds of the museum. Visits are restricted to a maximum of twenty-five people at a time and tickets have to be booked in advance – usually a minimum of three days beforehand.

The chapel was commissioned in 1303 by Enrico Scrovegni in atonement for his father's usury, which was so vicious that Dante allotted him a place in the *Inferno* – he died screaming "give me the keys to my strong box" and was denied a Christian burial. As soon as the walls were built, Giotto was commissioned to cover every inch of the interior with frescoed illustrations of the lives of Jesus, Mary and Joachim (Mary's father), and the story of the Passion; the finished cycle, arranged in three tightly knit tiers and painted against a backdrop of saturated blue, presents an artistic vision of the same order as that of the Sistine Chapel. Looking towards the altar, the tiers on the right depict (from top to bottom) *The History of Joachim, The Childhood of Christ* and *The Passion*; the tiers on the left comprise *The Life of the Virgin, Christ's Public Life* and *Christ's Death and Resurrection*.

Although Duccio and Cimabue, the two earliest major figures of Italian painting, had done much to relax the stylized, icon-like conventions of painting, it was in the work of Giotto that a consistent humanism first appeared. The Scrovegni series is a marvellous demonstration of this new attention to the inner nature of the protagonists – the exchange of looks between the two shepherds in *The Arrival of Joachim* is particularly powerful, as are *The Embrace of Joachim and Anna at the Golden Gate* and *The Visit of Mary to Elizabeth*. On occasion even the buildings and landscape have been manipulated to add to the drama, for example in the *Deposition* (immediately right of the *Crucifixion*), where a strong diagonal leads the eye straight to the faces of Jesus and Mary.

Beneath the main pictures are shown the vices and virtues in human (usually female) form, while on the wall above the door is the *Last Judgement*, with rivers of fire leading from God to hell, and two angels rolling back the painting to remind us that this is an imaginative scene and not an authoritative vision of eternity. An alleged self-portrait (fourth from the left at the bottom) places Giotto firmly amongst the redeemed, and directly above the door is a portrait of Scrovegni presenting the chapel; his tomb is at the far end, behind the altar with its statues by **Giovanni Pisano**.

The neighbouring **Musei Civici degli Eremitani**, formerly the monastery of the Eremitani, is a superbly presented museum complex that contains the Museo Archeologico, Museo d'Arte-Pinacoteca and the Museo Bottacin. There's a helpful information desk at the museums' entrance, which sells the *Padova Arte* card (see opposite) and has information on Padua's cultural events. The archeological collection, on the ground floor, has a vast array of pre-Roman, Roman and paleo-Christian objects, with an absorbing section on the unique language spoken in the Veneto before the establishment of Roman hegemony (but unfortunately no English translations). Upstairs, the vast Museo d'Arte houses extensive and varied collections of fourteenth- to nineteenth-century art from the Veneto and further afield, usually arranged in roughly chronological order. There are tracts of workaday stuff here, but names such as Titian, Tintoretto and Tiepolo leaven the mix, and spectacular highpoints are provided by the Giotto *Crucifixion* that was once in the Scrovegni chapel, and a fine *Portrait of a Young Senator* by Bellini. In the midst of the ranks of French, Flemish and miscellaneous Italian paintings you'll also happen upon a shockingly vivid sequence of pictures by Luca Giordano, featuring a repulsive and medically precise depiction of Job and his boils. The offshoot Capodilista collection contains a rich seam of sixteenth-century works, including four mysterious landscape allegories by Titian and Giorgione.

The Museo Bottacin, for more specialist tastes, was founded in 1865 and contains over 50,000 coins, medals and seals, making it one of the most important museums of its type in the world.

Padua

The Chiesa Eremitani is open summer Mon–Sat 8.15am–12.15 pm & 4–6pm, Sun 9.30am– 12.15pm & 4–6pm.

The Eremitani

The nearby church of the **Eremitani**, built at the turn of the four-teenth century, was almost completely wrecked by an Allied bomb-ing raid in 1944 and has been fastidiously rebuilt. (Photographs to the left and right of the apse show the bombs falling and the extent of the damage.) The worst aspect of the bombardment was the near total destruction of **Mantegna**'s frescoes of the lives of Saint James and Saint Christopher – during World War II, only the destruction of the Camposanto in Pisa was a comparably severe blow to Italy's artistic heritage.

Produced between 1454 and 1457, when Mantegna was in his mid-twenties, the frescoes were unprecedented in the thoroughness with which they exploited fixed-point perspective – a concept central to Renaissance humanism, with its emphasis on the primacy of individ-ual perception. Furthermore, Mantegna's compositions had to take into account the low viewpoint of the person in the chapel. The extent to which he overcame these complex technical problems can now be assessed only from the sad fragments preserved in the chapel to the right of the high altar. On the left wall is the *Martyrdom of St James*, put together from fragments found in the rubble; and on the right is the *Martyrdom of St Christopher*, which had been removed from the wall before the war.

The sanctuary and the second and fourth chapels of the right aisle contain frescoes by the late fourteenth-century Paduan painter Guariento, the *Madonna* in the fourth chapel being the best of them.

To Santa Sofia

The Museo della Terza Armata is open Mon–Fri 9am–noon & 3–4.30pm, Sat & Sun 9am–noon; free.

Straddling Via Altinate, the **Porta Altinate** was one of the gates of the medieval city, and bears a plaque recording its violent recapture from Ezzelino da Romano on June 20, 1256. More recent military history is recorded a short way east of here, at Via Altinate 59, in the former residence of Cardinal Pietro Bembo; once the HQ of the Italian Third Army (NE Division) and now the HQ of the artillery, the palace houses the **Museo della Terza Armata**, a collection of mili-taria primarily related to World War I.

Continuing past the dull sixteenth-century church of San Gaetano and a scattering of fine houses, you come to **Santa Sofia**, the oldest church in Padua. It dates back to the sixth century, though most of today's beautiful brick-built structure dates from the twelfth and thir-teenth centuries. The apse in particular shows Veneto-Byzantine influence, and is reminiscent of the cathedral at Torcello or Santi Maria e Donato on Murano.

Santa Sofia is open daily 9am–noon & 4–6.30pm.

The university and Palazzo Zabarella

A short distance south of the Porta Altinate stands the university's main block, the **Palazzo del Bò** – the name translates as "of the Ox", after an inn that used to stand here. Established in September 1221, the University of Padua is older than any other in Italy except that of Bologna, and the coats of arms that encrust the courtyard and Great Hall attest to the social and intellectual rank of its alumni. The first permanent **anatomy theatre** was built here in 1594, a facility that doubtless greatly helped William Harvey, who went on to develop the theory of blood circulation after taking his degree here in 1602. Galileo taught physics here from 1592 to 1610, declaiming from a lectern that is still on show. And in 1678 Elena Lucrezia Corner Piscopia became the first woman to collect a university degree when she was awarded her doctorate in philosophy here – there's a statue of her in the courtyard.

Piazza Antenore, at the back of the Bò, is the site of the **Tomba di Antenore**, alleged resting place of the city's legendary founder. If you cross the piazza you'll come to the **Palazzo Zabarella** on the corner of Via San Francesco and Via Zabarella. Founded in the twelfth century, it was owned by the Da Carrara family then the Zabarella family, who resided here for more than four hundred years from 1405. A fine example of a Paduan aristocratic town-house (the tower was characteristic of such houses), it has served various purposes since it ceased to be the Zabarella house: for a time it was the property of a local bank, and later became the salon of the Caffè Pedrocchi intellectuals when they moved out of their namesake after World War II. After an archeological exploration and restoration the Zabarelle opened in 1996 with an exhibition space upstairs and some stylish shops in the courtyard. When there is no art exhibition on, you can still get in to see the permanent collection belonging to the Palazzo Zabarella, including Roman relics unearthed on the site.

The central squares

The area north and west of the university forms the hub of the city. A little way up from the university, on the left, is the Neoclassical **Caffè Pedrocchi**, which used to be the city's main intellectual salon; it's no longer that, but it does have a multiplicity of functions – chic café, concert hall, conference centre and exhibition space.

Due west of the Pedrocchi, the **Piazza della Frutta** and **Piazza delle Erbe**, the sites of Padua's daily markets, are lined by bars, cafés and shops. Separating them is the extraordinary **Palazzo della Ragione** (or **Salone**, as it is more commonly known), which you enter up the grand stairs of the courtyard of the Palazzo Municipale in Via VIII Febbraio, opposite the Palazzo del Bò.

At the time of its construction in the 1210s, this vast hall was the largest room ever to have been built on top of another storey. Its decoration would once have been as astounding as its size, but the original frescoes by Giotto and his assistants were destroyed by fire in 1420, though some by **Giusto de' Menabuoi** have survived. Most of the extant frescoes, however, are by **Nicola Miretto** (1425–40), whose 333-panel astrological calendar has a fascination that

Padua

Guided tours of the Bò are held March–Oct Tues, Thurs, Sat 9, 10 & 11am, Mon Wed, Fri 3, 4 & 5pm; reduced hours in winter (varies); L5000/€2.58.

The Palazzo Zabarella is open Tues–Sun 10am–7pm, until 8pm in summer; L1000/€0.52 for permanent collection, L10,000/€5.16 for special exhibitions.

The Salone is open Tues–Sun: summer 9am–7pm; winter 9am–6pm; L7000/€3.62 – prices and times vary during exhibitions.

transcends the limitations of his workmanship. Each of the twelve sections begins with the apostle appropriate to that month (the larger panel) and progresses through the allegorical figures representing the month, the zodiacal sign, the planet and constellation, the type of work done in that month and the human figure representing the astrological type. The ceiling was originally frescoed as a deep blue starry sky but was rebuilt following a violent tornado in 1756 and has been letting in the wind and rain ever since; the consequent restoration work keeps at least part of the hall closed at all times, making it difficult to appreciate Miretto's grand scheme in its entirety.

Now used as an exhibition space and as the city council's assembly hall, the Salone was also a place where Padua's citizens could plead for justice – hence the appellation *della Ragione*, meaning "of reason". The black stone to the right inside the door, called the *pietra del vituperio* (stone of insults), also played a part in the judicial system: Thomas Coryat recorded that a bankrupt could dissolve some of his debts by sitting on it "with his naked buttocks three times in some public assembly". The gigantic wooden horse with disproportionately gigantic gonads (in a part of the hall closed to visitors at the time of writing) is modelled on Donatello's *Gattamelata*, and was made for a joust in 1466. Before leaving, take a stroll along the magnificent loggias on either side, which look out onto the Piazza della Frutta and Piazza delle Erbe.

Both the Piazza della Frutta and the Piazza delle Erbe have some attractive buildings around them, as does the **Piazza dei Signori**, which lies a little to the west. At the west end of the piazza, beyond the Lombard **Loggia della Gran Guardia** (c.1500), is the early fifteenth-century **Torre dell'Orologio**, a structure that predates even Venice's clock tower. Through the arch, under the clock, is the Corte Capitaniato, with two university buildings on the left. The first is the **Palazzo del Capitanio**, the sixteenth-century headquarters of the city's Venetian military commander; the second is the university's arts faculty, the **Liviano**. The frescoes in the Liviano's upstairs fourteenth-century **Sala dei Giganti** include a portrait of Petrarch, but there are no plans for public access once the current restoration is finished.

San Nicolò is open daily 8am–noon & 4–7pm.

Via dei Da Carrara runs north of the Piazza del Capitaniato straight up to the church of **San Nicolò** – basically an altered thirteenth-century building, though it retains an eleventh-century chapel.

The Duomo and Baptistery

The Baptistery is open daily: April–Sept 10am–7pm; Oct–March 10am–6pm; L3500/€1.81.

Immediately southwest of the Piazza dei Signori is Padua's **Duomo**, an unlovely church whose architect cribbed his design from drawings by Michelangelo; the adjacent Romanesque **Baptistery**, though, is one of the unproclaimed delights of Padua.

Built by the Da Carrara clan in the thirteenth century, and still used for baptisms today, it's lined with frescoes by **Giusto de'**

Menabuoi (c.1376), a cycle that makes a fascinating comparison with Giotto's in the Cappella degli Scrovegni. The influence of Giotto is plain, but in striving for greater naturalism Giusto has lost Giotto's monumentality and made some of his figures awkward and unconvincing. Yet many of the scenes are delightful – the *Marriage at Cana*, for instance – and the vibrancy of their colours, coupled with the size and relative quiet of the building, make the visit memorable. The polyptych **altarpiece**, also by Menabuoi, was stolen in 1972 but quickly recovered, minus some of its wooden framework. Don't overlook the **mausoleum of Fina Buzzaccharini** (on the wall opposite the altar), one of the Carrara family's most assiduous artistic patrons; she's shown on the front being presented to the Virgin by John the Baptist. The actual tomb was destroyed by the Venetians when they took control of the city in 1405.

Piazza del Santo and the Gattamelata monument

If you continue trudging south from the Porta Altinate you'll soon find yourself in Via del Santo, where an increasing density of shops selling garishly decorated candles and outsize souvenir rosaries will prepare you for the pilgrim-ensnaring stalls of the **Piazza del Santo**, dwarfed by the domes, towers and red brick bulk of the Basilica.

The main sight on the piazza is Donatello's **Monument to Gattamelata** ("The Honeyed Cat"), as the *condottiere* Erasmo da Narni was known. He died in 1443 and this monument was raised ten years later, the earliest large bronze sculpture of the Renaissance. It's a direct precursor to Verrocchio's equestrian monument to Colleoni in Venice (and Colleoni was under Gattamelata's command for a time), but could hardly be more different: Gattemelata was known for his honesty and dignity, and Donatello has given us an image of comparative sensitivity and restraint, quite unlike Verrocchio's image of power through force. The modelling of the horse makes a double allusion: to the equestrian statue of Marcus Aurelius in Rome, and to the horses of San Marco in Venice.

The Basilica di Sant'Antonio

Within eighteen months of his death in 1231, St Anthony of Padua had been canonized and his tomb was attracting enough pilgrims to warrant the building of the **Basilica di Sant'Antonio**, or **Il Santo**. It was not until the start of the fourteenth century that the church reached a state that enabled the saint's body to be placed in the chapel designated for it. The **exterior** is an outlandish mixture, with *campanili* like minarets, Byzantine domes and Romanesque and Gothic features on the facade and apse.

The Basilica is open daily: summer 6.30am–7.45pm; winter 6.30am–7pm.

The **interior** is similarly heterogeneous: the plan up to the transepts being much like that of Italian mendicant churches, whereas the complex ambulatory with radiating chapels is more like the layout of French pilgrimage churches of the period. St Anthony's chapel – the **Cappella del Santo** – is in the left transept, plastered

---

St Anthony

Born in 1195 in Lisbon, St Anthony (christened Fernando) was a canon of the Augustinian order in Coimbra before he donned the Franciscan habit in 1220 and set off for Morocco, having been inspired to undertake his mission by five Franciscan friars who had been martyred by the Moroccan infidels. Soon taken ill in Africa, he sailed back to Portugal but was blown off course and landed in Sicily. From there Anthony headed north to Assisi, thence to a hermitage near Forlì, where his oratorical skills and profound knowledge of the scriptures were discovered when he was called upon to speak at a service for which no-one had thought to prepare a sermon. After that he embarked on a career as a peripatetic preacher, addressing ever-increasing audiences in northern Italy and southern France, performing miracles (illustrated by the panels around his chapel) and bringing unbelievers into the fold. The "hammer of heretics" was esteemed both by St Francis and by Pope Gregory IX, who acclaimed him as the "*doctor optime*" upon hearing of Anthony's death in 1231. In 1263 the saint's relics were removed to the basilica that had been built in his honour. When his tomb was opened it was discovered that his flesh had turned to dust – except for the tongue.

St. Anthony's chaste life is symbolized by the lily that is his distinguishing feature in depictions of him. He is also often portrayed holding the infant Jesus, a reference to an incident when he was observed from afar cradling the Son of God. His popularity has continued to grow after his death, and the abundance of letters, photographs and gifts around his shrine confirms the endurance of the belief in Anthony's wonder-working powers. He is the patron saint of Portugal, lost property, and the less exalted animal species – the last honour comes from the legend that he preached to fishes when he could find no human audience.

---

with votive photographs of healed limbs, car crashes survived thanks to the saint's intervention, and other offerings irresistible to the voyeur. The chapel's more formal decoration includes a sequence of nine **panels** showing scenes from St Anthony's life; carved between 1505 and 1577, they are the most important series of relief sculpture created in sixteenth-century Italy. Reading from the left: St Anthony receives his Franciscan habit; a jealous husband stabs his wife, whom the saint later revived; St Anthony raises a man from the dead to prove the innocence of his father; he revives a drowned woman (panel by Sansovino); he revives a baby scalded to death in a cauldron (Sansovino and Minello); he directs mourners to find the heart of a miser in his coffer (Tullio Lombardo); he restores the severed foot of a boy (Tullio Lombardo); a heretic throws a glass which miraculously breaks the floor and remains intact; and a newborn baby tells of the innocence of its mother (Antonio Lombardo).

Adjoining the chapel is the **Cappella della Madonna Mora** (named after its fourteenth-century French altar statue), which in turn lets onto the **Cappella del Beato Luca**, where Saint Anthony's body was first placed. Dedicated to Luca Belludi, St Anthony's closest companion, the latter chapel contains a fine fresco cycle by **Giusto de'**

Menabuoi, including scenes from the lives of the Apostles Philip and James the Lesser (there's a lovely image of Saint James lifting a prison tower to free a prisoner), and *Saint Anthony revealing to Luca Belludi that Padua will be liberated from Ezzelino*, with an idealized version of the city, parts of it recognizable, as backdrop.

Back in the aisle, just before the Cappella del Santo, is Padua's finest work by **Pietro Lombardo**, the monument to Antonio Roselli (1467). More impressive still are the high altar's bronze sculptures and reliefs by **Donatello** (1444–45), the works which introduced Renaissance classicism to Padua. Unfortunately they are often inaccessible, though a word with one of the sacristans may get you a closer view. The neo-Gothic frescoes of the apse, choir and presbytery were begun by **Achille Casanova** in 1903, and took about forty years. Trying to imitate Giotto's use of blue, he ended up turning this end of the basilica into a gloomy cavern.

Built onto the furthest point of the ambulatory, the **Cappella del Tesoro** was designed in the 1690s by **Filippo Parodi**, a pupil of Bernini; its most important relics are some thorns from Christ's crown, and Il Santo's tongue and chin, kept in a head-shaped container.

The Cappella del Tesoro is open daily 8am–1pm & 2.30–7pm.

Most of the back wall of the **Cappella di San Felice**, occupying the right transept, is taken up by a glorious *Crucifixion*, frescoed in the 1370s by Altichiero da Zevio. Other things to seek out are the **monuments to Cardinal Pietro Bembo and Alessandro Contarini** on the nave's second pair of columns, both designed by Sanmicheli in the 1550s (with a bust by Danese Cattaneo), and the **tomb of Gattamelata**, in the first chapel on the right. The fresco on the interior wall of the facade is a more recent addition, *Saint Anthony preaching from the walnut tree* by **Annigoni** (1985). The painting above the altar in the first chapel on the left is also by him.

In the cloisters (on the south side of the basilica) you'll find the **Museo Antoniano** and **Mostra Antoniana**. The former, on the first floor, is a collection of paintings (including a fresco of *SS. Anthony and Bernardine* by **Mantegna**, which once adorned the basilica's facade), ornate incense-holders, ceremonial robes and other paraphernalia linked to the basilica; the latter, on the ground floor, is a history of votive gifts, with copious examples of the genre. A second component of the Mostra Antoniana, an audio-visual presentation (in Italian) of St Anthony and his work, is on perpetual show elsewhere in the cloister.

The Museo and Mostra are open Tues–Sun: summer 10am–1pm & 2.30–6pm; winter 10am–1pm & 2–5pm; L5000/€2.58 for the Museo, the Mostra is free.

The south side of the piazza

To the left as you leave the basilica are the joined Oratorio di San Giorgio and **Scoletta del Santo** (or Scuola di Sant'Antonio). The Scoletta, a confraternity run on the same lines as the scuole of Venice (see p.141), was founded soon after Anthony's canonization, though this building dates only as far back as the early fifteenth century. The

Padua

ground floor is still used for religious purposes, while upstairs is maintained pretty much as it would have looked in the sixteenth century, with its fine ceiling and paintings dating mainly from 1509–15. Four of the pictures are said to be by **Titian** – *The Jealous Husband Stabbing his Wife*, with an almost insignificant intervention by Il Santo in the background; *St Anthony Reattaching the Severed Foot of a Young Man*; *The Distribution of Blessed Bread*; and the *Newborn Infant Defends the Honour of its Mother*. If any of these are genuine, they would be the earliest known extant works by him. The *Miser's Heart Found in his Treasure Chest* is attributed to Titian's brother, Francesco Vecellio. Some of the other paintings are charming oddities, such as *St Anthony Confronting Ezzelino da Romano* – a perilous diplomatic exercise which may or may not have happened. Next door to the Scoletta, the **Museo al Santo** is used for one-off exhibitions, often drawing on the resources of the Musei Civici.

Following a visit to the Scoletta, the custodian takes you next door to the **Oratorio di San Giorgio**, which was founded in 1377 as a mortuary chapel – its frescoes by **Altichiero di Zevio** and **Jacopo Avanzi** were completed soon after. As pupils of the Giotto school, their work doesn't match the achievement of their master in the Scrovegni, but following a complete restoration the total effect is a winningly enthusiastic romp of story and colour. The *Crucifixion* on the altar wall shows the souls of the two thieves being received, one by a devil and one by an angel; the scenes from the life of Saint George on the left wall show not just the customary dragon-slaying, but also the saint being released by angels from a wheel of torture; and the opposite wall is adorned with the wonderfully titled *St Lucy Remains Immoveable at an Attempt to Drag Her with the Help of Oxen to a House of Ill Repute*.

A good way to relax after all this art is to stroll round the corner to the **Orto Botanico**, the oldest botanic gardens in Europe. Planted in 1545 by the university's medical faculty as a collection of medicinal herbs, the gardens are laid out much as they were originally, and the specimens on show haven't changed too much either. Goethe came here in 1786 to see a palm tree that had been planted in 1585; the selfsame tree still stands.

The Prato della Valle and Santa Giustina

A little to the south sprawls the **Prato della Valle**, claimed to be the largest town square in Italy; it's a generally cheerless area, ringed by over-wide roads, but the vast Saturday market and the summer funfair do a lot to make it jollier. The greenery in the centre follows the oval plan of the extinct Roman amphitheatre; the two rings of statues commemorate 78 worthy Paduans, both native and honorary.

One side is fronted by the sixteenth-century **Basilica di Santa Giustina** – at 120m long, one of the world's largest churches. A pair

The Oratorio and Scoletta are open daily: summer 9am–12.30pm & 2.30–7pm; winter 9am–12.30pm & 2.30–5pm; joint ticket L3000/€1.55.

The Orto Botanico is open summer daily 9am–1pm & 3–6pm; winter Mon–Sat 9am–1pm; L5000/€2.58.

of fifteenth-century griffins, one holding a knight and the other a lion, are the only notable adornments to the unclad brick facade; the freezing interior (scarves are worn by the Benedictine monks even when it's warm outside) is offputtingly clinical, with little of interest except a huge *Martyrdom of St Justina* by **Paolo Veronese**, some highly proficient carving on the choir stalls, and the sarcophagus that reputedly once contained the relics of Luke the Evangelist (in the left transept).

Far more appealing are the vestiges of the church's earlier incarnations, which have been the object of archeological research for some time. In the right transept a stone arch opens onto the **Martyrs' Corridor**, named after a well containing martyrs' bones, now part of the catacombs below the corridor. This part of the building is a composite of fifth- to twelfth-century architectural fragments, and leads to the **Sacellum di Santa Maria e San Prosdocimo**, burial place of Saint Prosdocimus. He was the first bishop of Padua back in the fourth century, when the church was founded, and is depicted here on a fifth-century panel. The fifteenth-century **old choir** is reached by a chain of corridors from the left-hand chapel of the right transept; the choir stalls are inset with splendid marquetry panels, and the **sacristy** beyond has an amusing painting of *St Maurus Rescuing St Placid from a Lake* by an artist glorying in the name of Toeput.

Finally, on the top floor of the Palazzo Angeli, at Prato della Valle 1, you'll find one of the Veneto's most engaging private museums, the **Collezione Minici Zotti**. Subtitled "un museo di magiche visione", this perfectly displayed collection of shadow puppets, magic lanterns and other optical instruments was assembled by Laura Minici Zotti in the course of thiry years of research into the precursors of cinematography. Gorgeous contraptions with names such as the Praxinoscope, Zogroscope, Priviliged Megalethoscope and the Panoptic Polyorama fill the rooms under the roof, from one of which you can survey the streets through a replica of the camera obscura that Canaletto used in creating a panoramic scene.

Padua

Santa Giustina is open: summer Mon–Sat 7.30am–noon & 3–7.45pm, Sun 7am–1pm & 3–7.45pm; winter closes Mon–Fri 5.30pm, Sat 6.45pm, Sun 7.30pm.

The Minici Zotti collection is open 10am–4pm; closed Tues; L5000/€2.58.

Eating, drinking and nightlife

As in any university city, there's plenty of choice when it comes to unpretentious bars and restaurants, and the student population guarantees a pretty active after-dark scene.

Catering for the midday stampede of ravenous students, Padua's bars generally produce weightier **snacks** than the routine *tramezzini* – slabs of pizza and sandwiches vast enough to satisfy a glutton are standard. There's also a surprisingly good choice of self-service restaurants offering good-value full menus – these are open for lunch and dinner but close earlier than other restaurants in the evening; the hot-plates could be turned off by 9pm. For a passeggiata and a place to sit and watch the world go by, the main areas to head for are

Piazza delle Erbe, Piazza Duomo and Piazza Cavour, but for the real action, the bars in the narrow streets around these piazzas and the university are the liveliest, with a student-based clientele.

Restaurants

Al Borgo, Via L. Belludi 56. Wood-fired-oven pizzeria with tables outside looking onto the Piazza del Santo; popular with locals and tourists alike. Closed Sun.

Al Cicheto, Via Savonarola 59 ☎049.871.9794. A stylish *osteria* where the atmosphere is young and friendly, and you can get inexpensive lunches and pizza, or go for the more luxurious evening menu. Try to book the conservatory section, which overlooks the canal. Closed Sun.

Anfora, Via Soncin 13 ☎049.656.629. Lively and very reasonable restaurant (around L40,000/€20) that doubles up as a bar between restaurant hours (12.30–3.15pm & 8–11.30pm). Get there early or book in advance. Closed Sun.

Antico Brolo, Corso Milano 22 ☎049.664.555. Located on a busy road but the garden is quite secluded. Expect to pay around L60,000/€30 for a full meal à la carte, or go for the pizza menu. Closed Mon.

Belle Parti, Via Belle Parti 11 ☎049.875.1822. On a tiny street running between Via Verdi and Via Santa Lucia; this is somewhere to go on a special occasion – it has an excellent menu (upwards of L70,000/€36 a head) and a relaxed atmosphere. Closed Sun.

Gastronomica al Portego, Via Dante 9. Self-service restaurant with local dishes. Closed Sun evening and all day Mon.

L'Isola di Capresa, via Marsilio di Padova 11–15 ☎049.876.0244. One of central Padua's best restaurants, situated just north of Piazza della Frutta and renowned for its fish and seafood dishes. A meal will cost you around L40,000/€20 per head, though there is a tourist menu for L35,000/€18.

Mappa, Via Matteotti 17. Another self-service restaurant, not far from the train station. Open until 9pm. Closed Sat.

Medina, Via S.G. Barbarigo 18. Small, bustling pizzeria, often packed with students enjoying excellent pizza and salads. Closed Tues.

Nane della Giulia, Via Santa Sofia 1. An unusual mix of trendy and unpretentious. Go for the reasonably priced Veneto and vegetarian specialities earlier in the evening and the bar atmosphere later. Live piano, tango or jazz Wed and Thurs. Closed Mon.

Osteria dei Fabbri, Via dei Fabbri 13 ☎049.650.336. Excellent mid-range trattoria; you'll be lucky to get a seat if you haven't booked. Closed Sun.

Pago Pago, Via Galilei 59. Simple, traditional pizzeria/trattoria, just off Via del Santo. Closed Sat.

Pepen, Piazza Cavour. With a wonderful range of pizzas and seats on the square in the summer, this is one of Padua's best-sited pizzerias. Closed Sun.

Bars

Ai Trani, Via Dante 26. Unpretentious bar, good for a restorative glass of wine.

Bar Nazionale, Piazza delle Erbe 40. Unmarked and unremarkable bar on the northeast corner of the piazza, mostly notable for the large, young crowd that gathers outside most evenings. Convenient *gelateria* next door. Closed Sun.

Joyce's Irish Pub, Riviera S. Benedetto 154. "Irish" pubs are all the rage in Italy and this one is particularly popular; situated to the west of the centre on an attractive part of the canal. Open until 2am. Closed Sun.

Limbo, via San Fermo, just south of Piazza Petrarca. A popular disco-pub. Open until 3am. Closed Sun.

Miniera, Via S. Francesco 144. Dimly lit, trendy bar in a part of town heavily populated by students. Open until 2am. Closed Wed.

Victoria Pub, via Savonarola, off Piazza Petrarca. Ghastly underground fake English pub, but pulls in the punters, has a central location and is open until 2am. Closed Sun.

Nightlife

Padua's main theatre, the **Teatro Verdi** on Corso Milano, hosts opera and big name dramatists; details of the season's events can be obtained from the tourist office or in the bilingual information booklet *Padova Today*, distributed at the tourist office, in some bars and in most hotels. Of the local newspapers, the most comprehensive for listings is *Il Mattino*, and for more offbeat events check the posters up around the city, particularly around the university. Padua's nightlife tends to fluctuate in synch with term time; during the summer vacation things tend to be a little somnolent and Padua's half-dozen regular clubs are all fairly low-octane places at the best of times, though things pick up after around 2am. The liveliest of the bunch, between Thursday and Saturday, at least, is *Extra Extra*, Via Ciamician, 145; take a taxi, as it's an inadvisable half-hour walk from the centre by way of Via Sório from Porta S. Giovanni.

Listings

Bookshop Feltrinelli International, Via San Francesco 12. Extensive and up-to-date selection of books in English.

Bus information City buses (ACAP): Piazzale Stazione ☎049.824.1111. Regional buses (SITA): Piazzale Boschetti ☎049.820.6844, with an information office at the left luggage office of the train station.

Car rental Avis, Piazzale Stazione 1 ☎049.664.198; Europcar, Piazzale Stazione 6 ☎049.875.8590.

Exchange Train station (tourist office; Mon–Sat 9.20am–5.45pm, Sun 9am–noon); Banco Ambrosiano Veneto, Piazza del Santo 14 (Mon–Fri 8.30am–1.15pm & 2.30–4pm).

Hospital Ospedale Civile, Via Giustiniani 1 ☎049.821.111.

Markets General daily markets are held every morning Mon–Fri and all day Saturday in Piazza delle Erbe, Piazza della Frutta and Piazza dei Signori. Other regular ones are held in Piazzale Azzurri d'Italia (Tues morning), Piazzale Cuoco-Guizza (Wed morning), Via Bajardi-Mortise (Fri morning) and Prato della Valle (all day Sat), which also hosts an antiques market every third Sunday of the month.

Police Questura, Riviera Ruzante 11 ☎049.833.111.

Post office Corso Garibaldi 33 (Mon–Fri 8.10am–6pm, Sat 8.15am–1pm).

Taxis Radio Taxi ☎049.651.333; night service (9.30pm–6am) ☎049.875.1666.

Telephones Telecom Italia, Riviera dei Ponti Romani 33 (Mon–Sat 8am–9.30pm).

Train information At the station (daily 8am–8pm; ☎8488.88.088).

The Colli Euganei

A few kilometres to the southwest of Padua the **Colli Euganei** (Euganean Hills) rise abruptly out of the plains, their slopes patched with vineyards between scattered villages, villas and churches. Between Padua and the hills lie the spa towns of **ÁBANO TERME** and **MONTEGROTTO TERME**, which for much of the year are crowded with people looking for cures or beauty treatment from the radioactive waters and mud baths. It's been like this for centuries, as the names of the towns indicate: *Ábano* comes from Aponeus, a Roman god of healing, while *Montegrotto* is said to derive from "mons aegratorum", meaning "mountain of the infirm". Largely composed of big and expensive modern hotels, these really are places to avoid unless you're hell-bent on trying to poach yourself in the hot springs – the cruellest one bubbles away at 87°C.

A car is a great advantage for exploring the Colli Euganei proper, as buses are few and far between, even to somewhere reasonably popular such as Arquà Petrarca (see below). The distances are not huge, however, and bikes can be hired in Montegrotto Terme from Brombin, Via Roma 10 (☎0429.793.491). The **villas** of the region are its major architectural attractions, but many of them remain in private hands and can only be viewed from a distance. An exception is the **Villa Barbarigo**, at Valsanzibio, which is famous for its extraordinary gardens; laid out in 1699, they feature a maze and fantastical Baroque gateways and fountains.

While touring the region, look out for the **wines** with the local DOC seal: a red circle round an image of Donatello's *Gattamelata*. The range includes a Pinot Bianco and Tocai Italico (whites), a Cabernet and Merlot (reds), and a sparkling Moscato.

Arquà Petrarca

The gem of the Colli Euganei is the medieval village of **ARQUÀ PETRARCA**, served by three daily buses from Este, though the two morning services leave impracticably early. A pleasant alternative is to walk along the back road from Monsélice, roughly an hour away: from the platform of the train station, cross over the tracks down Via S. Vio and after five minutes follow Via Isola Verso Monte all the way to the cemetery immediately below the village.

The Da Carrara family gave the poet **Francesco Petrarca** (Petrarch) a piece of land here on which to realize his dream of a "delightful house surrounded by an olive grove and a vineyard". He spent the last summers of his life (1369–74) in his idyllic home, at Via Valesella 4, and this is where he died. Not only does the **house** still stand, but his desk and chair are still intact, as are various parts of the original fabric of the interior – though the frescoes, illustrating his works, were retouched in the seventeenth century. Petrarch's sarcophagus is in the centre of the village, with one epitaph penned by him and another by his son-in-law, who placed it here. A short way up the hill, the church of **Santa Maria della Assunta** in Piazza Petrarca (founded in the tenth century, altered in the sixteenth) and the **Oratorio della Santissima Trinità**, in Piazza San Marco, both have interesting fresco fragments.

Arquà Petrarcha has a *Pro Loco* **tourist office** at Via Castello 6 (☎0429.777.240) and a park office for the Colli Euganei, the *Ente Parco Colli*, Via Fontana 2 (☎0429.777.145). The village centre, around Piazza San Marco, has a number of **restaurants** rather obviously directed at the tourist trade, but just down the hill, past the Oratorio, the family-run *La Pergola*, Via Roma 1 (☎0429.718.002; closed Mon evening & Tues), serves excellent and reasonably priced local specialities.

Monsélice

The Casa Petrarca is open Tues–Sun: Feb–Sept 9am–noon & 3–6.30pm; Oct–Jan 9am–noon & 2.30–5pm; L6000/€3.10.

Monsélice

In earlier times **MONSÉLICE** was perched on the pimple of volcanic rock around the foot of which it now winds. Of the five concentric walls that then protected it, all that remains of them and their towers is a small section of the outer ring and a citadel right on the hill's crest – the rest was demolished for building stone in the nineteenth century. The remnants make a powerful impression though, and the town possesses another fortress which is the equal of any in the Veneto. The town is easily accessible from Padua, from where there are nine trains a day and buses every half-hour, many of which head on to Este and Montagnana.

From the train station, the route to the centre of town crosses the Canale Bisato, from whose bridge you can look back to the **Villa Pisani** (sometimes open for exhibitions), which was a kind of stopover for the Pisani family as they travelled by water from Venice to their estates in Montagnana. The fragmentary town wall leads to the **Torre Civica**, built by Ezzelino da Romano in 1244 and repaired in 1504. Facing the Torre Civica across Piazza Mazzini, just beyond the wall, is the **Loggetta**, a seventeenth-century addition to the **Palazzo del Monte di Pietà**, the facade of which is on the road leading away from the square. Just behind, at the beginning of Via del Santuario, the **Antiquarium Longobardo** displays the contents of Lombard tombs discovered recently on the mountain above, including coins, weapons, some unusually complete sarcophagi and a beautiful gold cross.

This road bends round and up the hill to the Castello di Ezzelino, more often known as **Ca' Marcello** or the **Castello di Monsélice**.

The Antiquarium Longobardo is open Tues–Fri 10am–4pm; entrance with ticket for Ca' Marcello.

Monsélice

Guided tours of the Ca' Marcello are given April to mid-Nov Tues–Sun at 9am, 10am, 11am, 3pm, 4pm & 5pm; mid-Nov to March visits can be booked by phone ☎0429.72.931; L10,000/€5.16.

Dating back to the eleventh century, the house was expanded in the thirteenth century by Ezzelino, who added the square tower across the courtyard (the coat of arms was appended after the town came under Venetian rule in 1405). The interior was altered in the fourteenth century by the Da Carrara clan; linking the two main sections is a fifteenth-century annexe added by the Marcello family; a library (sixteenth-century) and family chapel (eighteenth-century) were the only later changes. The castle's immaculate appearance is down to **Count Vittorio Cini**, who inherited the derelict building after it had been in the tender care of the Italian army during World War I, and sank a fortune into restoring it and furnishing each section in the appropriate style, even down to the *marmorino* flooring, stained red with bull's blood in the traditional manner.

The tour begins in the **armoury**, three rooms of weaponry, some of it beautifully worked and decorated, occupying the ground floor of Ezzelino's tower. Up from here are the **Marcello family apartments**, an adaption of part of Ezzelino's tower, furnished in sixteenth- and seventeenth-century fashion. The family restyled the **courtyard** in the seventeenth century to mimic a Venetian campo, complete with well-head and drainage holes; it is still a source of local pride that the *tracchite* stone that paves much of Venice, including most of Piazza San Marco, came from the quarries of Monsélice.

Up the ramp, a gate leads to the upper storey of the Marcello building, the **anteroom** of which was added to the external wall of Ezzelino's palace and retains the original windows as internal features. The **great hall** was formed by the Carraresi; its fireplace was originally from Ferrara and the tapestries are from Brussels. Just off the hall is an example of a *becca di flauta* (flute-lipped) fireplace, an unusual style of chimney which the Carraresi left behind in many of the castles they controlled, proudly painted in their red and white chequerboard colours. The old part of the castle is quite domestic in feel: look for the fourteenth-century painted ceiling in the **Sala del Casteletto**. On the ground floor is the **kitchen**, set out with fifteenth-century furniture and copper plates up to seven hundred years old. The top part of this section contains the **council hall**, with delicate frescoes and fourteenth-century seating. The library, now minus its books, is used by the University of Padua and others as a conference room.

Continuing up the hill you see on the left the white, featureless **Palazzo Nani**, so called because of the stone dwarves (*nani*) on the surrounding wall: much more interesting than the palace itself are its steps up the garden (visible through the gate), flanked by mock Roman sculptures and leading to an imitation Roman temple.

The **Duomo Vecchio** is the next stop: fourteenth-century fresco fragments and a Romano-Gothic polyptych on the high altar are its principal attractions. Just beyond the duomo a gateway guarded by two Venetian lions gives onto the Via Sette Chiese, a private road leading up to the **Villa Duodo**. The seven churches of the road's name are a domesticated version of the seven pilgrimage churches of Rome, arranged as a line of six chapels leading up to the church of **San Giorgio** at the top.

Sinners could earn pardon for their misdemeanours by praying their penitential way up the hill to San Giorgio, where figures of martyred saints are arranged in wood and glass cabinets not unlike old bookcases. The chapels, church, triumphal arch and the main part of the villa were all designed in the late sixteenth century by **Vincenzo Scamozzi**. Now an international centre for the study of hydrology, the villa was commissioned by the son of Francesco Duodo, a hero of the battle of Lépanto; the land was donated by the Venetian state in thanks for services rendered.

Other than on a few exceptional days in the year, it's not possible to go up the steps to the **Rocca** – Ezzelino's citadel right at the summit – as it is undergoing restoration, but there is a chance that it will open to the public when the work is finally finished.

An alley running round the back of the duomo leads back to the centre; the most interesting building you'll pass on the descent is the Gothic **Ca' Bertana** in Via M. Carron, which has elegant fourteenth-century windows. There's no need to traipse over to the **Duomo Nuovo** – you'll have seen as much as you need to from the walk up the hill: its only remarkable aspect is its size.

Practicalities

The **tourist office** is in the Loggetta in Piazza Mazzini (daily 10am–12.30pm & 3–6pm, ☎0429.783.026). If you want to **stay**, the two-star *Cavallino*, Via Petrarca 2 (☎0429.72.242; ②) is central and decent enough, while the three-star *Ceffri*, Via Orti 7 (☎0429. 783.111, *www.ceffri.it*; ③), is further out but housed in the attractive Villa Corner. The brand-new **youth hostel**, Via S. Stefano 33 (reception closed 12.30–5pm; ☎0429.783.125; *ostellomonselice@libero .it*), occupies a beautifully restored sixteenth-century palace below the Duomo Vecchio.

By far the best options for **eating** are the trattoria-pizzeria *Al Campiello*, at Riviera G.B. Belzoni 2 (closed Wed), and the more formal *La Torre*, in Piazza Mazzini (closed Sun evening & Mon), where a good meal will set you back around L60,000/€31 a head. The atmospheric *Enoteca del Castello*, on the way up to the castle at Via del Santuario 22 (closed Mon) is good for a drink and there's a luscious pasticceria in Via Pellegrino (closed Tues).

Este

If you're using public transport, just about the best base from which to roam around the Colli Euganei is the ceramics-producing town of **ESTE**, on the southern edge of the outcrop, just a ten-minute train ride from Monsélice (9 daily). Sporadic buses run up into the hills from here and the chief **tourist office** of the Colli Euganei, the Pro Loco Sud-Est, is at Piazza Maggiore 9 (mid-April to mid-June & mid-Aug to mid-Oct Mon–Fri 10am–noon & 4–6pm, Sat & Sun 10am–noon; rest of year Mon–Fri 10am–noon & 4–6pm, Sat 10am–noon; ☎0429.3635).

From the train station a road runs straight to the central Piazza Maggiore, passing the blank-faced **Basilica di Santa Maria delle Grazie** (with a fourteenth-century Byzantine *Madonna*) and the Romanesque brick church of **San Martino**. The nearest thing to an alluring building in the piazza itself is the tatty thirteenth-century home of the *Società Gabinetto di Lettura*, a cultural organization and archive.

Turning to the right out of the piazza you come face to face with the walls of the ruined **Castello dei Carraresi**, a fortress founded by the Este dynasty and rebuilt by the Da Carrara family in 1340. Material salvaged from the walls was used in the construction of the *The Museo* sixteenth-century palace that now houses the **Museo Nazionale** *Nazionale* **Atestino**, Via G. Negri 9c.

Atestino is The Veneto's outstanding collection of pre-Roman artefacts is *open daily* installed on the museum's first floor (burial finds, Bronze Age tools *9am–8pm;* and Iron Age pots), while much of the ground floor is given over to *L4000/€2.07.* Roman remains. (Roman sites are still being excavated in the western part of the town.) The room devoted to medieval pieces includes a *Madonna and Child* by **Cima da Conegliano** that was once stolen from the church of Santa Maria della Consolazione and is now here for safe keeping. There's also a display of local pottery, a craft that Este has been famous for since before the Renaissance, and some curious tombstones from the fifth century BC which preserve the alphabet of the ancient language known as Venetico. The castle walls now enclose public gardens – useful on hot summer afternoons when everything is closed.

The privately owned **Villa de Kunkler**, round the back of the castle, was **Byron**'s residence in 1817–18, a stay commemorated by a plaque on the villa's wall. The house actually played a greater part in Shelley's life than Byron's – his daughter Clara fell ill while staying here, and died as a result of being carried by her father on an overnight gallop to see a doctor in Venice. When the Shelleys returned here a few days later, Percy wrote his poem of mourning for past splendour, "Lines Written Among the Euganean Hills".

Leading out of the Piazza Maggiore away from the castle, Via Matteotti passes under the **Porta Vecchia**, a restrained Baroque clock tower built on the site of a much earlier defensive tower. Over the river there's **Santa Maria della Consolazione**, a homely church containing nothing of special interest since its Cima painting went to the museum. Turn right instead of going through the tower and you come to the dull sixteenth-century church of San Francesco, beyond which (in the *Quartiere Augusteo*) is the main Roman archeological site in Este. The **Duomo** (turn right down Via Garibaldi) was rebuilt between 1690 and 1708 after an earthquake, the oval plan of its Baroque interior anticipating the design of the Pietà in Venice by several decades. The only painting of note is the huge altarpiece of *St Thecla Calling on God for the Cessation of the Plague*, an unusually bleak picture by **Giambattista Tiepolo**, which you'll need the sacristan to illuminate for you; the landscape in the background is a fairly accurate view of Este and the Colli Euganei.

Practicalities

There's a pair of good two-star **hotels** in Este: just beyond the Porta Vecchia is the homely *Leon d'Oro*, Viale Fiume 20 (☎0429.602.949; ②); the *Beatrice d'Este*, on the far side of the Castello, at Via Rimembranze 1 (☎0429.600.533, *beatrice@posta2000.com*; ②) is larger and more businesslike. Both have good **restaurants**, though you could also try *Al Gambero*, Via d'Azeglio 6 (closed Sat), or *Da Piero Ceschi*, Piazza Trento 16 (closed Thurs).

Montagnana

The pride of **MONTAGNANA**, fifteen minutes down the rail line from Este, is its **medieval city walls**, raised by the ubiquitous Ezzelino da Romano after he had virtually flattened the town in 1242. The walls were later strengthened by the Da Carrara family as Padua's first line of defence against the Scaligeri to the west. It was not until the Wars of the League of Cambrai in the early sixteenth century that the battlements were called upon to fulfil their function, and when the hour came they were found wanting – controlled by the Venetians at the start of hostilities, Montagnana changed hands no fewer than thirteen times in the course of the war. After that the walls were not used defensively again. With a circumference of nearly two kilometres and twenty-four polygonal towers spaced at regular intervals, these are among the finest medieval fortifications in the country, and the relatively sparse development around their perimeter makes them all the more impressive. (Appropriately enough, the town is the home of the *Istituto Internazionale dei Castelli*, a centre for historical research on military architecture.)

Gates pierce the walls at the cardinal points of the compass, the entrances to the east and west being further reinforced by fortresses. The **eastern** gate (Porta Padova) is protected by the **Castello di San Zeno**, built by Ezzelino in 1242, with a watchtower to survey the road to Padua; the Castello now houses the **Museo Civico e Archeologico**, which displays various rather dull objects uncovered around the town, from Neolithic arrowheads to medieval ceramics. The musical section shows off costumes and other memorabilia pertaining to Montagnana's favourite sons, the tenors Giovanni

Tours of the Museo Civico e Archeologico are given Mon–Fri at 11am, Sat at 10.30am, 11.30am, 3pm, 4pm & 5pm, and Sun at 11am, noon, 3pm, 4pm & 5pm; L4000/€2.07.

Montagnana

Martinelli and Aureliano Pertile – the custodian even plays scratchy recordings of their voices. On the **western** side of town, the **Rocca degli Alberi** was built by the Da Carrara family in 1362 to keep the roads from Mantua and Verona covered.

The centre of Montagnana is the Piazza Vittorio Emanuele, dominated by the late Gothic **Duomo**. The most arresting feature of its exterior, the marble portal, was a later addition, possibly designed by Sansovino. **Veronese's** altarpiece, a *Transfiguration*, is less engaging than the huge anonymous painting of the *Battle of Lépanto* on the left as you enter – it's said to represent accurately the ships and their positions at one point in the battle.

Outside the town, just beyond the Porta Padova, is the **Villa Pisani** by **Palladio** (closed to the public), its magnificent, if crumbling, facade at a right angle to the road. It was built as a summer residence and administrative centre for their mainland estates by a branch of the Pisani family of Venice. Also worth looking out for is the elegant facade of the **Palazzo Lombardesco** in Via Matteotti, with its five-lighted window.

Practicalities

The **tourist office** is in Castello San Zeno, on Piazza Trieste (daily: summer 9.30am–12.30pm & 4–7pm; winter 9.30am–12.30pm & 3–6pm; ☎0429.81.320). **Buses** run from Padua via Monsélice and Este roughly hourly (25 daily), departing and arriving at the stop on Viale Spalato, just short of Porta XX Settembre, which leads into the walled town.

The only **hotel** within the walls is the three-star *Aldo Moro*, Via Marconi 27 (☎0429.81.351; ③). Just outside, however, are two reasonable, two-star hotels: *Concordia*, Via San Zeno 148 (☎0429.81.673; ②), fifteen minutes' walk west from Porta Padova, and *Ezzelino*, Via Praterie 1 (☎0429.82.035; ①), a similar distance north of the historic centre, above the *Pizzeria Ezzelino*. The **youth hostel** is stunning, installed as it is in Rocca degli Alberi (April to mid-Oct; reception 7.30–9.30am & 3.30–11pm; ☎0429.81.076; L17,000/€8.78); if you don't have an HI card, you can join on the spot.

The most inexpensive decent **meal** in Montagnana is served at *Pizzeria al Palio* in the far corner of Piazza Trieste (closed Tues), but for just a little more you can eat delicious homemade dishes and try the local wines at *Da Stona*, Via Carrarese 51 (closed Mon), a hundred metres from the tourist office. The listed hotels have **restaurants** as well. If you're stopping for a picnic in Montagnana, be sure to sample the local *prosciutto*, which is so delicious it's exported all over the world.

Come to Montagnana on the first Sunday in September and you'll see its **Palio** – it may be but a poor relation of the costumed horse races in Siena, but it's enthusiastically performed, and the day finishes with a splendid fireworks display.

Rovigo and beyond

ROVIGO is the capital of the fertile and often flooded zone between the Adige and the Po, an area known as the Polésine (or "Little Mesopotamia"). Trains on their way to Ferrara and Bologna from Venice call here at least hourly (average journey 90min), crossing another line running east to west – and frankly there's little reason for coming to the town except to change trains. Should you be stuck for a couple of hours waiting for a connection, though, there are a couple of places you could visit. Maps are available from the **tourist office** at Via Dunant 10 (first floor), just off the Corso del Popolo (Mon–Sat 9.30am–12.30pm, plus Tues & Thurs 3–5pm; ☎0425. 361.481).

The two medieval towers in the centre were part of a castle re-fortified in 954 by the Bishop of Adria when the region was threatened by barbarian invasions. The **Pinacoteca dei Concordi** in Piazza Vittore Emanuele is the city's pride and joy. Eminent artists of the Veneto, in less than breathtaking form, comprise the main part of the collection: Palma il Vecchio, Giambattista Piazzetta and Rosalba Carriera are among those represented.

The Pinacoteca is open Mon–Fri 9.30am–noon & 3.30–7pm, Sat 9.30am–noon; L5000/€2.58.

About fifteen minutes' walk in the same direction is the **Museo Civico delle Civiltà in Polésine** in Piazza San Bartolomeo, the main archeological institute for the area. This is more an assemblage of pieces unearthed by the researchers than a regular museum, and you're shown round by one of the staff, whose informed commentary makes up for the uninspiring display techniques. Items relating to the Polésine's disappearing rural life are exhibited as well – tools of various trades, agricultural implements and so forth.

The Museo Civico delle Civiltà is open by appoint-ment only: ring ☎0425.262.70; free.

The only other thing worth hunting out is **La Rotonda**, as La Tempio Beata Vergine del Soccorso, in Piazza XX Settembre, is gen-erally known. An octagonal edifice built in 1594 by **Zamberlan**, a pupil of Palladio, it has a campanile by **Longhena** (1655) and a Baroque high altar of gilded wood.

The Villa Badoer at Fratta Polésine

A trip to **FRATTA POLÉSINE**, 18km southwest of Rovigo, will appeal to the more ardent fans of **Palladio**'s buildings. The **Villa Badoer**, designed in the 1560s, is one of his most eloquent flights of architectural rhetoric, with its distinctive curving colonnades linking the porticoed house to the storage spaces at the side. None of the original furnishings are left, but restorers have uncovered the villa's late sixteenth-century grotesque frescoes by **Giallo**, a recherché Florentine. Two **trains** a day from Rovigo will get you there for the afternoon session.

The Villa Badoer is open Tues–Sun: summer 10am–noon & 3–7pm, winter 9am–noon & 2–5pm; L10,000/€5.16.

Adria and the Po delta

Heading **eastward** from Rovigo, trains leave every couple of hours for the Po delta and Chioggia. **ADRIA**, a town of about twenty

Rovigo and
beyond

*The Museo
Archeologico is
open daily
9am–7.30pm;
L4000/€2.07.*

thousand inhabitants, is all that is left of the city from which the Adriatic Sea got its name. It's a sleepy little town sitting on a tributary of the Po some 25km inland now, owing to heavy silting in the lagoon. The only sight is the **Museo Archeologico** in Piazzale degli Etruschi, which has a collection of Greek and Etruscan pieces dating from the time when Adria was a major port. The **tourist office** is at Piazza Bocchi 1 (☎0426.21.675).

It's difficult to explore the **Po delta** properly unless you have a car, though bikes may be rented from Vittorio Cacciatori at Via Bologna 1 in Porto Tolle (☎0426.82.501) – you can get there by bus from Rovigo or Adria. Vittorio Cacciatori also rents out canoes, but if you prefer a less strenuous investigation of the waterways and islets, Marino Cacciatori, Via Varsarvia 12 (☎0426.81.508), runs half-day cruises in summer – an excellent way to observe the waterfowl and other birds of the delta's nature reserve.

The Po delta's waterways, swamps and mudflats constitute the finest **birdwatching** region in the country, with the prime sites being centred on Comacchio (buses from Venice) and the more southerly Punte Alberete, both of which lie outside the Veneto in Emilia-Romagna. Migratory birds fly into the delta from both north and south, with several wintering species of ducks and waders giving way after April to magnificent herons and egrets – and even, rarely, the exotic glossy ibis.

A few villages around the Veneto sector of the delta tout themselves as seaside resorts. Unfortunately for them, the Po is the filthiest river in Italy, carrying an unspeakable brew of chemical fertilizers and industrial toxins into the northern reaches of the Adriatic. Its annual load of around 250 tons of arsenic, 60 tons of mercury, 20,000 tons of phosphorus and 136,000 tons of nitrates is a major cause of the **algae slicks** that plagued the resorts of Italy's east coast in the 1990s. Faced with a drastic drop in bookings, the tourist boards tell everyone that the slime is harmless, blithely dismissing the Ministry of Health's warnings that children, old people, pregnant women, people with skin lesions – in fact, just about anyone with the slightest vulnerability – should stay out of the water. The fact is that the precise biochemistry of the algae has still not been determined, and even if it does turn out to be benign to humans, it still stinks and clings to the skin like glue. And if it were to disappear tomorrow, the water round here would still be foul.

Chapter 16

Vicenza, Verona and around

Lying almost midway between Padua and Verona, the orderly and affluent city of **Vicenza** tends to be overlooked in favour of its more charismatic neighbours – passengers getting off at the train station are more likely to be personnel from the local US armed forces base than tourists. Yet the streets of Vicenza form one of the most impressive urban landscapes in Italy, owing largely to

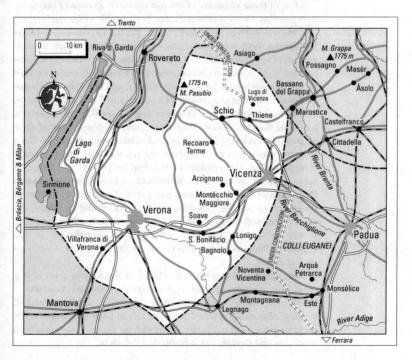

Vicenza, Verona and around

the activity of Andrea Palladio – the source of Western Europe's most influential architectural style. Buildings by Palladio and his acolytes are plentiful not only inside the city itself, but also out in the surrounding countryside, where the Venetian and Vicentine nobility built up their farming estates from the sixteenth century onwards.

A few of these **villas** are of interest only to cognoscenti like those who overrun Vicenza during September's architecture conference, but several – such as the **Villa Rotonda** and the Tiepolo-painted **Villa Valmarana**, both on the outskirts – make an impact on the un-initiated and the expert alike. And while Palladianism is the region's distinctive style, it doesn't monopolize the scene. Some of Vicenza's Gothic houses would look fine in Venice, and the **Palazzo Porto-Colleoni** at **Thiene** is as colourful a pile as you'll find in the Veneto.

Verona is perhaps best known to English speakers as the setting for Shakespeare's *Romeo and Juliet*, and supposed sites of their courtship are scattered over the city. Authentic remnants of the city's long and varied past are what make the place so memorable, though – in particular, the remains of the **Roman** period. Of these, the superb **Arena** is the most prominent, followed by the **Teatro Romano** and various archways and gates. Also high on the list of things to see are the monuments left by the **Scaligeri** family, the most celebrated rulers of medieval Verona. Their tombs are masterpieces of Gothic art, and scarcely less impressive is the **Castelvecchio**, once the Scaligeri fortress and now home of Verona's civic museum.

More good-quality wine is produced in the Veneto than in any other area of Italy, and the region's most productive vineyards – Soave, Valpolicella and Bardolino – lie within the hinterland of Verona. Also easily reached from the city is Lago di Garda, on the western edge of the Veneto – a resort as popular with southern Austrians and Germans as it is with the Veronese.

Vicenza

Europe's largest centre for the production of textiles, and the focus of Italy's "Silicon Valley", **VICENZA** is a very sleek city – by some estimates, one of the country's richest half-dozen. The wealth isn't as ostentatious as in Milan, for example, but if you took the banks and the clothes shops out of the centre's main street you'd be left with next to nothing, while the lower storey of the city's signature building – the Basilica – has become a corral of jewellers. The discreet Vicentine obsession with style pervades even the local clergy, who in the mid-1990s invited Italy's designers to improve the look of their priestly attire, prompting entries from big-league names such as Krizia and Laura Biagiotti. Asked what sort of outfit he would be likely to approve, Monsignor Don Giancarlo Santi was anxious not to be too restrictive: "We certainly wouldn't want *Valentino* written on our chests, but anything that is beautiful, well-made and serves its purpose is a gift of God."

Industrial estates and factories form a girdle round the city, and yet modern prosperity hasn't ruined the look of central Vicenza – still partly enclosed by medieval walls, it's an amalgam of Gothic and classical buildings that today looks much as it did when the last major phase of construction came to an end at the close of the eighteenth century. This historic core is compact enough to be explored in a day, but the city and its environs really require a short stay to do them justice.

Getting to Vicenza by public transport is very easy. More than twenty **trains** run daily from Venice (55min) through Padua, and are equally regular from Verona (30min); there's also an hourly service from Treviso (1hr) through Castelfranco Veneto. As with all Italian timetables, there are occasional gaps in the schedule, typically occurring just after the morning rush hour, when the interval between trains may be twice as long as normal.

Vicenza's history – and Palladio

The early history of Vicenza follows a course familiar in this part of northern Italy – development under Imperial Rome, destruction by Attila, Lombard occupation, attainment of a degree of independence followed by struggles with neighbouring towns, rule by the Scaligeri of Verona in the fourteenth century and finally absorption into the Venetian empire in 1404. The fifteenth-century palaces of Vicenza reflect its status as a Venetian satellite, with facades reminiscent of the Canal Grande, but in the latter half of the sixteenth century the city was transformed by the work of an architect who owed nothing to Venice but a lot to ancient Rome, and whose rigorous but flexible style was to influence every succeeding generation – Andrea di Pietro della Gondola, alias **Palladio**.

Born in Padua in 1508, Palladio came to Vicenza at the age of sixteen to work as a stonecutter. At thirty he became the protégé of a local nobleman, Count Giangiorgio Trissino, who directed his architectural training, gave him his classicized name, and brought him into contact with the dominant class of Vicenza. Some of these men were landowners, recently enriched now that peace had returned to the mainland after the War of the League of Cambrai, many were wealthy soldiers, and a decent percentage were well educated – it wasn't unknown for more than forty of the one hundred city councillors to possess doctorates. They turned to Palladio to design houses that would embody their financial and intellectual rank and their corporate superiority to their Venetian rulers. No architect in Western history has been more influential than Palladio, and although much of that influence derives from his *Quattro Libri dell'Architettura* or *Four Books of Architecture* (a survey of building techniques, classical structures and works by himself, both built and unbuilt), his buildings in and around Vicenza have been consistently studied by architects for the last four centuries. Between 1540 and his death in

Vicenza's museum passes

Four different types of museum pass are on offer in Vicenza. The simple **Biglietto Unico** costs L12,000/€6.20 and gives admission to the Teatro Olimpico, the Museo Civico and the less than enthralling Museo Naturalistico-Archeologico; a L14,000/€7.23 version of the ticket additionally gets you into the Museo del Risorgimento, a rather specialized museum that's a long way out of the city centre. The **Vicenza Musei e Palazzi Card**, costing L20,000/€10.32, gives admission to these four plus the Basilica, the Palazzo Barbaran da Porto and the Palazzo Leoni Montanari. The **Vicenza e le Ville Card**, costing L40,000/€20.64, gives admittance to all these plus the Villa Rotonda and Villa Valmarana; it is only available in the summer months, as the villas tend to close in winter. Each site individually charges L6000/€3.10 for admission, except Palazzo Barbaran da Porto and the two villas, which charge L10,000/€5.16. All three passes can be bought at the Museo Civico or the Teatro Olimpico, and are valid for one visit to each place within one month of the date of issue.

1580 Palladio created around a dozen palaces and public buildings in Vicenza plus an even larger number of villas on the Vicentine and Venetian farming estates in the surrounding countryside, and the variety of his designs will surprise anyone who associates Palladianism with blandness. Even if you've previously been inclined to agree with Herbert Read's opinion that "In the back of every dying civilization there sticks a bloody Doric column", you might well leave Vicenza converted.

The City

The main street of Vicenza, the **Corso Andrea Palladio**, is a vestige of the Roman street-plan and cuts right through the old centre from the Piazza Castello (overlooked by an eleventh-century tower, once part of the Scaligeri fort) down to the Piazza Matteotti. Nearly all cars are banned from the Corso, so the palaces that line it – now occupied by shops, offices and banks – can be admired with little risk, although you should keep your ears open for the occasional bus, and look out for cyclists.

The first major building comes just before the start of the Corso, on the far side of the Piazza Castello – it's the fragmentary **Palazzo Porto-Breganze**, Palladio's last palace in Vicenza. None of Palladio's town houses was completed to plan, but none of the others is as flagrantly unfinished as this one.

Particularly striking on the Corso itself are the following houses: no. 13, the **Palazzo Thiene Bonin-Longhare** (by Palladio's follower Scamozzi); no. 38–40, **Palazzo Pagello** (1780); no. 47, **Palazzo Thiene** (fifteenth-century); no. 67, **Palazzo Brunello** (fifteenth-century – have a look at the courtyard); no. 98, **Palazzo Trissino** (now the town hall; by Scamozzi); no. 147, **Palazzo da Schio** (fifteenth-century, restored), which is known as the Ca' d'Oro as it once had gilded decoration and bears a slight resemblance to the Ca' d'Oro in Venice; and no. 163, the **Casa Cogollo**, known as the Casa del Palladio even though he neither designed it (despite what the plaque says) nor lived there. None of the churches on the Corso repays the effort of pushing the door open.

The Museo Civico and Teatro Olimpico

The Corso Palladio ends with one of the architect's most imperious buildings, the **Palazzo Chiericati**. Begun in 1550 and completed about a hundred years later, this commission was a direct result of Palladio's success with the Basilica (see opposite), being a house for one of the Basilica's supervisors, Girolamo Chiericati. It's now the home of Vicenza's **Museo Civico**, many of whose pieces were gathered together in the 1810s to keep them out of the grasp of the marauding French.

The ground-floor archeological collection of locally excavated pieces from the fifth century BC to the seventh AD is neither more nor less interesting than such provincial collections usually are, but the art galleries are more ambitious. Celebrated names such as Memling, Tintoretto, Veronese, Giambattista Tiepolo, van Dyck, the Bassano family, Luca Giordano and Lorenzo Lotto punctuate a picture collection that is given its backbone by Vicentine artists – notably Montagna, Buonconsiglio, Fogolino (a tumultuous *Adoration of the Magi*), Maffei and Carpioni. Though none of these local artists is likely to knock you flat, there are some fine pieces amid the workaday stuff (the tiny bronze plaquettes made by Valerio Belli, for example), and the musuem has a smattering of oddities. Carpione's disgusting bubble-blowing cherub (an allegory of life's fragility) might tend to stick in the mind, as might Francesco del Cairo's orgasmic *Herodiade with the Head of the Baptist* and the ceiling fresco in one of the ground-floor rooms – a comically unflinching depiction of what you'd see if a group of horses steered by a stark naked charioteer flew overhead.

Across Piazza Matteotti is the one building in Vicenza you shouldn't fail to go into – the **Teatro Olimpico**, the oldest indoor theatre in Europe. Approached in 1579 by the members of the humanist Accademia Olimpica to produce a design for a permanent theatre, Palladio devised a covered amphitheatre derived from his reading of Vitruvius (architect to Augustus) and his studies of Roman structures in Italy and France. In terms of the development of theatre design, the Teatro Olimpico was not a progressive enterprise – contemporaneous theatres in Florence, for example, were far closer to the modern proscenium arch design – but it was the most comprehensive piece of classical reconstruction of its time, and the men responsible for it were suitably proud of their brainchild: the toga-clad figures above the stage are portraits of Palladio's clients.

Palladio died soon after work commenced, and the scheme was then overseen by Scamozzi, whose contribution to the design – a

The Museo Civico is open Tues–Sun 9am–5pm, (open until 7pm from June 19 to Aug 31); L6000/ €3.10 or combined ticket.

The Teatro Olimpico is open Tues–Sun 9am–5pm, (open until 7pm from June 19 to Aug 31); L6000/ €3.10 or combined ticket.

backstage perspective of an idealized Thebes – is its most startling feature. As is demonstrated by the theatre's guide (who'll give you a commentary in English on request), the illusion of long urban vistas is created by tilting the "streets" at an angle that demands chamois-like agility from the actors. The building was opened on March 3, 1585, with an extravagant production of *Oedipus Rex* that somehow had 108 performers on its roll-call, and it's still the main permanent theatre in Vicenza.

The Piazza dei Signori

At the hub of the city, the **Piazza dei Signori**, stands the most awesome of Palladio's creations – the Palazzo della Ragione, known to all but the irredeemably pedantic as the **Basilica**. Designed in the late 1540s, though not finished until the second decade of the next century, this was Palladio's first public project and secured his reputation. The architect himself, generally regarded as a mild and modest individual, had no doubt as to its merit: "this building can be compared to ancient ones and placed with the most beautiful of the major buildings that have been made by the ancients", he wrote in the *Quattro Libri*. The monumental regularity of the Basilica disguises the fact that the Palladian building is effectively a stupendous piece of buttressing – the Doric and Ionic colonnades, constructed in Istrian stone, enclose the fifteenth-century brick meeting hall of the city council, an unstable structure that had defied a number of attempts to prop it up before Palladio's solution was put into effect. And if you look closely you'll see that the colonnades aren't quite as regular as they first appear – Palladio had to vary the gaps between the columns and pillars to accommodate the passageways that go through the lower level. The vast Gothic hall, entered from the upper gallery, is often used for exhibitions, and discussions are taking place about the feasibility of converting the Basilica into an arts centre, but it's early days yet; at the moment there's a charge of L2000 for entry to the loggias of the upper storey, and another fee if you want to visit whatever exhibition is showing in the hall.

The hall of the Basilica is open Tues–Sun: summer 10am–7pm; winter 9am–5pm; fee varies.

Facing the Basilica across the Piazza dei Signori is a late Palladio building, the unfinished **Loggia del Capitaniato**. Built as accommodation for the Venetian military commander of the city (the *Capitano*), it's decorated with reliefs in celebration of the Venetian victory over the Turks at Lépanto in 1571. Had it been completed, the Loggia would have taken up much of the area now occupied by the terrace of the *Gran Caffè Garibaldi*; houses used to join onto the Loggia on that side, but they were demolished in the 1930s. Completing the enclosure of this side of the piazza is the **Monte di Pietà**, put up in two instalments in the first half of the sixteenth century, which brackets the seventeenth-century church of **San Vincenzo**. The worryingly slender **Torre di Piazza** reached its present altitude in 1444, having been started in the twelfth century and raised in 1311; its clock is claimed to have been the first such public timepiece in Italy. The obligatory lion of Saint Mark was deposited on top of its column in the mid-fifteenth century, not long after Venice took Vicenza to its bosom; the companion figure of the Redeemer dates from the mid-seventeenth century.

As in the sixteenth century, a daily fruit, vegetable and flower **market** is pitched at the back of the Basilica, in the Piazza dell'Erbe – glowered over by medieval **Torre del Tormento**, once the prison tower. On Tuesdays a vast general market hits town, spreading along the roads between the Basilica and the duomo.

In Contrà Pigafetta, just a few yards down the slope from the Piazzetta Palladio, on the duomo side of the Basilica, there's Vicenza's architectural oddity, the Spanish-influenced **Casa Pigafetta**. Built in 1481, it was the birthplace of Antonio Pigafetta, who set out with Magellan on his voyage of 1519 and kept a record of the expedition. Unlike his leader, Pigafetta lived to see his home town again. If you're puzzled by the street name, *contrà* – sometimes *contrada* – is the Vicentine dialect alternative to *via*.

The Duomo

The Duomo is open 10.30am–noon daily, plus 3.30–5.30pm Mon–Fri.

The **Duomo**, founded before the eighth century but substantially rebuilt, chiefly from the fourteenth to the sixteenth century, was bombed to bits in 1944 and carefully reconstructed after the war. It's a gloomy place, notable primarily as one of the few Italian cathedrals to be upstaged by its secular surroundings. A polyptych by **Lorenzo Veneziano** (fifth chapel on right) and a *Madonna* by **Montagna** (fourth chapel on left) are the best of its paintings.

Excavations in the crypt have uncovered Roman pavements and parts of a pre-ninth-century basilica, but there's no admission to the public. You can, however, visit the **Criptoporticus** – probably part of a first-century palace – that was unearthed beneath the Palazzo Proti on the other side of the Piazza Duomo. Access is only by appointment with the *Centro Turistico Giovanile*, nearby at Contrà San Francesco Vecchio 17; they conduct free tours of the site on Saturdays from 10 to 11.30am.

Santa Corona and Santo Stefano

Santa Corona is open daily 8.30am–noon & 2.30–6.30pm.

Far more interesting than the duomo is the Dominican church of **Santa Corona**, on the other side of the Corso Palladio, at the Piazza Matteotti end. Begun in 1261 to house a thorn from Christ's crown, it has what's said to be the oldest Gothic interior in the Veneto; the thorn itself, a gift from the beatified King Louis IX of France, is sometimes displayed in its fourteenth-century gold reliquary in the chapel on the left of the chancel. On permanent show are two of the three superlative church paintings in central Vicenza – *The Baptism of Christ*, a late work by **Giovanni Bellini** (fifth altar on left), and *The Adoration of the Magi*, painted in 1573 by **Paolo Veronese** (third chapel on right). Also well worth a look are the late fifteenth-century inlaid **choir stalls**, the simple and tranquil **Cappella Valmarana**, which was added to the crypt in 1576 by Palladio, and the anonymous *Madonna* near the Bellini picture, which includes at its base a view of Vicenza around 1500, added by **Fogolino**. One last item of interest: a plaque set into the pillar nearest to the steps for the crypt – to your right as you look at the Bellini – records that Palladio was buried at the foot of the pillar, from where his remains were removed to the civic cemetery in 1845.

The cloisters of Santa Corona, recently restored, now house a decidedly run-of-the-mill **Museo Naturalistico-Archeologico**, but a little further down the road, at no. 25, you'll find the newest addition to Vicenza's cultural landscape, the **Gallerie di Palazzo Leoni Montanari**. Owned by the Intesa banking group, this opulent Baroque palazzo has been fastidiously restored as a showcase for two art collections that the bank has accumulated over the years. Downstairs you'll find a thematic display of more than one hundred Russian icons (about a quarter of the bank's hoard), a remarkable assemblage that spans the period from the thirteenth century to the nineteenth; in the frescoed rooms of *piano nobile* paintings by Canaletto and Francesco Guardi feature in a survey of Veneto art that's interesting chiefly for the journalistic scenes of everyday life in eighteenth-century Venice created by Pietro Longhi and his workshop – only the Ca' Rezzonico and the Querini Stampalia museums in Venice have more extensive samples of Longhi's quirky output.

The nearby church of **Santo Stefano** merits a call for the city's third outstanding religious painting – **Palma il Vecchio**'s typically stolid and luscious *Madonna and Child with St George and St Lucy*. If you have hawk-like vision you could try to make out the church's trio of tiny monochrome paintings by Giandomenico Tiepolo (*The Resurrection, St Peter* and *St John the Baptist*) – they form the panels on the front and sides of the high altar's tabernacle.

The Museo Naturalistico-Archeologico is open the same hours as the Museo Civico & Teatro Olimpico; L6000/€3.10.

The Palazzo Leoni Montanari is open Fri–Sun 10am–6pm; L6000/€3.10.

Santo Stefano is open Mon–Sat 8.30am–noon & 5.30pm–7pm.

Contrà Porti and around

The entrance to Santo Stefano faces the immense **Palazzo Negri** and its mighty Gothic neighbour, the **Casa Fontana**, but more intimidating than either is Palladio's rugged **Palazzo Thiene**, on the Corso side of them. Had Palladio's plan been realized, this palace would have occupied the entire block down to the Corso and across to Contrà Porti; in the end, work progressed no further than the addition of this wing to the block built for the Thiene family at the end of the fifteenth century. The facade of the Gothic portion is in Contrà Porti. Palladio was not simply the most inventive and knowledgeable architect in the Veneto, he was also very cost-effective: his columns are usually made of brick covered with a skim of plaster, and, as an inspection of the Thiene residence will reveal, his rough-hewn stonework is just cunningly worked brick as well.

*Palazzo
Barbaran da
Porto is open
Tues–Sun
10am–6pm;
L10,000/€5.16
or Vicenza
Card.*

There's no better example than Contrà Porti of the way in which the builders of Vicenza skilfully grafted new houses onto old without doing violence to the line of the street: the palaces here span two centuries, yet the overall impression is one of cohesion. At no. 8 is the Gothic **Palazzo Cavalloni**, and over the road at no. 11 stands Palladio's **Palazzo Barbaran da Porto**, designed around 1570 and subsequently embellished by others; the Palazzo Barbaran regularly hosts architectural exhibitions under the auspices of its tenants, the *Centro Internazionale di Archittetura "A. Palladio"*, which organizes Vicenza's annual architectural conference and has plans to turn the building into a permanent museum devoted to Palladio. When there's no special exhibition on, the fee to view the profusely decorated but empty rooms of the Palazzo Barbaran might be thought a little steep, but admission is covered by both versions of the "Vicenza Card".

Back on the other side of the road, the Thiene palace is followed by the Renaissance **Palazzo Trissino-Sperotti** (no. 14), opposite which is a sweep of Gothic houses, the best being the fourteenth-century **Palazzo Colleoni Porto** (19); next door is Palladio's **Palazzo Iseppo Porto**, designed a few years after the Thiene and a couple of decades before the Barbaran da Porto. Luigi da Porto, the author of the story of Romeo and Juliet, died at no. 15 in 1529.

Contrà Porti takes you towards the Pusterla bridge and the **Parco Querini**, the biggest expanse of green in the city; with its backdrop of trees, its avenue of statuary and its tiny decorative hill (populated by ducks, rabbits and peacocks), it reminds you of the picturesque grounds of an eighteenth-century English country house. For those intent on doing a comprehensive Palladian tour, there's a palace by him on this side of the Bacchiglione river too – the **Palazzo Schio-Angaran** at Contrà San Marco no. 39.

Along Corso Fogazzaro

Connected to Contrà Porti by Contrà Riale (itself not short of grand houses) is Corso A. Fogazzaro, a busy road with a spread of architectural attractions. At the Corso Palladio end is the **Palazzo Valmarana** (no. 16), where Palladio's use of overlapping planes makes the design of the facade legible in the narrow street and at the same time integrates the palace with the flanking buildings. Take a peep at the uncompleted courtyard – the finished section constitutes no more than a third of the projected palace.

In the other direction you'll come across the Piazza San Lorenzo, on one side of which stands Francesco Muttoni's Palazzo Repeta, now the *Banca d'Italia*, with the thirteenth-century Franciscan church of **San Lorenzo** opposite. The fourteenth-century marble portal of the west front is the best feature of the church – the dimensions of the interior are impressive, but the church is rather barren in comparison with others of the same period in the Veneto, such as

*San Lorenzo is
open Mon–Sat
10.30am–noon
& 3.30–6pm,
Sun 3.30–6pm.*

San Nicolò at Treviso or San Zanipolo and the Frari in Venice. **Montagna**'s fresco of the *Beheading of St Paul*, in the chapel on the left side of the chancel, may once have been stunning, but it's now looking pretty tattered. The cloister is worth a visit, though, even if the monastic calm has given way to the noise of traffic and the neighbouring school.

Further along, where the arcades give out, is the church of **Santa Maria del Carmine**; founded in the fourteenth century but redone in the nineteenth, it has pictures by **Montagna**, **Veronese** and **Jacopo Bassano** that more than compensate for the peculiar decor – although you'll need infra-red vision to make them out on an overcast day.

The fringes of the centre

If the Museo Civico's collection has led to your acquiring a taste for **Francesco Maffei**'s superheated homages to Tintoretto, you'll not want to miss the **Oratorio di San Nicola**, which has a welter of paintings by him and his contemporary **Carpioni**. Maffei's delirious altarpiece – *The Trinity* – is an effective summary of what happened to painting in the Veneto after the golden age of the late Renaissance.

The Oratorio is open March–Dec Thurs 9am–noon.

The Oratorio stands by the side of Vicenza's other river, the Retrone, at the foot of its most picturesque bridge, the hump-backed **Ponte San Michele**, built in 1620. You can follow a pleasant loop on the south side of the river by going straight ahead off the bridge to the Piazza dei Gualdi, then basically following your nose (bear to the right), so that you go past the thirteenth-century gate called the **Portòn del Luzzo** and recross the Retrone by the **Ponte Furo**, from where there's a good view of the Basilica and Torre di Piazza. The long building on the opposite bank is Palladio's unexceptional first project in the city, the **Casa Civena** (c.1540).

Another area just out of the centre that's worth a look is on the far side of the Bacchiglione from the Teatro Olimpico. The bridge leads onto the major traffic confluence of Piazza Venti Settembre: the building with porticoes on two facades is the **Palazzo Angaran** – fifteenth-century, but rebuilt. In adjacent Contrà Venti Settembre there's the house with the best-preserved of Vicenza's exterior frescoes, the fifteenth-century **Palazzo Regaù**.

Don't miss the church of **Santi Felice e Fortunato** either. It's on the opposite side of town, about ten minutes' walk along the Corso of the same name, from the entrance to the **Giardino Salvi** (daily 7.30am–8pm), a compact little park whose winding gravel paths are punctuated by unconvincing replicas of great sculptures. Dating back to immediately after the Edict of Constantine (313 AD), the basilica is the oldest church in Vicenza, and is approached by a path littered with ancient sarcophagi and architectural fragments. Wrecked by barbarian invaders in 899 and then by earthquakes in 1117, it was largely reconstructed in the twelfth century, and recent

Santi Felice e Fortunato is open Mon–Sat 9am–noon & 3.30–6.30pm.

restorations have stripped away later accretions to reveal the form of the church at around that period. Remnants of the earliest building have survived – portions of fourth-century and fifth-century mosaics have been uncovered in the nave and right aisle, and a door off the right aisle leads into a fourth-century martyrs' shrine. Almost as remarkable as the mosaics and *martyrion* is the twelfth-century fortified campanile, which now looks as if it might have problems standing up to the next gale.

Practicalities

The **tourist office** is alongside the entrance to the Teatro Olimpico, at Piazza Matteotti 12 (Mon–Sat 9am–1pm & 2.30–6pm, Sun 9am–1pm; ☎0444.320.854, *www.ascom.vi.it/aptvicenza*). For **listings**, pick up a copy of the local papers – *Il Gazzettino* or *Il Giornale di Vicenza*. Culturally the busiest time of the year is from June to August, when there's a glut of concerts, opera productions and plays in town, many of the best being performed in the Teatro Olimpico.

The **post office** is in Piazza Garibaldi, between the duomo and Basilica; **banks** are strung out along the Corso Palladio.

Accommodation

Vicenza's one-star **hotels** are all on very noisy roads, or above bars or restaurants, or some way out of the centre – or some combination of these drawbacks. As with so many Veneto towns, the hotels in the upper categories are generally soulless bolt-holes for passing businesspeople, so the two-stars are the best on most fronts, as they are pretty well the same price as the one-stars. Of the two-stars within a few yards of the Piazza dei Signori, the following are all good choices – the capacious and friendly *Due Mori*, Contrà Do Rode 26 (☎0444.321.886; ②); the neighbouring and very similar *Vicenza*, Stradella dei Nodari 5/7 (☎0444.321.512; ②); and the *Palladio*, Via Oratorio dei Servi 25 (☎0444.321.072; ②). If centrality isn't an issue, consider the recently renovated two-star *Casa San Raffaele*, Viale X Giugno 10 (☎0444.545.767; ②), which enjoys a beautiful position on the slope of Monte Bèrico, about half an hour's walk from the centre (see p.342). Whichever hotel you decide to stay in, phone ahead to book a room if you're going in summer or early autumn – some places close down in August, and Vicenza's popularity as a conference centre can make it tricky to find rooms, especially in September.

The town's spruce ninety-bed **youth hostel**, the *Olimpico* (☎0444.540.222; L25,000/€12.90 per night), is at Viale Giuriolo 7–9, close to the Museo Civico and Teatro Olimpico.

Eating and drinking

The **restaurant** above the huge *Gran Caffè Garibaldi* (closed Wed), on Piazza dei Signori, offers low-cost meals and a good selection of colossal pizzas. The other budget choice is the *Antica Casa della Malvasia*, Contrà delle Morette 5 (closed Mon), a bustling, roomy inn just off the Piazza dei Signori: the food is variable but often very good, it has live music on Tuesday and Thursday, is open till at least 1am on Friday and Saturday, and the bar's excellent. Equally popular, and similarly priced at around L35,000 for three courses, is the *Vecchia Guardia*, close to the Basilica at Contrà Pescheria Vecchia 11 (☎0444.321.231; closed Thurs). Of the more upmarket places in the centre of town, *Tre Visi*, in the courtyard of Corso Palladio 25 (☎0444.324.868; closed Sun evening & Mon), and the *Allo Scudo di Francia*, which occupies part of a beautiful palazzo at Contrà Piancoli 4 (☎0444.323.322; closed Sun evening & Mon), have both been highly regarded for many years; bank on spending around L70,000/€36 per head at each.

As for **bars** in the centre of the city, the *Firenze* on Piazzetta A. Palladio is always friendly, as is the *Malvasia* (see above), but the most atmospheric is *Il Grottino*, under the Basilica at Piazza dell'Erbe 2 (closed Sun) – it has a good range of wines, a selection of cold food, and stays open till 2am. The nearby *Bar San Paolo*, on the far side of Ponte San Paolo (closed Mon), has a small riverside terrace and also keeps going until 2am.

There's a range of **cafés** and *pasticcerie* along the Corso and around the Basilica – try the excellent old-fashioned *Sorarù*, in the Piazzetta Andrea Palladio, the similarly elegant *Offelleria della Meneghina*, directly opposite the *Gran Caffè Garibaldi* at Contrà Cavour 20, or the *Gran Caffè Garibaldi* itself. The best **ice creams** in town are at *Tutto Gelato*, Contrà Frasche del Gambero 26 (between the Basilica and the duomo), though the *Gran Caffè Garibaldi* runs it close.

If you want to buy your own food, the *alimentari* of the Corso are excellent, especially *Il Ceppo* at no. 196; *Porro*, just south of the Basilica on Contrà Orefice, is also good.

Around Vicenza

The countryside around Vicenza is dotted with hundreds of **villas**, many of them the result of Venice's diversion of money into agriculture in the mid-sixteenth century, as a way of protecting the economy against the increasing uncertainties of shipping. The tourist office in Vicenza hands out a booklet and a map plotting the location of many of them, and if you have a hundred thousand lire to spare you can choose from a number of magnificently illustrated tomes on the subject. The trouble is, most of the villas are best seen as glossy photos, because some are in the middle of nowhere, others are falling to bits and many of the better-kept specimens are closed to the public. And of those that are open, accessible and in fair condition, some probably won't make much impression on the untrained

Other villas of
the Veneto are
dealt with in
the appropri-
ate sections of
this guide –
for example,
the entries on
The Brenta
(p.300), Masèr
(p.385) and
Castelfranco
Veneto (p.371).

eye – such as Palladio's **Villa Thiene** at Quinto Vicentino (a short journey on the #5 bus). Yet a number of the villas of wider interest lie within the orbit of Vicenza's public transport network; two of the best, indeed, are to be found right on Vicenza's doorstep, beneath the pilgrimage church of **Monte Bèrico**, the other big attraction of Vicenza's immediate surroundings. And for the ultimate villa experience, it's possible to rent Palladio's **Villa Saraceno** at Finale di Agugliaro, near Noventa Vicentina; the building has been immaculately restored by the Landmark Trust, whose office in England can give you the full details on prices and availability (phone no. in England ☎01628/825 925) – the waiting list is usually eighteen months long.

Monte Bèrico

Rising behind the rail line, **Monte Bèrico** is seen by everyone who comes to Vicenza, but not actually visited by many, which is a pity as an expedition up the hill has a number of attractions: an amazing view (on a clear day the horizon beyond Vicenza is a switchback of mountain peaks), a clutch of excellent paintings and one of Europe's most famous and imitated buildings.

Buses for Monte Bèrico leave the bus station (beside the train station) on average every ninety minutes; on foot it takes around half an hour from the centre of town. If you decide to walk, the most direct route from the Basilica is to cross the Ponte San Michele (see p.339), carry on past Piazza dei Gualdi to the Portòn del Luzzo, go through the gate and along Contrà San Silvestro, then cross Viale X Giugno (ignoring the road sign that directs cars up Viale Dante) to follow the **Portici**, an eighteenth-century arcade built to shelter the pilgrims on their way up to the church. Alternatively, soon after Ponte San Michele you could bear left along Contrà Pozzetto, then go straight along Contrà San Tommaso and Contrà Santa Caterina, which comes to an end opposite Palladio's **Arco delle Scalette**, the gateway to a steep flight of steps that leads you towards the upper part of the Portici, passing the road to the Villa Valmarana and Villa Rotonda. (If you take the latter route, cross to the left side of Contrà Santa Caterina at the end of the road, otherwise you'll find it impossible to get over the traffic intersection.)

The Basilica di Monte Bèrico and the Risorgimento museum

The Basilica di
Monte Bèrico is
open Mon–Sat
6.15am–
12.30pm &
2.30– 7.30pm,
Sun 6.15am–
8pm.

In 1426–28 Vicenza was struck by an outbreak of bubonic plague, in the course of which the Virgin appeared twice at the summit of Monte Bèrico to announce the city's deliverance. A chapel was raised on the spot that the Virgin had obligingly marked out for its construction, and it duly became a place of pilgrimage. It was enlarged later in the century, altered again in the sixteenth century, and then, at the end of the seventeenth, replaced by the present **Basilica di**

Monte Bèrico. (The church was extended in such a way that the nave of the fifteenth-century version became the transepts of the new church, leaving the old Gothic facade stuck onto the basilica's right side.) Pilgrims regularly arrive here by the busload, and the glossy interior of the church, all gilding and fake marble, is immaculately maintained to receive them. A well-stocked shop in the cloister sells devotional trinkets to the faithful, close to a cash desk displaying the current rates for customized Masses and other services.

The sceptical should nevertheless venture into the church for Montagna's *Pietà* (1500), in the chapel on the right side of the apse, and *The Supper of St Gregory the Great* by **Veronese** (1572), in the old refectory of the adjoining monastery, which it shares with the impressive fossil collection amassed by the resident Franciscans. The Veronese painting, the prototype of *The Feast in the House of Levi* in Venice's Accademia, was used for bayonet practice by Austrian troops in 1848 – a small reproduction on the adjoining wall shows what a thorough mess they made of it, and what a good job the restorers did. The repair was financed by the Austrian emperor Franz Josef, by way of apology for the vandalism.

The **Piazzale della Vittoria**, in front of the basilica, was built to commemorate the dead of World War I; today it's a parking lot and a belvedere for the best view across the city. Carry on towards the summit of the hill and you'll come to the **Museo del Risorgimento e della Resistenza**, some ten minutes' walk beyond the basilica. The museum is an impressively thorough display, paying particular attention to Vicenza's resistance to the Austrians in the mid-nineteenth century and to the efforts of the anti-Fascist Alpine fighters a century later, but for many visitors the main attraction will be the extensive wooded parkland laid out on the slopes below the **Villa Guiccioli**, the museum's main building.

The Villa Valmarana

Ten minutes' walk away from the basilica is the **Villa Valmarana ai Nani** – meaning "of the dwarves", after the figures on the garden wall. Still owned by the family for which it was built, it's an undistinguished eighteenth-century house made extraordinary by its gorgeous decoration, a cycle of frescoes created in 1757 by **Giambattista and Giandomenico Tiepolo**. To get there, go back to the elbow of the *Portici*, along Via M. D'Azeglio for about a hundred metres, then right into the cobbled Via S. Bastiano, which ends at the Villa Valmarana.

There are two parts to the house. The main block, the **Palazzina**, was frescoed with brilliant virtuosity by Giambattista, drawing his heroic imagery from Virgil, Tasso and Ariosto – you're handed a brief guide to the paintings at the entrance. Giambattista also painted one room of the **Foresteria**, the guest wing, but here the bulk of the work was done by his son Giandomenico; his scope was somewhat narrow-

Around Vicenza

The Risorgimento museum is open Tues–Sun 9am–5pm, (open until 7pm from June 19 to Aug 31); L6000/€3.10 or combined ticket. The park is open daily: April–Sept 9am–7.30pm; Oct–March 9am–5.30pm; free.

The Villa Valmarana is open March 15–April 30 Tues–Sat 2.30–5.30pm plus Wed, Thurs, Sat & Sun 10am–noon; May–Sept Tues–Sat 3–6pm plus same morning times; Oct–Nov 5 Tues–Sat 2–5pm plus same morning times; L10,000/€5.16.

er than his father's (carnivals and rustic pleasures were his favourite themes), but the same air of wistful melancholy pervades his scenes, and his apparently effortless fluency is very nearly as impressive.

La Rotonda

*The Rotonda is
open March
15–Nov 4 Wed
10am–noon &
3–6pm;
L10,000/€5.16,
including the
grounds. The
grounds are
open
Tues–Thurs,
same weeks
and hours;
L5000/€2.58.*

From the Valmarana house the narrow Stradella Valmarana descends the slope to **La Rotonda**, unique among Palladio's villas in that it was designed not as the main building of a farming estate but as a pavilion in which entertainments could be held and the landscape enjoyed. Begun in 1566, it was commissioned by Vicenza-born Paolo Almerico as his retirement home, after years in Rome in the service of the papacy, but was not finished until about 1620, by which time it had passed into the hands of the Capra family. (The Capra whose name appears on the main pediment of the villa finished the development of the site in the 1640s, when he commissioned the chapel that stands by the entrance gate.) Almerico chose a hill-top site "surrounded by other most pleasant hills, which present the appearance of a vast theatre" – and Palladio's design certainly makes the most of its centre-stage setting. The combination of the pure forms of the circle and square was a fundamental concern of many Renaissance architects (Leonardo, Bramante and Michelangelo all worked at it), and the elegance of Palladio's solution led to innumerable imitations – for example Mereworth and Chiswick in England, and Jefferson's rejected plan for the official residence of the US president, a near facsimile of the Rotonda.

Only a tour of the lavishly decorated rooms will fully reveal the subtleties of the Rotonda's design, which gives a strong impression of being as symmetrical as a square while in fact having a definite main axis. If you're here on a day when the interior's shut, try to get to see Joseph Losey's film of Mozart's *Don Giovanni* – the Rotonda was used as the remorseless seducer's residence. The grounds are open all year, but unless you're an architecture student and really want to scrutinize the walls from point-blank range, the garden can be given a miss, as it's just a narrow belt of grass and gravel.

The Villa Cordellina-Lombardi and Villa Pisani

*The Villa
Cordellina is
open April
1–Oct 15
Tues–Fri
9am–1pm, Sat
& Sun
9am–noon &
3–6pm;
L4000/€2.07.*

A must for admirers of Giambattista Tiepolo is the eighteenth-century **Villa Cordellina-Lombardi**, on the outskirts of the small town of **MONTECCHIO MAGGIORE**, 13km to the southwest of Vicenza. His frescoes in the entrance hall – *The Clemency of Scipio*, *The Clemency of Alexander* and, on the ceiling, *The Light of Reason Driving out the Fog of Ignorance* – are a touch less exuberant than the later ones at the Villa Valmarana, and show his debt to Paolo Veronese more plainly, but they will still make you feel better about life for the rest of the day.

Montecchio's other attractions, a pair of rebuilt fourteenth-century **Scaligeri forts** erected on a ridge overlooking the town, look their best from afar. They were made the strongholds of the Montague clan in Luigi da Porto's *Romeo and Juliet*.

A few **buses** from Vicenza go through Montecchio Maggiore, but there's a glut of services that pass through nearby Alte Ceccato on their way to Lonigo, Sossano and Noventa Vicentina – get off when you see the huge *Bertozzo* clothes supermarket, then follow the signs for the villa, which is about ten minutes' walk from the road. The journey takes about twenty minutes, through an unrelentingly grim landscape of shops, factories and commercial estates.

The Villa Pisani

About 20km to the south of Montecchio Maggiore, at **BAGNOLO**, stands Palladio's **Villa Pisani**. Dating from the early 1540s, the Villa Pisani is one of his less sophisticated designs, marking a transition from the traditional fortified villa to the fully classicized projects of the later sixteenth century. The division of the rooms follows a pattern found all over the Veneto: kitchens in the basement, highly decorated living quarters on the next level, and granary space on the upper storey. Only specialists will get a great deal out of this house, but if you've got a car you might want to give it a look – getting there by public transport involves a bus from Vicenza to Lonigo (almost hourly), then a four-kilometre walk, though at least the hike offers the diversion of a good view of Scamozzi's Villa Rocca-Pisani, a lineal descendant of the Rotonda. The last bus back from Lonigo to Vicenza leaves at 5.45pm (Mon–Fri).

The Villa Pisani is open April–Nov 4 Wed 10am– noon & 3–6pm, Sun 3–6pm; L10,000/€5.16, or L5000/€2.58 for the grounds only.

Thiene and Lugo di Vicenza

It was only with the ending of the War of the League of Cambrai in 1516 that the landowners of the Veneto were able to disregard defensive considerations when building homes out of the urban centres – prior to that, the great houses of the *terra firma* were a sort of cross-breed between a castle and a palace. The most imposing example of this genre still standing is the **Villa Porto-Colleoni**, built in the 1470s at **THIENE**, a bland textile town 20km north of Vicenza.

The crenellated corner towers, large central block and the encircling protective wall are all features that would have been common in this area in the fifteenth century, although this house, with its facade decorations and ornate Gothic windows, was probably more precious than most.

Guided tours of the Villa Porto-Colleoni are given March 12–Nov 12 Sun 3, 4 & 5pm; L10,000/€5.16.

Nowadays the buildings that most closely resemble it are to be found along Venice's Canal Grande (for example, the Fondaco dei Turchi) – which is not as strange as it first seems, as they belong to the same family tree, springing from the long-ruined provincial villas of the late Roman Empire. The mandatory guided tour of the interior makes the most of the workaday sixteenth-century frescoes by Giambattista Zelotti and G.A. Fasolo; the plethora of equine portraits

Verona

is explained by the fact that the Colleoni had a tradition of service in the Venetian cavalry.

To get to Thiene from Vicenza, take the Schio **train**; it leaves virtually every hour and takes 25 minutes.

Lugo di Vicenza

The next rung up the evolutionary ladder of the villas of the Veneto is represented 8km to the north of Thiene, on the edge of **LUGO DI VICENZA** (aka Lonedo di Lugo), where you'll find Palladio's first villa – the **Villa Godi Malinverni**, built in 1537–42. The plan of the Villa Godi Malinverni isn't all that different from that of the Villa Porto-Colleoni, but it's been shorn of fortified trappings and is clearly more of a country house than a castle; on the other hand, there's not a feature on the building that refers to the architecture of ancient Rome, and so it could be seen as occupying a position midway between the Gothic and Renaissance villas.

Professor Remo Malinverni restored the house in the early 1960s, and installed his collection of nineteenth-century Italian paintings in some of the rooms; elsewhere in the building you'll find a fossil museum – neither display can really compete with the sixteenth-century frescoes, some of which show the journeyman Giambattista Zelotti on top form.

Just above the Godi Malinverni stands the **Villa Piovene**, the central block of which was also built by Palladio around 1540; the Ionic portico was added later in the sixteenth century, and the external staircase and portal came in the eighteenth. Only the nineteenth-century landscaped garden is open to the public.

An infrequent **bus** service runs from Thiene to Lugo, on its way to Calvene – there's a stop by the Porto-Colleoni.

The Villa Godi Malinverni is open Tues, Sat & Sun: March–May & Oct–Nov 2–6pm; June–Sept 3–7pm; L10,000/€5.16.

The Piovene gardens are open daily 2.30–7pm; L8000/€4.16.

Verona

With its Roman sites and streets of pink-hued medieval buildings, the irresistible city of **VERONA** has more in the way of historic attractions than any other place in the Veneto except Venice itself. Unlike Venice, though, it's not a city overwhelmed by the tourist industry, important though that is to the local economy. Verona is the largest city of the mainland Veneto, its economic success largely due to its position at the crossing of the major routes from Germany and Austria to central Italy and from the west to Venice and Trieste.

Verona's initial development as a **Roman** settlement was similarly due to its straddling the main east–west and north–south lines of communication. A period of decline in the wake of the disintegration of the Roman Empire was followed by revival under the Ostrogoths, who in turn were succeeded by the Franks – Charlemagne's son, Pepin, ruled his kingdom from here. By the twelfth century Verona had become a city state, and in the following century approached the zenith of its independent existence with the rise of the **Scaligeri**. Ruthless in the exercise of power – they once employed Werner of Urlingea, self-styled "enemy of God and of compassion" – the Scaligeri were at the same time energetic patrons of the arts, and many of Verona's finest buildings date from the century of their rule. Both Giotto and Dante were guests of the family, the latter dedicating his *Paradiso* to Cangrande I, head of the family at the time.

With the fall of their dynasty a time of upheaval ensued, Gian Galeazzo Visconti of Milan emerging with control of the city. Absorption into the Venetian empire came in 1405, and Venice continued to govern Verona down to the arrival of Napoleon. Verona's history then shadowed that of Venice: a prolonged interlude of Austrian rule, brought to an end by the unification of Italy.

Arrival, information and accommodation

If you're flying in to Verona's Valerio Catullo **airport** at Villafranca, you can get into the city by a regular *APT* bus (every 20min 7am–midnight; L7000/€3.62) from the airport to the train station and Piazza Cittadella, near the city centre; flights from Verona's Brescia airport are served by a dedicated shuttle bus, which takes one hour. **Taxis** are available at the airport rank, or can be called through Radio Taxi Aeroporto (☎045.987.666).

From the train station it's a fifteen-minute walk to Piazza Brà, site of the Arena and the hub of Verona. Turn right out of the station (keeping to the right-hand side of the road – there are some busy junctions), then cross the main road to the Porta Nuova, from where Corso Porta Nuova brings you onto the south side of Piazza Brà. Otherwise, unless you're staying in the youth hostel, you're only likely to need a **bus** if you don't fancy the fifteen-minute walk from the train station to the centre. Orange local buses leave from the stands immediately opposite the train station: for Piazza Brà take any of the buses from bay A; buses for Castelvecchio leave from bay D; those for Piazza delle Erbe from bay F. Tickets must be bought before boarding, either from the ticket office and machines alongside bay A or from the *tabacchi* inside the train station ticket hall. Tickets cost L1600/€0.82 and are valid for any number of journeys within an hour; alternatively, a one-day ticket valid over the whole network costs L5000/€2.58.

The main **tourist office** is on the central Piazza Bra, within the old town walls beside the Palazzo Municipale (Mon–Sat 9am–6pm; ☎045.806.8680, *www.tourism.verona.it*). There is an additional office at the train station (daily 9am–6pm; ☎045.800.0861) and a **room-finding service**, Cooperativa Albergatori Veronesi (CAV), at Via Patuzzi 5 (Mon–Fri 9am–6.30pm; ☎045.800.9844): Via Patuzzi runs parallel to Via Leoncino off Piazza Gallieno in the southeast corner of Piazza Brà.

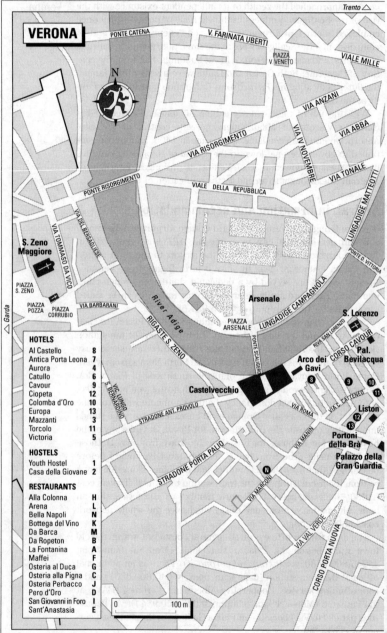

VERONA

Trento △

PONTE CATENA
V. FARINATA UBERTI
VIALE MILLE
PIAZZA V VENETO
VIA ANZANI
VIA ABBA
VIA RISORGIMENTO
VIA IV NOVEMBRE
VIA TONALE
PONTE RISORGIMENTO
VIALE DELLA REPUBBLICA
LUNGADIGE MATTEOTTI
VIA DEL BERSAGLIERE
PONTE D. VITTORIA
VIA TOMMASO DA VICO

S. Zeno Maggiore

PIAZZA S. ZENO
PIAZZA POZZA
PIAZZA CORRUBIO
VIA BARBARANI

△ Garda

River Adige
RIGASTE S. ZENO

Arsenale
LUNGADIGE CAMPAGNOLA
PIAZZA ARSENALE
PONTE SCALIGERO

S. Lorenzo
RIVA SAN LORENZO
CORSO CAVOUR

Arco dei Gavi
Pal. Bevilacqua

Castelvecchio
VIA ROMA
VIA C. CATTANEO
Liston
VIC. LUNGO S. BERNARDINO
STRADONE ANT. PROVOLO
VIA MANIN
Portoni della Brà
STRADONE PORTA PALIO
Palazzo della Gran Guardia
VIA MARCONI
CORSO PORTA NUOVA
VIA VAL VERDE

HOTELS

Al Castello	8
Antica Porta Leona	7
Aurora	4
Catullo	6
Cavour	9
Ciopeta	12
Colomba d'Oro	10
Europa	13
Mazzanti	3
Torcolo	11
Victoria	5

HOSTELS

Youth Hostel	1
Casa della Giovane	2

RESTAURANTS

Alla Colonna	H
Arena	L
Bella Napoli	N
Bottega del Vino	K
Da Barca	M
Da Ropeton	B
La Fontanina	A
Maffei	F
Osteria al Duca	G
Osteria alla Pigna	C
Osteria Perbacco	J
Pero d'Oro	D
San Giovanni in Foro	I
Sant'Anastasia	E

0 ————— 100 m

▽ Porta Nuova & Train Station

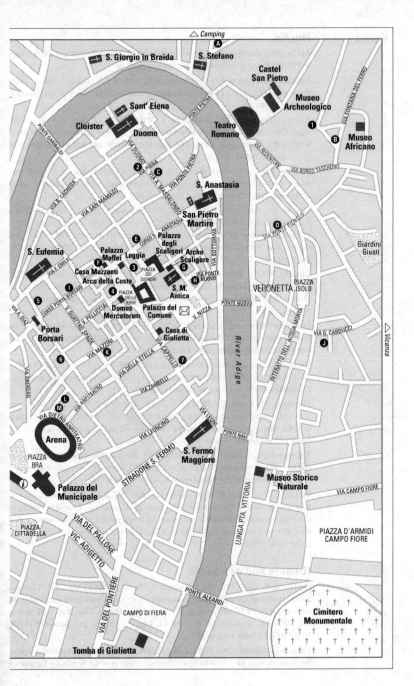

Verona

Hotels

Al Castello, Corso Cavour 43 ☎045.800.4403. Tiny one-star just off the central Corso Cavour, with simple but dark rooms. ②.

Antica Porta Leona, Via Corticella Leoni 3 ☎ & fax 045.595.499. A large three-star with plenty of singles, located close to the junction of Via Cappello and Via Leoni. ④.

Aurora, Piazzetta XIV Novembre 2 ☎045.594.717, fax 045.801.0860. Upmarket two-star hotel with a welcoming atmosphere and many rooms overlooking the Piazza delle Erbe. The staff are friendly and knowledgeable, and speak good English. ③.

Catullo, Via V. Catullo 1 ☎045.800.2786. The most economical hotel anywhere near the centre, just off the main shopping artery of Via Mazzini. Large rooms with shabby gentility and plenty of light. ①.

Cavour, Vicolo Chiodo 4 ☎045.590.166. A one-star, recently renovated, in a small street that runs south off Corso Cavour. Choose between cutesy rooms in blue and white, or the posher and slightly pricier annexe, which has been done up as a rural villa, with terracotta floors and beams. Rather eccentric management. ③.

Ciopeta, Vicolo Teatro Filarmonica 2 ☎045.800.6843, fax 045.803.3722, *ciopeta@iol.it*. Friendly, family-run one-star located in an alley parallel to Via Roma. Book ahead, as there are only eight rooms (with two shared bathrooms). ②.

Colomba d'Oro, via C. Catteneo 10 ☎045.595.300, *info@colombahotel.com*. Luxuriously appointed four-star, handily located for both Piazza delle Erbe and the Arena, with a garage (L30,000/€15.49 per day). ⑥.

Europa, Via Roma 8 ☎045.594.744, fax 045.800.1852. This reliable, if somewhat dull, three-star hotel is one of the city's biggest central establishments, so it's always worth a call if other places are full. ⑤.

Mazzanti, Via Mazzanti 6 ☎045.800.6813, fax 045.801.1262. A sizeable two-star with restaurant, just west of Piazza dei Signori. The rooms are less characterful than you'd think, given the rambling old building and location in the heart of the historic centre. ②.

Torcolo, Vicolo Listone 3 ☎045.800.7512, fax 045.800.4058. Nicely turned-out two-star hotel within 100m of the Arena. Extremely welcoming owners – and a favourite with the opera crowds, so book ahead. ③.

Victoria, Via Adua 8 ☎045.590.566, fax 045.590.155, *hotel.victoria @ifinet.it*. One of the quietest and most pleasantly run four-star hotels in the city – the one to pick if you want to treat yourself. In low season you can get a room for L330,000/€170, but in summer it'll be nearer L450,000/€232. ⑦.

Hostels and campsites

Ostello della Gioventù, Salita Fontana del Ferro 15 ☎045.590.360. A beautiful old building behind the Teatro Romano; it's quite a walk from the centre, so take bus #73 (# 90 on Sundays and at night) to Piazza Isolo then walk up the hill. Also has a campsite. Curfew 11.30pm; L23,000 per person/€11.88; L14,000/€7.23 evening meal.

Casa della Giovane, Via Pigna 7 ☎045.596.880. Spartan, convent-run hostel for women, with an 11pm curfew, although there is some flexibility for guests with opera tickets. L22,000/€11.36, plus some double rooms at L25,000/€12.91.

Campeggio Castel San Pietro, Via Castel S. Pietro 2 ☎045.592.037. Along with the hostel site, this is the most pleasant and convenient place to camp near Verona – take a bus to Via Marsala. Open mid-June to Sept.

The City

Set within the low amphitheatre that the wide River Adige has carved out of the hills, Verona conveys a sense of ease that you don't often find in the region's other cities. As you walk past the great Roman arena or along the embankments or over the bridges that span the broad curves of the Adige, you'll be struck by the spaciousness of Verona. And even in the narrow medieval lanes of the historic centre, around the beautiful Piazza delle Erbe, the atmosphere is quite distinct from that of busy Padua or sleek, efficient Vicenza. With cars and buses barred from many of the central squares and streets, it's a city that invites dawdling.

From the station to Piazza Brà

Coming from the station or the Verona Sud motorway exit, you pass Verona's south gate, the **Porta Nuova**, built in the sixteenth century by Michele Sanmicheli (though messed around with by the Austrians in the nineteenth century). From the wide Corso Porta Nuova, which begins here, the red roofs and towers of the city stand out on a clear day against the backdrop of the Torricelle and the Lessini mountains. At the other end of the Corso, the battlemented arches of the **Portoni della Brà** (1389), formerly part of the city walls, mark the entrance to the historic centre. Built by the Visconti family, the Portoni once carried a covered walk from the Castelvecchio (left down Via Roma) to their residence, of which only the **Torre Pentagona** remains, behind the **Palazzo della Gran Guardia** (1610) on the right. Ensconced in the left-hand wall of the Portoni lies the entrance to one of Verona's more obscure museums, the **Museo Lapidario Maffeiano**; the large

The Museo Lapidario Maffeiano is open Tues–Sun 9am–2pm; L4000/€2.07.

Combined tickets

A **biglietto unico**, costing L8000/€4.13, allows one visit to San Zeno, San Lorenzo, the Duomo (including the baptistry and archeological findings), Sant'Anastasia and San Fermo. The ticket can be bought at any of these churches, which individually charge L3000/€1.55 for admission. If you're planning to be very busy, it might be worth getting the **Verona Card**, which costs L22,000/€11.36 and gives access to all the sights listed above, plus the Arena, the Torre dei Lamberti, the Museo Lapidario, Castelvecchio and the roman theatre, as well as free travel on city buses. Be careful which day you buy it, however, as it's valid for just three days and almost everything shuts on a Monday. A third card, costing L52,000/€26.85, throws in entrance to Gardaland, Lake Garda's answer to Disney (*www.gardaland.it*).

---

courtyard and two upstairs rooms contain miscellaneous Greek, Etruscan and Roman statues and inscriptions, none of which is likely to grip the non-specialist, though the assembly of Greek inscriptions is the largest in the country.

Through these arches the broad expanse of **Piazza Brà** opens up, bordered on the south side by the disused Gran Guardia (formerly a sort of military gymnasium), on the east by the nineteenth-century **Palazzo del Municipio**, on the west by the **Liston**, and at the far end by the mightiest of Verona's Roman monuments, the **Arena**. (Brà, by the way, is the Veronese dialect version of *braida*, meaning 'meadow'.)

The Arena is open Tues–Sun 9am–6.30pm, but during the opera season it closes at 3.30pm; L6000/€3.10, free on first Sun of month.

Dating from the first century AD, the Arena has survived in remarkable condition, despite the twelfth-century earthquake that destroyed all but four of the arches of the outer wall. The interior was scarcely damaged by the tremor, and nowadays audiences come here to watch gargantuan opera productions where once crowds of around twenty thousand packed the benches for gladiatorial contests, mock naval battles and the like. Originally measuring 152m by 123m overall, and thus the third largest of all Roman amphitheatres – after the Colosseum and the amphitheatre at Capua – the Arena is still an awesome sight, and offers a fine panorama of the city and surrounding mountains from the topmost of the 44 pink marble tiers.

Piazza delle Erbe and Piazza dei Signori

Narrow, traffic-free Via Mazzini – the main route of Verona's *passeggiata* – leads north from the Arena, past expensive clothes and jewellery shops, to **Piazza delle Erbe**, a lively and handsome square tightly enclosed by medieval and Renaissance *palazzi*. Originally a major Roman crossroads and the site of the forum, the piazza is still the heart of the city, a place where people come to meet friends and see who's around. As the name suggests, the market used to sell mainly vegetables, but nowadays most of the stalls sell an assortment of clothes, souvenirs, antiques and fast food.

Lined along the square's central axis, and camouflaged by the stalls, are the **Colonna Antica** (a fifteenth-century lantern on a marble pillar), the **Capitello** (a fourteenth-century pavilion where public servants were invested with their office), the fountain of **Madonna Verona** (built in 1368 by Cansignorio della Scala) and finally the column of the lion of Saint Mark, demonstrating Verona's past links with Venice. This specimen is a nineteenth-century copy of one destroyed during the Pasqua Veronese (Veronese Easter), as the city's 1797 uprising against the French is known.

On the left as you look from the Via Cappello end, past the tall houses of the old Jewish ghetto, is the **Domus Mercatorum** (currently being restored), which was founded in 1301 as a merchants' warehouse and exchange and is now a bank and chamber of commerce. At the far end, the Baroque **Palazzo Maffei** has been taken over by shops, luxury apartments and an expensive restaurant; to the left of Palazzo Maffei rises the fourteenth-century **Torre del Gardello**, while to the right stands the **Casa Mazzanti**, whose sixteenth-century murals are best seen after dark, under enhancing spotlights. On the eastern side of the piazza, to your right, Verona's highest tower (83m), the twelfth-century **Torre dei Lamberti**, overlooks the **Palazzo del Comune** – a twelfth-century building with Renaissance additions and nineteenth-century alterations. Flanking the wing known as the **Sala della Ragione**, where justice was dispensed, the **Arco della Costa** (Arch of the Rib) hangs over the route through to the Piazza dei Signori. Cynical folklore has it that the whale's rib suspended under the arch will fall if an adult virgin passes underneath.

Piazza dei Signori, sometimes known as Piazza Dante after the grimly pensive statue of the poet in the centre, used to be the chief public square in Verona but is now often quiet and empty, a strong contrast with Piazza delle Erbe. Facing you as you come into the square is the **Palazzo degli Scaligeri**, residence of the Scaligeri. Extending from it at a right angle are the graceful arches of Verona's outstanding early Renaissance building, the late fifteenth-century **Loggia del Consiglio**, former assembly hall of the city council. The rank of Roman notables along the roof includes Verona's most illustrious native poet, Catullus. Opposite stands Sanmicheli's splendid gateway to the **Palazzo del Capitano**, which is separated from the Palazzo del Commune by a stretch of excavated Roman street.

A right turn at the entrance to the square leads into the courtyard known as the **Corte Mercato Vecchio**, dominated by a beautiful fifteenth-century staircase carved in roseate marble which leads to the Sala della Ragione. For a dizzying view, a lift ascends the **Torre dei Lamberti**, though masochists can take the steps – all 368 of them.

The Arche Scaligere

Passing under the arch linking the Palazzo degli Scaligeri to the Palazzo del Capitano, you come to the little twelfth-century Romanesque church of **Santa Maria Antica**, in front of which are ranged the **Arche Scaligere**, which are among the finest funerary monuments in Italy. The tombs are now surrounded by locked wrought-iron gates, but the elaborate Gothic stonework is still easily visible and the back-street location exudes an atmosphere of departed magnificence.

Over the side entrance to the church, an equestrian statue of **Cangrande I** ("Big Dog"; d.1329) grins on the summit of his tomb's pyramidal roof; the statue is a copy, the original being displayed in the Castelvecchio. The canopied tombs of the rest of the clan are enclosed within a wrought-iron palisade decorated with ladder motifs, the emblem of the Scaligeri – the family name was della Scala, "scala" meaning ladder. **Mastino I** ("Mastiff"; d.1277), founder of the dynasty, is buried in the simple tomb against the wall of the church;

Photographic exhibitions are often held in a room off the courtyard of the Palazzo del Capitano, alongside some smaller finds from the excavation of this area.

The Torre dei Lamberti is open Tues–Sun 9am–6.30pm; L4000/€2.07 by lift, L3000/€1.55 on foot.

Santa Maria Antica is open daily 7.30am–12.30pm & 3.30–7pm.

Mastino II (d.1351) is to the left of the entrance, opposite the most florid of the tombs, that of **Cansignorio** ("Top Dog"; d.1375). The unassuming tombs of the two who didn't take canine names, **Giovanni** (d.1359) and **Bartolomeo** (d.1304), are between Mastino II and Cansignorio.

Sant'Anastasia and San Pietro Martire

Sant'Anastasia is open March–Oct Mon–Sat 9.30am–6pm, Sun 1–6pm; Nov–Feb Tues–Sat 10am–1pm & 1.30–4pm, Sun 1–5pm; L3000/€1.55 (or biglietto unico).

To the east of the Arche Scaligere, you can walk parallel to the Adige along Via Sottoriva, where the majority of the houses date from the Middle Ages, making this one of Verona's most atmospheric areas. The street takes you to **Sant'Anastasia**, Verona's largest church. Started in 1290 and completed in 1481, it's mainly Gothic, with undertones of the Romanesque. The early fourteenth-century carvings of New Testament scenes around the doors are the most arresting feature of its bare exterior; the interior's highlight is **Pisanello's** delicately coloured fresco of *St George and the Princess* (above the chapel to the right of the altar), a work in which the normally martial saint appears as something of a dandy.

To the left of Sant'Anastasia's facade is an eye-catching tomb, the free-standing monument to Guglielmo di Castelbarco (1320) by Enrico di Rigino. To its left, on one side of the little piazza fronting Sant'Anastasia, stands the lovely church of **San Pietro Martire**, deconsecrated since its ransacking by Napoleon. Numerous little patches of fresco dot the walls, making for an atmospheric interior, though the highlight is the vast lunette fresco on the east wall. Easily the strangest picture in Verona, it is thought to be an allegorical account of the Virgin's Assumption, though the bizarre collection of animals appears to have little connection with a bemused-looking Madonna. Painted in 1480 by Giovanni Falconetti (and recently restored), it is thought to be a copy of a Swiss tapestry, and was commissioned by two knights in Emperor Maximilian's army. The two donors can be seen kneeling on either side of the fresco, against a background depicting an idealized Verona.

San Pietro Martire is open Tues–Sat 10am– 12.30pm & 4–7.30pm.

The Duomo

The Duomo, San Giovanni in Fonte and Sant'Elena are open March–Oct Mon–Sat 9.30am–6pm, Sun 1–6pm; Nov–Feb Tues–Sat 11am–1pm & 1.30–4pm, Sun 1.30–5pm; L3000/€1.55 (or biglietto unico).

Verona's red-and-white striped **Duomo** lies just round the river's bend, to the north of Sant'Anastasia and a short distance from the Roman **Ponte Pietra**, which was destroyed in 1945 by the retreating Germans, but rebuilt using mostly the original stones and bricks. Consecrated in 1187, the Duomo has been worked on constantly over the centuries and the campanile is still said to be incomplete, even though the bell-chamber wasn't added until 1927. As a whole it's Romanesque in its lower parts, developing into Gothic as it goes up; the two doorways are twelfth-century – look for the story of Jonah and a dragon-like whale on the south porch, and the figures of Roland and Oliver, two of Charlemagne's paladins, flanking the outstanding polychrome main west portal. The interior has a splendid organ, and fascinating architectural details around each chapel and on the columns – particularly fine is the **Cappella Mazzanti** (last on the right). In the first chapel on the left, an *Assumption* by **Titian** occupies an architectural frame by **Sansovino**, who also designed the choir.

The door at the end of the left aisle gives access to the churches of **San Giovanni in Fonte** and **Sant'Elena**, in front of which lie the remnants of the presbytery of a fourth-century basilica, the form of which Sant'Elena roughly follows. Mosaics from the second half of the fourth century can be seen in Sant'Elena itself, while the adjacent San Giovanni in Fonte contains a masterpiece of Romanesque sculpture – a baptismal font covered with carved panels of biblical scenes. The foundations of a larger, fifth-century basilica which was built nearby when the earlier one was partially destroyed can be seen in the cloister, reached by the gated alley immediately to the left of the duomo's facade.

The Casa di Giulietta and San Fermo

South of Piazza delle Erbe runs Via Cappello, a street named after the family that Shakespeare turned into the Capulets – and there on the left, at no. 23, is the **Casa di Giulietta**. Sadly for romantics, the association of the house with Juliet is based on nothing more than its picturesque courtyard and balcony, and even this latter feature is placed, as Arnold Bennett wrote, "too high for love, unless Juliet was a trapeze acrobat, accustomed to hanging downwards by her toes". Perhaps the most memorable thing about the house, however, is the extraordinary amount of lovers' graffiti that virtually obliterates the walls of the entrance to the courtyard.

In fact, although the "Capulets" (Capuleti) and the "Montagues" (Montecchi) did exist, Romeo and Juliet were entirely fictional creations; and although bloody feuds were common (the head of one family invited his enemy to a truce-making meal, informing him afterwards that he'd just dined off the liver of his son), there's no record of these two clans being at loggerheads. The cheerless facts notwithstanding, a bronze Juliet has been shoved into a corner of the courtyard, her right breast polished bright by the groping hands of pilgrims hoping for luck in love. The house itself, constructed at the start of the fourteenth century, is in a fine state of preservation, but is largely empty.

Via Cappello leads into Via Leoni with its Roman gate, the **Porta Romana dei Leoni**, and segment of excavated Roman street, exposed three metres below today's street level. At the end of Via Leoni and across the road stands the red-brick church of **San Fermo** (same price and hours as Sant'Anastasia), whose inconsistent exterior betrays the fact that it consists of two churches combined. The Benedictines built the original one in the eighth century, then rebuilt

The Casa di Giulietta is open Tues–Sun 9am–6.30pm; L6000/€3.10.

Verona has a couple of other spurious "Romeo and Juliet" shrines: the Tomba di Giulietta, in the southwest of the city, in the cloister of the deconsecrated San Francesco al Corso (Tues–Sun 9am–6.30pm; L6000/€3.10, free on first Sun of month); and "Romeo's house", a private dwelling at Via Arche Scaligere 4.

it in the eleventh to honour the relics of Saint Fermo and Saint Roch (the former supposedly martyred on this site); very soon after, flooding forced them to superimpose another church for day-to-day use, a structure greatly altered in the early fourteenth century by the Minorites. The Gothic upper church may have no outstanding works of art (though the *Annunciation* by Pisanello at the west end is the earliest surviving fresco by the artist), but the numerous fourteenth-century frescoes and the fine wooden keel vault make for a graceful interior – made in 1314, the ceiling is the oldest such vault left in the Veneto. The now subterranean Romanesque lower church, entered from the right transept, has some well-preserved twelfth-century frescoes on its columns, in particular the *Baptism of Jesus* halfway down on the left.

The Porta Borsari and Corso Cavour

After the Arena and the Teatro Romano, Verona's most impressive Roman remnant is the **Porta Borsari**, a structure that was as great an influence on the city's Renaissance architects as the amphitheatre. Now reduced to a monumental screen bestriding the road at the junction of Via Armando Diaz and Corso Porta Borsari (west of Piazza delle Erbe), it used to be Verona's largest Roman gate; the inscription dates it at 265 AD, but it's almost certainly older than that.

Busy **Corso Cavour**, which stretches away from the gate, is lined with bulky Renaissance palazzi, including two by **Michele Sanmicheli** (1484–1559) – the handsome **Palazzo Canossa**, at no. 44, and the **Palazzo Bevilacqua**, at no. 19. The two could hardly be more different: the former a handsome, restrainedly classical design with a shallow facade, the latter an ornately carved Mannerist effort. Sanmicheli, Verona's most illustrious native architect, left his mark elsewhere in the city too, most obviously in the shape of the great fortified gateways of the Porta Nuova and the Porta Palio (both near the train station), and in the Palazzo Pompei, now the home of the Museo Storico Naturale.

Opposite the Palazzo Bevilacqua is the Romanesque **San Lorenzo**, in the courtyard of which you'll see fragments dating back to the eighth century, the period of the church's foundation. The narrow, plain interior, which dates from the mid-twelfth century, is mostly notable for the women's galleries on the upper level and for a miscellany of columns, some banded in brick and soft *tufa* stone; atop the columns in the transept are two capitals which date back to Charlemagne and display his imperial eagle.

A short distance beyond the Palazzo Canossa, set back from the road on the right, stands the **Arco dei Gavi**, a first-century Roman triumphal arch; originally raised in the middle of the Corso, it was shifted to its present site overlooking the Adige in 1932. This is the best vantage point from which to admire the **Ponte Scaligero**; built by Cangrande II between 1355 and 1375, the bridge was blown up

San Lorenzo is open March–Oct Mon–Sat 9.30am–6pm & Sun 1–6pm; Nov–Feb Tues–Sat 10am–1pm & 1.30–4pm, Sun 1–5pm; L3000/€1.55 (or biglietto unico).

by the Germans in 1945 – the salvaged material was used for the plausible reconstruction. The stretch of shingle on the opposite bank is a popular spot for **picnics**, sunbathing and just watching the river flow by – the water's rich colour comes from minerals deposited by the glaciers upstream.

The Castelvecchio

The fortress from which the bridge springs, the **Castelvecchio**, was commissioned by Cangrande II at around the same time, and became the stronghold for Verona's subsequent rulers, all of whom altered it in some way – the last major addition, the small fort in the inner courtyard, was built by Napoleon. Opened as the city museum in 1925, it was damaged by bombing in World War II, but reopened in 1964 after scrupulous restoration by the modernist designer **Carlo Scarpa**. Scarpa's conversion of the Castelvecchio is one of his most impressive projects, leading the visitor through a labyrinthine succession of chambers, courtyards and open-air walkways – a route fascinating to explore in itself, particularly given Scarpa's subtle use of materials and textures. Halfway through the itinerary, you'll come face to face with the equestrian figure of **Cangrande I**, removed from his tomb and strikingly displayed on an outdoor pedestal; his expression is disconcerting from close range, his simpleton's grin difficult to reconcile with the image of the ruthless warlord.

The collection contains jewellery, sculpture, weapons and an array of other artefacts, but it's the paintings that stand out. Outstanding among them are two works by **Jacopo Bellini**, two *Madonnas* by **Giovanni Bellini**, another *Madonna* by **Pisanello**, **Mantegna**'s *Holy Family*, **Veronese**'s *Descent from the Cross*, a **Tintoretto** *Nativity*, a **Lotto** portrait and works by **Giambattista Tiepolo** and his son **Giandomenico**. The real joy of the museum, however, is in wandering round the fourteenth- and fifteenth-century pieces – beautiful sculptures and frescoes by the often nameless artists of the late Middle Ages. Exhibitions sometimes close parts of the gallery, but the major works are usually kept on view.

San Zeno Maggiore

A little over a kilometre northwest of the Castelvecchio stands the **Basilica di San Zeno Maggiore**, one of the most significant Romanesque churches in northern Italy. A church was founded here, above the tomb of the city's patron saint, as early as the fifth century (Zeno was the bishop of Verona in the 460s), but the present building and its campanile were put up in the first half of the twelfth century, with additions continuing up to the end of the fourteenth century. Its large **rose window**, representing the Wheel of Fortune, dates from around 1200, as does the magnificent **portal**, whose lintels bear relief sculptures representing the months and the miracles of Zeno, while the tympanum shows Zeno trampling the Devil. The reliefs to the side

The Castelvecchio is open Tues–Sun 9am–6.30pm; L6000/€3.10, free on first Sun of month.

San Zeno Maggiore is open March–Oct Mon–Sat 9.30am–6pm, Sun 1–6pm; Nov–Feb Tues–Sat 10am–1pm & 1.30–4pm, Sun 1–5pm; L3000/€1.55 (or biglietto unico).

of the portal, also from this period, show scenes from the Old and New Testaments and various allegorical scenes – notably *The Hunt of Theodoric*, in which the Ostrogoth king of Italy chases a stag down into Hell. (Theodoric, who ruled the peninsula from 493 to 526, based his court in Ravenna but so close was his attachment to Verona that for centuries the city was known in his native Germany as "Theodoric's city".) Extraordinary bronze panels on the **doors** depict scenes from the Bible and more miracles of Zeno, in a style influenced by Byzantine and Ottoman art; most of those on the left date from around 1100, most of the right-hand panels from a century later.

Areas of the lofty and simple **interior** are covered with frescoes, some superimposed upon others, some defaced by ancient graffiti. Diverting though these are, the one compulsive image in the church is the high altar's luminous *Madonna and Saints* by **Mantegna**. In the apse of the left aisle is a disarmingly cheerful fourteenth-century painted marble figure of Saint Zeno, typically represented as dark-skinned (it's believed he came from Africa) and with a fish on his crook (legend has it that when called upon to exorcize Emperor Gallienus' daughter, Saint Zeno was found fishing); the saint's tomb is in the beautifully colonnaded crypt beneath the raised choir.

Don't leave without a wander round the elegant, twin-columned arcades of the cloisters; a *Last Judgement* can be made out amid the fragmentary frescoes on the eastern wall, to which the tomb of an illegitimate Scaliger is also attached.

North and east of the Adige

On the other side of Ponte Garibaldi, and right along the embankments or through the public gardens, is **San Giorgio in Braida**, in terms of its artworks the richest of Verona's churches. A *Baptism* by **Jacopo Tintoretto** hangs over the door, while the third chapel on the right contains a *Descent of the Holy Ghost* by **Domenico Tintoretto**. The main altar, designed by **Sanmicheli**, incorporates a marvellous *Martyrdom of St George* by **Paolo Veronese**. If you're in need of a place to recuperate or picnic, the piazza in front of the church is your spot, providing a view along the river that must be the most photographed and painted scene in Verona. The park around the Arsenale is also a nice place for some time out, and is extremely convenient for the Castelvecchio and San Zeno Maggiore.

The Teatro Romano and Museo Archeologico are open Tues–Sun: July & Aug 9am–6.30pm; Sept–June 9am–3pm; L5000/€2.58, free on first Sun of month.

It's a short walk along the embankments, past the twelfth-century church of **Santo Stefano** and the Ponte Pietra, to the first-century BC **Teatro Romano**; much restored, the theatre is now used for concerts and plays (the entrance, which is a little hard to find, is 150m south of the Ponte Pietra). When the restorers set to work clearing later buildings away from the theatre, the only one allowed to remain was the tiny church of **Santi Siro e Libera** – built in the tenth century but altered in the fourteenth. Higher still, and reached by a lift, the **Museo Archeologico** (same ticket as the theatre) occupies the buildings of an old convent; its well-arranged collection features a number of Greek, Roman and Etruscan finds.

Steps to the side of the theatre lead to the **Castel San Pietro**, built by the Austrians on the site of a Visconti castle which had been destroyed by Napoleon. An uningratiating building, its sole appeal is the view away from it.

If you continue up the road from the Teatro Romano you'll come to one of the finest formal gardens in the country, the **Giardini Giusti** at Via Giardini Giusti 2. Full of fountains and shaded corners, the Giardini Giusti provides the city's most pleasant refuge from the streets, and was once an obligatory stop on any tour of Italy – Goethe and Mozart both paid a visit, and were much impressed. Two last spots on this side of the river might profitably fill an hour or so. The **Museo Storico Naturale**, opposite the church of San Fermo at Lungadige Porta Vittoria 9, is housed in Sanmicheli's earliest building in Verona, the Palazzo Pompei. As well as fossilized mammoths and tigers from local cave sites, the museum has an offbeat section on faked natural wonders – unicorn horns, monstrous animals and the like. If you've the energy to walk up the hill, you could call in at the **Museo Africano,** just off Via San Giovanni in Valle at Vicolo Pozzo 1; it contains musical instruments, fetishes and masks collected over the years by missionaries to the continent.

Eating, drinking and nightlife

Your money goes a lot further in Verona than it does in Venice: numerous **trattorias** offer full meals for around L25,000/€13 (especially in the Veronetta district, over the river on the east side), while on almost every street corner there's a bar where a glass of house wine (red Bardolino and Valpolicella, white Soave and Custoza) costs as little as L1000/€0.52. Verona's cuisine, meatier and richer than Venice's, can be sampled inexpensively in the city's many **osterie**, which typically serve fine wines and local specialities in the form of filling antipasti, though most do full meals too. **Nightlife** is more varied too, and genuinely goes on into the night, in contrast to Venice's general late-evening shutdown.

As the Veneto produces more DOC wine than any other region in Italy, it's not surprising that Italy's main wine fair, *Vinitaly*, is held in Verona; it takes place in April, and offers infinite sampling opportunities.

For a non-alcoholic indulgence, sit outside one of the *gelaterie* in Piazza delle Erbe and give a few minutes to an incredible concoction of fruit, cream and ice cream. If you want to follow the trend, the place to make for is *Gelateria Pampanin*, by Ponte Garibaldi.

Restaurants

Alla Colonna, Largo Pescheria Vecchia 4 ☎045.596.718. Almost impossible to get into, as the food is simple but superb, the prices excellent (L22,000/€11.36 menu) and the tables packed with savvy locals. Serves until 2am. Closed Sun.

The Giusti is open daily: summer 9am–8pm; winter 9am–sunset; L8000/€4.14.

The Museo Storico Naturale is open Mon– Thurs & Sat 8am–7pm, Sun 1.30–7pm; L4000/€2.07.

The Museo Africano is open Tues–Sat 9am–noon & 3–6pm, Sun 3–7pm; L5000/€2.58.

Verona

Arena, Vicolo Tre Marchetti 1. Large, raucous, canteen-like pizzeria, good for a late-night bite. Closed Mon.

Bella Napoli, Via Marconi 14. Serves the best pizza in Verona – in a distinctly Neapolitan atmosphere. Closed Mon.

Bottega del Vino, Vicolo Scudo di Francia 3a ☎045.597.945. One of the top restaurants in Verona, with flamboyant antique décor and one of the largest selection of wines you'll find anywhere in Italy – though it's slightly touristy. Open till midnight. Closed Tues.

Da Barca, Vicolo Tre Marchette 19b ☎045.803.0463. A couple of steps north of the Arena, with a classy ambience. The perfect spot for a pre- or post-opera meal of Veronese specialities. Closed Sun & Mon lunch.

Da Ropeton, Via Fontana del Ferro, Veronetta. Located just below the youth hostel, but worth the trip in any event. You can eat well for around L30,000/€15. Closed Tues.

La Fontanina, Piazzetta Fontanina, Veronetta. One of the best old-world *osterie* on the left bank of the Adige. Exclusive atmosphere (and prices to match), with tables hidden among crates of wine and decorated screens. A meal will cost upwards of L90,000/€46, including wine. Closed Sun & Mon lunch.

Maffei, Piazza delle Erbe 38 ☎045.801.015. Superb restaurant in a lovely Baroque palazzo, complete with courtyard. Wonderful menu for L60,000/€31, not including wine. Closed July & Aug, plus Sun (and Mon in winter).

Osteria al Duca, Via Arche Scaligere 2b ☎045.594.474. Small but extremely popular restaurant next door to "Romeo's house". Good menu at L23,000/€11.88. Closed Sun.

Osteria alla Pigna, Via Pigna 4. Elegant, traditional osteria between the duomo and Piazza delle Erbe. Closed Sun & Mon lunch.

Osteria Perbacco, Via Carducci 48, Veronetta. Moderately priced restaurant with a very attractive garden. Especially good fish and vegetarian dishes. Closed Wed.

Pero d'Oro, Via Ponte Pignolo 25, Veronetta ☎045.594.645. Friendly, family-run Veronetta trattoria. Serves inexpensive but genuine Veronese dishes. Closed Mon.

San Giovanni in Foro, Corte San Giovanni in Foro 4. Pizzas to rival *Bella Napoli*, with outside seating in a tiny courtyard just off Corso Porta Borsari. Closed Tues.

Sant'Anastasia, Corso Sant'Anastasia 27. Simple, atmospheric trattoria, offering a limited but consistently excellent menu and a small range of local wines. Around L40,000/€21, excluding drinks. Closed Wed & Sun.

Bars and snacks

Al Carro Armato, Vicolo Gatto 2a. One of the most atmospheric bars in the city, with delicious Veronese antipasti, and live music on Thursdays in winter. Open until 2am; closed Wed.

Al Mascaron, Piazza San Zeno 16. Fine wines and an urbane atmosphere early in the evening, popular disco-bar later. Five minutes' walk west from Castelvecchio. Open until 1am; closed Mon.

Al Ponte, Via Ponte Pietra. Sip a glass in the garden here and enjoy a marvellous view of Ponte Pietra and the Teatro Romano. Open until 3am; closed Wed.

Caffè delle Erbe, Piazza delle Erbe 32. Known universally as Mazzanti, this is the loudest, youngest and coolest of the late-opening bars on the square. Open until midnight.

El Tropico Latino, Via Pellicciai 20. Steer clear of the Tex-Mex food, and head for the cocktails and buzzing bar. One of the few late bars near the centre – open until 2am. Closed Tues.

Le Vecete, Via Pellicciai 32. Gracefully ordinary *osteria* with a delicious selection of the savoury tartlets known as *bocconcini*. Also serves good lunches. Open 8.30am–3pm & 5–9pm; closed Sun.

Osteria al Duomo, Via Duomo 7a. Best of the city's bars, little changed by modern fashion, and enlivened on Wednesday afternoons (5–8pm) and Friday nights in winter by a traditional singalong. Open 4pm–midnight; closed Thurs.

Osteria al Vino, Via Sottoriva 9. Rumbustious and full of locals: Verona's traditional *osterie* don't come much more authentic than this. Open daily.

Rivamancina, Vicolo Quadrelli 1, Veronetta. Lively late bar on the left bank of the Adige, with a trendy taste in music. Open 7pm–2am; closed Sun.

Nightlife

Music and **theatre** are the dominant art forms in the cultural life of Verona. In July and August an **opera** festival takes place in the **Arena**, always featuring a no-expense-spared production of *Aïda*. To get seats (from L50,000/€25.82), call in at the office at Via Dietro Anfiteatro 6b; if you can't make it in person you can now book by phone or online (☎045.800.5151, *www.arena.it*); big rock events crop up on the Arena's calendar too. A season of ballet and of Shakespeare and other dramatists in Italian is the principal summer fare at the **Teatro Romano**. Some of the Teatro events are free; for the rest, cheapskates who don't mind inferior acoustics can park themselves on the steps going up the hill alongside the theatre. The Teatro's box office also sells tickets for the Arena and vice versa.

Free performances by local dance and theatre groups in May can be surprisingly good, while the June **jazz festival** attracts international names, as does the **Canzone d'Autrice** festival for female singer-songwriters at the end of August. From October to May **English-language films** are shown every Tuesday at the Cinema Stimate in Piazza Cittadella. The **club** scene is livelier than in Venice, with venues coming and going; the *Spettacoli* section of the local paper, *L'Arena*, is the best source of up-to-date information on clubs and other entertainment in Verona.

Listings

American Express c/o Fabretto Viaggi, Corso Porta Nuova 11 (Mon–Fri 8.30am–12.30pm & 3–7pm; ☎045.594.700).

Airlines Alitalia (Venice) ☎041.521.6333; British Airways ☎045.595.699; Meridiana ☎045.808.9711.

Airport information ☎045.800.4129.

Bike rental From stalls on Piazza Brà, beside the Municipio.

Verona

Books The Bookshop, Via Interrato Acqua Morta 3a, near Ponte Navi. Well-stocked general bookshop with English-speaking staff.

Bus information Local AMT (orange) and provincial APT (blue) buses both at Piazzale XXV Aprile, opposite the train station: AMT Mon–Fri 6.30am–7.30pm ☎045.887.1111, *www.amt.it*; APT Mon–Fri 6am–8pm, Sat & Sun 6.30am–8pm ☎045.800.4125.

Car rental Combined office on Piazzale XXV Aprile, beside the train station: Europcar ☎045.592.759; Hertz ☎045.800.0832; Maggiore ☎147.67067.

Foreign exchange Porta Nuova station daily 7.30am–8.30pm; post office, Piazza Viviani (off Piazza dei Signori) Mon–Fri 8.30am–5pm, Sat 8.30am–1pm.

Hospital Ospedale Civile Maggiore, Borgo Trento, Piazza Stefani ☎045.931.111.

Internet access Head for the small shop on platform 1 at the train station (Mon–Sat 7.30am–7.30pm), Diesis, Via Sottoriva 15 (Mon–Thurs 11am–11pm, Fri & Sat 11am–midnight, Sun 3pm–8pm), or Internet Train, Via Roma 19 (Mon–Fri 11am–midnight, Sat & Sun 11am–8pm).

Lost property Buses ☎045.800.5825; trains ☎045.809.3827.

Police *Questura*, Lungoadige Porta Vittoria ☎045.809.0611. For the *Ufficio Stranieri*, which specifically deals with tourists, ring ☎045.809.0505.

Post office Via Teatro Filarmonico 11 (Mon–Fri 8.10am–6pm, Sat 8.10am–1.30pm); Piazza Viviani, near Ponte Nuovo (Mon–Sat 8.10am–6.30pm).

Taxis 24-hour: ☎045.532.666.

Telephones Telecom Italia, Via Leoncino 53.

Train information At the train station, daily 7am–9pm ☎147.888.088.

Chapter 17

The northern Veneto

Lacking a city of Verona's or Padua's appeal, the area extending from the Venetian lagoon to the southern edge of the Dolomites is the least visited part of the Veneto – most of those who pass through it are hurrying on to the ski-slopes of Cortina d'Ampezzo and its neighbouring winter resorts. This region's attractions might be generally on a smaller scale than those of the better-known Veneto towns, but they offer some of the most rewarding day trips from Venice.

The only city in the area covered by this chapter is prosperous **Treviso**, just 30km north of Venice. Some of the Veneto's finest medieval buildings and frescoes are to be seen here, and Treviso's position at the centre of the rail network makes it a good base from which to investigate the crannies of the region. To the west of Treviso, the beautiful little walled town of **Castelfranco Veneto** – the birthplace of Giorgione and home of one of his greatest paintings – also sits in the middle of a web of rail lines that connects Venice to the regional centres of Padua, Vicenza, Treviso and Belluno. A hop westward from Castelfranco brings you to another ancient walled town, **Cittadella**, while to the north lies **Bassano del Grappa**, source

---

Hotels in this guide are classified into nine price categories, indicating the minimum you can expect to pay for a double room in high season, including the cost of breakfast. For many Veneto hotels, high season is now an all-year phenomenon, but in those places that do reduce their prices for the quieter months of the winter, you can expect prices to be around ten percent lower on average.

   ① Under L100,000/€51.65.
   ② L100,000–150,000/€51.65–77.47.
   ③ L150,000–200,000/€77.47–103.29.
   ④ L200,000–250,000/€103.29–129.11.
   ⑤ L250,000–300,000/€129.11–154.94.
   ⑥ L300,000–400,000/€154.94–206.58.
   ⑦ L400,000–500,000/€206.58–258.23.
   ⑧ L500,000–600,000/€258.23–309.87.
   ⑨ Over L600,000/€309.87.

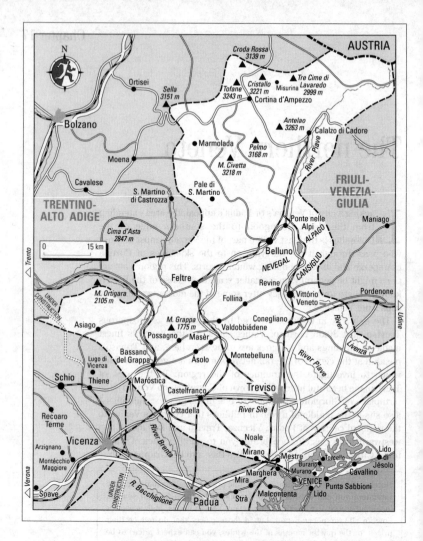

of the fiery grappa spirit and site of one of Italy's most spectacular bridges. Two other remarkable old towns lie within a short radius of Bassano: **Maróstica**, famous for its ceremonial chess game played with human "pieces"; and **Ásolo**, historically a rural retreat for the Venetian aristocracy, and just a few kilometres from the finest country house in all of Italy – the **Villa Barbaro** at **Masèr**. A short way to the north of Masèr, lodged on a ridge overlooking the valley of the Piave, **Feltre** boasts another historic centre that's been little changed by the last four centuries.

Due north of Treviso, the rail line into the far north of the Veneto runs through **Conegliano**, a town where life revolves round the production of wine, and of the sparkling Prosecco in particular. From there a service continues up through **Vittorio Veneto**, with its remarkably preserved Renaissance streets, and on to **Belluno**, in effect the mountains' border post.

Treviso

The local tourist board is pitching it a bit high when it suggests that the waterways of **TREVISO** may remind you of Venice, but you can't blame them for trying. To most tourists, Treviso is just the place that the cheap flights go to, and it does deserve a far better reputation than that – the old centre of the town is far more alluring than you might imagine from the modern suburbs you pass through on your way to or from the airport.

Treviso today is a brisk commercial centre and the capital of a province that extends to the north almost as far as Belluno. As with every settlement in the area, it used to be under Venetian control, but it was an important town long before its assimilation by Venice in 1389. As early as the eighth century it was minting its own coinage, and by the end of the thirteenth century, when it was ruled by the Da Camino family, Treviso was renowned as a refuge for artists and poets, and a model of good government. (Dante, in the *Purgatorio*, praises Gherardo da Camino as a man "left from a vanished race in reproof to these unruly times".) Plenty of evidence of the town's early stature survives in the form of Gothic churches, public buildings and, most dramatically of all, the paintings of **Tomaso da Modena** (1325–79), the dominant artist in northern Italy in the years immediately after Giotto's death. The general townscape within Treviso's sixteenth-century walls is often appealing too. A lack of local dressing stone led in the thirteenth century to the use of frescoes to decorate the houses, and these painted facades, along with the lengthy porticoes that shelter the pavements and the fast-running canals that cut through the centre (complete with waterwheels), give many of the streets an appearance quite distinct from that of other towns in the region.

Trains run at least hourly to Treviso from Venice (journey time 30min), and approximately hourly from Vicenza (1hr) via Castelfranco and Cittadella. Hourly buses from Padua and Venice arrive at the station in Lungosile Antonio Mattei, just before you cross the river going into the centre from the train station.

For online information on Treviso and Treviso province, go to: www .sevenonline .it/tvapt.

The City

Some of the best of Treviso's arcades and frescoes are in the main street of the historic centre, **Calmaggiore**, where modern commerce – epitomized by the locally based Benetton – has reached the sort of

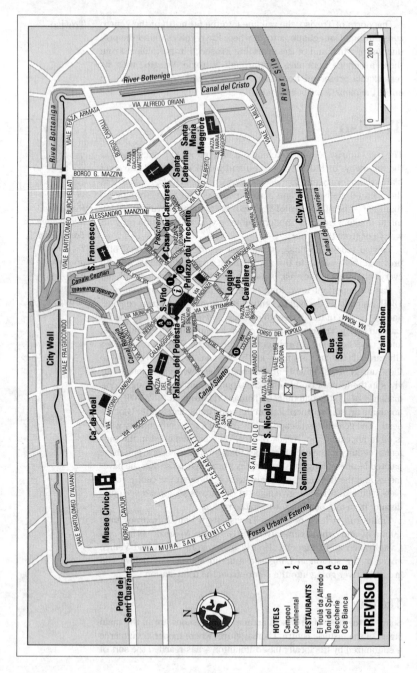

TREVISO

HOTELS
Campeol 1
Continental 2

RESTAURANTS
El Toulà da Alfredo D
Toni del Spin A
Beccherie C
Oca Bianca B

compromise with the past that the Italians seem to arrange better than anyone else. Modern construction techniques have played a larger part than you might think in shaping that compromise: Treviso was pounded during both world wars, and on Good Friday 1944 around half its buildings were destroyed in a single bombing raid.

The early thirteenth-century **Palazzo dei Trecento** (hall of the town council), at the side of the **Piazza dei Signori**, was one casualty of 1944 – a line of indented brick round the exterior shows the level at which the rebuilding began. Exhibitions are sometimes held in the main hall, which is generally open to the public each weekday from 8.30am to 12.30pm (free entry). The adjoining **Palazzo del Podestà**, with its high tower, is a late nineteenth-century structure, concocted in the appropriate style.

Incorporated into the back of this block are three buildings you could easily overlook: the Monte di Pietà (municipal pawnshop) and the churches of San Vito and Santa Lucia. The joined medieval churches of **San Vito** and **Santa Lucia** are tucked behind the Monte di Pietà, on the edge of Piazza San Vito. The latter is the more interesting – a tiny, dark chapel with extensive frescoes by **Tomaso da Modena** and his followers. San Vito has even earlier paintings (twelfth- and thirteenth-century) in the alcove through which you enter from Santa Lucia, but they are not in a good state.

San Vito and Santa Lucia are usually open daily 9am–noon & 4–6pm.

The **Monte di Pietà**, at the end of the piazzetta of the same name, is worth a visit for the Cappella dei Rettori, a chapel decorated in the sixteenth century with frescoes, panel paintings and gilded leather. In adjacent rooms you can see the scales used to assess the loans, and pictures by Luca Giordano and Sebastiano Ricci, with another labelled "attrib. Giorgione", one of countless highly dubious attributions scattered throughout Europe. Unfortunately access at the moment is solely through prior arrangement – if you're really keen to get in, the tourist office (in the same piazzetta) might be able to book a visit for you.

Another one of Treviso's ancient landmarks, the patricians' meeting place known as the **Loggia dei Cavalieri**, is close to the Palazzo dei Trecento, down Via Martiri della Libertà. Built in the early thirteenth century and pieced back together after the 1944 air raid, it was decorated first with a brick pattern and grotesque figures, and then with romanticized scenes from the Trojan wars, scraps of which you might be able to make out if you've got hawk-like vision. It's remarkable more for the fact of its survival than for its appearance, but it warrants a look if you're strolling down that way towards the Santa Caterina side of town (see p.369) – that's if the restoration of the building has finally been completed.

The Duomo

The Duomo of Treviso, **San Pietro**, stands at the end of Calmaggiore, rising above the squall of mopeds on the Piazza del Duomo. Founded

The Duomo is
open Mon–Sat
7.30am–noon
& 3.30–7pm,
Sun 7.30am–
1pm & 3.30–
8pm; the dioce-
san museum is
open Mon–
Thurs 9am–
noon, Sat
9am–noon &
3–6pm; free.

in the twelfth century, as were the **campanile** and perpetually closed **baptistery** alongside, San Pietro was much altered between the fifteenth and nineteenth centuries (when the huge portico was added), and then rebuilt to rectify the damage of 1944. The oldest clearly distinguishable feature of the exterior is the pair of eroded Romanesque lions at the base of the portico; fragments of Romanesque wall are embedded in the side walls too.

The interior is chiefly notable for the **crypt** – a thicket of twelfth-century columns with scraps of fourteenth- and fifteenth-century mosaics (if it's locked, ask the sacristan) – and the **Malchiostro Chapel**, with frescoes by **Pordenone** and a much restored *Annunciation* by Titian. Although Pordenone and Titian were the bitterest of rivals, their pictures were commissioned as part of a unified scheme, representing the conception and birth of Christ; the 1944 bombs annihilated the crowning piece of the ensemble – a fresco by Pordenone on the chapel dome, representing *God the Father*. Paintings by **Paris Bordone**, the most famous Treviso-born artist, hang in the vestibule of the chapel and in the sacristy. Other things to search out are the *Monument to Bishop Zanetti* by **Pietro Lombardo**, on the left wall of the chancel, the *Tomb of Bishop Nicolò Franco* by **Lorenzo and Giambattista Bregno**, in the chapel to the left of the chancel, and **Lorenzo Bregno's** figure of *St Sebastian*, on the first pillar of the left aisle. The **diocesan museum** – a typical jumble of functional paintings, ecclesiastical garb and silverware – is round the back of the duomo, in the angle of Via Canoniche del Duomo – you get to it by turning first left down the hill from the duomo.

San Nicolò

San Nicolò is
open Mon–Fri
8am–noon &
3.30–7pm. The
Seminario is
open: summer
Mon–Fri
8am–6pm;
winter
Mon–Fri
8am–12.30pm
& 3–5.30pm;
free.

The severe Dominican church of **San Nicolò**, dominating the corner of the old town just over the River Sile from the train station, upstages the duomo in every department. Wrapped round several of its massive pillars are delicate frescoes by **Tomaso da Modena** and his school, of which the freshest are the *SS. Jerome, Romuald, Agnes and John* by Tomaso himself, on the first column on your right as you enter. The towering *St Christopher* on the wall of the right aisle, with feet the size of sleeping bags, was painted around 1410, probably by **Antonio da Treviso**. Equally striking, but considerably more graceful, is the composite *Tomb of Agostino d'Onigo* on the left wall of the chancel, created in 1500 by **Antonio Rizzo** (who did the sculpture) and **Lorenzo Lotto** (who painted the attendant pages). The *Madonna and Saints* in the chancel is a collaboration between the little-known Marco Pensaben and Savoldo, painted twenty years after the Onigo tomb, and a third joint work, an *Incredulity of St Thomas*, stands on the altar of the Monigo chapel, on the right of the chancel – **Sebastiano del Piombo** is attributed with the upper section and **Lotto** with the lower gallery of portraits;

the frescoes on the side walls are by fourteenth-century Sienese and Riminese artists.

The figures of Agnes and Jerome are an excellent introduction to Tomaso da Modena, but for a comprehensive demonstration of his talent you should visit the neighbouring **Seminario**, where the **chapter house** is decorated with a series of portraits of members of the Dominican order, executed by the artist in 1352.

Although these are not portraits in the modern sense of the term, in that they don't attempt to reproduce the appearance of the men whose names they bear, the paintings are astonishingly advanced in their observation of idiosyncratic reality. Each shows a friar at study in his cell, but there is never a hint of the formulaic: one man is shown sharpening a quill, another checks a text through a magnifier, a third blows the surplus ink from his nib, a fourth scowls as if you've interrupted his work, and so on.

The east side of the city

On the other side of town from San Nicolò there's another brilliant fresco cycle by Tomaso da Modena – *The Story of the Life of Saint Ursula*. Painted for the now extinct church of Santa Margherita sul Sile, the frescoes were detached from the walls in the late nineteenth century and transported to the Museo Civico. From there they were dispatched in 1979 to Santa Caterina, a deconsecrated church maintained for the display of the frescoes by Tomaso and his school in its Cappella degli Innocenti. Unfortunately Santa Caterina has been only sporadically open since then, and in 1996 a full-blown restoration commenced that could still go on for years – the tourist office or the Museo Civico can give you the latest situation.

Two other churches in the Santa Caterina quarter are worth a call. To the north of Santa Caterina is the thirteenth-century church of **San Francesco**, which was reopened and restored early this century after years as a military depot. It's an immense hall of a church with a high ship's-keel ceiling and patches of fresco, including the top half of another vast *St Christopher* and a *Madonna and Saints* by **Tomaso da Modena** in the chapel to the left of the chancel. Close to the door on the right side of the church is the tomb of **Francesca, daughter of Petrarch**, who died in 1384, twenty years after **Dante's son**, Pietro, whose tomb is in the left transept.

San Francesco and Santa Maria Maggiore are both open daily 9am–noon & 3.30–6.30pm.

To the south, at the end of one of the most attractive streets in Treviso – Via Carlo Alberto – stands the largely fifteenth-century **Basilica di Santa Maria Maggiore**, which houses the most venerated image in Treviso, a fresco of the Madonna, originally painted by Tomaso da Modena but subsequently retouched.

This is the workshop and market area, a district in which Treviso has the feel of a rather smaller town. The antique sellers and furniture restorers of Treviso outnumber even the Benetton outlets, and it's over this side that you'll see most evidence of them; on a Saturday

Treviso

or Tuesday morning the northern part of this quarter, along Viale Bartolomeo Burchiellati and Borgo Mazzini, is overrun by a gigantic market.

Also in this area is the main market for fresh produce, the **Pescheria**, which occupies an island in the middle of Treviso's broadest canal. (As in Venice, health regulations dictated the siting of the fish market by a waterway.) Very close to the Pescheria, on Via Palestra, almost on the junction with Via Pescheria, stands the **Casa dei Carraresi**, a recently and beautifully restored palazzo that's Treviso's principal art exhibition venue.

The Museo Civico and city walls

The Museo Civico is open Tues–Fri 9am–12.30pm & 2.30–5pm, Sat & Sun 9am–noon & 3–7pm; L3000/€1.55.

From the duomo area the recommended route to the **Museo Civico** (or Musei Luigi Bailo) is along Via Riccati, which has a number of fine old houses. The ground floor of the museum is taken up by the archeological collection, predominantly late Bronze Age and Roman relics; the picture collection, on the upper floor, is typical of provincial collections all over Italy – acres of hackwork interrupted by a few paintings for which any gallery director would give a year's salary. In the first category there's a sequence of martyrdoms by Pietro Muttoni, a seventeenth-century Venetian whose obscurity is no mystery. In the second category are three paintings hanging cheek by jowl in room 9 – a *Crucifixion* by **Jacopo Bassano**, the *Portrait of Sperone Speroni* by **Titian**, and **Lorenzo Lotto**'s psychologically acute *Portrait of a Dominican*. Comparing the Titian and Lotto portraits, you can see some justice in Bernard Berenson's contrast between the two – "we might imagine Titian asking of every person he was going to paint: Who are you? What is your position in society? while Lotto would put the question: What sort of person are you? How do you take life?" Elsewhere in the galleries you'll find a roomful of Paris Bordone, a couple of pictures by Giandomenico Tiepolo, and a trio of pastel portraits by Rosalba Carriera, including one of her more illustrious contemporary, Antoine Watteau.

A couple of minutes away, in Via Antonio Canova, stands the fourteenth- to sixteenth-century Ca' da Noal, a building that used to house the **Museo della Casa Trevigiana**, Treviso's museum of the applied arts – furniture, dolls, architectural decorations, armour, musical instruments and, most impressive of all, wrought-iron work, a local speciality. It was a fine collection but it rarely attracted enough visitors to support permanent staffing; it's currently closed, undergoing a restoration that will be continuing for a long time to come.

The longest unbroken stretch of the **city walls** is in the vicinity of the Museo Civico, between the Porta dei Santi Quaranta and Porta San Tomaso. The fortification of Treviso was undertaken in 1509, at the start of the War of the League of Cambrai, and the work was finished around 1517, with the construction of these two monumental gates. If you fancy a walk away from the traffic, albeit only ten metres away, the path along the walls is your spot.

Practicalities

The **tourist office** is right in the centre, at Piazza Monte di Pietà 8 (Mon 9am–12.30pm, Tues–Fri 9am–12.30pm & 2.30–6pm, Sat & Sun 9am–12.30pm & 3.30–6pm,; ☎0422.547.632); it dispenses useful leaflets not just on Treviso but on attractions throughout Treviso province. The **post office** is in the Piazzale della Vittoria, over to your left shortly after crossing the river from the train station; for **banks** keep going straight along Corso del Popolo towards Calmaggiore – you'll pass most of them along this stretch.

Though the tourist office valiantly promotes Treviso as one of Italy's undervalued cities, the town isn't really geared up for tourists, its main problem being that the vast majority of Treviso's hotels are characterless or somewhat down-at-heel Eurobusiness places. The only reasonably priced and pleasant central hotel is the two-star *Campeol*, close to the tourist office at Piazza Ancilotto 4 (☎0422.56601, fax 0422.540871; ④); the reception is staffed only occasionally – if there's no-one at the desk, go to the *Beccherie* restaurant, opposite, which is run by the same management. Second choice would be the four-star *Continental*, a short walk from the train station at Via Roma 16 (☎0422.411.216, *www.sevenonline.it/continental/*; ⑤); it's not the most charismatic hotel in the Veneto, but it's conveniently located, well-maintained and, with eighty rooms, is almost certain to have space.

Treviso's **restaurants** have a far higher reputation than its hotels, the leader of the pack being *El Toulà da Alfredo*, at Via Collalto 26 (☎0422.540.275; closed Sun evening & Mon), where you shouldn't expect to see change from L100,000 per person. If that's too steep, you can enjoy excellent food at the homely *Toni del Spin*, a few steps from the church of San Vito at Via Inferiore 7 (☎0422.543.829; closed all Sun & Mon lunchtime), or the *Beccherie*, Piazza Ancilotto 10 (☎0422.540.871; closed Sun evening & Mon), both of which provide superb Trevisan cuisine at around L50,000 per head. Basic trattoria fare is available at *All'Oca Bianca*, Vicolo della Torre 7 (closed all Wed & Thurs lunchtime).

The most popular **bars and cafés** in Treviso are those clustered underneath the Palazzo dei Trecento and spread along Calmaggiore and Via XX Settembre. One of these, *Nascimben*, Via XX Settembre 3, serves perhaps the best **ice cream** in town – its main rival is the *Gelateria al Duomo*, opposite the duomo at Piazza del Duomo 25.

Castelfranco Veneto

In the twelfth century **CASTELFRANCO VENETO** stood on the western edge of Treviso's territory, and from the outside the old

Castelfranco Veneto

town – or **Castello** – looks much as it must have done when the Trevisans had finished fortifying the place against the Paduans. The battlemented and moated brick walls, raised in 1199, run almost right round the centre, and five of their towers still stand, the largest being the **Torrione**, the clock tower over the north gate. Of all the walled towns of the Veneto, only Cittadella and Montagnana bear comparison with Castelfranco, and the place would merit a call just for its brickwork, even though the Castello is so small that you can walk in through one gate and out through the opposite one in three minutes flat. And the place has one other attraction: it was the birthplace of Giorgio da Castelfranco – **Giorgione** – and possesses a painting which on its own is enough to vindicate Vasari's judgement that Giorgione's place in Venetian art is equivalent to Leonardo da Vinci's in that of Florence.

Castelfranco is well connected by **rail** with all parts of the Veneto, but it's most easily approached from Treviso (25min) or Vicenza (40min) – trains run along this line on average once an hour. Connections to Venice (50min) are more sporadic – during working hours it averages out at around one every two hours. In addition, there are hourly links to Padua and Bassano, and a train from Belluno every ninety minutes.

The Castelfranco Madonna

Known simply as the **Castelfranco Madonna**, Giorgione's *Madonna and Child with St Francis and St Liberale* hangs in the eighteenth-century **Duomo**, in a chapel to the right of the chancel; the bars of the iron grille across its entrance are far enough apart for you to be able to see the picture clearly, and there's a light-switch to the side (leave donation in nearby box).

The Duomo is open daily 9am–noon & 3–6pm.

Giorgione is the most elusive of all the great figures of the Renaissance: including the *Castelfranco Madonna*, only six surviving paintings can indisputably be attributed to him, and so little is known for certain about his life that legends have proliferated to fill the gaps – for instance, the story that his premature death in 1510, aged not more than 34, was caused by his catching bubonic plague from a mistress. The paintings themselves have compounded the enigma and none is more mysterious than this one, in which a boldly geometrical composition is combined with an extraordinary fidelity to physical texture and the effects of light, while the demeanour of the figures suggests, in the forgiveably lush words of one writer – "withdrawal . . . as if their spirit were preoccupied with a remembered dream". At first sight the scene appears naturalistic, but look more closely and you'll see that strange laws are in operation here. For one thing, the perspective isn't consistent – the Madonna's throne has one vanishing point, the chequered foreground another. And while the sun is rising or setting on the distant horizon, the shadow cast by the armoured saint suggest a quite different source of light, and the shadows of St Francis and the throne imply a third. To compound the mystery, even the identity of the armoured figure is far from clear: most favour Liberale, the local patron saint and co-dedicatee of the duomo, but he might be St George or even St Theodore, the first patron saint of Venice.

But some facts are known about the picture's origin. It was commissioned by Tuzio Costanzo, probably in 1505, to honour his son, Matteo, who had been killed in battle the previous year. The church for which the piece was painted was demolished long ago, but the present arrangement of this chapel (dating from 1935) recreates that devised by Giorgione's patron, in that the painting is placed so that the three figures look down at Matteo's tomb.

After perusing the Giorgione, you might spend a minute admiring the huge adjacent altarpiece, which was sculpted by Torretto, the master of Canova; Torretto's young apprentice is said to have carved the little castle at the feet of St Liberale. The only other paintings in the duomo likely to hold your attention are in the **sacristy**: fragments of the first fresco cycle painted by Paolo Veronese, they were removed from the Villa Soranza by Napoleon's troops, who demolished the entire building and carted the pictures off to Paris, whence they were later repatriated. The interior of the duomo itself was designed by the local architect **Francesco Maria Preti**, whose ashes are interred in the nave, underneath the dome (Preti's major contribution to the landscape of the Veneto is the Villa Pisani at Stra – see p.303); the facade is a late nineteenth-century hack job.

The rest of the town
Next to the duomo is the enticingly named **Casa Giorgione** – but it contains nothing of note except a chiaroscuro frieze in one of the first-floor rooms which has been hopefully attributed to Giorgione. The only other interior in Castelfranco that you might want to peep at is the **Teatro Accademico** (erratically open) in Via Garibaldi, opposite the duomo. Designed in the mid-eighteenth century by Preti, it has an auditorium that's considerably less modest than you might think from the sober outside. Of wider appeal, perhaps, is the **Parco Corner-Revedin-Bolasco**, a lovely wooded park that was laid out in the second half of the eighteenth century and has recently been meticulously groomed; the park lies behind the Villa Revedin-Bolasco (not open to the public), which is at Borgo Treviso 73, right opposite the top of the road that leads from the train station to the walled town.

Practicalities
Castelfranco's tiny **tourist office** is at no. 39 on the walled town's main street, Via F. M. Preti (Mon–Fri 8.30am–12.30pm & 3–7pm, Sat 8.30am–12.30pm & 3.30–6.30pm, Sun 9am–12.30pm & 3–6pm); it's not exactly the most clued-up information office in the Veneto. For an inexpensive **hotel** room in central Castelfranco go to the two-star *Alla*

The Casa Giorgione is open Tues–Sun 9am–noon & 3–6pm; often closed weekday mornings in winter; L2500/€1.29. The Bolasco park is open March 21–May 31 & Sept 21–Nov 2 Tues, Thurs & Sun 10am–12.30pm & 2.30–5.30pm; July 1–Sept 20 same days 10am–12.30pm & 4–7.30pm

Speranza, a few yards beyond the walls at Borgo Vicenza 13 (☎0423.494.480; ②) – Borgo Vicenza is the continuation of Via F. M. Preti, on the opposite side of the Castello from the train station. Should you want more comfort than this, go for either the modern three-star *Roma*, immediately outside the walls at Via F. Filzi 39 (☎0423.721.616, *www.sevenonline.it/albergoroma*; ③), or the four-star *Alla Torre* (☎0423.498.707, *www.sevenonline.it/hotelallatorre*; ④), which occupies a nicely restored palazzo on Piazza Trento e Trieste. There's a decent restaurant-pizzeria at the foot of the Torrione, *Alla Torre* (closed Tues), but the best restaurant in the historic centre is *Alle Mura*, Via Preti 69 (☎0423.498.098; closed Thurs), where you'll pay about L80,000 per person, with set menus beginning at around L90,000.

Around Castelfranco

The major attraction within a short radius of Castelfranco is the wonderfully preserved town of **Cittadella**, which can easily be reached by train, as it's a station on the Treviso–Vicenza line. Buses and the Venice–Castelfranco *locale* trains stop at the village of **Piombino Dese**, where you can see one of Palladio's most influential villas, while a more limited repertoire of public transport serves the hamlet of **Fanzolo**, site of Palladio's Villa Emo – in fact, buses and trains to Fanzolo are so sporadic that a visit isn't really feasible unless you have a car.

Buses from Castelfranco depart from Via Podgora, on the north side of Borgo Vicenza, and from Corso XXIX Aprile, which you cross to go into the Castello when coming from the station.

Cittadella

When Treviso turned Castelfranco into a garrison, the Paduans promptly retaliated by reinforcing the defences of **CITTADELLA**, 15km to the west. The **fortified walls** of Cittadella were built in the first quarter of the thirteenth century, and are even more impressive than those of its neighbour, forming an almost unbroken oval round the town.

You enter the town through one of four rugged brick gateways, built on the cardinal points of the compass; if you're coming from the train station it'll be the **Porta Padova**, the most daunting of the four, flanked as it is by the Torre di Malta. The tower was built as a prison and torture chamber by **Ezzelino da Romano III**, known to those he terrorized in this region in the mid-thirteenth century as the "Son of Satan". Basing his claim to power not on any dynastic or legalistic argument, but solely on the exercise of unrestrained military might, Ezzelino was the prototype of the despotic rulers of Renaissance Italy, and his atrocities earned him a place in the seventh circle of Dante's *Inferno*, where he's condemned to boil eternally in a river of blood. There's not much else to Cittadella, but it's definitely worth hopping off the train for a quick circuit of the walls.

The Villa Emo

Just 8km northeast of Castelfranco, in **FANZOLO**, stands one of the best-maintained and most sumptuous of Palladio's houses, the **Villa Emo**. In 1556 the Venetian government set up a department called the Board of Uncultivated Properties, to promote agricultural development on the terra firma and distribute subsidies to landowners. One of the first to take advantage of this initiative was Leonardo Emo, who commissioned the villa from Palladio around 1564, when he switched his financial interests to farming.

With its central accommodation and administration block and its arcaded wings for storage, stables, dovecots and so on, the building belongs to the same type as the earlier Villa Barbaro at Masèr (see p.385), and as at Masèr the main living rooms are richly frescoed. Nobody would claim that **Giambattista Zelotti**'s scenes and rubber-necked grotesques are in quite the same league as Veronese's work in the Barbaro house, but neither would anyone complain at having to look at them every morning over breakfast.

Bassano del Grappa

The Villa Emo is open Mon–Sat 3–7pm, Sun 10.30am–12.30pm & 3–7pm; L10,000/€5.

The Villa Cornaro

Palladio's villas fall into two broad types: the first was designed as the focus of a large, cohesive farm, and takes the form of a low central block with attached lateral buildings; the second was designed to be the living quarters of an estate that was scattered or where the farming land was unsuitable for building, and takes the form of a tall single building with a freestanding pedimented porch. The Villa Barbaro belongs to the first category, while to the second category belong the Villa Pisani at Montagnana, the Villa Fóscari at Malcontenta and the **Villa Cornaro**, built in the 1550s at **PIOMBINO DESE**, 9km southeast of Castelfranco. The majestic double-decker portico is the most striking element of the exterior, and when Palladian style was imported into colonial America, this became one of his most frequently copied devices. Unfortunately, the villa's decoration – frescoes by the obscure eighteenth-century artist Mattia Bortoloni – isn't anything to get excited about.

The Villa Cornaro is open May–Sept Sat 3.30–6pm; L6000/€3.10.

Bassano del Grappa

Situated on the River Brenta where it widens on its emergence from the hills, **BASSANO DEL GRAPPA** has expanded rapidly this century, though its historic centre remains largely unspoiled by twentieth-century mistakes. It's better known for its manufacturing and produce, and for the events of the two world wars (see below), than for any outstanding architecture or monuments, but its situation in the lee of the imposing Monte Grappa (1775m), with the Dolomites beyond, is impressive enough. For centuries a major producer of ceramics and wrought iron, Bassano is also renowned for its **grappa** distilleries and delicacies such as *porcini* (dried mushrooms), white asparagus and honey.

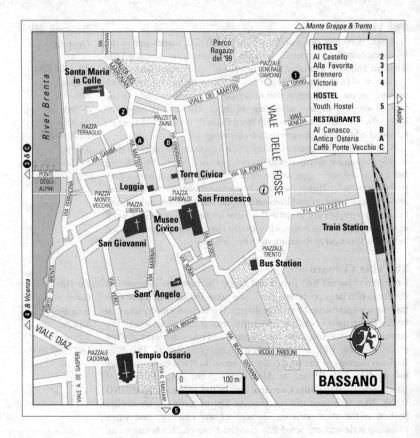

Trains run from Venice to Bassano fourteen times daily; the journey takes an hour. Buses, all of which run from Piazzale Trento, connect with Masèr (9 daily), Possagno (9 daily), Maróstica (roughly every 30min), Ásolo (9 daily) and Vicenza (at least hourly).

The Town

Almost all of Bassano's sights lie between the Brenta and the train station; go much further in either direction and you'll quickly come to recently developed suburbs. Walking away from the station, the orbital Viale delle Fosse stands between you and the town centre, following the line of the fourteenth-century outer walls. Cross the road, turn right then left to get to Via Da Ponte, which forms a main axis through the centre; the statue is of **Jacopo Da Ponte**, leader of the dynasty of Renaissance painters more commonly known simply as the Bassano family.

On the left of **Piazza Garibaldi**, one of the centre's two main squares, the fourteenth-century church of **San Francesco** carries a gold medal plaque in honour of the resistance fighters of World War II; a few fresco fragments remain inside, including an *Annunciation* of 1400 in the porch. The cloister now houses the **Museo Civico**, where the downstairs rooms are devoted to Roman and other archeological finds. Upstairs is a collection of sixteenth- to eighteenth-century work, including paintings by the **Bassano** family. Jacopo, the most highly regarded, plunges through a number of distinctive styles culminating in a late chiaroscuro manner, as in the *Adoration of the Shepherds*. Elsewhere in the museum are some huge frescoes detached from a palace in Piazzetta Montevecchio and a number of plaster works by **Canova** (see p.381), two thousand of whose drawings are owned by the museum. There's also a room devoted to the great baritone **Tito Gobbi**, who was born in Bassano.

Overlooking the other side of the piazza is the **Torre Civica**, once a lookout tower for the twelfth-century inner walls, now a clock tower with spurious nineteenth-century battlements and windows. Further in the same direction is **Piazza Libertà**, with its seventeenth-century sculpture of San Bassiano, the patron saint of Bassano, and the all-too-familiar winged lion of Venice. Dominating the left-hand side of the piazza, the church of **San Giovanni** was founded in 1308 but is now overbearingly Baroque in this relatively delicate city centre; the style continues within. Under the arches of the fifteenth-century **Loggia** on the other side are the frescoed coats of arms of the various Venetian governors of Bassano.

From the piazza's far right-hand corner, Piazzetta Montevecchio (the original core of the town), its frescoes now faded or removed, leads to a little jumble of streets and stairways running down to the river and the **Ponte degli Alpini** (which takes its name from the Alpine soldiers who last rebuilt the bridge in 1948). The river was first bridged at this point in the late twelfth century, and replacements or repairs have been needed at regular intervals ever since, mostly because of flooding. The present structure was designed by **Palladio** in 1568, and built in wood to make the bridge as flexible as possible – torrential meltwater would have demolished an unyielding stone version. Mined by the resistance during the last war, and badly damaged by the retreating German army, it was restored in accordance with Palladio's design, as has been the case with every repair since the day of its completion.

Nardini, a grappa distillery founded in 1779, stands at this end of the bridge. These days the distilling process takes place elsewhere, but the original shop and bar are still functioning here; you can also sample and buy the stuff in the so-called **Museo della Grappa** in nearby Via Gamba (it's open shop hours). Cross over the bridge to reach the **Taverna al Ponte**, home of the **Museo degli Alpini**, which also gives a good view of the underside of the bridge. The Alpine soldiers, who crossed the bridge many times during World War I on their way to Monte Grappa and Asiago, saw the bridge as a symbol of

Bassano del Grappa

The Museo Civico is open April–Oct Tues–Sat 9am–12.30pm & 3.30–6.30pm, Sun 3.30–6.30pm – June–Sept also Sun 10am–12.30pm; Nov Fri 9am–12.30pm, Sat & Sun 3.30–6.30pm; L8000/€4.12 (ticket also valid for the Palazzo Sturm).

The Museo degli Alpini is open Tues–Sun 8.30am–8pm; free.

*The Palazzo
Sturm is open
same hours as
Museo Civico;
entrance with
same ticket.*

their tenacity, and so adopted it as their emblem. They still have strong associations with Bassano, and take part in parades here, looking as though they've just stepped out of some nineteenth-century adventure yarn.

Back on the town side of the bridge again, if you follow Via Ferracina downstream for a couple of minutes you'll come to the eighteenth-century **Palazzo Sturm**, a showcase for the town's famed majolica ware. On the other side of the base of the Ponti degli Alpini, Via Gamba takes you up to the remnants of the **castle**; the huge, blank and none too safe-looking tower was built in the twelfth century by the Ezzelini. The campanile of **Santa Maria in Colle** is a conversion of another tower, while the church itself dates from around 1000; it contains two paintings by **Leandro Bassano**.

Go out of the castle enclosure, and spreading round to the right is the **Viale dei Martieri**, named after the resistance fighters who were rounded up in the hills and hanged from trees along here in September 1944. A telescope enables you to get the most out of the views of the Dolomites. To one end is the **Piazzale Generale Giardino**, with its Fascist-style memorial to the General, who died in 1935; a World War I monument in similar vein stands below in the **Parco Ragazzi del'99**, named after the "Lads of '99", born in just the right year to die by the thousand in the last phase of World War I.

If you cut across the town, through Piazza Libertà and south down Via Marinelli or Via Roma, then outside the city walls and right, you can't miss the vast **Tempio Ossario**. Begun in 1908 as a church, its function was changed in 1934, when it became a repository of over 5400 tombs, each containing the ashes of a soldier. The major **war memorial**, however, is out of town on **Monte Grappa**. A vast, circular, tiered edifice with a "Via Eroica" leading to a war museum, it holds 12,000 Italian and Austro-Hungarian dead; less a symbol of mourning and repentance than a declaration of future collaboration, it was built by the Fascists in 1935. Buses go up there from Bassano during the summer months.

Practicalities

The **tourist office** is opposite the train station at Largo Corona d'Italia 35 (Mon–Fri 9am–12.30pm & 2–5pm, Sat 9am–12.30pm; ☎0424.524.351); their free magazine called *Bassano News* gives up-to-date information about the city's facilities and events.

There's only one **hotel** actually in the old centre, *Al Castello*, Piazza Terraglio 19 (☎0424.228665; ③), right by the castle. The other hotels, also three-stars, are a short distance out, though the *Brennero*, at Via Torino 7, just east of the walls (☎0424.228.538; ③), and the *Victoria*, at Viale Diaz 33, on the west bank of the Brenta (☎0424.503.620, *victoriahotel@pn.itnet.it*; ②), are within easily walkable distance of the centre and are just as good. For a more budget stay there's a **hostel**, *Istituto Cremona*, Via Chini 6

(☎0424.522.032; L28,000/€14.46), or the two-star *Alla Favorita*, Via S. Giorgio 11 (☎0424.502.030; ②), which is a good fifteen minutes' walk from the centre.

Two highly popular *trattorie* come highly recommended for their **food**: the old-fashioned and classy *Trattoria del Borgo*, Via Margnan 7 (☎0424.522.155; closed Wed), which has a garden; and the more functional *Al Caneseo*, Via Vendramini 20 (☎0424.228.524; closed Mon). For pizza – and, surprisingly, authentic Cuban food – cross the old bridge to *Caffè Ponte Vecchio*, Via Angarano 14 (closed Mon). The *Antica Osteria*, Via Matteotti 7 (closed Wed), has good bar snacks, while the *Osteria Terraglio*, on Piazza Terraglio (closed Mon), has excellent wine (and jazz on Tuesdays), but for **drinking** it's perhaps best to head down to the old bridge, where you'll find the very popular *Birreria da Ponte*, Via Matteotti 50 (closed Mon) and the stylish *Nardini*, Ponte Vecchio 2 (closed Mon), which was once a distillery and is now a period-piece bar and **grappa** shop. Of all Bassano's *alimentari*, the one with the fullest range of local delicacies is on the corner of Salita B. Ferracina and Via B. Ferracina.

Maróstica

Seven kilometres to the west of Bassano, the walled town of **MARÓSTICA** was yet another stronghold of Ezzelino da Romano, whose fortress glowers down on the old centre from the crest of the hill of Pausolino. The fortress, the lower castle and the almost intact ramparts that connect them make a dramatic scene, but Maróstica's main claim to fame is the **Partita a Scacchi** – a chess game played every other September with human "pieces".

A **bus** service runs between Maróstica and Bassano (every 30min; 20min); the stop is outside the lower castle.

The Town

Maróstica was run by the Ezzelini for quite a time, the monstrous Ezzelino III being preceded by Ezzelino the Stutterer and Ezzelino the Monk. However, it was a slightly less hideous dynasty of despots, the Scaligeri of Verona, who constructed the **town walls** and the **Castello Inferiore** (lower castle): the castle was built by Cangrande della Scala, and the walls by his successor, Cansignorio, in the 1370s. An exhibition of costumes for the *Partita a Scacchi* is now housed in the castle.

Beyond the castle is **Piazza Castello**, the central square of the town, onto which is painted the board for the **Partita a Scacchi** (*www.marosticascacchi.it*). The game's origin was an everyday chivalric story of rival suitors, the only unusual aspect being that the matter was decided with chess pieces rather than swords. In 1454

Guided tours of the Castello Inferiore's costume exhibition are given Mon–Sat 10am, 10.45am, 11.30am, 3.30pm, 4.15pm, 5pm & 5.45pm, Sun 10am, 10.45am, 11.30am, 3.30pm & 6pm; L2000/€1.03

two men, Vieri da Vallonara and Rinaldo d'Angarano, both petitioned the *podestà* of Maróstica, Taddeo Parisio, for the hand of his daughter. Parisio decreed that the matter should be decided by a chess match, with the winner marrying Lionora and the loser being consoled with the prize of Parisio's younger sister – who seems to have had as little say in the proceedings as Parisio's daughter. The game was played with live pieces here in the square, and is re-enacted biennially with great pomp – five hundred people in the costume of the time, with music, dancing and fireworks.

The **Doglione**, behind the inevitable lion of Saint Mark (Venice ruled Maróstica from 1404 to 1797), is a much-altered fifteenth-century building; once the castle armoury, it's now owned by a bank. To the left of it, Via San Antonio runs past the church of the same name to the forgettable church of the **Carmine**, looking like a Baroque palace with the windows missing. A path round to the left of the Carmine winds up through an olive grove to the **Castello Superiore** (upper castle), which was built by Ezzelino and later expanded by the Scaligeri. Only the walls remain but within them a restaurant has been built, which has a marvellous view. It's only when you're at the top that you realize there's a road up, much less steep than the stony path but longer; if you take this route back down, look out for the cyclists who train on the hill – they whizz through the hair-pins with scarcely a sound to warn of their approach. Near the bottom a little junk shop sells war memorabilia scavenged from the mountains around.

The oldest church in Maróstica, **Santa Maria**, is outside the city walls on the other side – go through the eastern gate, turn left, then second right. Unfortunately it was rebuilt in the eighteenth century, but it has some quirky attractions: modern votive paintings on the ceiling, for instance, and an altarpiece that's a copy of the top half of Titian's *Assumption* in Venice's Frari.

Practicalities

The *pro loco* **tourist office** is in the lower castle at Piazza Castello 1 (daily 10am–noon & 3.30–6pm; ☎0424.72.127). Maróstica has one superb **hotel** in the walled centre, the *Due Mori*, which occupies a stylishly modernised seventeenth-century building just above the piazza at Corso Mazzini 73 (☎0424.471.777, *www.duemori.it*; ④). The tourist office can give details of alternatives in the modern town, but it's better to stay in Bassano if the *Due Mori* is full.

For **food**, *L'Angelo e il Diavolo*, Piazza Castello 41a (closed Mon), is a reasonable pizzeria and enoteca, while the expensive *Ristorante al Castello Superiore*, in the upper castle (closed Wed and Thurs lunch), is surprisingly good. The best places, however, are outside the old town: *All'Angelo d'Oro*, at Via Monte Grappa 20, beyond the Porta Bassano (open daily), is a popular trattoria with home cooking, while the *Dama Bianca*, 1km down the road heading towards Bassano at Via Montello 16/c (☎0424.470.239; closed Sun all day and Sat lunch), is excellent, but more expensive and often fully booked at weekends. The *Osteria Madonetta*, just off the main piazza at Via Vajenta 21, is perhaps the most genuine **osteria** in the Veneto – virtually unchanged since it opened in 1904, it looks like a handsome rustic living room. It has been run by the same family for generations, and sells its wine not from a bar but from an ordinary table set with bottles.

Regular **events** include first and foremost the **Partita a Scacchi**, played in the second weekend of September on even-numbered years. An exhibition of **cartoonists** specializing in political and social comment takes place every May and June, followed in July and August by a **crafts fair**. An **antiques market** is held the first Sunday of every month.

Possagno

As you approach **POSSAGNO**, a small town lodged at the base of Monte Grappa, one of the strangest sights in the Veneto hits you: a huge temple that rises above the houses like a displaced chunk of ancient Rome. It was built by **Antonio Canova**, one of the dominant figures of Neoclassicism and the last Italian sculptor to be generally regarded as the most accomplished living practitioner of his art. He was born here in 1757, and his family home now houses a magnificent museum of his work. Just as you can't come to grips with Tintoretto until you've been to Venice, so an excursion to Possagno is essential to an understanding of Canova. You can reach Possagno easily by **bus** from Bassano (9 daily; 1hr) or Ásolo (7 daily; 40min); an infrequent service runs from Castelfranco Veneto.

Shortly after Canova's death in 1822, all the working models that had accumulated in his studio in Rome were transported to Possagno, and here, from 1831 to 1836, an annexe (the Gipsoteca) was built onto the Canova house for the display of the bulk of the collection. A second addition was built in 1957, and the Gipsoteca is now one of only two complete displays of an artist's working models in Europe – the other being Copenhagen's collection of pieces by Thorvaldsen.

The Gipsoteca and Casa Canova

The process by which Canova worked towards the final form of his sculptures was a painstaking one, involving the creation of a series of rough clay models (*bozzetti*) in which the general shape would be refined, then a full-scale figure in gypsum plaster (*gesso*), and finally the replication of the plaster figure in marble, using small nails to map the proportions and contours from the plaster model to the marble statue. Preparatory works from all stages of Canova's career are shown in the **Gipsoteca** in Piazza Canova, and even if you're repelled

The Gipsoteca is open Tues–Sun: May–Sept 9am–noon & 3–6pm; Oct–April 9am–noon & 2–5pm; L5000/€2.58.

by the polish of the finished pieces, you'll be won over by the energy and spontaneity of the first versions – such as the tiny terracotta model for the tomb of Pope Clement XIV, or the miniature group of Adam and Eve weeping over the body of Abel.

Canova's range will probably be as much of a surprise as his technique. Among the works collected in the serene main hall, for example, you'll find portraits, images of classical heroes, the funerary monument for Maria Christina of Austria (adapted by Canova's pupils for his own tomb in Venice's Frari), and a large *Deposition*, a bronze version of which is to be found in the Tempio (see below). Notions of Canova as a bloodless pedant are dispelled by two overpowering tableaux of violence, each over ten feet high – *Hercules and Lichas* and *Theseus and the Centaur* – while the adjoining room, tastefully added in 1957 by Carlo Scarpa, displays a more intimate and even erotic side, including a *Sleeping Nymph* and the famous *Graces*. More models are kept in the house, but the pleasure of this section of the museum is weakened by Canova's paintings – a parade of winsome Venuses and frolicking nymphs, which will not dispose you to disagree with the artist's own low opinion of his pictorial talents.

The Tempio

The Tempio is open Tues–Sat: April–Oct 9am–noon & 3–6pm; Nov–March 9am–noon & 2–5pm.

Donated to the town to serve as its new parish church, the **Tempio** was designed by Canova with assistance from **Giannantonio Selva** (architect of La Fenice in Venice) and constructed from 1819 to 1832. Both Roman and Greek classical sources were plundered for its composition – the body of the building is derived from the Pantheon, but its portico comes from the Parthenon. The cool precision of the interior is disrupted by a sequence of dreadful paintings of the Apostles, and an appalling altarpiece for which Canova himself was the culprit. To the right is the bronze version of the *Deposition* in the Gipsoteca (cast posthumously in 1829), and opposite is the **tomb of Canova** and his half-brother Monsignor G.B. Sartori, with a self-portrait bust to the right. Designed by Canova for a different occupant, this tomb is not the Veneto's only memorial to the sculptor – the other one, infinitely more interesting, is in the Frari in Venice. In good weather the sacristan opens the stairs to the top of the dome (L2000/€2.03) – the view of the Asolean hills and the plain of the Piave is marvellous.

Ásolo

Known as "la città dei cento orizzonti" (the city with a hundred horizons), the medieval walled town of **ÁSOLO** presides over a tightly grouped range of twenty-seven gentle peaks in the foothills of the Dolomites. Fruit trees and pastures cover the lower slopes of the Asolean hills, and a feature of life in the town itself are the festivals that take place at the various harvest times.

Paleolithic settlements have been found in the region, but the earliest documented settlement here was the Roman town called Acelum, which thrived from the second century BC until its destruction by Attila. Following resettlement, a succession of feudal lords ruled Ásolo, culminating with the vile **Ezzelino da Romano**, whose parents were born in the town. Ezzelino wrested Ásolo from the Bishop of Treviso in 1234, and a network of castles over much of the Veneto shows the extent of his conquests in the years that followed. On his death in 1259 the townspeople of Ásolo ensured that the dynasty died with him by butchering the rest of his family, who were at that time in nearby San Zenone.

The end of the fifteenth century was marked by the arrival of **Caterina Cornaro**; her celebrated court was attended by the likes of Cardinal Bembo, one of the most eminent literary figures of his day, who coined the verb *asolare* to describe the experience of spending one's time in pleasurable aimlessness. Later writers and artists found the atmosphere equally convivial: Gabriele d'Annunzio wrote about the town, and Robert Browning's last published work – *Asolando* – was written here.

There are regular **buses** to Ásolo from Bassano; if you want to get there from Venice, the quickest route is to take a train to Treviso (there's at least one an hour), where you won't have to wait more than an hour for a bus to Ásolo (some change at Montebelluna) – in addition to the direct services, all the buses to Bassano go through Ásolo and Masèr. The bus drops you at the foot of the hill, a connecting minibus (L1500/€0.77 return) taking you up into the town.

The Town

The main road into town from Bassano enters the southern Porta Loreggia, with a fifteenth-century fountain on the left and on the right **Casa Freia**, home of the traveller and writer Freya Stark. Via Browning continues up the hill; no. 151, formerly the house of Pen Browning, bears a plaque recording his father's stay in 1889. At the top is the hub of the town, **Piazza Garibaldi** (otherwise known as Piazza Maggiore), to the south of which stands the **Duomo** – not an attraction itself, but containing a couple of good pictures by Jacopo Bassano and Lorenzo Lotto. A well-known antiques fair is held in and around Piazza Maggiore on the second weekend of each month; prices are steep, but browsing is fun.

Also on the Piazza Maggiore, in the fifteenth-century Loggia del Capitano, is the **Museo Civico**, which has long been in the throes of restoration but should soon be open again. The main interest of the art collection is provided by a pair of dubiously attributed Bellinis, a portrait of Ezzelino painted a good couple of centuries after his death, and a brace of large sculptures by **Canova**. More diverting are the memorabilia of Ásolo's residents, especially the portraits, photos and personal effects of **Eleonora Duse**. An actress in the Sarah

Bernhardt mould, Duse was almost as well known for her tempestuous love-life as for her roles in Shakespeare, Hugo and Ibsen, and she came to Ásolo to seek refuge from public gossip. Although she died in Pittsburgh while on tour in 1924, her wish was to be buried in Ásolo, and so her body was transported back here, to the church of Sant'Anna.

The Teatro Duse occupies a large part of the **Castello**, which has been largely restored, though there's little to see other than the view down to the plain. From 1489 to 1509 this was the home of **Caterina Cornaro**, one of the very few women to have played a decisive part in Venetian history. Born into one of Venice's most powerful families, Caterina was betrothed at the age of fourteen to the philandering Jacques II, king of the strategically vital island of Cyprus. The prospective groom then prevaricated for a while, until the scheming of his half-sister (who wanted him overthrown) and the Venetian promises of help against the belligerent Turks finally pushed him into marriage. Within a year Jacques was dead, in all likelihood poisoned by Marco Venier, the Venetian governor of Famagusta harbour. A few weeks later Caterina gave birth to a son, after whose christening the Venetian fleet set sail for home. No sooner had the detested Venetians left than the city was taken over by men of the Royal Council, Caterina jailed, and her son handed over to her mother-in-law, Marietta. (Marietta's hatred of Caterina was to an extent due to resentment of the latter's beauty: when Marietta was the mistress of Jacques' father she had been caught making love to him by the king's wife, who bit her nose off in the ensuing mêlée.)

While Caterina refused to surrender Famagusta to the rebels, news of the insurrection reached the Venetian galleys, who promptly returned and overpowered the city. Their reappearance was a mixed blessing. The death of her son at the age of one was taken by Venier as a cue to propose marriage; spurned, he plotted to kill her instead, but was discovered and hanged. For nine years Caterina resisted Venice's political pressure until at last, in 1489, she was forced to abdicate in order to gain much-needed weapons and ships against a new Turkish attack. Brought back to Venice to sign a deed "freely giving" Cyprus to the Republic, she was given the region of Ásolo as a sign of Venice's indebtedness, and a joust was held on the frozen Canal Grande in her honour. In Ásolo her court was constantly under the eye of the Council of Ten, who dispatched any man rumoured to be her lover for fear that a new dynasty should be started. Eventually Ásolo, too, was taken away from her by the Emperor Maximilian, and she returned to seek asylum in Venice, where she died soon after, in 1510.

The Rocca is open Sat 10am– 12.30pm & 2–7pm, Sun 10am– 7pm; L3000/€1.55.

Ásolo's ruined medieval fortress, the **Rocca**, is reached by taking Via Collegio up the hill from the back of Piazza Brugnoli (right by Piazza Garibaldi) and going through the Porta Colmarian. You have to be fairly fit to tackle it in the heat of the midday sun, but the views on both sides are worth the sweat. Built on Roman foundations, the Rocca stands 350m above sea level.

Via Canova leads west away from the town centre past Eleonora Duse's house (no. 306), near the Porta Santa Caterina. The church of **Santa Caterina**, next to the *Carabinieri*, is deconsecrated but open to allow visitors to see its fifteenth-century frescoes. Some way further on, at the junction of the road, is the enchanting fifteenth-century **Lombard house**, with allegorical figures carved in soft stone; the architect was Francesco Graziolo, who worked for Caterina Cornaro. Taking the central of the three roads at this junction you will arrive at the pedestrian Franciscan church of **Sant'Anna**; the **cemetery** on the right, from which there are splendid views, is where Eleonora Duse and Pen Browning are buried.

The Villa
Barbaro

*Santa Caterina
is open daily
11am–1pm &
3–7pm.*

Practicalities

The *pro loco* **tourist office** is at Piazza G. D'Annunzio 2 (Mon–Sat 9am–12.30pm & 3–6pm; ☎0423.529.046); if it's closed, you might find the boss in the bar opposite. The office (and sometimes the bar) gives out a map of the town which is quite handy, even if it isn't exactly a model of clarity.

Accommodation is all but impossible. The cheapest of the three hotels is the *Duse*, a reasonable-quality three-star at Via Browning 190 (☎0423.55.241; ③); the place is booked solid on the second weekend of every month, when the antiques fair takes over the centre of town. The new four-star *Albergo al Sole*, Via Collegio 33 (☎0423. 528.399, *www.albergoalsole.com*; ⑥) has impeccable facilities and a breathtaking view from the breakfast terrace, but top of the price range is the sybaritic *Villa Cipriani*, Via Canova 298 (☎0423. 523.411, *www.sheraton.com/villacipriani*; ⑦), long a favourite with Europe's crowned heads and showbiz types.

Ásolo has a handful of **bars and restaurants**. For around L45,000/€23.24 you'll get a fine meal at the best restaurant in town – *Ca' Derton*, Piazza G. D'Annunzio (☎0423.529.648; closed Sun evening & Mon); the more basic *Cornaro* just off Piazza Garibaldi in Via Regina Cornaro (closed Mon), has a good range of pizzas plus the standard *primi* and *secondi*. The large and popular *Caffè Centrale* on Piazza Garibaldi (closed Tues) is fine for a snack and a drink, but not as friendly as the *Enoteca Marcello Agnoletto*, an excellent wine bar in Via Browning (closed Wed).

The Villa Barbaro

Most people come away from the **Villa Barbaro** at **MASÈR**, 7km east of Ásolo, persuaded that this is the most beautiful house in Europe. Touring the villas of the mainland, you become used to discrepancies between the quality of the architecture and the quality of

*The Villa
Barbaro is
open Tues, Sat
& Sun: sum-
mer 3–6pm;
winter
2.30–5pm;
closed Dec 24–
Jan 6;
L10,000/
€4.90;
www.tvol.it
/villadimaser.*

the decoration, but at Masèr you'll see the best of two of the central figures of Italian civilization in the sixteenth century – **Palladio** and **Paolo Veronese**, whose careers crossed here and nowhere else. If you're reliant on public transport, a visit is best made by bus from Bassano via Ásolo (8 daily), or from Treviso – the services from Treviso to Ásolo and Bassano all pass the villa.

The villa was built in 1557–58 for **Daniele and Marcantonio Barbaro**, men whose diverse cultural interests set them apart from most of the other wealthy Venetians who were then beginning to farm the Veneto. Both were prominent figures in the society of Venice. Marcantonio served as the Republic's ambassador to Constantinople and became one of the Procurators of San Marco, a position that enabled him to promote Palladio's scheme for the church of the Redentore. Daniele, the more scholarly of the pair, edited the writings of Vitruvius, wrote on mathematics and perspective, and founded the botanical gardens in Padua; he was also Venice's representative in London and was later elected Patriarch of Acquileia, as well as becoming the official historian of Venice. The association between Palladio and the brothers was very close by the time the villa was begun – in 1554 Daniele and Palladio had visited Rome, and they'd worked together on Barbaro's edition of Vitruvius – and the process of designing the house was far more of a collaborative venture than were most of Palladio's projects.

The interior and the Tempietto

The Villa Barbaro was a working farm in which was embodied a classical vision – derived from writers such as Livy – of the harmony of architectural form and the well-ordered pastoral life. Farm functions dominated the entire ground floor – dovecots in the end pavilions, stables and storage space under the arcades, administrative offices on the lower floor of the central block. It's in the living quarters of the piano nobile that the more rarefied aspect of the brothers' world is expressed, in a breathtaking series of **frescoes** by Veronese (1566–68) that has no equal anywhere in northern Italy. You need to be a student of Renaissance iconography to decode unassisted the allegorical figures in the amazing trompe l'oeil ceiling of the **Hall of Olympus** – the scheme was devised by Daniele Barbaro and centres on the figure of Eternal Wisdom – but an excellent guidebook is on sale in the villa, and most of the other paintings require no footnotes. The walls of the Villa Barbaro are the most resourceful display of visual trickery you'll ever see – servants peer round painted doors, a dog sniffs along the base of a flat balustrade in front of a landscape of ruins, illusory statues throw counterfeit shadows, flagstaffs lean in alcoves that aren't there. At the end of an avenue of doorways, a huntsman (probably Veronese himself) steps into the house through an entrance that's a solid wall – inevitably it's speculated that the woman facing the hunter at the other end of the house was

Veronese's mistress. On top of all this, there's some remarkable architectural sculpture by **Alessandro Vittoria**: chimneypieces in the living rooms, figures in the tympanum of the main block, and the ornate **nymphaeum** in the garden at the back. The last incorporates a pond that used to be the house's fish-tank, and whose waters were channelled through the kitchens and out into the orchards.

In the grounds in front of the villa stands Palladio's **Tempietto**, the only church by him outside Venice and one of his last projects – commissioned by Marcantonio a decade after his brother's death, it was built in 1580, the year Palladio himself died. From the outside it's clear that the circular domed temple is based on the Pantheon, but the interior (currently closed for restoration) reveals a different form, the tiny side chapels creating a modified Greek-cross plan – thus combining the mathematically pure form of the circle with the liturgically perfect form of the cross. Another surprise is the richness of the stucco decoration, much of which is again by Vittoria.

There's also a **carriage museum** in the grounds, for which there's an extra entrance charge; it contains a few curiosities – such as a boat-shaped nineteenth-century ice-cream cart with a voluptuous mermaid on its prow – but it's difficult to whip up much interest after the villa and Veronese. Just by the bus stop and crossroads, 300m from the villa, the *Locanda di Masèr* (closed Wed) is a gem of a **restaurant**, serving superb local cuisine at very reasonable prices – perfect for a late lunch before the villa opens.

Feltre

The historic centre of **FELTRE**, spread along a narrow ridge about 20km north of Masèr, owes its beguiling appearance to a disaster. At the outbreak of the War of the League of Cambrai, Feltre declared its allegiance to Venice – and so, when the army of Emperor Maximilian I swept into town in 1509, it was decided to punish Feltre by wiping its buildings and a hefty number of its inhabitants from the face of the planet. The Venetians took care of the reconstruction, and within a few decades the streets had been rebuilt. They still look pretty much as they did when the scaffolding came down. You're not going to find the town crawling with students making notes on the architecture of the Renaissance, and neither will you want to stay over, but you'll have to travel a long way to get a better idea of how an ordinary town looked in sixteenth-century Italy. And on top of that, there's the beauty of Feltre's position – the Dolomites in one direction, the valley of the Piave in the other. The last stretch of the train journey from the south, along the Piave from Valdobbiádene, is on its own worth the price of the ticket.

There are no direct **trains** to Feltre from Venice, but Feltre is a stop on the **Padua–Belluno** line (12 daily) – you can intercept these trains at Castelfranco. The journey from Padua to Feltre takes ninety minutes, and it's a further thirty to Belluno. There's an alternative route from Venice via Treviso, which involves a change of trains there and at Montebelluna; because this route covers fewer kilometres the ticket is slightly cheaper, but the connections can be less convenient than going via Castelfranco.

The Old Town

From the station, down in the modern part of town, the shortest route to the old quarter is to cross straight over into Viale del Piave, over Via Garibaldi and along Via Castaldi, which brings you to the **Duomo** and **Baptistery**, at the foot of the ridge. The oldest section of the much-altered duomo is the fifteenth-century apse; its main objects of interest are a tomb by Tullio Lombardo (on the right wall of the chancel) and the *Pala della Misericordia* (second altar of right aisle), by local sixteenth-century painter Pietro de Marascalchi, who also painted the *John the Baptist* on the fourth altar of the right aisle, and possibly the altarpiece in the chapel to the right of the chancel. At the top of the steps going past the side of the porticoed baptistery, on the other side of the road, is the discreet south gate (1494), from under which a long covered flight of steps rises into the heart of the old town.

You come out by the sixteenth-century **Municipio**, which has a sturdy portico by Palladio. Goldoni's earliest plays, first performed in 1729 in the old Palazzo Pretorio (the building at a right-angle to the Municipio), were soon afterwards staged in the Municipio's own theatre, the exquisite little **Teatro della Senna**, which was redesigned at the start of the nineteenth century. Recently restored, it fully merits its nickname of "La piccola Fenice.".

The Teatro della Senna is open July–Sept Thurs–Sat 4–7pm, Sun 10am–1pm & 4–7pm; L4000/€2.06.

Under the gaze of the inescapable Venetian lion, two Feltrian luminaries face each other across the stage-like **Piazza Maggiore**: **Panfilo Castaldi** and Vittorino de' Rambaldoni, usually known as **Vittorino da Feltre**. The former was instrumental in the development of printing in Italy, and according to some it was Castaldi rather than Gutenberg who was the first European to develop moveable type – the inscription on the plinth categorically declares him to be its inventor. Vittorino's fame rests on the school he ran in Mantua in the first half of the fifteenth century, under the financial patronage of the Gonzaga family, which took in pupils from aristocratic families and unprivileged backgrounds alike, and put them through a regimen in which, for the first time, a broad liberal education was combined with a programme of physical training.

Behind Piazza Maggiore rises the keep of the medieval castello, just below which stands the church of **San Rocco** – go round the back for a good view of the mountains. The carved wall between the steps going up to the church is a fountain by Tullio Lombardo.

To the left as you look across at San Rocco, the main street of Feltre, **Via Mezzaterra**, slopes down to the fifteenth-century Porta

Imperiale. Nearly all the houses here are sixteenth-century, and several are decorated with external frescoes by **Lorenzo Luzzo** (1467–1512) and his pupils. Feltre's most important artistic figure, Luzzo is more widely known as **Il Morto da Feltre** (The Dead Man . . .), a nickname prompted by the pallor of his complexion. Having begun with spells in Rome and Florence, Il Morto's career received something of a boost when he was called in to help Giorgione on the Fondaco dei Tedeschi in Venice.

The **Museo Civico**, at the end of Via L. Luzzo, the equally decorous continuation of Via Mezzaterra on the other side of the piazza, contains Il Morto's *Madonna with St Vitus and St Modestus* and other pieces by him, plus paintings by Cima and Gentile Bellini, and a display of Roman and Etruscan finds. Il Morto's finest work is generally held to be the fresco of the *Transfiguration* in the **Ognissanti** church; this building is very unlikely to be open in the foreseeable future, but if you want to try your luck, go out of the Porta Oria, right by the Museo, down the dip and then along Borgo Ruga for a couple of hundred metres.

The Museo Civico is open Tues–Sun 10am–1pm & 3–6pm; L8000/€4.12.

Feltre has another, more unusual museum – the **Museo Rizzarda** at Via del Paradiso 8, parallel to Via Mezzaterra. This doubles as the town's collection of modern art and an exhibition of wrought-iron work, most of it by **Carlo Rizzarda** (1883–1931), the former owner of the house. It might not sound appetizing, but the finesse of Rizzarda's pieces is remarkable. The frescoed building at the piazza end of Via del Paradiso is the **Monte di Pietà**, one of the few fifteenth-century buildings to escape the wrath of the Imperial hordes.

The Museo Rizzarda is open June–Sept Tues–Sun 10am–1pm & 4–7pm; L3000/€1.55.

Practicalities

It's not very likely that you'll want to stay overnight in Feltre, but if you do, choose between the three-star *Nuovo*, Vicolo Fornere Pazze 5 (☎0439.2110; ②), and the four-star *Doriguzzi*, Viale del Piave 2 (☎0439.2902; ③). Feltre has an excellent **restaurant**, the *Osteria Novecento* (☎0439.80.193; closed Mon), at Via Mezzaterra 24a; reckon on L60,000 per person.

Conegliano

Travelling north from Treviso, it's at the amiable town of **CONEGLIANO** that the landscape ceases to be as boring as a polder, as the terrain begins to rise towards the Dolomites. It markets itself to tourists as *La Città Murata* (Walled City), on the strength of fortifications that bear witness to its medieval history, most notably the six decades of occupation by the Da Carrara and Della Scala (Scaliger) warlords, prior to annexation by Venice in 1389. But to the untrained eye the vestigial walls of Conegliano aren't especially remarkable, and in truth what this town is really about is **wine**

Conegliano

– the surrounding hills are patched with vineyards, and the production of wine is central to the economy of the district. Italy's first wine-growers' college was set up in Conegliano in 1876, and today there are a couple of well-established **wine routes**: the **Strada del Vino Rosso**, which follows a looping 68-kilometre course southeast to Oderzo, and the more rewarding **Strada del Prosecco**, a straighter 42-kilometre journey west to Valdobbiádene. The former takes you through Merlot, Cabernet and Raboso country; the latter passes the Bianco dei Colli, Prosecco and Cartizze producers – the last, a more refined version of Prosecco, could be mistaken for champagne with a small effort of will.

Getting to Conegliano on public transport from Venice is easy – nearly all the thirty-odd Venice to Udine **trains** stop there; the journey from Venice takes a little under an hour.

The Town

The old centre of Conegliano, adhering to the slope of the Colle di Giano and presided over by the castello on its summit, is right in front of you as you come out of the station. After crossing the principal street of the modern town (Corso V. Emanuele–Corso G. Mazzini) you pass through a portico and into the original high street – **Via XX Settembre**. Lined with fifteenth- to eighteenth-century houses, this is an attractive street on any day, but to see it at its best you should turn up on a Friday morning, when the weekly **market** sets up camp.

The Duomo is generally closed noon–3pm.

The most decorative feature of Via XX Settembre is the unusual facade of the **Duomo** – a fourteenth-century portico, frescoed at the end of the sixteenth century by **Ludovico Pozzoserrato**, which joins seamlessly the buildings on either side. The interior of the church has been rebuilt, but retains fragments of fifteenth-century frescoes; the major adornment of the church, though, is the magnificent altarpiece of *The Madonna and Child with Saints and Angels*, painted in 1493 by **Giambattista Cima** (c.1459–c.1517), the most famous native of Conegliano.

The Cima museum is open summer Thurs 9am– noon & 3.30– 7pm, Sat 3.30– 7pm, Sun 10am–noon & 3.30–7pm; winter Thurs 9am–noon & 3–6pm, Sat 3–6pm, Sun 10am–noon & 3–6pm; L2000/€1.03.

Alongside the duomo, at the top of the steps facing the door off the right-hand aisle of the church, is the **Sala dei Battuti** (Hall of the Flagellants), the frescoed meeting place of a local confraternity (Sun 3–7pm; at other times ask the sacristan for admission). The pictures are mostly sixteenth-century and depict scenes from the Creation to the Last Judgement, incorporating the weirdest *Ascension* you'll ever see, with the ascendant Christ half out of the frame and a pair of footprints left behind at the point of lift-off. Individually the frescoes are nothing much to write home about, but the room as a unit is quite striking.

Cima's birthplace, no. 24 Via G.B. Cima, at the rear of the duomo, has been restored and converted into the **Casa Museo di G.B. Cima**. Formally unadventurous, Cima exemplifies the conservative strand in Venetian painting of the early sixteenth century, but at their best his paintings have something of the elegiac tone of Giovanni Bellini's later works. The museum's pictures present clearly his strengths and his weaknesses; not one of them, though, is a painting by Cima – they're all high-class reproductions.

The **Palazzo Sarcinelli**, at Via XX Settembre 130–134, sometimes stages good art exhibitions, but the only permanent display is that in the Museo Civico, which is housed in the tallest surviving tower of the reconstructed tenth-century castello on top of the hill. It's reached most quickly by the steep and cobbled Calle Madonna della Neve, which begins at the end of Via Accademia, the street beside the palatial *Accademia* cinema, and follows the town's most impressive stretch of ancient wall. (The Scaligeri raised the wall in the 1330s, and half a century later the Carraresi made it higher.) The **Museo Civico** has some damaged frescoes by Pordenone and a small bronze horse by Giambologna, but most of the paintings are "Workshop of . . . " or "School of . . . ", and the displays of coins, maps, war memorabilia, armour and so forth are no more fascinating than you'd expect. To pad things out there's a section devoted to famous people with local connections, complete with terracotta busts of Arturo Toscanini, who got married in Conegliano, and Mozart's great librettist Lorenzo da Ponte, who was born in nearby Cèneda (see p.393). But it's a lovingly maintained museum, and the climb through the floors culminates on the tower's roof, from where you get a fine view across the vine-clad landscape. (If you'd like to savour the panorama in more comfort, you could sip a drink on the terrace of the neighbouring *Al Castello* bar, which looks towards the Dolomites.) The castello shares the summit of the hill with the heavily restored **Santa Orsola**, the minuscule remnant of the ancient church of San Leonardo, which was Conegliano's main church from its foundation in the twelfth century until the demolition of everything but the apse (where some scrappy frescoes survive) and a single chapel in the middle of the eighteenth.

The Museo Civico is open Tues–Sun: summer 10am–12.30pm & 3.30–7pm; winter 10am–12.30pm & 3–6.30pm; open Sun only for most of Nov; L3000/ €1.55.

Practicalities

Conegliano's **tourist office** is at Via XX Settembre 61, on the corner of Piazza G.B. Cima (Tues–Fri 9am–12.30pm & 3–6pm, Sat 9am–12.30pm & 3.30–6pm, Sun 9.30am–12.30pm & 3.30–6pm; ☎0438.21.230). Via XX Settembre has all you'll need in the way of cafés, bars and food shops, and it has what's clearly the first-choice **hotel** – the three-star *Canon d'Oro* at no. 129 (☎0438.34.246, *www.sevenonline.it/canondoro*; ③); the town's one-stars are nowhere near the centre, and not very plesant anyway. Top recommendation for low-cost **eating** is the *Alla Corona* trattoria, Via Beato Ongaro 29 (closed Mon), where a meal of genuine local dishes should cost around L40,000; you get to it by continuing along Via XX Settembre past the *Canon d'Oro*. The fish menu at the excellent

Vittorio Veneto

Città di Venezia, Via XX Settembre 77 (☎0438.23.186; closed Sun evening & all Mon), will take you into the region of L60,000, about the same as a meal at the very good restaurant of the *Canon d'Oro* itself (closed Sun June–Aug, Fri rest of year).

Prosecco is the chief wine of the Conegliano district, and its producers compile a list of recommended outlets: the tourist office should have the latest list, plus details of the wine routes. If you want to sample the stuff at source, exploration of the Strada del Prosecco by public transport isn't a problem – **buses** run frequently from Conegliano to Valdobbiádene (1hr), leaving from Piazzale Santa Caterina (follow Via Colombo).

Conegliano has some kind of **festival** – musical, literary, culinary – on each weekend in September, a sequence that's brought to a close on the first weekend of October by the **Dama Castellana**, a gigantic draughts game played with human pieces. Initiated in 1241 to mark a victory over the troops of Treviso, the game is nowadays preceded by a costumed procession and flag-twirling, and followed by a gruelling ritual in which the losers have to shove the winners up the hill to the castle in a cart. In traditional style, fireworks bring the fun to a full stop.

Vittorio Veneto

The name **VITTORIO VENETO** first appeared on the map in 1866 when, to mark the unification of Italy and honour Vittorio Emanuele II, the first king of the new country, the neighbouring towns of Cèneda and Serravalle, which hadn't previously been the best of friends, were knotted together and rechristened. A new town hall was built midway along the avenue connecting the two, and the train station constructed opposite, in the hope that the towns would grow closer together. To an extent they have, but the visitor emerging from the station still steps straight into a sort of no-man's-land.

The old quarter of Serravalle is very alluring, but if anything will tempt you to stay in Vittorio Veneto it's the environs rather than the town itself. From the centre of town there are paths leading up into the encircling wooded hills, such as the one that takes you up to Monte Altare, immediately to the west. Further out, there are watersports facilities on the reservoir to the north and ski centres on both sides of the gorge to the north of the town, on the Alpago and Nevegàl slopes, the nearest ski resorts to Venice. However, the most rewarding area for walkers is to be found to the northeast of Vittorio Veneto – the **Bosco del Cansiglio**, a plateau forested with beech and pine which was once husbanded by the Venetian state as a source of timber for oars. Although the area has been developed as a holiday resort, you can still roam here for hours without seeing a soul. A good base from which to explore this vast expanse of woodland is Fregona, which is connected by regular buses to Vittorio Veneto.

Four **trains** a day run direct to Vittorio Veneto from Venice; otherwise it's a short hop **from Conegliano**. There are fifteen northward connections a day from Conegliano (25min) – sometimes these connections are by *autocorsa*, a bus service on which train tickets alone are valid. Read the timetable carefully when checking your connection back to Conegliano – if it's an *autocorsa* you'll probably have to skip over to the bus station behind Piazza del Popolo, which is opposite the train station. From Vittorio Veneto four trains carry on to Belluno, and six connect with a Belluno shuttle at Ponte delle Alpi. The remaining services chug north from Ponte delle Alpi to Calalzo, in the heart of the eastern Dolomites.

Cèneda

CÈNEDA, overlooked by the seventh-century Lombard castle of San Martino (now the bishop's residence), is the less appealing of the town's halves; having a more open situation than Serravalle, it has inevitably developed as the commercial centre of Vittorio Veneto. It is, nonetheless, worth a visit for the **Museo della Battaglia** in the sixteenth-century Loggia Cenedese, which is possibly by Sansovino. It's on the same piazza as the nondescript duomo, which you get to by turning right out of the station and keeping going until you come to the road junction of Piazza San Francesco di Assisi, where you turn right, a fifteen-minute walk in total. The battle of Vittorio, which lasted from October 24 to November 3, 1918, was the final engagement of World War I for the Italian army (which is why most towns in Italy have a Via Vittorio Veneto) and the museum is dedicated to the climactic engagement.

The Museo della Battaglia is open Tues–Sun: May–Sept 10am–noon & 4.30–6.30pm; Oct–April 10am–noon & 3–5pm; L5000/€2.58.

The only other building that merits a look in Cèneda is the church of **Santa Maria del Meschio**, where you'll find a luscious *Annunciation* by Andrea Previtali (c.1470–1528), a pupil of Giovanni Bellini. If you turn left off the Cèneda–Serravalle road down Via Armando Diaz, instead of going right for the cathedral square, you'll quickly come across it.

Serravalle

The Romanesque church of **Sant'Andrea di Bigonzo** will catch your attention as you walk from Cèneda to Serravalle, at the end of an avenue to the right; it's decorated with Renaissance frescoes, but unless you've a bit of time to spare, content yourself with the view from a distance.

SERRAVALLE, wedged in the neck of the gorge between the Col Visentin and the Cansiglio (the name means "Valley Lock"), is an entirely different proposition from its partner. Once through its southern gate – to the left of which the ruined walls disappear into the trees on the valley side – you are into a town that has scarcely seen a demolition since the sixteenth century. Franco Zeffirelli

Vittorio Veneto

The Museo del Cenedese is open same hours as Museo della Battaglia, but closed Tues; same ticket.

San Lorenzo is open daily except Tues: May–Sept 3–4pm; Oct–April 2–3pm; same ticket as museums.

exploited the place's charm to the full when he used it as one of the locations for his soft-focus *Romeo and Juliet*. Most of the buildings along Via Martiri della Libertà, Via Roma and Via Mazzini, and around the stage-like Piazza Marcantonio Flaminio, date from the fifteenth and sixteenth centuries – the handsomest being the finely painted and shield-encrusted Loggia Serravallese (rebuilt c.1460). This is now the home of the **Museo del Cenedese**, a jumble of sculptural and archeological bits and pieces, detached frescoes and very minor paintings.

Time is more profitably spent in the churches of Serravalle than in its museum. One of the best-preserved fresco cycles in the Veneto covers the interior of **San Lorenzo dei Battuti**, immediately inside the south gate. Painted around 1450, the frescoes were damaged when Napoleon's louts used the chapel as a kitchen, but restoration subsequent to the uncovering of the cycle in 1953 has rectified the situation.

The **Duomo**, across the swift-flowing River Meschio on the far side of the Piazza Flaminio from the Museo, is a dull eighteenth-century building with a medieval campanile; an altarpiece of *The Virgin with St Peter and St Andrew*, produced in 1547 by **Titian** and his workshop, is the sole reason to go inside.

Follow the road past the duomo and you'll immediately come to a flight of steps. This leads to a path that winds through the woods to the **Santuario di Santa Augusta** – go for the walk, not for the building. If you're in town on August 21, the festival of Saint Augusta's martyrdom, you'll be treated to a huge fireworks display and all-night party. Carry on up Via Roma instead of veering across Piazza Flaminio and you'll pass the remnant of the castello and, eventually (outside the walls), the partly frescoed church of **San Giovanni Battista**, which has beautiful cloisters (ask the sacristan for admission, as the cloisters belong to the adjacent Carmelite monastery). Further out still, and a few yards over the river (turn right about 400m after San Giovanni), stands **Santa Giustina**, which was founded in 1226 by the Camino clan, who for around three hundred years were the rulers of Treviso province. It contains a superb funerary monument, the **tomb** erected in 1336 by Verde della Scala (ie Scaliger) for her husband, Rizzardo VI da Camino, who had been killed in battle. The four praying warriors that support the Gothic sarcophagus were probably purloined from an older pulpit or other such structure.

Practicalities

The **tourist office**, at Piazza del Popolo 18 (Mon–Fri 9am–12.30pm & 3–6pm, Sat & Sun closes 5.30pm; ☎0438.57.243), is good for information on the ski resorts and walking terrain around the town. Most homely of the local **hotels** is the *Locanda Leon d'Oro*, a small three-star at Via Cavour 8 (☎0438.940.740; ③), opposite the gate into

Serravalle. The competing hotels are mainly geared towards business-people; the three-star *Terme*, on the Serravalle–Cèneda road at Via delle Terme 4 (☎0438.554.345, *www.sevenonline.it/hotelterme*; ④), is as comfortable as any of them. The *Leon d'Oro* has a fine and moderately priced **restaurant**, but the best food in town is served at *Al Postiglione*, Via Cavour 39 (☎0438.556.924; closed Tues), where wild boar and mushrooms feature prominently on a very reasonably priced menu – you'll pay in the region of L50,000.

Belluno

The most northerly of the major towns of the Veneto, **BELLUNO** stands at the point where the tiny River Ardo flows into the Piave, in the shadow of the eastern Dolomites. Once a strategically important ally of Venice, which took the town under its wing in 1404, it is today a provincial capital, and attached more firmly to the mountainous region to the north than to the urban centres to the south: the net-work of the Dolomiti-Bus company radiates out from Belluno, trains run fairly regularly to the terminus at Calalzo, and the tourist office's handouts are geared mostly to hikers and skiers. Many visitors to the town use the place simply for its access to the mountains, and miss out on its attractions – of which there are quite a few, besides its breathtaking position.

At present there's just one **train** a day that runs straight from Venice to Belluno (around 1.30pm), and only one afternoon train back, but it's just as quick anyway to take an Udine-bound train and change at Conegliano (see p.389) – the complete expedition takes just over two hours. You can get to Belluno from Padua (via Castelfranco) as well – there are twelve trains a day, also taking two hours.

The Town

Belluno has two distinct but adjacent centres, reached by walking straight ahead from the train station. The hub of the modern town, the spot where you'll find its most popular bars and cafés, is the wide **Piazza dei Martiri** (named after a group of partisans executed in the square by the Nazis in 1944). Off the south side, a road leads to the **Piazza del Duomo**, the kernel of the old town. The sixteenth-century **Duomo** (or Santa Maria Assunta), a Gothic-classical amalgam built in the pale yellow stone that's a distinctive feature of Belluno, was designed by **Tullio Lombardo**; it has had to be reconstructed twice after earthquake damage, in 1873 and 1936. The elegant inte-rior – a long barrel vault ending in a single dome, with flanking aisles – has a couple of good paintings: one by Andrea Schiavone (first altar on the right), and one by Palma il Giovane (fourth altar on the right). If the restoration of the stately **campanile** has at last been finished, you might be able to climb up to the bell-chamber, from where you'll get a glorious view of the Dolomites in one direction and the Venetian plain in the other (allegedly you can even see Venice if your binoculars are powerful enough); the tower was designed in 1743 by **Filippo Juvarra**, best known for his rebuilding of central Turin.

Occupying one complete side of the Piazza del Duomo, at a right angle to the duomo itself, is the residence of the Venetian administrators of the town, the **Palazzo dei Rettori**, a frilly late fifteenth-century building dolled up with Baroque trimmings. A relic of more independent times stands on the right – the twelfth-century **Torre Civica**, all that's left of Belluno's medieval castle. Continuing round the piazza, in Via Duomo, along the side of the nineteenth-century town hall, you'll find the **Museo Civico**. It's strongest on the work of Belluno's three best-known artists, all of whom were working at the end of the seventeenth and beginning of the eighteenth centuries: the painters Sebastiano and Marco Ricci, and the virtuoso sculptor-woodcarver Andrea Brustolon, who features prominently in Venice's Ca' Rezzonico. For those who prefer a touch less agitation in their art, the placid Paduan artist Bartolomeo Montagna is represented here as well.

The Museo Civico is open Mon–Sat 10am–noon, plus 3–6pm Tues & Thurs; L4000/€2.06.

Via Duomo ends at the **Piazza del Mercato**, a tiny square hemmed in by porticoed Renaissance buildings; until the Venetians shifted the administrative offices to the Piazza del Duomo, this was the nerve-centre of Belluno, and even after the Venetian alterations it remained the commercial centre. Its fountain dates from 1410 and the **Monte di Pietà** (no. 26) from 1501, making it one of the oldest pawnshops in Italy. One of the prime claimants to the honour of being the originator of pawnshops is Martino Tomitani (later Saint Bernardine of Feltre), a Franciscan friar from the village of Tomo, in the vicinity of nearby Feltre. The principal street of the old town, **Via Mezzaterra**, goes down from the Piazza del Mercato to the fourteenth-century Porta Ruga (veer left along the cobbled Via S. Croce about 100m from the end), from where the view along the mountain-backed valley of the Piave will provide some compensation if you haven't managed to find the campanile open.

The unprepossessing and rarely open church of **San Pietro**, just off Via Mezzaterra at the end of Vicolo San Pietro, is worth trying to look into for pieces by **Sebastiano Ricci** (main altarpiece), **Brustolon** (carved altarpieces on the second altars on both sides, and angels over baldachin) and **Andrea Schiavone** (paintings over the door and to the sides of the high altar).

Leaving the Piazza del Mercato in the other direction, you pass through the sixteenth-century **Porta Dojona** and into Piazza Vittorio Emanuele II, an extension of the main square of the modern town. Belluno's other major church, **Santo Stefano**, is to the right, on Via Roma. A bright Gothic building (1486) with banded arches and alternating brown and white columns, it has yet more carvings by

Brustolon (in the left aisle, a Crucifix resting on figures in Purgatory) and restored frescoes by **Jacopo da Montagnana** (chapel to the right of the main altar), painted within a year or so of the church's construction.

Practicalities

The **tourist office**, at Piazza dei Martiri 7 (Mon–Sat 9am–12.30pm & 3–6pm, Sun 9am–12.30pm; ☎0437.940.083), is a good source of leaflets on Belluno and its province, but if you want specialized information on mountain pursuits you should also call at ASVI Viaggi, Piazza dei Martiri 27e (Mon–Fri 9am–12.30pm & 3–7pm, Sat 9am–12.30pm).

The cheapest **hotels** in town are the *Taverna*, Via Cipro 7 (☎0437.25.192; ①), and *Centrale*, Via Loreto 2 (☎0437.943.349; ①); both are basic (only the *Centrale* has private bathrooms) but are very close to Piazza dei Martiri. *Alle Dolomiti*, just off the piazza at Via Carrera 46 (☎0437.941.660; ②), and *Astor*, Piazza dei Martiri 26/e (☎0437.942.094; ③), are the pick of the central three-stars. The best **restaurant** in town is *Terracotta*, near the train station at Borgo Garibaldi 61 (☎0437.942.644; closed Sat.); a three-course meal should cost around L45,000. Its only rival is the similarly priced *Al Borgo*, Via Anconetta 8 (☎0437.926.755; closed Mon evening & Tues); it's in an eighteenth-century villa surrounded by beautiful parkland on the road to Feltre.

Mountain excursions

Apart from *Dolomiti Neve* leaflets on the ski resorts of the area, ASVI can supply you with details of the **Alte Vie** (High Trails) of the eastern Dolomites – these are six mountain-top routes, up to nearly 200km in length, punctuated by alpine refuges. Most popular is the **Alta Via no. 1**, a north–south route right across the Dolomites from Braies to Belluno. The **Club Alpino Italiano**, at Via Ricci 1, runs several of the refuges, and is another good source of information for intrepid hikers.

If a two-week trek across the vertiginous peaks of northern Italy doesn't appeal, but you feel like a quick burst of alpine exertion, it's best to head south, to the ski centre of **Nevegàl** (11km), easily reached by bus. From there you can take a chairlift up to the *Rifugio Brigata Alpina Cadore*, and then embark on the climb up the mountain ridge to the refuge of **Col Visentin** (1761m), from where you can survey the crags of the Dolomites in one direction, and the waters of Venice in the other. Allow at least two and a half hours for the walk to the refuge.

The train will take you up the Piave valley only as far as Calalzo (10 daily; journey time 1hr), so you'll probably find the **buses** more useful for trips north. All the **Dolomiti-Bus** services depart from the train station forecourt, and there's an information office there too.

The Contexts

A brief history of Venice

In the midst of the waters, free, indigent, laborious, and inaccessible, they gradually coalesced into a Republic.

Edward Gibbon

Beginnings

Though the Venetian lagoon supported small groups of fishermen and hunters at the start of the Christian era, it was only with the barbarian invasions of the fifth century and after that sizeable communities began to settle on the mudbanks. The first mass migration was provoked by the arrival in the Veneto of **Attila the Hun**'s hordes in **453**, but a large number of the refugees struck camp and returned to dry land once the danger seemed to be past. Permanent settlement was accelerated a century later, when, in **568**, the Germanic **Lombards** (or Longobards), led by **Alboin**, swept into northern Italy.

A loose conglomeration of island communes arose, each cluster of islands drawing its population from one or two clearly defined areas of the Veneto: the fugitives from Padua went to **Malamocco** and **Chioggia**; the inhabitants of **Grado** mainly came from Aquileia; and Altino supplied many of the pioneers of **Torcello**, **Burano** and **Murano**. Distinct economic, ecclesiastical and administrative centres quickly evolved: Torcello was the focal point of trading activity; Grado, the new home of the Bishop of Aquileia, was the Church's base; and Heraclea

(now extinct) was the seat of government. The lagoon confederation was not autonomous, though – it owed **political allegiance to Byzantium**, and until the end of the seventh century its senior officials were the **maritime tribunes**, who were effectively controlled by the Imperial hierarchy of Ravenna.

The refugee population of the islands increased steeply as the Lombard grip on the Veneto strengthened under the leadership of **Grimoald** (667–71), and shortly after this influx the confederation took a big step towards independence. This is one of the many points at which Venetian folklore has acquired the status of fact: tradition has it that a conference was convened at Heraclea in 697 by the Patriarch of Grado, and from this meeting sprang the election of the **first doge**, to unify the islands in the face of the Lombard threat. (John Julius Norwich adroitly disentangles the myth in his history of Venice – see "Books" p.433.) In fact, it was not until **726** that the lagoon settlers chose their first leader, when a wave of dissent against Emperor Leo III throughout the Byzantine Empire spurred them to elect **Orso Ipato** as the head of their provincial council.

After a period during which the old system of government was briefly reinstituted, Orso Ipato's son **Teodato** became the second doge in 742. Yet the lagoon administration – which was now moved from Heraclea to **Malamocco** – was still not autonomous. Teodato's relationship to the emperor was less subservient than his father's had been, yet he nonetheless took orders from the capital, and the **fall of Ravenna to the Lombards in 751** did not alter the constitutional relationship between Byzantium and the confederation.

At the close of the eighth century, the Lombards were overrun by the Frankish army of **Charlemagne**, and in **810** the emperor's son **Pepin** sailed into action against the proto-Venetians. Malamocco was quickly taken, but Pepin's fleet failed in its attempt to pursue the settlers when they withdrew to the better-protected islands of **Rivoalto**, and retreated with heavy losses. Now the seat of government in the lagoon was shifted for the second and last time, to Rivoalto, the name by which the central cluster of islands was known until the late twelfth century, when it became generally known as **Venice**. The **Rialto** district, in the core of the city, perpetuates the old name.

From independence to empire

In the **Treaty of Aix-la-Chapelle**, signed by Charlemagne and the Byzantine emperor shortly after Pepin's defeat, Venice was declared to be a dukedom within the Eastern Empire, despite the fact that by now the control of Byzantium was little more than nominal. The traders and boatmen of the lagoon were less and less inclined to acknowledge the precedence of the emperor, and they signalled their recalcitrance through one great symbolic act – **the theft of the body of**

Saint Mark from Alexandria in 828. Saint Mark, whose posthumous arrival in Venice was held to be divinely ordained (see the "Basilica di San Marco" entry, p.47), was made the patron saint of the city in place of the Byzantine patron, Saint Theodore, and a basilica was built alongside the doge's castle to accommodate the holy relics. These two buildings – the **Basilica di San Marco** and the **Palazzo Ducale** – were to remain the emblems of the Venetian state and the repository of power within the city for almost one thousand years.

By the end of the ninth century the population of the islands of central Venice was increasing steadily. The city was comprehensively protected against attack, with chains slung across the entrance to the major channels and fortified walls shielding the waterfront between the Palazzo Ducale and the area in which the

Andrea Contarini 1368–1382
Michele Morosini 1382
Antonio Venier 1382–1400
Michele Steno 1400–1413
Tommaso Mocenigo 1414–1423
Francesco Fóscari 1423–1457
Pasquale Malipiero 1457–1462
Cristoforo Moro 1462–1471
Nicolò Tron 1471–1473
Nicolò Marcello 1473–1474
Pietro Mocenigo 1474–1476
Andrea Vendramin 1476– 1478
Giovanni Mocenigo 1478–1485
Marco Barbarigo 1485–1486
Agostino Barbarigo 1486–1501
Leonardo Loredan 1501–1521
Antonio Grimani 1521–1523
Andrea Gritti 1523–1538
Pietro Lando 1539–1545
Francesco Donà 1545–1553
Marcantonio Trevisan 1553–1554
Francesco Venier 1554–1556
Lorenzo Priuli 1556–1559
Girolamo Priuli 1559–1567
Pietro Loredan 1567–1570
Alvise Mocenigo I 1570–1577
Sebastiano Venier 1577–1578
Nicolò da Ponte 1578–1585
Pasquale Cicogna 1585–1595
Marino Grimani 1595–1605
Leonardo Donà 1606–1612

Marcantonio Memmo 1612–1615
Giovanni Bembo 1615–1618
Nicolò Donà 1618
Antonio Priuli 1618–1623
Francesco Contarini 1623–1624
Giovanni Corner I 1625–1629
Nicolò Contarini 1630-1631
Francesco Erizzo 1631–1646
Francesco Molin 1646–1655
Carlo Contarini 1655–1656
Francesco Corner 1656
Bertucci Valier 1656–1658
Giovanni Pésaro 1658–1659
Domenico Contarini 1659–1675
Nicolò Sagredo 1675–1676
Alvise Contarini 1676–1684
Marcantonio Giustinian 1684–1688
Francesco Morosini 1688–1694
Silvestro Valier 1694–1700
Alvise Mocenigo II 1700–1709
Giovanni Corner II 1709–1722
Alvise Mocenigo III 1722–1732
Carlo Ruzzini 1732–1735
Alvise Pisani 1735–1741
Pietro Grimani 1741–1752
Francesco Loredan 1752–1762
Marco Foscarini 1762–1763
Alvise Mocenigo IV 1763–1778
Paolo Renier 1779–1789
Lodovico Manin 1789–1797

church of Santa Maria Zobenigo now stands. Before the close of the following century, the Venetian **trading networks** were well established – military assistance given to their former masters in Byzantium had earned concessions in the markets of the East, and the Venetian economy was now prospering from the distribution of eastern goods along the waterways of northern Italy.

Slav pirates, operating from the shelter of the Dalmatian coast, were the greatest hindrance to Venetian trade in the northern Adriatic, and in the year **1000** a fleet set out under the command of **Doge Pietro Orseolo II** to subjugate the troublemakers. The successful expedition was commemorated each subsequent year in the ceremony of the **Marriage of Venice to the Sea**, in which the city's lordship of the Adriatic was ritually confirmed (see p.236). However, although

the Doge of Venice could now legitimately claim the title "Duke of Dalmatia", there remained the problem of the **Normans** of southern Italy, whose navy threatened to confine the Venetians to the upper part of the Adriatic. The breakthrough came in the 1080s. In **1081** the Byzantine emperor Alexius Comnenus, himself endangered by Norman expansion, appealed to Venice for aid. The result was a series of naval battles costing thousands of lives, at the end of which Venice had strengthened its shipping lanes, established itself as the protector of the Eastern Empire's seaboard, and earned invaluable commercial rights for its traders. In a charter of 1082, known as the Crisobolo (Golden Bull), the emperor declared Venetian merchants to be exempt from all tolls and taxes within his lands. In the words of one historian – "On that day Venetian world trade began".

Venice and the Crusades

In 1095 Pope Urban II called for a Christian army to wrest the Holy Land from the Muslims, and within four years Jerusalem had been retaken by the **First Crusade**. Decades of chaos ensued, which the Venetians, typically, managed to turn to their commercial advantage. Offering to transport armies and supplies to the East in return for grants of property and financial bonuses, Venice extended its foothold in the Aegean, the Black Sea and Syria, battling all the time (sometimes literally) against its two chief maritime rivals in Italy – Pisa and Genoa. While it was consolidating its overseas bases, Venice was also embroiled in the political manoeuvrings between the papacy, the Western Emperor and the cities of northern Italy, the conclusion of which was one of Venice's greatest diplomatic successes: **the reconciliation of Emperor Frederick Barbarossa and Pope Alexander III** in 1177, in Venice.

Now a major European power, Venice was about to acquire an empire. In November 1199 Count Tibald of Champagne proposed a **Fourth Crusade** to regain Jerusalem, which twelve years earlier had fallen to Saladin. It came about that Venice was commissioned, for a huge fee, to provide the ships for the army. In 1202 the forces gathered in Venice, only to find that they couldn't raise the agreed sum. In the negotiations that followed, the doge obtained a promise from the French commanders that the Crusade would stop off to reconquer the colony of Zara, recently captured from Venice by the King of Hungary. No sooner was that accomplished than the expedition was diverted, after Venetian persuasion, to Constantinople, where the succession to the Imperial throne was causing problems. The eventual upshot was the **Sack of Constantinople in 1204**, one of the most disgusting episodes in European history. Thousands were massacred by the Christian soldiers and virtually every precious object that could be lifted was stolen from the city, mainly by the Venetians. So vast was the scale of the destruction and murder that a contemporary historian regretted that the city had not fallen instead to the Infidel. Ultimately its consequences were disastrous – not only did no help reach the forces in the Holy Land, but the Eastern Empire was fatally divided between the native Greeks and the barbaric Westerners. The Ottoman conquest of Constantinople in 1453, and the consequent peril of Western Europe,

were distant but direct results of the Fourth Crusade. Venice got what it wanted, though – "one quarter and half a quarter" of the Roman Empire was now under its sway, with an almost uninterrupted chain of ports stretching from the lagoon to the Black Sea.

The Genoese Wars

The enmities created within the Eastern Empire by the Fourth Crusade were soon to rebound on Venice. The Genoese were now the main opposition in the eastern markets, maintaining a rivalry so violent that some Venetian historians refer to their succession of conflicts as the **Five Genoese Wars**. Genoa's hatred of Venice led to an alliance with the dethroned Byzantine dynasty, whose loathing of the Venetians was no less intense; within months of the Pact of Ninfeo (1261), **Michael Palaeologus VIII** was installed as emperor in Constantinople. Venice now faced a struggle to hold onto its commercial interests against the favoured Genoese.

For the rest of the century, and almost all the fourteenth century, the defeat of Genoa was the primary aim of Venice's rulers. Both sides suffered terrible defeats: at the battle of **Curzola** (1298) 65 ships out of a Venetian fleet of 95 were lost, and 5000 Venetians taken captive; at the Sardinian port of **Alghero** (1353) the Genoese navy lost a similar proportion of its vessels. The climax came with the Fourth War of Genoa, better known as the **War of Chioggia**. Following a victory over the Venetians at Zara in 1379, the Genoese fleet sailed on to Venice, supported by the Paduans and the Austrians, and quickly took Chioggia. This was the zenith of Genoa's power – in August **1380** the invaders were driven off, and although the treaty signed between the two cities seemed inconclusive, within a few decades it was clear that Venice had at last won the battle for economic and political supremacy.

Political upheaval

It was during the Genoese campaigns that the **constitution** of Venice arrived at a state that was to endure until the fall of the Republic, the most significant step in this evolution being the **Serrata del Maggior Consiglio of 1297**, a measure which basically allowed a role in the government of the city only to those families already involved in it. (See the "Palazzo Ducale" entry, p.404.) Not surprisingly, many of those disenfranchised by the Serrata resented its instigator, **Doge Pietro Gradenigo**, and when Venice lost its tussle with the papacy for possession of Ferrara in 1309, it seemed that Gradenigo had scarcely a single supporter in the city. Yet the insurrection that came the following year was a revolt of a patrician clique, not an uprising of the people; its leader – **Bajamonte Tiepolo** – had personal reasons for opposing the doge and appears to have wanted to replace the new system not with a more democratic one but with a despotic regime headed by himself. Tiepolo's private army was routed in a battle in the centre of the city, but his rebellion had a permanent effect upon the history of Venice, in that it led to the creation in 1310 of the **Council of Ten**, a committee empowered to supervise matters of internal security. Though the Council was intended to be an emergency measure, its tenure was repeatedly extended until, in 1334, it was made a permanent institution.

The most celebrated attempt to subvert the Venetian government followed a few years later, in **1355**, and this time the malefactor was the doge himself – **Marin Falier**, who ironically had played a large part in the sentencing of Bajamonte Tiepolo. Falier's plot to overthrow the councils of Venice and install himself as absolute ruler seems to have been prompted by his fury at the lenient treatment given to a young nobleman who had insulted him. Exploiting the grievances felt against certain noble families by, among others, the director of the Arsenale, Falier gathered together a group of conspirators, many of whom were drawn from the working class, a section of Venetian society that was particularly affected by the economic demands of the rivalry with Genoa. (Open war had recently broken out again after a long but tense period of truce, and to make the situation worse, the **Black Death of 1348–49** had killed around 60 percent of the city's population.) Details of the planned coup leaked out, Falier was arrested, and on April 17, eight months after becoming doge, he was beheaded on the steps of the Palazzo Ducale.

Terra firma expansion

The sea lanes of the eastern Mediterranean were the foundation of Venice's wealth, but its dominance as a trading centre clearly depended on free access to the rivers and mountain passes of northern Italy. Thus, although Venetian foreign policy was predominantly eastward-looking from the start, a degree of intervention on the mainland was inevitable, especially with the rise in the fourteenth century of ambitious dynasties such as the **Scaligeri** in Verona and the **Visconti** in Milan. Equally inevitable was the shift from a strategy to preserve Venice's commercial interests, to a scheme that was blatantly imperialistic.

The unsuccessful battle for Ferrara was Venice's first territorial campaign; the first victory came thirty years later, when the combined forces of Venice, Florence and a league of Lombard cities defeated the Scaligeri, allowing Venice to incorporate **Castelfranco**, **Conegliano**, **Sacile**, **Oderzo** and, most importantly, **Treviso** into the domain of the Republic. Having thus made safe the roads to Germany, the Venetians set about securing the territory to the west. The political and military machinations of northern Italy in this period are extremely complicated, with alliances regularly made and betrayed, and cities changing hands with bewildering frequency – Treviso, for example, was lost and won back before the close of the fourteenth century. The bare outline of the story is that by **1405** Venice had eradicated the most powerful neighbouring dynasty, the **Carrara** family of Padua, and had a firm hold on **Bassano**, **Belluno**, **Feltre**, **Vicenza**, **Verona** and **Padua** itself. The annexation in **1420** of the **Friuli** and **Udine**, formerly ruled by the King of Hungary, virtually doubled the area of the terra firma under Venetian control, and brought the border of the empire right up to the Alps.

Many Venetians thought that any further expansion would be foolish. Certainly this was the view of **Doge Tommaso Mocenigo**, who on his deathbed urged his compatriots to "refrain . . . from taking what belongs to others or making unjust wars". Specifically, he warned them against the ambitions of **Francesco Fóscari** – "If he becomes doge, you will be constantly at war . . . you will become the slaves of your masters-at-arms and their captains". Within a fortnight of Mocenigo's funeral in 1423, Fóscari was elected as his successor, and Venice was soon on the offensive against the mightiest prince of northern Italy – **Filippo Maria Visconti** of Milan. In the first phase of the campaign nothing except a tenuous ownership of Bergamo and Brescia was gained, a failure for which the Venetian mercenary captain, **Carmagnola**, served as the scapegoat. He was executed in 1432 for treason, and his place taken by Erasmo da Narni, better known as **Il Gattamelata**. The **Treaty of Cremona** (1441) confirmed Venetian control of **Peschiera**, **Brescia**, **Bergamo** and part of the territory of **Cremona**, and by now **Ravenna** was also officially part of the Venetian dominion, but still the fighting did not stop. Peace on the mainland finally came in **1454**, with the signing of a treaty between Venice and the new ruler of Milan, **Francesco Sforza**, Venice's erstwhile ally against the Visconti. Ravenna didn't stay Venetian for long; the rest of its mainland empire, though, remained intact until the coming of Napoleon.

The Turkish threat

The other Italian states might have taken concerted action against Venice had it not been for the fact that the entire peninsula now faced the common threat of the Ottoman Turks, as was acknowledged in the pact drawn up at **Lodi** later in 1454 between Venice, Milan, Naples, Florence and the Papal States. Open conflict between Venice and the Turks had broken out early in the century – the Republic winning the naval battle of Gallipoli in 1416 – but the policy of terra firma expansion kept the majority of Venice's warships on the rivers of the north, so reliance had to be placed in diplomatic measures to contain the Turkish advance. They were ineffective. Reports of a Turkish military build-up under the command of the young **Sultan Mahomet II** were not treated with the necessary urgency, and the consequence was that Western troops sent to defend **Constantinople** against the Sultan's army were insufficient to prevent the fall of the city in **1453**.

The trade agreement which the Venetians managed to negotiate with the Sultan could not arrest the erosion of its commercial empire in the East. The Turkish fleets penetrated into the northern Aegean and many times in the last years of the century the Turkish cavalry came so close to Venice that the fires from the villages it destroyed could be seen from the top of the Campanile of San Marco. In 1479 Venice was forced to sign away the vital port of **Negroponte** and a batch of other Aegean islands; the defeat of the Venetian navy at **Sapienza** in 1499 led to the loss of the main fortresses of the **Morea** (Peloponnese), which meant that the Turks now controlled the so-called "door to the Adriatic". Virtually the only bright spot in all the gloom came about through the marriage of the Venetian **Caterina Cornaro** to

the King of **Cyprus** in 1468. In 1473 the king died, and the ensuing political pressure on the widow paid off in **1489**, when Caterina handed over the island to the government of Venice.

The sixteenth century

In **1494** Italy was invaded by **Louis XII of France**, an intervention which Venice lost no time in exploiting. By playing the various territorial contenders off against each other (mainly France and the Habsburgs), Venice succeeded in adding bits and pieces to the terra firma empire, and in 1503 signed a disadvantageous treaty with the Turks so as to be able to concentrate its resources on the mainland. Given the accumulated hostility to Venice, it was a dangerous game, and when the Republic began to encroach on the papal domain in Romagna, it at last provoked a unified response from its opponents. The **League of Cambrai**, formed in **1508** with Pope Julius II, Louis XII, Emperor Maximilian and the King of Spain at its head, pitted almost every power in Europe against the Venetians, in a pact that explicitly declared its intention of destroying Venice's empire as a prelude to conquering the Turks.

The ensuing war began calamitously for Venice – its army was crushed by the French at **Agnadello**, city after city defected to the League, and Venice prepared for a siege. The siege never came, and in the end the conflicting interests of the League enabled the Venetians, through subtle diplomacy, to repossess nearly everything they had held at the start of the war. Nonetheless, when the fighting finished in **1516** many of the cities of the Veneto had been sacked, great swathes of the countryside ruined, and the Venetian treasury bled almost dry.

Worse was to come. Clearly **the discovery of the New World** was going to have significant repercussions for Venice, but the most catastrophic of the voyages of discovery from Venice's point of view was that of **Vasco da Gama**. In September **1499**, da Gama arrived back in Lisbon having reached India by the Cape of Good Hope. The slow and expensive land routes across Asia to the markets and docks of Venice could now be bypassed by the merchants of northern Europe – from the moment of da Gama's return, the economic balance of Europe began to tilt in favour of the Portuguese, the English and the Dutch.

In **1519**, with the accession of the 19-year-old **Charles V**, the Habsburg Empire absorbed the massive territories of the Spanish kingdom, and after the **sack of Rome in 1527** the whole Italian peninsula, with the sole exception of Venice, was under the young emperor's domination. Meanwhile, the **Turks** were on the move again – **Syria** and **Egypt** had been taken in **1517**; **Rhodes** had fallen to **Suleiman the Magnificent** in **1522**; and by 1529 the Ottoman Empire had spread right along the southern Mediterranean to Morocco. To survive, Venice had to steer a path between these two empires and France, the other superpower of the period. It did survive, but at a cost. When a combined Christian fleet took on the Turks at **Prevesa** in **1538**, the supreme commander, acting under Charles V's instructions, was so concerned to prevent the Venetians profiting from an allied victory that his tactics ensured a Turkish victory; the Venetians were obliged to accept a punitive treaty shortly after. Even the great allied success at **Lépanto** in **1571** didn't work to Venice's advantage, as the Habsburg commander of the fleet, Don John of Austria, refused to consolidate the Venetian position by sailing east after the victory. In the subsequent negotiations, Venice was forced formally to surrender **Cyprus**, whose brutal capture by the Turks had been the reason for the allied offensive in the first place.

The seventeenth century

Relations between Rome and Venice were always fractious. Venice's expansion on the mainland was a source of irritation, especially when it turned its attention to areas over which the Vatican claimed sovereignty, but papal animosity was also caused by the restrictions imposed on the pope's authority within the Republic's boundaries, restrictions which led to Venice's being regarded in some quarters as a crypto-Protestant state. The pope was Venice's spiritual overlord, the Venetians agreed, but the doge and his officers were the masters in temporal affairs. The problem for the papacy was that the doge's notion of what constituted temporal affairs was far too broad, and at the start of the seventeenth century **Pope Paul V** and the Republic came to a head-on clash.

Two incidents provoked the row: Venice's insistence that the pope should routinely approve its candidate for the office of Patriarch; and its deter-

mination not to hand over to papal jurisdiction two clerics it had decided to prosecute. Matters came to a head with the **Papal Interdict of 1606** and the excommunication of the whole city. Venice's resistance, orchestrated by the scholar-priest **Paolo Sarpi**, was fierce – the Jesuits were expelled, priests within Venetian territory ordered to continue in their duties, and pamphlets printed putting the Venetian case. One year later the Interdict was lifted, damaging the prestige of the papacy throughout Europe.

No sooner was the Interdict out of the way than the Spanish and Austrian **Habsburgs** entered the fray again. The Austrian branch was the first to cause trouble, by encouraging the piratical raids of the **Uskoks**, a loosely defined and regularly obstreperous community living along the Dalmatian coast. Venice took retaliatory action, Archduke Ferdinand objected, and a half-hearted war dragged on until **1617**, when, under the peace terms, the benighted Uskoks were removed completely from their sea-ports.

The Spanish wing was more devious, attempting, in **1618**, to subvert the Venetian state with a wildly ambitious scheme that has always been known as **The Spanish Conspiracy**. Masterminded by the Spanish Viceroy of Naples, the **Duke of Osuna**, and the Spanish ambassador to Venice, the **Duke of Bedmar**, the plot involved smuggling a Spanish army into the city in disguised groups of two or three, and then inciting a mutiny among a contingent of Dutch mercenaries already lodged there. Just how convoluted the conspiracy was can be gathered from the fact that its betrayal resulted in the execution of around 300 people.

And then, after half a century of ceasefire, the **Turks** renewed their harassment of the Venetian colonies, concentrating their attention now on the one remaining stronghold in the eastern Mediterranean, **Crete**. The campaign lasted for 25 years, ending in **1669** with the inevitable fall of the island. Even then the war with the Turks was not over – in **1699**, under the military command of **Doge Francesco Morosini**, the Venetians embarked on a retaliatory action in the **Morea** (Peloponnese), and succeeded in retaking the islands. By 1715, however, all the gains had been turned to losses once more, and in the **Treaty of Passarowitz** in **1718** Venice was forced to accept a definition of its Mediterranean empire drawn up by the Austrians and the Turks. It was left with just the Ionian islands and the

Dalmatian coast, and its power in these colonies was little more than hypothetical.

Collapse

Venice in the eighteenth century became a political nonentity, pursuing a foreign policy of unarmed neutrality of which one historian wrote "she sacrifices everything with the single object of giving no offence to other states". When the **Treaty of Aix-la-Chapelle** in **1748** confirmed Austrian control of the neighbouring areas of the mainland, the Venetians felt compelled to send ambassadors to the Austrian court in a humiliating attempt to wheedle guarantees of their possessions on the terra firma. At home, the economy remained strong, but the division between the upper stratum of the aristocracy and the ever-increasing poorer section was widening, and all attempts to dampen discontent within the city by democratizing its government were stifled by the conservative elite.

Politically trivial and constitutionally ossified, Venice was now renowned not as one of the great powers of Europe, but rather as its playground. Hester Thrale observed in 1789 that no other place was "so subservient to the purposes of pleasure", and William Beckford recorded the effects of a life spent between the ballroom and casino – "Their nerves unstrung by disease and the consequence of early debaucheries, allow no natural flow of lively spirits . . . they pass their lives in one perpetual doze."

The conflict between Austria and post-revolutionary France quickly brought about the end of the Venetian Republic. Having mollified the Austrians by handing over the Veneto to them, **Napoleon** waited for a pretext to polish off the Republic itself. On April 20, 1797, the Venetians duly provided him with one, by attacking a French naval patrol off the Lido. "I will have no more Inquisitors. I will have no more Senate; I shall be an Attila to the state of Venice," Bonaparte proclaimed; war was declared on Venice, and on May 9 an ultimatum was sent to the city's government, demanding the dissolution of its constitution.

On Friday, **May 12, 1797**, the Maggior Consiglio met for the last time. By 512 votes to 20, with 5 abstentions, the Council voted to accede to every one of Napoleon's demands; the vote cast, the last Doge of Venice, **Lodovico Manin**, handed to his valet the linen cap worn beneath the ducal crown, saying – "Take it, I shall not be needing it again." The Venetian Republic was dead.

Within days a provisional democratic council had been formed and there were French troops in the city, many of them occupied with wrecking the Arsenale or stripping the place of its art treasures and shipping them off to Paris. On this occasion, the French didn't stay long, because in the **Treaty of Campo Formio**, signed in October, Napoleon relinquished Venice to the Austrians. They were soon back, though – in **1805** Napoleon joined the city to his Kingdom of Italy, and it stayed under French domination until the aftermath of Waterloo, ten years later. It then passed back to the Austrians again, and remained a Habsburg province for the next half-century, the only break in Austrian rule coming with the **revolt of March 1848**, when the city was reinstituted as a republic under the leadership of **Daniele Manin**, the last heroic figure in Venetian history. The rebellion lasted until **August 1849**, when a combination of starvation, disease and relentless bombardment forced the Venetians to surrender. Liberation finally arrived in the wake of Prussia's defeat of the Austrians at Sadowa in **1866**. Soon after, Venice was absorbed into the Kingdom of United Italy.

To the present

In many respects the Austrians were better for Venice than the French had been. Although the French initiated modernization schemes such as the creation of public gardens and the cemetery of San Michele, not all of the fifty or so religious buildings and forty palaces that they demolished were destroyed in a good cause; in addition to which, they also wrecked the shipyards and confiscated hundreds of works of art. The Austrians' urban improvements were less ruthless: they filled in some of the more unhygienic canals (the origin of the rio terrà), built a rail link with the mainland, and undertook two major, albeit controversial, restoration projects – the Fondaco dei Turchi and the church of Santi Maria e Donato on Murano.

Yet Venice went through most of the nineteenth century in a state of destitution. There were no more government jobs to provide a source of income, and Trieste was the Austrians' preferred port on the Adriatic. By 1820 begging was the main means of support for about one quarter of its population. Families that had once been among the city's wealthiest were obliged to sell their most treasured possessions: the Barbarigo family sold seventeen paintings by Titian to the Tsar, for example. Later in the century, even the churches were selling their property to pay for their upkeep. It's been calculated that of the moveable works of art that were to be found in Venice at the fall of the Republic, only four percent remains.

Manufacturing activity within the city revived towards the end of the nineteenth century: there were flour mills on Giudecca, glass factories on Murano, lace workshops on Burano. The opening of the Suez Canal in 1869 brought a muted revival to the Arsenale docks. Already, though, **tourism** had emerged as the main area of economic expansion, with the development of the **Lido** as Europe's most fashionable resort. It was the need for a more substantial economic base than bathing huts, hotels and a few pockets of industrial production that led, in the wake of World War I, to the development of the industrial complex on the marshland across the lagoon from Venice, at **Porto Marghera**.

As recently as 1913 the Baedeker guide could describe Venice as a "shipbuilding, cotton spinning and iron working centre", but by the end of World War I Venice was finished as a maritime centre. Battleships had been built in the Arsenale, but the proximity of enemy forces persuaded the navy to dismantle the docks in 1917 and switch its yards to Genoa and Naples. The new port of Marghera was not a shipyard but a processing and refining centre to which raw materials would be brought by sea. In 1933 a **road link** was built to carry the workforce between Venice and the steadily expanding port, whose progress was of special concern to Mussolini's government. (Venice was the second city in Italy in which organized Fascism appeared; as early as 1919 the local newspaper published an appeal for the formation of Fascist squads.) After World War II (from which Venice emerged undamaged) Marghera's growth accelerated even more rapidly. The consequences were not those that had been predicted.

What happened was that the factory workers of Marghera, instead of commuting each day from Venice, simply decamped to the mainland. Housing in Marghera's neighbour, **Mestre**, is drier, roomier, warmer and cheaper to maintain than the apartments in Venice, and as a result

the population of Mestre-Marghera is today more than three times that of the historic centre of Venice, which is now around the 70,000 mark and falling by around 1500 with each passing year. (Immediately after the last war it was around 170,000.) Apart from polluting the environment of the lagoon, Mestre has siphoned so many people of working age from the islands that the average age of Venice's population (44) is now the highest of any major European city. Moreover, the percentage of native Venetians in the city is declining as the place becomes a favourite second base or retirement home for the wealthy of Milan, Turin and other more prosperous Italian cities – only the wealthy can afford to maintain the fragile fabric of many of the city's houses, most of which are listed as historic monuments. When a flat is sold in Venice, the odds are now around 2/1 that the buyer will not be a Venetian.

Venice's future?

No city has suffered more from the tourist industry than Venice. Nearly fifteen million tourists invade the city each year, with a daily average of around 80,000 in high season (on so-called "Black Sunday", July 15, 1989, the figure hit 150,000) – and half of those don't even stay a night. It costs in excess of 18 billion lire to clear up all the litter the visitors leave behind. Only 8 plumbers are registered in Venice, while the number of souvenir shops has risen to around 400.

Yet Venice at the moment is dependent on tourism, which generates almost 70 percent of the city's income, and every year proposals are put forward to break that dependency. A science park, a national library, a conservation and marine technology centre, a national institute for restoration research – all have been suggested as projects that could give Venice a more active role in the life of twentieth-century Italy. Some dismiss such ideas as mere gestures, and prefer to see the political shifts in Eastern Europe as the harbingers of Venice's revival. Should political realignment lead to the development of a market economy in these countries, Venice will once again be sitting on a major European trade route – or so the argument ran, until the wars in former Yugoslavia placed Italy's immediate neighbours in a rather different perspective.

Perhaps the craziest scheme for the renewal of Venice was the proposal that it should be the venue for **Expo 2000**, the trade jamboree that ushered in the new millennium. The project envisaged the drainage of a large part of the lagoon to build the Expo site, and it was anticipated that 45 million people would come to the city over the four months of the show – in other words, four times the city's population daily. Despite the evident idiocy of the idea, it was vociferously championed by Venice-born Gianni de Michelis, then Foreign Minister and, quite coincidentally, owner of a lot of property in the city, where he is known unaffectionately as "The Doge". By a combination of blatant threats and bribery, de Michelis and his brother secured the backing of a majority among the 43 member states of the Bureau International des Expositions, and it seemed that the BIE's meeting in June 1990 would be nothing more than a formal ratification of Venice's disastrous application.

But the forces of reason were making themselves heard in the upper reaches of the Italian government. Environmentalists from all over the world lobbied the Italians to reconsider, and the upper house of the Italian parliament passed a motion deploring the scheme – as did the European Parliament, by 195 to 14. The near-unanimity of this latter vote was decisive. Two days before the BIE meeting the Italian government cancelled the city's application.

Mr de Michelis's career has followed a sharp downward trajectory since the rejection of his pet project. In the latter half of 1992 a huge scandal broke in Venice. It was alleged that the de Michelis faction of the Socialist party and their Christian Democrat allies had shared out bribes from major civil contractors, splitting the kickbacks on a percentage related directly to the parties' representation on the city council. Known as a "**theorem**", this system of wealth redistribution had been unearthed a few months earlier in Milan, where it had destroyed the Socialists' reputation for honesty and wrecked the career of the party's former Mr Fixit, Bettino Craxi. The Venetian scandal, said to have involved some £7 billion worth of contracts, has done the same to Gianni de Michelis – in 1995 he received a suspended four-year prison sentence, which now has been set aside.

It's quite possible that much of the money for the lagoon barrier (see p.425) has found its way into the bank accounts of various politicians. It remains to be seen whether corruption or sound sense will wreck one spectacularly crack-brained

idea about how to propel Venice into the twenty-first century. In 1992 Venice was granted metropolitan status, which enabled the town council to apply for central funding for an **urban rail system**. It has seriously been proposed that an underground train line be excavated to link central Venice and the islands of San Giorgio Maggiore, Giudecca, the Lido, San Michele and Murano to the mainland rail network at Marco Polo airport and Mestre. Apologists for the metro project insist that it will enable those of the city's inhabitants who work on the mainland to get quickly to their desks and back home again. Its opponents, led by the conservation group Italia Nostra, argue that the enthusiasm of the politicians for the train plan had a lot to do with the 700 billion lire set aside for its development, some of which would doubtless percolate into the corridors of the town hall. What's more, they say, the metro will increase the tourist deluge of Venice and undermine the delicate substructures of the city's buildings.

There are plans to deal with the tourism problem by building a massive coach park on the mainland, and it's been proposed that the Arsenale might become a sort of processing centre for tourists, in which the daily inundation will be briefed on the city's attractions (and allocated accommodation if necessary) before being sent on their way. There's even been talk of Venice as a Winter Olympics host, with the events being staged up in the Dolomites at Cortina d'Ampezzo, where the Games were held back in 1956 – though it's not clear quite how Venice would gain from its involvement in an event that doesn't exactly ignite global interest.

Though too many of Venice's politicians seem enamoured of such high-profile schemes, more modest and sensible ideas do occasionally emerge. Some have proposed that efforts should be concentrated on furthering the city's reputation for crafts and restoration work – a good idea, but one that received a setback when the European Centre for the Training of Craftspeople was not permitted to extend its occupancy of the island of San Servolo. Others see the advent of the Internet and global information technologies as offering an opportunity for Venice to redeem itself economically. One person who has championed this notion, and consistently propounded a clear vision of how Venice might find a role for itself in the twenty-first century, is **Massimo Cacciari**, who was mayor of the city from 1993 to

2000. Taking time out from his career as professor of philosophy at the University of Venice, Cacciari rapidly became a hugely respected politician, both for his energetic commitment and his incorruptibility – when Gianni de Michelis invited him to join his socialist party, Cacciari fended him off with the words "No thanks, I already come from a wealthy family". As he sees it, Venice's best hope lies in its being classified as an area of special economic need by the European Union, which would give it access to funds for major infrastucture repairs and improvements, such as the laying of fibre-optic cables in tandem with the dredging of canals. To complement this strategy, hi-tech companies could also be given tax incentives to open offices in Venice, a location which has plenty of very desirable and unoc-cupied real estate to offer potential investors. In an attempt to tackle the enduring problem of depopulation, Cacciari tried to get the municipality and conservation groups to apply themselves to the restoration of old houses rather than old churches and other such monuments, so that the historic centre could provide housing at prices comparable with those in Mestre. As Cacciari pointed out, no project for Venice's future has any chance of succeeding if there are no young Venetians living there. Cacciari commanded broad support on the city council, but he is no longer at the helm and Venice is a city of considerable political inertia, where urgent measures typically take years to initiate, and often fizzle away into half-measures. Inertia could be fatal this time.

Venetian painting and sculpture

After just a day in Venice you notice that the light is softer than that on the mainland and changes more during the course of a day. Reflecting off the water and the white stone facades, it gives shifting impressions of places that would otherwise be shadowed, and adds shimmering highlights to solid brickwork. In view of the specific qualities of Venetian light, it's scarcely surprising that the city's painters emphasized colour and texture rather than structure and perspective. The political and social peculiarities of Venice were equally influential on the development of its art, as will become apparent in the following thumbnail account.

Byzantine Venice

The close political and commercial ties between the early Venetian state and the Byzantine Empire (see the "History" section) led to a steady exchange of works of art between the two, and to the creation of the most important work of art from that period – the **Pala d'Oro** on the high altar of San Marco. Begun as a collaboration between Venetian and Byzantine craftsmen, it epitomizes the Venetian taste for elaborate decoration and creates the impression of a complex content unified by a dazzlingly rich surface. The

Pala was later expanded with panels stolen from Constantinople during the sack of 1204, a wholesale plundering which provided Venice with a hoard of artefacts that was to nourish its craftsmen and artists for centuries.

It is notable that the earliest Venetian painter of renown, **Paolo Veneziano** (working from the 1330s to at least 1358), shows far stronger affinities with Byzantine work than with the frescoes created by Giotto at the start of the century in nearby Padua. He generally employs a flat, gold background and symmetrical arrangements of symbolic figures, rather than attempting a more emotional representation of individuals. Two paintings in the Accademia show these characteristics: a *Madonna and Child Enthroned* and a polyptych that achieves the same overall effect as that of the Pala d'Oro – and indeed it was he who was commissioned to paint the **cover of the Pala d'Oro**, now in San Marco's museum. A work believed to be by Paolo Veneziano has recently been revealed during restoration of an altarpiece in the church of San Zaccaria.

The first room of the Accademia is full of work displaying this indebtedness to Byzantine art, and Byzantium remained a living influence in the city up to the seventeenth and eighteenth centuries, sustained in part by the influx of refugees following the **fall of Constantinople** in 1453. The neo-Byzantine *Madoneri* (the main school of the Greek community) are represented in the **Museo Dipinti Sacri Bizantini**, where the paintings show a complete indifference to the post-Renaissance cult of the artist and to notions of aesthetic novelty. The young Cretan **El Greco** (1545–1614) worked with the *Madoneri* for a while, before setting out for fame and fortune in Spain.

Gothic painting and sculpture

Deemed to be relics of a barbaric age, a huge number of Gothic paintings and sculptures were destroyed in the seventeenth and eighteenth centuries. The reinstatement of the Gothic is in large part due to the determination of John

Ruskin, whose preoccupation was the Gothic architecture and sculpture of Venice. His meticulous work on **Santi Giovanni e Paolo** (San Zanipolo), mapping the change from Gothic to Renaissance through a study of the **funerary sculpture**, is still a useful analysis.

Santi Giovanni e Paolo's main apse contains the **tomb of Doge Michele Morosini** (d. 1382), described by Ruskin as "the richest monument of the Gothic period in Venice", although its figures (apart from those at the head and foot of the doge) have an awkward, un-Gothic stiffness. More interesting sculpturally is the **tomb of Doge Marco Corner** (d. 1368) opposite, which was carved in the workshop of the non-Venetian **Nino Pisano**. Slightly later is San Marco's **rood screen**, by the two brothers **Pierpaolo and Jacobello Dalle Masegne**, who made a study of the work of Pisano and northern European Gothic sculpture. The other high points of Gothic sculpture in Venice are also architecturally related – the **Palazzo Ducale's capitals**, **corner sculptures** and **Porta della Carta** (though the main figures on the Porta are nineteenth-century replicas of fifteenth-century originals).

Paolo Veneziano's unrelated namesake, **Lorenzo Veneziano** (working 1356–72) marries a distinctly Gothic element to the Byzantine elements in Venetian painting. The large polyptych in the Accademia is a fine example of his work, showing a roundedness in the face and hands and in the fall of the drapery, and a sinuousness of pose in the figures that suggests the influence of Gothic painters such as Simone Martini of Siena.

Around 1409 **Gentile de Fabriano**, the exemplar of the style known as **International Gothic**, frescoed parts of the Palazzo Ducale with the help of his pupil **Pisanello**. These frescoes are all now destroyed, and the nearest example of Pisanello's work is his *St George* (1438–42) in Verona's church of Sant'Anastasia. Even in this one piece it's possible to see what the Venetians would have found congenial in his art: chiefly an all-over patterning that ties the content of the painting to the picture plane and eschews the illusion of receding space.

The work of Gentile and Pisanello was most closely studied in Venice by **Michele Giambono** (working 1420–62), represented in the Accademia by a *Coronation of the Madonna in Paradise* (1447) and in the church of San Trovaso by *St Chrysogonus* (c.1450). These claustrophobic paintings are of the same date as Padua's frescoes by Mantegna and sculptures by Donatello – Giambono and others in Venice were happily working in a sophisticated high Gothic style at a time when the Renaissance was elsewhere into its maturity.

Early Renaissance painting

Petrarch, who lived in Venice in the 1360s, described the Republic as "a world apart", and nothing illustrates this insularity better than the reception of Renaissance ideas in the city. Venetians were chary of overemphasizing the individual, a tendency implicit in the one-point perspective of Renaissance painting; in addition, the use of abstract mathematical formulas in the depiction of form was alien to the pragmatic Venetian temperament. When the principles of the Florentine Renaissance did belatedly filter into the art of Venice, they were transformed into a way of seeing that was uniquely Venetian.

Key figures in this period of absorption were the **Vivarini** family – **Antonio** (c.1419–c.1480), his brother **Bartolomeo** (c.1430–c.1491) and son **Alvise** (c.1445–1505). Antonio's work, though still part of the Gothic tradition, marks a shift away from it, with his more angular line and construction of pictorial spaces consistent with the rules of one-point perspective – as in the *Madonna and Child* triptych in the Accademia, painted in collaboration with Giovanni d'Alemagna. A more humanistic temperament is embodied in the paintings of **Alvise**, manifested less through his depiction of space than through his representation of people. He individualizes his figures, giving an emotional charge to narratives which had to that point functioned symbolically. The *St Clare* in the Accademia is an excellent example of his work, establishing an unprecedentedly intimate contact between the saint and the viewer.

The pre-eminent artistic dynasty of this transitional period was that of **Jacopo Bellini** (c.1400–70), once a pupil of Gentile da Fabriano, and his sons **Gentile** (c.1429–1507) and **Giovanni** (c.1430–1516). Jacopo suffered from the anti-Gothic zealotry of later years, and his two major cycles of paintings – at the Scuola di San Marco and the Scuola di San Giovanni Evangelista – were destroyed. From descriptions of these works, it would appear that the two Madonnas in the Accademia are rather restrained in their decoration; other pieces by him can be seen in the Museo Correr.

Giovanni is the one that people mean when they refer simply to "Bellini". In the Accademia he's represented by a number of Madonnas, a series of allegorical panels and a couple of large altarpieces. Other works around Venice include altarpieces in San Zaccaria, San Pietro (Murano), the Frari, Madonna dell'Orto and San Zanipolo. In the majority of these paintings the attention is concentrated on the foreground, where the arrangement of the figures or a device such as a screen or throne turns the background into another plane parallel to the surface, rather than a receding landscape. That this was a conscious choice which had nothing to do with his perspectival skills is demonstrated by the **San Giobbe altarpiece** (in the Accademia), in which a meticulously worked-out illusionistic space would have suggested the presence of an extra chapel. A fundamental humanism pervades much of Giovanni's output – although his Madonnas show an idealized version of motherhood, each possesses an immediacy which suggests to the viewer that this ideal could be attainable.

Meanwhile, **Gentile** was pursuing a form of painting that was also a specifically Venetian Renaissance phenomenon – the *istoria* or narrative painting cycle. At least ten of these were commissioned by public bodies between around 1475 and 1525: the three remaining cycles in Venice are the *Miracles of the Relic of the True Cross* (Accademia), by five artists including Gentile and **Carpaccio**, and the *St Ursula* cycle (Accademia) and the *St George and St Jerome* cycle (Scuola di San Giorgio degli Schiavoni), which are both by Carpaccio. To the modern observer the story line of the *Relic* and *St Ursula* cycles in particular can seem to be naive pretexts for precise renditions of the pageant of Venetian social life and a wealth of domestic minutiae. The details of the paintings were not mere incidentals to the narrative, however – a person hanging out washing or mending a roof would have been perceived as an enhancement of the physical reality of the miracle, and not as a distraction from the central event.

High Renaissance painting

While these narrative cycles were being produced Giovanni Bellini was beginning to experiment with oil paint, which was soon to displace tempera (pigment in egg yolk) as the preferred medium. Whereas tempera had to be applied in layers, the long drying time of oil allowed colours to be mixed and softened, while its thick consistency enabled artists to simulate the texture of the objects depicted. Close examination of later paintings by Bellini shows he used his fingers to merge colours and soften light, and two of his young assistants at the time – **Giorgione** and **Titian** – were to explore even further the potential of the new material, developing a specifically Venetian High Renaissance style.

Giorgione (1475–1510) seems custom-built for myth: little is known about him other than that he was tall and handsome and he died young (possibly of plague). The handful of enigmatic works he created were innovative in their imaginative self-sufficiency – for instance, the Venetian collector Michiel, writing in 1530, was unable to say precisely what the subject was of *The Tempest* (Accademia), perhaps Giorgione's most famous image. His only altarpiece, still in the cathedral at Castelfranco (his home town), isolates the Madonna and the two saints from each other by manipulating perspective and by placing the Madonna against a landscape while the attendant saints stand against a man-made background. Despite the serenity of the individual figures, the painting instils in the viewer a disquieting sense of elusiveness.

Given his long life and huge output, **Titian** (c.1485–1576) is very badly represented in his home town: a *Presentation in the Temple*, a *Pietà* left unfinished at his death, and a couple of minor works in the Accademia; a handful in the Salute; the *Assumption* and *Pésaro Altarpiece* in the Frari, and that's more or less it. (Napoleon made off with a good crop of Titians, including a *Venus* which he hung in his tent; the Louvre now has a fine collection.)

Titian, like Giorgione, used the qualities of oils to evoke a diffuse light and soften contours – in contrast with the contemporaneous art of Rome, the city of Michelangelo, where the emphasis was on the solidity and sculptural aspects of the objects depicted. Artists in Florence were answerable to an imperious ruling family, in Rome they had to comply with the wishes of successive popes, but Titian's success was so great that he could virtually pick and choose from a host of clients from all over the continent, and the diversity of works he produced – portraits, allegories, devotional paintings, mythologies – remains unsurpassed in Western art. His technical range is as impressive as the range of subject matter; the earliest works are highly polished and precisely drawn, but in the later pieces he tested the possibilities of oil paint to their limit, using his bare hands to scrape the canvas and add great gobbets of paint (see the Accademia *Pietà*).

Giorgionesque is an adjective used to describe a number of early sixteenth-century Venetian painters, in reference to the enrichment of colour popular at the time and to the increasingly oblique and suggestive approach to content. **Sebastiano del Piombo**, who studied under Giovanni Bellini with Titian and Giorgione, before moving to Rome in 1611, is one of the artists to whom the term is applied: his altarpiece of **San Giovanni Crisostomo** in the eponymous church is his best work still in Venice. Another is **Palma il Vecchio** (1480–1528); although he was often frivolous in a way that Giorgione and Titian rarely were – ponds of frothy nymphs and the like – his strongest work in Venice is a redoubtable *St Barbara* in Santa Maria Formosa. The most interesting painter of this period and type is **Lorenzo Lotto** (c.1480–1556), represented in the Accademia by the almost metaphysical *Portrait of a Young Man*. The rivalries of other painters eventually drove Lotto from Venice, and it's not too fanciful to see a reflection of the artist's anxieties in his restless, wistful paintings.

Born three years after Bellini's death and nine years after that of Giorgione, **Tintoretto** (1519–94) grew up during the period in which the ascendancy of Titian became established. Princes were sending agents to Venice to buy the latest Titian, no matter what the subject, and every visiting dignitary would want to be painted by him. Titian's exploratory attitude to paint and the increasing Venetian receptivity to individual style were both exploited by the energetic and competitive younger artist. The painting that made his reputation, the *Miracle of the Slave* (Accademia; 1548), shows how he learned from Titian's experiments and distanced himself from them. Tintoretto's palette is as rich as Titian's, but is aggressively vivid rather than sensuous, and uses far stronger lighting. And while Titian is concerned with the inner drama of an event, Tintoretto's attention is given to the drama of gesture.

Tintoretto's dynamic style was not universally acclaimed. Pietro Aretino, Titian's close friend and most vociferous champion, disparaged the speed and relative carelessness of Tintoretto's tech-

nique, and one member of the **Scuola di San Rocco** said he would give his money towards the decoration of the scuola's building as long as Tintoretto was not commissioned. He didn't get his way, and San Rocco's cycle is the most comprehensive collection of paintings by the artist. Dramatic perspectival effects, bizarre juxtapositions of images and extraordinarily fluid brushwork here make the substantial world seem otherworldly – the converse of the earlier *istorie* cycles.

In contrast, the art of **Paolo Veronese** (1528–88), who moved to Venice from Verona in his twenties, conveys worldly harmony rather than spiritual turbulence. This is particularly evident in his work for architectural settings (San Sebastiano in Venice and the Villa Barbaro at Masèr), where he constructed logical spaces that complement the form of the buildings. More urbane than Tintoretto, he nonetheless attracted controversy: in his *Christ in the House of Levi* (Accademia) the naturalistic representation of German soldiers was interpreted as a gesture of support for Protestantism. Veronese's response to his accusers revealed a lot about the changing attitude towards the status of the artist: claiming licence to depict what he wanted, he simply changed the title of the work from *The Last Supper* to the title by which it's now known.

Renaissance sculpture

Venetian **sculpture** in the Renaissance was conditioned by the society's ingrained aversion to the over-glorification of the individual and by the specific restrictions of the city's landscape. Freestanding monumental work of the sort that was being commissioned all over Italy is conspicuous by its absence. The exception to prove the rule, the **monument to Colleoni**, was made by the Florentine artist **Verrocchio**. Venetian sculptors worked mainly to decorate tombs or the walls of churches, and up to the late Renaissance no clear distinction was made between sculptors, masons and architects. Beyond the Renaissance, sculpture was generally commissioned as part of an architectural project, and it's usually futile to try to disentangle the sculpture from its architectural function.

Pietro Lombardo (c.1438–1515) was born in Cremona and went to Rome before arriving in Venice around 1460. His development can be charted in the church of San Zanipolo: his first major monument, the **tomb of Doge Pasquale Malipiero**, is pictorially flat and smothered with carved decoration, but the **monument to Doge Pietro Mocenigo**, with its classicized architectural elements and figures, is a fully Renaissance piece. In true Venetian style the latter glorifies the State through the man, rather than stressing his individual salvation – the image of Christ is easily overlooked. Pietro's sons **Antonio** (c.1458–c.1516) and **Tullio** (c.1460–1532) were also sculptors and assisted him on the Mocenigo monument. Tullio's independent work is less pictorial: his **monument to Doge Andrea Vendramin** (also in San Zanipolo) is a complex architectural evocation of a Roman triumphal arch, though again the whole is encrusted with decorative figures.

Jacopo Sansovino, who went on to become the Republic's principal architect, was known as a sculptor when he arrived in Venice from Rome in 1527. More of a classicist than his predecessors, he nonetheless produced work remarkably in tune with Venetian sensibilities – his figures on the logetta of the Campanile, for example, animate the surface of the building rather than draw attention to themselves. **Alessandro Vittoria** was the major sculptor of the middle and later part of the century; originally a member of Sansovino's workshop, Vittoria developed a more rhetorical style, well demonstrated in the figures of St Jerome in the Frari and San Zanipolo.

Seventeenth and eighteenth centuries

The High Baroque style in painting and sculpture was largely a Roman phenomenon and the Venetians, whose distrust of Rome led in 1606 to a Papal Interdict (see "History" section), remained largely untouched by it. Suitably enough, the only Venetian interior that relates to Roman Baroque is the Jesuit church, the **Gesuiti**.

After the hyper-productive **Palma il Giovane**, who seems to have contributed something to the majority of the city's church interiors, it was up to foreign painters – **Johann Lys**, for instance – to keep painting alive in the city. Much the same is true of sculpture: the Venetian **Baldassare Longhena** early in his career turned from sculpture to architecture, leaving the field to the Bolognese **Giuseppe Mazza** (bronze reliefs in San Zanipolo) and the Flemish **Juste Le Court** (high altar of the Salute), although Le Court's

Venetian pupil **Orazio Marinelli** (portrait busts in the Querini-Stampalia) did achieve a measure of celebrity. A particularly successful artist towards the end of the seventeenth century was **Andrea Brustolon** of Belluno, best known for his sculptural furniture (Ca' Rezzonico).

The last efflorescence of Venetian art began around the start of the eighteenth century, as Venice was degenerating into the playground of Europe. The highly illusionistic decorative paintings of **Giambattista Piazzetta** (1682–1752) mark the first step and foreshadow the work of **Giambattista Tiepolo** (1696–1777), whose ever-lightening colours and elegant, slightly disdainful Madonnas typified the sensuous but melancholy climate of the declining Republic. There's a similarity of mood to most of Tiepolo's work – from the dizzying trompe l'oeil ceiling painted in the Ca' Rezzonico to celebrate a marriage, to the airy *Virgin in Glory* painted for the Carmini.

Another major figure of the period was **Rosalba Carriera** (1675–1758), the first artist to use pastel as a medium in its own right. She was known chiefly as a portraitist, and the Ca' Rezzonico and the Accademia both contain a fine selection of her work – the latter featuring a *Self-Portrait in Old Age* which expresses a melancholy temperament usually suppressed from her pictures. (Incidentally, Carriera was not Venice's only woman artist: Marietta Robusti, Tintoretto's daughter, was known as a fine portraitist and Carriera's contemporary Giulia Lama has a *Judith and Holofernes* in the Accademia.)

By this time, Venetian art was being siphoned out of the city in large quantities, with people such as the English consul Joseph Smith sending pictures home by the crateful. Aristocrats on the Grand Tour were particularly interested in topographical work – kind of upmarket postcards – and in this area the pre-eminent artist was **Canaletto** (1695–1768), whose work was copied and engraved to make further saleable items. Don't be misled into believing he showed the "real" Venice – he idealized the city, changing spatial arrangements in order to suit a harmonious composition and sometimes even altering individual buildings. Canaletto's work in Venice is as sparse as Titian's – there's only one painting by him in the Accademia and a couple in the Ca' Rezzonico.

More sombre is the work of **Francesco Guardi** (1712–93), whose images of the lagoon and imaginary architectural scenes are frequently swathed in atmospheric mist and dotted with a few prophetic ruins. Genre painters were also popular at this time, none more so than **Pietro Longhi** (1708–85), whose wonderful illustrations of Venetian life (painted with a technique that is at best adequate) can also be seen in the Accademia and the Ca' Rezzonico. Longhi's production line was as busy as Canaletto's, as his workshop churned out copies of his most popular paintings to meet demand.

The last word on the painting of the Venetian Republic should be devoted to **Giandomenico Tiepolo** (1727–1804), seen at his best in the cycle of frescoes painted for his home and now installed in the Ca' Rezzonico. Freed from the whims of clients, he produced here a series of images that can with hindsight be seen as symbolic of the end of an era, with Sunday crowds gawping at a peepshow and clowns frittering away their time flirting and playing.

Nineteenth and twentieth centuries

After the fall of the Republic, art in Venice became the domain of outsiders. **Turner**, who visited the city three times, was its supreme painter in the nineteenth century, but as Ruskin said, you'd only have to stay in Venice for a few days to learn about it what Turner had learned. **Whistler, Monet** and **Sargent** were among other visitors. The only Venetian nineteenth-century artist of note is **Frederico Zandomeneghi** (1841–1917), and he decamped for Paris in 1874 to join the Impressionists' circle.

This century the story of art in Venice is no more cheerful. The internationally known artists who stayed as guests of **Peggy Guggenheim** between 1949 and 1979 came and left without making an impact on its cultural life. Every two years the **Biennale** brings in the hot-shots of the international art world, but does little to help young Venetian artists. The few Italian artists who have worked here have not exactly galvanized the city: the painter **Lucio Fontana** lived in Venice in the 1950s, and **Emilio Vedova** – a founder member of the avant-garde groups *Fronte Nuovo* and *Gruppo degli Otto* – taught at the Accademia until his death in the mid-1980s. Today the best-known artists at work in Venice are the video/installation artist **Fabrizio Plessi** and the American painter **Judith Harvest**.

An outline of Venetian architecture

This is just a brief chronology of Venetian architectural styles, intended simply as a means of giving some sense of order to the city's jumble of buildings. For more detailed accounts, refer to the "Books" section.

Byzantine Venice

Although settlement of the lagoon began as far back as the fifth century, no building has survived intact from earlier than the start of the eleventh century. The very first houses raised on the mudflats were "built like birds' nests, half on sea and half on land . . . the solidity of the earth . . . secured only by wattle-work", according to a letter written in 523 by a Roman official named Cassiodorus. Many of the earliest shelters were only temporary, constructed as refuges from the barbarian hordes of the mainland and abandoned as soon as the threat had receded, but with the Lombard invasions of the second half of the sixth century, communities uprooted from northern Italy began to construct more durable buildings on the islands. Some of the materials for these buildings were scavenged from Roman temples and dwellings, and a few of these fragments – used over and over again in succeeding centuries – can still be seen embedded in the walls of some of Venice's oldest structures. The great majority of the lagoon's buildings were still made of wood, however, and of these nothing is left.

From the twelfth century onwards the houses of the richest families were made from brick and stone, raised on foundations that rested on wooden piles hammered deep into the impacted clay and sand of the islands (a technique that has remained basically unchanged ever since). Prior to this period, such materials were reserved for the most important public buildings, and so it is that the **oldest structure in the lagoon** is a church – the **cathedral at Torcello**. Founded in 639 but altered in 864 and again, comprehensively, in **1008**, it takes its form from such early Christian basilicas as Sant'Apollinare in Ravenna. The prototypes of the Western Empire influenced other lagoon churches either founded or rebuilt in the eleventh and twelfth centuries – for example **Sant'Eufemia** on Giudecca, **Santi Maria e Donato** on Murano, and **San Giovanni Decollato** and **San Nicolò dei Mendicoli** in central Venice – but the predominant cultural influence on the emergent city was **Byzantium**, on which the lagoon confederation was originally dependent.

Santa Fosca on Torcello and **San Giovanni di Rialto**, traditionally the oldest church in Venice, are Byzantine in their adherence to a Greek-cross plan, but the building in which the Byzantine ancestry of Venice is most completely displayed is the **Basilica di San Marco**. Like the cathedral of Torcello, San Marco was extensively rebuilt in the eleventh century, but the basic layout – an elongated version of the five-domed Greek-cross design of Constantinople's Church of the Apostles – didn't change much between the consecration of the first Basilica in 832 and the completion of the final version in 1094. As much as its architectural form, the mosaic decoration of San Marco betrays the young city's Eastern affiliations – and it was in fact begun, as soon as the shell of the church was completed, by artists from Constantinople.

Byzantium has also left its mark on the **domestic architecture** of Venice, even though the oldest specimens still standing date from the late twelfth century or early thirteenth, by which time the political ties between the two cities had been severed. The high and rounded Byzantine arch can be seen in a number of Canal Grande palaces – the **Ca' da Mosto**, the **Donà** houses, the neighbouring **Palazzo Loredan** and **Palazzo Farsetti**, and the **Fondaco dei Turchi**. All of these buildings have been altered greatly over the years, but paradoxically it's the one that's been most drastically reconstructed – the Fondaco dei Turchi – which bears the closest resemblance to the earliest merchants' houses. Descended from the Roman villas of the mainland, they had an arcade at water level to permit the unloading of cargo, a long gallery on the upper storey, and lower towers at each end of the facade. Frequently they were embellished with relief panels (*paterae*) and insets of multicoloured marble – another Byzantine inheritance, and one that was to last, in modified form, for hundreds of years (for example in the predilection for heraldic devices on the fronts of houses).

Gothic Venice

Building land is scarce in Venice, and the consequent density of housing imposed certain restrictions on architectural inventiveness – ground plans had to make the fullest possible use of the available space (hence the rarity of internal courtyards and the uniformly flat facades) and elevations had to maximize the window areas, to make the most of the often limited natural light. Thus architectural evolution in the domestic buildings of Venice is to be observed not so much in the development of overall forms but rather in the mutations of surface detail, and in particular in the arches of the main facades. Nearly all the rich families of Venice derived their wealth from trade, and the predominant shipping lanes from Venice ran to the East – so it was inevitable that **Islamic features** would show through in Venetian architecture. As the thirteenth century progressed, the pure curve of the Byzantine arch first developed an upper peak and then grew into a type of ogival arch – as at the **Palazzo Falier** near Santi Apostoli, and **Porta dei Fiori** on the north side of the Basilica. This Islamicized Byzantine shape was in turn influenced in the fourteenth century by contact with the Gothic style of the mainland, so producing a repertoire that was uniquely Venetian.

The masterpiece of Venetian Gothic is also the city's greatest civic structure – the **Palazzo Ducale**. Begun in 1340, possibly to designs by **Filippo Calendario**, the present building was extended in a second phase of work from 1423 onwards, culminating in the construction of the most elaborate Gothic edifice in Venice – the **Porta della Carta**, by **Giovanni and Bartolomeo Bon**.

Imitations and variations of the Palazzo Ducale's complex tracery can be seen all over the city, most strikingly in the **Ca' d'Oro**, begun by Giovanni Bon at much the same time as work began on the extension of the Palazzo Ducale. The Ca' d'Oro represents the apex of Gothic refinement in Venice's domestic architecture; for monumental grandeur, on the other hand, none can match the adjoining Gothic palaces on the Volta del Canal – the **Palazzi Giustinian** and the **Ca' Fóscari**.

Ecclesiastical architecture in fourteenth- and fifteenth-century Venice is not as idiosyncratic as its secular counterpart – the religious communities who built the churches, affiliated to orders on the mainland, tended to follow the architectural conventions that had been established by those orders. In some of Venice's Gothic churches the old basilical plan prevailed over the cruciform (eg at **Madonna dell'Orto**), but the two most important churches of the period, the immense **San Zanipolo** (Dominican) and the **Frari** (Franciscan), display many of the basic features of contemporaneous churches in the Veneto: the Latin-cross plan, the pointed arches, the high nave with flanking aisles, and the chapels leading off from the transepts. Yet even these churches have distinctively Venetian characteristics, such as the use of tie-beams and the substitution of lath and plaster vaulting for vaults of stone – both necessary measures in a place with no bedrock for its foundations to rest on. In a few Gothic churches the builders capitalized on the availability of skilled naval carpenters to produce elegant and lightweight ceilings in the shape of an inverted **ship's keel** – for example at **Santo Stefano** and **San Giacomo dell'Orio**.

Early Renaissance

The complicated hybrid of Venetian Gothic remained the city's preferred style well into the second half of the fifteenth century, long after the classical precepts of Renaissance architecture had gained currency elsewhere in Italy. The late work of **Bartolomeo Bon** contains classical elements mixed with Gothic features (for example the portal of **San Zanipolo** and the incomplete **Ca' del Duca**, both from c.1460), but the first architect in Venice to produce something that could be called a classical design was **Antonio Gambello**, with his land gate for the **Arsenale** (1460). Gambello was not a committed proponent of the new ideas, however, and had work on his church of **San Zaccaria** not been interrupted by his death in 1481, it would have resembled a northern European Gothic church more closely than any other in Venice.

In the 1470s another dynasty of stonemason-architects succeeded the Bon family as the leading builders in Venice – **Pietro Solari** and his sons **Antonio and Tullio**, otherwise known as the **Lombardi**. Having worked with followers of Donatello in Padua in the 1460s, Pietro Lombardo was familiar with the latest principles of Tuscan architecture, but the chief characteristics of his own work – the elaborately carved pilasters and friezes, and the inlaid marble panels of various shapes and sizes – are not so much architectonic as decorative. The chancel of **San Giobbe**, the courtyard screen of the **Scuola di San Giovanni Evangelista**, the tiny church of **Santa Maria dei Miracoli** and the facade of the **Scuola di San Marco** represent the best of the Lombardi's architecture. Over-ornate though much of their building projects were, their style was closely imitated by numerous Venetian architects: nobody is certain, for example, whether the **Palazzo Dario** (on the Canal Grande) was designed by Pietro Lombardo or one of his "Lombardesque" acolytes.

Antonio Rizzo, a contemporary of Pietro Lombardo, was similarly esteemed as both a sculptor and architect. After the fire of 1483, Rizzo was put in charge of the rebuilding of the entire **east wing of the Palazzo Ducale**, and it was he who designed the **Scala dei Giganti**, a work which displays a typically Venetian delight in heavy ornamentation.

Codussi and his successors

The most rigorous and inventive Venetian architect of the early Renaissance was the man who took over the design and supervision of San Zaccaria after the death of Gambello – **Mauro Codussi** (sometimes spelled Coducci). His first commission in the city, the church of **San**

Michele in Isola (1469), is not purely classical – the huge lunette and inset roundels are Venetian idiosyncracies – but its proportions and clarity, and the use of classical detail to emphasize the structure of the building, entitle it to be known as the **first Renaissance church in Venice**. Codussi reintroduced the traditional Greek-cross plan in his other church designs (**Santa Maria Formosa** and **San Giovanni Crisostomo**), his impetus coming in part from a scholarly revival of interest in the culture of Byzantium and in part from the work of Renaissance theorists such as Alberti, whose *De Re Aedificatoria* proclaimed the superiority of centrally planned temples. In his secular buildings the influence of Alberti is even more pronounced, especially in his **Palazzo Vendramin-Calergi**, which is strongly reminiscent of Alberti's Palazzo Rucellai in Florence. Codussi was employed by the Venetian nobility, the scuole (he designed staircases for both the **Scuola di San Giovanni Evangelista** and the **Scuola di San Marco**) and the religious foundations, yet despite his pre-eminence it was only after archival research in the nineteenth century that he was identified as the author of all these buildings – a fact indicative of the difference between the status of the architect in Renaissance Florence and in Venice.

The economic effects of the War of the League of Cambrai limited the amount of building work in Venice at the start of the sixteenth century, but it was nonetheless a period of rapid transformation in the centre of the city: the **Campanile** of San Marco was completed, and the **Torre dell'Orologio** and **Procuratie Vecchie** were built – the last two being commenced to designs by Codussi. In the aftermath of serious fires, major projects were undertaken in the Rialto district as well – notably the **Fabbriche Vecchie** and the **Fondaco dei Tedeschi** – but the architects of the generation after Codussi (who died in 1504) were generally undistinguished. **Guglielmo dei Grigi** designed the **Palazzo dei Camerlenghi** at the foot of the Ponte di Rialto and went on to add the **Cappella Emiliana** to Codussi's San Michele in Isola. **Bartolomeo Bon the Younger** took over the supervision of the Procuratie Vecchie after Codussi's death, and began the **Scuola di San Rocco** in 1515 – a project that was completed by **Scarpagnino** (Antonio Abbondi), the man in charge of the rebuilding of the Rialto markets after the fire of 1514. **Giorgio Spavento**, described by the diarist Marin Sanudo as "a man of great genius", was the most talented architect of this period, and with **San Salvatore** he produced its best church design. By joining together three Greek-cross plans, Spavento created a building which reconciled the long open nave required by modern liturgy with the traditional Byzantine centralized plan.

High Renaissance

The definitive classical authority for the architectural theorists of Renaissance Italy was **Vitruvius**, architect to the Emperor Augustus, and it was in Venice in 1511 that the first printed edition of his *De Architectura* was produced. However, the consistent application of classical models was not seen in Venice until after the sack of Rome by the Imperial army in 1527. A large number of Roman artists then sought refuge in Venice, and it was with this influx that the advances of such figures as Raphael, Michelangelo and Bramante were absorbed into the practice of Venice's architects.

Of all the exiles, the one who made the greatest impact was **Jacopo Sansovino**. Despite his limited architectural experience – he was known mainly as a sculptor when he arrived in Venice – Sansovino was appointed Proto of San Marco on the death of Bartolomeo Bon in 1529, a position that made him the most powerful architect in the city, and which he was to hold for the next forty years. From 1537 onwards a group of buildings by Sansovino went up around the Piazzetta, completely changing the appearance of the area: the **Zecca** (Mint) was the first, then the **Loggetta** at the base of the Campanile, and then the most celebrated of all his designs – the **Libreria Sansoviniana**. Showing a familiarity with the architecture of ancient Rome that was unprecedented in Venice, the Libreria is still unmistakeably Venetian in its wealth of surface detail, and the rest of Sansovino's buildings similarly effect a compromise between classical precision and Venetian convention. Thus his palace designs – the **Palazzo Dolfin-Manin** (1538) and **Palazzo Corner della Ca' Grande** (1545) – are clearly related to the houses of the Roman Renaissance, but perpetuate the traditional Venetian division of the facade into a central bay with symmetrically flanking windows. Though principally a secular architect, Sansovino did also design churches; the religious buildings by him that still stand are **San Francesco della Vigna**, **San Martino di Castello**, **San Giuliano** and the apse of **San Fantin**.

Of Sansovino's contemporaries, the only one of comparable stature was **Michele Sanmicheli**. More proficient as an engineer than Sansovino, he was employed early in his career by Pope Clement VII to improve the military defences of Parma and Piacenza, and in 1535 was taken on as Venice's military architect. The **Fortezza di Sant'Angelo** (1543), protecting the Lido entrance to the lagoon, was his largest public project, and in addition to this he built two of the most grandiose palaces in the city – the **Palazzo Corner Mocenigo** at San Polo (1545) and the **Palazzo Grimani** (c.1559) on the Canal Grande.

Andrea Palladio, Italy's most influential architect in the second half of the sixteenth century (indeed, one of the most influential architects of any epoch), was based in nearby Vicenza yet found it difficult to break into Venice's circle of patronage. In the 1550s his application for the position of *Proto* to the Salt Office (supervisor of public buildings) was turned down, and his project for the Palazzo Ducale's Scala d'Oro rejected; later schemes for the Ponte di Rialto and the rebuilding of the entire Palazzo Ducale were no more successful. He was never asked to undertake a private commission in the city. The facade of **San Pietro in Castello** was his first contract (eventually built in a much altered form), and it was the religious foundations that were to provide him with virtually all his subsequent work in Venice. Palladio's churches of **San Giorgio Maggiore** (1565) and the **Redentore** (1576) are the summit of Renaissance classicism in Venice: the scale on which they were composed, the restraint of their decoration, the stylistic unity of exterior and interior, the subtlety with which the successive spaces were combined, and the correctness of their quotations from the architecture of Imperial Rome – all these factors distinguished them from all previous designs and established them as reference points for later churches.

Once Palladio's churches had been finished, the islands of San Giorgio Maggiore and Giudecca presented much the same face to the main part of the city as they do today. The work of his closest follower, **Vincenzo Scamozzi**, brought the landscape of the Piazza very close to its present-day state – it was Scamozzi who completed the Campanile end of the Libreria Sansoviniana and began the construction of the **Procuratie Nuove** in 1582. Another Venetian landmark, the **Ponte di Rialto**, was built at this time; its creator, **Antonio da Ponte**, was also in charge of the repair and redesign of the Palazzo Ducale after the fire of 1577, and designed the new prisons on the opposite bank of the Rio di Palazzo. The bridge connecting the prisons to the Palazzo Ducale – the **Ponte dei Sospiri** (Bridge of Sighs) – was the work of **Antonio Contino** (1600).

Baroque

Although there are a few sixteenth-century Venetian buildings that could be described as proto-Baroque – **Alessandro Vittoria**'s **Palazzo Balbi** (1582), with its encrusted decoration and broken pediments, is one example – the classical idiom remained entrenched for some time as the stylistic orthodoxy in Venice, as is demonstrated by the appointment of the unadventurous **Bartolomeo Monopola** to complete the final stages of the **Palazzo Ducale** in the first decades of the seventeenth century. The colossal **Palazzo Pisani** at Santo Stefano, possibly by Monopola, is further evidence of the city's aesthetic conservatism.

It was not until the maturity of Venice's finest native architect, **Baldassare Longhena**, that the innovations of the Baroque made themselves fully felt. Longhena's early work – for example the **Palazzo Giustinian-Lolin** and the **Duomo** at **Chioggia** (both 1624) – continues the Palladianism of the previous century, but with his design for the votive church of **Santa Maria della Salute** (1631) he gave the city its first Baroque masterpiece. In its plan the Salute is indebted to Palladio's Redentore, but in its use of multiple vistas, and devices such as the huge volutes round the base of the dome, it introduces a dynamism that was completely alien to Palladio's architecture. In 1640 Longhena became the Proto of San Marco, and between then and his death in 1682 he occupied a position in Venetian architectural circles as commanding as Sansovino's had been. Among his major projects were the completion of the **Procuratie Nuove**, the addition of a grand staircase and library to the monastic complex of **San Giorgio Maggiore**, and the design of two of the Canal Grande's most spectacular palaces – the **Ca' Pésaro** and the **Ca' Rezzonico**.

When compared to much of the work being produced in other parts of Italy at this time, Longhena's brand of Baroque was quite sober. Yet it was the chief exception in his output – the

grotesque facade of the **Ospedaletto** – which proved in the short term to be specially influential. Its most direct descendant was **Alessandro Tremignon**'s facade for the church of **San Moisè** (1668), which is choked with sculpture by Heinrich Meyring. **Giuseppe Sardi**'s church of **Santa Maria del Giglio** (1680) can also be traced back to the Ospedaletto, but on the other hand Sardi's work is equally redolent of the architecture of the sixteenth century – his facade for Scamozzi's **San Lazzaro dei Mendicanti** could be seen as a deliberate rejection of the excesses of the Baroque. His other prominent designs are the **Scuola di San Teodoro** and the facades of **San Salvatore** and **Santa Maria di Nazareth** (the Scalzi), all of them rather routine efforts.

The eighteenth century

The concerted reaction against Baroque began with the work of Sardi's nephew, **Domenico Rossi**. Rossi's facade for the church of **San Stae** (1709) is essentially a neo-Palladian design enlivened by the addition of some exuberant pieces of sculpture, and his rebuilding of the **Palazzo Corner della Regina** is closer to the palace projects of Sansovino than to such works as Longhena's nearby Ca' Pésaro. **Andrea Tirali**, Rossi's exact contemporary (1657–1737), was an even more faithful adherent to the principles of the sixteenth century – the portico he added to the church of **San Nicolò da Tolentino** is strictly classical, and his facade for **San Vitale** is a straight plagiarism of San Giorgio Maggiore. Another church of this period – **San Simeone Piccolo** – is one of the most conspicuous in Venice, standing as it does right opposite the train station. Designed in 1718 by **Giovanni Scalfarotto** (Rossi's son-in-law), its facade and plan are derived from the Pantheon, but the vertical exaggeration of its dome makes it closer in spirit to Longhena's Salute.

The most significant architect of the period was **Giorgio Massari** (1687–1766), whose church of the **Gesuati**, begun in 1726, combines Palladian forms (for example the facade and the arrangement of the interior bays) with understated Rococo details (the ceiling frames). His later church of the **Pietà**, based on Sansovino's destroyed Incurabili church, is more sober in its use of decoration, and his design for the last of the great palaces of the Canal Grande, the **Palazzo Grassi** (1748), is the severest of all his buildings.

The Palladian creed was kept alive in late eighteenth-century Venice through innumerable academic and polemical publications. Two of the leading figures in this movement were **Antonio Visentini** (1688–1782) and Scalfarotto's nephew, **Tommaso Temanza** (1705–89), both of whom taught architecture at the Accademia. Temanza was the more important architect, and his **Santa Maria Maddalena** was the first uncompromisingly Neoclassical building in Venice.

To the present

With the work of **Giannantonio Selva**, a pupil of Visentini and Temanza, Neoclassicism entered its most spare and fastidious phase. His first large scheme was **La Fenice** opera house (1790), where exterior adornment was reduced to the minimum necessary to signify the building's function and importance. Selva's career was undisturbed by the subsequent collapse of the Venetian Republic, and his other main works – the churches of **San Maurizio** (1806) and **Nome del Gesù** (1815) – were created under French rule.

During the second period of French occupation (1806–15) a large number of buildings were demolished to facilitate urban improvement schemes. Four churches were knocked down to make space for the **Giardini Pubblici**, for instance, and by the time the French were ejected by the Austrians a total of nearly fifty religious buildings had been demolished. The most celebrated loss was that of Sansovino's **San Geminiano**, pulled down in 1807 to make room for the construction of the **Ala Napoleonica**, a ballroom wing added to the Procuratie Nuove, which was then serving as a royal palace. In the 1830s the designer of the ballroom, **Lorenzo Santi**, went on to build the now abandoned coffee house (**Palazzetto Bucintoro**) by the Giardinetti Reali, and the **Palazzo Patriarcale** alongside the Basilica.

Alterations to Venice's network of canals and streets, which had been started by the French with schemes such as the creation of **Via Garibaldi**, were accelerated under Austrian rule. Most of Venice's *rii terrà* (infilled canals) originated in the period of Austrian occupation, and a number of new bridges were constructed at this time too – including the ones at the **Accademia** and **Scalzi**, the first bridges to be put across the Canal Grande since the Ponte di Rialto. It was the Austrians who connected Venice by rail with the mainland (1846), and in 1860 they expanded the train station, demolishing Palladio's church of **Santa Lucia** in the process. And the first major **restoration projects** were carried out under Austrian supervision – at the **Fondaco dei Turchi**, at **Santi Maria e Donato** on **Murano**, and on the north facade of **San Marco**.

Major town planning schemes continued after Venice joined the Unified Kingdom of Italy. In the 1870s two wide thoroughfares were completed – the **Strada Nova** in Cannaregio and **Calle Larga XXII Marzo** between San Moisè and Santa Maria Zobenigo – and **Campo Manin** was opened up in 1871. The brief industrialization of central Venice in the late nineteenth century has left behind one prominent hulk – the **Mulino Stucky**, built on Giudecca in 1895. The hotels and middle-class housing developments of the **Lido** – which became a fashionable resort in this period – have outlived the city's industrial sites.

In 1933 Venice was joined by road to the mainland, and five years later the Rio Nuovo was cut from the recently created Piazzale Roma towards the Canal Grande. The chief buildings of the Fascist era are the **fire station** on the Rio di Ca' Fóscari (which continues the Rio Nuovo), and the **Palazzo del Casinò** and **Palazzo del Cinema** on the Lido. Few buildings worth a mention have been put up in Venice since then – the least objectionable are, perhaps, the **train station** (1954) and the **Cassa di Risparmio di Venezia** in Campo Manin, designed in 1964 by **Pier Luigi Nervi** and **Angelo Scattolin**. The density and antiquity of most of Venice's urban fabric makes intervention particularly problematic for the modern architect. Understandable Venetian resistance to new developments, hardened by such insensitive twentieth-century efforts as the extension to the **Hotel Bauer-Grünwald**, adds further difficulties, and accounts for the fact that two of the most interesting modern schemes, **Frank Lloyd Wright**'s Ca' Masieri and **Le Corbusier**'s plan for a civic hospital in Cannaregio, never left the drawing-board. Though small items are occasionally added to the assortment box of architectural styles that is the **Biennale** site, major new schemes will always be rare; of the two big building contracts awarded in the late 1990s, one is for the reconstruction of a destroyed structure (**La Fenice**), and the other is for a site that will have no living occupants – David Chipperfield's extension to the **San Michele cemetery**.

Conservation and restoration

In 1818 Byron published the fourth section of *Childe Harold's Pilgrimage*, in which is encapsulated the Romantic notion that if Venice isn't actually sinking, then it ought to be:

Venice, lost and won,
Her thirteen hundred years of freedom done
Sinks, like a sea-weed into whence she rose!

Ever since, it's been a commonplace that Venice is doomed to an aquatic extinction. In reality, Venice as a whole was not sinking in Byron's day and is not sinking today – but this is not to say that alarmists have no reason to panic. The city is threatened by water, by salt, by air pollution and by local subsidence, and faces massive problems of conservation and restoration. In the decade from 1984 the Italian government set aside some £2000 million under the so-called Special Laws, to underwrite projects ranging from schemes to restore single paintings or architectural details through to grandiose plans to control the industrialization of the mainland and the encroachments of the Adriatic. In addition to the intrinsic difficulties of each project, the major interventions prompt interminable arguments about the very purpose of restoration – should Venice be turned into even more of a museum piece, its buildings preserved in the aspic of contemporary restoration techniques, or should parts of the city be rebuilt, reintroducing industry and modern housing? On the one hand, Venice desperately needs the income from tourism, and on the other its population has halved since the war and its houses are in such a state that 45 percent of them don't have adequate bathrooms.

Flooding

On November 4, 1966, the waters of the Adriatic, already dangerously high after two successive high tides had been prevented from receding by gale-force southeasterly winds, were disturbed by an earth tremor. The resulting tidal wave breached Venice's *Murazzi* (the sea walls), and for the next 48 hours the sea level remained an average of six feet above mean high tide – in other words, nearly four feet above the pavement of the Piazza, the lowest point of the city. Venice was left with no power or telephone lines, and buildings were awash with filthy water, mud and oil from broken storage tanks.

Outside Venice, the flooding did not immediately provoke extreme concern, partly because floods in Venice were nothing new (at the height of the crisis national radio simply announced "high water in the Piazza San Marco"), and partly because attention was focused on the same day's disaster in Florence. A reservoir above Florence had become swollen by a month of heavy rain, and in order to relieve pressure on the dam the reservoir gates had been opened, causing a flash-flood that killed several people and caused serious damage – some of it irreparable – to numerous works of art. Nobody was hurt in the Venice flood and no artefacts were lost, but the photographs of water swirling through the doors of San Marco and around the courtyard of the Palazzo Ducale did highlight the perilous condition of the city. When floods almost as bad occurred in the following year, the international campaign to save Venice was already gathering strength, and similarly severe floods in 1979 and 1986 kept the situation in the public eye.

Called the **acqua alta** (high water), the winter flooding of the city is caused by a combination of seasonal tides and persistent southeasterly winds, and has always been a feature of Venetian life. With a surface area of some 550 square kilometres, the Venetian lagoon is the largest in Italy, and with an average depth of just 1.2m this large body of water is very sensitive to the vagaries of the climate. In recent years, however, its sensitivity has increased markedly. Between 1931 and 1945 there were 8 serious *aque alte*; in the 14 years following 1971 there were 49. By 1996 the number of annual floods had risen to 100 – not all of them were major, but the statistic is nonetheless indicative of a relentlessly rising trend. This may in part be due to shifts in global weather conditions, or to the effect of the gradual melting of the polar ice cap, but at least one independent study points the finger firmly at avoidable factors. In a nutshell, the argument is as follows. At the ancient port of Aquileia, at the head of the Adriatic, the height of the Roman wharves relative to the water seems to indicate that there has been no major change in sea level since they were built. Excavations of building foundations in various parts of the city indicate that the notion of a general subsidence is unfounded. Therefore the increased flooding is a local phenomenon related to recent changes in the balance of the lagoon.

It is certainly a fact that the workings of the lagoon have been interfered with in an unprecedented way during this century. Land has been reclaimed, both for industrial sites on the mainland and in central Venice itself – around the docks, for instance. Nowadays only about 70 percent of the area that was under water in 1900 remains that way. At the same time, channels have been deepened to allow modern industrial and commercial vessels to pass through the lagoon, and smaller motor boats within the city also churn up the sea bed and cause erosion. Consequently, both the speed and depth of the tides have been affected.

Bodies such as the centuries-old Magistrato alle Acque and the Consiglio di Nazionale Ricerca Venezia have studied the workings of the lagoon in detail, and the construction of a **tidal barrier** across the three entrances to the lagoon has often emerged as a possible solution to the problem. In early November 1988 the first component of just such a barrier was towed into place close to the Porto di Lido. Nicknamed **Moisè** (Moses) after the Old Testament's great manipulator of the waters (and because MOSE was an approximate acronym for the prototype of the barrier, the Modulo Sperimentale Elettromecanico), it was put together by the Consorzio Venezia Nuova, a consortium of engineering companies, all eager for international publicity. Colossal sums of money were set aside for the project, which basically involves laying 79 300-tonne steel flaps on the floor of the lagoon, forming a submerged barrage some two kilometres long in total; when the water level rises, air is pumped into the flaps and the barrier rises to protect the city – or at least, that's the theory.

Predictably enough, the relationship between the government and the consortium has run into difficulties. The official auditors criticized the Consorzio Venezia Nuova for taking a cut of up to 25 percent from contractors, and for ignoring

technical criticisms of the barrier's design "for reasons of political opportunism". The original deadline for the completion of Moisè was 1995; come the deadline, there was little more to show than a forlorn segment of the barrier anchored off the Arsenale. In 1998 the project was stalled by political wrangling, a development that pleased many conservationists, who had always maintained that the abandonment of the barrier would be more beneficial to Venice than its completion. Some experts have objected that Moses has been designed as though the waters of the lagoon moved vertically but not laterally – in the event of a sudden tidal surge, they claim, the barrier will simply not be strong enough to resist the push of the water. Italia Nostra, Italy's national heritage group, insists that the alteration of the shipping channels and the cessation of land reclamation would be cheaper and more effective responses to the situation, to which proponents of the barrier reply that these non-mechanical interventions won't offer any protection against the effects of global warming, which could raise the level of the Mediterranean by as much as 30cm.

While Consorzio Venezia Nuova continues to proclaim the virtues of Moisè, a host of less extravagant projects are making progress all over the lagoon. Embankments and pavements have been rebuilt and raised at numerous points (particularly in the settlements between the Lido and Chioggia), the jetties at the Lido, Malamocco and Chioggia inlets are being strengthened, and tracts of land reclaimed for industrial use but never built on have been allowed to flood again. The largest of these schemes involves the reinforcement of the 60km of the lagoon's outer coastline: the beaches at Jesolo, Cavallino, the Lido, Pellestrina, Sottomarina and Isola Verde have been extended within a grid of stone groynes and artifical reefs, thereby dissipating the energy of the waves, while the sand dunes at Cavallino have been planted with marram grass, which binds the sand and thus makes the dunes a more effective windbreak. As for the problem of tanker traffic, it's intended that the Marghera refineries will eventually be scaled down as a consequence of extending the Genoa–Cremona oil pipeline to Mantua (at the moment Mantua's oil comes from Marghera), and the remaining tankers will be diverted to less damaging routes across the lagoon, or even be banned from the lagoon entirely. The petrochemical companies have not exactly been enjoying good PR of late. In the summer of 1998 the Italian press was in a state of high excitement when a secret chemical waste dump was discovered on the edge of the lagoon; the creators of the toxic reservoir, Enichem, offered to clear up the mess they'd made, on condition they were allowed to carry on their operations at Marghera – a response that didn't win many friends.

With global warning now beginning to make a tangible impact on the climate, the stabilization of the lagoon has become a more urgent problem than ever. On November 6, 2000, as freakish rainfall continued over much of Western Europe and whole regions of Italy were classified as disaster areas, Venice was inundated by the worst *acqua alta* since 1966, with more than one and a half metres of water lying over the Piazza. Two weeks later the *acqua alta* surged to more than 120cm, putting more than a third of the city's pavements under water. This was the fifth time the tide had passed the 110cm mark that winter. The warnings could not be clearer, but still the barrier remains on the drawing board.

Water pollution

A major objection to the barrier is that it will further inhibit the cleansing effects of the tides, already diminished in parts of the lagoon by the creation of firm land out of mudflats. Twice-daily tidal movements and the activity of waste-digesting marine life were enough until fairly recently to keep the water relatively fresh – fresh enough, until the 1980s, for fastidious Venetians to swim in certain deep spots at high tides.

Much of the **pollution** is the fault of the industrial complexes of Mestre-Marghera, which, though in decline, have dumped thousands of tons of zinc, copper, iron, lead and chrome into the lagoon, creating a toxic sludge so dangerous that nobody has yet devised a safe way of dredging the stuff out. Chemical fertilizers seeping into the water from the mainland add to the accumulation of phosphates in the water, a situation exacerbated by the heavy use of phosphate-rich detergents in Venetian homes. (Although Venice treats its sewage in sumps before emptying it into the sea, all household sinks and baths drain straight into the canals.) Plants, fishes and other forms of marine life are being suffocated by algae that thrive on these phosphates, forming a foul-smelling scum that is thickened by the rotting animal and vegetable matter.

When photographs of gondoliers and tourists in face masks brought adverse publicity abroad, it was finally acknowledged that a crisis had been reached, and in 1988 the Ministry of the Environment earmarked £175 million to clean up the lagoon. Moreover, the town hall has now banned the sale of phosphate-enriched detergents – Venice's boat-restorers will be pleased about this too: their work has steadily diminished as the bottoms of boats have remained relatively unencumbered by weeds.

In order to restore the equilibrium of the lagoon's ecosystem, salt marshes and fish farms are being reconstructed at various places in the lagoon, wetlands are being created on the periphery and waste disposal sites are being consolidated (there are seventeen such dumps in the lagoon). But local action such as this will still not be enough. Venice's lagoon is threatened by the grossly polluted water of the whole upper Adriatic, into which the Po and numerous other waterways disgorge their effluents. In 1989 the Italian government assigned a sum of £500 million to the cleansing of the Adriatic, but the complexity of the problem is terrifying. It has even been proposed that the techniques used to purify sewage may be actually contributing to the proliferation of the algae by feeding them with vitamin-saturated fluids. In the 1950s and 1960s Lake Erie was threatened with the same sort of marine disaster as now faces the Venice region; regulations imposed in the 1970s seem to have rescued the lake. If drastic action is taken now, the Po might be a moderately clean river within a decade.

Air pollution

The other environmental problem facing Venice is that of **air pollution**, which worsened in phase with the growing industrial complexes on the mainland. Sulphur dioxide combines with the salty and humid air of the lagoon to make a particularly vicious corrosive which eats at brick, stone and bronze alike. An experiment carried out in the 1970s showed that stone covered with pigeon droppings stayed in better condition than stone exposed to the Venetian air. The conversion of domestic heating systems from oil to gas has helped to cut down the amount of sulphur dioxide in the atmosphere, and expenditure on industrial filtration has had an effect too, but Marghera's factories still pump around 50,000 tons of the gas into the atmosphere each year. Some observers point out that the prevailing winds carry the fumes from the Marghera stacks inland, but even though the bulk of the emissions are someone else's problem, the ambient air of Venice was one of the factors the Italian trades union congress had in mind when they christened the city "the capital of pollution".

In the years immediately after the 1966 flood, as Venice attracted ever more attention from outside the country, the city authorities were often criticized for their tardiness in commissioning restoration work on Venice's crumbling stonework. Their cautiousness was to an extent vindicated when it became apparent that the restoration work on Sansovino's Loggetta – initially hailed as an unqualified success – had in fact done as much damage as it had repaired. The resins used to protect the restored marble have now begun to discolour the building, and it may prove impossible to sluice the resins out. A major restoration of the Miracoli church has turned out to be similarly ill-advised, with salt eating at the walls from inside and excreting white crusts onto the marble cladding. The cleaning and strengthening of the Porta della Carta was undertaken with far greater circumspection, and so far it seems that all is well; the lessons learned on that project are being employed on the continuous restoration of the Basilica di San Marco and the Palazzo Ducale.

Subsidence

The industries at Marghera used to threaten Venice from below as well as from above. Drawing millions of gallons of water directly from the ground, they caused a dramatic fall in the water table and threatened to cause the subsidence of the entire city. Calamity was averted in 1973, when the national government built two aqueducts to pipe water from inland rivers to the refineries and factories of Marghera and the houses of Venice. In 1975 the artesian wells at Marghera were sealed, and by the late 1990s there was evidence that this measure had resulted in a rise of two centimetres in the land level of some parts of the historic centre.

Local subsidence will continue to be a problem, though. The majority of buildings in Venice are built on wooden pilings driven deep into the mudbanks of the lagoon. Interference with the lagoon's equilibrium has resulted in an increase in the number of extremely low tides as well as the number of floods, and occasionally the water falls so far that air gets at the pilings, causing them to decay. Furthermore, those people unable to afford proper wood-piled foundations would have used rubbish and rubble instead, which through the years slowly compresses. Another crucial factor is the erosive effect of the city's water-buses: a study in the 1990s showed that the foundations of sixty percent of the buildings on the Canal Grande had been damaged by the wash from the vaporetti, and the situation along the Rio Novo (which was created expressly as a short-cut for the water-buses) has become so bad that it has now been closed to vaporetti. Projects to consolidate the houses and churches of Venice against erosion by the water will never cease to be necessary, and recently a new potential source of subsidence has emerged: AGIP have been probing for gas about 20km offshore of Chioggia, and there is considerable concern that full-scale exploitation of any gas reserves in this part of the Mediterranean might disturb the sea-bed, with very unpleasant consequences for Chioggia and possibly even for central Venice.

Aid groups

Restoration in Venice is principally a collaborative venture between UNESCO and the city's Superintendancies of Art and of Monuments. The former co-ordinates the fund-raising and restoration proposals from the multitude of aid groups set up in various countries after the 1966 floods; the latter pair oversee the restoration centres in Venice, the cataloguing of endangered buildings and objects and the deployment of restoration teams.

The first top-to-toe makeover for a Venetian building was that of Madonna dell'Orto, undertaken by the British Italian Art and Archives Rescue Fund (transformed in 1971 into **Venice in Peril**). The church's facade statue of St Christopher was the first Istrian stone sculpture to be cleaned in Venice, and the techniques used were taken up by later restorers. Since then, the organization has financed scores of restorations, ranging from single pictures to the Loggetta at the base of the Campanile di San Marco, the Porta della Carta (the ceremonial gateway of the

Books

A comprehensive Venetian reading-list would run on for dozens of pages, and would include a vast number of out-of-print titles. Most of our recommendations are in print, and those that aren't shouldn't be too difficult to track down. Wherever a book is in print, the UK publisher is given first in each listing, followed by the publisher in the US – unless the title is available in one country only, in which case we have specified which country, or is published by the same company in both territories, in which case only the publisher is specified.

Fiction

Italo Calvino, *Invisible Cities* (Minerva; Harcourt, Brace). Characteristically subtle variations on the idea of the City, presented in the form of tales told by Marco Polo to Kublai Khan. No explicit reference to Venice until well past halfway, when Polo remarks – "Every time I describe a city I am saying something about Venice."

James Cowans, *A Mapmaker's Dream* (Sceptre; Warner). Engaging historical-philosophical fantasy based on the creation of Fra Mauro's famous map of the world, one of the great exhibits in the Libreria Sansoviniana.

Michael Dibdin, *Dead Lagoon* (Faber; Vintage). Superior detective story starring Venice-born Aurelio Zen, a cop entangled in the political maze of 1990s Italy.

Ernest Hemingway, *Across the River and into the Trees* (Arrow; Scribner). Hemingway at his most square-jawed and most mannered: our hero fights good, drinks good, loves good, and could shoot a duck out of the skies from the hip at a range of half a mile. Target of one of the funniest parodies ever written: E.B. White's *Across the Street and into the Grill* – "'I love you,' he said, "and we are going to lunch together for the first and only time, and I love you very much.'"

E.T.A. Hoffmann, *Doge and Dogaressa* (in *Tales of Hoffmann*, Penguin). Fanciful reconstruction of events surrounding the treason of Marin Falier, by one of the pivotal figures of German Romanticism. Lots of passion and pathos, narrated at headlong pace.

Hugo von Hofmannsthal, *Andreas* (Pushkin Press; Turtle Point Press). The last novel by a writer nowadays best known for his collaborations with the composer Richard Strauss. An interesting example of the use of Venice as a metaphor for moral decay, it charts the corruption of a naïve Viennese aristocrat in the slippery city – or, rather, it would have done, had Hofmannsthal finished it. As it is, most of the text consists of notes, which makes it something of an esoteric pleasure.

Henry James, *The Aspern Papers* & *The Wings of the Dove* (both Penguin). The first, a 100-page tale about a biographer's manipulative attempts to get at the personal papers of a deceased writer, is one of James's most tautly constructed longer stories. The latter, one of the three vast and circumspect late novels, was likened to caviar by Ezra Pound, and is likely to put you off James for life if you come to it without acclimatizing yourself with the earlier stuff.

Donna Leon, *Acqua Alta* (Pan; Harper o/p). Liberally laced with an insider's observations on daily life in Venice, this is the most atmospheric of Leon's long sequence of highly competent Venice-set detective novels.

Thomas Mann, *Death in Venice* (Minerva; Penguin). Profound study of the demands of art and the claims of the flesh, with the city itself thematically significant rather than a mere exotic backdrop. Richer than most stories five times its length and infinitely more complex than Visconti's sentimentalizing film.

Ian McEwan, *The Comfort of Strangers* (Vintage). A modern Gothic yarn in which an ordinary young

English couple fall foul of a sexually ambiguous predator. Venice is never named as the locality, but is evoked with some subtlety and menace.

Caryl Phillips, *The Nature of Blood* (Faber; Vintage). Principally set during the Holocaust, this exploration of persecution and alienation interweaves the twentieth century with re-creations of sixteenth-century Venetian society, particularly the Ghetto.

Marcel Proust, *Albertine Disparue*. The Venetian interlude, occurring in the penultimate novel of Proust's massive novel sequence, can be sampled in isolation for its acute dissection of the sensory experience of the city – but to get the most from it, you've got to knuckle down and commit yourself to the preceding ten volumes of *À la Recherche*. The best English translation is D.J. Enright's revision of the pioneering Kilmartin/Scott-Moncrieff version, published in six paperback volumes (Vintage; Modern Library).

William Rivière, *A Venetian Theory of Heaven* (Sceptre in UK). Pleasant, undemanding story of marital woes and emotional confusion, with expertly evoked Venetian setting.

Frederick Rolfe (Baron Corvo), *The Desire and Pursuit of the Whole* (Da Capo, o/p). A transparent exercise in self-justification, much of it taken up with venomous ridicule of the English community in Venice, among whom Rolfe moved while writing the book in 1909. (Its libellous streak kept it unpublished for 25 years.) Snobbish and incoherent, redeemed by hilarious character-assassinations and gorgeous descriptive passages. One of the few books by an Anglophone to be saturated with a knowledge of the place. Unfortunately, the Da Capo paperback is currently out of print, leaving a very expensive hardback as the only one in the catalogue.

Arthur Schnitzler, *Casanova's Return to Venice* (Pushkin Press in UK). Something of a Schnitzler revival followed the release of Kubrick's *Eyes Wide Shut*, which was adapted from a novella by this contemporary and compatriot of Freud. This similarly short and intense book also explores the dynamics of desire, but from the perspective of a desperate man who is rapidly approaching the end of his life.

Michel Tournier, *Gemini* (Johns Hopkins). Venice is just one of the localities through which the identical twins Jean and Paul (known to their parents as Jean-Paul) are taken in this amazingly inventive exploration of the concept of twinship. It might be flashy in places, yet Tournier throws away more ideas in the course of a novel than most writers dream up in a lifetime.

Barry Unsworth, *Stone Virgin* (Penguin; Norton). Yet another story of the uncanny repetitions of history – this time an English expert in stone conservation begins to suspect that his emotional entanglement with a sculptor's wife is a recapitulation of a past liaison. The gobbets of scholarly detail sit uncomfortably alongside the melodrama of the plot.

Salley Vickers, *Miss Garnet's Angel* (HarperCollins/Carroll & Graf). Desiccated spinster (a Marxist as well, to make matters worse) is awakened by Venice to the finer things in life – a somewhat hackneyed tale, but Vickers has a sound knowledge of the city and its art, and displays a light touch in her recreation of the place.

Jeanette Winterson, *The Passion* (Vintage; Grove). Whimsical little tale of the intertwined lives of a member of Napoleon's catering corps and a female gondolier. Acclaimed as a masterpiece in some quarters.

Art and architecture

James S. Ackerman, *Palladio* (Penguin; Viking). Concise introduction to the life, works and cultural background of the Veneto's greatest architect. Especially useful if you're visiting Vicenza or any of the villas.

Svetlana Alpers and Michael Baxandall, *Tiepolo and the Pictorial Intelligence* (Yale). This brilliant book analyzes with exhilarating precision the way in which Tiepolo perceived and re-created the world in his paintings, and demolishes the notion that Tiepolo was merely a "decorative" artist. Though they devote most space to the frescoes at Würzburg, Alpers and Baxandall discuss many of the Tiepolo paintings in Venice and the Veneto, and their revelatory readings will enrich any encounter with his art. The reproductions maintain Yale's customary high standards.

Patricia Fortini Brown, *Venetian Narrative Painting in the Age of Carpaccio* (Yale). Rigorously researched study of a subject central to Venetian culture yet often overlooked in more general accounts. Fresh reactions to the works discussed are combined with a penetrating analysis of the ways they reflect the ideals of the Republic at the time. Worth every penny.

Richard Goy, *Venice: The City and its Architecture* (Phaidon). Published in 1997, this superb book instantly became the benchmark. Eschewing the linear narrative adopted by previous writers on the city's architecture, Goy goes for a multi-angled approach, devoting one part to the growth of the city and its evolving technologies, another to its "nuclei" (the Piazza, Arsenale, Ghetto and Rialto), and the last to its building types (palazzi, churches, etc). The result is a book that does full justice to the richness and density of the Venetian cityscape – and the design and choice of pictures are exemplary.

Alastair Grieve, *Whistler's Venice* (Yale). Bankrupted after his libel action against Ruskin, Whistler took himself off to Venice to lick his wounds. He ended up staying for a year, having been inspired by the city to produce some of his finest work. Grieve's methodical and deeply researched book – yet another beautifully produced Venetian title from Yale – reproduces the fifty etchings and one hundred pastels that Whistler created in that year, juxtaposing them with photographs and other images of the locales in a way that elucidates the artist's way of working, and builds up an absorbing portrait of the city in the late ninetheenth century.

Paul Hills, *Venetian Colour* (Yale). Seductive colour has always been seen as a pre-eminent characteristic of Venetian painting and applied art, but this handsome book, subtitled "Marble, mosaic, painting and glass 1250–1550", has some interesting angles on a subject you might have thought had been exhausted long ago. Hills discusses the production of dyes, pigments and works of art in the context of the Republic's mercantile culture, relating aspects of pictorial style to the social history of Venetian costume, for example, and explaining how black came to be the most luxurious of hues. First-class illustrations, as is usually the case with this publisher.

Paul Holberton, *Palladio's Villas* (John Murray). Excellent survey of the architectural principles underlying Palladio's country houses, and the social environment within which they were created.

Deborah Howard, *The Architectural History of Venice* (o/p); *Jacopo Sansovino: Architecture and Patronage in Renaissance Venice* (Yale); *Venice & the East* (Yale). The former is a fine introduction to the subject (and should soon be back in print), while the latter's analysis of the environment

within which Sansovino operated is of wider interest than you might think. Howard's latest book, *Venice & the East*, is a fascinating and characteristically rigorous examination of the ways in which the fabric of the city was conditioned by the close contact between Venice's merchants and the Islamic world in the period 1100–1500. It's a truism that San Marco and the Palazzo Ducale are hybrids of Western and Islamic styles, but this splendidly illustrated study not only has illuminating things to say about those two great monuments – it makes you look freshly at the texture of the whole city.

Peter Lauritzen and Alexander Zielcke, *The Palaces of Venice* (Laurence King, o/p). Lauritzen knows Venice as intimately as anyone currently writing. This is a rich blend of social and architectural history, and Zielcke's photographs are outstanding.

Michael Levey, *Painting in Eighteenth Century Venice* (Yale). On its appearance in 1959 this book was the first detailed discussion of its subject. Now in its third edition, it's still the most thorough exposition of the art of Venice's last golden age, though it shows its age in concentration on heroic personalities – Giambattista Tiepolo in particular.

Ralph Lieberman, *Renaissance Architecture in Venice* (Abbeville, o/p). Lieberman illustrates the complex development of architecture in fifteenth- and sixteenth-century Venice through a chronological survey of key buildings, but annoyingly calls a halt at 1540. Authoritative without being pedantic.

John McAndrew, *Venetian Architecture of the Early Renaissance* (o/p). Definitive study of its subject by one of the very few writers to have studied Venice's buildings with anything like Ruskin's concentration. A beautiful book, but expensive even second-hand.

Tom Nichols, *Tintoretto* (Reaktion Books). Ever since Vasari wrote his life of the artist, Tintoretto has been presented as an artist who flouted all the conventions of Venetian painting. This in-depth study overturns that somewhat romanticised notion, to reveal a figure who was both a radical and a populist. By far the best monograph on Tintoretto in English.

Filippo Pedrocco and M.A. Chiara Moretto Wiel, *Titian – The Complete Paintings* (Thames & Hudson). The text is worthy rather than stimulating (there's a lot of discussion of technique, but little social context), but every surviving picture in Titian's colossal oeuvre is reproduced in colour, and the interpretations of individual paintings are as sound as you'd expect from two of the world's leading experts on the subject.

Terisio Pignatti and Filippo Pedrocco, *Giorgione* (Rizzoli). Expensive monograph on the most enigmatic of the great Venetian painters. Not especially acute in its observations, but very thorough, very nicely produced, and better than the other in-print titles devoted to Giorgione.

Sarah Quill, *Ruskin's Venice: The Stones Revisited* (Ashgate). Prefaced by four brief but informative essays on Ruskin and Venice, the core of this book is a judicious selection of short passages from *The Stones of Venice* and other works by Ruskin, with excellent illustrations for every excerpt. Most of the pictures are crisp colour photographs of buildings and architectural details, but the book also includes some of Ruskin's own watercolours and drawings.

David Rosand, *Painting in Sixteenth-Century Venice* (Cambridge University Press). Covers the century of Giorgione, Titian, Tintoretto and Veronese as thoroughly as most readers will want; especially good on the social networks and artistic conventions within which the painters worked.

John Ruskin, *The Stones of Venice*. Enchanting, enlightening and infuriating in about equal measure, this is still the most stimulating book written about Venice by a non-Venetian. Sadly, you'll have to scour the second-hand bookshops to get hold of the full three-volume edition, as the only editions in print are abridgements, the best of which is published by Da Capo.

John Steer, *A Concise History of Venetian Painting* (Thames & Hudson). Whistle-stop tour of Venetian art from the fourteenth to the eighteenth century. Skimpy and undemanding, but a useful aid to sorting your thoughts out after the visual deluge of Venice's churches and museums, and the plentiful pictures come in handy when your memory needs a prod.

Anchise Tempestini, *Giovanni Bellini* (Abbeville). Deeply knowledgeable overview of the work of the first great Venetian Renaissance artist, with copious full-colour plates. No other currently available book does justice to him.

John Unrau, *Ruskin and St Mark's* (o/p). Ruskin discarded around 600 pages of notes and drawings of San Marco when he came to prepare the text of *The Stones of Venice*; using this material, Unrau has produced a book that is as illuminating about Ruskin as it is about the building. A fine selection of watercolours, paintings and photographs complements the text.

Ettore Vio (ed.), *St Mark's Basilica in Venice* (Thames & Hudson). Edited by the man who is the current *proto* of San Marco (ie the person in overall charge of the building's conservation), this lusciously illustrated paperback gives you an informative close-up tour of the fabric and contents of Europe's most ornate cathedral, from the carvings of the façade to the goldwork of the treasury.

History

Fernand Braudel, *The Mediterranean in the Age of Philip II* (University of California). Vast, magisterial analysis of the economics and politics of the Mediterranean in the second half of the sixteenth century, with Venice rarely off the stage. Braudel's deployment of masses of raw material (population statistics, contemporary chronicles, trade documents) requires prolonged and unwavering attention.

Patricia Fortini Brown, *Venice and Antiquity* (Yale). Subtitled "The Venetian Sense of the Past", this fascinating book explores a subject that strangely no-one has tackled in depth before – the ways in which an imperialist city with no pre-Christian past went about classicizing its self-image. Drawing on a vast range of cultural artefacts, from the great monuments to private manuscripts and medals, Brown adds a new dimension to the history of Venice between the thirteenth and the sixteenth centuries, the city's Golden Age. It's not easy going but the effort is worthwhile, and superlative pictures go some way to leaven the text.

David Chambers and Brian Pullen (eds.), *Venice: A Documentary History, 1450–1630* (Blackwell, o/p). A fine anthology of contemporary chronicles and documents, virtually none of which have previously been translated. Invaluable for getting the feel of the city in its heyday.

Robert Finlay, *Politics in Renaissance Venice* (o/p). Subverts a few received ideas about the political tranquillity of La Serenissima, and is laced with anecdotes about the squabbling, scheming aristocracy. Though not the first book you'd read after your holiday, it explains the mechanics of power in Venice with great clarity.

Christopher Hibbert, *Venice, The Biography of a City* (Grafton, o/p; Norton, o/p). The usual highly proficient Hibbert synthesis of a vast range of secondary material. Very good on the changing social fabric of the city, with more on twentieth-century Venice than most others. Excellent illustrations too – but, bafflingly, it's currently out of print on both sides of the Atlantic.

Frederic C. Lane, *Venice, A Maritime Republic* (Johns Hopkins, o/p). The most authoritative one-volume socio-economic history of the city in English, based on decades of research. Excellent on the infrastructure of the city, and on the changing texture of everyday life. A rather more arduous read than John Julius Norwich's populist history (see below), which is presumably why it's slipped out of print.

Jan Morris, *The Venetian Empire: A Sea Voyage* (Penguin). Anecdotal survey of the Republic's Mediterranean empire, with excursions on the evidence left behind. More a sketch than an attempt to give the full picture, it bears the usual Morris stylistic imprint – ie, a touch too rich for some tastes.

John Julius Norwich, *A History of Venice* (Penguin; Vintage). Although it's far more reliant on secondary sources than Lane, and nowhere near as compendious – you won't learn much, for example, about Venice's finances, which is a major omission in a history of the quintessential mercantile city – this book is unbeatable for its grand narrative sweep.

A Venetian miscellany

Pietro Aretino, *Selected Letters* (Penguin, o/p). Edited highlights from the voluminous correspondence of a man who could be described as the world's first professional journalist. Recipients include Titian, Michelangelo, Charles V, Francis I, the pope, the doge, Cosimo de' Medici – virtually anybody who was anybody in sixteenth-century Europe.

Helen Barolini, *Aldus and his Dream Book* (Italica Press). The innovative printer and typographer Aldus Manutius was a crucial figure in the culture of Renaissance Europe, but for every thousand visitors to Venice who have heard of Titian there's perhaps one who knows anything of Aldus. This concise, elegant and scholarly study

deserves to rectify that situation, and is copiously illustrated with pages from the *Hypnerotomachia Poliphili*, a recondite allegory that was the most beautiful book Aldus – or anyone else for that matter – ever published. The complete *Hypnerotomachia* is now available in English from Thames & Hudson, in an edition that's in the same format as the original and reproduces all 174 of its woodcuts; it's a fine piece of publishing, but the lay reader is likely to find the text somewhat abstruse.

Joseph Brodsky, *Watermark* (Hamish Hamilton, o/p; Noonday). Musings on the wonder of being in Venice and the wonder of being Joseph Brodsky, Nobel laureate and friend of the great. Flashes of imagistic brilliance vitiated by some primitive sexual politics.

Giacomo Casanova, *History of My Life* (Johns Hopkins). For pace, candour and wit, the insatiable seducer's autobiography ranks with the journals of James Boswell, a contemporary of similar sexual and literary stamina. The twelve-volume sequence (here handsomely repackaged into six paperbacks) takes him right across Europe, from Madrid to Moscow. His Venetian escapades are covered in volumes two and three of Willard Trask's magnificent translation.

Roberta Curiel and Bernard Dov Cooperman, *The Ghetto Of Venice* (Tauris Parke, o/p). Prefaced by a concise history of the Jewish community in Venice, the main part of this lavishly produced book is a synagogue-by-synagogue tour of the ghetto.

Milton Grundy, *Venice: An Anthology Guide* (De la Mare). A series of itineraries of the city fleshed out with appropriate excerpts from a huge range of travellers and scholars. Doesn't cover every major sight in Venice, but the choice of quotations couldn't be bettered.

Henry James, *Italian Hours* (Penguin). Urbane travel pieces from the young Henry James, including five essays on Venice. Perceptive observations on the paintings and architecture of the city, but mainly of interest in its evocation of the tone of Venice in the 1860s and 70s.

Henry James, *Letters from the Palazzo Barbaro* (Pushkin Press; Turtle Point Press). Palazzo Barbaro was the home of the Curtis family, whose circle of friends included not just Henry James (who was a frequent guest in the house) but also John Singer Sargent, James Whistler and

Robert Browning. Consisting primarily of letters by James (some of them previously unpublished), this engaging little book also contains correspondence from the Curtis family, and creates a vivid composite portrait of life among the city's expatriate American community a hundred years ago.

Ian Littlewood, *Venice: A Literary Companion* (Penguin; St Martin's Press). Wide-ranging anthology of writings on the city, including many pieces that will be unfamiliar to all but the most scholarly devotees of Venice.

Giulio Lorenzetti, *Venice and its Lagoon* (Lint). The most thorough cultural guide ever written to any European city – Lorenzetti seems to have researched the history of every brick and every canvas. Though completely unmanageable as a guidebook (it even has an index to the indexes), it's indispensable for all those besotted with the place. Almost impossible to find outside Venice, but every bookshop in the city sells it.

Mary McCarthy, *Venice Observed* (Penguin; Harcourt, Brace). Originally written for the *New Yorker*, McCarthy's clear-eyed and brisk report is a refreshing antidote to the gushing enthusiasm of most first-hand accounts from foreigners in Venice. The UK Penguin edtion combines it with her equally entertaining *The Stones of Florence*.

James Morris, *Venice* (Faber; published in the US as Jan Morris's *The World of Venice*, Harcourt, Brace). To some people this is the most brilliant book ever written about Venice; to others it's revoltingly fey and self-regarding. But if you can't stomach the style, Morris's knowledge of Venice's folklore provides some compensation.

Tim Parks, *Italian Neighbours* (Vintage; Fawcett). One of the more worthwhile additions to the genre defined by *A Year in Provence*, Parks's

book is a sharp and engaging account of ex-pat life in a village near Verona.

John Pemble, *Venice Rediscovered* (Oxford University Press). This is one of the most engrossing academic studies of the city to have appeared in recent years, concentrating on the ever-changing perceptions of Venice as a cultural icon since it ceased to exist as a political power. An eloquent writer, totally uninfected by the preciousness that overcomes so many writers on Venice, Pemble unearths stories missing from all other histories.

Dorothea Ritter, *Venice in Old Photographs 1841–1920* (Laurence King, o/p; Little, Brown, o/p). A well-researched and beautifully presented book, packed with rare images of Venice spanning the years from the birth of photography to the birth of mass tourism. The cityscapes have barely altered, but the scenes of everyday Venetian life come from another world.

A.J.A. Symons, *The Quest for Corvo* (Quartet; Ecco, o/p). Misanthropic, devious and solitary, Frederick Rolfe was a tricky subject for a biographer to tackle, and Symons' book, subtitled *An Experiment in Biography*, makes the difficult process of writing Rolfe's life the focus of its narrative. An engrossing piece of literary detective work, and a perfect introduction to Rolfe's Venetian novel, *The Desire and Pursuit of the Whole*.

Stefan Zweig, *Casanova: A Study in Self-Portraiture* (Pushkin Press; Turtle Point Press). A fascinating study of Casanova's life and autobiography, offering a persuasive analysis that differs strikingly from the clichéd image of Casanova as a real-life Don Juan – in fact, Zweig presents him as the very antithesis of Don Juan the misogynistic seducer. Though brief, this is the best book on its subject.

Language

Although it's not uncommon for the staff of Venetian hotels and restaurants to speak some English, you'll make a lot more friends by attempting the vernacular. Outside the city, you might be able to get by in English at tourist offices, but in the depths of the Veneto you shouldn't expect to encounter fluency in English.

Some tips

You'd do well to master at least a little **Italian**, a task made more enjoyable by the fact that your halting efforts will often be rewarded by smiles and genuine surprise that an English-speaker should make an attempt to learn Italian. In any case, it's one of the easiest European languages to learn, especially if you already have a smattering of French or Spanish, both extremely similar grammatically.

Easiest of all is the **pronunciation**, since every word is spoken exactly as it's written, and usually enunciated with exaggerated, open-mouthed clarity. The only difficulties you're likely to encounter are the few **consonants** that are different from English:

c before **e** or **i** is pronounced as in **ch**urch, while **ch** before the same vowels is hard, as in **c**at.

sci or **sce** are pronounced as in **sh**eet and **sh**elter respectively.

G is soft before **e** and **i**, as in **g**eranium; hard when followed by **h**, as in **g**arlic.

gn has the ni sound of our "on**io**n".

gl in Italian is softened to something like li in English, as in stal**li**on.

h is not aspirated, as in **h**onour.

When **speaking** to strangers, the third person is the polite form (ie Lei instead of Tu for "you"); using the second person is a mark of disrespect or stupidity. Also remember that Italians don't use "please" and "thank you" half as much as we do: it's all implied in the tone, though if you're in any doubt, err on the polite side.

All Italian words are **stressed** on the penultimate syllable unless an **accent** (´ or `) denotes otherwise, although written accents are often left out in practice. Note that the ending **-ia** or **-ie** counts as two syllables, hence trattoria is stressed on the **i**. We've put accents on names throughout the text wherever it isn't immediately obvious how a word should be pronounced: for example, in Maríttima, the accent is on the first **i**; similarly the stress in Pésaro is not on the **a**, where you'd expect it, but on the **e**. We've omitted accents on some of the more common exceptions (like Isola, stressed on the I), some names (Domenico), and words that are stressed similarly in English, such as archeologico and Repubblica.

The **Venetian dialect** virtually qualifies as a separate language, with its own rules of spelling and grammar, and distinctive pronunciation. However, you'll probably encounter it only in the form of the words given in the Glossary, in dialect proper names (which are deciphered in the text) or the occasional shop sign – eg Venexiana rather than Veneziana.

ITALIAN WORDS AND PHRASES

BASICS

Good morning	*Buon giorno*	Day after tomorrow	*Dopodomani*
Good afternoon/evening	*Buona sera*	Yesterday	*Ieri*
Good night	*Buona notte*	Now	*Adesso*
Hello/goodbye	*Ciao (informal; to strangers use phrases above)*	Later	*Più tardi*
		Wait a minute!	*Aspetta!*
		In the morning	*Di mattina*
Goodbye	*Arrivederci*	In the afternoon	*Nel pomeriggio*
Yes	*Sì*	In the evening	*Di sera*
No	*No*	Here/there	*Qui/La*
Please	*Per favore*	Good/bad	*Buono/cattivo*
Thank you (very much)	*Grázie (molte/ mille grazie)*	Big/small	*Grande/Píccolo*
		Cheap/expensive	*Económico/Caro*
You're welcome	*Prego*	Early/late	*Presto/Ritardo*
Alright/that's OK	*Va bene*	Hot/cold	*Caldo/Freddo*
How are you?	*Come stai/sta? (informal/formal)*	Near/far	*Vicino/Lontano*
		Vacant/occupied	*Líbero/Occupato*
I'm fine	*Bene*	Quickly/slowly	*Velocemente/ Lentamente*
Do you speak English?	*Parla inglese?*		
I don't understand	*Non ho capito*	Slowly/quietly	*Piano*
I don't know	*Non lo so*	With/without	*Con/Senza*
Excuse me	*Mi scusi/Prego*	More/less	*Più/Meno*
Excuse me (in a crowd)	*Permesso*	Enough, no more	*Basta*
I'm sorry	*Mi dispiace*	Mr . . .	*Signor . . .*
I'm here on holiday	*Sono qui in vacanza*	Mrs . . .	*Signora . . .*
I'm English/Scottish/ American/Irish/Welsh	*Sono inglese/scozzese americano/ irlandese/gallese*	Miss . . .	*Signorina . . . (il Signor, la Signora, la Signorina when speaking about someone else)*
I live in . . .	*Abito a . . .*		
Today	*Oggi*		
Tomorrow	*Domani*		

NUMBERS

1	*uno*	14	*quattordici*	70	*settanta*
2	*due*	15	*quindici*	80	*ottanta*
3	*tre*	16	*sedici*	90	*novanta*
4	*quattro*	17	*diciassette*	100	*cento*
5	*cinque*	18	*diciotto*	101	*centuno*
6	*sei*	19	*diciannove*	110	*centodieci*
7	*sette*	20	*venti*	200	*duecento*
8	*otto*	21	*ventuno*	500	*cinquecento*
9	*nove*	22	*ventidue*	1000	*mille*
10	*dieci*	30	*trenta*	5000	*cinquemila*
11	*undici*	40	*quaranta*	10,000	*diecimila*
12	*dodici*	50	*cinquanta*	50,000	*cinquantamila*
13	*tredici*	60	*sessanta*		

SOME SIGNS

Entrance/exit	*Entrata/Uscita*	Gentlemen/ladies	*Signori/Signore*
Free entrance	*Ingresso líbero*	WC	*Gabinetto*

Vacant/engaged	*Libero/Occupato*	Cash desk	*Cassa*
Open/closed	*Aperto/Chiuso*	Go/walk	*Avanti*
Arrivals/departures	*Arrivi/Partenze*	Stop/halt	*Alt*
Closed for restoration	*Chiuso per restauro*	Customs	*Dogana*
Closed for holidays	*Chiuso per ferie*	Do not touch	*Non toccare*
Pull/push	*Tirare/Spingere*	Danger	*Perícolo*
Out of order	*Guasto*	Beware	*Attenzione*
Drinking water	*Acqua potabile*	First aid	*Pronto soccorso*
To let	*Affitasi*	Ring the bell	*Suonare il campanello*
Platform	*Binario*	No smoking	*Vietato fumare*

DRIVING

Left/right	*Sinistro/Destro*	No entry	*Senso vietato*
Go straight ahead	*Sempre diritto*	Slow down	*Rallentare*
Turn to the right/left	*Gira a destra/sinistra*	Road closed/up	*Strada chiusa/guasta*
Parking	*Parcheggio*	No through road	*Vietato il transito*
No parking	*Divieto di sosta/ Sosta vietata*	No overtaking	*Vietato il sorpasso*
		Crossroads	*Incrocio*
One way street	*Senso único*	Speed limit	*Limite di velocità*

TRAVELLING

Aeroplane	*Aeroplano*	What time does it leave?	*A che ora parte?*
Bus	*Autobus/pullman*		
Train	*Treno*	When is the next bus/ train/ferry to . . . ?	*Quando parte il prossimo pullman /treno/traghetto per. . .?*
Car	*Macchina*		
Taxi	*Taxi*		
Bicycle	*Bicicletta*		
Ferry	*Traghetto*	Do I have to change?	*Devo cambiare?*
Ship	*Nave*	Where does it leave from?	*Da dove parte?*
Hydrofoil	*Aliscafo*		
Hitch-hiking	*Autostop*	What platform does it leave from?	*Da quale binario parte?*
On foot	*A piedi*		
Bus station	*Autostazione*	How many kilometres is it?	*Quanti chilometri sono?*
Train station	*Stazione ferroviaria*		
Ferry terminal	*Stazione maríttima*	How long does it take?	*Quanto ci vuole?*
Port	*Porto*	What number bus is it to . . . ?	*Che numero di autobus per . . . ?*
A ticket to . . .	*Un biglietto a . . .*	Where's the road to . . .?	*Dovè la strada per . . .?*
One-way/return	*Solo andata/ andata e ritorno*	Next stop please	*La prossima fermata, per favore*
Can I book a seat?	*Posso prenotare un posto?*		

ACCOMMODATION

Hotel	*Albergo*	for one/two/three nights	*per una/due/tre nott(e/i)*
Is there a hotel nearby?	*C'è un albergo qui vicino?*		
		for one/two weeks	*per una/due setti- man(a/e)*
Do you have a room . . . for one/two/three people	*Ha una cámera . . . per una/due/tre person(a/e)*		
		with a double bed	*con un letto matrimoniale*

continued overleaf

continued from previous page

with a shower/bath	*con una doccia/ un bagno*	I'll take it	*La prendo*
with a balcony	*con una terrazza*	I'd like to book a room	*Vorrei prenotare una cámera*
hot/cold water	*acqua calda/fredda*		
How much is it?	*Quanto costa?*	I have a booking	*Ho una prenotazione*
It's expensive	*È caro*		
Is breakfast included?	*È compresa la prima colazione?*	Can we camp here?	*Possiamo campeggiare qui?*
Do you have anything cheaper?	*Ha niente che costa di meno?*	Is there a campsite nearby?	*C'è un camping qui vicino?*
Full/half board	*Pensione completa/ mezza pensione*	Tent	*Tenda*
		Cabin	*Cabina*
Can I see the room?	*Posso vedere la cámera?*	Youth hostel	*Ostello per la gioventù*

QUESTIONS AND DIRECTIONS

Where? (where is/are . . . ?)	*Dove?* *(Dov'è/Dove sono)*	Can you give me a lift to . . . ?	*Mi può dare un passaggio a . . . ?*
When?	*Quando?*	Can you tell me when to get off?	*Mi può dire scendere alla fermata giusta?*
What? (what is it?)	*Cosa? (Cos'è?)*		
How much/many?	*Quanto/Quanti?*		
Why?	*Perché?*	What time does it open?	*A che ora apre?*
It is/there is (is it/is there . . . ?)	*È/C'è* *(È/C'è . . . ?)*	What time does it close?	*A che ora chiude?*
What time is it?	*Che ora è/ Che ore sono?*	How much does it cost (. . . do they cost?)	*Quanto costa? (Quanto cóstano?)*
How do I get to . . . ?	*Come arrivo a . . . ?*	What's it called in Italian?	*Come si chiama in italiano*
How far is it to . . . ?	*Quant'è lontano a . . . ?*		

PHRASEBOOKS AND DICTIONARIES

The best phrasebook is *Italian: A Rough Guide Dictionary Phrase Book* (Penguin), which has a huge but accessible vocabulary, a detailed menu reader and useful dialogues. As for dictionaries, Collins publish a comprehensive series: their Gem or Pocket dictionaries are fine for travelling purposes, while their Concise is adequate for most language needs.

A MENU GLOSSARY

This glossary should allow you to decode most menus; it concludes with a summary of Venetian specialities – for more detail on Venetian food and drink, see p.261.

BASICS AND SNACKS

Aceto	Vinegar	Pane	Bread
Aglio	Garlic	Pane integrale	Wholemeal bread
Biscotti	Biscuits	Panino	Bread roll
Burro	Butter	Patatine	Crisps
Caramelle	Sweets	Patatine fritte	Chips
Cioccolato	Chocolate	Pepe	Pepper
Focaccia	Oven-baked snack	Pizzetta	Small cheese and tomato pizza
Formaggio	Cheese	Riso	Rice
Frittata	Omelette	Sale	Salt
Gelato	Ice-cream	Tramezzini	Sandwich
Grissini	Bread sticks	Uova	Eggs
Marmellata	Jam	Yogurt	Yoghurt
Olio	Oil	Zúcchero	Sugar
Olive	Olives	Zuppa	Soup

STARTERS (ANTIPASTI)

Antipasto misto	Mixed cold meats and cheese (and a selection of other things in this list)	Melanzane in parmigiana	Fried aubergine in tomato and parmesan cheese
Caponata	Mixed aubergine, olives, tomatoes and celery	Mortadella	Salami-type cured meat
		Pancetta	Bacon
Caprese	Tomato and mozzarella salad	Peperonata	Grilled green, red or yellow peppers stewed in olive oil
Insalata di mare	Seafood salad	Pomodori ripieni	Stuffed tomatoes
		Prosciutto	Ham
Insalata di riso	Rice salad	Salame	Salami

PIZZAS

Biancaneve	"Black and white": mozzarella and oregano	Frutti di mare	Seafood, usually mussels, prawns, squid and clams
Calzone	Folded pizza with cheese, ham and tomato	Margherita	Cheese and tomato
		Marinara	Tomato and garlic
Capricciosa	Literally "capricious": topped with whatever they've got in the kitchen, usually including baby artichoke, ham and egg	Napoli/ Napoletana	Tomato, anchovy and olive oil (and sometimes mozzarella)
		Quattro formaggi	"Four cheeses", usually including mozzarella, fontina, gorgonzola and gruyère
Diavolo	Spicy, with hot salami or Italian sausage	Quattro stagioni	"Four seasons": the toppings split into four sections, usually including ham, peppers, onion, mushrooms, artichokes, olives and egg
Funghi	Mushroom; tinned, sliced button mushrooms unless it specifies fresh mushrooms, either funghi freschi or porcini		
		Romana	Anchovy and olives

continued overleaf

continued from previous page

THE FIRST COURSE (IL PRIMO)

Soups

Brodo	Clear broth
Minestrina	Any light soup
Minestrone	Thick vegetable soup
Pasta e fagioli	Pasta soup with beans
Pastina in brodo	Pasta pieces in clear broth
Stracciatella	Broth with egg

Pasta

Cannelloni	Large tubes of pasta, stuffed
Farfalle	Literally "bow"-shaped pasta; the word also means "butterflies"
Fettuccine	Narrow pasta ribbons
Gnocchi	Small potato and dough dumplings
Lasagne	Lasagne
Maccheroni	Tubular spaghetti
Pasta al forno	Pasta baked with minced meat, eggs, tomato and cheese
Penne	Smaller version of rigatoni
Ravioli	Small packets of stuffed pasta
Rigatoni	Large, grooved tubular pasta
Risotto	Cooked rice dish, with sauce
Spaghetti	Spaghetti
Spaghettini	Thin spaghetti

Tagliatelle	Pasta ribbons, another word for fettucine
Tortellini	Small rings of pasta, stuffed with meat or cheese
Vermicelli	Very thin spaghetti (literally "little worms")

Pasta sauces

Aglio e olio (e peperoncino)	Tossed in garlic and olive oil (and hot chillies)
Arrabiata	Spicy tomato sauce
Bolognese	Meat sauce
Burro e salvia	Butter and sage
Carbonara	Cream, ham and beaten egg
Frutta di mare	Seafood
Funghi	Mushroom
Matriciana	Cubed pork and tomato sauce
Panna	Cream
Parmigiano	Parmesan cheese
Pesto	Ground basil, pine nut, garlic and pecorino sauce
Pomodoro	Tomato sauce
Ragù	Meat sauce
Vóngole	Clam and tomato sauce

THE SECOND COURSE (IL SECONDO)

Meat (carne)

Agnello	Lamb
Bistecca	Steak
Cervello	Brains
Cinghiale	Wild boar
Coniglio	Rabbit
Costolette	Chops
Cotolette	Cutlets
Fegatini	Chicken livers
Fégato	Liver
Involtini	Steak slices, rolled and stuffed
Lingua	Tongue
Maiale	Pork
Manzo	Beef
Ossobuco	Shin of veal
Pollo	Chicken
Polpette	Meatballs (or minced balls of anything)
Rognoni	Kidneys
Salsiccia	Sausage
Saltimbocca	Veal with ham
Spezzatino	Stew
Tacchino	Turkey
Trippa	Tripe
Vitello	Veal

Fish (pesce) and shellfish (crostacei)

Acciughe	Anchovies
Anguilla	Eel
Aragosta	Lobster
Baccalà	Dried salted cod
Bronzino/Branzino	Sea-bass
Calamari	Squid
Cape lungue	Razor clams
Cape sante	Scallops
Caparossoli	Shrimps
Coda di rospo	Monkfish
Cozze	Mussels
Dentice	Dentex (like sea bass)
Gamberetti	Shrimps
Gámberi	Prawns
Granchio	Crab
Merluzzo	Cod
Moleche	Soft-shelled crabs
Nasello	Hake
Orata	Bream
Ostriche	Oysters
Pescespada	Swordfish
Pólipo	Octopus
Ricci di mare	Sea urchins
Rombo	Turbot

San Pietro	John Dory	Ceci	Chickpeas
Sarde	Sardines	Cetriolo	Cucumber
Schie	Shrimps	Cipolla	Onion
Seppie	Cuttlefish	Fagioli	Beans
Sógliola	Sole	Fagiolini	Green beans
Tonno	Tuna	Finocchio	Fennel
Triglie	Red mullet	Funghi	Mushrooms
Trota	Trout	Insalata verde/	Green salad/
Vóngole	Clams	insalata mista	mixed salad

Vegetables (contorni) and salad (insalata)

		Melanzana	Aubergine/eggplant
		Orígano	Oregano
Asparagi	Asparagus	Patate	Potatoes
Basílico	Basil	Peperoni	Peppers
Bróccoli	Broccoli	Piselli	Peas
Cápperi	Capers	Pomodori	Tomatoes
Carciofi	Artichokes	Radicchio	Chicory
Carciofini	Artichoke hearts	Spinaci	Spinach
Carotte	Carrots	Zucchini	Courgettes
Cavolfiori	Cauliflower	Zucca	Pumpkin
Cávolo	Cabbage		

DESSERTS (DOLCI), CHEESES (FORMAGGI), FRUIT (FRUTTA) AND NUTS (NOCE)

Desserts

Amaretti	Macaroons
Cassata	Ice-cream cake with candied fruit
Gelato	Ice-cream
Macedonia	Fruit salad
Torta	Cake, tart
Zabaglione	Dessert made with eggs, sugar and marsala wine
Zuppa Inglese	Trifle

Cheese

Caciocavallo	A type of dried, mature mozzarella cheese
Fontina	Northern Italian cheese used in cooking
Gorgonzola	Soft blue-veined cheese
Mozzarella	Bland soft white cheese used on pizzas
Parmigiano	Parmesan cheese
Pecorino	Strong-tasting hard sheep's cheese
Provolone	Hard strong cheese

Ricotta	Soft white cheese made from ewe's milk, used in sweet or savoury dishes

Fruit and nuts

Ananas	Pineapple
Anguria/Coccómero	Water melon
Arance	Oranges
Banane	Bananas
Ciliegie	Cherries
Fichi	Figs
Fichi d'India	Prickly pears
Frágole	Strawberries
Limone	Lemon
Mándorle	Almonds
Mele	Apples
Melone	Melon
Pere	Pears
Pesche	Peaches
Pignoli	Pine nuts
Pistacchio	Pistachio nut
Uva	Grapes

COOKING TERMS

Affumicato	Smoked	Al forno	Baked
Al dente	Firm, not overcooked	Al Marsala	Cooked with marsala wine
Al ferro	Grilled without oil	Al vapore	Steamed

continued overleaf

continued from previous page

Alla brace	Barbecued	*Fritto*	Fried
Alla griglia	Grilled	*Grattugiato*	Grated
Allo spiedo	On the spit	*In úmido*	Stewed
Arrosto	Roasted	*Lesso*	Boiled
Ben cotto	Well done	*Milanese*	Fried in egg and breadcrumbs
Bollito	Boiled	*Pizzaiola*	Cooked with tomato sauce
Brasato	Cooked in wine	*Ripieno*	Stuffed
Cotto	Cooked (not raw)	*Sangue*	Rare
Crudo	Raw	*Surgelato*	Frozen

DRINKS

Acqua minerale	Mineral water	*Succo*	Concentrated fruit juice with sugar
Aranciata	Orangeade		
Bicchiere	Glass	*Tè*	Tea
Birra	Beer	*Tónico*	Tonic water
Bottiglia	Bottle	*Vino*	Wine
Caffè	Coffee	*Rosso*	Red
Cioccolata calda	Hot chocolate	*Bianco*	White
Ghiaccio	Ice	*Rosato*	Rosé
Granita	Iced coffee or fruit drink	*Secco*	Dry
Latte	Milk	*Dolce*	Sweet
Limonata	Lemonade	*Litro*	Litre
Selz	Soda water	*Mezzo*	Half
Spremuta	Fresh fruit juice	*Quarto*	Quarter
Spumante	Sparkling wine	*Salute!*	Cheers!

VENETIAN SPECIALITIES

Antipasti e Primi

Acciughe marinate	Marinated anchovies with onions
Bigoli in salsa	Spaghetti with butter, onions and sardines
Brodetto	Mixed fish soup, often with tomatoes and garlic
Castraura	Artichoke hearts
Granseola alla Veneziana	Crab cooked with oil, parsley and lemon
Pasta e fasioi	Pasta and beans
San Prosciutto Daniele	The best quality prosciutto
Risotto di mare	Mixed seafood risotto
Risotto di cape	Risotto with clams and shellfish
Risotto alla sbirraglia	Risotto with chicken, vegetables and ham
Risotto alla trevigiana	Risotto with butter, onions and chicory
Sopa de peoci	Mussel soup with garlic and parsley

Secondi

Anguilla alla Veneziana	Eel cooked with lemon and tuna
Baccalà mantecato	Salt cod simmered in milk
Fegato veneziana	Sliced calf liver cooked in olive oil with onion
Peoci salati	Mussels with parsley and garlic
Risi e bisi	Rice and peas, with parmesan and ham
Sarde in saor	Marinated sardines
Seppie in nero	Squid cooked in its ink
Seppioline nere	Baby cuttlefish cooked in its ink

Dolci

Frittole alla Veneziana	Rum- and anise-flavoured fritters filled with pine nuts, raisins and candied fruit
Tiramisù	Dessert of layered chocolate and cream, flavoured with rum and coffee

Glossary of Italian words and acronyms

Italian words

ANFITEATRO Amphitheatre.

AUTOSTAZIONE Bus station.

AUTOSTRADA Motorway.

BELVEDERE A look-out point.

CAPPELLA Chapel.

CASTELLO Castle.

CENTRO Centre.

CHIESA Church.

COMUNE An administrative area; also, the local council or the town hall.

CORSO Avenue/boulevard.

DUOMO/CATTEDRALE Cathedral.

ENTRATA Entrance.

FESTA Festival, carnival.

FIUME River.

LAGO Lake.

MARE Sea.

MERCATO Market.

MUNICIPIO Town Hall.

PALAZZO Palace, mansion or block (of flats).

PARCO Park.

PASSEGGIATA The customary early evening walk.

PIAZZA Square.

PONTE Bridge.

SANTUARIO Sanctuary.

SENSO ÚNICO One-way street.

SOTTOPASSAGGIO Subway.

SPIAGGIA Beach.

STAZIONE Station.

STAZIONE FERROVIARIA Train station.

STAZIONE MARÍTTIMA Ferry terminal.

STRADA Road/street.

TEATRO Theatre.

TEMPIO Temple.

TORRE Tower.

TRAGHETTO Ferry.

USCITA Exit.

VIA Road.

Venetian words

CALLE Main alleyway.

CAMPO Square, generally named after a church.

CAMPIELLO Small square.

CORTE Courtyard.

FONDACO (or FONTEGO) Warehouse/hostel used by foreign traders.

FONDAMENTA Pavement along a stretch of water.

PISCINA Former site of a pool.

PUNTA Point, the extremity of an island.

RAMO Small side street.

RIO (pl. Rii) Canal.

RIO TERRÀ Infilled canal.

RIVA A major fondamenta.

RUGA Usually a main shopping street.

SACCA Inlet.

SALIZZADA (or SALIZADA) Main street of a parish. Means "paved street" – originally only main thoroughfares were paved.

SOTTOPORTICO (or SOTTOPORTEGO) Small alleyway running under a building.

Acronyms

ACI Italian Automobile Club.

APT Azienda Promozionale Turismo (local tourist office).

DC Democrazia Cristiana; the Christian Democrats.

EPT Ente Provinciale di Turismo (provincial tourist office).

FS Italian State Railways.

IVA Imposta Valore Aggiunto (VAT).

MSI Movimento Sociale d'Italia; the Fascist party.

PDS Partito Democratico della Sinistra; the former Communist party.

PSI Partito Socialista d'Italia; the Socialist party.

RAI The state TV and radio network.

SS Strada Statale; major carriageway.

Glossary of artistic and architectural terms

AMBULATORY Corridor round the back of the altar formed by a continuation of the aisles.

APSE Recess at the altar end of a church.

ARCHITRAVE The lowest part of the entablature.

BALDACHIN Canopy over an altar or tomb.

BAPTISTERY Chapel for baptisms, often detached from church.

BAROQUE Dynamic architectural and sculptural style of seventeenth century and early eighteenth century.

CAMPANILE Belltower, sometimes detached.

CAPITAL Top of a column.

CHANCEL Part of church containing the altar and sanctuary.

CHOIR Part of church in which the service is sung; often raised or screened, usually near the altar.

CRYPT Burial place, usually under the choir.

CUPOLA Dome.

ENTABLATURE The part above the capital on a classical building.

EX-VOTO Painting or some other object presented as thanksgiving to a saint.

FRESCO Painting applied to wet plaster so that pigments are absorbed into the wall.

FRIEZE Decorative strip along top of wall or on an entablature.

ICONOSTASIS Screen between the sanctuary and nave in Eastern churches.

LUNETTE Semicircular panel above a door or window.

NAVE Central space in a church, usually flanked by aisles.

PANTOCRATOR An image of Christ, portrayed with outstretched arms in the act of blessing.

PIANO NOBILE Main floor, usually the first.

POLYPTYCH Painting or carving on several joined wooden panels.

PORTICO The covered entrance to a building.

ROCOCO Florid eighteenth-century style.

RELIQUARY Receptacle for a saint's relics.

ROMANESQUE General term for plain architectural style of eleventh century to late thirteenth century.

ROOD SCREEN Screen between sanctuary and nave, bearing a rood (crucifix).

RUSTICATION Large blocks of stone with deep joints, or brick designed to simulate them.

SANCTUARY Area immediately surrounding the high altar.

STELE Inscribed stone slab.

STUCCO Heavy plaster made from water, sand, lime and powdered marble, used for decorative work.

TESSERA Small square piece of stone or glass used in mosaics.

TRACERY Geometrical or patterned stonework.

TRANSEPT Part of church at ninety degrees to the nave.

TROMPE L'OEIL Painting designed to trick the viewer into seeing a three-dimensional image.

TRIPTYCH Painting or carving on three joined panels.

TYMPANUM Panel enclosed by lintel of a door and the arch above it.

Index

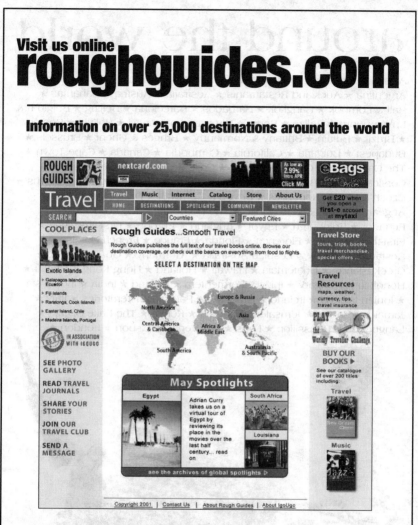

around the world

Alaska ★ Algarve ★ Amsterdam ★ Andalucía ★ Antigua & Barbuda ★
Argentina ★ Auckland Restaurants ★ Australia ★ Austria ★ Bahamas ★
Bali & Lombok ★ Bangkok ★ Barbados ★ Barcelona ★ Beijing ★ Belgium &
Luxembourg ★ Belize ★ Berlin ★ Big Island of Hawaii ★ Bolivia ★ Boston
★ Brazil ★ Britain ★ Brittany & Normandy ★ Bruges & Ghent ★ Brussels ★
Budapest ★ Bulgaria ★ California ★ Cambodia ★ Canada ★ Cape Town ★
The Caribbean ★ Central America ★ Chile ★ China ★ Copenhagen ★
Corsica ★ Costa Brava ★ Costa Rica ★ Crete ★ Croatia ★ Cuba ★ Cyprus ★
Czech & Slovak Republics ★ Devon & Cornwall ★ Dodecanese & East
Aegean ★ Dominican Republic ★ The Dordogne & the Lot ★ Dublin ★
Ecuador ★ Edinburgh ★ Egypt ★ England ★ Europe ★ First-time Asia ★
First-time Europe ★ Florence ★ Florida ★ France ★ French Hotels &
Restaurants ★ Gay & Lesbian Australia ★ Germany ★ Goa ★ Greece ★
Greek Islands ★ Guatemala ★ Hawaii ★ Holland ★ Hong Kong & Macau ★
Honolulu ★ Hungary ★ Ibiza & Formentera ★ Iceland ★ India ★ Indonesia
★ Ionian Islands ★ Ireland ★ Israel & the Palestinian Territories ★ Italy ★
Jamaica ★ Japan ★ Jerusalem ★ Jordan ★ Kenya ★ The Lake District ★
Languedoc & Roussillon ★ Laos ★ Las Vegas ★ Lisbon ★ London ★

in twenty years

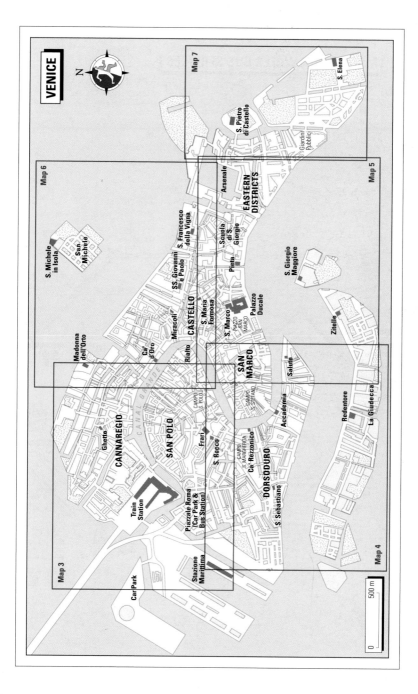

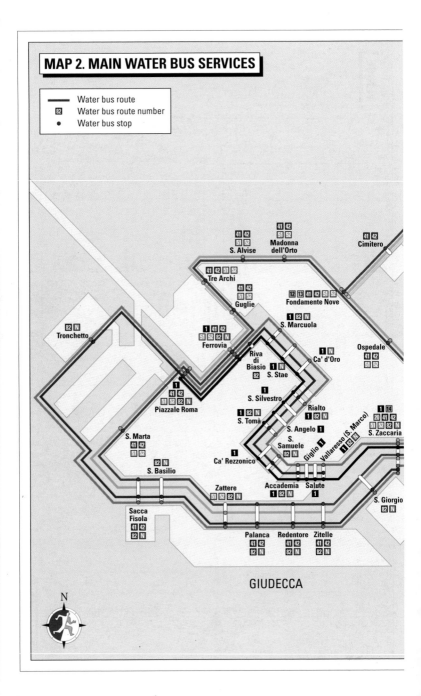

MAP 2. MAIN WATER BUS SERVICES

— Water bus route
82 Water bus route number
• Water bus stop

S. Alvise 41 42 51 52
Madonna dell'Orto 41 42 51 52
Cimitero 41 42
Tre Archi 41 42 51 52
Guglie 41 42 51 52
Fondamente Nove 12 13 41 42 51 52
S. Marcuola 1 82 N
Tronchetto 82 N
Ferrovia 1 41 42 51 52 82 N
Riva di Biasio 1 N
S. Stae 82
Ca' d'Oro 1 N
Ospedale 41 42 51 52
S. Silvestro 1
Piazzale Roma 1 41 42 51 52 82 N
Rialto 1
S. Tomà 1 82 N
S. Angelo 1
Vallaresso (S. Marco) 1 82 N
S. Zaccaria 1 14 20 41 42 51 52 82 N
S. Marta 41 42 51 52
S. Samuele 82 N
Giglio 1
Ca' Rezzonico 1
S. Basilio 82 N
Zattere 51 52 82 N
Accademia 1 82 N
Salute 1
S. Giorgio 82 N
Sacca Fisola 41 42 82 N
Palanca 41 42 82 N
Redentore 41 42 82 N
Zitelle 41 42 82 N

GIUDECCA

N

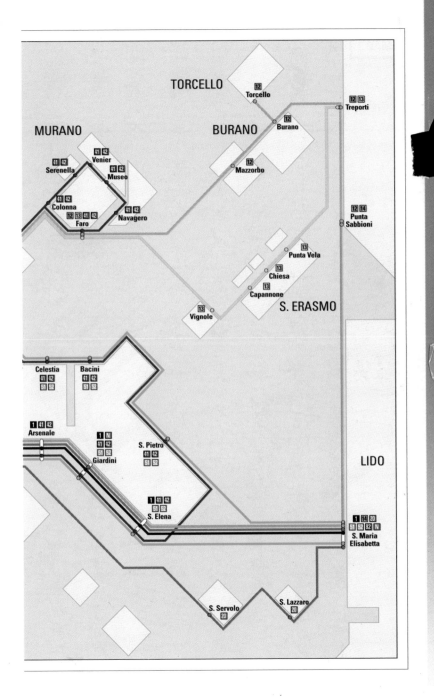

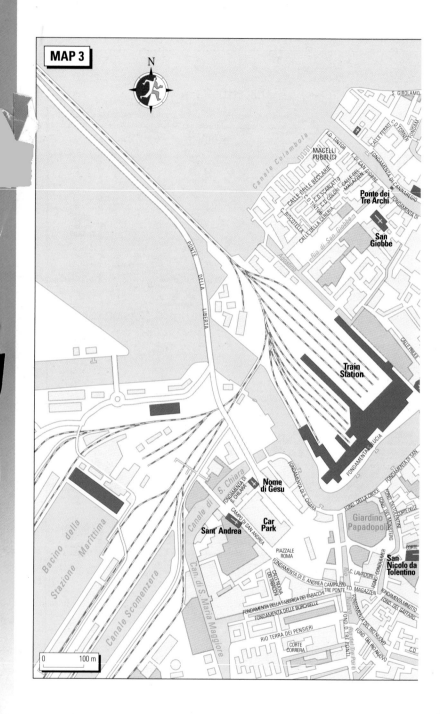

MAP 3

N

S. GIROLAMO

MACELLI PUBBLICI

CALLE DELLE BECCARIE

Canale Colombola

Ponte dei Tre Archi

San Giobbe

PONTE DELLA LIBERTA

Rio di San Giobbe

Train Station

Bacino della Stazione Marittima

Nome di Gesu

S. Chiara

Car Park

Sant' Andrea

CAMPO DI SAN ANDREA

PIAZZALE ROMA

Giardino Papadopoli

San Nicolo da Tolentino

Canale di S. Maria Maggiore

Canale Scomenzera

FONDAMENTA DELLA FABBRICA DEI TABACCHI

FONDAMENTA DELLE BURCHIELLE

RIO TERRA DEI PENSIERI

CORTE CORRERA

0   100 m

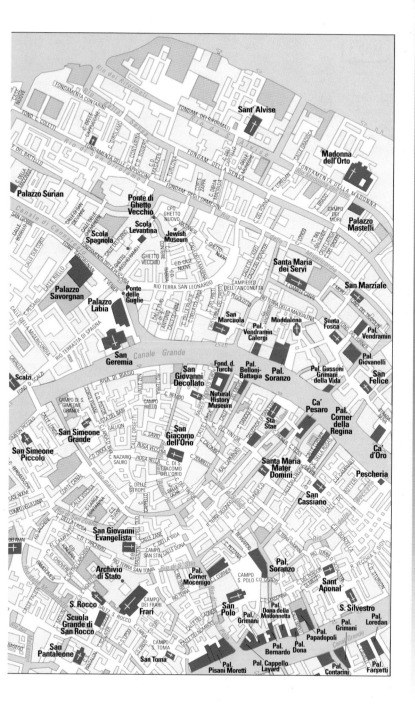

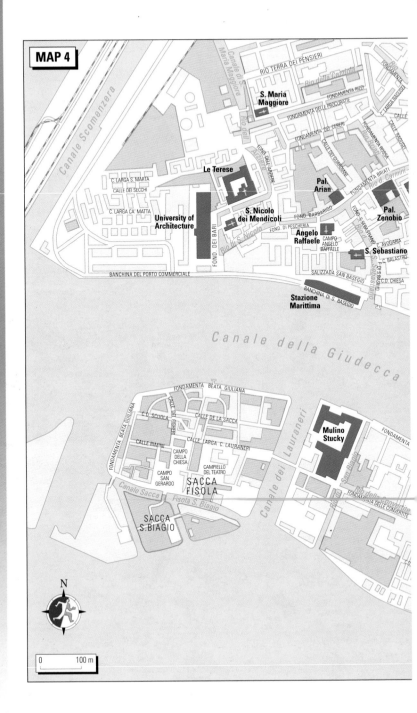

MAP 4

Canale Scomenzera

RIO TERRA DEI PENSIERI
Rio della Cazziola
FONDAMENTA RIZZI

S. Maria Maggiore

FONDAMENTA DELLE PROCURATIE

FONDAMENTA DE' CERERI

C. LARGA BAGATIN
CALLE
CALLE BAGOSSI

FONDAMENTA ROSSA

CALLE DEI CHIOVERETTE

FONDAMENTA BRIATI

C. LARGA S. MARTA
CALLE DEI SECCHI

Le Terese

Pal. Arian

Rio di S. Carmini

Pal. Zenobio

C. LARGA CA' MATTA

University of Architecture

S. Nicolo dei Mendicoli

FOND. DEI BARI

FOND. BARBARIGO

FOND. DI PESCHERIA

Angelo Raffaele

CAMPO ANGELO RAFFAELE

FOND. S. SEBASTIANO

C. AVOGARIA

S. Sebastiano

C. BALASTRO

RIO DI S. NICOLO

BANCHINA DEL PORTO COMMERCIALE

SALIZZADA SAN BASEGIO

C.D. CHIESA

C. DI S BASILIO

BANCHINA DI S. BASEGIO

Stazione Marittima

Canale della Giudecca

FONDAMENTA BEATA GIULIANA

C.D. SCUOLA

CALLE DEL FORNER

CALLE DE LA SACCA

FONDAMENTA BEATA GIULIANA

CALLE RIMINI

CALLE LARGA C. LAURANERI

Mulino Stucky

FONDAMENTA

CAMPO DELLA CHIESA

CAMPIELLO DEL TEATRO

Canale dei Lauraneri

Rio della Convertite

FONDAMENTA DELLE CONVERTITE

CAMPO SAN GERARDO

SACCA FISOLA

Canale Sacca

Fisola S. Biagio

SACCA S. BIAGIO

C.D.

N

0   100 m

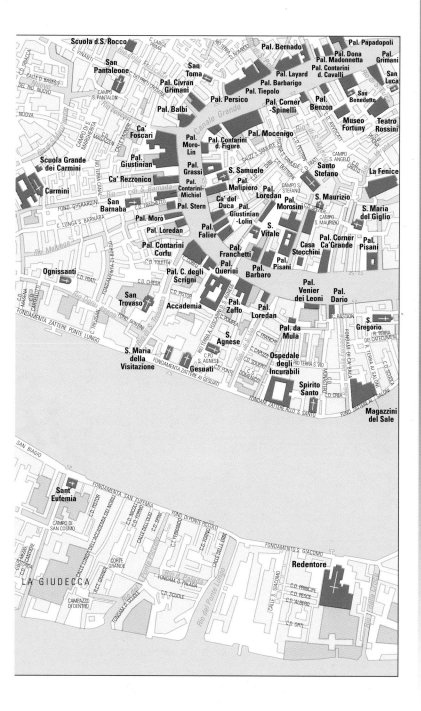

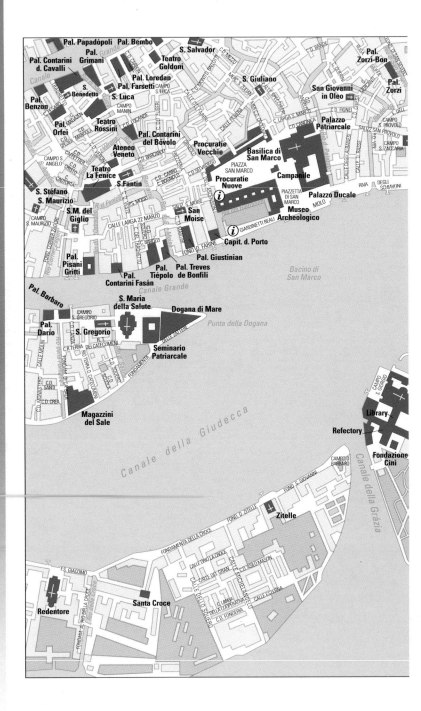

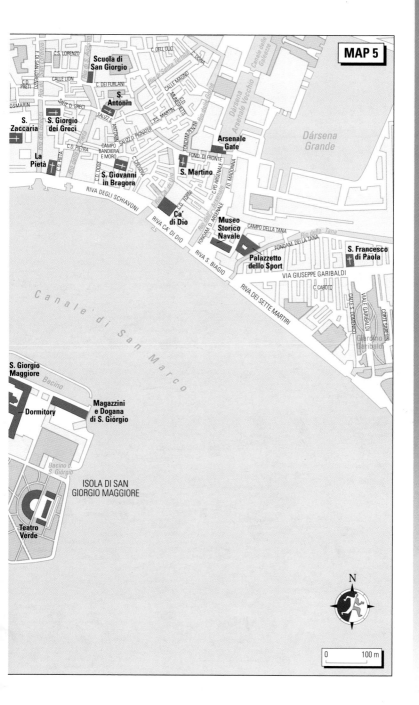

MAP 5

C.S. LORENZO
C. DELL'OLIO
Scuola di
San Giorgio
CALLE LION
C. DEI FURLANI
C.D. PRETI
OSMARIN
S. Antonin
S. Zaccaria
S. Giorgio dei Greci
La Pietà
C.D. PIETA
S. Giovanni in Bragora
RIVA DEGLI SCHIAVONI
RIVA CA' DI DIO
Ca' di Dio
S. Martino
Arsenale Gate
FOND. DI FRONTE
FOND. DELLA MADONNA
Arsenale Vecchio
Dársena Grande
Museo Storico Navale
CAMPO DELLA TANA
RIVA S. BIAGIO
Palazzetto dello Sport
Rio della Tana
FONDAM. DELLA TANA
S. Francesco di Paola
VIA GIUSEPPE GARIBALDI
C. CABOTO
RIVA DEI SETTE MARTIRI
VIALE GARIBALDI
CORTE SARESIN
Giardino Garibaldi

Canale di San Marco

S. Giorgio Maggiore
Bacino
Dormitory
Magazzini e Dogana di S. Giórgio
Bacino di S. Giórgio

ISOLA DI SAN GIORGIO MAGGIORE

Teatro Verde

N

0   100 m

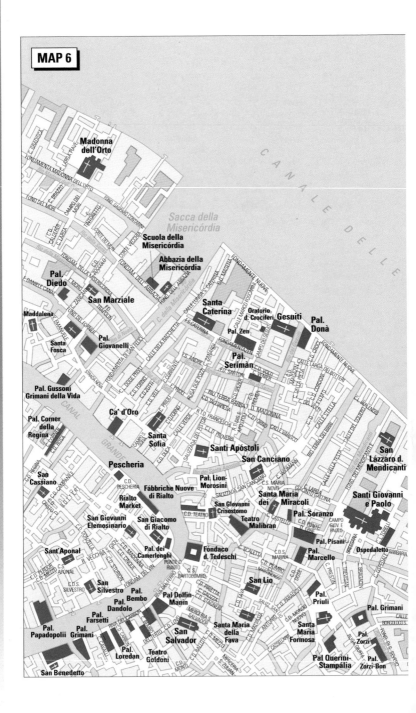

MAP 6

Madonna dell'Orto

Sacca della Misericórdia

CANALE DELLE

Scuola della Misericórdia

Abbazia della Misericórdia

Pal. Diedo

San Marziale

Santa Caterina

Oratorio d. Crociferi

Gesuiti

Pal. Donà

Maddalena

Santa Fosca

Pal. Giovanelli

Pal. Zen

Pal. Serimàn

Pal. Gussoni Grimani della Vida

Ca' d'Oro

Pal. Corner della Regina

Santa Sofia

Santi Apóstoli

San Canciano

San Lázzaro d. Mendicanti

Pescheria

Pal. Lion-Morosini

San Cassiano

Fábbriche Nuove di Rialto

Santa Maria dei Miracoli

Santi Giovanni e Paolo

Rìalto Market

San Giovanni Crisostomo

San Giacomo di Rialto

Pal. Soranzo

San Giovanni Elemosinario

Teatro Malibran

Sant'Aponal

Pal. dei Camerlenghi

Fóndaco d. Tedeschi

Pal. Pisani

Ospedaletto

Pal. Marcello

San Lio

San Silvestro

Pal Dolfin-Manin

Pal. Bembo

Pal. Dandolo

Pal. Priuli

Pal. Grimani

Pal. Farsetti

Pal. Papadopolii

Pal. Grimani

Santa Maria della Fava

Santa Maria Formosa

Pal. Zorzi

San Salvador

Pal. Loredan

Teatro Goldoni

Pal Querini-Stampália

Zorzi-Bon

San Benedetto

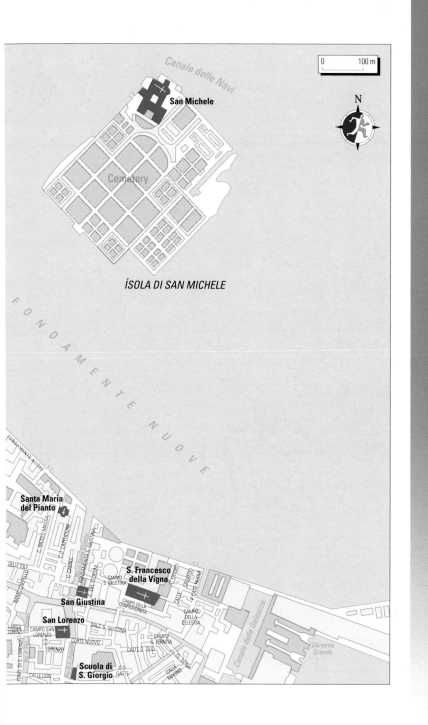

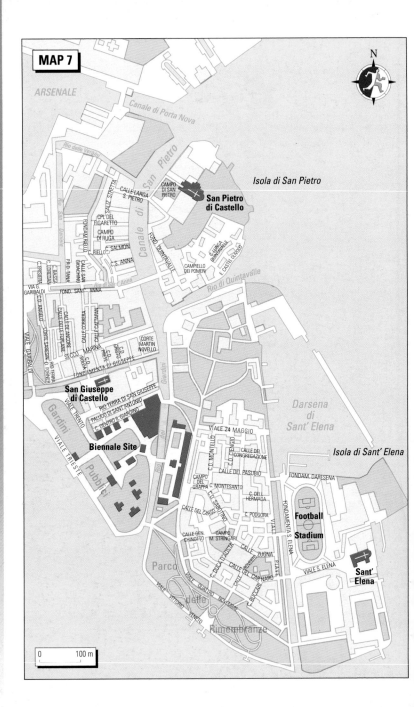